Everyday Air Fryer Perfection Cookbook

~1001~

Recipes to Turn Your Appliance into an All-Purpose Cooking Machine of Healthy Comfort Food and Quick-Yet-Homey Family Meals

© by Marion Bartolini

TABLE OF CONTENTS

CHRISTMAS MEAL RECIPES BONUS 194

CONCLUSION 195

I

INDEX

Air Fryer Cooking Guide

Fahrenheit	Celsius	oz	g	lb
250 F	130 C	1/6	5	...
275 F	140 C	1/2	15	...
300 F	150 C	1	28	...
325 F	165 C	2	58	...
350 F	177 C	4	114	...
375 F	190 C	6	170	...
400 F	200 C	8	226	1/2
425 F	220 C	12	340	...
450 F	230 C	16	454	...
475 F	245 C			
500 F	260 C			

tsp	tbsp	fl oz	cup	pint	liter	quart	gallon
3	1	1/2	1/16	1/32	15 ml	...	...
6	2	1	1/8	1/16	30 ml	1/32	...
12	4	2	1/4	1/8	60 ml	1/16	...
18	6	3	3/8	...	...	...	...
24	8	4	1/2	1/4	120 ml	1/8	1/32

SPECIAL BONUS FOR YOU

Thank you for buying this book!

Only for the <u>paperback version</u> you can get your **"Special Full-Color Recipes Selection Bonus"** by typing the link or by simply scanning with any QR & Barcode Scanner app on any of your devices Android or IOS.

After you got your gift and joined my newsletter, you will receive a notification when my books are to download for FREE on Amazon, no charge.

You will also receive an email when I publish new books and they will be available to you in promotion price or big discount.

As promised, I want to provide you the special gift absolutely FREE, it will help you to prepare delicious dinner with ingredients, directions and nutritional values, and it will also help you to be loved by your partner and friends. ☺

This file will be sent to your email in PDF and can be opened in any digital device such as tablet, smartphone and laptop.

You can find it at the beginning of the cookbook (page 18).

You will definitely love it!

Thank you for staying with me!

INTRODUCTION

An air fryer is a small type of oven. It is an innovative countertop kitchen gadget that fries or cook's food by circulating hot air via convection current.

The air fryer has a heating ring that produces hot air. There is also a mechanical fan that circulates the hot air all over the food at high speed. This hot air cook or fries the food to give the same crispy product as the oil fried variety. The difference between air frying and oil frying is that while oil frying involves immersion of the food into the hot oil to cook, the air fryer doesn't. It means that you can achieve the same cooking results as in oil frying but with little to no oil.

The air fryer works great for foods like roasted vegetables, especially roasted garlic, bacon, whole chicken, wings, eggs, meat, and fish. Most air fryers come with timers and temperature adjustments to make for more precise cooking. There is an opening at the top that takes in air, heated up by the heating rings, and subsequently blown over the food, thereby efficiently cooking them. A cooking basket also sits on top of a drip tray inside which the food is cooked. This basket needs to be shaken frequently to ensure even mixing of oil and a better cooking result. While most models have agitators that initiate this shaking at regular intervals, most others do not, and the shaking should be done manually.

Since air fryers don't require as much oil as oil frying does, they are generally considered healthier. An air fryer reduces the oil content of food to nearly 80% less than oil frying. It is because the food does not absorb as much oil as with oil frying. However, this difference has led to arguments about the taste of air fried food compared to the oil fried variety. Since oil adds more flavor to fried food as it is being absorbed, it comes as no surprise if an air fried food tastes slightly different from oil fried ones. An excellent example is French fries that may taste a lot different when air fried than the usual oil fried delicacy. Chicken, however, turns out pretty great whether sprinkled with oil or not before air frying.

Moreover, spraying the food with oil before air frying gives it an added crispiness compared to the one that was not sprinkled before air frying. Oil on its own is also one of the essential macronutrients and will come in handy in the right proportion.

There are many heart friendly oils out there, which you can spread over your food before air frying to achieve that fabulous taste. These oils can be used to sprinkle your food before air frying to maintain a healthier diet.

Just like most innovative appliances, the air fryer might come with an initial dread on how to use it effectively. Once mastered, the art of air frying is what many people find themselves resorting to more often than not.

Even though air frying is a convenient hands-off cooking method, using the air fryer is more than just turning on the device and leaving your kitchen.

THE BENEFITS OF AN AIR FRYER

As you are aware, an air fryer is a great appliance to have in your kitchen. Not only does it save on the time taken to cook, but it also produces healthy meals. It's worthwhile looking at some of the health benefits provided by it.

Healthy foods

The air fryer is quite popular, owing to producing healthy meals. It reduces oils and fats, thereby making the result relatively healthy. The same cannot be said about standard cooking techniques where you must add in lots of oils and fats. These can adversely affect your health and be the reason for obesity and illnesses. Therefore, an air fryer is best suited for improving their health by making changes in their cooking habits.

Time

The time crunch is one of the most significant issues people face today and age, as everybody is preoccupied with one thing or another. The air fryer effectively solves this problem, as you can prepare foods within a short period. It works by cutting down on 20% of the time taken to cook foods the traditional way. This feature comes in handy for many people, including working professionals, students, and the elderly. If you are always short of time, then it is best to invest in an air fryer as soon as you get a chance.

Usage

The air fryer is extremely easy to use and can be used by just about anyone. The machine is supplied with a manual that can be used to operate the appliance. The manual will also provide you with the right temperatures and times to cook different meals. With time, you will know the exact measures and be able to cook meals much faster. However, it will take a certain level of trial and error to stumble upon the right temperatures and times until you get used to using it. Remember, your ideas center around traditional cooking.

Effort required

The air fryer is designed to be a very efficient machine that pretty much works by itself. It means that you don't have to put in too much effort to operate it. You just have to prepare the ingredients and add them to the appliance, and it will take it from there. You don't have to sauté, season, cover or keep an eye on the foods you place into the oven. All these steps are eliminated, thereby reducing both your effort and time taken to cook a meal. It makes it ideal for all those who are usually too lazy to cook up a meal and prefer takeout.

Nutritional content

An air fryer helps maintain food's nutritional value. Cooking foods at higher temperatures can cause nutritional value to deplete. This issue is solved with an air fryer as it retains the nutritional content of foods placed into it.

Cost of cooking

The air fryer helps in cutting down on the overall costs of cooking. It cuts down on the use of oils and fats, thereby reducing the overall costs of providing your family with food. Another advantage of cooking with an air fryer is that it tends to expand the food item, thereby decreasing the quantity required to cook a meal, reducing cooking costs. You will be surprised by the reduction in your budget and overall cooking costs.

Variety in cooking

Throwing parties and cooking big meals will now be quite easy thanks to the air fryer's multitasking ability. One of the most advantages of using an air fryer is that it can be used for many different cooking purposes. Right from roasting to frying to baking, the air fryer can be put to many uses. You can also use it to grill foods, making it a truly versatile appliance to have in your kitchen. What's more, you will have the choice of cooking several dishes at the same time by using the separator provided with the fryer.

Maintaining the fryer

It is easy to maintain the air fryer, as you do not have to do too much to stay clean. You can eliminate the need to clean several appliances and get away with cleaning, just one that servings many purposes. The machine is easy to clean from the outside. The basket and catching utensil are dishwasher friendly.

Cost saving

The air fryer is quite cheap, price wise, considering the utility that it can provide. You don't need to buy different appliances like an oven, a grill, a chip fryer, etc. It can be done through the air fryer alone. Think of it as a onetime investment that is sure to last you a lifetime if taken care of following manufacturer instructions. Always read these, as the maintenance of each fryer will differ.

These descriptions show the different benefits of using air fryer. Each one of these contributes towards making it an ideal appliance to have in your kitchen.

TIPS ON USING AIR FRYER

10 Tips on Using Air Fryer

An air fryer is a little device that has rapidly grown in popularity in the last few years. It is supposed to help you bake food. Some people call them air fryer ovens. You may remember when you saw your first Indian dish inspired by food fried in oil. Now, it's time to take you on a tour of the world and in a healthier way!

In the last few years, air fryers have become more and more popular. A lot of websites and blogs are now making them out to be the new microwave oven or rice cooker. The fine folks at Amana, pioneers in air fryers, sent me one of their most hot selling models.

Frying has become a bad word lately. As a result, we try to cut down on it in as many of our recipes as possible. Fortunately, air fryers are a great way to make food taste like it's been fried when it hasn't. So, here are some tips on cooking with air fryers:

Air fryers are available in multiple sizes. Look for one that fits the amount of food you want to make. Some air fryers are small enough that you would only use them for a snack or a single person. Others could make enough food for a whole family. There's also a market for commercial sized air fryers, and they're quite large. They could make enough food for a dozen people easily. They're also versatile in that they can be used for baking and as steamers.

Your new air fryer comes with a lot of accessories. You don't need to worry too much about them at the moment. Here are a few tips.

1. No matter what your air fryer comes with, you'll also need a pan and a spatula. The pan is for use as a defroster and a catch-all for when you take out the food. The spatula is to get food out of the air fryer. Remember that the food comes out very hot, so use caution.

2. Look at the shape of your air fryer. It may be a square or a circle. You can do a lot of things to a square air fryer, but few to a circle one. Look at your recipe and decide what you want to use it for.

3. The air fryer's controls are arguably the most important part. The air fryer has a lot of temperature controls that are quite precise. Unlike a microwave oven, an air fryer can give you a wide range of temperatures. You can cook things at really low temperatures, and you can cook things at incredibly hot temperatures that you couldn't use otherwise. Of course, you can also use it at the default temperature. Use the recommendations for your model in the instruction manual to help figure out which temperature is best for your needs.

4. You can make very unique recipes using the air fryer. The temperature and the food you use set the tone of the meal. The temperature you want to use should depend mostly on the type of food you're making, or even how you want it to come out. Low temperature cooking is helpful when you want to cook things slowly. You also want foods with a lot of moisture to be cooked at a high temperature because they cook through faster. You can make dishes with vegetables and meats evenly. You can also make quick breads since they would take less time and the other ingredients are easier to get.

5. Air fryers are very inexpensive. No matter what your budget is, there is an air fryer that fits it. They're mainly used for snacks. However, you can use the air fryer for other recipes if you want. They're a great alternative to the waffle iron, and you can cook a wide range of foods with them.

6. There are different components to an air fryer, and you can use each of them for different purposes. The top is traditionally used for eggs and for steaming. The middle can be used for both frying foods and steaming them. The bottom is typically for fries and other fried foods.

7. Air fryers are very versatile. It's hard to find a recipe that can't be used in an air fryer. It's possible to make chicken legs, wings, and even drumsticks. You can even make foods with breading. People can even make grills and pizzas in air fryers.

8. If you're looking for the best air fryer, you can't go wrong with a Norpro. This is a great air fryer that is affordable and very easy to use. It has multiple functions and will work in no time.

9. Most air fryers have a filter. You need to make sure you always keep the filter cleaned. As much as you don't want to clean your air fryer, you have to clean the filter. This is very important because all the cooking oil is retained in the filter.

10. There are different types of air fryers. The ones that are made of glass and stainless steel are the most expensive. They're also more attractive. There are the ones that are made of plastic. Finally, there are the ones that are made from nonstick surfaces. These are the cheapest and also the most commonly sold air fryers.

"GET YOUR SPECIAL FULL-COLOR RECIPES SELECTION BONUS"

Please Note: you can get your bonus by typing the link below or by simply scanning with any QR & Barcode Scanner app on any of your devices Android or IOS.

Link: https://qrgo.page.link/13YX4

DENSO WAVE INCORPORATED

BREAKFAST RECIPES

1. Cinnamon banana muffins

Preparation time: 10 minutes
Cooking time: 15 minutes
Servings: 4
Ingredients:

- 1 large egg, whisked
- 1 ripe banana, peeled and mashed
- 1/4 cup butter, melted
- 1/4 cup agave nectar
- 1/2 cup all-purpose flour
- 1/4 almond flour
- 1 teaspoon baking powder
- 1/4 cup brown sugar
- 1/2 teaspoon vanilla essence
- 1 teaspoon cinnamon powder
- 1/4 teaspoon ground cloves

Directions:

1. Start by preheating your air fryer to 320° f.
2. Mix all ingredients in a bowl.
3. Scrape the batter into silicone baking molds; place them in the air fryer basket.
4. Bake your muffins for about 15 minutes or until a tester comes out dry and clean. Allow the muffins to cool before unmolding and serving.

Nutrition: Calories 236; Fat 13g; Carbs 26g; Protein 7g; Sugars 10g; Fiber: 2g

2. Mixed berry breakfast muffins

Preparation time: 5 minutes
Cooking time: 10 minutes
Servings: 6
Ingredients:

- 3/4 cup all-purpose flour
- 1/4 cup honey
- 1/2 teaspoon ground cinnamon
- 1/4 teaspoon ground cloves
- 1/4 cup buttermilk
- 1 egg
- 4 tablespoons olive oil
- 1 teaspoon vanilla extract
- 1/2 cup fresh mixed berries

Directions:

1. Start by preheating your air fryer to 320° f.
2. Mix all ingredients in a bowl. Scrape the batter into silicone baking molds; place them in the air fryer basket.
3. Bake your muffins for about 15 minutes or until a tester comes out dry and clean.
4. Allow the muffins to cool before unmolding and serving. Bon appétit!

Nutrition: Calories: 200 Fat 10g Carbs 25g Protein 3g Sugars 13g Fiber 1g

3. Apple oat muffins

Preparation time: 10 minutes
Cooking time: 15 minutes
Servings: 6
Ingredients:

- 1/2 cups self-rising flour
- 1/2 cup rolled oats
- 1/2 cup agave syrup
- 1/4 teaspoon grated nutmeg
- 1/2 teaspoon cinnamon powder
- A pinch of coarse salt
- 1/2 cup milk
- 1/4 cup coconut oil, room temperature
- 2 eggs
- 1 teaspoon coconut extract
- 1 cup apples, cored and chopped

Directions

1. Start by preheating your air fryer to 320° f.
2. Mix all ingredients in a bowl.
3. Scrape the batter into silicone baking molds; place them in the air fryer basket.
4. Bake your muffins for about 15 minutes or until a tester comes out dry and clean.
5. Allow the muffins to cool before unmolding and serving.

Nutrition: Calories 290; Fat 12g; Carbs 41g; Protein 3g

4. Easy cornbread bites

Preparation time: 10 minutes
Cooking time: 20 minutes
Servings: 6
Ingredients:

- 1/2 cup all-purpose flour
- 1/2 cup yellow cornmeal
- 1 ½ teaspoons baking powder
- 4 tablespoons honey
- A pinch of sea salt
- A pinch of grated nutmeg
- 4 tablespoons coconut oil, room temperature
- 2 eggs, whisked
- 1/2 cup milk

Directions:

1. Preheat air fryer to 360° f.
2. Prepare and mix all ingredients until everything is well incorporated.
3. Scrape the batter into baking molds and place them in the air fryer basket.
4. Bake your mini cornbread for about 22 minutes or until a tester comes out dry and clean.
5. Allow your mini cornbread to cool before unmolding and serving. Bon appétit!

Nutrition: Calories 243; Fat 11g; Carbs 32g; Protein 4g; Sugars 13g; Fiber 8g

5. Classic British scones

Preparation time: 5 minutes
Cooking time: 17 minutes
Servings: 6
Ingredients:

- 1 cup all-purpose flour
- 1 teaspoon baking powder
- 1/4 teaspoon salt
- 1/4 teaspoon grated nutmeg
- 1/2 cup brown sugar
- 2 egg, beaten
- 1/4 cup buttermilk
- 1/2 teaspoon vanilla extract
- 6 tablespoons raisins, soaked for 15 minutes

Directions

1. Prepare your air fryer and set it to 360° f.
2. Mix well all the ingredients.
3. Spoon the batter into baking cups; lower the cups into the air fryer basket.
4. Bake your scones for about 17 minutes or until a tester comes out dry and clean.

Nutrition: Calories 177; Fat 34g; Carbs 4g; Protein 19g

6. Breakfast banana oatmeal

Preparation time: 5 minutes
Cooking time: 12 minutes
Servings: 4
Ingredients:

- 1 cup old-fashioned oats
- 1 cup of coconut milk
- 1 cup of water
- 1 banana, mashed
- 1/2 teaspoon vanilla extract
- 1/2 teaspoon ground cinnamon

- A pinch of grated nutmeg
- A pinch of sea salt

Directions
1. Thoroughly combine all ingredients in a mixing bowl. Spoon the mixture into lightly greased mugs.
2. Then, place the mugs in the air fryer cooking basket.
3. Bake your oatmeal at 380° f for about 12 minutes.

Nutrition: Calories 217; Fat 7g; Carbs 34g; Protein 8g

7. Classic baked oatmeal

Preparation time: 5 minutes
Cooking time: 10 minutes
Servings: 4
Ingredients:

- 1 cup old-fashioned oats
- 1/4 cup agave syrup
- 1 cup milk
- 1 egg, whisked
- 1 cup apple, chopped
- 1/2 teaspoon baking powder
- 1/2 teaspoon ground cinnamon
- A pinch of grated nutmeg
- A pinch of salt

Directions:
1. Thoroughly combine all ingredients in a mixing bowl. Spoon the mixture into four lightly greased ramekins.
2. Then, place the ramekins in the air fryer cooking basket.
3. Bake your oatmeal at 380° f for about 12 minutes.
4. Enjoy!

Nutrition: Calories 277; Fat 6g; Carbs 45g; Protein 9g; Sugars 20g; Fiber 4g

8. Old-fashioned granola

Preparation time: 5 minutes
Cooking time: 15 minutes
Servings: 6
Ingredients:

- 1/2 cup rolled oats
- 1/4 cup wheat germ, toasted
- 1/2 cup dried cranberries
- 1/4 cup pumpkin seeds
- 1/4 cup sunflower seeds
- 1/4 cup pecans, chopped
- 1/4 cup walnuts, chopped
- 1/2 teaspoon vanilla extract
- 1/4 cup agave syrup
- 4 tablespoons coconut oil
- 1 teaspoon pumpkin pie

Directions
1. Start by preheating your air fryer to 350° f.
2. Thoroughly combine all ingredients in a lightly greased baking pan.
3. Then, place the pan in the air fryer cooking basket. Bake your granola for about 15 minutes, stirring every 5 minutes.
4. Stock in a closed container for up to three weeks.

Nutrition: Calories 332; Fat 19g; Carbs 38g; Protein 7g

9. Mushroom and rice bake

Preparation time: 5 minutes
Cooking time: 10 minutes
Servings: 4
Ingredients:

- 1 pound brown mushrooms, chopped
- 1 small onion, peeled and chopped
- 2 tablespoons butter, room temperature
- 2 garlic cloves, minced
- Ground black pepper
- Sea salt, to taste
- 1 cup vegetable broth
- 1 ½ cups brown rice, cooked

Directions:
1. Put your air fryer to 360° f.
2. Thoroughly combine all ingredients in a lightly greased baking pan.
3. Lower the pan into the air fryer cooking basket.

4. Cook for about 10 minutes or until cooked through.

Nutrition: Calories 192; Fat 28g; Carbs 6g; Protein 3g

10. Dried berry bread pudding

Preparation time: 15 minutes
Cooking time: 20 minutes
Servings: 6
Ingredients:

- 2 cups sweet raisin bread, cubed
- 2 eggs, whisked
- 1 cup milk
- 1/2 teaspoon vanilla extract
- 1/4 cup agave syrup
- 1/4 cup dried cherries
- 1/4 cup dried cranberries

Directions
1. Place the bread cubes in a lightly greased baking pan.
2. In a mixing bowl, thoroughly combine the remaining ingredients.
3. Pour the egg/milk mixture over the bread cubes; set aside for 15 minutes to soak.
4. Bake your bread pudding at 350° f for about 20 minutes or until the custard is set but still a little unsteady.
5. Serve at room temperature.

Nutrition: Calories 152; Fat 3g; Carbs 21g; Protein 3g; Sugars 15g

11. Decadent bread pudding

Preparation time: 15 minutes
Cooking time: 20 minutes
Servings: 5
Ingredients:

- 8 slices bread, cubed
- 1 cup of coconut milk
- 1/4 cup coconut oil
- 1 egg, beaten
- 1/4 cup honey
- 1/2 teaspoon ground cinnamon
- 1/4 teaspoon ground cloves
- A pinch of kosher salt
- 1/2 cup prunes, pitted and chopped

Directions
1. Place the bread cubes in a lightly greased baking pan.
2. In a mixing bowl, thoroughly combine the milk, coconut oil, egg, honey, cinnamon, cloves, and salt.
3. Pour the custard mixture over the bread cubes. Fold in the prunes and set aside for 15 minutes to soak.
4. Bake the bread pudding at 350° f for about 20 minutes or until the custard is set but still a little wobbly.

Nutrition: Calories 317; Fat 44g; Carbs 6g; Protein 18g

12. Bourbon ciabatta bread pudding

Preparation time: 10 minutes
Cooking time: 15 minutes
Servings: 5
Ingredients:

- 1 1/2 cups ciabatta bread, cubed
- 2 eggs, whisked
- 1/2 cup double cream
- 1/2 cup milk
- 1/2 teaspoon vanilla extract
- 1 tablespoon bourbon
- 1/4 cup honey
- 1/2 cup golden raisins

Directions:
1. Place the ciabatta bread in a lightly greased baking pan.
2. In a mixing bowl, thoroughly combine the eggs, double cream, milk, vanilla, bourbon, and honey.
3. Pour the egg/cream mixture over the bread cubes. Fold in the raisins and set aside for 15 minutes to soak.
4. Bake your bread pudding at 350° f for about 20 minutes or until the custard is set but still a little wobbly.
5. Serve at room temperature. Enjoy!

Nutrition: Calories 217; Fat 7g; Carbs 35g; Protein 1g; Sugars 26g; Fiber 1g

13. Cheesy cauliflower risotto

Preparation time: 5 minutes
Cooking time: 10 minutes
Servings: 4
Ingredients:

- 2 cups rice, cooked
- 2 tablespoons olive oil
- 1/2 cup cauliflower, chopped
- 1/2 cup vegetable broth
- 4 tablespoons mozzarella cheese, shredded

Directions:

1. Prepare your air fryer to 360° f.
2. Thoroughly combine all ingredients in a lightly greased baking pan.
3. Lower the pan into the air fryer cooking basket.
4. Cook for about 10 minutes or until cooked through.

Nutrition: Calories 218; Fat 11g; Carbs 25g; Protein 5g; Sugars 2g; Fiber 2g

14. Autumn walnut porridge

Preparation time: 5 minutes
Cooking time: 10 minutes
Servings: 4
Ingredients:

- 1/2 cup rolled oats
- 1/2 cup rye flakes
- 1 cup milk
- 1 cup applesauce, unsweetened
- 1/2 cup walnuts, chopped
- A pinch of coarse sea salt
- A pinch of freshly grated nutmeg

Directions:

1. Thoroughly combine all ingredients in a mixing bowl.
2. Spoon the mixture into a lightly greased casserole dish.
3. Lower the dish into the air fryer cooking basket.
4. Bake your oatmeal at 380° f for about 12 minutes.

Nutrition: Calories 249; Fat 10g; Carbs 33g; Protein 3g; Sugars 9g; Fiber 5g

15. Traditional French toast

Preparation time: 5 minutes
Cooking time: 5 minutes
Servings: 3
Ingredients:

- 2 eggs
- 1/2 cup milk
- 2 tablespoons butter, room temperature
- 1 teaspoon vanilla extract
- 1/4 teaspoon grated nutmeg
- 1/2 teaspoon cinnamon powder
- 3 slices challah bread

Directions:

1. In a mixing bowl, thoroughly combine the eggs, milk, butter, vanilla, nutmeg, and cinnamon.
2. Then dip each piece of bread into the egg mixture; place the bread slices in a lightly greased baking pan.
3. Air fry the bread slices at 330° f for about 4 minutes.
4. Turn them over and cook for more minutes. Enjoy!

Nutrition: Calories 194; Fat 12g; Carbs 13g; Protein 7g; Sugars 3g; Fiber 1g

16. Egg stuffed buns

Preparation time: 10 minutes
Cooking time: 25 minutes
Servings: 4
Ingredients:

- 3 eggs, whisked
- 4 ounces pizza dough
- 3 bacon slices
- 1 ounce cream cheese softened
- 1 tablespoon fresh chive, chopped
- Cooking spray

Directions:

1. Place a suitable nonstick skillet over medium heat and add bacon to sauté for 10 minutes.
2. Transfer the cooked crispy bacon to a plate lined with a paper towel and crumble it.

3. Crack eggs in the same pan and stir cook for 1 minute, then transfer to a bowl.
4. Add chives, bacon, and cream cheese to the egg and whisk well.
5. Divide the pizza dough into 4 equal pieces and roll each into 5inch circles.
6. Add 1/4 of the egg mixture to the center of each dough circle.
7. Brush the edges of the circle with water and pinch the edges to seal together.
8. Set air fryer on poultry mode for 15 minutes at 350° f, then press preheat.
9. Once preheated, place the prepared dumplings in the basket, return it to the fryer, and press start. Enjoy.

Nutrition: Calories 284; Fat 9g; Carbs 46g; Fiber 6g; Sugar 5g; Protein 9g

17. Ham and cheese sandwiches

Preparation time: 10 minutes
Cooking time: 18 minutes
Servings: 2
Ingredients:

- 1 egg
- 2 ounces deli ham, sliced
- Salt and black pepper, to taste
- 2 ounces deli turkey, sliced
- 2 bread slices
- 2 1/2 ounces swiss cheese, sliced
- 1 teaspoon butter, melted
- 3 tablespoons half & half cream

Directions:

1. Whisk egg with salt, black pepper, and a half and half cream in a bowl.
2. Put one bread slice on a working surface and top each slice with ham, turkey, and swiss cheese slice. Place the remaining bread slice on top.
3. Press each sandwich, then dip them in the egg mixture.
4. Place the dipped sandwiches in an aluminum sheet greased with butter.
5. Set on poultry mode for 10 minutes at 350° f, then press preheat.
6. Once preheated, place the prepared sandwiches in the air fryer basket, return it to the fryer, and press start.
7. Flip the sandwiches and continue cooking for 8 minutes. Enjoy.

Nutrition: Calories 412; Fat 28g; Carbs 48g; Fiber 9g; Sugar 5g; Protein 19g

18. Cheese sausage pockets

Preparation time: 10 minutes
Cooking time: 10 minutes
Servings: 6
Ingredients:

- 5 eggs
- 1/2 cup sausage crumbles, cooked
- 1/2 cup bacon, cooked
- 1 box puff pastry sheet
- 1/2 cup cheddar cheese, shredded

Directions:

1. Place a suitable nonstick skillet on medium heat and crack eggs one by one.
2. Stir cook until set then adds bacon and sausages.
3. Spread the puff pastry on a cutting board, then slice it into equal sized rectangles.
4. Add a spoonful of egg mixture and cheese to the center of half of the rectangle.
5. Place the remaining rectangles to cover the filling and pinch the edges together.
6. Set on poultry mode for 10 minutes at 370° f, then press "preheat."
7. Once preheated, place the prepared pockets in the basket, return it to the fryer, and press "start."
8. Serve right away.

Nutrition: Calories 387; Fat 6g; Carbs 34g; Fiber 9g; Sugar 13g; Protein 6g

19. Sausage wraps

Preparation time: 10 minutes
Cooking time: 3 minutes
Servings: 4
Ingredients:

- 8 mini sausages

- 2 pieces American cheese, cut into 4 pieces
- 8 refrigerated crescent roll dough
- Ketchup, for dipping

Directions:
1. Spread the crescent rolls on a working surface.
2. Place cheese and sausage over a wide portion of each crescent roll.
3. Wrap the rolls around the sausage and tuck the ends.
4. Set air fryer on poultry mode for 3 minutes at 380 °f, then press preheat.
5. Once preheated, place the prepared wraps in the basket, return it to the fryer, and press start.
6. Enjoy.

Nutrition: Calories 331; Fat 5g; Carbs 69g; Fiber 12g; Sugar 15g; Protein 7g

20. Avocado flautas
Preparation time: 10 minutes
Cooking time: 24 minutes
Servings: 8
Ingredients:
- 1 tablespoon butter
- 8 eggs, whisked
- 1/2 teaspoon salt
- 1/4 teaspoon black pepper
- 1 1/2 teaspoon cumin
- 1 teaspoon chili powder
- 8 fajita size tortillas
- 4 ounces cream cheese, softened
- 8 cooked bacon slices
- 1/2 cup Mexican cheese, shredded
- 1/2 cup cotija cheese, crumbled
- Avocado crème
- 2 small avocados, peeled
- 1/2 cup sour cream
- 1 lime, juiced
- 1/2 teaspoon salt
- 1/4 teaspoon black pepper

Directions:
1. Place a skillet with butter over medium heat.
2. Add eggs and stir cook for 4 minutes, then stir in salt, chili powder, pepper, and cumin.
3. Spread cream cheese over each tortilla and place a piece of bacon over it.
4. Top the bacon with an egg scramble and cheese shreds.
5. Roll each tortilla tightly, then place 4 of them in the fryer basket.
6. Set the air fryer on poultry mode for 12 minutes at 400 ° f, then press preheat.
7. Once preheated, place the prepared flautas in the air fryer basket, return it to the fryer, and press start.
8. Cook the remaining tortillas using the same steps.
9. Blend avocado crème ingredients in a blender until smooth.
10. Enjoy with baked flautas with avocado cheese and cotija cheese.

Nutrition: Calories 212; Fat 18g; Carbs 16g; Fiber 4g; Sugar 8g; Protein 13 g

21. Sausage burritos
Preparation time: 10 minutes
Cooking time: 12 minutes
Servings: 6
Ingredients:
- 6 medium tortillas
- 6 scrambled eggs
- 1/2pound ground sausage, browned
- 1/2 bell pepper, minced
- 1/3 cup bacon bits
- 1/2 cup cheddar cheese, shredded
- Oil for spraying

Directions:
1. Toss scrambled eggs with bacon bits, sausage, cheese, and bell pepper in a large bowl.
2. Place one tortilla on a working surface at a time.
3. Add 1/2 cup of the prepared egg mixture to the center of this tortilla.
4. Fold its two sides and roll it tightly.

5. Repeat the same cooking steps with the remaining tortillas and egg mixture.
6. Set poultry mode for 6 minutes at 330° f, then press preheat.
7. Once preheated, place 3 burritos in the air fryer basket, return it to the fryer, and press start.
8. Cook the remaining burritos in the air fryer using the same steps. Enjoy fresh.

Nutrition: Calories 319; Fat 3g; Carbs 18g; Sugar 49g; Fiber 6g; Protein 2 g

22. Morning potatoes
Preparation time: 10 minutes
Cooking time: 18 minutes
Servings: 4
Ingredients:
- 2 medium russet potatoes, diced
- 1/2 teaspoon salt
- 1 tablespoon olive oil
- 1/4 teaspoon garlic powder
- Chopped parsley for garnish

Directions:
1. Dice the washed potatoes into half inch cubes.
2. Soak the potatoes in ice-cold water for 45 minutes.
3. Drain the potatoes and pat them dry.
4. Toss the potatoes with salt, garlic powder, and olive oil in a large bowl.
5. Set air fryer on fries mode for 18 minutes at 400 ° f, then press preheat.
6. Once preheated, place the prepared potatoes in the basket, return it to the fryer, and press start.
7. Shake the potatoes when cooked halfway through, then resume cooking.
8. Garnish with parsley, then enjoy.

Nutrition: Calories 134; Fat 7g; Carbs 51g; Fiber 7g; Sugar 3g; Protein 2g

23. Avocado boats
Preparation time: 10 minutes
Cooking time: 10 minutes
Servings: 4
Ingredients:
- 2 avocados, halved and pitted
- 2 tomatoes, seeded and diced
- 1/4 cup red onion, diced
- 2 tablespoons fresh cilantro, chopped
- 1 tablespoon jalapeno, diced
- 1 tablespoon lime juice
- 1/2 teaspoon salt
- 1/4 teaspoon black pepper
- 4 eggs

Directions:
1. Remove the avocado flesh from its outer shell and keep the shells aside.
2. Mash avocado flesh in a bowl and stir in jalapeno, cilantro, tomato, onion, salt, pepper, and lime juice.
3. Cover this avocado mixture and refrigerate.
4. Set on poultry mode for 10 minutes at 350° f, then press preheat.
5. Arrange all the avocado shells on a foil sheet, crack one egg into each shell carefully.
6. Once preheated, place the prepared shells in the air fryer basket, return it to the fryer, and press start.
7. Drizzle salt and black pepper on top.
8. Serve with avocado salsa.

Nutrition: Calories 322; Fat 18;g Carbs 16g; Dietary Fiber 4g; Sugar 8g; Protein 13g

24. Chicken omelet
Preparation time: 10 minutes
Cooking time: 18 minutes
Servings: 4
Ingredients:
- 4 eggs
- 1/2 cup cooked chicken breast, diced
- 2 tablespoons cheddar cheese, shredded
- 1/2 teaspoon salt
- 1/4 teaspoon black pepper
- 1/4 teaspoon garlic powder

- 1/4 teaspoon onion powder

Directions:
1. Grease two 4 oz. Ramekins with olive oil and keep them aside.
2. Crack two eggs into each of the greased ramekins.
3. Drizzle seasonings and cheese into each of the ramekins.
4. Whisk well gently and stir in ¼ cup chicken to each ramekin.
5. Set air fryer on poultry mode for 18 minutes at 330 ° f, then press preheat.
6. Once preheated, place the ramekins in the basket, return it to the fryer, and press start.
7. Enjoy.

Nutrition: Calories 197; Fat 14g; Sugar 1g; Fiber 4g; Protein 9g

25. Cajun sausages
Preparation time: 10 minutes
Cooking time: 16 minutes
Servings: 3
Ingredients:
- 1 1/2 lbs. Ground sausage
- 1 teaspoon chili flakes
- 1 teaspoon dried thyme
- 1 teaspoon onion powder
- 1/2 teaspoon each paprika and cayenne
- Sea salt and black pepper to taste
- 2 teaspoons brown sugar
- 3 teaspoons minced garlic
- 2 teaspoons tabasco
- Herbs to garnish

Directions:
1. Mix the ground sausage with herbs and spices in a bowl.
2. Stir in tabasco sauce and mix well.
3. Make 3 inches wide and 5inchthick patties out of the sausage mixture.
4. Place 4 patties in the air fryer basket and spray them with cooking oil.
5. Set air fryer on poultry mode for 16 minutes at 370° f, then press preheat.
6. Once preheated, put patties in the air fryer basket, return it to the fryer, and press start.
7. Flip the patties when cooked halfway through.
8. Cook the remaining patties in the air fryer using the same steps.
9. Enjoy with your favorite sauce.

Nutrition: Calories 138; Fat 7g; Carbs 5g; Fiber 3g; Sugar 7g; Protein 13g

26. Kale potato nuggets
Preparation time: 15 minutes
Cooking time: 18 minutes
Serving: 4
Ingredients:
- 2 cups potatoes, chopped
- 1 teaspoon olive oil
- 1 garlic clove, minced
- 4 cups kale, chopped
- 1/8 cup almond milk
- 1/4 teaspoon sea salt
- 1/8 teaspoon ground black pepper
- Vegetable oil spray as needed

Directions:
1. Set a cooking pot filled with water over medium heat.
2. Add potatoes to this boiling water and cook for 30 minutes until soft.
3. Meanwhile, sauté garlic with oil in a skillet over medium high heat until golden.
4. Stir in kale and sauté for 3 minutes., then transfer this mixture to a bowl.
5. Drain the boiled potatoes and add them to the kale.
6. Mix the potatoes with a potato masher.
7. Stir in salt, black pepper, and milk them, mix well.
8. Make 1inch potato nuggets out of this mixture.
9. Place these nuggets in the air fryer basket.
10. Return the air fryer basket to the air fryer.
11. Select the air fry mode at 390° f for 15 minutes.
12. Flip the nuggets once cooked halfway through, then resume cooking. Serve warm.

Nutrition: Calories 113 Fat 3g Carbs 20g Fiber 3g Sugar 1g Protein 5g

27. Air fried falafel
Preparation time: 15 minutes
Cooking time: 10 minutes
Serving: 6
Ingredients:
- 1 1/2 cups dry garbanzo beans
- 1/2 cup fresh parsley, chopped
- 1/2 cup fresh cilantro, chopped
- 1/2 cup white onion, chopped
- 7 garlic cloves, minced
- 2 tablespoons all-purpose flour
- 1/2 teaspoons sea salt
- 1 tablespoon ground cumin
- 1/8 teaspoons ground cardamom
- 1 teaspoon ground coriander
- 1/8 teaspoons cayenne pepper

Directions:
1. Soak garbanzo beans in a bowl filled with water for 24 hours.
2. Drain and transfer the beans to a cooking pot filled with water.
3. Cook the beans for 1 hour or more on simmer until soft.
4. Add cilantro, onion, garlic, and parsley to a food processor and blend until finely chopped.
5. Drain the cooked garbanzo beans and transfer them to the food processor.
6. Add salt, cardamom, cayenne, coriander, cumin, and flour.
7. Blend until it makes a rough dough.
8. Transfer this falafel mixture to a bowl, cover with a plastic wrap and refrigerate for 2 hours.
9. Make 1 ½ inches balls out of this bean's mixture.
10. Lightly press the balls and place them in the air fryer basket.
11. Return the air fryer basket to the air fryer.
12. Select the air fry mode at 400° f for 10 minutes.
13. Flip the falafels once cooked halfway through the resume cooking.
14. Serve warm.

Nutrition: Calories 206; Fat 4g; Carbs 35g; Fiber 4g; Sugar 9g; Protein 16g

28. Veggie bites
Preparation time: 10 minutes
Cooking time: 45 minutes
Serving: 6
Ingredients:
- 1 large broccoli, cut into florets
- 6 large carrots, diced
- A handful of garden peas
- 1/2 cauliflower, riced
- 1 large onion, peeled and diced
- 1 small zucchini, diced
- 2 leeks, sliced
- 1 can coconut milk
- 2 oz. Plain flour
- 1 cm cube ginger peeled and grated
- 1 tablespoon garlic puree
- 1 tablespoon olive oil
- 1 tablespoon Thai green curry paste
- 1 tablespoon coriander
- 1 tablespoon mixed spice
- 1 teaspoon cumin
- Salt and black pepper, to taste

Directions:
1. Place leek and courgette in a steamer basket and steam them for 20 minutes.
2. Sauté onion, ginger, and garlic with olive oil in a skillet until soft.
3. Add steamed leek and courgette to the skillet and sauté for 5 minutes.
4. Stir in coconut milk and the rest of the spices.
5. Mix well, then add the cauliflower rice then cook for 10 minutes.
6. Remove the hot skillet from the heat and allow it to cool.
7. Cover and refrigerate this mixture for 1 hour.
8. Slice the mixture into bite size pieces and place these pieces in the air fryer basket.

9. Return the air fryer basket to the air fryer.
10. Select the air fry mode at 350° f for 10 minutes.
11. Carefully flip the bites once cooked halfway through, then resume cooking. Serve warm.

Nutrition: Calories 270; Fat 16g; Carbs 33g; Fiber 5g; Sugar 7g; Protein 4g

29. Fried mushrooms

Preparation time: 15 minutes
Cooking time: 25 minutes
Serving: 6
Ingredients:

- 2 cups oyster mushrooms
- 1 cup buttermilk
- 1 ½ cups all-purpose flour
- 1 teaspoon salt
- 1 teaspoon black pepper
- 1 teaspoon garlic powder
- 1 teaspoon onion powder
- 1 teaspoon smoked paprika
- 1 teaspoon cumin
- 1 tablespoon oil

Directions:

1. At 375° f, preheat your air fryer on air fry mode.
2. Clean the mushrooms and then soak them in buttermilk for 15 minutes.
3. Mix all-purpose flour with onion powder, garlic powder, black pepper, salt, smoked paprika, and cumin in a suitable bowl.
4. Coat the mushrooms with flour mixture and then dip again with buttermilk.
5. Coat the mushrooms again with flour and buttermilk.
6. Place the coated mushrooms in the air fryer basket.
7. Return the air fryer basket to the air fryer and cook for 10 minutes.
8. Flip the mushrooms once cooked halfway through. Serve warm.

Nutrition: Calories 166; Fat 2g; Carbs 28g; Fiber 8g; Sugar 7g; Protein 8g

30. General Tso's cauliflower

Preparation time: 15 minutes
Cooking time: 28 minutes
Serving: 4
Ingredients:

- Cauliflower
- 1/2 head cauliflower, cut into florets
- 1/2 cup flour
- 2 large eggs, whisked
- 1 cup panko breadcrumbs
- 1/4 teaspoons salt
- 1/4 teaspoons black pepper
- General Tso's sauce
- 1 tablespoon sesame oil
- 2 garlic cloves, minced
- 1 tablespoon fresh ginger, grated
- 1/2 cup vegetable broth
- 1/4 cup of soy sauce
- 1/4 cup of rice vinegar
- 1/4 cup brown sugar
- 2 tablespoons tomato paste
- 2 tablespoons cornstarch
- 2 tablespoons cold water

Directions:

1. At 400° f, preheat your ninja air fryer on air fry mode.
2. Whisk egg in one bowl spread panko in another bowl and add flour to another bowl.
3. Dredge the cauliflower through the flour, dip in the egg and then coat with breadcrumbs.
4. Place the prepared cauliflower florets in the air fryer basket.
5. Return the air fryer basket to the air fryer and cook for 20 minutes.
6. Flip the florets once cooked halfway through, then resume cooking.
7. Meanwhile, sauté ginger, garlic, and sesame oil in a saucepan for 2 minutes.
8. Stir in the rest of the sauce ingredients except cornstarch.

9. Mix cornstarch with 2 tablespoons water in a bowl.
10. Pour the slurry into the sauce, mix, and cook until the sauce thickens.
11. Get the sauce from the heat and allow it to cool.
12. Toss in the baked cauliflower and mix well to coat. Serve warm.

Nutrition: Calories 288; Fat 9g; Sodium 761mg; Carbs 46g; Fiber 4g; Sugar 12g; Protein 6g

31. Parmesan eggplant

Preparation time: 15 minutes
Cooking time: 15 minutes
Serving: 4
Ingredients:

- 1/2 cup flour
- 1/2 cup almond milk
- 1/2 cup panko breadcrumbs
- 2 tablespoons parmesan, grated
- Onion powder to taste
- Garlic powder to taste
- 1 large eggplant, stems removed and sliced
- Salt and black pepper, to taste
- Eggplant parmesan:
- 1 cup marinara sauce
- 1/2 cup mozzarella shreds
- Parmesan, grated

Directions:

1. Mix panko crumbs with garlic powder, black pepper, salt, onion powder, and vegan parmesan in a bowl.
2. First coat the eggplant slices with flour, then dip in the almond milk and finally coat with breadcrumbs mixture.
3. Place the coated eggplant slices in the air fryer basket.
4. Put the basket back to the air fryer.
5. Select the air fry mode at 390° f for 15 minutes.
6. Flip the eggplant slices once cooked halfway through.
7. Place the eggplant slices on the serving plate and top them with marinara sauce and cheese. Serve warm.

Nutrition: Calories 231; Fat 9g; Carbs 38g; Fiber 4g; Sugar 7g; Protein 3g

32. Black bean burger

Preparation time: 15 minutes
Cooking time: 15 minutes
Serving: 6
Ingredients:

- 1 1/3 cups rolled oats
- 16 ounces canned black bean
- 3/4 cup salsa
- 1 tablespoon soy sauce
- 1 1/4 teaspoon mild chili powder
- 1/41/2 teaspoon chipotle chile powder
- 1/2 teaspoon garlic powder
- 1/2 cup corn kernels

Directions:

1. Add all the rolled oats to a food processor and pulse to get a coarse meal.
2. Add black beans, salsa, soy sauce, chili powder, chile powder, and garlic powder.
3. Blend again for 1 minute, then transfer to a bowl.
4. Stir in corn kernel, then make six patties out of this mixture.
5. Place the black bean patties in the air fryer basket.
6. Return the air fryer basket to the air fryer.
7. Select the air fry mode at 375° f for 15 minutes.
8. Flip the patties once cooked halfway through and resumed cooking.
9. Serve warm.

Nutrition: Calories 350; Fat 6g; Carbs 66g; Fiber 14g; Sugar 3g; Protein 19g

33. Potato cakes

Preparation time: 10 minutes
Cooking time: 35 minutes
Serving: 4
Ingredients:

- 4 cups potatoes, diced
- 1 bunch green onions, chopped
- 1 lime, zest, and juice

- 11/2inch knob of fresh ginger
- 1 tablespoon tamari
- 4 tablespoons red curry paste
- 4 sheets nori, chopped
- 1 can heart of palm, drained
- 3/4 cup canned artichoke hearts, drained
- Black pepper, to taste
- Salt, to taste

Directions:
1. Add potato cubes to a pot filled with water.
2. Place it over medium heat and cook until potatoes are soft.
3. Clear the potatoes and transfer them to a suitable bowl.
4. Mash the potatoes with a masher, then add green onions, lime juice, and remaining ingredients.
5. Mix well and stir in artichoke shreds.
6. Stir well and make 4 patties out of this mixture.
7. Place the patties in the air fryer basket.
8. Return the basket to the air fryer.
9. Select the air fry mode at 375° f for 10 minutes.
10. Flip the patties once cooked halfway through and resume cooking. Serve warm.

Nutrition: Calories 208; Fat 5g; Carbs 31g; Fiber 8g; Sugar 5g; Protein 9g

34. Veggie wontons
Preparation time: 15 minutes
Cooking time: 8 minutes
Serving: 15
Ingredients:
- 30 wonton wrappers
- 3/4 cup cabbage, grated
- 1/2 cup white onion, grated
- 1/2 cup carrot, grated
- 1/2 cup mushrooms, chopped
- 3/4 cup red pepper, chopped
- 1 tablespoon chili sauce
- 1 teaspoon garlic powder
- 1/2 teaspoon white pepper
- Pinch of salt
- 1/4 cup water
- Spray olive oil

Directions:
1. Sauté cabbage, onion, carrot, mushrooms, and red pepper with olive oil in a skillet until soft.
2. Mix chili sauce, white pepper, salt, and garlic powder, then pour in the vegetables.
3. Stir and cook for 2 minutes until well mixed.
4. Remove the filling from the heat and allow it cool.
5. Spread the wonton wrappers on the working surface.
6. Add 1 tablespoon of vegetable filling on top of each wrapper.
7. Wet their edges, then fold each wrapper in half and roll them in a wonton.
8. Place the wrapped wontons in the air fryer basket.
9. Return the basket to the air fryer.
10. Select the air fry mode at 320° f for 6 minutes. Serve warm.
11. You can serve with red chunky salsa or chili sauce.
12. Add ground chicken to the filling.

Nutrition: Calories 193; Fat 1g; Carbs 37g; Fiber 6g; Sugar 9g; Protein 6g

35. Garlic mogo chips
Preparation time: 20 minutes
Cooking time: 25 minutes
Serving: 4
Ingredients:
- Mogo chips
- 1 lb. Mogo chips
- Salt to taste
- 1/2 teaspoon turmeric powder
- 1/2 teaspoon garlic powder
- 1 tablespoon lime juice
- 1/2 teaspoon oil
- 8 cups of water
- Masala mix
- 1 teaspoon red chili powder

- Pinch dried chili flakes
- 1/2 teaspoon garlic powder
- Salt to taste
- 1 teaspoon lime juice
- 1/2 teaspoon lime zest
- 1 teaspoon oil

Directions:
1. Mix water with oil, lime juice, turmeric powder, garlic powder, and salt in a saucepan.
2. Stir in mogo chips and cook for 8-10 minutes until the chips are boiled.
3. Drain and allow the chips to cool.
4. Mix all the spices for masala mix in a suitable bowl.
5. Toss in mogo chips and mix well to coat.
6. Spread the chips in the air fryer basket.
7. Return the air fryer basket to the air fryer.
8. Select the air fry mode at 400° f for 5 minutes.
9. Toss the chips once cooked halfway through, then resume cooking. Serve warm.

Nutrition: Calories 212; Fat 18g; Carbs 26g; Fiber 4g; Sugar 8g; Protein 3g

36. Simple and easy croutons
Preparation time: 5 minutes
Cooking time: 8 minutes
Servings: 4
Ingredients:
- 2 slices friendly bread
- 1 tablespoon olive oil
- Hot soup, for serving

Directions:
1. Cut the slices of bread into medium-sized chunks.
2. Brush the air fryer basket with the oil and place the chunks inside.
3. Select the air fry function and cook at 390°f (199°cfor 8 minutes.
4. Serve with hot soup.

Nutrition: Calories 120; Fat 9g; Carbs 10g; Protein 2g; Sugars 2g; Fiber 0g

37. Sweet corn and carrot fritters
Preparation time: 10 minutes
Cooking time: 8 11 minutes
Servings: 4
Ingredients:
- 1 medium-sized carrot, grated
- 1 yellow onion, finely chopped
- 4 ounces (113g) canned sweet corn kernels, drained
- 1 teaspoon sea salt flakes
- 1 tablespoon chopped fresh cilantro
- 1 medium-sized egg, whisked
- 2 tablespoons plain milk
- 1 cup grated parmesan cheese
- 1/4 cup flour
- 1/3 teaspoon baking powder
- 1/3 teaspoon sugar
- Cooking spray

Directions:
1. Select the bake function and preheat to 350°f (177°c).
2. Place the grated carrot in a colander and press down to squeeze out any excess moisture. Dry it with a paper towel.
3. Combine the carrots with the remaining ingredients.
4. Mold 1 tablespoon of the mixture into a ball and press it down with your hand or a spoon to flatten it. Repeat with the remaining mixture.
5. Spritz the balls with cooking spray.
6. Arrange in the air fryer basket, taking care not to overlap any balls. Bake for 8 to 11 minutes, or until they're firm. Serve warm.

Nutrition: Calories 260; Fat 14g; Carbs 26g; Protein 9g; Sugars 2g; Fiber 8g

38. Simple pea delight
Preparation time: 5 minutes
Cooking time: 15 minutes
Servings: 4
Ingredients:
- 1 cup flour

- 1 teaspoon baking powder
- 3 eggs
- 1 cup of coconut milk
- 1 cup cream cheese
- 3 tablespoons pea protein
- 1/2 cup chicken or turkey strips
- Pinch of sea salt
- 1 cup mozzarella cheese

Directions:
1. Select the bake function and preheat to 390°f (199°c).
2. Mix all ingredients using a large wooden spoon.
3. Spoon equal amounts of the mixture into muffin cups and bake for 15 minutes.
4. Serve immediately.

Nutrition: Calories 188; Fat 10g; Carbs 19g; Protein 8g; Sugars 2g

39. Cheesy sausage balls

Preparation time: 5 minutes
Cooking time: 15 minutes
Servings: 6
Ingredients:

- 12 ounces (340g) jimmy dean's sausage
- 6 ounces (170g) shredded cheddar cheese
- 10 cheddar cubes

Directions:
1. Mix the shredded cheese and sausage.
2. Divide the mixture into 12 equal parts to be stuffed.
3. Add a cube of cheese to the center of the sausage and roll into balls.
4. Select the air fry function and cook at 375°f (191°c) for 15 minutes, or until crisp.
5. Serve immediately.

Nutrition: Calories 109; Fat 8g; Carbs 7g; Protein 5g; Sugars 4g; Fiber 2g

40. Air fried broccoli

Preparation time: 5 minutes
Cooking time: 6 minutes
Servings: 1
Ingredients:

- 4 egg yolks
- 1/4 cup butter, melted
- 2 cups coconut flour
- Salt and pepper, to taste
- 2 cups broccoli florets

Directions:
1. Whisk the egg yolks and melted butter together. Throw in the coconut flour, salt, and pepper, then stir again to combine well.
2. Dip each broccoli floret into the mixture and place it in the air fryer basket. Select the air fry function and cook at 400°f (204°c) for 6 minutes.
3. Work in batches if necessary. Take care when removing them from the air fryer oven and serve immediately.

Nutrition: Calories 43; Fat 1g; Carbs 8g; Protein 3g; Sugars 2g; Fiber 3g

41. Cheesy potato patties

Preparation time: 5 minutes
Cooking time: 10 minutes
Servings: 8
Ingredients:

- 2 pounds (907g) white potatoes
- 1/2 cup finely chopped scallions
- 1/2 teaspoon ground black pepper
- 1 tablespoon fine sea salt
- 1/2 teaspoon hot paprika
- 2 cups shredded colby cheese
- 1/1 cup canola oil
- 1 cup crushed crackers

Directions:
1. Select the bake function and preheat to 360°f (182°c.)
2. Boil the potatoes until soft. Dry them off and peel them before mashing thoroughly, leaving no lumps.
3. Combine the mashed potatoes with scallions, pepper, salt, paprika, and cheese.

4. Mold the mixture into balls with your hands and press with your palm to flatten them into patties.
5. In a shallow dish, combine the canola oil and crushed crackers. Coat the patties in the crumb mixture.
6. Bake the patties for about 10 minutes, in multiple batches if necessary. Serve hot.

Nutrition: Calories 245; Fat 15g; Carbs 22g; Protein 7g; Sugars 5g; Fiber 2g

42. Spinach and carrot balls

Preparation time: 10 minutes
Cooking time: 10 minutes
Servings: 4
Ingredients:

- 2 slices of toasted bread
- 1 carrot, peeled and grated
- 1 package fresh spinach, blanched and chopped
- 1/2 onion, chopped
- 1 egg, beaten
- 1/2 teaspoon garlic powder
- 1 teaspoon minced garlic
- 1 teaspoon salt
- 1/2 teaspoon black pepper
- 1 tablespoon nutritional yeast
- 1 tablespoon flour

Directions:
1. In a food processor, pulse the toasted bread to form breadcrumbs. Transfer into a shallow dish or bowl.
2. Mix well all the other ingredients.
3. Shape the mixture into small sized balls using hands. Roll the balls in the breadcrumbs, ensuring to cover them well.
4. Put in the air fryer basket. Select the air fry function and cook at 390°f (199°c) for 10 minutes.
5. Serve immediately.

Nutrition: Calories 139; Fat 7g; Carbs 13g; Protein 3g; Sugars 7g; Fiber 1g

43. Bangbang chicken

Preparation time: 10 minutes
Cooking time: 15 minutes
Servings: 6
Ingredients:

- 1/2 cup mayonnaise
- 2 tablespoons honey
- 1/2 tablespoon sriracha sauce
- 1 cup buttermilk
- 3/4 flour
- 1/2 cup cornstarch
- Egg 1
- Oil

Directions:
1. Add all ingredients in a mixing bowl to create bang bang chicken sauce. Whisk before it's all mixed.
2. In the air fryer, first create buttermilk batter by mixing flour, egg, corn starch, pepper, salt, sriracha sauce, and buttermilk to produce bang bang meat. And whisk until mixed.
3. Before inserting the poultry, grease your air fryer with some oil of your choosing.
4. Drop bits of chicken in buttermilk batter, and then apply breadcrumbs to the air fryer. Air fried for 8-10 minutes at 375°f or until chicken is boiling thru. When on the other hand, rotate the chicken bits.
5. Drizzle over the chicken with the sauce and serve with leafy greens or egg.

Nutrition: Calories 480; Fat 33g; Carbs 35g; Protein 21g; Sugars 7g; Fiber 1g

44. Baconwrapped beef hot dog

Preparation time: 5 minutes
Cooking time: 10 minutes
Servings: 4
Ingredients:

- 4 slices sugar free bacon
- 4 beef hot dogs

Directions:
1. Select the bake function and preheat to 370°f (188°c).

2. Get a slice of bacon and wrap it around the hot dog, securing it with a toothpick. Repeat with the other bacon and hot dogs, placing each wrapped dog in the air fryer basket.
3. Bake for 10 minutes, turning halfway through.
4. Once hot and crispy, the hot dogs are ready to serve.

Nutrition: Calories 230; Fat 10g; Carbs 26g; Protein 8g; Sugars 3g; Fiber 1g

45. Carrot and celery croquettes

Preparation time: 10 minutes
Cooking time: 6 minutes
Servings: 4
Ingredients:

- 2 medium-sized carrots, trimmed and grated
- 2 medium-sized celery stalks, trimmed and grated
- 1/2 cup finely chopped leek
- 1 tablespoon garlic paste
- 1/4 teaspoon freshly cracked black pepper
- 1 teaspoon fine sea salt
- 1 tablespoon finely chopped fresh dill
- 1 egg, lightly whisked
- 1/4 cup flour
- 1/4 teaspoon baking powder
- 1/2 cup breadcrumbs
- Cooking spray
- Chive mayo, for serving

Directions:
1. Clear the excess liquid from the carrots and celery by placing them on a paper towel.
2. Stir together the vegetables with all of the other ingredients, save for the breadcrumbs and chive mayo.
3. Use your hands to mold 1 tablespoon of the vegetable mixture into a ball and repeat with all of the mixtures.
4. Flatten each ball using a palette knife or your hand. Cover completely with breadcrumbs. Spritz the croquettes with cooking spray.
5. Arrange the croquettes in a single layer in the air fryer basket. Select the air fry function and cook at 360°f (182°c) for 6 minutes.
6. Serve warm with the chive mayo on the side.

Nutrition: Calories 90; Fat 4g; Carbs 11g; Protein 2g; Sugars 3g; Fiber: 3g

46. Bistro potato wedges

Preparation time: 10 minutes
Cooking time: 13 minutes
Servings: 4
Ingredients:

- 1 pound (454g) fingerling potatoes, cut into wedges
- 1 teaspoon extra virgin olive oil
- 1/2 teaspoon garlic powder
- Salt and pepper, to taste
- 1/2 cup raw cashews, soaked in water overnight
- 1/2 teaspoon ground turmeric
- 1/2 teaspoon paprika
- 1 tablespoon nutritional yeast
- 1 teaspoon fresh lemon juice
- 2 tablespoons to 1/4 cup water

Directions:
1. Get a bowl and put the potato wedges, olive oil, garlic powder, and salt and pepper, making sure to coat the potatoes well.
2. Move potatoes to the air fryer basket. Select the air fry function and cook at 400°f (204°c) for 10 minutes).
3. In the meantime, prepare the cheese sauce. Pulse the cashews, turmeric, paprika, nutritional yeast, lemon juice, and water together in a food processor. You can put more water to achieve your desired consistency.
4. When the potatoes are finished cooking, transfer to a bowl and add the cheese sauce on top. Air fry for an additional 3 minutes.
5. Serve hot.

Nutrition: Calories 100; Fat 5g; Carbs 18g; Protein 2g; Sugars 1g; Fiber 2g

47. Baked chorizo scotch eggs

Preparation time: 10 minutes
Cooking time: 15 – 20 minutes
Servings: 4

Ingredients:

- 1 pound (454g) Mexican chorizo or other seasoned sausage meat)
- 4 soft boiled eggs plus 1 raw egg
- 1 tablespoon water
- 1/2 cup all-purpose flour
- 1 cup panko breadcrumbs
- Cooking spray

Directions:
1. Divide the chorizo into 4 equal portions. Flatten each portion into a disc. Put the soft boiled egg in the center of each disc.
2. Wrap the chorizo around the egg, encasing it completely. Place the encased eggs on a plate and chill for at least 30 minutes.
3. Select the bake function and preheat to 360°f (182°c).
4. Beat the raw egg with 1 tablespoon of water. Place the flour on a small plate and the panko on a second plate.
5. Work with 1 egg at a time, roll the encased egg in the flour, and then dip it in the egg mixture. Dredge the egg in the panko and place on a plate. Repeat with the remaining eggs.
6. Spray the eggs with oil and place them in the air fryer basket. Bake for 10 minutes.
7. Rotate and cook for an additional 5 to 10 minutes, or until browned and crisp on all sides. Serve immediately.

Nutrition: Calories 268; Fat 17g; Carbs 9g; Protein 18g; Sugars 1g; Fiber 0g

48. Buttery sweet potatoes

Preparation time: 5 minutes
Cooking time: 10 minutes
Servings: 4
Ingredients:

- 2 tablespoons butter, melted
- 1 tablespoon light brown sugar
- 2 peeled sweet potatoes, cut into ½inch cubes
- Cooking spray

Directions:
1. Line the air fryer basket with parchment paper.
2. Stir the brown sugar and melted butter until blended in a bowl. Toss the sweet potatoes in the butter mixture until coated.
3. Place the sweet potatoes on the parchment and spritz with oil.
4. Select the air fry function and cook at 400°f (204°c) for 5 minutes. Shake the basket, spritz the sweet potatoes with oil, and air fry for 5 minutes more.
5. Serve immediately.

Nutrition: Calories 260; Fat 3g; Carbs 55g; Protein 3g; Sugars 1g; Fiber 8g

49. Pomegranate avocado fries

Preparation time: 5 minutes
Cooking time: 8 minutes
Servings: 4
Ingredients:

- 1 cup panko breadcrumbs
- 1 teaspoon kosher salt
- 1 teaspoon garlic powder
- 1/2 teaspoon cayenne pepper
- 2 ripe but firm avocados
- 1 egg, beaten with 1 tablespoon water
- Cooking spray
- Pomegranate molasses, for serving

Directions:
1. Select the bake function and preheat to 375°f (191°c).
2. Whisk together the panko, salt, and spices on a plate. Cut up the avocado in half and remove the pit. Cut each avocado half into 4 slices and scoop the slices out with a large spoon, taking care to keep the slices intact.
3. Dip each avocado slice in the egg wash and then dredge it in the panko. Place the breaded avocado slices on a plate.
4. Working in 2 batches, arrange half of the avocado slices in a single layer in the air fryer basket. Spray lightly with oil.
5. Bake the slices for 7 to 8 minutes, turning once halfway through. Remove the cooked slices to a platter and repeat with the remaining avocado slices.

6. Sprinkle the warm avocado slices with salt and drizzle with pomegranate molasses. Serve immediately.

Nutrition: Calories 132; Fat 11g; Carbs 7g; Protein 4g; Sugars 1g; Fiber 4g

50. Baked cheese sandwich

Preparation time: 5 minutes
Cooking time: 8 minutes
Servings: 2
Ingredients:

- 2 tablespoons mayonnaise
- 4 thick slices sourdough bread
- 4 thick slices brie cheese
- 8 slices hot capicola

Directions:
1. Select the bake function and preheat air fryer to 350°f (177°c.)
2. Put mayonnaise on one side of each slice of bread. Place 2 slices of bread in the air fryer basket, mayonnaise side down.
3. Place the slices of brie and capicola on the bread and cover with the remaining two slices of bread, mayonnaise side up.
4. Bake until the cheese has melted.
5. Serve immediately.

Nutrition: Calories 271; Fat 12g; Carbs 32g; Protein 9g; Sugars 4g; Fiber 1g

51. Avocado taco fry

Preparation time: 5 minutes
Cooking time: 20 minutes
Servings: 12 slices
Ingredients:

- 1 peeled avocado, sliced
- 1 beaten egg
- 1/2 cup panko breadcrumbs
- Salt
- Tortillas and toppings

Directions:
1. Using a bowl, add in the egg.
2. Using a separate bowl, set in the breadcrumbs.
3. Dip the avocado into the bowl with the beaten egg and coat with the breadcrumbs. Sprinkle the coated wedges with a bit of salt.
4. Arrange them in the cooking basket in a single layer.
5. Set the air fryer to 392°f and cook for 15 minutes. Shake the basket halfway through the cooking process.
6. Put them on tortillas with your preferred toppings.

Nutrition: Calorie 140 kcal; Carbs 12g; Fat 8g; Protein 6g

52. Cinnamon and cheese pancake

Preparation time: 7 minutes
Cooking time: 20 minutes
Servings: 4
Ingredients:

- 2 eggs
- 2 cups reduced-fat cream cheese
- 1/2 tsp. Cinnamon
- 1 pack stevia

Directions:
1. Adjust the air fryer to 330°f.
2. In a blender, mix cream cheese, cinnamon, eggs, and stevia.
3. Pour a quarter of the mixture into the air fryer basket. Cook for 2 minutes on all sides. Repeat the process with the remaining portion of the mixture. Serve.

Nutrition: Calories 140 kcal; Carbs 4g; Fat 16g; Protein 27g

53. Scallion sandwich

Preparation time: 10 minutes
Cooking time: 15 minutes
Servings: 1
Ingredients:

- 2 slices wheat bread
- 2 tsps. Low-fat butter
- 2 sliced scallions
- 1 tbsp. Grated parmesan cheese
- 3/4 cup low-fat, grated cheddar cheese

Directions:
1. Adjust the air fryer to 356°f.
2. Apply butter to a slice of bread. Then place it inside the cooking basket with the butter side facing down.

3. Place cheese and scallions on top. Spread the rest of the butter on the other slice of bread. Then put it on top of the sandwich and sprinkle with parmesan cheese.
4. Allow to cook for 10 minutes. Serve.

Nutrition: Calories 154 kcal; Carbs 9g; Fat 5g; Protein 6g

54. Cinnamon pancake

Preparation time: 15 minutes
Cooking time: 20 minutes
Servings: 4
Ingredients:

- 2 eggs
- 2 cups low-fat cream cheese
- 1/2 tsp. Cinnamon
- 1 tsp stevia

Directions:
1. Adjust the temp. To 330°f.
2. Combine cream cheese, cinnamon, eggs, and stevia in a blender.
3. Pour a quarter of the mixture in the air fryer basket.
4. Allow to cook for 2 minutes on both sides.
5. Repeat the process with the rest of the mixture. Serve.

Nutrition: Calories 106 kcal; Carbs 10g; Fat 2g; Protein 9g;

55. Fried egg

Preparation time: 5 minutes
Cooking time: 4 minutes
Servings: 1
Ingredients:

- 1 pastured egg
- 1/8 tsp. Salt
- 1/8 tbsp. Cracked black pepper

Directions:
1. Grease the fryer pan with olive oil then crack the egg in it.
2. Insert the fryer pan into the air fryer, close the lid. Then adjust the fryer to 370°f.
3. After 3minutes, open the air fryer to check if the egg needs more cooking. If yes, leave it for an extra 1 minute.
4. Serve the egg. Add salt and black pepper to season it.

Nutrition: Calories 90 kcal; Carbs 6g; Fat 7g; Protein 3g

56. Breakfast cheese bread cups

Preparation time: 6 minutes
Cooking time: 15 minutes
Servings: 2
Ingredients:

- 2 eggs
- 2 tbsps. Grated cheddar cheese
- Salt and pepper
- 1 ham slice cut into 2 pieces
- 4 bread slices flatted with a rolling pin

Directions:
1. Spray both sides of the ramekins with cooking spray.
2. Place two slices of bread into each ramekin.
3. Add the ham slice pieces into each ramekin.
4. Crack an egg in each ramekin then sprinkle with cheese.
5. Season with salt and pepper.
6. Place the ramekins into air fryer at 300°f for 15-minutes.
7. Serve warm.

Nutrition: Calories 162 kcal; Total Fat 8g; Carbs 10g; Protein 11g

57. Cheese & egg breakfast sandwich

Preparation time: 3 minutes
Cooking time: 6 minutes
Servings: 1
Ingredients:

- 1 egg
- 2 slices cheddar or swiss cheese
- A bit of butter
- 1 roll either English muffin or Kaiser bun, halved

Directions:
1. Butter the sliced rolls on both sides.
2. Whisk the eggs in an oven-safe dish.
3. Place the cheese, egg dish, and rolls into the air fryer. Make sure the buttered sides of the roll are facing upwards.
4. Adjust the air fryer to 390°f. Cook for 6 minutes.

5. Place the egg and cheese between the pieces of roll. Serve warm.

Nutrition: Calories 212 kcal; Total Fat 12g; Carbs 3g; Protein 14g

58. Peanut butter & banana breakfast sandwich

Preparation time: 4 minutes
Cooking time: 6 minutes
Servings: 1
Ingredients:

- 2 slices whole-wheat bread
- 1 tsp. Sugar-free maple syrup
- 1 sliced banana
- 2 tbsps. Peanut butter

Directions:

1. Evenly coat each side of the sliced bread with peanut butter.
2. Add the sliced banana and drizzle with some sugar-free maple syrup.
3. Adjust the air fryer to 330°f then cook for 6 minutes. Serve warm.

Nutrition: Calories 211 kcal; Total Fat 2g; Carbs 3g; Protein 12g

59. Morning mini cheeseburger sliders

Preparation time: 5 minutes
Cooking time: 10 minutes
Servings: 6
Ingredients:

- 1 lb. Ground beef
- 6 slices cheddar cheese
- 6 dinner rolls
- Salt and black pepper

Directions:

1. Adjust the air fryer to 390°f.
2. Form 6 beef patties each about 5 oz. and season with salt and black pepper.
3. Add the burger patties to the cooking basket and cook them for 10 minutes.
4. Remove the burger patties from the air fryer; place the cheese on top of burgers and return to the air fryer and cook for another minute.
5. Remove and put burgers on dinner rolls and serve warm.

Nutrition: Calories 262 kcal; Total Fat 4g; Carbs 2g; Protein 12g

60. Cinnamon sugar muffins

Preparation time: 20 minutes
Cooking time: 12 minutes
Servings: 6
Ingredients

- 1 - 3/4 cups all-purpose flour
- 1 - 1/2 teaspoon baking powder
- 1/3 cup oil
- 1/2 teaspoon salt
- 1/2 teaspoon nutmeg
- 1/2 teaspoon cinnamon
- 1/2 teaspoon vanilla extract
- 3/4 cup sugar
- 1 egg
- 3/4 cup milk
- Mini cupcake liners

Instructions

1. Mix together flour, nutmeg, cinnamon, and salt in a medium bowl.
2. In a large bowl combine oil, sugar, egg, milk, and vanilla.
3. Pour the dry ingredients into the larger bowl and fold over until combined but not completely smooth.
4. Pour the mixture into your cupcake liners and transfer them to the basket.
5. Cook at 350 °f for 12 minutes, check a few times to make sure they are not baking too fast.

Nutrition: Calories 306; Sodium 220 mg; Dietary Fiber7g; Fat 17g; Carbs 41g; Protein 1g

61. Banana bites

Preparation time: 10 minutes
Cooking time: 10 minutes
Servings: 6
Ingredients

- 3 bananas

- 1 cup dry pancake mix
- 1 cup milk
- 1 egg
- 1 teaspoon vanilla
- 1/4 cup powdered sugar

Instructions

1. Combine the egg, milk, vanilla, and pancake mix in a medium bowl.
2. Cut each banana into 1/2-inch slices.
3. Use a fork or slotted spoon to dip each banana slice in the pancake mix allowing extra batter to drip off.
4. Cook in your basket at 320 °f for 10 minutes, tossing 1 or 2 times.
5. Serve with a side of maple syrup for dipping.

Nutrition: Calories 114; Sodium 60 mg; Dietary Fiber 6g; Fat 9g; Carbs 23g; Protein 1g

62. Apple fritter rings

Preparation time: 20 minutes
Cooking time: 10 minutes
Servings: 6
Ingredients

- 2 cups all-purpose flour
- 1/2 teaspoon baking powder
- 1/4 teaspoon ground nutmeg
- 1 teaspoon cinnamon
- 1/4 cup sugar
- 1/4 teaspoon salt
- 2 eggs
- 1 1/4 cups buttermilk
- 6 red apples

Instructions

1. Peel and core the apples then cut each one into 6 rings.
2. Combine all of your dry ingredients in a bowl and mix well.
3. Add the eggs and buttermilk into the dry ingredients bowl and mix well.
4. Dip the apple rings in a batter and let any excess batter drip off.
5. Transfer rings to a sheet of parchment paper.
6. Lay about 6 rings depending on size in your basket and cook at 320 °f for 10 minutes, flipping at the halfway point.

Nutrition: Calories 342; Sodium 174 mg; Dietary Fiber 8g; Fat 8g; Carbs 74g; Protein 5g

63. Cinnamon rolls

Preparation time: 20 minutes
Cooking time 10 minutes
Servings: 8
Ingredients

- Rolls
- 1-pound frozen bread dough
- 1/4 cup melted butter
- 3/4 cup brown sugar
- 1-1/2 tablespoons ground cinnamon
- Cream cheese glaze
- 4 ounces cream cheese
- 2 tablespoons butter
- 1 1/4 cups powdered sugar
- 1/2 teaspoon vanilla

Instructions

1. Allow dough to thaw before use. Roll the dough into a 13 x 11-inch rectangle with the wider part facing you.
2. Mix the brown sugar and cinnamon together. Melt the butter for the rolls and brush it evenly over the dough.
3. Sprinkle the brown sugar mix evenly over the dough. Roll the dough into a tight tube starting at your end and rolling away from you.
4. Cut the tube into 8 pieces and lay them flat on a clean surface with a kitchen towel over them. Allow the dough to rise for 2 hours. Pull out your cream cheese and butter for the glaze to let it soften.
5. Preheat your fryer to 350°f. Bake the rolls for 10 minutes, flipping them halfway through.
6. While the rolls bake, mix together all of the ingredients for the cream cheese glaze.

Nutrition: Calories 246; Sodium 298 mg; Dietary Fiber 5g; Fat 3g; Carbs 44g; Protein 2g

64. Chocolate filled donut holes
Preparation time: 10 minutes
Cooking time: 12 minutes
Servings: 6
Ingredients:

- 1 (8-countcan refrigerated biscuits)
- 1 bag semi-sweet chocolate chips
- 3 tablespoons melted butter
- 1/4 cup powdered sugar

Directions:

1. Cut each biscuit on into thirds.
2. Flatten each third with your hands and put a small dimple in the center with your thumb.
3. Place 2 – 3 chocolate chips inside each dimple and wrap the dough around the chocolate chips creating a ball.
4. Brush each ball with butter.
5. Cook at 320 °f for 10 minutes tossing at least once to ensure even baking throughout.
6. Place powdered sugar in bowl.
7. As soon as your donut holes are done put them in the powdered sugar and toss before serving.

Nutrition: Calories 297; Sodium 705 mg; Dietary Fiber 6g; Fat 15g; Carbs 34g; Protein 7g

65. Bacon egg and cheese eggroll
Preparation time: 15 minutes
Cooking time: 10 minutes
Servings: 5
Ingredients:

- 4 eggs
- 4 slices bacon
- 1/2 cup shredded cheddar cheese
- 5 egg roll wrappers

Directions:

1. In a big pan, fry the bacon until crispy and set aside.
2. Drain the bacon fat but leave a little left behind in the skillet.
3. Using the bacon fat, scramble your eggs.
4. Roll out your eggroll wrappers.
5. In a separate bowl, crumble, the bacon into tiny pieces, then mix in the eggs and the cheese.
6. Scoop in equal amounts of the mixture to the center of each wrapper.
7. Pull the bottom left corner of the wrapper over the mixture, then fold each side in.
8. Wet the remaining edge and roll the eggroll shut.
9. Preheat the air fryer to 360°f and cook for 10 minutes flipping eggrolls halfway through.

Nutrition: Calories 302; Sodium 483 mg; Dietary Fiber 6g; Fat 15g; Carbs 12g; Protein 18g

66. Blueberry lemon muffins
Preparation time: 10 minutes
Cooking time: 10 minutes
Servings: 6
Ingredients

- 2 1/2 cups self-rising flour
- 1/2 cup sugar
- 1/2 cup cream
- 1/4 cup olive oil
- 2 eggs
- 1 cup blueberries
- 2 tablespoons lemon juice
- 1 teaspoon vanilla

Instructions

1. Mix flower and sugar together in a small bowl.
2. In another large bowl combine cream, oil, lemon juice, eggs, and vanilla.
3. Add the flour mix to the large bowl and mix well.
4. Put 6 cupcake holders in the fryer basket and fill each with batter.
5. Cook at 320°f for 10 minutes.

Nutritional info: Calories 375; Sodium 29 mg; Dietary Fiber 2g; Fat 16g; Carbs 68g; Protein 6g

67. Hash browns
Preparation time: 35 minutes
Cooking time: 15 minutes
Servings: 8
Ingredients

- 4 russet potatoes
- 2 tablespoons corn flour
- 1 teaspoon garlic powder
- 1 teaspoon onion powder
- 2 teaspoons olive oil, separated
- Salt and pepper to taste

Instructions

1. Peel and shred your potatoes.
2. Soak potatoes in water, then drain and repeat to remove excess starch.
3. Heat 1 teaspoon olive oil in a pan and sauté the potatoes for a few minutes.
4. Mix the potatoes and all the dry ingredients until well mixed.
5. Flatten them out over a plate and refrigerate for 20 minutes.
6. Preheat the fryer to 360°f.
7. Cut your hash browns into squares and place them in the basket brushing them with a little oil.
8. Cook for 15 minutes, flipping halfway through.

Nutritional info: Calories 92; Sodium 7 mg; Dietary Fiber 7g; Fat 4g; Carbs 16g; Protein 2g

68. Ham and egg toast cups
Preparation time: 10 minutes
Cooking time: 15 minutes
Servings: 2
Ingredients

- 2 ramekins
- 2 eggs
- 4 slices of bread
- 1 slice of ham
- Melted butter
- Salt and pepper to taste

Instructions

1. Brush the inside of the ramekin with melted butter.
2. Toast bread and flatten it with a rolling pin.
3. Press 1 piece of toast into the bottom of the ramekin to create a bread bowl.
4. Press another piece of toast onto the first one to create a double layer.
5. Cut the ham into 4 slices then line the inside of the toast cups with 2 strips of ham each.
6. Crack an egg into the center of each cup and season with salt and pepper.
7. Cook in the air fryer for 15 minutes at 320° f, if you like your eggs less runny, you may want to add a few minutes to the cooking time.

Nutritional info: Calories202; Sodium 488 mg; Dietary fiber 6g; Fat 6 g; Carbs 16g; Protein 2g

69. Breakfast Spinach Quiche
Preparation time: 10 minutes
Cooking time: 15 minutes
Servings: 4
Ingredients:

- 7 ounces whole wheat flour
- 7ounces spinach, torn
- 2 tablespoons olive oil
- 2 tablespoons flax meal mixed with 3 tablespoons water
- 2 tablespoons almond milk
- 3 ounces soft tofu, crumbled
- Salt and black pepper to the taste
- 1 yellow onion, chopped

Directions:

1. In your food processor, mix flour with half of the oil, flax meal, milk, salt and pepper and pulse well.
2. Transfer to a bowl, knead a bit, cover and keep in the fridge for 10 minutes.

3. Heat up a pan with the rest of the oil over medium-high heat, add onion, spinach, tofu, salt and pepper, stir, cook for a few minutes and take off heat.
4. Divide dough in 4 pieces, roll each piece, place on the bottom of a ramekin, divide spinach mix into the ramekins, place all ramekins in your air fryer's basket and cook at 360° f for 15 minutes.
5. Leave quiche aside to cool down a bit and then serve them for breakfast.
6. Enjoy!

Nutrition: Calories 250; Fat 12g; Fiber 2g; Carbs 13g; Protein 9g

70. Greek Veggie Mix
Preparation time: 10 minutes
Cooking time: 45 minutes
Servings: 4
Ingredients:
- 8 ounces eggplant, sliced
- 8 ounces zucchini, sliced
- 8 ounces bell peppers, chopped
- 2 garlic cloves, minced
- 5 tablespoons olive oil
- 1 bay leaf
- 1 thyme spring
- 2 onions, chopped
- 8 ounces tomatoes, cut into quarters
- Salt and black pepper to the taste

Directions:
1. Heat up a pan that fits your air fryer with 2 tablespoons oil over medium-high heat, add eggplant, salt and pepper, stir, cook for 5 minutes and transfer to a bowl.
2. Heat up the pan with 1 more tablespoon oil, add zucchini, cook for 3 minutes and transfer over eggplant pieces.
3. Heat up the pan again, add bell peppers, stir, cook for 2 minutes and pour over the other veggies.
4. Heat up the pan with 2 tablespoons oil, add onions, stir and cook for 3 minutes.
5. Add tomatoes, the rest of the veggies, bay leaf, thyme, garlic, salt and pepper, stir, transfer to your air fryer and cook at 300° f for 30 minutes.
6. Divide between plates and serve for breakfast.
7. Enjoy!

Nutrition: Calories 200; Fat 1g; Fiber 3g; Carbs 7g; Protein 6g

71. Tofu Casserole
Preparation time: 10 minutes
Cooking time: 20 minutes
Servings: 4
Ingredients:
- 1 teaspoon lemon zest, grated
- 14 ounces tofu, cubed
- 1 tablespoon lemon juice
- 2 tablespoons nutritional yeast
- 1 tablespoon apple cider vinegar
- 1 tablespoon olive oil
- 2 garlic cloves, minced
- 10 ounces spinach, torn
- ½ cup yellow onion, chopped
- ½ teaspoon basil, dried
- 8 ounces mushrooms, sliced
- Salt and black pepper to the taste
- ¼ teaspoon red pepper flakes
- Cooking spray

Directions:
1. Spray your air fryer with some cooking spray, arrange tofu cubes on the bottom, add lemon zest, lemon juice, yeast, vinegar, olive oil, garlic, spinach, onion, basil, mushrooms, salt, pepper and pepper flakes, toss, cover and cook at 365° f for 20 minutes.
2. Divide between plates and serve for breakfast.
3. Enjoy!

Nutrition: Calories 246; Fat 6g; Fiber 8g; Carbs 12g; Protein 4g

72. Simple Granola
Preparation time: 10 minutes

Cooking time: 15 minutes
Servings: 3
Ingredients:
- ½ cup granola
- ½ cup bran flakes
- 2 green apples, cored, peeled and roughly chopped
- ¼ cup apple juice
- 1/8 cup maple syrup
- 2 tablespoons cashew butter
- 1 teaspoon cinnamon powder
- ½ teaspoon nutmeg, ground

Directions:
1. In your air fryer, mix granola with bran flakes, apples, apple juice, maple syrup, cashew butter, cinnamon and nutmeg, toss, cover and cook at 365° f for 15 minutes.
2. Divide into bowls and serve for breakfast.
3. Enjoy!

Nutrition: Calories 188; Fat 6g; Fiber 9g; Carbs 11g; Protein 6g

73. Greek Veggie with Thyme
Preparation time: 10 minutes
Cooking time: 45 minutes
Servings: 4
Ingredients:
- 8 ounces eggplant, sliced
- 8 ounces zucchini, sliced
- 8 ounces bell peppers, chopped
- 2 garlic cloves, minced
- 5 tablespoons olive oil
- 1 bay leaf
- 1 thyme spring
- 2 onions, chopped
- 8 ounces tomatoes, cut into quarters
- Salt and black pepper to the taste

Directions:
1. Heat up a pan that fits your air fryer with 2 tablespoons oil over medium-high heat, add eggplant, salt and pepper, stir, cook for 5 minutes and transfer to a bowl.
2. Heat up the pan with 1 more tablespoon oil, add zucchini, cook for 3 minutes and transfer over eggplant pieces.
3. Heat up the pan again, add bell peppers, stir, cook for 2 minutes and pour over the other veggies.
4. Heat up the pan with 2 tablespoons oil, add onions, stir and cook for 3 minutes.
5. Add tomatoes, the rest of the veggies, bay leaf, thyme, garlic, salt and pepper, stir, transfer to your air fryer and cook at 300°f for 30 minutes.
6. Divide between plates and serve for breakfast.
7. Enjoy!

Nutrition: Calories 200; Fat 1g; Fiber 3g; Carbs 7g; Protein 6g

74. Tomatoes Breakfast Salad
Preparation time: 10 minutes
Cooking time: 20 minutes
Servings: 2
Ingredients:
- 2 tomatoes, halved
- Cooking spray
- Salt and black pepper to the taste
- 1 teaspoon parsley, chopped
- 1 teaspoon basil, chopped
- 1 teaspoon oregano, chopped
- 1 teaspoon rosemary, chopped
- 1 cucumber, chopped
- 1 green onion, chopped

Directions:
1. Spray tomato halves with cooking oil, season with salt and pepper, place them in your air fryer's basket and cook at 320°f for 20 minutes.
2. Transfer tomatoes to a bowl, add parsley, basil, oregano, rosemary, cucumber and onion, toss and serve for breakfast.
3. Enjoy!

Nutrition: Calories 100; Fat 1g; Fiber 3g; Carbs 8g; Protein 1g

75. Veggie Casserole with Cashew

Preparation time: 10 minutes
Cooking time: 16 minutes
Servings: 4
Ingredients:

- 2 teaspoons onion powder
- ¾ cup cashews, soaked for 30 minutes and drained
- ¼ cup nutritional yeast
- 1 teaspoon garlic powder
- ½ teaspoon sage, dried
- Salt and black pepper to the taste
- 1 yellow onion, chopped
- 2 tablespoons parsley, chopped
- 3 garlic cloves, minced
- 1 tablespoon olive oil
- 4 red potatoes, cubed
- ½ teaspoon red pepper flakes

Directions:

1. In your blender, mix cashews with onion powder, garlic powder, nutritional yeast, sage, salt and pepper and pulse really well.
2. Add oil to your air fryer's pan and preheat the machine to 370°f.
3. Arrange potatoes, pepper flakes, garlic, onion, salt, pepper and parsley in the pan,
4. Add cashews sauce, toss, cover and cook for 16 minutes
5. Divide between plates and serve for breakfast.
6. Enjoy!

Nutrition: Calories 218; Fat 6g; Fiber 6g; Carbs 14g; Protein 5g

76. Easy Breakfast Oats

Preparation time: 10 minutes
Cooking time: 15 minutes
Servings: 4
Ingredients:

- 2 cups almond milk
- 1 cup steel cut oats
- 2 cups water
- 1/3 cup cherries, dried
- 2 tablespoons cocoa powder
- ¼ cup stevia
- ½ teaspoon almond extract
- For the sauce:
- 2 tablespoons water
- 1 and ½ cups cherries
- ¼ teaspoon almond extract

Directions:

1. In your air fryer's pan, mix almond milk with oats, water, dried cherries, cocoa powder, stevia and ½ teaspoon almond extract, stir, cover and cook at 360°f for 15 minutes.
2. Meanwhile, in a small pot, mix 2 tablespoons water with 1 and ½ cups cherries and ¼ teaspoon almond extract, stir, bring to a simmer over medium heat and cook for 10 minutes.
3. Divide oats into bowls, drizzle cherry sauce all over and serve for breakfast.
4. Enjoy!

Nutrition: Calories 172; Fat 7g; Fiber 7g; Carbs 12g; Protein 6g

77. Pear Vanilla Oatmeal

Preparation time: 10 minutes
Cooking time: 15 minutes
Servings: 3
Ingredients:

- 2 cups coconut milk
- ½ cup steel cut oats
- ½ teaspoon vanilla extract
- 1 pear, chopped
- ½ teaspoon maple extract
- 1 tablespoon stevia

Directions:

1. In your air fryer's pan, mix coconut milk with oats, vanilla, pear, maple extract and stevia, stir, cover and cook at 360° f for 15 minutes.
2. Divide into bowls and serve for breakfast.
3. Enjoy!

Nutrition: Calories 200; Fat 5g; Fiber 7g, Carbs 14g, Protein 4g

78. Pumpkin Oatmeal

Preparation time: 10 minutes
Cooking time: 20 minutes
Servings: 4
Ingredients:

- 1 and ½ cups water
- ½ cup pumpkin puree
- 1 teaspoon pumpkin pie spice
- 3 tablespoons stevia
- ½ cup steel cut oats

Directions:

1. In your air fryer's pan, mix water with oats, pumpkin puree, pumpkin spice and stevia, stir, cover and cook at 360°f for 20 minutes
2. Divide into bowls and serve for breakfast.
3. Enjoy!

Nutrition: Calories 211; Fat 4g; Fiber 7g; Carbs 8g; Protein 3g

79. Veggie Burrito with Tofu

Preparation time: 10 minutes
Cooking time: 15 minutes
Servings: 8
Ingredients:

- 16 ounces tofu, crumbled
- 1 green bell pepper, chopped
- ¼ cup scallions, chopped
- 15 ounces canned black beans, drained
- 1 cup vegan salsa
- ½ cup water
- ¼ teaspoon cumin, ground
- ½ teaspoon turmeric powder
- ½ teaspoon smoked paprika
- A pinch of salt and black pepper
- ¼ teaspoon chili powder
- 3 cups spinach leaves, torn
- 8 vegan tortillas for serving

Directions:

1. In your air fryer, mix tofu with bell pepper, scallions, black beans, salsa, water, cumin, turmeric, paprika, salt, pepper and chili powder, stir, cover and cook at 370°f for 20 minutes
2. Add spinach, toss well, divide this on your vegan tortillas, roll, wrap them and serve for breakfast.
3. Enjoy!

Nutrition: Calories 211; Fat 4g; Fiber 7g; Carbs 14g; Protein 4g

80. Apple Steel Cut Oats

Preparation time: 10 minutes
Cooking time: 15 minutes
Servings: 6
Ingredients:

- 1 and ½ cups water
- 1 and ½ cups coconut milk
- 2 apples, cored, peeled and chopped
- 1 cup steel cut oats
- ½ teaspoon cinnamon powder
- ¼ teaspoon nutmeg, ground
- ¼ teaspoon allspice, ground
- ¼ teaspoon ginger powder
- ¼ teaspoon cardamom, ground
- 1 tablespoon flaxseed, ground
- 2 teaspoons vanilla extract
- 2 teaspoons stevia
- Cooking spray

Directions:

1. Spray your air fryer with cooking spray, add apples, milk, water, cinnamon, oats, allspice, nutmeg, cardamom, ginger, vanilla, flaxseeds and stevia, stir, cover and cook at 360°f for 15 minutes
2. Divide into bowls and serve for breakfast.
3. Enjoy!

Nutrition: Calories 172; Fat 3g; Fiber 7g; Carbs 8g; Protein 5g

81. Lemony Tofu Casserole

Preparation time: 10 minutes
Cooking time: 20 minutes
Servings: 4
Ingredients:

- 1 teaspoon lemon zest, grated
- 14 ounces tofu, cubed
- 1 tablespoon lemon juice
- 2 tablespoons nutritional yeast
- 1 tablespoon apple cider vinegar
- 1 tablespoon olive oil
- 2 garlic cloves, minced
- 10 ounces spinach, torn
- ½ cup yellow onion, chopped
- ½ teaspoon basil, dried
- 8 ounces mushrooms, sliced
- Salt and black pepper to the taste
- ¼ teaspoon red pepper flakes
- Cooking spray

Directions:

1. Spray your air fryer with some cooking spray, arrange tofu cubes on the bottom, add lemon zest, lemon juice, yeast, vinegar, olive oil, garlic, spinach, onion, basil, mushrooms, salt, pepper and pepper flakes, toss, cover and cook at 365°f for 20 minutes.
2. Divide between plates and serve for breakfast.
3. Enjoy!

Nutrition: Calories 246, Fat 6g; Fiber 8g; Carbs 12g; Protein 4g

82. Carrot Mix

Preparation time: 10 minutes
Cooking time: 15 minutes
Servings: 4
Ingredients:

- 2 cups coconut milk
- ½ cup steel cut oats
- 1 cup carrots, shredded
- 1 teaspoon cardamom, ground
- ½ teaspoon agave nectar
- A pinch of saffron
- Cooking spray

Directions:

1. Spray your air fryer with cooking spray, add milk, oats, carrots, cardamom and agave nectar, stir, cover and cook at 365°f for 15 minutes
2. Divide into bowls, sprinkle saffron on top and serve for breakfast.
3. Enjoy!

Nutrition: Calories 202; Fat:7g; Fiber 4g; Carbs 8g; Protein 3g

83. Blueberries Vanilla Oats

Preparation time: 10 minutes
Cooking time: 15 minutes
Servings: 4
Ingredients:

- 1 cup blueberries
- 1 cup steel cut oats
- 1 cup coconut milk
- 2 tablespoons agave nectar
- ½ teaspoon vanilla extract
- Cooking spray

Directions:

1. Spray your air fryer with cooking spray, add oats, milk, agave nectar, vanilla and blueberries, toss, cover and cook at 365°f for 10 minutes.
2. Divide into bowls and serve for breakfast.
3. Enjoy!

Nutrition: Calories 202; Fat 6g; Fiber 8g; Carbs 9g; Protein 6g

84. Apple and Pears Mix

Preparation time: 10 minutes
Cooking time: 15 minutes
Servings: 6
Ingredients:

- 4 apples, cored, peeled and cut into medium chunks
- 1 teaspoon lemon juice
- 4 pears, cored, peeled and cut into medium chunks
- 5 teaspoons stevia
- 1 teaspoon cinnamon powder
- 1 teaspoon vanilla extract
- ½ teaspoon ginger, ground
- ½ teaspoon cloves, ground
- ½ teaspoon cardamom, ground

Directions:

1. In your air fryer, mix apples with pears, lemon juice, stevia, cinnamon, vanilla extract, ginger, cloves and cardamom, stir, cover, cook at 360°f for 15 minutes
2. Divide into bowls and serve for breakfast.
3. Enjoy!

Nutrition: Calories; 161; Fat 3g; Fiber 7g; Carbs 9g; Protein 4g

85. Bell Pepper and Beans Oatmeal

Preparation time: 10 minutes
Cooking time: 15 minutes
Servings: 2
Ingredients:

- 1 cup steel cut oats
- 2 tablespoons canned kidney beans, drained
- 2 red bell peppers, chopped
- 4 tablespoons coconut cream
- A pinch of sweet paprika
- Salt and black pepper to the taste
- ¼ teaspoon cumin, ground

Directions:

1. Heat up your air fryer at 360°f, add oats, beans, bell peppers, coconut cream, paprika, salt, pepper and cumin, stir, cover and cook for 16 minutes.
2. Divide into bowls and serve for breakfast.
3. Enjoy!

Nutrition: Calories 173; Fat 4g; Fiber 6g; Carbs 12g; Protein 4g

86. Banana and Walnuts Oats

Preparation time: 10 minutes
Cooking time: 15 minutes
Servings: 4
Ingredients:

- 1 banana, peeled and mashed
- 1 cup steel cut oats
- 2 cups almond milk
- 2 cups water
- ¼ cup walnuts, chopped
- 2 tablespoons flaxseed meal
- 2 teaspoons cinnamon powder
- 1 teaspoon vanilla extract
- ½ teaspoon nutmeg, ground

Directions:

1. In your air fryer mix oats with almond milk, water, walnuts, flaxseed meal, cinnamon, vanilla and nutmeg, stir, cover and cook at 360°f for 15 minutes.
2. Divide into bowls and serve for breakfast.
3. Enjoy!

Nutrition: Calories 181; Fat 7g; Fiber 6g; Carbs 12g; Protein 11g

87. Cinnamon Granola

Preparation time: 10 minutes
Cooking time: 15 minutes
Servings: 3
Ingredients:

- ½ cup granola
- ½ cup bran flakes
- 2 green apples, cored, peeled and roughly chopped
- ¼ cup apple juice
- 1/8 cup maple syrup
- 2 tablespoons cashew butter
- 1 teaspoon cinnamon powder
- ½ teaspoon nutmeg, ground

Directions:

1. In your air fryer, mix granola with bran flakes, apples, apple juice, maple syrup, cashew butter, cinnamon and nutmeg, toss, cover and cook at 365°f for 15 minutes
2. Divide into bowls and serve for breakfast.
3. Enjoy!

Nutrition: Calories 188; Fat 6g; Fiber 9g; Carbs 11g; Protein 6g

88. Zucchini Oatmeal

Preparation time: 10 minutes
Cooking time: 15 minutes
Servings: 4
Ingredients:

- ½ cup steel cut oats
- 1 carrot, grated
- 1 and ½ cups almond milk
- ¼ zucchini, grated
- ¼ teaspoon nutmeg, ground
- ¼ teaspoon cloves, ground
- ½ teaspoon cinnamon powder
- 2 tablespoons maple syrup
- ¼ cup pecans, chopped
- 1 teaspoon vanilla extract

Directions:
1. In your air fryer, mix oats with carrot, zucchini, almond milk, cloves, nutmeg, cinnamon, maple syrup, pecans and vanilla extract, stir, cover and cook at 365°f for 15 minutes.
2. Divide into bowls and serve.
3. Enjoy!

Nutrition: Calories 175; Fat 4g; Fiber 7g; Carbs 12g; Protein 7g

89. Almond and Cranberry Quinoa

Preparation time: 10 minutes
Cooking time: 13 minutes
Servings: 4
Ingredients:

- 1 cup quinoa
- 3 cups coconut water
- 1 teaspoon vanilla extract
- 3 teaspoons stevia
- 1/8 cup coconut flakes
- ¼ cup cranberries, dried
- 1/8 cup almonds, chopped

Directions:
1. In your air fryer, mix quinoa with coconut water, vanilla, stevia, coconut flakes, almonds and cranberries, toss, cover and cook at 365°f for 13 minutes.
2. Divide into bowls and serve for breakfast.
3. Enjoy!

Nutrition: Calories 146; Fat 5g; Fiber 5g; Carbs 10g; Protein 7g

90. Sweet Quinoa Mix

Preparation time: 10 minutes
Cooking time: 14 minutes
Servings: 6
Ingredients:

- ½ cup quinoa
- 1 and ½ cups steel cut oats
- 4 tablespoons stevia
- 4 and ½ cups almond milk
- 2 tablespoons maple syrup
- 1 and ½ teaspoons vanilla extract
- Strawberries, halved for serving
- Cooking spray

Directions:
1. Spray your air fryer with cooking spray, add oats, quinoa, stevia, almond milk, maple syrup and vanilla extract, toss, cover and cook at 365°f for 14 minutes
2. Divide into bowls, add strawberries on top and serve for breakfast.
3. Enjoy!

Nutrition: Calories 207; Fat 5g; Fiber 8g; Carbs 14g; Protein 5g

BRUNCH RECIPES

91. Spicy cauliflower rice

Preparation time: 10 minutes
Cooking time: 22 minutes
Servings: 2
Ingredients:

- 1 cauliflower head, cut into florets
- 1/2 tsp cumin
- 1/2 tsp chili powder
- 6 onion spring, chopped
- 2 jalapenos, chopped
- 4 tbsp olive oil
- 1 zucchini, trimmed and cut into cubes
- 1/2 tsp paprika
- 1/2 tsp garlic powder
- 1/2 tsp cayenne pepper
- 1/2 tsp pepper
- 1/2 tsp salt

Directions:
1. Preheat the air fryer to 370° f.
2. Prepare food processor and put the cauliflower florets. Process until it looks like rice.
3. Transfer cauliflower rice into the air fryer baking pan and drizzle with half oil.
4. Place pan in the air fryer and cook for 12 minutes, stir halfway through.
5. Heat remaining oil in a small pan over medium heat.
6. Add zucchini and cook for 58 minutes.
7. Add onion and jalapenos and cook for 5 minutes.
8. Add spices and stir well. Set aside.
9. Add cauliflower rice to the zucchini mixture and stir well.
10. Serve and enjoy.

Nutrition: Calories 254; Fat 28 g; Carbs 13g; Sugar 5g; Protein 3g

92. Sausage egg cups

Preparation time: 10 minutes
Cooking time: 10 minutes
Servings: 2
Ingredients:

- 1/4 cup egg beaters
- 1/4 sausage, cooked and crumbled
- 4 tsp jack cheese, shredded
- 1/4 tsp garlic powder
- 1/4 tsp onion powder
- 4 tbsp spinach, chopped
- Pepper
- Salt

Directions:
1. Mix well all ingredients in a large bowl.
2. Pour batter into the silicone muffin molds and place in the air fryer basket.
3. Cook at 330° f for 10 minutes.
4. Serve and enjoy.

Nutrition: Calories 90; Fat 5g; Carbs 1g; Sugar 2g; Protein 7 g

93. Vegetable egg cups

Preparation time:10 minutes
Cooking time:20 minutes
Servings:4
Ingredients:

- 4 eggs
- 1 tbsp cilantro, chopped
- 4 tbsp half and half

- 1 cup cheddar cheese, shredded
- 1 cup vegetables, diced
- Pepper
- Salt

Directions:
1. Put cooking sprays on four ramekins and set aside.
2. In a mixing bowl, whisk eggs with cilantro, half and half, vegetables, 1/2 cup cheese, pepper, and salt.
3. Pour egg mixture into the four ramekins.
4. Place ramekins in the air fryer basket and cook at 300° f for 12 minutes.
5. Top with remaining 1/2 cup cheese and cook for 2 minutes more at 400° f.
6. Serve and enjoy.

Nutrition: Calories 194 Fat 15 g Carbohydrates 6 g Sugar 5 g Protein 13 g

94. Radish hash browns
Preparation time: 10 minutes
Cooking time: 13 minutes
Servings: 4
Ingredients:
- 1 lb. Radishes, washed and cut off roots
- 1 tbsp olive oil
- 1/2 tsp paprika
- 1/2 tsp onion powder
- 1/2 tsp garlic powder
- 1 medium onion
- 1/4 tsp pepper
- 3/4 tsp sea salt

Directions:
1. Slice onion and radishes using a mandolin slicer.
2. Add sliced onion and radishes in a large mixing bowl and tossed with olive oil.
3. Transfer onion and radish slices to air fryer basket and cook at 360° f for 8 minutes. Shake basket twice.
4. Return onion and radish slices in a mixing bowl and toss with seasonings.
5. Again, cook onion, and radish slices in air fryer basket for 5 minutes at 400° f. Shake basket halfway through.
6. Serve and enjoy.

Nutrition: Calories 62; Fat 7g Carbohydrates 1 g Sugar 5 g Protein 2 g

95. Broccoli frittata
Preparation time: 10 minutes
Cooking time: 17 minutes
Servings: 2
Ingredients:
- 3 eggs
- 1/2 cup bell pepper, chopped
- 1/2 cup broccoli florets
- 2 tbsp parmesan cheese, grated
- 1/4 tsp garlic powder
- 1/4 tsp onion powder
- 2 tbsp coconut milk
- Pepper
- Salt

Directions:
1. Mist cooking spray to air fryer baking dish.
2. Place bell peppers and broccoli in the prepared baking dish.
3. Cook broccoli and bell pepper in the air fryer at 350 °f for 7 minutes.
4. Beat together eggs, milk, and seasoning in a bowl.
5. Once veggies are cooked, then pour egg mixture over vegetables and sprinkle cheese on top.
6. Cook frittata in the air fryer for 10 minutes. Serve and enjoy.

Nutrition: Calories 155 Fat 3 g Carbohydrates 1 g Sugar 3 g Protein 18 g

96. Spinach frittata
Preparation time: 5 minutes
Cooking time: 8 minutes
Servings: 1
Ingredients:
- 3 eggs
- 1 cup spinach, chopped

- 1 small onion, minced
- 2 tbsp mozzarella cheese, grated
- Pepper
- Salt

Directions:
1. Preheat the air fryer to 350° f.
2. Spray air fryer pan with cooking spray.
3. In a bowl, whisk eggs with remaining ingredients until well combined.
4. Pour egg mixture into the prepared pan and place pan in the air fryer basket.
5. Cook frittata for 8 minutes or until set.
6. Serve and enjoy.

Nutrition: Calories 384 Fat 23 g Carbohydrates 17 g Sugar 1 g Protein 33 g

97. Omelet frittata
Preparation time: 10 minutes
Cooking time: 6 minutes
Servings: 2
Ingredients:
- 3 eggs, lightly beaten
- 2 tbsp cheddar cheese, shredded
- 2 tbsp heavy cream
- 2 mushrooms, sliced
- 1/4 small onion, chopped
- 1/4 bell pepper, diced
- Pepper
- Salt

Directions:
1. In a bowl, whisk eggs with cream, vegetables, pepper, and salt.
2. Preheat the air fryer to 400° f.
3. Pour egg mixture into the air fryer pan. Place pan in the air fryer basket and cook for 5 minutes.
4. Add shredded cheese on top of the frittata and cook for 1 minute more. Serve and enjoy.

Nutrition: Calories 160 Fat 10 g Carbohydrates 4 g Sugar 2 g Protein 12 g

98. Asparagus frittata
Preparation time: 10 minutes
Cooking time: 10 minutes
Servings: 4
Ingredients:
- 6 eggs
- 3 mushrooms, sliced
- 10 asparagus, chopped
- 1/4 cup half and half
- 2 tsp butter, melted
- 1 cup mozzarella cheese, shredded
- 1 tsp pepper
- 1 tsp salt

Directions:
1. Toss mushrooms and asparagus with melted butter and add into the air fryer basket.
2. Cook mushrooms and asparagus at 350°f for 5 minutes. Shake basket twice.
3. Meanwhile, in a bowl, whisk together eggs, half and half, pepper, and salt.
4. Transfer cook mushrooms and asparagus into the air fryer baking dish.
5. Pour egg mixture over mushrooms and asparagus.
6. Put the dish in the air fryer and cook at 350° f for 5 minutes or until eggs are set.
7. Slice and serve.

Nutrition: Calories 211 Fat 13 g Carbohydrates 4 g Sugar 1 g Protein 16 g

99. Mushroom leek frittata
Preparation time: 10 minutes
Cooking time: 32 minutes
Servings: 4
Ingredients:
- 6 eggs
- 6 oz mushrooms, sliced
- 1 cup leeks, sliced
- Salt

Directions:

1. Prepare the air fryer to 325 °f.
2. Spray cooking oil to air fryer baking dish and set aside.
3. Heat another pan over medium heat. Spray pan with cooking spray.
4. Add mushrooms, leeks, and salt in a pan sauté for 6 minutes.
5. Break eggs in a bowl and whisk well.
6. Transfer sautéed mushroom and leek mixture into the prepared baking dish.
7. Pour egg over mushroom mixture.
8. Arrange the mixture in the air fryer and cook for 32 minutes. Serve and enjoy.

Nutrition: Calories 116 Fat 7 g Carbohydrates 1 g Sugar 1 g Protein 10 g

100. Mushroom frittata

Preparation time: 10 minutes
Cooking time: 13 minutes
Servings: 1
Ingredients:

- 1 cup egg whites
- 1 cup spinach, chopped
- 2 mushrooms, sliced
- 2 tbsp parmesan cheese, grated
- Salt

Directions:

1. Add a cooking spray to a pan and heat over medium heat.
2. Add mushrooms and sauté for 23 minutes. Put the spinach and cook for 12 minutes or until wilted.
3. Transfer mushroom spinach mixture into the air fryer pan.
4. Whip the egg whites in a mixing bowl—season with a pinch of salt.
5. Pour egg white mixture into the spinach and mushroom mixture. Sprinkle with parmesan cheese.
6. Put the pan with the mixture in the air fryer basket and cook frittata at 350° f for 8 minutes.
7. Slice and serve.

Nutrition: Calories 176 Fat 3 g Carbohydrates 4 g Sugar 5 g Protein 31 g

101. Tomato mushroom frittata

Preparation time: 10 minutes
Cooking time: 15 minutes
Servings: 2
Ingredients:

- 1 cup egg whites
- 1/4 cup tomato, sliced
- 2 tbsp coconut milk
- 2 tbsp chives, chopped
- 1/4 cup mushrooms, sliced
- Pepper
- Salt

Directions:

1. Preheat the air fryer to 320° f.
2. In a bowl, whisk together all ingredients.
3. Spray air fryer baking pan with cooking spray.
4. Pour egg mixture into the prepared pan and place it in the air fryer.
5. Cook frittata for 15 minutes.
6. Serve and enjoy.

Nutrition: Calories 75 Fat 6 g Carbohydrates 3 g Sugar 1 g Protein 13 g

102. Crab cheese frittata

Preparation time: 10 minutes
Cooking time: 14 minutes
Servings: 2
Ingredients:

- 5 eggs
- ¼ tsp fresh lemon juice
- 2 tbsp fresh mint, chopped
- 1/3 cup goat cheese, crumbled
- ¼ cup onion, minced
- ¼ tsp pepper
- ¼ tsp salt

Directions:

1. Preheat the air fryer to 325° f.

2. In a bowl, whisk eggs with pepper and salt. Add remaining ingredients and stir well.
3. Drizzle cooking spray to air fryer baking dish.
4. Add egg mixture into the prepared dish, place it in the air fryer, and cook for 14 minutes.
5. Serve and enjoy.

Nutrition: Calories 325° f at 25 g Carbohydrates 9 g Sugar 5 g Protein 24 g

103. Zucchini noodles

Preparation time: 10 minutes
Cooking time: 44 minutes
Servings: 3
Ingredients:

- 1 egg
- 1/2 cup parmesan cheese, grated
- 1/2 cup feta cheese, crumbled
- 1 tbsp thyme
- 1 garlic clove, chopped
- 1 onion, chopped
- 2 medium zucchinis, trimmed and spiralized
- 2 tbsp olive oil
- 1 cup mozzarella cheese, grated
- 1/2 tsp pepper
- 1/2 tsp salt

Directions:

1. Preheat the air fryer to 350° f.
2. Add spiralized zucchini and salt in a colander and set aside for 10 minutes.
3. Wash zucchini noodles and pat dry with a paper towel.
4. Get a pan and add oil over medium heat.
5. Add garlic and onion and sauté for 34 minutes.
6. Add zucchini noodles and cook for 45 minutes or until softened.
7. Add zucchini mixture into the air fryer baking pan. Add egg, thyme, cheeses. Mix well and season.
8. Place pan in the air fryer and cook for 30-35 minutes. Serve and enjoy.

Nutrition: Calories 435 Fat 29 g Carbohydrates 14 g Sugar 5 g Protein 25 g

104. Mushroom cheese salad

Preparation time: 10 minutes
Cooking time: 15 minutes
Servings: 3
Ingredients:

- 10 mushrooms, halved
- 1 tbsp fresh parsley, chopped
- 1 tbsp olive oil
- 1 tbsp mozzarella cheese, grated
- 1 tbsp cheddar cheese, grated
- 1 tbsp dried mixed herbs
- Pepper
- Salt

Directions:

1. Toss well all ingredients into the bowl.
2. Transfer bowl mixture into the air fryer baking dish.
3. Put the mixture in the air fryer and cook at 380° f for 15 minutes.
4. Serve and enjoy.

Nutrition: Calories 90 Fat 7 g Carbohydrates 2 g Sugar 1 g Protein 5 g

105. Creamy cabbage

Preparation time: 10 minutes
Cooking time: 20 minutes
Servings: 4
Ingredients:

- 1 cabbage head, shredded
- 1 cup heavy cream
- 4 bacon slices, chopped
- 1 onion, chopped
- Pepper
- Salt

Directions:

1. Stir well all ingredients into the air fryer baking dish.
2. Place dish in the air fryer and cook at 400 f for 20 minutes.
3. Serve and enjoy.

Nutrition: Calories 163 Fat 11 g Carbohydrates 13 g Sugar 7 g Protein 3 g

106. Indian cauliflower

Preparation time: 10 minutes
cooking time: 20 minutes
servings: 2
Ingredients:

- 3 cups cauliflower florets 2 tbsp water
- 2 tsp fresh lemon juice
- ½ tbsp ginger paste 1 tsp chili powder
- ¼ tsp turmeric
- ½ cup vegetable stock pepper
- Salt

Directions:
1. Add all ingredients into the air fryer baking dish and mix well.
2. Place dish in the air fryer and cook at 400 f for 10 minutes.
3. Stir well and cook at 360° f for 10 minutes more.
4. Stir well and serve.

Nutrition: Calories 49 Fat 5 g Carbohydrates 9 g Sugar 3 g Protein 3 g Cholesterol 0 mg

107. Lunch gnocchi

Preparation time: 10 minutes
Cooking time: 17 minutes
servings: 4
Ingredients:

- 1 yellow onion, chopped
- 1 tablespoon olive oil
- 3 garlic cloves, minced
- 16 ounces gnocchi
- ¼ cup parmesan, grated
- 8 ounces spinach pesto

Directions:
1. Grease your air fryer's pan with olive oil, add gnocchi, onion and garlic, toss, put pan in your air fryer and cook at 400 °f for 10 minutes.
2. Add pesto, toss and cook for 7 minutes more at 350 °f.
3. Divide among plates and serve for lunch.

Nutrition: Calories 113 Fat 2 g Carbohydrates 3 g Sugar 2 g Protein 4 g Cholesterol 18 mg

108. Chicken and corn casserole

Preparation time: 10 minutes
Cooking time: 30 minutes
servings: 6
Ingredients:

- 1 cup clean chicken stock
- 2 tsps. Garlic powder
- Salt and black pepper to the taste
- 6 ounces canned coconut milk
- 1 and ½ cups green lentils
- 2 pounds chicken breasts, skinless, boneless and cubed 1/3 cup cilantro, chopped
- 3 cups corn
- 3 handfuls spinach
- 3 green onions, chopped

Directions:
1. In a pan that fits your air fryer, mix stock with coconut milk, salt, pepper, garlic powder, chicken and lentils.
2. Add corn, green onions, cilantro and spinach, stir well, introduce in your air fryer and cook at 350 °f for 30 minutes.

Nutrition: Calories: 292 Fat: 5g Carbs: 31g Protein: 32g

109. Tomato mushroom mix

Preparation time: 10 minutes
Cooking time: 15 minutes
Servings: 4
Ingredients:

- 6 oz tomatoes, chopped 2 tbsp olive oil
- ½ tsp ground nutmeg 1 onion, chopped
- 15 oz mushrooms, sliced pepper
- Salt

Directions:
1. Add all ingredients into the air fryer baking dish and mix well.
2. Place dish in the air fryer and cook at 380° f for 15 minutes.

3. Serve and enjoy.

Nutrition: Calories 103 Fat 5 g Carbohydrates 9 g Sugar 4 g Protein 4 g Cholesterol 0 mg

110. Herb carrots

Preparation time: 10 minutes
Cooking time: 20 minutes
Servings: 4
Ingredients:

- 1 Lb. baby carrots, trimmed
- 2 tbsp fresh lime juice
- 1 Tsp herb de Provence
- 2 tsp olive oil
- Pepper salt

Directions:
1. Add carrots into the bowl and toss with remaining ingredients.
2. Transfer carrots into the air fryer basket and cook at 320° f for 20 minutes.
3. Serve and enjoy.

Nutrition: Calories 60 Fat 5 g Carbohydrates 4 g Sugar 4 g Protein 7 g Cholesterol 0 mg

111. Asian popcorn chicken

Preparation time: 30 minutes
cooking time: 15 minutes
servings: 2
Ingredients

- 1 lbs. Chicken breast chicken thigh, boneless
- 1 clove garlic, medium, minced
- 1 tablespoon soy sauce
- 2 green onions, minced
- ¼ tsp. Of pepper
- ¼ tsp. Of chili pepper
- ¼ t tsp. Of five spice
- ½ tsp. Of sweet potato starch or corn starch
- 1 egg
- ¼ cup water breadcrumbs

Directions:
1. Wash the chicken and dice. Put the washed and minced green onions and garlic in a medium bowl.
2. Add the chili pepper, five spice powder, pepper, soy sauce and starch, mixing well.
3. Place chicken into the bowl and ensure the pieces are fully coated on all the sides. Leave the chicken to marinate in the bowl for at least 30 minutes or overnight if you like.
4. Preheat the air fryer to 390°f. Beat 1 egg with water in a small ball, add starch and mix thoroughly.
5. Coat the chicken with the starch, pressing with hands, so it does not fall off. Place in the air fryer and cook for 12 minutes. Served, tossed with salt and pepper.

Nutrition: Calories: 153 Fat: 3g Carbs: 6g Protein: 24g

112. Onion and parsley turkey rolls

Preparation time: 15 minutes
Cooking time: 40 minutes
Servings: 4
Ingredients

- 1 pound of turkey breast fillets 6 tsp. of olive oil
- 1 tsp. Of cinnamon 1 clove of garlic, crushed
- 1 small sized onion, finely chopped 1 tsp. Of salt
- 1½ ounces of parsley, finely chopped
- 1½ tsp. Of ground cumin
- ½ tsp. Of ground chili

Directions:
1. Place the turkey fillets on a chopping board with the smaller side facing you and cut through horizontally up to about 2/3 of the length. Fold open the slit and cut through again to form a long strip of meat.
2. Mix the chili, garlic, cumin, pepper, cinnamon and salt together in a large bowl. Stir in the olive oil. Remove 1 tablespoon of the mixture and set aside in a small bowl.
3. Add the parsley and onion to the mixture in the large bowl and stir.
4. heat your air fryer to 356°f.

5. spread the herb mixture on the surface of the meat and roll firmly beginning from the shorter end. Tie the roll with a string at about an inch interval. Coat the outside of the meat rolls with the spice mixture that was set aside.
6. place in the air fryer and cook for 40 minutes.

Nutrition: Calories: 200 Fat: 12g Carbs: 4g Protein: 18g

113. Mushroom & chicken noodles with glasswort and sesame

Preparation time: 30 minutes
Cooking time: 17 minutes
Servings: 4
Ingredients

- 14 ounces of chicken thigh fillets, cut to pieces
- 14 ounces of noodles, cooked
- 2 cloves of garlic
- 2/3 cup of chestnut mushrooms
- 2/3 cup of shiitake mushrooms
- 1/4 cup of soy sauce
- 6 tsp. of sesame oil
- 3 tsp. of sesame seeds
- 7 ounces of glasswort
- 3 ounces of bean sprouts
- 1 tsp. Sambal
- 1 medium sized onion, thinly sliced krupuk

Directions:
1. Mix the soy sauce, garlic and sambal to form a marinade and soak the chicken pieces in it to absorb.
2. Add 3 tsps. Of oil to the cooked noodles.
3. Heat the air fryer to 392°f. Place the chicken pieces in the fryer basket and sprinkle with oil. Cook for 6 minutes, shaking at intervals.
4. Add the onion, mushrooms, glasswort and bean sprouts. Cook for another 5 minutes. Put in the noodles and cook further for 5 minutes. Finally, add the krupuk at the last minute.
5. remove from the air fryer and sprinkle with sesame seed.

Nutrition: Calories: 186 Fat: 0g Carbs: 33g Protein: 8g

114. Easy cheesy broccoli

Preparation Time: 15 minutes
Cooking Time: 20 minutes
Servings: 4
Ingredients

- 1/3 cup grated yellow cheese
- large-sized head broccoli, stemmed and cut small florets
- 2 1/2 tbsp. canola oil
- 1 tsp. dried rosemary
- 2 tsp. dried basil
- Salt and ground black pepper, to taste

Directions:
1. Bring a medium pan filled with a lightly salted water to a boil. Then, boil the broccoli florets for about 3 minutes.
2. Then, drain the broccoli florets well; toss them with the canola oil, rosemary, basil, salt and black pepper.
3. Set your air fryer to 390 °f; arrange the seasoned broccoli in the cooking basket; set the timer for 17 minutes. Toss the broccoli halfway through the cooking process.
4. Serve warm topped with grated cheese and enjoy!

Nutrition: 103 Calories; 1g Fat; 9g Carbs; 9g Protein; 2g Sugars

115. Potato and kale croquettes

Preparation Time: 5 minutes
Cooking Time: 7 minutes
Servings: 6
Ingredients

- 2 eggs, slightly beaten
- 1/3 cup flour
- 1/3 cup goat cheese, crumbled
- 1/2 tsp. fine sea salt 4 garlic cloves, minced
- 1 cup kale, steamed
- 1/3 cup breadcrumbs
- 1/3tsp. red pepper flakes
- 2 potatoes, peeled and quartered
- 1/3 tsp. dried dill weed

Directions:
1. Firstly, boil the potatoes in salted water. Once the potatoes are cooked, mash them; add the kale, goat cheese, minced garlic, sea salt, red pepper flakes, dill and one egg; stir to combine well.
2. Now, roll the mixture to form small croquettes.
3. Grab three shallow bowls. Place the flour in the first shallow bowl.
4. Beat the remaining 3 eggs in the second bowl. After that, throw the breadcrumbs into the third shallow bowl.
5. Dip each croquette in the flour; then, dip them in the eggs bowl; lastly, roll each croquette in the breadcrumbs.
6. Air fry at 335 °f for 7 minutes or until golden. Adjust for seasonings and serve warm.

Nutrition: 309 Calories; 9g Fat; 48g Carbs; 11g Protein; 2g sugars

116. Meat, corn and potato barbecue

Preparation time: 3 minutes
Cooking time: 27 minutes
Servings: 4
Ingredients

- 2 Pancetta belly bacon slices
- 2 sausages
- 1 corn on the cob
- 1 mealy potato
- 2 spareribs
- 2 shasliks
- Salt and pepper to taste
- Barbecue sauce

Directions:
1. Heat the air fryer to 392°f. Put the potato in it and cook for 15 minutes.
2. Put in the corn and meat-shasliks, pancetta bacons, sausages and spareribs and grill for 12 minutes.
3. Remove and sprinkle with salt and pepper. Serve with barbecue sauce and vegetable salad.

Nutrition: Calories 113 Fat 2 g Carbohydrates 3 g Sugar 2 g Protein 4 g Cholesterol 18 mg

117. Creamed asparagus and egg salad

Preparation Time: 10 minutes
Cooking Time: 20 minutes
Servings: 4
Ingredients

- 2 eggs
- 1-pound asparagus, chopped
- 2 cup baby spinach
- 1/2 cup mayonnaise
- 1 tsp. Mustard
- 1 tsp. Fresh lemon juice
- Sea salt and ground black pepper, to taste

Directions:
1. Place the wire rack in the air fryer basket; lower the eggs onto the wire rack. Cook at 270 °f for 15 minutes.
2. Transfer them to an ice-cold water bath to stop the cooking. Peel the eggs under cold running water; coarsely chop the hard-boiled eggs and set aside.
3. Increase the temperature to 400 °F. Place your asparagus in the lightly greased air fryer basket.
4. Cook for 5 minutes or until tender. Place in a nice salad bowl. Add the baby spinach.
5. in a mixing dish, thoroughly combine the remaining ingredients. Drizzle this dressing over the asparagus in the salad bowl and top with the chopped eggs.

Nutrition: 245 Calories; 29g Fat; 3g Carbs; 6g Protein; 4g Sugars

118. Red currant cupcakes

Preparation time: 10 minutes
Cooking Time: 12 minutes
Servings: 3
Ingredients

- 1 cup all-purpose flour
- 1/2 cup sugar
- 1 tsp. baking powder
- A pinch of kosher salt
- A pinch of grated nutmeg

- 1/4 cup coconut, oil melted
- 1 egg
- 1/4 cup full-fat coconut milk
- 1/4 tsp. ground cardamom
- 1/4 tsp. ground cinnamon
- 1 tsp. vanilla extract
- 6 ounces red currants

Directions:

1. Mix the flour with the sugar, baking powder, salt, and nutmeg. In a separate bowl, whisk the coconut oil, egg, milk, cardamom, cinnamon, and vanilla.
2. Add the egg mixture to the dry ingredients; mix to combine well.
3. Now, fold in the red currants; gently stir to combine. Scrape the batter into lightly greased 6 standard-size muffin cups.
4. Bake your cupcakes at 360 °f for 12 minutes or until the tops are golden brown. Sprinkle some extra icing sugar over the top of each muffin if desired. Enjoy!

Nutrition: 346 Calories; 5g Fat; 59g Carbs; 7g Protein; 22g Sugars

LUNCH RECIPES

119.   Sweet chili chicken wings

Preparation time: 10 minutes
Cooking time: 50 minutes
Servings: 12
Ingredients:

- 12 chicken wings
- 1/2 tbsp baking powder
- 1 tsp black pepper
- 1/2 tsp sea salt
- 1 tsp garlic powder
- 1/4 tsp onion powder
- 1/4 tsp paprika

Directions:

1. Dry the chicken wings. Add the chicken wings to a zip-lock container with baking powder and seasoning. Cover the bag and chuck it around until it covers the wings.
2. Spray with cooking spray on the metal rack and place the chicken wings into a single layer. Close the lid and press air crisp, then set the temp to 400 ° F, set the period to 20 minutes, and then press start.
3. Open the cover for 10 minutes and toss/flip the chicken wings with tongs to keep them from sticking. Cover the lid and allow the remaining 10 minutes to cook for them.
4. In a shallow saucepan, mix all ingredients and cook over medium heat on the burner.
5. Let the sauce boil and then reduce heat until it has decreased and thickened gradually to a simmer, stirring.
6. In the gravy, toss or drop the fried chicken wings.
7. Put a single layer of the sauced chicken wings on a greased baking sheet with a wire rack cover. Broil the chicken wings for 24 minutes at high on the top rack.
8. Remove them from the oven till the sauce is crispy and the wings have some flavor. Serve immediately.

Nutrition: Calories: 648 Fat: 35g Carbs: 25g Protein: 48g Sugars: 13g Fiber: 3

120.   Chicken chimichangas

Preparation time: 15 minutes
Cooking time: 20 minutes
Servings: 4
Ingredients:

- 1 rotisserie chicken white meat
- 1 1/2 cups cooked rice
- 1 cup salsa
- 1/2 tsp salt
- 8 inches soft taco size flour tortillas
- 2 tbsp vegetable oil

Directions:

1. Rub the bottom of the basket with vegetable oil for the air fryer. The air fryer should be preheated to 360°F.
2. Mix the rice, chicken, salt, and salsa in a big bowl until well mixed.
3. In the middle of each tortilla, position about 1/2 cup of the chicken filling. With the ends bent in to lock in the lining, firmly wrap them back.
4. Place the chimichangas in the oiled bowl, two at a time, and seam side down. With vegetable oil, gently clean the tops of the chimichangas.

5. Air fry the chimichangas at 360°F for around 4 minutes. To flip the chimichangas, open an air fryer and use metal tongs.
6. The filling will be stored for up to two days in the refrigerator in an airtight container.
7. Placed sour cream, white cheese sauce, onion, spinach, and guacamole on top of the chimichangas.

Nutrition: Calories: 390 Fat: 18g Carbs: 30g Protein: 40g Sugars: 5g Fiber: 16g

121.   Simple chicken burrito bowls

Preparation time: 20 minutes
Cooking time: 20 minutes
Servings: 4
Ingredients:

- 1 rotisserie chicken
- 1 15 oz black beans
- 1 15 oz corn
- 1 8 oz packet taco skillet sauce
- 1 tbsp vegetable oil
- 1 cup white rice
- 1 tsp salt
- 1 3/4 cup water
- 2 tbsp taco sauce
- 1 cup iceberg lettuce
- 1 avocado
- 4 lime wedges
- 6 oz medium cheddar cheese
- 1/2 cup sour cream
- 4 oz jalapenos

Directions:

1. Add the corn, chicken, taco skillet sauce, and black beans to a wide saucepan. Mix, cover, and heat until simmering, over medium low heat.
2. On over medium high pressure, heat the oil in a different saucepan. Put rice and cook for a minute.
3. Add the sauce to the water, salt and taco and bring it to a boil. Cover and boil the rice for 15 to 20 minutes or until the water is absorbed—lower the pressure.
4. Put a large scoop of rice to the cups and then cover with the mixture of meat, beans, and maize.
5. Add lime wedge, diced avocado, shredded lettuce, shredded cheese, sliced jalapeños, and sour cream to the option. Immediately serve.

Nutrition: Calories: 253 Fat: 7g Carbs: 19g Protein: 28g Sugars: 4g

122.   Southern style chicken

Preparation time: 20 minutes
Cooking time: 20 minutes
Servings: 6
Ingredients:

- Crushed Ritz crackers 2 cups
- Fresh parsley 1 tablespoon
- Garlic salt 1 teaspoon
- Paprika 1 teaspoon
- Pepper 1/2 teaspoon
- Cumin 1/4 teaspoon
- Rubbed sage 1/4 teaspoon
- Egg 1 large

- 2 lbs. Chicken legs
- Cooking spray

Directions:
1. Heat an air fryer at 375 °F. Blend the first seven ingredients in a small dish. Put the egg in a different shallow bowl.
2. Dip the chicken in the shell, then pat in the cracker combination to help adhere to the coating.
3. Place the chicken in batches in a thin layer on the oiled tray in the air fryer bowl and sprinkle with the cooking mist.
4. Cook for 10 minutes. With cooking oil, transform the spritz and chicken; cook until the chicken is lightly browned, and the juices are transparent, 1520 mins longer.

Nutrition: Calories: 318 Fat: 15g Carbs: 21g Protein: 21g Sugars: 2g Fiber: 1g

123. Chickpea fritters with sweet spicy sauce
Preparation time: 15 minutes
Cooking time: 5 minutes
Servings: 12
Ingredients:
- 1 cup yogurt
- 2 tablespoons sugar
- 1 tablespoon honey
- 1/2 teaspoon salt
- 1/2 teaspoon pepper
- 1/2 teaspoon red pepper flakes
- 15 ounces garbanzo beans
- Cumin 1 teaspoon
- 1/2 teaspoon salt
- 1/2 teaspoon garlic powder
- 1/2 teaspoon ginger
- 1 large egg
- 1/2 teaspoon baking soda
- 1/2 cup cilantro
- 2 onions

Directions:
1. Heat an air fryer at 400 °F. Integrate the ingredients in a small bowl; refrigerate before they are eaten.
2. Put in a food processor with seasonings and chickpeas; pulse unless finely ground. Also include baking soda and egg, pulse until combined. Then shift to a bowl, whisk in the green onions and cilantro.
3. Drop rounded teaspoons of bean combination on the greased tray in the air fryer basket in batches. For 56 minutes, fry till golden brown. Serve with the gravy.

Nutrition: Calories: 46 Fat: 2g Carbs: 5g Protein: 1g Sugars: 3g Fiber: 1g

124. Nashville hot chicken
Preparation time: 20 minutes
Cooking time: 30 minutes
Servings: 6
Ingredients:
- 2 tablespoons pickle juice
- 2 tablespoons hot pepper sauce
- 1 teaspoon salt
- 2 pounds chicken tenderloins
- 1 cup flour
- 1/2 teaspoon pepper
- 1 large egg
- 1/2 cup buttermilk
- Cooking spray
- 1/2 cup olive oil
- 2 tablespoons cayenne pepper
- 2 tablespoons dark brown sugar
- 1 teaspoon paprika
- 1 teaspoon chili powder
- 1/2 teaspoon garlic powder
- Pickle slices

Directions:
1. Combine 1 tablespoon pickle juice, 1 tablespoon hot sauce, and 1/2 teaspoon salt in a cup or shallow bath. Connect the chicken, then switch the coat over. Freeze, sealed, for 1 hour. Drain, tossing out some marinade.
2. Heat an air fryer at 375°F. Mix the starch, the remaining 1/2 teaspoon salt, and the pepper in a small dish.
3. Whisk together the bacon, buttermilk, 1 tablespoon of pickle juice, and 1 tablespoon of hot sauce in another small cup. To cover all ends, dip the chicken in flour; shake off the waste.
4. Dip in the egg mixture, then the flour mixture again.
5. Organize the chicken in batches on a well-greased tray in the air fryer bowl in a single layer; spritz with cooking spray.
6. Cook for 56 minutes until it is golden brown. Turn; spritz with spray for cooking. Cook until golden brown, for 56 more minutes.
7. Mix milk, cayenne pepper, brown sugar, seasonings, spillover warm chicken, and cover with the flip. With pickles, eat.

Nutrition: Calories: 413 Fat: 20g Carbs: 20g Protein: 39g Sugars: 5g Fiber: 1g

125. Fiesta chicken fingers
Preparation time: 20 minutes
Cooking time: 15 minutes
Servings: 4
Ingredients:
- Boneless skinless chicken breasts 3/4 pound
- Buttermilk 1/2 cup
- Pepper 1/4 teaspoon
- Flour 1 cup
- Corn chips 3 cups
- Taco seasoning 1 envelope
- Salsa

Directions:
1. Heat an air fryer at 400 °F. Pound the chicken breasts with a 1/2in meat mallet. Slice into 1in. Strips big.
2. Whisk together the buttermilk and pepper in a small dish. Place flour in a different shallow bowl. In the third bowl, combine the corn chips with the taco seasoning.
3. To cover all ends, dip the chicken in flour; shake off the waste. Dip in the buttermilk combination, then pat in the corn chip mixture to help adhere to the coating.
4. Arrange the chicken in batches on an oiled tray in the air fryer bowl in a single layer; spritz with olive oil.
5. Cook for 78 minutes on either side until the covering is lightly browned and the chicken is no longer pink. Repeat for the chicken that remains.
6. Serve with dip or salsa from the ranch.

Nutrition: Calories: 670 Fat: 35g Carbs: 60g Protein: 24g Sugars: 4g Fiber: 3g

126. Bagel chicken strips
Preparation time: 10 minutes
Cooking time: 10 minutes
Servings: 4
Ingredients:
- 1dayold bagel
- 1/2 cup panko breadcrumbs
- 1/2 cup parmesan cheese
- 1/4 teaspoon red pepper flakes
- 1/4 cup butter
- 1pound chicken tenderloins
- 1/2 teaspoon salt

Directions:
1. Heat an air fryer at 400 °F. In a food processor, pulse the broken bagel until coarse crumbs develop.
2. In a shallow bowl, put 1/2 cup bagel crumbs; toss with panko, pepper flakes, and cheese.
3. Microwave the butter once molten in a microwave safe small dish. Sprinkle salt on the chicken.
4. To aid bind, dip in hot butter, then cover with crumb mixture, patting.
5. Place the chicken in a thin layer on an oiled tray in the air fryer bowl in batches.
6. Cook for 7 minutes; switch the chicken around. Continue to cook for 78 minutes until the covering is lightly browned and the chicken is no longer yellow.

Nutrition: Calories: 350Fat: 15g Carbs: 10g Protein: 40g Sugars: 3g Fiber: 3g

127. Peach bourbon wings

Preparation time: 20 minutes
Cooking time: 15 minutes
Servings: 6
Ingredients:

- 1/2 cup peach preserving
- 1 tablespoon brown sugar
- 1 garlic clove
- 1/4 teaspoon salt
- 2 tablespoons white vinegar
- 2 tablespoons bourbon
- 1 teaspoon cornstarch
- 11/2 teaspoons water
- 2 pounds chicken wings

Directions:

1. Heat an air fryer at 400°F. In a food processor, put the preserving, brown garlic, sugar, and salt, until blended. Move it to a tiny casserole.
2. Remove bourbon and vinegar; heat it. Reduce heat; boil, uncovered, for 46 minutes, until lightly thickened.
3. Mix the cornstarch and water in a small bowl until smooth. Whisk in the mixture of preserving.
4. Return to a boil, continuously stirring; cook and stir for 12 minutes or until thickened. For serving, save 1/4 cup sauce.
5. Breakthrough the 2 joints on each chicken wing with a sharp knife; cut the wings' tips. Place wing parts in a single layer on an oiled tray in the air fryer bowl in batches.
6. Cook for 6 minutes, switch and spray with a blend of preserving. Cooked 68 minutes longer, before browned and juices run free.
7. Serve the wings with the reserved sauce immediately.

Nutrition: Calories: 145 Fat: 8g Carbs: 7g Protein: 9g Sugars: 5g Fiber: 1g

128. Classic Greek chicken

Preparation time: 10 minutes
Cooking time: 30 minutes
Servings: 4
Ingredients:

- 1 lb. Chicken breasts, skinless & boneless
- For marinade:
- 1/2 tsp dill
- 1 tsp onion powder
- 1/4 tsp basil
- 1/4 tsp oregano
- 3 garlic cloves, minced
- 1 tbsp lemon juice
- 3 tbsp olive oil
- 1/4 tsp pepper
- 1/2 tsp salt

Directions:

1. Add all marinade ingredients into the mixing bowl and mix well.
2. Add chicken into the marinade and coat well. Put a cover in the bowl and place it in the refrigerator overnight.
3. Insert wire rack. Select bake, set temperature 390° F, timer for 30 minutes. Press start to preheat the oven.
4. Arrange marinated chicken on a roasting pan and bake for 25-30 minutes.
5. Serve and enjoy.

Nutrition: Calories 313 Fat 19 g Carbohydrates 5 g Sugar 3 g Protein 31 g

129. Crispy chicken thighs

Preparation time: 10 minutes
Cooking time: 35 minutes
Servings: 6
Ingredients:

- 6 chicken thighs
- 1 tbsp olive oil
- For rub:
- 1/2 tsp basil
- 1/2 tsp oregano
- 1/2 tsp pepper
- 1 tsp garlic powder
- 1 tsp onion powder
- 1/2 tsp salt

Directions:

1. Insert wire rack in rack position select bake, set temperature 390° F, timer for 35 minutes. Press start to preheat the oven.
2. Brush chicken thighs with olive oil. In a small bowl, mix rub ingredients and rub all over the chicken.
3. Arrange chicken on a roasting pan and bake for 30-35 minutes.
4. Serve and enjoy.

Nutrition: Calories 49 Fat 4 g Carbohydrates 9 g Sugar 3 g Protein 1 g

130. Perfect juicy chicken breast

Preparation time: 10 minutes
Cooking time: 15 minutes
Servings: 8
Ingredients:

- 4 chicken breasts, skinless and boneless
- 1 tbsp olive oil
- For rub:
- 1 tsp garlic powder
- 1 tsp onion powder
- 4 tsp brown sugar
- 4 tsp paprika
- 1 tsp black pepper
- 1 tsp salt

Directions:

1. Insert wire rack in rack position select bake, set temperature 390° F, timer for 30 minutes. Press start to preheat the oven.
2. Brush chicken breasts with olive oil. In a small bowl, mix rub ingredients and rub all over chicken breasts.
3. Put the chicken breasts on a roasting pan and bake for 12-15 minutes or until internal temperature reaches 165° F.
4. Serve and enjoy.

Nutrition: Calories 165 Fat 3 g Carbohydrates 7 g Sugar 8 g Protein 24 g

131. Crispy & tasty chicken breast

Preparation time: 10 minutes
Cooking time: 35 minutes
Servings: 4
Ingredients:

- 4 chicken breasts, skinless and boneless
- 1/2 cup butter, cut into pieces
- 1 cup cracker crumbs
- 2 eggs, lightly beaten
- Pepper
- Salt

Directions:

1. Insert wire rack. Select bake, set temperature 375 F, timer for 35 minutes. Press start to preheat the oven.
2. Add cracker crumbs and eggs in 2 separate shallow dishes.
3. Mix cracker crumbs with pepper and salt.
4. Dip chicken in the eggs and then coat with cracker crumb.
5. Arrange coated chicken into the 9*13inch baking dish.
6. Spread butter pieces on top of the chicken and bake for 30-35 minutes. Serve and enjoy.

Nutrition: Calories 590 Fat 40 g Carbohydrates 7 g Sugar 5 g Protein 44 g

132. Broccoli bacon ranch chicken

Preparation time: 10 minutes
Cooking time: 30 minutes
Servings: 4
Ingredients:

- 4 chicken breasts, skinless and boneless
- 1/3 cup mozzarella cheese, shredded
- 1 cup cheddar cheese, shredded
- 1/2 cup ranch dressing
- 5 bacon slices, cooked and chopped
- 2 cups broccoli florets, blanched and chopped

Directions:

1. Select bake, set temperature 375° F, timer for 30 minutes. Press start to preheat the oven.
2. Add chicken into the 13*9inch casserole dish. Top with bacon and broccoli.
3. Pour ranch dressing over chicken and top with shredded mozzarella cheese and cheddar cheese.
4. Bake chicken for 30 minutes.
5. Serve and enjoy.

Nutrition: Calories 551 Fat 38 g Carbohydrates 4 g Sugar 7 g Protein 64 g

133. Jerk chicken legs

Preparation time: 10 minutes
Cooking time: 50 minutes
Servings: 10
Ingredients:

- 10 chicken legs
- 1/2 tsp ground nutmeg
- 1/2 tsp ground cinnamon
- 1 tsp ground allspice
- 1 tsp black pepper
- 1 tbsp fresh thyme
- 1 1/2 tbsp brown sugar
- 1/4 cup soy sauce
- 1/3 cup fresh lime juice
- 1 tbsp ginger, sliced
- 2 habanera peppers, remove the stem
- 4 garlic cloves, peeled and smashed
- 6 green onions, chopped

Directions:

1. Add chicken into the large zip-lock bag.
2. Put the remaining ingredients into the food processor and process until coarse.
3. Pour mixture over chicken. Shake to coat the chicken and refrigerate overnight.
4. Insert wire rack. Select bake, set temperature 375° F, timer for 50 minutes. Press start to preheat the oven.
5. Line baking sheet with foil. Arrange marinated chicken legs on a baking sheet and bake for 45-50 minutes.
6. Serve and enjoy.

Nutrition: Calories 232 Fat 12 g Carbohydrates 8 g Sugar 2 g Protein 29 g

134. Creamy cheese chicken

Preparation time: 10 minutes
Cooking time: 45 minutes
Servings: 4
Ingredients:

- 4 chicken breasts, skinless, boneless & cut into chunks
- 1 cup mayonnaise
- 1 tsp garlic powder
- 1 cup parmesan cheese, shredded
- Pepper
- Salt

Directions:

1. Add chicken pieces into the bowl of buttermilk and soak overnight.
2. Select bake, set temperature 375° F, timer for 45 minutes. Press start to preheat the oven.
3. Add marinated chicken pieces into the 9*13inch baking dish.
4. Mix mayonnaise, garlic powder, 1/2 cup parmesan cheese, pepper, and salt and pour over chicken.
5. Put some cheese on top of the chicken and bake for 40-45 minutes. Serve and enjoy.

Nutrition: Calories 581 Fat 33 g Carbohydrates 14 g Sugar 9 g Protein 51 g

135. Baked chicken breasts

Preparation time: 10 minutes
Cooking time: 25 minutes
Servings: 6
Ingredients:

- 6 chicken breasts, skinless & boneless
- 1/4 tsp paprika
- 1/2 tsp garlic salt
- 1 tsp Italian seasoning
- 2 tbsp olive oil
- 1/4 tsp pepper

Directions:

1. Select bake, set temperature 390° F, timer for 25 minutes. Press start to preheat the oven.
2. Brush chicken with oil. Mix Italian seasoning, garlic salt, paprika, and pepper and rub all over the chicken.
3. Arrange chicken breasts on a roasting pan and bake for 25 minutes or until internal temperature reaches 165° F.
4. Slice and serve.

Nutrition: Calories 321 Fat 17 g Carbohydrates 4 g Sugar 1 g Protein 43 g

136. Bbq chicken wings

Preparation time: 10 minutes
Cooking time: 55 minutes
Servings: 8
Ingredients:

- 32 chicken wings
- 1 1/2 cups BBQ sauce
- 1/4 cup olive oil
- Pepper
- Salt

Directions:

1. Get and line a baking sheet with parchment paper. Set aside.
2. Select bake, set temperature 375° F, timer for 55 minutes. Press start to preheat the oven.
3. In a mixing bowl, toss chicken wings with olive oil, pepper, and salt.
4. Put the chicken wings on a baking sheet and bake for 50 minutes.
5. Toss chicken wings with BBQ sauce and bake for 5 minutes more. Serve and enjoy.

Nutrition: Calories 173 Fat 3 g Carbohydrates 17 g Sugar 12 g Protein 4 g

137. Honey mustard sauce chicken

Preparation time: 10 minutes
Cooking time: 40 minutes
Servings: 6
Ingredients:

- 6 chicken thighs, bone in & skin on
- 1/4 cup yellow mustard
- 1/2 cup honey
- Pepper
- Salt

Directions:

1. Insert wire rack. Select bake, set temperature 350° F, timer for 30 minutes. Press start to preheat the oven.
2. Put salt and pepper on the chicken. Place it into the baking dish.
3. Mix together yellow mustard and honey and pour over chicken and bake the chicken for 30 minutes.
4. Spoon honey mustard mixture over chicken and bake chicken 10 minutes more.
5. Serve and enjoy.

Nutrition: Calories 119 Fat 4 g Carbohydrates 29 g Sugar 23 g Protein 5 g

138. Baked chicken & potatoes

Preparation time: 10 minutes
Cooking time: 60 minutes
Servings: 5
Ingredients:

- 5 chicken thighs
- 1 lemon juice
- 1/2 cup olive oil
- 1 tbsp fresh rosemary, chopped
- 1 tsp dried oregano
- 2 lbs. Potatoes, cut into chunks
- 4 garlic cloves, minced
- Pepper
- Salt

Directions:

1. Put in the wire rack. Select bake, set temperature 375° F, timer for 60 minutes. Press start to preheat the oven.
2. In a large mixing bowl, add chicken and remaining ingredients and mix well.
3. Place chicken in the baking dish and spread potatoes around the chicken.
4. Bake chicken for 60 minutes.
5. Serve and enjoy.

Nutrition: Calories 333 Fat 26 g Carbohydrates 31 g Sugar 3 g Protein 3 g

139. Curried chicken

Preparation time: 10 minutes
Cooking time: 40 minutes
Servings: 4
Ingredients:

- 4 chicken breasts, skinless and boneless
- 4 tsp curry powder

- 1/4 cup mustard
- 1/3 cup butter
- 1/3 cup honey

Directions:
1. Select bake, set temperature 375° F, timer for 40 minutes. Press start to preheat the oven.
2. Add butter and honey in a small saucepan and heat over low heat until butter is melted.
3. Remove saucepan from heat and stir in curry powder and mustard.
4. Arrange chicken in a casserole dish and pour butter mixture over chicken and bake for 40 minutes.
5. Serve and enjoy.

Nutrition: Calories 552 Fat 23 g Carbohydrates 29 g Sugar 29 g Protein 42 g

140. Chicken meatballs
Preparation time: 10 minutes
Cooking time: 25 minutes
Servings: 4
Ingredients:
- 1 lb. Ground chicken
- 1/4 tsp red pepper flakes
- 1/2 tsp dried oregano
- 1 tsp dried onion flakes
- 1 garlic clove, minced
- 1 egg, lightly beaten
- 2 tbsp olive oil
- 1 tbsp parsley, chopped
- 1/2 cup breadcrumbs
- 1/2 cup parmesan cheese, grated
- 1/4 tsp pepper
- 1/2 tsp sea salt

Directions:
1. Line baking sheet and set aside.
2. Insert wire rack. Select bake, set temperature 390° F, timer for 25 minutes. Press start to preheat the oven.
3. Get all ingredients and put them into the mixing bowl. Mix until well combined.
4. Make small balls from the meat mixture and arrange on a baking sheet.
5. Bake meatballs for 25 minutes. Serve and enjoy.

Nutrition: Calories 385 Fat 17 g Carbohydrates 11 g Sugar 1 g Protein 38 g

141. Korean gochujang chicken wings
Preparation time: 15 minutes
Cooking time: 25 minutes
Servings: 4
Ingredients:
- 2 pounds chicken wings, thawed
- 2 tbsp olive oil
- 1 tsp salt
- 1 tsp black pepper
- 2 tbsp gochujang (Korean red chili paste)
- 1 tbsp rice vinegar
- 1 tbsp maple syrup or honey
- 2 tbsp light soy sauce
- 1 tbsp toasted sesame oil
- 1 garlic clove, minced
- 1 tbsp fresh ginger, minced
- 1 tbsp sesame seeds
- 1/4 cup scallions, chopped

Directions:
1. Preheat the air fryer to 400°F.
2. Using a large bowl, toss the wings with the olive oil, and season with salt and black pepper.
3. Prepare the wings in the air fryer basket and cook for 20 minutes, turning it halfway through.
4. Meanwhile, using a small bowl, combine the gochujang, rice vinegar, maple syrup or honey, soy sauce, sesame oil, garlic, and ginger.
5. Remove the wings and put to a large bowl.
6. Pour about half of the gochujang sauce on the wings and toss to coat well.
7. Put the wings back to the air fryer basket and cook for 5 minutes more, until the sauce has glazed.
8. Get a serving plate and put the wings. Dust with the sesame seeds and scallions.
9. Serve with the remaining sauce.

Nutrition: Calories: 380 Fat: 20g Carbs: 23g Protein: 25g Sugars: 16g Fiber: 1g

142. Herbed Cornish hen
Preparation time: 15 minutes
Cooking time: 30 minutes
Servings: 4
Ingredients:
- 1 Cornish game hens (about 2 lb.)
- 1 tbsp unsalted butter, melted
- 1/2 tsp dried thyme
- 1/2 tsp ground cumin
- 1/2 tsp garlic powder
- 1/2 tsp paprika
- 1/2 tsp kosher salt
- 1/8 tsp freshly ground black pepper

Directions:
1. Remove the backbone by of hens through the ribs using sharp kitchen scissors or shear. Discard the giblets from the hen.
2. Trim any excess fat, then cut the hen in half along the breastbone. Trim off the wingtips.
3. Rinse each hen and pat dry.
4. Get a bowl and put butter, thyme, cumin, garlic powder, paprika, salt, and pepper.
5. Coat game hen thoroughly with the mixture.
6. Preheat the air fryer to 380°F.
7. Transfer the hen to the air fryer basket, skin side down.
8. Cook for about 30 minutes, flipping halfway, until golden.
9. Transfer to the serving plates and enjoy!

Nutrition: Calories: 400 Fat: 30g Carbs: 1g Protein: 29g

143. Chicken burgers
Preparation time: 5 minutes
Cooking time: 10 minutes
Servings: 4
Ingredients:
- 1 lb. Ground chicken
- 1 egg, beaten
- 1/2 cup breadcrumbs
- 1/2 onion, diced
- 2 garlic cloves, minced
- 1/2 tsp paprika
- 1/2 cup fresh parsley, finely chopped
- 1/2 tsp salt
- 1/2 tsp pepper
- 4 burger buns, split
- 1/4 cup mayonnaise
- 4 slices cheddar cheese
- 4 fresh lettuce leaves

Directions:
1. Preheat the air fryer to 380°F.
2. Put the chicken, egg, breadcrumbs, onion, garlic, paprika, parsley, salt, and black pepper in a bowl. Mix until just combined. Form into 4 patties.
3. Arrange on a greased air fryer basket.
4. Cook patties for 10 minutes and turn once halfway through.
5. Generously spread mayonnaise on burger buns.
6. Place chicken patties on the bottom of the buns and top with cheddar cheese and lettuce leaves.
7. Place tops of the buns on top.
8. Divide between serving plates and enjoy!

Nutrition: Calories: 320 Fat: 12g Carbs: 27g Protein: 19g Sugars: 4g

144. Garlic roasted chicken with baby potatoes
Preparation time: 10 minutes
Cooking time: 25 minutes
Servings: 4
Ingredients:
- 2 tbsp olive oil
- 1 tbsp fresh lemon juice

- 5 garlic cloves, minced
- 1/2 tsp garlic salt
- 1 tbsp Italian seasoning
- 1/2 tsp thyme, dried
- 1/2 tsp rosemary, dried
- 2 1/2 lbs. chicken thighs, bone in, skin on
- 1 lb. baby potatoes, halved
- 1/2 cup minced parsley leaves (for garnish)

Directions:
1. Preheat the Air Fryer to 380 °F.
2. Put olive oil, lemon juice, garlic, garlic salt, Italian seasoning, thyme, and rosemary in a large mixing bowl. Mix well.
3. Put the chicken and potatoes. Toss to coat.
4. Transfer the chicken skin side up and potatoes to the Air Fryer basket.
5. Cook for 25 minutes.
6. Let the chicken and potatoes rest for 5 minutes before serving.
7. Transfer to the serving plates and enjoy!

Nutrition: Calories: 110 Fat: 1g Carbs: 21f Protein: 4g Fiber: 4g

145. Homemade chicken nuggets

Preparation time: 10 minutes
Cooking time: 10 minutes
Servings: 4
Ingredients:

- 2 chicken breasts, cut into nugget size pieces
- 1/2 tsp seasoned salt
- 1/2 tsp black pepper
- 1/2 tsp garlic powder
- 1/2 tsp paprika
- 1/2 cup all-purpose flour
- 2 eggs
- 2 cups breadcrumbs
- Olive oil spray
- Ketchup, for serving

Directions:
1. Preheat the air fryer to 360°F.
2. Prepare a large bowl then add salt, pepper, garlic powder, and paprika on the chicken. Mix well.
3. Add flour and toss to coat well.
4. Beat egg and set aside.
5. Transfer the breadcrumbs to a rimmed plate.
6. Working in batches, dip chicken pieces in the egg, shaking off the excess, and then roll in the breadcrumbs to coat.
7. Arrange the nuggets on the greased air fryer basket and lightly spray with olive oil spray.
8. Cook for 10 minutes, until golden brown, turning once halfway through.
9. Transfer to a plate and serve with ketchup if desired!

Nutrition: Calories: 188 Fat: 4g Carbs: 8g Protein: 25g

146. Chicken fajitas

Preparation time: 15 minutes
Cooking time: 25 minutes
Servings: 6
Ingredients:

- 1 lb. Boneless skinless chicken breasts
- 2 tbsp vegetable oil
- 4 1/2 tsp taco seasoning
- 1 medium onion, thinly sliced
- 1 red cored bell pepper, sliced into strips
- 1 green bell pepper, cored and sliced into strips
- 1 tbsp vegetable oil
- 1 garlic clove, minced
- 1/2 tsp salt
- 1/4 tsp ground cumin
- 1/4 tsp chili powder
- For serving:
- 6 flour tortillas, 8inch size
- Salsa
- Guacamole
- Sour cream
- Shredded cheese

Directions:
1. Preheat the air fryer to 375°F.
2. Chop the chicken breast into half inch-thick strips.
3. Using a large bowl, toss together the chicken strips, vegetable oil, and taco seasoning to coat.
4. Put to the air fryer basket and cook for 10 minutes.
5. Meanwhile, using a separate bowl, combine the onion, bell peppers, vegetable oil, garlic, salt, ground cumin, and chili powder. Toss to coat well.
6. Put vegetables to the air fryer basket and toss everything together to blend the seasonings.
7. Cook for 15 minutes more.
8. Transfer to a serving plate.
9. Serve with warmed tortillas, salsa, guacamole, sour cream, and shredded cheddar (if you wish).

Nutrition: Calories: 184 Fat: 6g Carbs: 17g Protein: 15g Sugars: 3g Fiber: 2g

147. Maple mustard glazed turkey

Preparation time: 10 minutes
Cooking time: 25 minutes
Servings: 4
Ingredients:

- 1 turkey breast (about 1½2 lbs.
- 1 tbsp olive oil
- 1/4 tsp paprika
- 1/2 tsp thyme
- 1/8 tsp dry mustard
- 1/4 tsp garlic powder
- 1/2 tsp salt
- 1/4 tsp freshly ground black pepper
- 1 tbsp maple syrup
- 1 tbsp Dijon mustard
- 1 tbsp unsalted butter, melted

Directions:
1. Preheat the air fryer to 350°F.
2. Combine paprika, olive oil, thyme, dry mustard, garlic powder, salt, and freshly ground black pepper in a bowl.
3. Massage turkey breast with the oil mixture.
4. Put the turkey in the fryer basket. Cook for 15 minutes.
5. Once done, turn the turkey breast using tongs and cook for 10 minutes more.
6. Using a separate bowl, mix the maple syrup, Dijon mustard, and unsalted butter.
7. Turn the turkey breast and brush the glaze all over the turkey breast.
8. Cook for 3 minutes more.
9. Transfer to a serving plate and enjoy!

Nutrition: Calories: 350 Fat: 6g Carbs: 33g Protein: 40g Sugars: 16g Fiber: 3g

148. Turkey and vegetables kabobs

Preparation time: 15 minutes
Cooking time: 20 minutes
Servings: 4
Ingredients:

- 1/4 cup of soy sauce
- 1 tbsp honey
- 2 garlic cloves, minced
- 1 lb. Boneless skinless turkey breast tenderloins, cut into large chunks
- 1 large zucchini, cut into chunks
- 1 yellow bell pepper, chunks
- 1 red onion, cut into large chunks
- 1 cup cherry tomatoes
- Cooking or olive oil spray

Directions:
1. Rinse skewers in water for at 30 minutes if using wooden ones.
2. Preheat the air fryer to 350°F.
3. Place turkey, zucchini, bell pepper, onion, and tomatoes in a large bowl.
4. Using a small mixing bowl, combine soy sauce, honey, garlic, and rosemary. Mix well.
5. Pour prepared sauce over turkey and vegetables and toss to coat well.
6. Thread the turkey and vegetables onto skewers.

7. Transfer to the air fryer and spray with cooking spray.
8. Cook for 15 minutes, flipping once halfway through.
9. Transfer to the serving plates.
10. Serve and enjoy!

Nutrition: Calories: 405 Fat: 19g Carbs: 60g Protein: 7g Sugars: 41g Fiber: 9g

149. Turkey meatloaf
Preparation time: 15 minutes
Cooking time: 25 minutes
Servings: 4
Ingredients:
- 1 lb. 99% lean ground turkey
- 1/2 cup breadcrumbs
- 1 large egg, beaten
- 1 tbsp tomato paste
- 1/3 cup of frozen corn
- 1/4 cup onion, minced
- 1/4 cup red bell pepper, chopped
- 1/4 cup scallions, chopped
- 1 garlic clove, minced
- 2 tbsp fresh cilantro, chopped
- 1 tsp salt
- 1/2 tsp ground cumin
- 1/4 tsp chili powder
- Olive oil spray
- 2 tbsp ketchup
- 1 tsp Worcestershire sauce
- 1 tsp honey

Directions:
1. Coat the inside of a loaf pan that fits in your air fryer with cooking spray or oil. Set aside.
2. Preheat the air fryer to 350°F.
3. Prepare the turkey, breadcrumbs, egg, tomato paste, corn, onion, bell pepper scallions, garlic and fresh cilantro in large mixing bowl.
4. Season with salt, ground cumin, chili powder and gently mix until just combined.
5. Place in the prepared loaf pan.
6. Using a separate bowl, mix ketchup, Worcestershire sauce and honey.
7. Brush the meatloaves with the ketchup mixture.
8. Transfer the meatloaf to the air fryer and cook for 20 minutes.
9. Let cool for 10 minutes before slicing.
10. Transfer to a serving plate and enjoy!

Nutrition: Calories: 297 Fat: 19g Carbs: 6g Protein: 25g Sugars: 3g Fiber: 1g

150. Turkey cordon bleu
Preparation time: 15 minutes
Cooking time: 20 minutes
Servings: 4
Ingredients:
- 1 lb. Turkey breast
- 1 tsp salt
- 1/4 tsp thyme, dried
- 1/4 tsp freshly ground black pepper
- 1 tbsp cream cheese
- 4 slices ham
- 4 slices swiss cheese
- 1 egg, beaten
- 1/4 cup all-purpose flour
- 1 cup breadcrumbs

Directions:
1. Preheat the air fryer to 360°F.
2. Slice turkey breast into four equal pieces.
3. Pound each piece slightly with a rolling pin or the smooth side of a meat mallet or heavy skillet until they are about ½inch thick.
4. Season with salt, thyme, and pepper.
5. Lay out cream cheese evenly over one side of each piece of meat.
6. Top with ham slices and swiss cheese.
7. Roll the breast and secure with toothpicks.
8. Whisk egg in a small bowl.
9. Place flour on a shallow plate.
10. Spread breadcrumbs in a bowl.

11. Coat the cordon bleu with the flour and then dip in egg.
12. Sprinkle with breadcrumbs and place in the greased air fryer basket.
13. Cook for 20 minutes, turning once halfway through.
14. Transfer to a serving plate and remove toothpicks.
15. Serve and enjoy!

Nutrition: Calories: 208 Fat: 6g Carbs: 11g Protein: 26g Sugars: 5g Fiber: 9g

151. Provencal pork
Preparation time: 10 minutes
Cooking time: 15 minutes
Servings: 2
Ingredients:
- 1, sliced red onion
- 1, cut into strips yellow bell pepper
- 1, cut into strips green bell pepper
- Salt and black pepper to taste
- 2 tsp. Provencal herbs
- 1/2 tsp. Mustard
- 1 tbsp. Olive oil
- 7 ounces pork tenderloin

Directions:
1. In a dish, mix salt, pepper, onion, green bell pepper, yellow bell pepper, half the oil, and herbs, then toss well.
2. Season pork with mustard, salt, pepper, and rest of the oil.
3. Toss well and add to veggies.
4. Cook in the air fryer at 370°F for 15 minutes. Serve.

Nutrition: Calories 300 Carbs 21g Fat 8g Protein 23g

152. Indian pork
Preparation time: 10 minutes
Cooking time: 12 minutes
Servings: 4
Ingredients:
- Ginger powder – 1 tsp.
- Chili paste – 2 tsp.
- Garlic cloves – 2, minced
- Pork chops – 14 ounces, cubed
- Shallot – 1, chopped
- Coriander – 1 tsp. Ground
- Coconut milk – 7 ounces
- Olive oil – 2 tbsps.
- Peanuts – 3 ounces, ground
- Soy sauce 3 tbsps.
- Salt and black pepper to taste

Directions:
1. In a bowl, mix ginger with half the oil, half of the soy sauce, half of the garlic, and 1 tsp. Chili paste.
2. Whisk and add meat. Coat and marinate for 10 minutes.
3. Cook the meat at 400°F in the air fryer for 12 minutes.
4. Meanwhile, heat the pan with the rest of the oil and add the rest of the peanuts, coconut milk, coriander, rest of the garlic, rest of the chili paste, rest of the soy sauce, and shallot.
5. Stir-fry for 5 minutes. Divide pork on plates, spread coconut mix on top, and serve.

Nutrition: Calories 423 Carbs 42g Fat 11g Protein 18g

153. Creamy pork
Preparation time: 10 minutes
Cooking time: 22 minutes
Servings: 6
Ingredients:
- Pork meat – 2 pounds, boneless and cubed
- Yellow onions – 2, chopped
- Olive oil – 1 tbsp.
- Garlic – 1 clove, minced
- Chicken stock – 3 cups
- Sweet paprika – 2 tbsps.
- Salt and black pepper to taste
- White flour – 2 tbsps.
- Sour cream – 1 1/2 cups
- Dill – 2 tbsp. Chopped

Directions:
1. In a pan, mix pork with oil, salt, and pepper.
2. Mix and place in the air fryer. Cook at 360°F for 7 minutes.

3. Add the sour cream, dill, flour, paprika, stock, garlic, and onion and mix.
4. Cook at 370°F for 15 minutes more. Serve.

Nutrition: Calories 300 Carbs 26g Fat 4g Protein 34g

154. Pork chops with onions

Preparation time:
Cooking time: 25 minutes
Servings: 2
Ingredients:

- Pork chops – 2
- Olive oil – ¼ cup
- Yellow onions – 2, sliced
- Garlic cloves – 2, minced
- Mustard – 2 tsp.
- Sweet paprika – 1 tsp.
- Salt and black pepper to taste
- Oregano – ½ tsp. Dried
- Thyme – ½ tsp. Dried
- A pinch of cayenne pepper

Directions:

1. In a bowl, mix oil with cayenne, thyme, oregano, black pepper, paprika, mustard, and garlic. Whisk well.
2. Combine onions with meat and mustard mix.
3. Mix well to coat, cover and marinate in the refrigerator for 1 day.
4. Transfer meat and onions mix to a pan and cook in the air fryer at 360F for 25 minutes. Serve.

Nutrition: Calories 384 Carbs 17g Fat 4g Protein 25g

155. Braised pork

Preparation time: 15 minutes
Cooking time: 40 minutes
Servings: 4
Ingredients:

- Pork loin roast – 2 pounds, boneless and cubed
- Butter – 4 tbsps. Melted
- Salt and black pepper to taste
- Chicken stock – 2 cups
- Dry white wine – ½ cup
- Garlic – 2 cloves, minced
- Thyme – 1 tsp. Chopped
- Thyme spring – 1
- Bay leaf – 1
- Yellow onion – ½, chopped
- White flour – 2 tbsps.
- Red grapes – ½ pound

Directions:

1. Season pork cubes with salt and pepper. Rub with 2 tablespoons melted butter and put in the air fryer.
2. Cook at 370°F for 8 minutes.
3. Meanwhile, heat a pan with 2 tablespoons of butter over medium heat. Put the onion and garlic—stir fry for 2 minutes.
4. Add a bay leaf, flour, thyme, salt, pepper, stock, and wine. Mix well. Bring to simmer, then remove from the heat.
5. Add grapes and pork cubes.
6. Put in the air fryer at 360°F and cook for 30 minutes. Serve.

Nutrition: Calories 320 Carbs 29g Fat 4g Protein 38g

156. Pork with couscous

Preparation time: 10 minutes
Cooking time: 35 minutes
Servings: 6
Ingredients:

- Pork loin – 2 1/2 pounds, boneless, and trimmed
- Chicken stock – 3/4 cup
- Olive oil – 2 tbsps.
- Sweet paprika – 1/2 tbsp.
- Dried sage – 2 1/4 tsps.
- Garlic powder – 1/2 tsp.
- Dried rosemary – 1/4 tsp.
- Dried marjoram – 1/4 tsp.
- Dried basil – 1 tsp.
- Dried oregano – 1 tsp.
- Salt and black pepper to taste

- Couscous – 2 cups, cooked

Directions:

1. In a bowl, mix oil with stock, salt, pepper, oregano, marjoram, thyme, rosemary, sage, garlic powder, and paprika.
2. Whisk well and add pork loin. Mix and marinate for 1 hour.
3. Cook in the air fryer at 370°F for 35 minutes.
4. Divide among plates and serve with couscous on the side.

Nutrition: Calories 310 Carbs 37g Fat 4g Protein 34g

157. Pulled pork

Preparation time: 10 minutes
Cooking time: 2 hours and 30 minutes
Servings: 8
Ingredients:

- Chili powder – 2 tbsps.
- Garlic powder – 1 tsp.
- Onion powder – 1/2 tsp.
- Ground black pepper – 1/2 tsp.
- Cumin – 1/2 tsp.
- Pork shoulder – 1 (4pound

Directions:

1. In a bowl, mix cumin, pepper, onion powder, garlic powder, and chili powder.
2. Put the spice mixture over the pork shoulder.
3. Place the pork shoulder into the air fryer basket.
4. Cook at 350F for 150 minutes.
5. Shred the meat with forks and serve.

Nutrition: Calories 537 Carbs 1g Fat 35g Protein 43g

158. Juicy pork chops

Preparation time: 10 minutes
Cooking time: 15 minutes
Servings: 2
Ingredients:

- Chili powder – 1 tsp.
- Garlic powder – 1/2 tsp.
- Cumin – 1/2 tsp.
- Ground black pepper – 1/4 tsp.
- Dried oregano – 1/4 tsp.
- Boneless pork chops – 2 (4ounce
- Unsalted butter – 2 tbsps. Divided

Directions:

1. Mix oregano, pepper, cumin, garlic powder, and chili powder in a bowl. Rub dry rub onto pork chops.
2. Add pork chops into the air fryer basket.
3. Cook at 400°F for 15 minutes.
4. Serve each chop topped with 1 tbsp. Butter.

Nutrition: Calories 313 Carbs 1g Fat 26g Protein 24g

159. Pork salad

Preparation time: 10 minutes
Cooking time: 8 minutes
Servings: 2
Ingredients:

- Coconut oil – 1 tbsp.
- Pork chops – 2 (4ouncechopped into 1inch cubes
- Chili powder – 2 tsp.
- Paprika – 1 tsp.
- Garlic powder – 1/2 tsp.
- Onion powder – 1/4 tsp.
- Chopped romaine – 4 cups
- Roma tomato – 1 medium, diced
- Shredded Monterey jack cheese – 1/2 cup
- Avocado – 1, diced
- Full fat ranch dressing – 1/4 cup
- Chopped cilantro – 1 tbsp.

Directions:

1. Drizzle coconut oil over the pork and sprinkle with onion powder, garlic powder, paprika, and chili powder.
2. Place pork into the air fryer basket. Cook at 400°F for 8 minutes.
3. In a bowl, place crispy pork, tomato, and romaine. Top with shredded cheese and avocado.
4. Pour ranch dressing around the bowl and toss to coat. Top with cilantro. Serve.

Nutrition: Calories 526 Carbs 2g Fat 37g Protein 34g

160. Beef with peas and mushrooms

Preparation time: 10 minutes
Cooking time: 22 minutes
Servings: 2
Ingredients:

- Beef steaks – 2, cut into strips
- Salt and black pepper to taste
- Snow peas – 7 ounces
- White mushrooms – 8 ounces, halved
- Yellow onion – 1, cut into rings
- Soy sauce – 2 tbsps.
- Olive oil – 1 tsp.

Directions:
1. In a bowl, mix soy sauce and olive oil, and whisk. Add beef strips and coat.
2. In another bowl, mix mushrooms, onion, snow peas with salt, pepper, and the oil. Toss well.
3. Place in pan and cook in the air fryer at 350°F for 16 minutes.
4. Add beef strips to the pan as well and cook at 400°F for 6 minutes more. Serve.

Nutrition: Calories 235 Carbs 22g Fat 8g Protein 24g

161. Beef and green onions

Preparation time: 10 minutes
Cooking time: 20 minutes
Servings: 4
Ingredients:

- Green onion 1 cup, chopped
- Soy sauce – 1 cup
- Water – 1/2 cup
- Brown sugar – 1/4 cup
- Sesame seeds – 1/4 cup
- Garlic – 5 cloves, minced
- Black pepper – 1 tsp.
- Lean beef – 1 pound

Directions:
1. In a bowl, mix the onion with water, soy sauce, garlic, sugar, sesame seeds, and pepper.
2. Whisk and add meat. Marinate for 10 minutes. Drain beef.
3. Cook in the preheated 390°F air fryer for 20 minutes. Serve.

Nutrition: Calories 329 Carbs 26g Fat 8g Protein 22g

162. Beef and broccoli

Preparation time: 10 minutes
Cooking time: 20 minutes
Servings: 2
Ingredients:

- Sirloin steak – 1/2 pound, thinly sliced
- Liquid aminos – 2 tbsps.
- Grated ginger – 1/4 tsp.
- Finely minced garlic – 1/4 tsp.
- Coconut oil – 1 tbsp.
- Broccoli florets – 2 cups
- Crushed red pepper – 1/4 tsp.
- Xanthan gum – 1/8 tsp.
- Sesame seeds – 1/2 tsp.

Directions:
1. In a bowl, add coconut oil, garlic, ginger, liquid aminos, and beef.
2. Put a cover and marinate 1 hour in the refrigerator.
3. Remove beef from the marinade, reserving marinade, and place the beef into the air fryer basket.
4. Cook at 320°F for 20 minutes. After 10 minutes, add broccoli and sprinkle red pepper into the air fryer basket and shake.
5. Let the marinade boil in a skillet, then reduce heat to simmer. Stir in xanthan gum and allow to thicken.
6. When cooking is done, add the beef and broccoli from the air fryer to the skillet and toss.
7. Sprinkle with sesame seeds and serve.

Nutrition: Calories 342 Carbs 9g Fat 19g Protein 27g

163. Marinated beef

Preparation time: 15 minutes
Cooking time: 45 minutes
Servings: 6

Ingredients:

- Bacon strips – 6
- Butter – 2 tbsps.
- Garlic – 3 cloves, minced
- Salt and black pepper to taste
- Horseradish – 1 tbsp.
- Mustard – 1 tbsp.
- Beef roast – 3 pounds
- Beef stock – 1 3/4 cups
- Red wine – 3/4 cup

Directions:
1. In a bowl, mix butter with horseradish, salt, pepper, garlic, and mustard.
2. Whisk and rub the beef with this mix.
3. Arrange bacon strips on a cutting board. Place beef on top and fold bacon ground beef.
4. Place in the air fryer basket and cook at 400°F for 15 minutes and transfer to a pan. Add stock and wine to the beef.
5. Place pan in the air fryer and cook at 360F for 30 minutes.
6. Carve beef, divide among plates, and serve.

Nutrition: Calories 500 Carbs 29g Fat 9g Protein 36g

164. Beef with mayo

Preparation time: 15 minutes
Cooking time: 40 minutes
Servings: 8
Ingredients:

- Mayonnaise – 1 cup
- Sour cream – 1/3 cup
- Garlic – 3 cloves, minced
- Beef fillet – 3 pounds
- Chives – 2 tbsps. Chopped
- Mustard – 2 tbsp.
- Tarragon – ¼ cup, chopped
- Salt and black pepper to taste

Directions:
1. Rub salt and pepper on the beef before placing it in the air fryer.
2. Cook at 370°F for 20 minutes. Transfer to a plate and set aside.
3. In a bowl, mix garlic with salt, pepper, mayo, chives, and sour cream. Whisk and set aside.
4. In another bowl, mix mustard with tarragon and Dijon mustard. Whisk, and add beef. Mix well.
5. Put it back to the air fryer and cook at 350°F for 20 minutes more.
6. Divide beef on plates spread garlic mayo on top and serve.

Nutrition: Calories 400 Carbs 27g Fat 12g Protein 19g

165. Egg crusted beef schnitzel

Preparation time: 10 minutes
Cooking time: 15 minutes
Servings: 1
Ingredients:

- 1/2 cup almond flour
- One egg, beaten
- One slice of lemon, to serve
- 1/2pound beef schnitzel
- Two tablespoons vegetable oil

Directions:
1. Place the instant pot air fryer lid on and preheat the instant pot at 370°F for 5 minutes.
2. In a baking dish, mix the oil and almond flour.
3. Dip the schnitzel into the egg and dredge in the almond flour mixture.
4. Press the almond flour so that it sticks on to the beef. Place the baking dish in the instant pot.
5. The air fryer should close the lid and cook for 15 minutes at 350°F.
6. Serve with a slice of lemon.

Nutrition: Calories: 732 Carbs: 1g Protein: 56g Fat: 51g

166. Easy beef jerky

Preparation time: 15 minutes
Cooking time: 1 hour
Servings: 4

Ingredients:
- 1 cup beer
- 1/2 cup tamari sauce
- 1 teaspoon liquid smoke
- 2 garlic cloves, minced
- Sea salt and ground black pepper
- 1 teaspoon ancho chili powder
- 2 tablespoons honey
- 3/4pound flank steak, slice into strips

Directions:
1. Place all ingredients in a ceramic dish; let it marinate for 3 hours in the refrigerator. Slice the beef into thin strips
2. Marinate the meat in the fridge overnight.
3. Now, discard the marinade, and hang the meat in the cooking basket by using skewers.
4. Air fry at 190 °F for 1 hour.

Nutrition: Calories: 284 Fat: 14g Carbs: 15g Protein: 23g

167. Beef brisket in spices
Preparation time: 30 minutes
Cooking time: 1 hour and 30 minutes
Servings: 8
Ingredients:
- 1 1/2 cup beef stock
- 1 bay leaf
- 1 tablespoon garlic powder
- 1 tablespoon onion powder
- 2 pounds beef brisket, trimmed
- 2 tablespoons chili powder
- 2 teaspoons dry mustard
- 4 tablespoons olive oil
- Salt and pepper to taste

Directions:
1. Place the instant pot air fryer lid on and preheat the instant pot at 390°F for 5 minutes.
2. Put all ingredients in a deep baking dish that will fit in the instant pot.
3. Put the baking dish in the instant bowl and close the air fryer lid—cook for 1 hour and 30 minutes at 400F.
4. Stir the beef every after 30 minutes to soak in the sauce.

Nutrition: Calories: 306 Carbs: 8g Protein: 13g Fat: 21g

168. Texas rodeo style beef
Preparation time: 2 hours
Cooking time: 1 hour
Servings: 6
Ingredients:
- 1/2 cup honey
- 1/2 cup ketchup
- 1/2 teaspoon dry mustard
- 1 clove of garlic, minced
- 1 tablespoon chili powder
- 2 onion, chopped
- 2 pounds beef steak sliced
- Salt and pepper to taste

Directions:
1. Place ingredients in a zip-loc bag together and marinate in the fridge for at least 2 hours.
2. Place the instant pot air fryer lid on and preheat the instant pot at 390°F.
3. Place the grill pan accessory in the instant bowl.
4. Close the air fryer lid and grill the beef for 15 minutes per batch, making sure that you flip it every 8 minutes for even roasting.
5. Meanwhile, pour the marinade into a saucepan and allow to simmer over medium heat until the sauce thickens.
6. Baste the beef with the sauce before serving.

Nutrition: Calories:542 Carbs: 49g Protein: 37g Fat: 22g

169. Cheesy beef Spanish rice casserole
Preparation time: 10 minutes
Cooking time: 50 minutes
Servings: 3
Ingredients:
- 2 tablespoons chopped green bell pepper
- 1 tablespoon chopped fresh cilantro

- 1/2pound lean ground beef
- 1/2 cup water
- 1/2 teaspoon salt
- 1/2 teaspoon brown sugar
- 1/2 pinch ground black pepper
- 1/3 cup uncooked long grain rice
- 1/4 cup finely chopped onion
- 1/4 cup chile sauce
- 1/4 teaspoon ground cumin
- 1/4 teaspoon Worcestershire sauce
- 1/4 cup shredded Cheddar cheese
- 1/2 (14.5 ounces) can canned tomatoes

Directions:
1. Place the instant pot air fryer lid on and lightly grease the instant pot's baking pan with cooking spray.
2. Add ground beef and place the baking pan in the instant bowl.
3. Close the air fryer lid and cook for 10 minutes at 360°F. Halfway through cooking time, stir and crumble beef. Discard excess fat,
4. Stir in pepper, Worcestershire sauce, cumin, brown sugar, salt, chile sauce, rice, water, tomatoes, green bell pepper, and onion. Mix well.
5. Cover pan with foil and cook for 25 minutes. Stirring occasionally.
6. Give it one last good stir, press down firmly, and sprinkle cheese on top.
7. Cook uncovered for 15 minutes at 390°F until tops are lightly browned.
8. Serve and enjoy with chopped cilantro.

Nutrition: Calories: 346 Carbs: 29g Protein: 15g Fat: 11g

170. Bone in beef in spices
Preparation time: 10 minutes
Cooking time: 2 hours
Servings: 8
Ingredients:
- 1 large onion, quartered
- 1 tablespoon fresh rosemary
- 1 tablespoon fresh thyme
- 2 tablespoons Worcestershire sauce
- 3 cups beef broth
- 3 pounds bone in beef roast
- 4 tablespoons olive oil
- Salt and pepper to taste

Directions:
1. Place the instant pot air fryer lid on and preheat the instant pot at 325° F for 5 minutes.
2. Place ingredients all together in a baking dish and place the baking dish in the preheated instant pot.
3. The air fryer should close the lid 1 hour and 30 minutes at 325F.

Nutrition: Calories: 574 Carbs: 1g Protein: 31g Fat:49g

171. Beef pie
Preparation time: 10 minutes
Cooking time: 1 hour and 5 minutes
Servings: 4
Ingredients:
- 3 tablespoons soy sauce
- 1 tablespoon Worcestershire sauce
- 1/4 cup plain flour
- 1/4 teaspoon salt
- 1/2 teaspoon pepper
- 3 bay leaves
- 3 sprigs thyme
- 2 lbs. Lean beef, cubed
- 3 garlic cloves
- 1carrot, sliced
- 1onion, sliced
- 6new potatoes halved
- 2 celery ribs, sliced
- 1 cup red wine
- 1 cup beef stock
- 2 tablespoons parsley

Directions:

1. Whisk seasonings with flour, soy, Worcestershire sauce, thyme, and bay leaves in a pot.
2. Stir cook this sauce for 5 minutes, then add carrot, garlic, onion, stock, red wine, and beef.
3. Mix well then spread this beef mixture into the instant pot duo.
4. Put on the air fryer lid and seal it.
5. Hit the "bake button" and select 60 minutes of cooking time, then press "start."
6. Once the instant pot duo beeps, remove its lid.
7. Serve

Nutrition: Calories: 535g Fat: 18g Carbs: 47g Protein: 52g

172. Spicy pulled beef
Preparation time: 10 minutes
Cooking time: 8 hours
Servings: 6
Ingredients:
- 2 lbs. Lean beef eye round, trimmed
- 2 tbsp fresh lime juice
- 1 tbsp Worcestershire sauce
- 1 cup can tomato, diced
- 1/4 cup beef broth
- 2 jalapeno peppers
- 2 onion, diced
- 1/4 tsp coriander
- 1/4 tsp oregano
- 1/2 tsp cumin
- 1 tsp garlic, sliced
- 2 red bell pepper, diced

Directions:
1. Season meat with pepper and salt and place into the inner pot of instant pot duo crisp.
2. Add garlic, red pepper, onion, and jalapeno peppers around the beef.
3. Mix coriander, lime juice, Worcestershire sauce, tomatoes, oregano, cumin, and broth and pour over meat.
4. Seal the pot with a pressure-cooking lid and select slow cook mode and cook on low for 8 hours.
5. Remove meat from pan and shred using a fork.
6. Return shredded meat to the pot and stir well.
7. Serve and enjoy.

Nutrition: Calories: 278 Fat: 4 g Carbs: 6 g Protein: 45 g

173. Grilled steak with butter
Preparation time: 10 minutes
Cooking time: 45 minutes
Servings: 2
Ingredients:
- 2 top sirloin steaks
- 3 tablespoons butter, melted
- 3 tablespoons olive oil
- Salt and pepper to taste

Directions:
1. Place the instant pot air fryer lid on and preheat the instant pot at 350 ° F for 5 minutes.
2. Season the sirloin steaks with olive oil, salt, and pepper.
3. Arrange the beef in the air fryer basket and place the air fryer basket in the instant pot.
4. The air fryer should close the lid and cook for 45 minutes at 350 ° F.
5. Once cooked, serve with butter.

Nutrition: Calories: 250 Carbs: 1g Protein: 23g Fat: 17g

174. Steak a la mushrooms
Preparation time: 10 minutes
Cooking time: 18 minutes
Serving: 2
Ingredients:
- 1 lb. Steaks, cubed
- 8 oz. Mushrooms washed and halved
- 2 tablespoons butter, melted
- 1 teaspoon Worcestershire sauce
- 1/2 teaspoon garlic powder, optional
- Salt, to taste
- Fresh cracked black pepper, to taste

- Minced parsley, garnish

Directions:
1. Toss the steak cubes with mushrooms, melted butter, garlic powder, salt, black, Worcestershire sauce, black pepper, and salt in a bowl.
2. Spread the steak cubes and mushrooms in the basket.
3. Put on the air frying lid and seal it.
4. Hit the "air fryer button" and select 18 minutes of cooking time, then press "start."
5. Once the instant pot duo beeps, remove its lid.
6. Garnish with parsley.
7. Serve.

Nutrition: Calories: 582 Fat: 22g Carbs: 8g Protein: 87g

175. Lime garlic steak carnitas
Preparation time: 10 minutes
Cooking time: 6 hours
Servings: 4
Ingredients:
- 1 1/2 lbs. Beef chuck, cut into small pieces
- 1 fresh lime juice
- 1 lime zest
- 2 chilies in adobo sauce
- 1 tbsp garlic, minced
- 1 orange juice
- 1 jalapeno pepper halved

Directions:
1. Adding all ingredients into the inner pot of instant pot duo crisp and stir well.
2. Seal the pot with a pressure-cooking lid and select slow cook mode and cook on low for 6 hours.
3. Serve and enjoy.

Nutrition: Calories: 346 Fat: 12 g Carbs: 8 g Protein: 52 g Cholesterol: 152 mg

176. Duo crisp ribs
Preparation time: 10 minutes
Cooking time: 50 minutes
Servings: 2
Ingredients:
- 1 rack of pork ribs
- Spice rub
- 1 1/2 cup broth
- 3 tablespoons liquid smoke
- 1 cup barbecue sauce

Directions:
1. Rub the rib rack with spice rub generously.
2. Pour the liquid into the instant pot duo crisp.
3. Set an air fryer basket into the pot and place the rib rack in the basket.
4. Put on the pressure-cooking lid and seal it.
5. Hit the "pressure button" and select 30 minutes of cooking time, then press "start."
6. Once the instant pot duo beeps, do a quick release and remove its lid.
7. Remove the ribs and rub them with barbecue sauce.
8. Empty the pot and place the air fryer basket in it.
9. Set the ribs in the basket and air fry them for 20 minutes.
10. Serve.

Nutrition: Calories: 306 Fat: 4g Carbs: 46g Protein: 17g

177. Smoky ribs
Preparation time: 30 minutes
Cooking time: 30 minutes
Servings: 4
Ingredients:
- 1 slab baby back rib, cut into individual pieces
- 1/2 tsp. Smoked paprika
- 1/2 cup barbecue sauce

Directions:
1. Place ribs in a mixing bowl and add the paprika and salt, mixing to coat thoroughly.
2. Coat ribs with barbecue sauce and allows ribs to marinate for 30 minutes.
3. Take the ribs out of the marinade. We are leaving space to

arrange the bones so that air can get all around bones inside the basket.
4. Fry at 350° F for 10 minutes for thin separated ribs, or 20 mins for thicker bones.
5. Turn ribs once halfway through the cooking time.

Nutrition: Calories: 147 Carbs: 9 g Fat: 7 g Protein: 9 g

178. Broiled tilapia
Preparation time: 5 minutes
Cooking time: 10 minutes
Servings: 4
Ingredients:

- 1 lb. Tilapia fillets
- 1/2 tsp. Lemon pepper
- Salt to taste

Directions:
1. Spritz the air fryer basket with some cooking spray.
2. Put the tilapia fillets in a basket and sprinkle on the lemon pepper and salt.
3. Cook at 400°F for 7 minutes.
4. Serve with a side of vegetables.

Nutrition: Calories: 98 Fat: 1g Carbs: 0g Protein: 21g

179. Hot tilapia
Preparation time: 5 minutes
Cooking time: 9 minutes
Servings: 2
Ingredients:

- 1 chili pepper, chopped
- 1 teaspoon chili flakes
- 1 tablespoon sesame oil
- 1/2 teaspoon salt
- 10 oz tilapia fillet
- 1/4 teaspoon onion powder

Directions:
1. In the shallow bowl, mix up chili pepper, chili flakes, salt, and onion powder.
2. Gently churn the mixture and add sesame oil. After this, slice the tilapia fillet and sprinkle with chili mixture.
3. Massage the fish with the help of the fingertips gently and leave for minutes to marinate. Preheat the air fryer to 390° F.
4. Put the tilapia fillets in the air fryer basket and cook for 5 minutes.
5. Then flip the fish on another side and cook for 4 minutes more.

Nutrition: Calories: 98 Fat: 1g Carbs: 0g Protein: 21g

180. Ham tilapia
Preparation time: 5 minutes
Cooking time: 10 minutes
Servings: 4
Ingredients:

- 16 oz tilapia fillet
- 4 ham slices
- 1 teaspoon sunflower oil
- 1/2 teaspoon salt
- 1 teaspoon dried rosemary

Directions:
1. Cut the tilapia into 4 servings. Sprinkle every fish serving with salt, dried rosemary, and sunflower oil.
2. Then carefully wrap the fish fillets in the ham slices and secure with toothpicks. Preheat the air fryer to 400F.
3. Put the wrapped tilapia in the air fryer basket in one layer and cook them for minutes.
4. Gently flip the fish on another side after 5 minutes of cooking.

Nutrition: Calories: 213 Fat: 10g Carbs: 7g Protein: 22g

181. Tarragon and spring onions salmon
Preparation time: 10 minutes
Cooking time: 15 minutes
Servings: 4
Ingredients:

- 12 oz salmon fillet
- 2 spring onions, chopped
- 1 tablespoon ghee, melted
- 1 teaspoon peppercorns
- 1/2 teaspoon salt
- 1/2 teaspoon ground black pepper

- 1 teaspoon tarragon
- 1/2 teaspoon dried cilantro

Directions:
1. Cut the salmon fillet into 4 servings. Then make the parchment pockets and place the fish fillets in the parchment pockets.
2. Add salt, ground black pepper, tarragon and dried cilantro on the salmon.
3. After this, top the fish with spring onions, peppercorns, and ghee.
4. Preheat the air fryer to 385° F.
5. Arrange the salmon pockets in the air fryer in one layer and cook them for minutes.

Nutrition: Calories: 140 Fat: 8g Carbs: 0g Protein: 21g

182. Salmon and garlic sauce
Preparation time: 5 minutes
Cooking time: 15 minutes
Servings: 4
Ingredients:

- 3 tablespoons parsley, chopped
- 4 salmon fillets, boneless
- 1/4 cup ghee, melted
- 2 garlic cloves, minced
- 4 shallots, chopped
- Salt and black pepper to the taste

Directions:
1. Heat a pan that fits the air fryer with the ghee over medium high heat, add the garlic, shallots, salt, pepper, and the parsley, stir and cook for 5 minutes.
2. Add the salmon fillets, toss gently, introduce the pan in the air fryer and cook at 380 ° F for 15 minutes.
3. Divide between plates and serve.

Nutrition: Calories: 409 Fat: 26g Carbs: 12g Protein: 29g

183. Creamy salmon
Preparation time:
Cooking time: 20 minutes
Servings: 2
Ingredients:

- 3/4 lb. Salmon, cut into 6 pieces
- 1/4 cup yogurt
- 1 tbsp. Olive oil
- 1 tbsp. Dill, chopped
- 3 tbsp. Sour cream
- Salt to taste

Directions:
1. Sprinkle some salt on the salmon.
2. Put the salmon slices in the air fryer basket and add a drizzle of olive oil.
3. Air fry the salmon at 285°F for 10 minutes.
4. In the meantime, combine the cream, dill, yogurt, and salt.
5. Plate up the salmon and pour the creamy sauce over it. Serve hot.

Nutrition: Calories: 217 Fat: 11g Carbs: 6g Protein: 24g

184. Pistachio crusted salmon
Preparation time: 10 minutes
Cooking time: 15 minutes
Servings: 4
Ingredients:

- 1 tsp mustard
- 3 tbsp pistachios
- A pinch of sea salt
- A pinch of garlic powder
- A pinch of black pepper
- 1 tsp lemon juice
- 1 tsp grated parmesan cheese
- 1 tsp olive oil
- 4 salmon fillets

Directions:
1. Set and preheat the air fryer to 350 ° F, and whisk mustard and lemon juice together.
2. Season the salmon with pepper, salt, and garlic powder.
3. Brush the olive oil on all sides. Brush also the mustard mixture onto salmon.

4. Chop the pistachios finely, combine them with the parmesan cheese, sprinkle on the salmon.
5. Add the salmon in the basket with the skin side down—cook for 15 minutes, or to your liking.

Nutrition: Calories: 372 Fat: 28g Carbs: 9g Protein: 35g

185. **Lemon chili salmon**

Preparation time: 10 minutes
Cooking time: 17 minutes
Servings: 4
Ingredients:

- 2 lbs. Salmon fillet, skinless and boneless
- 2 lemon juice
- 1 orange juice
- 1 tbsp olive oil
- 1 bunch fresh dill
- 1 chili, sliced
- Pepper
- Salt

Directions:
1. Preheat the air fryer to 325° F.
2. Place salmon fillets in air fryer baking pan and drizzle with olive oil, lemon juice, and orange juice.
3. Sprinkle chili slices over salmon and season with pepper and salt.
4. Place pan in the air fryer and cook for 15-17 minutes.
5. Garnish with dill and serve.

Nutrition: Calories: 269 Fat: 7g Carbs: 10g Protein: 38g

186. **Beer battered cod fillet**

Preparation time: 10 minutes
Cooking time: 15 minutes
Servings: 2
Ingredients:

- 1/2 cup all-purpose flour
- 3/4 teaspoon baking powder
- 1 1/4 cup lager beer
- 2 cod fillets
- 2 eggs, beaten
- Salt and pepper to taste

Directions:
1. Preheat the air fryer to 390° F.
2. Pat the fish fillets dry, then set aside.
3. In a bowl, combine the rest of the ingredients to create a batter.
4. Dip the fillets on the batter and place on the double layer rack.
5. Cook for 1 minute.

Nutrition: Calories: 250 Fat: 12g Carbs: 20g Protein: 14g

187. **Golden cod fish nuggets**

Preparation time: 5 minutes
Cooking time: 20 minutes
Servings: 4
Ingredients:

- 2 tbsp olive oil
- 2 eggs, beaten
- 1 cup breadcrumbs
- A pinch of salt
- 1 cup flour
- 4 cod fillets

Directions:
1. Preheat air fryer to 390° F. Mix breadcrumbs, olive oil, and salt in a bowl until combined.
2. In another bowl, place the eggs and the flour into a third bowl.
3. Toss the cod fillets in the flour, then in the eggs, and then in the breadcrumb mixture.
4. Arrange in the fryer basket and cook for 9 minutes. At the 5minute mark, quickly turn the nuggets over.
5. Once done, remove to a plate to serve.

Nutrition: Calories: 230 Fat: 9g Carbs: 20g Protein: 16g

188. **Basil and paprika cod**

Preparation time: 10 minutes
Cooking time: 15 minutes
Servings: 4
Ingredients:

- 4 cod fillets, boneless
- 1 teaspoon red pepper flakes
- 1/2 teaspoon hot paprika
- 2 tablespoon olive oil
- 1 teaspoon basil, dried
- Salt and black pepper to the taste

Directions:
1. In a bowl, mix the cod with all the other ingredients and toss.
2. Put the fish in your air fryer's basket and cook at 380 ° F for 10 – 15 minutes.
3. Divide the cod between plates and serve.

Nutrition: Calories: 280 Fat: 16g Carbs: 6g Protein: 29g

189. **Saucy garam masala fish**

Preparation time: 10 minutes
Cooking time: 20 minutes
Servings: 2
Ingredients:

- 2 teaspoons olive oil
- 1/4 cup coconut milk
- 1/2 teaspoon cayenne pepper
- 1 teaspoon garam masala
- 1/4 teaspoon kala namak (Indian black salt)
- 1/2 teaspoon fresh ginger, grated
- 1 garlic clove, minced
- 2 catfish fillets
- 1/4 cup coriander, roughly chopped

Directions:
1. Preheat air fryer to 390 ° F. Then, spritz the baking dish with a nonstick cooking spray.
2. Prepare a mixing bowl, then whisk the olive oil, milk, cayenne pepper, garam masala, kala namak, ginger, and garlic.
3. Coat the catfish fillets with the garam masala mixture.
4. Cook the catfish fillets in the preheated air fryer for approximately 18 minutes, turning over halfway through the cooking time.
5. Garnish with fresh coriander and serve over hot noodles if desired.

Nutrition: Calories: 134 Fat: 6g Carbs: 26g Protein: 4g

190. **Saltine fish fillets**

Preparation time: 10 minutes
Cooking time: 15 minutes
Servings: 4
Ingredients:

- 1 cup crushed saltines
- 1/4 cup extra virgin olive oil
- 1 tsp. Garlic powder
- 1/2 tsp. Shallot powder
- 1 egg, well whisked
- 4 white fish fillets
- Salt and ground black pepper to taste
- Fresh Italian parsley to serve

Directions:
1. Put the crushed saltines and olive oil in a bowl.
2. Get another bowl, then mix the garlic powder, shallot powder, and the beaten egg.
3. Put some salt and pepper over the fish before dipping each fillet into the egg mixture.
4. Coat the fillets with the crumb mixture.
5. Air fry the fish at 370° F for 10 - 12 minutes.
6. Serve with fresh parsley.

Nutrition: Calories: 148 Fat: 7g Carbs: 14g Protein: 2g

191. **Curried halibut fillets**

Preparation time: 10 minutes
Cooking time: 20 minutes
Servings: 4
Ingredients:

- 2 medium-sized halibut fillets
- 1 teaspoon curry powder
- 1/2 teaspoon ground coriander
- Kosher salt and freshly cracked mixed peppercorns, to taste
- 1 1/2 tablespoon olive oil
- 1/2 cup parmesan cheese, grated
- 2 eggs
- 1/2 teaspoon hot paprika

- A few drizzles of tabasco sauce

Directions:
1. Set your air fryer to cook at 365 ° F.
2. Then, grab two mixing bowls. In the first bowl, combine the parmesan cheese with olive oil.
3. In another shallow bowl, thoroughly whisk the egg. Then evenly drizzle the halibut fillets with tabasco sauce, add hot paprika, curry, coriander, salt, and cracked mixed peppercorns.
4. Dip each fish fillet into the whisked egg; now, roll it over the parmesan mix.
5. Put single layer in the air fryer cooking basket. Cook for 10 minutes, working in batches.
6. Serve over creamed salad if desired. Enjoy!

Nutrition: Calories: 355 Fat: 13g Carbs: 22g Protein: 34g

192. Parmesan walnut salmon

Preparation time: 10 minutes
Cooking time: 12 minutes
Servings: 4
Ingredients:

- 4 salmon fillets
- 1/4 cup parmesan cheese, grated
- 1/2 cup walnuts
- 1 tsp olive oil
- 1 tbsp lemon rind

Directions:
1. Preheat the air fryer to 370° F.
2. Spray an air fryer baking dish with cooking spray.
3. Place salmon on a baking dish.
4. Add walnuts into the food processor and process until finely ground.
5. Mix ground walnuts with parmesan cheese, oil, and lemon rind. Stir well.
6. Spoon walnut mixture over the salmon and press gently.
7. Place in the air fryer and cook for 12 minutes.
8. Serve and enjoy.

Nutrition: Calories 420 Fat 24 g Carbs 2 g Sugar 3 g Protein 43 g Cholesterol 98 mg

193. Lemony and spicy coconut crusted salmon

Preparation time: 10 minutes
Cooking time: 6 minutes
Servings: 4
Ingredients:

- 1pound salmon
- 1/2 cup flour
- 2 egg whites
- 1/2 cup breadcrumbs
- 1/2 cup unsweetened coconut, shredded
- 1/4 teaspoon lemon zest
- Salt
- Freshly ground black pepper
- 1/4 teaspoon cayenne pepper
- 1/4 teaspoon red pepper flakes, crushed
- Vegetable oil, as required

Directions:
1. Ready the air fryer to 400° F and grease an air fryer basket.
2. Mix the flour, salt, and black pepper in a dish.
3. Beat egg whites in a shallow dish.
4. Mix the breadcrumbs, coconut, lime zest, salt, and cayenne pepper in a third shallow dish.
5. Coat salmon in the flour, then dip in the egg whites and then into the breadcrumb mixture evenly.
6. Put salmon in the basket and drizzle with vegetable oil.
7. Cook for about 6 minutes and dish out to serve warm.

Nutrition: Calories: 558 Fat: 22g Carbs: 16g Sugar: 7g Protein: 43g

194. Salmon jerky

Preparation time: 2 hours
Cooking time: 4 hours 5 minutes
Servings: 4
Ingredients:

- 1 lb. Salmon, skin and bones removed
- 1/4 cup of soy sauce
- 1/2 tsp. Ground ginger
- 1/4 tsp. Red pepper flakes

- 1/2 tsp. Liquid smoke
- 1/4 tsp. Ground black pepper
- Juice of 1/2 medium lime

Directions:
1. Slice salmon into 1/4inchthick slices, 4inch long
2. Place strips into a large storage bag or a covered bowl and add remaining ingredients. Allow marinating for 2 hours in the refrigerator.
3. Place each strip into the air fryer basket in a single layer. Adjust the temperature to 140 ° F and set the timer for 4 hours.
4. Cool then store in a sealed container until ready to eat.

Nutrition: Calories: 108 Fiber: 2g Fat: 1g Carbs: 0g Protein: 11g

195. Hawaiian salmon recipe

Preparation time: 10 minutes
Cooking time: 10 minutes
Servings: 2
Ingredients:

- 20ounce canned pineapple pieces and juice
- 2 medium salmon fillets; boneless
- 1/2 tsp. Ginger; grated
- 2 tsp. Garlic powder
- 1 tsp. Onion powder
- 1 tbsp. Balsamic vinegar
- Salt and black pepper to the taste

Directions:
1. Season salmon with garlic powder, onion powder, salt, and black pepper, rub well.
2. Transfer to a heatproof dish that fits your air fryer, add ginger and pineapple chunks and toss them gently
3. Drizzle the vinegar all over, put in your air fryer, and cook at 350°F for 10 minutes.
4. Divide everything among plates and serve

Nutrition: Calories: 261 Fat: 12g Carbs: 5g Protein: 29g

196. Salmon thyme and parsley

Preparation time: 10 minutes
Cooking time: 12 minutes
Servings: 4
Ingredients:

- 4 salmon fillets; boneless
- 4 thyme sprigs
- 4 parsley sprigs
- 3 tbsp. Extra virgin olive oil
- 1 yellow onion; chopped
- 3 tomatoes; sliced
- Juice from 1 lemon
- Salt and black pepper to the taste

Directions:
1. Drizzle 1 tablespoon oil in a pan that fits your air fryer; add a layer of tomatoes, salt, and pepper.
2. Drizzle 1 more tablespoon oil, add fish, season them with salt and pepper, drizzle the rest of the oil, add thyme and parsley springs, onions, lemon juice, salt and pepper, place in your air fryer's basket
3. Cook at 360°F for 12 minutes, shaking once.
4. Divide everything on plates and serve right away

Nutrition: Calories: 469 Fat: 34g Carbs: 2g Protein: 36g

197. Miso fish

Preparation time: 10 minutes
Cooking time: 10 minutes
Servings: 2
Ingredients:

- 2 cod fish fillets
- 1 tbsp garlic, chopped
- 2 tsp swerve
- 2 tbsp miso

Directions:
1. Add all ingredients to the zip-lock bag. Shake well place in the refrigerator overnight.
2. Place marinated fish fillets into the air fryer basket and cooked at 350° F for 10 minutes.
3. Serve and enjoy.

Nutrition: Calories 229 Fat 6 g Carbs 19 g, Sugar 1 g Protein 44 g Cholesterol 99 mg

198.   Tilapia fish fillets
Preparation time: 10 minutes
Cooking time: 7 minutes
Servings: 2
Ingredients:

- 2 tilapia fillets
- 1 tsp old bay seasoning
- 1/2 tsp butter
- 1/4 tsp lemon pepper
- Pepper
- Salt

Directions:
1. Spray air fryer basket with cooking spray.
2. Place fish fillets into the air fryer basket and season with lemon pepper, old bay seasoning, pepper, and salt.
3. Spray fish fillets with cooking spray and cook at 400 °F for 7 minutes.
4. Serve and enjoy.

Nutrition: Calories 80 Fat 2 g Carbs 2 g Sugar 0 g Protein 15 g Cholesterol 45 mg

199.   Fish sticks
Preparation time: 10 minutes
Cooking time: 25 minutes
Servings: 4
Ingredients:

- 1 lb. Cod fillet; cut into 3/4inch strips
- 1 oz. Pork rinds, finely ground
- 1 large egg.
- 1/4 cup blanched finely ground almond flour.
- 1 tbsp. Coconut oil
- 1/2 tsp. Old bay seasoning

Directions:
1. Put the ground pork rinds, almond flour, old bay seasoning, and coconut oil into a large bowl and mix. Take a medium bowl, whisk the egg
2. Soak each fish stick into the egg and slowly roll into the flour mixture. Make sure to coat evenly.
3. Arrange the fish sticks into the air fryer basket
4. Adjust the temperature to 400 °F and set the timer for 10 minutes or until golden. Serve immediately.

Nutrition: Calories: 205 Protein: 24g Fiber: 8g Fat: 17g Carbs: 6g

200.   Lime trout and shallots
Preparation time: 10 minutes
Cooking time: 17 minutes
Servings: 4
Ingredients:

- 4 trout fillets; boneless
- 3 garlic cloves; minced
- 6 shallots; chopped.
- 1/2 cup butter; melted
- 1/2 cup olive oil
- Juice of 1 lime
- A pinch of salt and black pepper

Directions:
1. In a pan that fits the air fryer, combine the fish with the shallots and the rest of the ingredients toss gently
2. Place the pan in the fryer and cook at 390°F for 12 minutes, flipping the fish halfway.
3. Arrange in the plates and serve with a side salad.

Nutrition: Calories: 270 Fat: 12g Fiber: 4g Carbs: 6g Protein: 12g

201.   Trout and zucchinis
Preparation time: 5 minutes
Cooking time: 15 minutes
Servings: 4
Ingredients:

- 3 zucchinis, cut in medium chunks
- 4 trout fillets; boneless
- 1/4 cup tomato sauce
- 1 garlic clove; minced
- 1/2 cup cilantro; chopped.

- 1 tbsp. Lemon juice
- 2 tbsp. Olive oil
- Salt and black pepper to taste

Directions:
1. In a pan that fits your air fryer mix the fish with the other ingredients toss, introduce in the fryer, and cook at 380°F for 15 minutes.
2. Divide everything between plates and serve right away

Nutrition: Calories: 220 Fat: 12g Fiber: 4g Carbs: 6g Protein: 9g

202.   Crumbed cod
Preparation time: 15 minutes
Cooking time: 7 minutes
Servings: 4
Ingredients:

- 1 cup flour
- 4: 4ounce skinless codfish fillets, cut into rectangular pieces
- 6 eggs
- 2 green chilies, finely chopped
- 6 scallions, finely chopped
- 4 garlic cloves, minced
- Salt and black pepper, to taste
- 2 teaspoons soy sauce

Directions:
1. Prepare the air fryer to 375 ° F and grease an air fryer basket.
2. Place the flour in a shallow dish and mix remaining ingredients except cod in another shallow dish.
3. Coat each cod fillet into the flour and then dip in the egg mixture.
4. Arrange the cod fillets in the air fryer basket and cook for about 7 minutes.
5. Dish out and serve warm.

Nutrition: Calories: 462 Fat: 19g Carbohydrates: 53g Sugar: 3g Protein: 24g

203.   Spicy cod
Preparation time: 5 minutes
Cooking time: 10 minutes
Servings: 4
Ingredients:

- 4 cod fillets; boneless
- 2 tbsp. Assorted chili peppers
- 1 lemon; sliced
- Juice of 1 lemon
- Salt and black pepper to taste

Directions:
1. In your air fryer, mix the cod with the chili pepper, lemon juice, salt, and pepper
2. Arrange the lemon slices on top and cook at 360°F for 10 minutes.
3. Divide the fillets between plates and serve.

Nutrition: Calories: 102 Fat: 8g Carbs: 1g Protein: 8g

204.   Haddock with cheese sauce
Preparation time: 15 minutes
Cooking time: 8 minutes
Servings: 4
Ingredients:

- 4: 6ounce haddock fillets
- 6 tablespoons fresh basil, chopped
- 4 tablespoons pine nuts
- 2 tablespoons parmesan cheese, grated
- 2 tablespoons olive oil
- Salt and black pepper, to taste

Directions:
1. Ready the air fryer to 360 ° F and grease an air fryer basket.
2. Season the haddock fillets with salt and black pepper and coat evenly with olive oil.
3. Transfer the haddock fillets to the air fryer basket and cook for about 8 minutes.
4. Put the remaining ingredients in a food processor and pulse until smooth to make cheese sauce.
5. Dish out the haddock fillets in the bowl and top with cheese sauce to serve.

Nutrition: Calories: 354 Fat: 15g Carbohydrates: 7g Sugar: 3gn Protein: 47g

205. Swordfish steaks and tomatoes

Preparation time: 10 minutes
Cooking time: 10 minutes
Servings: 2
Ingredients:

- 30 oz. Canned tomatoes; chopped.
- 2 1inch thick swordfish steaks
- 2 tbsp. Capers, drained
- 1 tbsp. Red vinegar
- 2 tbsp. Oregano; chopped.
- A pinch of salt and black pepper

Directions:

1. In a pan that fits the air fryer, combine all the ingredients, toss, put the pan in the fryer and cook at 390°F for 10 minutes, flipping the fish halfway
2. Divide the mix between plates and serve

Nutrition: Calories: 280 Fat: 12g Fiber: 4g Carbs: 6g Protein: 11g

206. Roasted red snapper

Preparation time: 5 minutes
Cooking time: 15 minutes
Servings: 4
Ingredients:

- 4 red snapper fillets; boneless
- 2 garlic cloves; minced
- 1 tbsp. Hot chili paste
- 2 tbsp. Olive oil
- 2 tbsp. Coconut aminos
- 2 tbsp. Lime juice
- A pinch of salt and black pepper

Directions:

1. Take a bowl and mix all the ingredients except the fish and whisk well
2. Rub the fish with this mix, place it in your air fryer's basket and cook at 380°F for 15 minutes
3. Serve with a side salad.

Nutrition: Calories: 220 Fat: 13g Fiber: 4g Carbs: 6g Protein: 11g

207. Lemony flounder fillets

Preparation time: 5 minutes
Cooking time: 12 minutes
Servings: 2
Ingredients:

- 2 flounder fillets; boneless
- 2 garlic cloves; minced
- 2 tbsp. Olive oil
- 2 tbsp. Lemon juice
- 2 tsp. Coconut aminos
- 1/2 tsp. Stevia
- A pinch of salt and black pepper

Directions:

1. In a pan that fits your air fryer mix all the ingredients, toss, and cook at 390 ° F for 12 minutes.
2. Divide into bowls and serve.

Nutrition: Calories: 251 Fat: 13g Fiber: 3g Carbs: 5g Protein: 10g

208. Sea bass paella

Preparation time: 10 minutes
Cooking time: 25 minutes
Servings: 4
Ingredients:

- 1 lb. Sea bass fillets; cubed
- 1 red bell pepper; deseeded and chopped.
- 6 scallops
- 8 shrimp; peeled and deveined
- 5 oz. Wild rice
- 2 oz. Peas
- 14 oz. Dry white wine
- 3 1/2 oz. Chicken stock
- A drizzle of olive oil
- Salt and black pepper to taste

Directions:

1. In a heatproof dish that fits your air fryer, place all the ingredients and toss.

2. Place the dish in your air fryer and cook at 380°F for 25 minutes, stirring halfway.
3. Divide between plates and serve.

Nutrition: Calories: 710 Fat: 37g Carbs: 68g Protein: 51g

209. Shrimp with lime and tequila

Preparation time: 10 minutes
Cooking time: 20 minutes
Servings: 4
Ingredients:

- 1 lime large
- 12 big shrimps
- 2 oz of tequila
- 2 tablespoons of oil
- 1/2 teaspoon of salt
- 1/2 teaspoon of pepper
- 1/2 teaspoon of onion powder
- 1/2 teaspoon of garlic powder
- 1 medium-sized onion

Directions

1. Mix 1 tablespoon of oil, salt, pepper, onion powder, tequila, garlic powder, and blend all well.
2. Then chop the onion into pieces and mix again.
3. Wash and clean mint.
4. Rub them with spices.
5. Leave in the marinade for 10 minutes.
6. Sprinkle the frying basket with oil.
7. Preheat the air fryer to 350°F.
8. Then put mint in the air fryer.
9. Cook mint for 10 minutes.
10. 1after that put them on the other side and cook for 5 minutes more.
11. 1sprinkle with lime juice and serve hot.
12. 1you can eat them with sauces.

Nutrition: Calories: 348 Fat: 16g Carbs: 19g Protein: 27g

210. Fried shrimps with celery

Preparation time: 15 minutes
Cooking time: 13 minutes
Serving: 3
Ingredients:

- 6 to 8 stalks celery
- 1/2 large carrot, chopped
- 10 to 12 fresh shrimps (quantity depending on your choice
- 3 clove garlic, finely chopped
- 1 tablespoon olive oil
- 1 tablespoon oyster sauce
- 1 tablespoon soy sauce
- 1 teaspoon sugar
- 1 teaspoon cornstarch
- 3/4 to 1 cup of water

Directions:

1. Put chopped garlic, sliced celery, and sliced carrot diagonally into the air fryer, pour with oil, and cook for 7 minutes.
2. Mix oyster sauce, soy sauce, sugar, cornstarch, and water in a bowl. Add this mixture into the air fryer and cook for another 1 minute.
3. Add shrimps and cook for another 5 minutes.

Nutrition: Calories: 190 Fat: 12g Carbs: 4g Protein: 17g

211. Crispy nachos shrimps

Preparation time: 25 minutes
Cooking time: 10 minutes
Servings: 2
Ingredients:

- 20 shrimps
- 2 eggs
- 7 oz nacho flavored chips

Directions

1. Prepare the shrimps. Remove the shells and veins. Clean and wash them, dry with a paper towel.
2. Place eggs in the bowl and whisk.
3. Crush nacho chips in another bowl.
4. Dip each shrimp in the whisked egg and then in the chips' crumbs.

5. Preheat the air fryer to 370°F.
6. Place the crumbed shrimps to the air fryer basket and cook for 8 minutes, or until they cooked through.
7. Serve with your favorite sauce

Nutrition: Calories: 463 Fat: 29g Carbs: 24g Protein: 26g

212. Tender coconut shrimps

Preparation time: 5 minutes
Cooking time: 20 minutes
Servings: 4
Ingredients:

- 2 pounds (12-15raw shrimps)
- 1 cup egg white
- 1 cup dried coconut, unsweetened
- 1 cup breadcrumb
- 1 cup all-purpose flour
- 1/2 tsp salt

Directions

1. Prepare shrimps and set aside
2. In the large mixing bowl, combine breadcrumbs and coconut. Season with salt lightly.
3. In another bowl, place flour, and in the third bowl, place egg whites.
4. Meanwhile, preheat the air fryer to 340°F.
5. Put each shrimp into the flour, then into egg whites, and then into breadcrumbs mixture.
6. Transfer shrimps to a fryer and cook for about 10 minutes, shaking occasionally.
7. Serve with dipping sauce you prefer.

Nutrition: Calories: 310 Fat: 16g Carbs: 31g Protein: 9g

213. Quick shrimp recipe

Preparation time: 10 minutes
Cooking time: 20 minutes
Servings: 4
Ingredients:

- 1 tbsp vegetable oil
- 1 tbsp curry paste
- 1 lb. Shrimps
- 1 tbsp fish sauce
- 1 tbsp lemon juice
- 1 cup cilantro, chopped
- 1 onion, chopped
- 2 tomatoes, chopped
- 1 bell pepper, strips
- 1/2 tbsp olive oil

Directions

1. Add curry paste to the round baking tray.
2. Add shrimps and place it in the air fryer for 10 minutes on 300°F.
3. Make sure the chicken is cooked well before you add any other ingredient.
4. Now add bell pepper, onion, fish sauce, tomatoes, and lemon juice.
5. Stir well and make sure that the shrimps absorb all the sauces
6. Cook it for about 20 minutes and, when done, sprinkle the cilantro to serve immediately.

Nutrition: Calories: 228 Fat: 3g Carbs: 0 Protein: 46g

214. Yummy shrimps with bacon

Preparation time: 20 minutes
Cooking time: 7 minutes
Servings: 4
Ingredients:

- 1 1/4 pound peeled and deveined tiger shrimp (16 pieces)
- 1 pound thinly sliced pound bacon (also 16 slices at room temperature)

Directions

1. Wrap each shrimp in bacon.
2. To make the job easy and cover the whole shrimp, start from the head and finish at the tail. Put shrimps in the refrigerator for 20 minutes
3. Cook in the air fryer at 390°F for 5-7 minutes. Then just dry shrimps on a paper towel.
4. Serve and enjoy!

Nutrition: Calories: 208 Fat: 2g Carbs: 1g Protein: 23g

215. Spring rolls stuffed with shrimps

Preparation time: 10 minutes
Cooking time: 15 minutes
Servings: 4
Ingredients:

- 4 oz shrimps, cooked
- 12 spring roll wrappers
- 1 teaspoon root ginger, freshly grated
- 2 oz mushrooms, sliced
- 1 egg, beaten
- 1 teaspoon Chinese five spice powder
- 1 oz bean sprouts
- 1 spring onion
- 1 small carrot, cut into matchsticks
- 1 tablespoon groundnut oil
- 1 tablespoon soy sauce

Directions:

1. In the large skillet or wok, heat the oil over medium high heat. Add ginger and mushrooms and cook for 2 minutes.
2. Add the soy sauce, Chinese five spice powder, bean sprouts, spring onions, and carrots.
3. Cook for 1 minute and then set aside to chill. Add the shrimps and toss.
4. Preheat the Air fryer to 370-390° F. Roll up the shrimp mixture in spring roll wrappers, sealing with beaten egg. Brush each roll with oil.
5. Cook in batches in the air fryer basket for 5 minutes.

Nutrition: Calories: 80 Fat: 5g Carbs: 0g Protein: 3g

216. Delicious crab pillows

Preparation time: 15 minutes
Cooking time: 20 minutes
Servings: 4
Ingredients:

- 2 beaten egg whites
- 1pound lump crab meat
- 2 tablespoons finely chopped celery
- 1/4 finely chopped red bell pepper
- 1/4 teaspoon finely chopped tarragon
- 1/2 teaspoon finely chopped parsley
- 1/4 teaspoon finely chopped chives
- 1 tablespoon olive oil
- 1/4 cup red onion
- 1/2 teaspoon cayenne pepper
- 1/4 cup sour cream
- 1/4 cup mayonnaise
- Ingredients for breading
- 3 beaten eggs
- 1 cup breadcrumbs
- 1 cup flour
- 1/2 teaspoon salt

Directions:

1. Mix onions, celery, peppers, and olive oil in a small pan heat on medium high. Cook for a couple of minutes until the onion is translucent.
2. Blend breadcrumbs with olive oil and salt to a fine paste.
3. In three bowls, prepare eggs, breadcrumbs, and flour. In a separate bowl, mix mayonnaise, crab meat, sour cream, and egg whites.
4. Crab meat mold into balls, roll in flour, eggs, and breadcrumbs and put in the air fryer, heated to 390°F, and cook 8-10 minutes.

Nutrition: Calories: 11 Fat: 2g Carbs: 4g Protein: 1g

217. Air fried crab herb croquettes

Preparation time: 5 minutes
Cooking time: 20 minutes
Servings: 4
Ingredients:

- 1 lb. Crab meat
- 1 cup breadcrumbs
- 2 egg whites
- 1/2 tsp parsley
- 1/4 tsp chives

- 1/4 tsp tarragon
- 2 tbsp celery, chopped
- 1/4 cup red pepper, chopped
- 1 tsp olive oil
- 1/2 tsp lime juice
- 4 tbsp sour cream
- 4 tbsp mayonnaise
- 1/4 cup onion, chopped
- 1/4 tsp salt

Directions

1. Place breadcrumbs and salt in a bowl.
2. In a small bowl, add egg whites.
3. Get the remaining ingredients and put them into the bowl. Mix well to combine.
4. Make croquettes from the mixture and dip in egg white, and coat with breadcrumbs.
5. Place in the basket and air fry for 18 minutes.
6. Serve and enjoy.

Nutrition: Calories: 185 Fat: 13g Carbs: 2g Protein: 13g

218. Cod fish teriyaki with oyster mushrooms

Preparation time: 5 minutes
Cooking time: 12 minutes
Servings: 3
Ingredients:

- 1pound cod fish cut into 1inch thickness pieces
- 6 pieces oyster mushrooms, sliced
- 1 Wong bok leaf, sliced
- 2 garlic cloves, coarsely chopped
- 1 tablespoon olive oil
- A pinch of salt
- Steamed rice for serving
- Ingredients for teriyaki sauce
- 2 tablespoon mirin
- 2 tablespoon soy sauce
- 2 tablespoon sugar

Directions

1. Take a large baking pan suitable for your air fryer and grease it with a little oil.
2. Toss your mushroom, garlic, and salt with 1 tablespoon of oil in a baking pan. Lay the codfish slices on top of mushrooms.
3. Preheat the air fryer at 360° F and place the baking pan into the air fryer. Cook for 5 minutes. Then, stir the mushrooms to prevent sticking and burning.
4. Drizzle teriyaki sauce over codfish slices. Fry for another 5 minutes.
5. When ready, transfer codfish slices to a serving plate.
6. Stir the mushrooms with the remaining sauce in the baking pan.
7. Serve with steamed rice.

Nutrition: Calories: 120 Fat: 7g Carbs: 11g Protein: 1g

219. Grilled stuffed lobster

Preparation time: 10 minutes
Cooking time: 15 minutes
Servings: 3
Ingredients:

- 1 lobster
- 2 tablespoons freshly chopped basil
- 1 medium-sized zucchini
- 1 lemon
- 2 tablespoons butter
- Olive oil
- Salt, to taste

Directions

1. Boil the lobster for 5 minutes until nice and red.
2. To cut the lobster in half: put the knife between the lobster's eyes.
3. Get the intestinal tract, liver, and stomach.
4. Slice zucchini in long and coat them with a little olive oil.
5. Mix chopped basil with butter. Season the mixture with salt, to taste.
6. Prepare the air fryer to 360 ° F. Add lobster halves, brush with butter and cook for about 68 minutes.
7. Get lobster from the grill pan and let it rest.

8. Grill zucchini slices at 390 ° F for 4 to 5 minutes.
9. Arrange the lobster and the zucchini slices in a dish. Add little lemon juice.

Nutrition: Calories: 313 Fat: 26g Carbs: 3g Protein: 18g

220. Tender tuna nuggets

Preparation time: 10 minutes
Cooking time: 10 minutes
Serving: 3
Ingredients:

- 2 cans tuna (10-12 oz)
- 1/2 cup breadcrumbs
- 3 tablespoon olive oil
- 2 tablespoon parsley, chopped
- 1 egg
- 2 teaspoon Dijon mustard
- Ground pepper and salt to taste

Directions

1. Mix tuna, olive oil, parsley, egg, and mustard in a large bowl.
2. Form tuna mixture into nuggets and place them on the baking sheet.
3. Cool nuggets in the fridge for 2 hours
4. Preheat the air fryer to 350°F.
5. Put frozen nuggets in the fryer and cook for 10 minutes.

Nutrition: Calories: 100 Fat: 3g Carbs: 5g Protein: 13g

221. Cod fish bites

Preparation time: 10 minutes
Cooking time: 8 minutes
Servings: 3
Ingredients:

- 2 cod fish fillets
- 1/2 cup all-purpose flour
- 3 eggs
- 2 garlic cloves, minced
- 2 small chili peppers, chopped
- 2 spring onions, chopped
- 1/4 teaspoon black pepper
- A pinch of salt

Directions

1. Whisk 3 eggs and add chopped green onion, garlic, and chili. Season with salt and black pepper.
2. Cut the fillets into 2inch pieces.
3. Coat codpieces with flour and then dip into the egg mixture.
4. Cook codpieces into the air fryer for 78 minutes at 390 F

Nutrition: Calories: 292 Fat: 17g Carbs: 12g Protein: 8g

222. Buttery shrimp

Preparation time: 5 minutes
Cooking time: 10 minutes
Servings: 2
Ingredients:

- 1 tablespoon butter, melted
- A drizzle of olive oil
- 1pound shrimp, peeled and deveined
- 1/4 cup heavy cream
- 8 ounces mushrooms, roughly sliced
- A pinch of red pepper flakes
- Salt and black pepper to taste
- 2 garlic cloves, minced
- 1/2 cup beef stock
- 1 tablespoon parsley, chopped
- 1 tablespoon chives, chopped

Directions:

1. Put salt and pepper on the shrimp. Grease with the oil.
2. Place the shrimp in your air fryer, cook at 360 ° F for 7 minutes and divide between plates.
3. Heat a pan with the butter over medium heat. Add the mushrooms, stir, and cook for 34 minutes.
4. Add all remaining ingredients; stir and then cook for a few minutes more.
5. Drizzle the butter/garlic mixture over the shrimp and serve.

Nutrition: Calories 225 Fat 8g Carbs 14g Protein 22g

223. Shrimp and veggie mix

Preparation time: 10 minutes

Cooking time: 20 minutes
Servings: 4
Ingredients:

- 1/2 cup red onion, chopped
- 1 cup red bell pepper, chopped
- 1 cup celery, chopped
- 1pound shrimp, peeled and deveined
- 1 teaspoon Worcestershire sauce
- Salt and black pepper to taste
- 1 tablespoon butter, melted
- 1 teaspoon sweet paprika

Directions:
1. Get a mixing bowl and put all the ingredients. Mix well.
2. Transfer everything to your air fryer and cook 320 ° F for 20 minutes, shaking halfway.
3. Divide between plates and serve.

Nutrition: Calories 220 Fat 14g Carbs 17g Protein 20g

224.   Tiger shrimp mix
Preparation time: 5 minutes
Cooking time: 10 minutes
Servings: 2
Ingredients:

- 20 tiger shrimp, peeled and deveined
- Salt and black pepper to taste
- 1/2 teaspoon Italian seasoning
- 1 tablespoon extra-virgin olive oil
- 1/4 teaspoon smoked paprika

Directions:
1. Toss well all the ingredients to a bowl.
2. Put the shrimp in the air fryer's basket and cook at 380 ° F for 10 minutes.
3. Divide into bowls and serve.

Nutrition: Calories 219 Fat 6g Carbs 14g Protein 15g

225.   Paprika and tabasco shrimp mix
Preparation time: 2 hours
Cooking time: 10 minutes
Servings: 4
Ingredients:

- 1pound large shrimp, peeled and deveined
- 1 teaspoon red pepper flakes
- 2 tablespoons olive oil
- 1 teaspoon tabasco sauce
- 2 tablespoons water
- 1 teaspoon basil, dried
- Salt and black pepper to taste
- 1 tablespoon parsley, chopped
- 1/2 teaspoon garlic powder
- 1/2 teaspoon sweet paprika

Directions:
1. Mix shrimp with all ingredients except the parsley; toss to coat the shrimp well.
2. Place shrimp in the fridge for 2 hours.
3. Transfer the shrimp to your air fryer's basket and cook at 370 ° F for 10 minutes.
4. Arrange into bowls, top with parsley, and serve.

Nutrition: Calories 210 Fat 7g Carbs 13g Protein 8g

226.   Red pepper shrimps
Preparation time: 10 minutes
Cooking time: 10 minutes
Servings: 4
Ingredients:

- 1½ pounds shrimp, peeled and deveined
- 2 cups corn
- A drizzle of olive oil
- ¼ cup chicken stock
- 1 tablespoon old bay seasoning
- Salt and black pepper to taste
- 1 teaspoon red pepper flakes, crushed
- 2 sweet onions, cut into wedges
- 8 garlic cloves, crushed

Directions:
1. Grease a pan that fits your air fryer with the oil.
2. Add all other ingredients to the oiled pan and toss well.
3. Place the pan in the fryer and cook at 390 degrees F for 10 minutes.
4. Divide everything into bowls and serve.

Nutrition: Calories 350 Fat 6g Carbs 47g Protein 25g

227.   Shrimp and peas mix
Preparation time: 10 minutes
Cooking time: 8 minutes
Servings: 4
Ingredients:

- 1pound shrimp, peeled and deveined
- 2 tablespoons soy sauce
- ½ pound pea pods
- 3 tablespoons balsamic vinegar
- ¾ cup pineapple juice
- 3 tablespoons sugar

Directions:
1. Mix all the ingredients in a pan that fits your air fryer.
2. Place the pan in the fryer and cook at 380° F for 8 minutes.
3. Divide into bowls and serve.

Nutrition: Calories 251 Fat 4 Fiber 3 Carbs 14 Protein 5

228.   Parmesan shrimp
Preparation time: 10 minutes
Cooking time: 12 minutes
Servings: 4
Ingredients:

- 2 tablespoons olive oil
- 2 garlic cloves, minced
- 1 yellow onion, chopped
- 2 tablespoons dry white wine
- ½ cup chicken stock
- Salt and black pepper to taste
- 1pound shrimp, peeled and deveined
- 3/4 cup parmesan cheese, grated
- 1/4 cup tarragon, chopped

Directions:
1. Prepare a pan and add all ingredients except the parmesan cheese and stir well.
2. Place a pan that fits in the air fryer and cook at 380 ° F for 12 minutes.
3. Add the parmesan and toss.
4. Divide everything between plates.

Nutrition: Calories 307 Fat 16g Carbs 12g Protein 28g

229.   Bell pepper shrimp skewers
Preparation time: 10 minutes
Cooking time: 6 minutes
Servings: 2
Ingredients:

- 8 shrimps, peeled and deveined
- 4 garlic cloves, minced
- Salt and black pepper to the taste
- 8 green bell pepper slices
- 1 tablespoon rosemary, chopped
- 1 tablespoon butter, melted

Directions:
1. Mix shrimp with butter, garlic, salt, pepper, rosemary, and bell pepper slices. Make sure to coat and leave aside for 10 minutes.
2. Get a skewer, then set out 2 shrimp and 2 bell pepper slices. Repeat with the remaining.
3. Place them all in your air fryer's basket and cook at 360 ° F for 6 minutes.
4. Divide among plates and serve right away.
5. Enjoy!

Nutrition: Calories 142 Fat 4g Carbs 6g Protein 21g

230.   Creamy shrimp and veggies
Preparation time: 10 minutes
Cooking time: 30 minutes

Servings: 4
Ingredients:

- 8 ounces mushrooms, chopped
- 1 asparagus bunch, cut into medium pieces
- 1 pound shrimp, peeled and deveined
- Salt and black pepper to the taste
- 1 spaghetti squash, cut into halves
- 2 tablespoons olive oil
- 2 teaspoons Italian seasoning
- 1 yellow onion, chopped
- 1 teaspoon red pepper flakes, crushed
- ¼ cup butter, melted
- 1 cup parmesan cheese, grated
- 2 garlic cloves, minced
- 1 cup heavy cream

Directions:

1. Place squash halves in air fryer's basket, cook at 390 ° F for 17 minutes, transfer to a cutting board, scoop insides and transfer to a bowl.
2. Add water in a pot and add some salt. Bring to a boil over medium heat, add asparagus, steam for a couple of minutes.
3. Once done, move to a bowl filled with ice water, drain and leave aside as well.
4. Get a pan that fits the air fryer with the oil and heat over medium heat.
5. Add onions and mushrooms, stir and cook for 7 minutes.
6. Add pepper flakes, Italian seasoning, salt, pepper, squash, asparagus, shrimp, melted butter, cream, parmesan, and garlic, toss and cook in your air fryer at 360 ° F for 6 minutes.
7. Divide everything on plates and serve. Enjoy!

Nutrition: Calories 325 Fat 15g Carbs 24g Protein 31g

231. Air fried shrimps and cauliflower

Preparation time: 10 minutes
Cooking time: 12 minutes
Servings: 2
Ingredients:

- 1 tablespoon butter
- Cooking spray
- 1 cauliflower head, riced
- 1 pound shrimp, peeled and deveined
- 1/4 cup heavy cream
- 8 ounces mushrooms, roughly chopped
- A pinch of red pepper flakes
- Salt and black pepper to the taste
- 2 garlic cloves, minced
- 4 bacon slices, cooked and crumbled
- 1/2 cup beef stock
- 1 tablespoon parsley, finely chopped
- 1 tablespoon chives, chopped

Directions:

1. Season shrimp with salt and pepper, spray with cooking oil, place in the air fryer and cook for 7 minutes at 360 ° F.
2. Meanwhile, heat a pan with the butter over medium heat, add mushrooms, stir and cook for 34 minutes.
3. Add garlic, cauliflower rice, pepper flakes, stock, cream, chives, parsley, salt, and pepper. Cook for a few minutes and take off the heat.
4. Divide shrimp on plates, add cauliflower mix on the side, sprinkle bacon on top, and serve. Enjoy!

Nutrition: Calories 245 Fat 7g Carbs 6g Protein 20g

232. Ginger squid

Preparation time: 10 minutes
Cooking time: 25 minutes
Servings: 4
Ingredients:

- 1 pound cleaned squid, cut into small pieces
- 10 garlic cloves, minced
- 1 teaspoon ginger piece, grated
- 2 green chilis, chopped
- 2 yellow onions, chopped
- 1/2 tablespoon lemon juice

- 1 tablespoon coriander powder
- 3/4 tablespoon chili powder
- Salt and black pepper to taste
- 1 teaspoon mustard seeds, toasted
- ½ cup chicken stock
- 3 tablespoons olive oil

Directions:

1. Place all ingredients into a pan that fits your air fryer and toss.
2. Put the pan in the air fryer and cook at 380 ° F for 25 minutes.
3. Divide between plates and serve.

Nutrition: Calories 251 Fat 10g Carbs 9g Protein 30g

233. Squid and guacamole

Preparation time: 10 minutes
Cooking time: 6 minutes
Servings: 2
Ingredients:

- 2 medium squids, tentacles separated, and tubes scored lengthwise
- 1 tablespoon olive oil
- Juice from 1 lime
- Salt and black pepper to the taste
- For the guacamole:
- 2 avocados, pitted, peeled, and chopped
- 1 tablespoon coriander, chopped
- 2 red chilies, chopped
- 1 tomato, chopped
- 1 red onion, chopped
- Juice from 2 limes

Directions:

1. Season squid and squid tentacles with salt, pepper, drizzle the olive oil all over.
2. Put in the air fryer's basket and cook for 3 minutes on each side at 360 ° F.
3. Transfer squid to a bowl, drizzle lime juice all over and toss.
4. Meanwhile put avocado in a bowl, mash with a fork, add coriander, chilies, tomato, onion, and juice from 2 limes and toss.
5. Divide squid on plates, top with guacamole and serve.
6. Enjoy!

Nutrition: Calories 230 Fat 16g Carbs 15g Protein 10g

234. Spicy mussels

Preparation time: 5 minutes
Cooking time: 12 minutes
Servings: 4
Ingredients:

- 2 pounds mussels, scrubbed
- 12 ounces black beer
- 1 tablespoon olive oil
- 1 yellow onion, chopped
- 8 ounces spicy sausage, chopped
- 1 tablespoon paprika

Directions:

1. Combine all the ingredients in a pan that fits your air fryer.
2. Put the pan in the air fryer and cook at 400 °F for 12 minutes.
3. Divide the mussels into bowls, serve, and enjoy!

Nutrition: Calories 101 Fat 6g Carbs 3g Protein 6g

235. Clams and potatoes

Preparation time: 5 minutes
Cooking time: 15 minutes
Servings: 4
Ingredients:

- 15 small clams, shucked
- 2 chorizo links, sliced
- 1 pound baby red potatoes, scrubbed
- 1 yellow onion, chopped
- 10 ounces beer
- 2 tablespoons cilantro, chopped
- 1 teaspoon olive oil

Directions:

1. Get a pan that fits in the air fryer and toss all of the ingredients.
2. Place the pan in the fryer and cook at 390 ° F for 15 minutes.
3. Divide into bowls and serve.

Nutrition: Calories 231 Fat 6 Carbs 16 Protein 16

236. Seafood medley

Preparation time: 10 minutes
Cooking time: 15 minutes
Servings: 4
Ingredients:

- 12 mussels
- 1½ pounds large shrimp, peeled and deveined
- 2 tablespoons butter, melted
- 2 yellow onions, chopped
- 3 garlic cloves, minced
- ½ cup parsley, chopped
- 20 ounces canned tomatoes, chopped
- 8 ounces clam juice
- ½ teaspoon marjoram, dried
- 1 tablespoon basil, dried
- Salt and black pepper to taste

Directions:
1. Toss all the ingredients in a pan that fits your air fryer.
2. Put the pan into the fryer and cook at 380 degrees F for 15 minutes.
3. Divide into bowls and serve right away.

Nutrition: Calories 261 Fat 7g Carbs 45g Protein 18g

237. Air fried brussels sprouts

Preparation time: 5 minutes
Cooking time: 10 minutes
Servings: 1
Ingredients:

- 1pound brussels sprouts
- 1 tablespoon coconut oil, melted
- 1 tablespoon unsalted butter, melted

Directions:
1. Preheat the air fryer oven to 400°F (204C).
2. Prepare the Brussels sprouts by halving them, discarding any loose leaves.
3. Combine with the melted coconut oil and transfer to the air fryer basket. Set and cook for 10 minutes. Shake the basket once cooking. The sprouts are ready when they are partially caramelized.
4. Remove from the oven and serve with a topping of melted butter.

Nutrition: Calories: 45g Fat: 0g Carbs: 9g Protein: 2g

238. Saltine wax beans

Preparation time: 10 minutes
Cooking time: 7 minutes
Servings: 4
Ingredients:

- 1/2 cup flour
- 1 teaspoon smoky chipotle powder
- 1/2 teaspoon ground black pepper
- 1 teaspoon sea salt flakes
- 2 eggs, beaten
- 1/2 cup crushed saltines
- 10 ounces wax beans
- Cooking spray

Directions:
1. Preheat the air fryer oven to 360°F (182C).
2. Combine the flour, chipotle powder, black pepper, and salt in a bowl. Put the eggs in second bowl. Put the crushed saltines in third bowl.
3. Wash the beans with cold water and discard any tough strings.
4. Coat the beans with the flour mixture before dipping them into the beaten egg. Cover them with the crushed saltines.
5. Spritz the beans with cooking spray, then transfer to the air fryer basket.
6. Move the baking pan to the fryer basket and set time to 4 minutes.
7. Give the air fryer basket a good shake and continue to air fry for 3 minutes. Serve hot.

Nutrition: Calories: 35 Fiber: 3g Carbs: 7g Protein: 2g

239. Easy rosemary green beans

Preparation time: 5 minutes

Cooking time: 5 minutes
Servings: 1
Ingredients:

- 1 tablespoon butter, melted
- 2 tablespoons rosemary
- 1/2 teaspoon salt
- 3 cloves garlic, minced
- 3/4 cup chopped green beans

Directions"
1. Preheat the air fryer oven to 390°F (199C).
2. Combine the melted butter with the rosemary, salt, and minced garlic.
3. Toss in the green beans, coating them well. Transfer to the air fryer basket. Set air fryer time to 5 minutes.
4. Serve immediately.

Nutrition: Calories: 32 Fat: 3g Carbs: 8g Protein: 2g

240. Simple buffalo cauliflower

Preparation time: 5 minutes
Cooking time: 5 minutes
Servings: 1
Ingredients:

- ½ packet dry ranch seasoning
- 2 tablespoons salted butter, melted
- 1 cup cauliflower florets
- ¼ cup buffalo sauce

Directions:
1. Preheat the air fryer oven to 400°F (204C).
2. In a bowl, combine the dry ranch seasoning and butter. Toss with the cauliflower florets to coat and transfer them to the air fryer basket.
3. Put the baking pan in the air fryer basket onto the baking pan and set time to 5 minutes. Shake the basket occasionally to ensure the florets cook evenly.
4. Get the cauliflower and arrange it on a platter.
5. Pour the buffalo sauce over it and serve warm.

Nutrition: Calories: 129 Fat: 1g Carbs: 24g Protein: 7g

241. Sriracha golden cauliflower

Preparation time: 5 minutes
Cooking time: 17 minutes
Servings: 4
Ingredients:

- 1/4 cup vegan butter, melted
- 1/4 cup sriracha sauce
- 4 cups cauliflower florets
- 1 cup breadcrumbs
- 1 teaspoon salt

Directions:
1. Preheat the air fryer oven to 375° F (191C).
2. Mix the sriracha and vegan butter in a bowl and pour this mixture over the cauliflower, taking care to cover each floret entirely.
3. Get another bowl. Mix the breadcrumbs and salt.
4. Dip the cauliflower florets in the breadcrumbs, coating each one well. Put them in the air fryer basket and set time to 17 minutes. Serve hot.

Nutrition: Calories: 469 Fat: 34g Carbs: 35g Protein: 15g

242. Cauliflower tater tots

Preparation time: 15 minutes
Cooking time: 16 minutes
Servings: 12
Ingredients:

- 1pound (454 g) cauliflower, steamed and chopped
- ½ cup nutritional yeast
- 1 tablespoon oats
- 1 tablespoon desiccated coconuts
- 3 tablespoons flaxseed meal
- 3 tablespoons water
- 1 onion, chopped
- 1 teaspoon minced garlic
- 1 teaspoon chopped parsley
- 1 teaspoon chopped oregano
- 1 teaspoon chopped chives

- Salt and ground black pepper, to taste
- ½ cup breadcrumbs

Directions:
1. Preheat the air fryer oven to 375°F (191C).
2. Drain any excess water out of the cauliflower by wringing it with a paper towel.
3. Mix the cauliflower with the remaining ingredients, save the breadcrumbs. Using the hands, shape the mixture into several small balls.
4. Coat the balls in the breadcrumbs and transfer to the air fryer
5. Change temperature to 400 ° F and air fry for an additional 10 minutes.
6. Serve immediately.

Nutrition: Calories: 147 Fat: 6g Carbs: 20g Protein: 3g

243.   Chili fingerling potatoes

Preparation time: 10 minutes
Cooking time: 16 minutes
Servings: 4
Ingredients:
- 1pound (454 g) fingerling potatoes, rinsed and cut into wedges
- 1 teaspoon olive oil
- 1 teaspoon salt
- 1 teaspoon black pepper
- 1 teaspoon cayenne pepper
- 1 teaspoon nutritional yeast
- ½ teaspoon garlic powder

Directions:
1. Preheat the air fryer oven to 400°F (204C).
2. Coat the potatoes with the rest of the ingredients. Transfer to the air fryer basket.
3. Place in the air fryer basket set time to 16 minutes, shaking the basket halfway through the cooking time.
4. Serve immediately.

Nutrition: Calories: 120 Fat: 4g Carbs: 20g Protein: 4g

244.   Potato with creamy cheese

Preparation time: 5 minutes
Cooking time: 15 minutes
Servings: 2
Ingredients:
- 2 medium potatoes
- 1 teaspoon butter
- 3 tablespoons sour cream
- 1 teaspoon chives
- 1½ tablespoons grated parmesan cheese

Directions:
1. Preheat the air fryer oven to 350 ° F.
2. Stick the potatoes with a fork and boil them in water until they are cooked. Transfer to the air fryer basket and cook for 15 minutes.
3. In the meantime, combine the sour cream, cheese, and chives in a bowl.
4. Cut the potatoes halfway to open them up and fill with the butter and sour cream mixture.
5. Serve immediately.

Nutrition: Calories: 184 Fat: 2g Carbs: 38g Protein: 5g

245.   Golden pickles

Preparation time: 10 minutes
Cooking time: 15 minutes
Servings: 4
Ingredients:
- 14 dill pickles, sliced
- ¼ cup flour
- ⅛ teaspoon baking powder
- Pinch of salt
- 2 tablespoons cornstarch plus 3 tablespoons water
- 6 tablespoons panko breadcrumbs
- ½ teaspoon paprika
- Cooking spray

Directions:
1. Preheat the air fryer oven to 400°F (204C).
2. Drain any excess moisture out of the dill pickles on a paper towel.
3. In a bowl, combine the flour, baking powder, and salt.
4. Throw in the cornstarch and water mixture and combine well with a whisk.
5. Put the panko breadcrumbs in a shallow dish along with the paprika. Mix thoroughly.
6. Dip the pickles in the flour batter before coating in the breadcrumbs. Spritz all the pickles with the cooking spray.
7. Transfer to the air fryer basket. Choose air fry and set time to 15 minutes, or until golden brown. Serve immediately.

Nutrition: Calories: 195 Fat: 13g Carbs: 20g Protein: 26g

246.   Garlic eggplant slices

Preparation time: 5 minutes
Cooking time: 15 minutes
Servings: 1
Ingredients:
- 1 large eggplant, sliced
- 2 tablespoons olive oil
- ¼ teaspoon salt
- ½ teaspoon garlic powder

Directions:
1. Preheat the air fryer oven to 390°F (199C).
2. Put eggplant slices with the olive oil, salt, and garlic powder in a mixing bowl until evenly coated.
3. Put the slices in the air fryer basket. Place the baking pan and cook for 15 minutes.
4. Serve immediately.

Nutrition: Calories: 66 Fat: 7g Carbs: 1g

247.   Zucchini balls

Preparation time: 5 minutes
Cooking time: 10 minutes
Servings: 4
Ingredients:
- 4 zucchinis
- 1 egg
- ½ cup grated parmesan cheese
- 1 tablespoon Italian herbs
- 1 cup grated coconut

Directions:
1. Thinly grate the zucchinis and dry with a cheesecloth, ensuring to remove all the moisture.
2. Blend zucchinis with the egg, parmesan, Italian herbs, and grated coconut in a bowl. Mix well to incorporate everything.
3. Using the hands, mold the mixture into balls.
4. Preheat the air fryer oven to 400°F (204C).
5. Lay the zucchini balls in the air fryer basket and cook for 10 minutes.
6. Serve hot.

Nutrition: Calories: 105 Fat: 3g Carbs: 16g Protein: 6g

248.   Lemony falafel

Preparation time: 10 minutes
Cooking time: 15 minutes
Servings: 8
Ingredients:
- 1 teaspoon cumin seeds
- ½ teaspoon coriander seeds
- 2 cups chickpeas, drained and rinsed
- ½ teaspoon red pepper flakes
- 3 cloves garlic
- ¼ cup chopped parsley
- ¼ cup chopped coriander
- ½ onion, diced
- 1 tablespoon juice from freshly squeezed lemon
- 3 tablespoons flour
- ½ teaspoon salt
- Cooking spray

Directions:
1. Cook the cumin and coriander seeds over medium heat.
2. Grind using a mortar and pestle.
3. Put all ingredients, except for the cooking spray, in a food processor and blend until a fine consistency is achieved.
4. Use the hands to mold the mixture into falafels and spritz with the cooking spray.
5. Preheat the air fryer oven to 400° F (204C).

6. Transfer the falafels to the air fryer basket in a single layer. Cook until golden brown. Serve warm.

Nutrition: Calories: 56 Fat: 1g Carbs: 9g Protein: 3g

249. Sweet and sour tofu

Preparation time: 15 minutes
Cooking time: 20 minutes
Servings: 2
Ingredients:

- 2 teaspoons apple cider vinegar
- 1 tablespoon sugar
- 1 tablespoon soy sauce
- 3 teaspoons lime juice
- 1 teaspoon ground ginger
- 1 teaspoon garlic powder
- ½ block firm tofu pressed to remove excess liquid and cut into cubes
- 1 teaspoon cornstarch
- 2 green onions, chopped
- Toasted sesame seeds, for garnish

Directions:

1. In a bowl, thoroughly combine the apple cider vinegar, sugar, soy sauce, lime juice, ground ginger, and garlic powder.
2. Cover the tofu with this mixture and leave to marinate for at least 30 minutes.
3. Preheat the air fryer oven to 400°F (204C).
4. Transfer the tofu to the air fryer basket, keeping any excess marinade for the sauce.
5. Cook the tofu for 20 minutes, or until crispy.
6. In the meantime, thicken the sauce with the cornstarch over medium low heat.
7. Serve the cooked tofu with the sauce, green onions, and sesame seeds.

Nutrition: Calories: 207 Fat: 11g Carbs: 13g Protein: 18g

250. Crispy chickpeas

Preparation time: 5 minutes
Cooking time: 15 minutes
Servings: 4
Ingredients:

- 1 can (15ounces / 425g) chickpeas, drained but not rinsed
- 2 tablespoons olive oil
- 1 teaspoon salt
- 2 tablespoons lemon juice

Directions:

1. Preheat the air fryer oven to 400°F (204°C).
2. Put and mix all ingredients in a bowl. Transfer this mixture to the air fryer basket.
3. Put mixture into baking pan and slide into rack position 2, select air fry, and set time to 15 minutes, ensuring the chickpeas become nice and crispy.
4. Serve immediately.

Nutrition: Calories: 132 Fat: 6g Carbs: 14g Protein: 5g

251. Winter vegetable braise

Preparation time:
Cooking time:
Servings: 2
Ingredients:

- 4 peeled potatoes, cut into 1inch pieces
- 1 peeled celery root, cut into 1inch pieces
- 1 cup winter squash
- 2 tablespoons unsalted butter, melted
- 1/2 cup chicken broth
- 1/4 cup tomato sauce
- 1 teaspoon parsley
- 1 teaspoon rosemary
- 1 teaspoon thyme

Directions

1. Prepare the air fryer by preheating to 370 ° F.
2. Add all ingredients in a lightly greased casserole dish. Stir to combine well.
3. Bake in the preheated air fryer for 10 minutes.
4. Gently stir the vegetables with a large spoon and increase the temperature to 400° F; cook for 10 minutes more.

5. Serve in individual bowls with a few drizzles of lemon juice. Enjoy!

Nutrition: Calories: 192 Fat: 1g Carbs: 41g Protein: 7g

252. Spicy roasted potatoes

Preparation time: 10 minutes
Cooking time: 12 minutes
Servings: 2
Ingredients:

- 4 potatoes, peeled and cut into wedges
- 2 tablespoons olive oil
- Sea salt
- Ground black pepper, to taste
- 1 teaspoon cayenne pepper
- 1/2 teaspoon ancho chili powder

Directions

1. Get a bowl and mix all ingredients until the potatoes are well covered.
2. Transfer them to the air fryer basket and cook at 400 ° F for 6 minutes. Shake the basket and cook for a further 6 minutes.
3. Serve warm with your favorite sauce for dipping. Enjoy!

Nutrition: Calories 299 Fat 16gCarbs 49g Protein 8g

253. Skinny pumpkin chips

Preparation time: 10 minutes
Cooking time: 13 minutes
Servings: 2
Ingredients:

- 1pound pumpkin, cut into sticks
- 1 tablespoon coconut oil
- 1/2 teaspoon rosemary
- 1/2 teaspoon basil
- Salt and ground black pepper, to taste

Directions

1. Start by preheating the air fryer to 395 ° F. Brush the pumpkin sticks with coconut oil.
2. Put the spices and combine well.
3. Cook for 13 minutes, shaking the basket halfway through the cooking time.
4. Serve with mayonnaise. Bon appétit!

Nutrition: Calories 118 Fat 7g Carbs 17g Protein 2g

254. Classic onion rings

Preparation time: 5 minutes
Cooking time: 5 minutes
Servings: 1
Ingredients:

- 1 medium-sized onion, slice into rings
- 1 cup all-purpose flour
- 1 teaspoon baking powder
- Coarse sea salt
- Ground black pepper, to taste
- 1/2 cup yogurt
- 2 eggs, beaten
- 3/4 cup breadcrumbs
- 1 teaspoon onion powder
- 1 teaspoon garlic powder
- 1/2 teaspoon celery seeds

Directions

1. Place the onion rings in the bowl with cold water; let them soak approximately 20 minutes; drain the onion rings and pat dry using a pepper towel.
2. In an empty bowl, put the flour, baking powder, salt, and black pepper. Add the yogurt and eggs and mix well to combine.
3. In another, mix the breadcrumbs, onion powder, garlic powder, and celery seeds.
4. Dip the onion rings in the flour/egg mixture; then, dredge in the breadcrumb mixture.
5. Spritz the air fryer basket with cooking spray; arrange the breaded onion rings in the basket.
6. Cook at 400 ° F for 4 to 5 minutes, turning them over halfway through the cooking time. Enjoy!

Nutrition: Calories: 114 Fat: 1g Carbs: 18g Protein: 5g

255. Rainbow vegetable fritters

Preparation time: 10 minutes

Cooking time: 12 minutes
Servings: 2
Ingredients:

- 1 zucchini, grated and squeezed
- 1 cup corn kernels
- 1/2 cup canned green peas
- 4 tablespoons all-purpose flour
- 2 tablespoons fresh shallots, minced
- 1 teaspoon fresh garlic, minced
- 1 tablespoon peanut oil
- Sea salt
- Ground black pepper, to taste
- 1 teaspoon cayenne pepper

Directions
1. Combine well all ingredients in a mixing bowl until everything is incorporated.
2. Shape the mixture into patties. Put cooking spray in the air fryer basket.
3. Cook in the preheated air fryer at 365 °F for 6 minutes. Turn and cook the other side for additional 6 minutes.
4. Serve immediately and enjoy!

Nutrition: Calories: 215 Fat: 32g Carbs: 6g Protein: 4g

256. Sweet corn fritters with avocado
Preparation time: 5 minutes
Cooking time: 7 minutes
Servings: 1
Ingredients:

- 2 cups sweet corn kernels
- 1 small sized onion, chopped
- 1 garlic clove, minced
- 2 eggs, whisked
- 1 teaspoon baking powder
- 2 tablespoons chopped fresh cilantro
- Sea salt
- Ground black pepper, to taste
- 1 avocado, peeled, pitted, and diced
- 2 tablespoons sweet chili sauce

Directions
1. In a mixing bowl, thoroughly combine the corn, onion, garlic, eggs, baking powder, cilantro, salt, and black pepper.
2. Shape the corn mixture into 6 patties and transfer them to the lightly greased air fryer basket.
3. Cook in the preheated air fry at 370 ° F for 8 minutes; turn them over and cook for 7 minutes longer.
4. Serve the cakes with the avocado and chili sauce.

Nutrition: Calories: 132 Fat: 6g Carbs: 17g Protein: 4g

257. Three cheese stuffed mushrooms
Preparation time: 10 minutes
Cooking time: 7 – 10 minutes
Servings: 9
Ingredients:

- 9 large button mushrooms, stems removed
- 1 tablespoon olive oil
- Salt and ground black pepper, to taste
- 1/2 teaspoon dried rosemary
- 6 tablespoons swiss cheese shredded
- 6 tablespoons Romano cheese, shredded
- 6 tablespoons cream cheese
- 1 teaspoon soy sauce
- 1 teaspoon garlic, minced
- 3 tablespoons green onion, minced

Directions
1. Graze the mushroom caps with olive oil. Add salt, pepper, and rosemary.
2. Combine the remaining ingredients in a bowl, mix it well, and divide the filling mixture among the mushroom caps.
3. Cook in the preheated air fryer at 390 ° F for 7 minutes.
4. Let the mushrooms cool slightly before serving. Bon appétit!

Nutrition: Calories: 104 Fat: 8g Carbs: 3g Protein: 5g

258. Spicy ricotta stuffed mushrooms
Preparation time: 10 minutes

Cooking time: 18 minutes
Servings:
Ingredients:

- 1/2pound small white mushrooms
- Sea salt
- Ground black pepper, to taste
- 2 tablespoons ricotta cheese
- 1/2 teaspoon ancho chili powder
- 1 teaspoon paprika
- 4 tablespoons all-purpose flour
- 1 egg
- 1/2 cup fresh breadcrumbs

Directions
1. Get and chop the stems from the mushroom caps.
2. Mix the chopped mushrooms stems with salt, black pepper, cheese, chili powder, and paprika.
3. Stuff the mushroom caps with the cheese filling.
4. Prepare the flour in a mixing bowl and beat the egg in another bowl.
5. Get a third bowl and put the breadcrumbs.
6. Dip the mushrooms in the flour, then dip in the egg mixture; finally, dredge in the breadcrumbs and press to adhere. Spritz the stuffed mushrooms with cooking spray.
7. Cook at 360 degrees F for 18 minutes. Enjoy!

Nutrition: Calories: 214 Fat: 6g Carbs: 30g Protein: 12g

259. Mediterranean vegetable skewers
Preparation time: 15 minutes
Cooking time: 13 minutes
Servings: 4
Ingredients:

- 2 medium-sized zucchinis
- 2 red bell peppers
- 1 green bell pepper
- 1 red onion, cut into 1inch pieces
- 2 tablespoons olive oil
- Sea salt, to taste
- 1/2 teaspoon black pepper, preferably freshly cracked
- 1/2 teaspoon red pepper flakes

Directions:
1. Cut the zucchinis, red and green bell peppers into 1inch pieces
2. Rinse the wooden skewers in water for 15 minutes.
3. Thread the vegetables on skewers; drizzle olive oil all over the vegetable skewers; sprinkle with spices.
4. Preheat at 400° F and cook for 13 minutes. Serve warm and enjoy!

Nutrition: Calories 138Fat 12g Carbs 12g Protein 2g

260. Fried peppers with sriracha mayo
Preparation time: 10 minutes
Cooking time: 14 minutes
Servings: 2
Ingredients:

- 4 bell peppers, seeded and sliced (1inch pieces)
- 1 onion, sliced (1inch pieces)
- 1 tablespoon olive oil
- 1/2 teaspoon dried rosemary
- 1/2 teaspoon dried basil
- Kosher salt, to taste
- 1/4 teaspoon ground black pepper
- 1/3 cup mayonnaise
- 1/3 teaspoon sriracha

Directions
1. Mix the onions and bell peppers with the olive oil, rosemary, basil, salt, and black pepper.
2. Place the peppers and onions on an even layer in the cooking basket.
3. Cook at 400° F for 12 to 14 minutes.
4. Meanwhile, make the sauce by whisking the mayonnaise and sriracha. Serve immediately.

Nutrition: Calories: 15 Fiber: 5g Carbs: 5g Protein: 5g

261. Balsamic root vegetables
Preparation time: 10 minutes
Cooking time: 15 minutes

Servings: 1
Ingredients:
- 2 potatoes, cut into 1 1/2inch piece
- 2 carrots, cut into 1 1/2inch piece
- 2 parsnips, cut into 1 1/2inch piece
- 1 onion, cut into 1 1/2inch piece
- Pink Himalayan salt and ground black pepper, to taste
- 1/4 teaspoon smoked paprika
- 1 teaspoon garlic powder
- 1/2 teaspoon dried thyme
- 1/2 teaspoon dried marjoram
- 2 tablespoons olive oil
- 2 tablespoons balsamic vinegar

Directions
1. Toss all ingredients in a large mixing dish.
2. Roast in the preheated air fryer at 400 ° F for 10 minutes. Shake the basket and cook for 7 minutes more.
3. Serve with some extra fresh herbs if desired. Bon appétit!

Nutrition: Calories: 164 Fat: 4g Carbs: 32g Protein: 3g

262.   Asian fennel and noodle salad

Preparation time: 10 minutes
Cooking time: 15 minutes
Servings: 3
Ingredients:
- 1 fennel bulb, quartered
- Salt and white pepper, to taste
- 1 clove garlic, finely chopped
- 1 green onion, thinly sliced
- 2 cups Chinese cabbage, shredded
- 2 tablespoons of rice wine vinegar
- 1 tablespoon honey
- 2 tablespoons sesame oil
- 1 teaspoon ginger, freshly grated
- 1 tablespoon soy sauce
- 1 cup chow Mein noodles, for serving

Directions
1. Preheat air fryer to 370 ° F.
2. Now, cook the fennel bulb in the lightly greased cooking basket for 15 minutes, shaking the basket once or twice.
3. Let it cool completely and toss with the remaining ingredients. Serve well chilled.

Nutrition: Calories: 173 Fat: 11g Carbs: 18g Protein: 4g

263.   Sweet potato and chickpea tacos

Preparation time: 15 minutes
Cooking time: 10 minutes
Servings: 8
Ingredients:
- 2 cups sweet potato puree
- 2 tablespoons butter, melted
- 14 ounces canned chickpeas, rinsed
- 1 cup Colby cheese, shredded
- 1 teaspoon garlic powder
- 1 teaspoon onion powder
- Salt
- Freshly cracked black pepper
- 8 corn tortillas
- 1/4 cup Pico de Gallo
- 2 tablespoons fresh coriander, chopped

Directions
1. Mix the sweet potatoes with the butter, chickpeas, cheese, garlic powder, onion powder, salt, black pepper.
2. Split the sweet potato mixture between the tortillas.
3. Bake in the preheated Air Fryer at 390° F for 7 minutes.
4. Garnish with Pico de Gallo and coriander. Enjoy!

Nutrition: Calories: 314 Fat: 13g Carbs: 41g Protein: 9g

264.   Charred asparagus and cherry tomato salad

Preparation time: 10 minutes
Cooking time: 10 minutes
Servings: 4
Ingredients:
- 1/4 cup olive oil

- 1pound asparagus, trimmed
- 1pound cherry tomatoes
- 1/4 cup balsamic vinegar
- 2 garlic cloves, minced
- 2 scallion stalks, chopped
- 1/2 teaspoon oregano
- Coarse sea salt
- Ground black pepper
- 2 hardboiled eggs, sliced

Directions
1. Brush the cooking basket with 1 tablespoon of olive oil. Preheat to 400 ° F.
2. Add the asparagus and cherry tomatoes to the cooking basket. Drizzle 1 tablespoon of olive oil all over your veggies.
3. Cook for 5 minutes, shaking the basket halfway through the cooking time. Let it cool slightly.
4. Add the remaining olive oil, balsamic vinegar, garlic, scallions, oregano, salt, and black pepper.
5. Afterward, add the hardboiled eggs on the top of your salad and serve.

Nutrition: Calories: 153 Fat: 11g Carbs: 6g Protein: 10g

265.   Vietnamese pork rolls

Preparation time: 20 minutes
Cooking time: 20 minutes
Servings: 4
Ingredients:
- 2 tablespoons vegetable oil
- ½ cup yellow onion, chopped
- 1 tablespoon garlic, minced
- ¼ lb. Ground pork
- 1 tablespoon scallions, chopped
- 1 cup carrot, sliced into thin strips
- 1 cup bean sprouts
- 1 cup mint
- 1 cup cilantro
- 24 spring roll wrappers
- ¼ cup lime juice
- 2 tablespoon fish sauce
- 1 tablespoon chili garlic sauce

Directions:
1. Cook onion, garlic and ground pork for 8 to 10 minutes, stirring frequently. Stir in the scallions, carrot, bean sprouts, mint and cilantro.
2. Cook for 3 minutes, stirring often. Drain the mixture.
3. Top the wrappers with the mixture.
4. Roll up the wrappers and seal.
5. Add the rolls to the crisper tray.
6. Choose air fry setting.
7. Cook at 380 ° F for 7 minutes.
8. Mix lime juice and fish sauce.
9. Serve rolls with lime juice mixture and chili garlic.

Nutrition: Calories: 74 Fat: 3g Carbs: 7g Protein: 4g

266.   Breaded pork chops

Preparation time: 5 minutes
Cooking time: 12 minutes
Servings: 4
Ingredients:
- 4 pork chops
- Salt and pepper to taste
- 1 egg, beaten
- Cooking spray
- Breading
- 1 cup breadcrumbs
- 2/3 cups cornflakes, crushed
- 2 teaspoons sweet paprika
- 1 teaspoon garlic powder
- 1 teaspoon onion powder
- 1 teaspoon chili powder

Directions:
1. Season the pork chops with salt and pepper.
2. Dip in egg.

3. In a bowl, mix the breading ingredients.
4. Cover the pork chops with the breading.
5. Spray with oil.
6. Add the pork chops to the air crisper tray.
7. Cook at 360 ° F for 6 minutes per side.

Nutrition: Calories: 315 Fat: 21g Carbs: 11g Protein: 20g

267. Bacon pudding with corn

Preparation time: 20 minutes
Cooking time: 25 minutes
Servings: 6
Ingredients:

- 4 slices bacon
- 1 onion, chopped
- 2 teaspoons garlic, minced
- 1 red bell pepper, diced
- ¼ cup celery, chopped
- 1 cup corn kernels
- ¾ teaspoon creole seasoning
- Pinch cayenne pepper
- Salt to taste
- 3 eggs, beaten
- ½ cup heavy cream
- 1 ½ cups milk
- 1 tablespoon butter
- 3 cups day old bread, sliced into cubes
- 1 cup Monterey jack cheese, grated

Directions:

1. Warm up a pan over medium heat and cook the bacon.
2. Stir in the onion, garlic, red bell pepper, celery, corn, Creole seasoning, cayenne pepper and salt.
3. Cook for 5 minutes, stirring often.
4. In a bowl, mix the eggs, cream and milk.
5. Fold in butter, bread, cheese and onion mixture.
6. Pour the pudding into a casserole dish.
7. Slide it into the pizza rack. Choose bake setting.
8. Cook for 25 minutes at 325 ° F.

Nutrition: Calories: 125 Fat: 7g Carbs: 13g Protein: 4g

268. Spicy short ribs

Preparation time: 20 minutes
Cooking time: 8 hours
Servings: 5
Ingredients:

- 6 lb. Beef short ribs
- Salt and pepper to taste
- 14 oz. Ketchup
- 12 oz. Beer
- 1 tablespoon molasses
- 1 tablespoon mustard
- 2 cloves garlic, minced
- ½ cup onions, chopped
- ¼ cup brown sugar
- 1 teaspoon hot pepper sauce
- 1 teaspoon cayenne pepper

Directions:

1. Season ribs with salt and pepper.
2. Add the ribs to a Dutch oven.
3. Add the rest of the ingredients to a food processor.
4. Pulse until smooth.
5. Coat the ribs with the mixture.
6. Place the ribs and sauce in the pizza rack.
7. Choose slow cook setting.
8. Cook at 225 ° F for 8 hours.

Nutrition: Calories: 220 Fat: 16g Carbs: 1g Protein: 16g

269. Pork teriyaki

Preparation time: 10 minutes
Cooking time: 20 minutes
Servings: 4
Ingredients:

- 1 tablespoon vegetable oil
- 2 tablespoons soy sauce
- 1 tablespoon brown sugar

- 1 tablespoon dry sherry
- 1 clove garlic, minced
- 1 tablespoon vinegar
- 1 teaspoon ginger, grated
- Salt and pepper to taste
- 1 lb. Pork tenderloin

Directions:

1. Add all the ingredients except pork in a bowl.
2. Mix well.
3. Add pork to the bowl.
4. Cover and marinate overnight.
5. Cook at 400 ° F for 20 to 30 minutes, flipping once.

Nutrition: Calories: 105 Fat: 3g Carbs: 2g Protein: 18g

270. Ham with apricot sauce

Preparation time: 5 minutes
Cooking time: 10 minutes
Servings: 2
Ingredients:

- 1 teaspoon lemon juice
- 1 teaspoon lemon juice
- ¼ cup apricot preserving
- ½ teaspoon ground cinnamon
- 1 teaspoon mustard
- 2 ham steaks

Directions:

1. Mix the ingredients in a bowl except the ham.
2. Brush ham with the sauce.
3. Place the ham steaks in the air crisper tray.
4. Select air fry setting.
5. Cook at 350 ° F for 5 minutes per side, basting with the sauce.

Nutrition: Calories: 273 Fat: 12gb Carbs: 13g Protein: 33g

271. Pork & veggies

Preparation time: 20 minutes
Cooking time: 20 minutes
Servings: 4
Ingredients:

Veggies

- ½ cup onion, diced
- 10 oz. Mushrooms, diced
- 2 red peppers, diced
- 1 lb. Cabbage, shredded
- 1 tablespoon olive oil
- 1 tablespoon Cajun seasoning

Pork

- 1 lb. Pork tenderloin
- Salt and pepper to taste

Directions:

1. Toss the veggies in oil and seasoning.
2. Add to the air crisper tray.
3. Select air fry setting.
4. Cook at 350 ° F for 5 minutes.
5. Stir and cook for another 5 minutes.
6. Transfer to a serving plate.
7. Season pork with salt and pepper.
8. Set it inside the air fryer oven.
9. Cook at 350 ° F for 10 minutes, flipping once.
10. Serve pork with veggies.

Nutrition: Calories: 398 Fat: 11g Carbs: 43g Protein: 33g

272. Blackened pork chops

Preparation time: 5 minutes
Cooking time: 15 minutes
Servings: 4
Ingredients:

- 1 lb. Pork loins
- Dry rub
- 1 teaspoon chili powder
- 1 teaspoon paprika
- 1 teaspoon cayenne pepper
- 1 teaspoon garlic powder
- 1 teaspoon dried thyme
- 1 teaspoon sugar
- Salt to taste

Directions:
1. Mix rub ingredients in a bowl.
2. Season both sides of pork with this mixture.
3. Add the pork loin to the air crisper tray.
4. Cook at 360 ° F for 7 minutes per side.

Nutrition: Calories: 341 Fat: 15g Carbs: 4g Protein: 46g

273. Pork roast

Preparation time: 10 minutes
Cooking time: 1 hour
Servings: 6
Ingredients:

- 2 tablespoons orange juice
- 1 tablespoon orange zest
- ½ cup brown sugar
- ½ cup honey
- Salt and pepper to taste
- 4 lb. Pork loin roast

Directions:
1. Add all the ingredients except pork in a bowl.
2. Mix well.
3. Attach the rotisserie spit through the pork.
4. Place it in the air fryer oven.
5. Coat the pork with the mixture.
6. Choose rotisserie setting.
7. Cook at 350 ° F for 1 hour, basting the pork every 15 minutes.

Nutrition: Calories: 150 Fat: 6g Carbs: 0g Protein: 31g

274. Savory pork loin

Preparation time: 5 minutes
Cooking time: 5 minutes
Servings: 4
Ingredients:

- 4 slices pork loin
- Garlic salt to taste
- Pepper to taste

Directions:
1. Season pork loin with garlic salt and pepper.
2. Place pork loin in the air crisper tray.
3. Choose air fry setting.
4. Set it to 320 ° F.
5. Cook for 5 to 8 minutes.

Nutrition: Calories: 211 Fat: 6g Carbs: 2g Protein: 36g

275. Spicy green crusted chicken

Servings: 4
Preparation time: 10 minutes
Cooking time: 40 minutes
Temperature: 360° F
Ingredients:

- 4 whole eggs, beaten
- 4 teaspoons parsley
- 3 teaspoons thyme
- 3 teaspoons paprika
- ¾ pound chicken pieces
- Salt and pepper, to taste
- 4 teaspoons oregano

Directions:
1. Preheat your air fryer to 360 ° F.
2. Grease the air fryer cooking basket.
3. Crack eggs in a bowl and whisk well, take another bowl and mix all of the ingredients except chicken pieces.
4. Dip chicken in eggs and then into the dry mixture.
5. Transfer half of the chicken pieces to your air fryer and cook for 20 minutes.
6. Keep repeating until all ingredients are used up.
7. Enjoy!

Nutrition: Calories: 393, Fat: 22g, Carbs: 7g, Fiber: 1g, Carbs: 4g, protein: 39g

276. Jamaican pork roast

Servings: 8
Preparation time: 10 minutes
Cooking time: 50 minutes
Temperature: 440 ° F
Ingredients:

- 2 tablespoons olive oil
- 2 pounds pork shoulder
- ¼ cup beef broth
- ¼ cup Jamaican jerk spice blend

Directions:
1. Marinate pork using the Jamaican jerk spice blend and olive oil, let it sit for 10 minutes.
2. Preheat your air fryer to 440 ° F.
3. Add marinated pork to air fryer and cook for 2 minutes.
4. Add beef broth, cook for 45 minutes more.
5. Serve and enjoy!

Nutrition: Calories: 362, total fat: 27g, total carbs: 10g, fiber: 2g, net carbs: 6g, protein: 26g

277. Cheesy chicken drumsticks

Servings: 2
Preparation time: 18 minutes
Cooking time: 15 minutes
Temperature: 370 ° F
Ingredients:

- 1-pound small chicken drumsticks, bone in
- 2 tablespoons almond flour
- 1 cup mixed cheese, grated
- 1 teaspoon dried rosemary
- 1 teaspoon dried oregano
- ½ teaspoon chili flakes
- ½ teaspoon salt
- ½ teaspoon pepper
- Chopped green onion for garnish

Directions:
1. Rinse drumsticks thoroughly and pat them dry.
2. Take a medium-sized bowl and add flour, mixed cheese, herbs, chili flakes, salt, and pepper.
3. Dip drumsticks in the mixture and turn them well, keep in the freezer for 5 minutes.
4. Spray air fryer cooking basket with cooking spray and preheat your fryer to 370 °F.
5. Transfer drumsticks to your fryer and cook for 15 minutes, making sure to shake the basket halfway through.
6. Transfer to a serving plate and enjoy with your garnish!

Nutrition: Calories: 226, Fat: 10g, Carbs: 4g, Fiber: 1g, Carbs: 2g, Protein: 16g

278. Swiss bacon pork chops

Servings: 8
Preparation time: 5 minutes
Cooking time: 40 minutes
Temperature: 450 ° F
Ingredients:

- 2 tablespoons butter
- Salt and pepper to taste
- 12 bacon strips, cut in half
- 8 pork chops, bone in
- 1 cup swiss cheese, shredded

Directions:
1. Preheat your air fryer to 450 ° F.
2. Grease air fryer cooking basket.
3. Season pork chops with salt and pepper, top with bacon strips and swiss cheese.
4. Transfer to air fryer cooking basket and cook for 40 minutes.
5. Serve and enjoy!

Nutrition: Calories: 483, Fat: 40g, Carbs: 4g, Fiber: 1g, Carbs: 2g, Protein: 28g

279. Buttery scallops

Servings: 6
Preparation time: 10 minutes
Cooking time: 10 minutes
Temperature: 390 ° F
Ingredients:

- 2 pounds sea scallops
- 3 tablespoons butter, melted
- 2 tablespoons fresh thyme, minced
- Salt and pepper, to taste

Directions:
1. Preheat your air fryer to 390° F, grease air fryer cooking basket with butter.

2. Take a bowl, mix in all of the remaining ingredients, and toss well to coat the scallops.
3. Transfer scallops to the air fryer cooking basket and cook for 5 minutes.
4. Repeat if any ingredients are left, serve and enjoy!

Nutrition: Calories: 186, Fat: 24g, Carbs: 4g, Protein: 20g

280. Coconut crusted prawns

Servings: 3
Preparation time: 5 minutes
Cooking time: 6 minutes
Temperature: 400 ° F
Ingredients:

- 12 large raw prawns, peeled and deveined
- Salt and pepper, to taste
- 1 cup egg white
- 1 cup dried unsweetened coconut
- ½ cup almond flour
- 4 tablespoons butter

Directions:

1. Preheat your air fryer to 400 ° F for 5 minutes.
2. Season prawns with salt and pepper.
3. Transfer all ingredients to zip-loc bag and shake until combined well.
4. Transfer the ingredients to your air fryer cooking basket.
5. Cook for 6 minutes at 400 ° F.
6. Serve and enjoy!

Nutrition: Calories: 497, Fat: 43g, Carbs: 11g, Protein: 19g

281. Turmeric beef

Servings: 4
Preparation time: 10 minutes
Cooking time: 30 minutes
Temperature: 450 ° F
Ingredients:

- 2 pounds beef, steak pieces
- 2 cups yogurt
- 4 tablespoons salt
- 6 tablespoons olive oil
- 4 tablespoons turmeric powder
- 4 tablespoons coriander powder
- 4 tablespoons cumin powder
- 4 tablespoons red chili powder
- 4 tablespoons lemon juice

Directions:

1. Marinate beef pieces overnight in a mixture of cumin, yogurt, red chili powder, salt, lemon juice, coriander, vinegar, turmeric, and oil.
2. Preheat your air fryer to 450 ° F.
3. Transfer marinated beefsteaks to air fryer.
4. Cook for 30 minutes.
5. Serve and enjoy!

Nutrition: Calories: 362, Fat: 28g, Carbs: 8g, protein: 40g

282. Keto beef tongue

Servings: 3
Preparation time: 10 minutes
Cooking time: 20 minutes
Temperature: 350 ° f
Ingredients:

- 1-pound beef tongue
- 1 teaspoon paprika
- 1 tablespoon butter
- Pinch of salt
- Pinch of pepper

Directions:

1. Rinse the beef tongues thoroughly under cold water.
2. Take a pot and add 4 cups of water, place it over a stove and add the tongues.
3. Simmer over low heat for 30 minutes.
4. Remove tongues from water and let them cool, slice into strips.
5. Take a microwave proof bowl and melt butter, add the tongues to the butter.
6. Season with salt, paprika, and pepper.
7. Preheat your air fryer to 350 ° F.
8. Transfer beef tongues to the air fryer and cook for 20 minutes.

9. Transfer to a platter, serve and enjoy!

Nutrition: Calories: 234, Fat: 18g, Carbs: 6g, Protein: 16g

283. Pork carnitas

Servings: 6
Preparation time: 10 minutes
Cooking time: 40 minutes
Temperature: 450 ° F
Ingredients:

- 2 oranges, juiced
- 2 pounds pork shoulder
- 1 teaspoon garlic powder
- Salt and pepper, to taste
- 2 tablespoons butter

Directions:

1. Preheat your air fryer to 450° F.
2. Grease the air fryer cooking basket with butter.
3. Season pork with garlic powder, pepper, and salt.
4. Transfer to air fryer cooking basket and top with orange juice
5. Cook for 40 minutes.
6. Serve by shredding with forks, serve and enjoy!

Nutrition: Calories: 506, Fat: 36g, Carbs: 7g, Protein: 18g

284. Ginger chicken thighs

Servings: 3
Preparation time: 5 minutes
Cooking time: 15 minutes
Temperature: 350 ° F
Ingredients:

- 3 boneless, skinless chicken thighs, diced into bite size portions
- 1 shallot, thinly sliced
- ½ cup apple cider
- 1 tablespoon ginger, grated
- Pinch of salt

Directions:

1. Rinse chicken thoroughly under cold water, pat it dry.
2. Take a small bowl and add apple cider, ginger, salt, pepper, and shallot.
3. Pour the mixture into Ziploc bag and add chicken thighs, massage to coat it well.
4. Let it chill for 2 hours.
5. Preheat your air fryer to 350 ° F and lightly spray the cooking basket.
6. Transfer chicken thigh to air fryer and cook for 15 minutes, making sure to turn them halfway through.
7. Serve and enjoy!

Nutrition: Calories: 726, total Fat: 48g, total Carbs: 9g, Fiber: 2g, net Carbs: 6g, Protein: 64g

285. Lemon fish fillet

Servings: 4
Preparation time: 5 minutes
Cooking time: 15 minutes
Temperature: 400 ° F
Ingredients:

- 4 salmon fish fillets
- 1 lemon
- Salt and pepper, to taste
- 2 tablespoons olive oil
- 1 large egg, beaten
- ½ cup almond flour

Directions:

1. Preheat your air fryer to 400 ° F for 5 minutes.
2. Season salmon fillets with oil, lemon, salt, and pepper.
3. Soak the fillets in beaten egg and dredge them in almond flour.
4. Transfer fillets to the air fryer cooking basket and cook for 15 minutes.
5. Serve and enjoy!

Nutrition: Calories: 628, Fat: 23g, Carbs: 11g, Protein: 43g

286. Garlic pork roast

Servings: 8
Preparation time: 10 minutes
Cooking time: 45 minutes
Temperature: 470 ° F
Ingredients:

- 2 pounds pork shoulder

- 1½ tablespoons olive oil
- 2 teaspoons dried thyme
- 8 garlic cloves, minced
- Salt and pepper, to taste

Directions:
1. Preheat your air fryer to 470 ° F.
2. Take a bowl and mix in olive oil, salt, pepper, thyme, and garlic.
3. Marinate pork with oil mixture for about 30 minutes.
4. Transfer pork to the air fryer cooking basket and cook for 40 minutes.
5. Serve and enjoy!

Nutrition: Calories: 359, Fat: 26g, Carbs: 7g, protein: 26g

287. Ribeye steaks
Servings: 3
Preparation time: 10 minutes
Cooking time: 13 minutes
Temperature: 350 ° F
Ingredients:
- 2 pounds ribeye steaks
- Salt and pepper, as needed

Directions:
1. Preheat your air fryer to 350 ° F.
2. Lightly spray cooking backset with nonstick keto cooking spray.
3. Bring the steaks to room temperature and season with salt and pepper.
4. Transfer steaks to air fryer and cook for 7 minutes, turn the steak and cook for 6 minutes more.
5. Transfer to a serving platter and let it sit for 5 minutes, slice and serve.
6. Enjoy!

Nutrition: Calories: 703, Fat: 58g, Carbs: 4g, Protein: 46g

288. Mustard pork chops
Servings: 6
Preparation time: 10 minutes
Cooking time: 40 minutes
Temperature: 450 ° F
Ingredients:
- 3 tablespoons Dijon mustard
- Salt and pepper to taste
- 6 pork chops
- 1½ tablespoons fresh rosemary, coarsely chopped
- 3 tablespoons butter

Directions:
1. Preheat your air fryer to 450 °F.
2. Grease air fryer cooking basket with butter.
3. Marinate pork chops with Dijon mustard, fresh rosemary, salt, pepper and let it marinate for 3 hours.
4. Transfer the chops to the air fryer cooking basket and cook for 40 minutes.
5. Serve and enjoy!

Nutrition: Calories: 315, Fat: 26g, carbs: 4g, Protein: 20g

289. Turkey Cakes
Preparation Time: 10 minutes
Cooking Time: 10 minutes
Servings: 4
Ingredients:
- mushrooms, chopped
- 1 teaspoon garlic powder
- 1 teaspoon onion powder
- Salt and black pepper to the taste
- 1 and ¼ pounds turkey meat, ground
- Cooking spray
- Tomato sauce for serving

Direction:
1. In your blender, mix mushrooms with salt and pepper, pulse well and transfer to a bowl.
2. Add turkey, onion powder, garlic powder, salt and pepper, stir and shape cakes out of this mix.
3. Spray them with cooking spray, transfer them to your air fryer and cook for 10 minutes at 320 degrees F.
4. Serve.

Nutrition: Calories: 200 Fat: 6g Carbs: 2g Protein: 35g

290. Cheese Ravioli and Marinara Sauce
Preparation Time: 10 minutes
Cooking Time: 8 minutes
Servings: 6
Ingredients:
- 20 ounces cheese ravioli
- ounces marinara sauce
- 1 tablespoon olive oil
- 1 cup buttermilk
- 2 cups breadcrumbs
- ¼ cup parmesan, grated

Directions:
1. Put buttermilk in a bowl and breadcrumbs in another bowl.
2. Dip ravioli in buttermilk, then in breadcrumbs and place them in your air fryer on a baking sheet.
3. Drizzle olive oil over them, cook at 400 ° F for 5 minutes, divide them on plates, sprinkle parmesan on top and serve for lunch.

Nutrition: Calories: 260 Fat: 6g Carbs: 40g Protein: 12g

291. Meatballs Sandwich
Preparation Time: 10 minutes
Cooking Time: 22 minutes
Servings: 4
Ingredients:
- baguettes, sliced more than halfway through
- ounces beef, ground
- ounces tomato sauce
- 1 small onion, chopped
- 1 egg, whisked
- 1 tablespoon breadcrumbs
- 2 tablespoons cheddar cheese, grated
- 1 tablespoon oregano, chopped
- 1 tablespoon olive oil
- Salt and black pepper to the taste
- 1 teaspoon thyme, dried
- 1 teaspoon basil, dried

Directions:
1. In a bowl, combine meat with salt, pepper, onion, breadcrumbs, egg, cheese, oregano, thyme and basil, stir, shape medium meatballs and add them to your air fryer after you've greased it with the oil.
2. Cook them at 375 ° F for 12 minutes, flipping them halfway.
3. Add tomato sauce, cook meatballs for 10 minutes more and arrange them on sliced baguettes.
4. Serve them right away.

Nutrition: Calories: 300 Fat: 12g Carbs: 38g Protein: 10g

292. Scallops and Dill
Preparation Time: 10 minutes
Cooking Time: 5 minutes
Servings: 4
Ingredients:
- 1-pound sea scallops, debearded
- 1 tablespoon lemon juice
- 1 teaspoon dill, chopped
- 2 teaspoons olive oil
- Salt and black pepper to the taste

Directions:
1. In your air fryer, mix scallops with dill, oil, salt, pepper and lemon juice, cover and cook at 360 ° F for 5 minutes.
2. Discard unopened ones, divide scallops and dill sauce on plates and serve for lunch.

Nutrition: Calories: 280 Fat: 21g Carbs: 6g Protein: 24g

293. Hot Bacon Sandwiches
Preparation Time: 10 minutes
Cooking Time: 7 minutes
Servings: 4
Ingredients:

- 1/3 cup BBQ sauce
- 2 tablespoons honey
- bacon slices, cooked and cut into thirds
- 1 red bell pepper, sliced
- 1 yellow bell pepper, sliced
- pita pockets, halved
- 1 and ¼ cup butter lettuce leaves, torn
- 2 tomatoes, sliced

Directions:
1. In a bowl, mix BBQ sauce with honey and whisk well.
2. Brush bacon and all bell peppers with some of this mix, place them in your air fryer and cook at 350 ° F for 4 minutes.
3. Shake fryer and cook them for 2 minutes more.
4. Stuff pita pockets with bacon mix, also stuff with tomatoes and lettuce, spread the rest of the BBQ sauce and serve for lunch.

Nutrition: Calories: 484 Fat: 0g Carbs:0g Protein: 12g

294. Chicken Pie
Preparation Time: 10 minutes
Cooking Time: 16 minutes
Servings: 4
Ingredients:
- 2 chicken thighs, boneless, skinless and cubed
- 1 carrot, chopped
- 1 yellow onion, chopped
- 2 potatoes, chopped
- 2 mushrooms, chopped
- 1 teaspoon soy sauce
- Salt and black pepper to the taste
- 1 teaspoon Italian seasoning
- ½ teaspoon garlic powder
- 1 teaspoon Worcestershire sauce
- 1 tablespoon flour
- 1 tablespoon milk
- 2 puff pastry sheets
- 1 tablespoon butter, melted

Directions:
1. Cook potatoes, carrots and onion in a heated pan, stir for 2 minutes.
2. Add chicken and mushrooms, salt, soy sauce, pepper, Italian seasoning, garlic powder, Worcestershire sauce, flour and milk, stir really well and take off heat.
3. Place 1 puff pastry sheet on the bottom of your air fryer's pan and trim edge excess.
4. Add chicken mix, top with the other puff pastry sheet, trim excess as well and brush pie with butter.
5. Place in your fryer and cook at 360 ° F for 6 minutes.
6. Leave pie to cool down, slice and serve for breakfast.

Nutrition: Calories: 531 Fat: 28g Carbs: 45g Protein: 24g

295. Hash Brown Toasts
Preparation Time: 10 minutes
Cooking Time: 7 minutes
Servings: 4
Ingredients:
- hash brown patties, frozen
- 1 tablespoon olive oil
- ¼ cup cherry tomatoes, chopped
- tablespoons mozzarella, shredded
- 2 tablespoons parmesan, grated
- 1 tablespoon balsamic vinegar
- 1 tablespoon basil, chopped

Directions:
1. Put hash brown patties in your air fryer, drizzle the oil over them and cook them at 400 ° F for 7 minutes.
2. In a bowl, mix tomatoes with mozzarella, parmesan, vine gar and basil and stir well.
3. Divide hash brown patties on plates, top each with tomatoes mix and serve for lunch.

Nutrition: Calories: 150 Fat: 9g Carbs: 15g Protein:1g

296. Delicious Beef Cubes
Preparation Time: 10 minutes
Cooking Time: 12 minutes
Servings: 4
Ingredients:
1. 1-pound sirloin, cubed
2. ounces jarred pasta sauce
3. 1 and ½ cups breadcrumbs
4. 2 tablespoons olive oil
5. ½ teaspoon marjoram, dried
6. White rice, already cooked for serving

Directions:
1. In a bowl, mix beef cubes with pasta sauce and toss well.
2. In another bowl, mix breadcrumbs with marjoram and oil and stir well.
3. Dip beef cubes in this mix, place them in your air fryer and cook at 360 ° F for 12 minutes.
4. Divide among plates and serve with white rice on the side.

Nutrition: Calories: 140 Fat: 6g Carbs: 0g Protein: 25g

297. Pasta Salad
Preparation Time: 15 minutes
Cooking Time: 12 minutes
Servings: 6
Ingredients:
- 1 zucchini, sliced in half and roughly chopped
- 1 orange bell pepper, roughly chopped
- 1 green bell pepper, roughly chopped
- 1 red onion, roughly chopped
- ounces brown mushrooms, halved
- Salt and black pepper to the taste
- 1 teaspoon Italian seasoning
- 1-pound penne, already cooked
- 1 cup cherry tomatoes, halved
- ½ cup kalamata olive, pitted and halved
- ¼ cup olive oil
- tablespoons balsamic vinegar
- 2 tablespoons basil, chopped

Directions:
1. In a bowl, mix zucchini with mushrooms, orange bell pepper, green bell pepper, red onion, salt, pepper, Italian seasoning and oil.
2. Toss well, transfer to preheated air fryer at 380 ° F and cook them for 12 minutes.
3. In a large salad bowl, mix pasta with cooked veggies, cherry tomatoes, olives, vinegar and basil, toss and serve for lunch.

Nutrition: Calories: 172 Fat: 5g Carbs:26g Protein: 6g

298. Philadelphia Chicken Lunch
Preparation Time: 10 minutes
Cooking Time: 30 minutes
Servings: 4
Ingredients:
- 1 teaspoon olive oil
- 1 yellow onion, sliced
- 2 chicken breasts, skinless, boneless and sliced Salt and black pepper to taste
- 1 tablespoon Worcestershire sauce
- ounces pizza dough
- 1 and ½ cups cheddar cheese, grated
- ½ cup jarred cheese sauce

Directions:
1. Heat up air fryer at 400 ° F, add half of the oil and onions and fry them for 8 minutes, stirring once.
2. Add chicken pieces, Worcestershire sauce, salt and pepper, toss, air fry for 8 minutes more, stirring once and transfer everything to a bowl.
3. Roll pizza dough on a working surface and shape a rectangle.

4   Spread half of the cheese all over, add chicken and onion mix and top with cheese sauce.

5   Roll your dough and shape into a U.

6   Place your roll in your air fryer's basket, brush with the rest of the oil and cook at 370 ° For 12 minutes, flipping the roll halfway.

7   Slice your roll when it's warm and serve for lunch.

Nutrition: Calories: 570 Fat: 20g Carbs: 59g Protein: 38g

299. Quick Lunch Pizzas

Preparation Time: 10 minutes
Cooking Time: 7 minutes
Servings: 4
Ingredients:

- pitas
- 1 tablespoon olive oil
- ¾ cup pizza sauce
- 2 ounces sliced, jarred mushrooms
- ½ teaspoon basil, dried
- 2 green onions, chopped
- 2 cup mozzarella, grated
- 1 cup grape tomatoes, sliced

Direction:

1   Spread pizza sauce on each pita bread, sprinkle green onions and basil, divide mushrooms and top with cheese.

2   Arrange pita pizzas in your air fryer and cook them at 400 ° F for 7 minutes.

3   Top each pizza with tomato slices, divide among plates and serve. Enjoy!

Nutrition: Calories: 302 Fat: 7g Carbs: 41g Protein: 25g

300. Tuna and Zucchini Tortillas

Preparation Time: 10 minutes
Cooking Time: 10 minutes
Servings: 4
Ingredients:

- corn tortillas
- tablespoons butter, soft
- ounces canned tuna, drained
- 1 cup zucchini, shredded
- 1/3 cup mayonnaise
- 2 tablespoons mustard
- 1 cup cheddar cheese, grated

Directions:

1   Spread butter on tortillas, place them in your air fryer's basket and cook them at 400° F for 3 minutes.

2   Meanwhile, in a bowl, mix tuna with zucchini, mayo and mustard and stir.

3   Divide this mix on each tortilla, top with cheese, roll tortillas, place them in your air fryer's basket again and cook them at 400 ° F for 4 minutes more.

4   Serve for lunch.

Nutrition: Calories: 119 Fat: 8g Carbs: 3g Protein: 10g

301. Squash Fritters

Preparation Time: 10 minutes
Cooking Time: 7 minutes
Servings: 4
Ingredients:

- ounces cream cheese
- 1 egg, whisked
- ½ teaspoon oregano, dried
- A pinch of salt and black pepper
- 1 yellow summer squash, grated
- 1/3 cup carrot, grated
- 2/3 cup breadcrumbs
- 2 tablespoons olive oil

Directions:

1   In a bowl, mix cream cheese with salt, pepper, oregano, egg, breadcrumbs, carrot and squash and stir well.

2   Shape medium patties out of this mix and brush them with the oil.

3   Place squash patties in your air fryer and cook them at 400 ° F for 7 minutes.

4   Serve them for lunch.

Nutrition: Calories: 32 Fat: 0g Carbs: 6g Protein: 2g

302. Prosciutto Sandwich

Preparation Time: 10 minutes
Cooking Time: 5 minutes
Servings: 1
Ingredients:

- 2 bread slices
- 2 mozzarella slices
- 2 tomato slices
- 2 prosciutto slices
- 2 basil leaves
- 1 teaspoon olive oil
- A pinch of salt and black pepper

Directions:

1   Arrange mozzarella and prosciutto on a bread slice.

2   Season with salt and pepper, place in your air fryer and cook at 400 ° F for 5 minutes.

3   Drizzle oil over prosciutto, add tomato and basil, cover with the other bread slice, cut sandwich in half and serve.

Nutrition: Calories: 132 Fat: 6g Carbs: 0g Protein: 0g

303. Bacon and Garlic Pizza

Preparation Time: 10 minutes
Cooking Time: 10 minutes
Servings: 4
Ingredients:

- dinner rolls, frozen
- garlic cloves minced
- ½ teaspoon oregano dried
- ½ teaspoon garlic powder
- 1 cup tomato sauce
- bacon slices, cooked and chopped
- 1 and ¼ cups cheddar cheese, grated
- Cooking spray

Directions:

1   Place dinner rolls on a working surface and press them to obtain 4 ovals.

2   Spray each oval with cooking spray, transfer them to your air fryer and cook them at 370 degrees F for 2 minutes.

3   Spread tomato sauce on each oval, divide garlic, sprinkle oregano and garlic powder and top with bacon and cheese.

4   Return pizzas to your heated air fryer and cook them at 370 ° F for 8 minutes more.

5   Serve them warm for lunch.

Nutrition: Calories: 660 Fat: 27g Carbs: 54g Protein: 15g

304. Pasta chips

Preparation Time: 15 minutes
Cooking Time: 40 minutes
Servings: 2
Ingredients:

- Whole wheat bow tie pasta (2 c., dry)
- Olive oil (1 Tbsp.)
- Yeast (1 Tbsp.)
- Italian seasoning (1 1/2 tsp)
- Salt (pinch)

Directions:

1.   Prepare the pasta for half the time instructed in packaging. Drain. Mix with other ingredients.

2.   Place in fryer basket and cook for 5 minutes at 390 °F.

3.   Shake basket to remove excess and cook until crunchy.

Nutrition: Calories: 294 Carb: 49g Fat: 8g Protein: 10g

305. Tofu nuggets with ginger soy marinade

Preparation Time: 10 minutes
Cooking Time: 25 minutes

Servings: 4
Ingredients:
- Extra firm tofu (14 oz)
- Arrowroot flour (0.25 c.)
- Garlic powder (1 tsp)
- Smoked paprika (0.5 tsp)
- Ground cumin (0.5 tsp)
- Salt (1 tsp)
- Soy Sauce (3 Tbsp.)
- Coconut sugar (2 Tbsp.)
- Agave nectar (2 Tbsp.)
- Ginger (1 Tbsp., freshly grated)
- Garlic powder (1 tsp)
- White sesame seeds (1 tsp)
- Scallion (1, chopped)
- Avocado oil

Directions:
1. Slice tofu to preferred bite sized squares. Remove excess moisture by pressing with a towel or paper towel.
2. Place tofu squares in a bowl. Mix in the arrowroot flour, smoked paprika, salt, cumin, and garlic powder. Coat tofu evenly.
3. Spray avocado oil in fryer and place cubes in a single layer. Spray tops of tofu squares with oil as well—Cook at 350 °F for 10 minutes.
4. Toss tofu and settle back to one layer to cook for another 15 minutes.
5. In a large bowl, whisk soy sauce, coconut sugar, avocado oil, ginger, agave nectar, pepper, sesame seeds, and garlic powder.
6. Place fried tofu into the bowl with the sauce and toss to coat evenly.
7. Once plated, pour remaining sauce on meal and garnish with sesame seeds and scallion.

Nutrition: Calories: 139 Carb: 18g Fat: 4g Protein: 10g

306. Sushi rolls
Preparation Time: 20 minutes
Cooking Time: 1 hour and 20 minutes
Servings: 3
Ingredients:
- Kale (1 0.5 c., chopped, ribs removed)
- Rice vinegar (0.5 tsp)
- Sesame oil (0.75 tsp)
- Garlic powder (0.125 tsp)
- Ginger (0.25 tsp, ground)
- Soy sauce (0.75 tsp)
- Sesame seeds (1 Tbsp.)
- Sushi rice (1 0.5 c. white rice, prepped with 1 Tbsp. rice vinegar and 1 Tbsp. agave nectar)
- Sushi nori (3 sheets)
- Avocado (half, sliced)
- Vegan mayonnaise (0.25 c.)
- Sriracha sauce (to taste)
- Panko (0.5 c.)

Directions:
1. Mix kale, sesame oil, vinegar, ground ginger, garlic powder, and soy sauce in a bowl. Toss in sesame seeds and stir.
2. Spread out one sheet of the nori. Plays a handful of rice and spread it on the nori. Leave one edge naked, about 00.5 inch—opposite of the naked edge, dab few dollops of the kale mixture and top with avocado slices.
3. Using the side with the filling, roll up the nori tightly and seal using the naked seaweed. Moisten, if need to stick, it closed. Repeat this process with remaining nori sheets.
4. Blend in bowl, the mayonnaise with sriracha to taste.
5. Place panko into a bowl. Coat your sushi rolls evenly with the spicy mayo, then with the panko. Place the rolls into the fryer basket.
6. Fry at 390°F for 10 minutes, shake at 5 minutes to fry evenly.
7. Allow rolls to cool, then slice each roll into 6 to 8 pieces.
8. Serve with soy sauce to dip.

Nutrition: Calories: 241 Carb: 23g Fat: 15g Protein: 5g

307. Thai veggie bites
Preparation Time: 10 minutes

Cooking Time: 25 minutes
Servings: 4
Ingredients:
- Broccoli crown (1)
- Cauliflower (1 0.5, half a crown used as cauliflower rice)
- Large carrots (6)
- Garden peas (1 c.)
- Large onion (1)
- Zucchini (1)
- Leeks (2, washed and sliced thin)
- Coconut milk (1 can)
- Flour (50g)
- Ginger (1cm cube, peeled then grated)
- Garlic puree (1 Tbsp.)
- Olive oil (1 Tbsp.)
- Thai green curry paste (1 Tbsp.)
- Coriander (1 Tbsp.)
- Mixed spice (1 Tbsp.)
- Cumin (1 tsp)
- Salt (to taste)
- Pepper (to taste)

Directions:
1 In a skillet, pan fry onion, ginger, and garlic until brown.
2 Place vegetables save from the zucchini and leek, in a steamer until they are almost cooked through.
3 Add the leek, zucchini, and curry paste to the skillet and cook for 5 minutes on medium heat.
4 Add coconut milk and the seasoning mix. Mix in the cauliflower rice. Simmer for 10 minutes.
5 Add in the steamed veggies and stir. Stick in the fridge and allow the mixture to cool.
6 Once cooled, form bite sized lumps and place in the fryer—Cook for 10 minutes at 350 °F.

Nutrition: Calories: 117 Carb: 12g Fat: 7g Protein: 2g

308. Coconut French toast
Preparation Time: 5 minutes
Cooking Time: 4 minutes
Servings: 1
Ingredients:
- Gluten free bread (2 slices)
- Lite culinary coconut milk (0.5 c.)
- Baking powder (1 tsp)
- Unsweetened shredded coconut (0.5 c.)

Directions:
1. In a bowl, mix the coconut milk and baking powder.
2. Take the shredded coconut and spread it on a plate.
3. Take both slices of bread and soak in the coconut milk, then coat with shredded coconut.
4. Place the slices of bread in the fryer—fry for 4 minutes at 350° F.

Nutrition: Calories: 627 Carb: 56g Fat: 42g Protein: 83g

309. Beignets
Preparation Time: 15 minutes
Cooking Time: 2 hours
Servings: 24
Ingredients:
- Powdered sugar (1 c.)
- Full fat coconut milk (1 c.)
- Baking yeast (1 0.5 tsp)
- Coconut oil (2 Tbsp.)
- Aquafaba (2 Tbsp.)
- Vanilla extract (2 tsp)
- Unbleached white flour (3 c.)

Directions:
1 Warm the coconut milk just enough to be tolerable with your finger. Pour in a bowl or stand mixer with the yeast. Let stand for 10 minutes.
2 Mix in warmed coconut oil (to avoid clumping) vanilla extract,

and aquafaba. Add only a cup. of flour at a time. The paddle attachment is recommended.

3 Switch to a dough hook when the dough no longer sticks to the sides and knead for 3 minutes.

4 Remove the dough and let sit, covered, in a bowl for 1 hour to allow it to rise.

5 Sprinkle flour on a cutting board and form dough into a rectangle about a third of an inch thick. Cut into 24 squares and proof for 30 more minutes.

6 Set air fryer to 390 °F and place 1 layer of beignets at a time. Cook for one side, then flip and continue cooking for 2 minutes or until golden brown.

7 Remove beignets and coat them with powdered sugar.

Nutrition: Calories: 106 Carb: 17g Fat: 3g Protein: 2g

310.   Potato wedges in cashew sauce
Preparation Time: 10 minutes
Cooking Time: 35 minutes
Servings: 4
Ingredients:
- Fingerling potatoes (1 lb.)
- Olive oil (1 tsp)
- Salt (1 tsp)
- Ground black pepper (1 tsp)
- Garlic powder (0.5 tsp)
- Raw cashews (0.5 c.)
- Turmeric (0.5 tsp)
- Paprika (0.5 tsp)
- Nutritional yeast (2 Tbsp.)
- Lemon juice (1 tsp)

Directions:
1. Set fryer to 400 °F. Wash and cut the potatoes into wedges. Mix in oil, pepper, salt, and garlic powder. Coat evenly.
2. Cook for 16 minutes, shake at the 8minute mark.
3. To create the sauce, combine the cashews, yeast, paprika, turmeric, and lemon juice in a blender. Add water as needed, no more than 25 c. Should be necessary.
4. Place the potato wedges into a compatible pan or parchment paper. Drizzle the sauce of the wedges and stick back into the fryer to cook for 2 minutes.

Nutrition: Calories 182 Carb 21g Fat 9g Protein 7g

311.   Fruit crumble
Preparation Time: 10 minutes
Cooking Time: 30 minutes
Servings: 2
Ingredients:
- Apple (1, diced finely)
- Frozen fruit of choice (0.5 c., we'll go with strawberries)
- Brown rice flour (0.25 c.)
- Sugar (2 Tbsp.)
- Cinnamon (0.5 tsp, ground)
- Nondairy butter (2 Tbsp.)

Directions:
1 Set fryer to 350 °F. Pour the apple bits and frozen strawberries in a compatible pan.
2 Get another bowl and mix well all other ingredients.
3 Pour over the fruit and fry for 15 minutes.

Nutrition: Calories: 310 Carb: 50g Fat: 19g Protein: 2g

312.   Cajun French fry sandwich with mushroom gravy
Preparation Time: 10 minutes
Cooking Time: 35 minutes
Servings: 4
Ingredients:
- Russet potatoes (4, cut into wedges or fries)
- Olive oil (1 Tbsp. & 2 tsp)
- Cajun seasoning (1 tsp)
- Smoked paprika (0.5 tsp)
- Salt (pinch)
- Granulated garlic (pinch)
- Black pepper (pinch, ground)
- Mushrooms (3 c., chopped)
- Soy sauce (2 tsp)
- Vegan Worcestershire sauce (2 tsp)
- Tapioca starch (1 Tbsp.)
- Bread of choice
- Sandwich condiments of choice (lettuce, tomatoes, etc.)

Directions:
1 Pour boiling water onto the fries and let soak for roughly 15 minutes. Strain.
2 Mix fries with oil, seasoning, salt, garlic, paprika, and black pepper.
3 Take fries and cook in air fryer basket for 5 minutes at 350 degrees. Shake and then cook another 5 minutes.
4 Increase heat to 400 °F and cook for 5 minutes. Shake and cook another 5.
5 During downtime, add 1 Tbsp. of oil to a skillet. On medium heat, add mushrooms and sauté until dehydrated. Add Worcestershire & soy sauces and cook for approximately 2 minutes.
6 Add roughly half a cup of water and whisk tapioca starch into the mix. Cook until thick, raising temperature as necessary.
7 Take fries, and gravy, and assemble sandwich as you wish.

Nutrition: Calories: 555 Carb: 104g Fat: 10g Protein: 20g

313.   Vegan French toast
Preparation Time: 5 minutes
Cooking Time: 10 minutes
Servings: 4
Ingredients:
- Rolled oats (1 c.)
- Pecans (1 c.)
- Ground flax seed (2 Tbsp.)
- Ground cinnamon (1 tsp)
- Whole grain vegan bread (8 pieces)
- Nondairy milk (0.75 c.)
- Maple Syrup

Directions:
1 Throw oats, nuts, flaxseed, and cinnamon into a blender or food processor and process into a coarse grind. Pour mixture into a pan.
2 Pour the nondairy milk into a separate container and soak bread slices for approximately 15 seconds on each side.
3 Coat both slides of bread slices with the previously ground mixture and fit into the fryer basket. Do not overlap. Cook for 3 minutes at 350 °F, then flip and cook another 3 minutes.
4 Top with maple syrup.

Nutrition: Calories: 183 Carb: 32g Fat: 4g Protein: 6g

314.   Beef fajitas
Preparation Time: 5 minutes
Cooking Time: 20 minutes
Servings: 4-6
Ingredients:
Beef:
- 1/8 C. carne asada seasoning
- 2 pounds beef flap meat
- Diet 7-Up

Fajita veggies:
- 1 tsp. chili powder
- 1-2 tsp. pepper
- 1-2 tsp. salt
- 2 bell peppers, your choice of color
- 1 onion

Directions:
1 Slice flap meat into manageable pieces and place into a bowl. Season meat with carne seasoning and pour diet soda over meat. Cover and chill overnight.
2 Ensure your air fryer is preheated to 380 °F.

3   Place a parchment liner into air fryer basket and spray with olive oil. Place beef in layers into the basket.

4   Cook 8 to 10 minutes, flipping halfway through. Remove and set to the side.

5   Slice up veggies and spray air fryer basket. Add veggies to the fryer and spray with olive oil. Cook 10 minutes at 400 °F, shaking 1-2 times during cooking process.

6   Serve meat and veggies on wheat tortillas and top with favorite fillings!

Nutrition: Calories: 412 Fat: 21g Protein: 13g Sugar: 1g

315.   Cheeseburger egg rolls

Preparation time: 15 minutes
Cooking Time: 10 minutes
Servings: 6
Ingredients:

- 6 egg roll wrappers
- 6 chopped dill pickle chips
- 1 tbsp. Yellow mustard
- 3 tbsp. Cream cheese
- 3 tbsp. Shredded cheddar cheese
- ½ c. Chopped onion
- ½ c. Chopped bell pepper
- ¼ tsp. Onion powder
- ¼ tsp. Garlic powder
- 8 ounces of raw lean ground beef

Directions:

1.   In a skillet, add seasonings, beef, onion, and bell pepper. Stir and crumble beef till fully cooked, and vegetables are soft.
2.   Take skillet off the heat and add cream cheese, mustard, and cheddar cheese, stirring till melted.
3.   Pour beef mixture into a bowl and fold in pickles.
4.   Lay out egg wrappers and place 1/6th of beef mixture into each one. Moisten egg roll wrapper edges with water. Fold sides to the middle and seal with water.
5.   Repeat with all other egg rolls.
6.   Place rolls into air fryer, one batch at a time. Cook 7-9 minutes at 392 °F.

Nutrition: Calories: 153 Fat: 4g Protein: 12g Sugar: 3g

316.   Crispy Mongolian beef

Preparation time: 10 minutes
Cooking time: 12 minutes
Servings: 6-10
Ingredients:

- Olive oil
- ½ c. Almond flour
- 2 pounds beef tenderloin or beef chuck, sliced into strips

Sauce:

- ½ c. Chopped green onion
- 1 tsp. Red chili flakes
- 1 tsp. Almond flour
- ½ c. Brown sugar
- 1 tsp. Hoisin sauce
- ½ c. Water
- ½ c. Rice vinegar
- ½ c. Low-sodium soy sauce
- 1 tbsp. Chopped garlic
- 1 tbsp. Finely chopped ginger
- 2 tbsp. Olive oil

Directions:

1.   Toss strips of beef in almond flour, ensuring they are coated well.
2.   Add to air fryer and cook 10 minutes at 300 °F.
3.   Meanwhile, add all sauce ingredients to the pan and bring to a boil. Mix well.
4.   Add beef strips to the sauce and cook 2 minutes.
5.   Serve over cauliflower rice!

Nutrition: Calories: 290 Fat: 14g Protein: 22g Sugar: 1g

317.   Copycat taco bell crunch wraps

Preparation time: 5 minutes
Cooking time: 5 minutes
Servings: 6

Ingredients:

- 6 wheat tostadas
- 2 c. Sour cream
- 2 c. Mexican blend cheese
- 2 c. Shredded lettuce
- 12 ounces low-sodium nacho cheese
- 3 roman tomatoes
- 6 12-inch wheat tortillas
- 1 1/3 c. Water
- 2 packets low-sodium taco seasoning
- 2 pounds of lean ground beef

Directions:

1.   Ensure your air fryer is preheated to 400 °F.
2.   Make beef according to taco seasoning packets.
3.   Place 2/3 c. Prepared beef, 4 tbsp. Cheese, 1 tostada, 1/3 c. Sour cream, 1/3 c. Lettuce, 1/6th of tomatoes and 1/3 c. Cheese on each tortilla.
4.   Fold up tortillas edges and repeat with remaining ingredients.
5.   Lay the folded sides of tortillas down into the air fryer and spray with olive oil.
6.   Cook 2 minutes till browned.

Nutrition: Calories: 311 Fat: 9g Protein: 22g Sugar: 2g

318.   Beef taco fried egg rolls

Preparation Time: 15 minutes
Cooking Time: 10 minutes
Servings: 8
Ingredients:

- 1 tsp. cilantro
- 2 chopped garlic cloves
- 1 tbsp. olive oil
- 1 C. shredded Mexican cheese
- ½ packet taco seasoning
- ½ can cilantro lime
- ½ chopped onion
- egg roll wrappers
- 1-pound lean ground beef

Directions:

1.   Ensure that the air fryer is turn on to 400 °F.
2.   Add onions and garlic to a skillet, cooking till fragrant. Then add taco seasoning, pepper, salt, and beef, cooking till beef is broke up into tiny pieces and cooked thoroughly.
3.   Add cilantro and stir well.
4.   Lay out egg wrappers and brush with water to soften a bit.
5.   Load wrappers with beef filling and add cheese to each.
6.   Fold diagonally to close and use water to secure edges.
7.   Brush filled egg wrappers with olive oil and add to the air fryer.
8.   Cook 8 minutes, flip, and cook another 4 minutes.
9.   Served sprinkled with cilantro.

Nutrition: Calories: 348 Fat: 11g Protein: 24g Sugar: 1g

319.   Pub style corned beef egg rolls

Preparation time: 5 minutes
Cooking time: 15 minutes
Servings: 10
Ingredients:

- Olive oil
- ½ c. Orange marmalade
- 5 slices of swiss cheese
- 4 c. Corned beef and cabbage
- 1 egg
- 10 egg roll wrappers
- Brandy mustard sauce:
- 1/16th tsp. Pepper
- 2 tbsp. Whole grain mustard
- 1 tsp. Dry mustard powder
- 1 c. Heavy cream
- ½ c. Chicken stock
- ¼ c. Brandy
- ¾ c. Dry white wine
- ¼ tsp. Curry powder
- ½ tbsp. Cilantro
- 1 minced shallot

- 2 tbsp. Ghee

Directions:
1. To make mustard sauce, add shallots and ghee to skillet, cooking until softened. Then add brandy and wine, heating to a low boil. Cook 5 minutes for liquids to reduce. Add stock and seasonings. Simmer 5 minutes.
2. Turn down heat and add heavy cream. Cook on low till sauce reduces and it covers the back of a spoon.
3. Place sauce in the fridge to chill.
4. Crack the egg in a bowl and set to the side.
5. Lay out an egg wrapper with the corner towards you. Brush the edges with egg wash.
6. Place 1/3 cup of corned beef mixture into the center along with 2 tablespoons of marmalade and ½ a slice of swiss cheese.
7. Fold the bottom corner over filling. As you are folding the sides, make sure they are stick well to the first flap you made.
8. Place filled rolls into prepared air fryer basket. Spritz rolls with olive oil.
9. Cook 10 minutes at 390 °F, shaking halfway through cooking.
10. Serve rolls with brandy mustard sauce and devour!

Nutrition: Calories: 415 Fat: 13g Protein: 38g Sugar: 4g

320.   Reuben egg rolls
Preparation time: 5 minutes
Cooking time: 15 minutes
Servings: 10
Ingredients:
- Swiss cheese
- Can of sauerkraut
- Sliced deli corned beef
- Egg roll wrappers

Directions:
1. Cut corned beef and swiss cheese into thin slices.
2. Drain sauerkraut and dry well.
3. Take egg roll wrapper and moisten edges with water.
4. Stack center with corned beef and cheese till you reach desired thickness. Top off with sauerkraut.
5. Fold corner closest to you over the edge of filling. Bring up sides and glue with water.
6. Add to air fryer basket and spritz with olive oil.
7. Cook 4 minutes at 400 °F, then flip and cook another 4 minutes.

Nutrition: Calories: 251 Fat: 12g Protein: 31g Sugar: 4g

321.   Beef empanadas
Preparation time: 15 minutes
Cooking time: 15 minutes
Servings: 8
Ingredients:
- 1 tsp. water
- 1 egg white
- 1 C. picadillo
- Goya empanada discs (thawed)

Directions:
1. Ensure your air fryer is preheated to 325. Spray basket with olive oil.
2. Place 2 tablespoons of picadillo into the center of each disc. Fold disc in half and use a fork to seal edges. Repeat with all ingredients.
3. Whisk egg white with water and brush tops of empanadas with egg wash.
4. Add 2-3 empanadas to air fryer, cooking 8 minutes until golden. Repeat till you cook all filled empanadas.

Nutrition: Calories: 183 Fat: 5g Protein: 11g Sugar: 2g

322.   Lamb fritters
Preparation time: 10 minutes
Cooking time: 30 minutes
Servings: 8
Ingredients:
- 2 ½ lb. lamb meat, ground
- 2 spring onions; chopped
- ½ cup almond meal
- eggs, whisked
- 1 tbsp. garlic; minced
- 2 tbsp. cilantro; chopped
- Zest of 1 lemon

- Juice of 1 lemon
- Cooking spray
- 2 tbsp. mint; chopped
- A pinch of salt and black pepper

Directions:
1. Take bowl and mix all the ingredients except the cooking spray, stir well and shape medium cakes out of this mix
2. Put the cakes in your air fryer, grease them with cooking spray and cook at 390°F for 15 minutes on each side
3. Split between plates and serve with side salad

Nutrition: Calories: 283; Fat: 13g; Fiber: 4g; Carbs: 6g; Protein: 15g

323.   Lasagna casserole
Preparation time: 15 minutes
Cooking time: 15 minutes
Servings: 4
Ingredients:
- ¾ cup low-carb no-sugar-added pasta sauce
- 1 lb. 80/20 ground beef; cooked and drained
- ½ cup full-fat ricotta cheese
- ¼ cup grated parmesan cheese.
- ½ tsp. Garlic powder.
- 1 tsp. Dried parsley.
- ½ tsp. Dried oregano.
- 1 cup shredded mozzarella cheese

Directions:
1. In a 4-cup round baking dish, pour ¼ cup pasta sauce on the bottom of the dish. Place ¼ of the ground beef on top of the sauce.
2. In a small bowl, mix ricotta, parmesan, garlic powder, parsley and oregano. Place dollops of half the mixture on top of the beef
3. Sprinkle with ⅓ of the mozzarella. Repeat layers until all beef, ricotta mixture, sauce and mozzarella are used, ending with the mozzarella on top
4. Cover dish with foil and place into the air fryer basket. Adjust the temperature to 370 °F and set the timer for 15 minutes. In the last 2 minutes of cooking, remove the foil to brown the cheese. Serve immediately.

Nutrition: Calories: 371; Protein: 34g; Fiber: 6g; Fat: 24g; Carbs: 8g

324.   Beef and chorizo burger
Preparation Time: 10 minutes
Cooking Time: 15 minutes
Servings: 4
Ingredients:
- 5 slices pickled jalapeños; chopped
- ¼ lb. Mexican-style ground chorizo
- ¾lb. 80/20 ground beef.
- ¼ cup chopped onion
- ¼ tsp. Cumin
- 1 tsp. Minced garlic
- 2 tsp. Chili powder

Directions:
1. Take a large bowl, mix all ingredients. Divide the mixture into four sections and form them into burger patties.
2. Place burger patties into the air fryer basket, working in batches if necessary. Adjust the temperature to 375 °F and set the timer for 15 minutes
3. Flip the patties halfway through the cooking time. Serve warm.

Nutrition: Calories: 291; Protein: 26g; Fiber: 9g; Fat: 13g; Carbs: 7g

325.   Filet mignon with chili peanut sauce
Preparation Time: 2 hours
Cooking Time: 20 minutes
Servings: 4
Ingredients
- 2 pounds filet mignon, sliced into bite-sized strips
- 1 tablespoon oyster sauce
- 2 tablespoons sesame oil
- 2 tablespoons tamari sauce
- 1 tablespoon ginger-garlic paste
- 1 tablespoon mustard

- 1 teaspoon chili powder
- 1/4 cup peanut butter
- 2 tablespoons lime juice
- 1 teaspoon red pepper flakes
- 2 tablespoons water

Directions
1. Place the beef strips, oyster sauce, sesame oil, tamari sauce, ginger-garlic paste, mustard, and chili powder in a large ceramic dish.
2. Cover and allow it to marinate for 2 hours in your refrigerator.
3. Cook in the preheated air fryer at 400 °F for 18 minutes, shaking the basket occasionally.
4. Mix the peanut butter with lime juice, red pepper flakes, and water. Spoon the sauce onto the air fried beef strips and serve warm.

Nutrition: 420 Calories; 21g Fat; 5g Carbs; 50g Protein; 7g Sugars; 1g Fiber

326. Irish whisky steak
Ingredients Preparation Time: 2 hours
Cooking Time: 22 minutes
Servings: 6
Ingredients
- 2 pounds sirloin steaks
- 1 ½ tablespoons tamari sauce
- 1/3 teaspoon cayenne pepper
- 1/3 teaspoon ground ginger
- 2 garlic cloves, thinly sliced
- 2 tablespoons Irish whiskey
- 2 tablespoons olive oil
- Fine sea salt, to taste

Directions
1. Firstly, add all the ingredients, minus the olive oil and the steak, to a resealable plastic bag.
2. Throw in the steak and let it marinate for a couple of hours. After that, drizzle the sirloin steaks with 2 tablespoons olive oil.
3. Roast for approximately 22 minutes at 395 °F, turning it halfway through the time. Bon appétit!

Nutrition: 260 Calories; 17g Fat; 8g Carbs; 35g Protein; 2g Sugars; 1g Fiber

327. Hungarian beef goulash
Preparation Time: 10 minutes
Cooking Time: 1 hour
Servings: 4
Ingredients
- Sea salt and cracked black pepper, to taste
- 1 teaspoon Hungarian paprika
- 1 ½ pounds beef chuck roast, boneless, cut into bite-sized cubes
- 2 teaspoons sunflower oil
- 1 medium-sized leek, chopped
- 2 garlic cloves, minced
- 2 bay leaves
- 1 teaspoon caraway seeds.
- 2 cups roasted vegetable broth
- 1 ripe tomato, pureed
- 2 tablespoons red wine
- 2 bell peppers, chopped
- 1 celery stalk, peeled and diced

Directions
1. Add the salt, black pepper, Hungarian paprika, and beef to a resealable bag; shake to coat well.
2. Heat the oil in a Dutch oven over medium-high flame; sauté the leeks, garlic, bay leaves, and caraway seeds about 4 minutes or until fragrant. Transfer to a lightly greased baking pan.
3. Then, brown the beef, stirring occasionally, working in batches. Add to the baking pan.
4. Add the vegetable broth, tomato, and red wine. Lower the pan onto the air fryer basket. Bake at 325 °F for 40 minutes.
5. Add the bell peppers and celery. Cook an additional 20 minutes. Serve immediately and enjoy!

Nutrition: 306 Calories; 11g Fat; 8g Carbs; 36g Protein; 6g Sugars; 8g Fiber

328. Saucy beef with cotija cheese
Preparation Time: 5 minutes
Cooking Time: 22 minutes
Servings: 3
Ingredients
- 2 ounces cotija cheese, cut into sticks
- 2 teaspoons paprika
- 2 teaspoons dried thyme
- 1/2 cup shallots, peeled and chopped
- 3 beef tenderloins, cut in half lengthwise
- 2 teaspoons dried basil
- 1/3 cup homemade bone stock
- 2 tablespoon olive oil
- 3 cloves garlic, minced
- 1 ½ cups tomato puree, no sugar added
- 1 teaspoon ground black pepper, or more to taste
- 1 teaspoon fine sea salt, or more to taste

Directions
1. Firstly, season the beef tenderloin with the salt, ground black pepper, and paprika; place a piece of the cotija cheese in the middle.
2. Now, tie each tenderloin with a kitchen string; drizzle with olive oil and reserve.
3. Stir the garlic, shallots, bone stock, tomato puree into an oven safe bowl; cook in the preheated air fryer at 375 °F for 7 minutes.
4. Add the reserved beef along with basil and thyme. Set the timer for 14 minutes. Eat warm and enjoy!

Nutrition: 589 Calories; 47g Fat; 3g Carbs; 31g Protein; 5g Sugars; 2g Fiber

329. Coconut beef and broccoli
Preparation Time: 5 minutes
Cooking Time: 25 minutes
Servings: 4
Ingredients:
- 1 lb. Beef; cubed
- 1 broccoli head, florets separated
- 1/3 cup balsamic vinegar
- 2 garlic cloves; minced
- 2 tbsp. Olive oil
- 1 tsp. Coconut aminos
- 1 tsp. Stevia

Directions:
1. In a pan that fits your air fryer, mix the beef with the rest of the ingredients, toss, put the pan in the fryer and cook at 390°F for 225 minutes
2. Divide into bowls and serve hot.

Nutrition: Calories: 274; Fat: 12g; Fiber: 4g; Carbs: 6g; Protein: 16g

330. Roasted spareribs
Preparation time: 10 minutes
Cooking time: 45 minutes
Servings: 4
Ingredients:
- 2 racks of ribs
- 1 tbsp. Coriander; chopped
- 2 tbsp. Cocoa powder
- ½ tsp. Chili powder
- ½ tsp. Cumin, ground
- ½ tsp. Cinnamon powder
- Cooking spray
- A pinch of salt and black pepper

Directions:
1. Grease the ribs with the cooking spray, mix with the other ingredients and rub very well.
2. Put the ribs in your air fryer's basket and cook at 390°F for 45 minutes. Divide between plates and serve with a side salad

Nutrition: Calories: 284; Fat: 14g; Fiber: 5g; Carbs: 7g; Protein: 20g

331. Ground beef and eggplants mix
Preparation time: 10 minutes
Cooking time: 30 minutes
Servings: 4
Ingredients:
- 2 pounds beef, ground
- 2 tablespoons butter, melted
- 2 eggplants, cubed

- 1 cup tomato passata
- 1 red onion, chopped
- Salt and black pepper to the taste
- 6 garlic cloves, chopped
- 2 teaspoons chili powder
- 1 tablespoon chives, chopped

Directions:
1. Heat up the air fryer with the butter at 380 °F, add the onion, meat and the other ingredients, toss and cook for 30 minutes.
2. Divide everything into bowls and serve.

Nutrition: Calories; 300 Fat; 8 Fiber; 6 Carbs; 20 Protein; 17

332.   Baby back ribs
Preparation time: 15 minutes
Cooking Time: 25 minutes
Servings: 4
Ingredients:

- 2 lb. Baby back ribs
- ½ cup low-carb, sugar-free barbecue sauce
- 2 tsp. Chili powder
- 1 tsp. Paprika
- ¼ tsp. Ground cayenne pepper
- ½ tsp. Onion powder.
- ½ tsp. Garlic powder.

Directions:
1. Rub ribs with all ingredients except barbecue sauce. Place into the air fryer basket.
2. Adjust the temperature to 400 °F and set the timer for 25 minutes
3. When done, ribs will be dark and charred with an internal temperature of at least 190 °F.
4. Brush ribs with barbecue sauce and serve warm.

Nutrition: Calories: 650; Protein: 41g; Fiber: 8g; Fat: 55g; Carbs: 6g

333.   Moroccan lamb
Preparation time: 10 minutes
Cooking time: 30 minutes
Servings: 4
Ingredients:

- 8 lamb cutlets
- ½ cup mint leaves
- 6 garlic cloves
- 3 tbsp. Lemon juice
- 1 tbsp. Coriander seed
- 4 tbsp. Olive oil
- 1 tbsp. Cumin, ground
- Zest of 2 lemons, grated
- A pinch of salt and black pepper

Directions:
1. In a blender, combine all the ingredients except the lamb and pulse well.
2. Rub the lamb cutlets with this mix, place them in your air fryer's basket and cook at 380°F for 15 minutes on each side. Serve with a side salad.

Nutrition: Calories: 284; Fat: 13g; Fiber: 3g; Carbs: 5g; Protein: 15g

334.   Crusted lamb cutlets
Preparation time: 10 minutes
Cooking time: 30 minutes
Servings: 4
Ingredients:

- 8 lamb cutlets
- ¼ cup parmesan, grated
- ½ cup coconut flakes
- 2 tbsp. Parsley; chopped
- 2 tbsp. Chives; chopped
- 3 tbsp. Olive oil
- 1 tbsp. Rosemary; chopped
- 3 tbsp. Mustard
- A pinch of salt and black pepper

Directions:
1. Take a bowl and mix the lamb cutlets with all the ingredients except the parmesan and the coconut flakes and toss well.

2. Dredge the cutlets in parmesan and coconut flakes, put them in your air fryer's basket and cook at 390°F for 15 minutes on each side
3. Divide between plates and serve.

Nutrition: Calories: 284; Fat: 13g; Fiber: 3g; Carbs: 6g; Protein: 17g

335.   Lamb and corn
Preparation time: 5 minutes
Cooking time: 30 minutes
Servings: 4
Ingredients

- 2pounds lamb stew meat, cubed
- 1cup corn
- 1cup spring onions, chopped
- ¼ cup beef stock
- 1tablespoon olive oil
- A pinch of salt and black pepper
- 2tablespoons rosemary, chopped

Directions
1. in the air fryer's pan, mix the lamb with the corn, spring onions and the other ingredients, toss and cook at 380 °F for 30 minutes.
2. divide the mix between plates and serve.

Nutrition: Calories 274; Fat 12; Fiber 3; Carbs 5; protein 15

336.   Nutmeg lamb
Preparation time: 5 minutes
Cooking time: 30 minutes
Servings: 4
Ingredients

- 1pound lamb stew meat, cubed
- 2teaspoons nutmeg, ground
- 1teaspoon coriander, ground
- 1cup heavy cream
- 2tablespoons olive oil
- 2tablespoons chives, chopped
- Salt and black pepper to the taste

Directions
1. in the air fryer's pan, mix the lamb with the nutmeg and the other ingredients, put the pan in the air fryer and cook at 380 °F for 30 minutes.
2. divide everything into bowls and serve.

Nutrition: Calories 287; Fat 13; Fiber 2; Carbs 6; Protein 12

337.   Lamb and eggplant meatloaf
Preparation time: 5 minutes
Cooking time: 35 minutes
Servings: 4
Ingredients

- 2pounds lamb stew meat, ground
- 2eggplants, chopped
- 1yellow onion, chopped
- A pinch of salt and black pepper
- ½ teaspoon coriander, ground
- Cooking spray
- 2tablespoons cilantro, chopped
- 1egg
- 2tablespoons tomato paste

Directions
1. in a bowl, mix the lamb with the eggplants of the ingredients except the cooking spray and stir.
2. grease a loaf pan that fits the air fryer with the cooking spray, add the mix and shape the meatloaf.
3. put the pan in the air fryer and cook at 380 °F for 35 minutes.
4. slice and serve with a side salad.

Nutrition: Calories 263; Fat 12; Fiber 3; Carbs 6; Protein 15

338.   Homemade flamingos
Preparation time: 10 minutes
Cooking Time: 20 minutes
Servings: 6
Ingredients

- 6pieces of serrano ham, thinly sliced
- 454g pork, halved, with butter and crushed
- 6g of salt
- 1g black pepper

- 227g fresh spinach leaves, divided
- 4slices of mozzarella cheese, divided
- 18g sun-dried tomatoes, divided
- 10ml of olive oil, divided

Direction:
1. place 3 pieces of ham on baking paper, slightly overlapping each other. Place 1 half of the pork in the ham. Repeat with the other half.
2. season the inside of the pork rolls with salt and pepper.
3. place half of the spinach, cheese, and sun-dried tomatoes on top of the pork loin, leaving a 13 mm border on all sides.
4. roll the fillet around the filling well and tie with a kitchen cord to keep it closed.
5. repeat the process for the other pork steak and place them in the fridge.
6. select preheat in the air fryer and press start/pause.
7. brush 5 ml of olive oil on each wrapped steak and place them in the preheated air fryer.
8. select steak. Set the timer to 9 minutes and press start/pause.
9. allow it to cool for 10 minutes before cutting.

339. Pork fillets
Preparation time: 10 minutes
Cooking time: 20 minutes
Servings: 4
Ingredients
- 400g of very thin sliced pork fillets c / n
- 2boiled and chopped eggs
- 100g chopped serrano ham
- 1beaten egg
- Breadcrumbs

Direction:
1. make a roll with the pork fillets. Introduce half cooked egg and serrano ham. So that the roll does not lose its shape, fasten with a string or chopsticks.
2. pass the rolls through beaten egg and then through the breadcrumbs until it forms a good layer.
3. preheat the air fryer a few minutes at 180° c.
4. insert the rolls in the basket and set the timer for about 8 minutes at 180o c.
5. serve right away.

Nutrition: Calories 424; Fat 115g; Carbohydrates 347g; Protein 384g; Sugar 37g; Cholesterol 157mg

340. Katsu pork
Preparation time: 10 minutes
Cooking time: 14 minutes
Servings: 2
Ingredients
- 170g pork chops, boneless
- 56g of breadcrumbs
- 3g garlic powder
- 2g onion powder
- 6g of salt
- 1g white pepper
- 60g all-purpose flour
- 2eggs, shakes
- Nonstick spray oil

Direction:
1. place the pork chops in an airtight bag or cover them with a plastic wrap.
2. crush the pork with a meat roller or hammer until it is 13 mm thick.
3. combine the crumbs and seasonings in a bowl. Leave aside.
4. pass each pork chop through the flour, then soak them in the beaten eggs and finally pass them through the crumb mixture.
5. preheat the air fryer set the temperature to 180°c.
6. spray pork chops on each side with cooking oil and place them in the preheated air fryer.
7. cook the pork chops at 180°c for 4 minutes.
8. remove them from the air fryer when finished and let them sit for 5 minutes.
9. cut them into pieces and serve them.

Nutrition: Calories 820; Fat 275g; Carbohydrates 117g; Protein 375g; Sugar 0g; Cholesterol 120mg

341. Garlic & honey chicken wings
Preparation time: 10 minutes
Cooking time: 15 minutes
Servings: 4
Ingredients:
- 16 chicken wings
- ¼ cup honey
- 4 garlic cloves, minced
- ¼ cup butter, melted
- ¾ cup potato starch
- Salt and pepper to taste

Directions:
1. Preheat your air fryer to 370° F. Place wings in bowl and coat with potato starch.
2. Grease a baking dish with cooking spray.
3. Place wings inside of air fryer and cook for 5-minutes.
4. Whisk together remaining ingredients. Pour sauce over chicken wings and cook for an additional 10-minutes.

Nutrition: Calories 296; Total Fat 14g; Carbs 6g; Protein 17g

342. Crunchy chicken strips
Preparation Time: 5 minutes
Cooking Time: 5 minutes
Servings: 8
Ingredients:
- 1 chicken breast, cut into strips
- ¾ cup breadcrumbs
- 1 teaspoon mix spice
- 1 tablespoon plain oats
- Salt and pepper to taste
- 1 tablespoon dried coconut
- ¼ cup almond flour
- 1 egg, beaten

Directions:
1. In a bowl, mix oats, mix spice, coconut, pepper, salt, and breadcrumbs.
2. Add beaten egg to another bowl. Add the flour to a third dish.
3. Take the flour and coat chicken strips with it, then dip in egg and roll in breadcrumb mixture.
4. Place the coated chicken strips in air fryer basket and air fry at 350°F and cook for 4-minutes. Serve hot!

Nutrition: Calories 286; Total Fat 18g; Carbs 7g; Protein 12g

343. Turkey & cheese calzone
Preparation Time: 10 minutes
Cooking time: 10 minutes
Servings: 4
Ingredients:
- 1 free-range egg, beaten
- ¼ cup mozzarella cheese, grated
- 1 cup cheddar cheese, grated
- 1-ounce bacon, diced, cooked
- Cooked turkey, shredded
- 4 tablespoons tomato sauce
- Salt and pepper to taste
- 1 teaspoon thyme
- 1 teaspoon basil
- 1 teaspoon oregano
- 1 package frozen pizza dough

Directions:
1. Roll the pizza dough out into small circles, the same size as a small pizza. Add thyme, oregano, basil into a bowl with tomato sauce and mix well.
2. Pour a small amount of sauce onto your pizza bases and spread across the surface. Add the turkey, bacon, and cheese.
3. Brush the edge of dough with beaten egg, then fold over and pinch to seal. Brush the outside with more egg.
4. Place into air fryer and cook at 350°F for 10-minutes. Serve warm.

Nutrition: Calories 289; Total Fat 12g; Carbs 13g; Protein 14g

344. Turkey & avocado burrito
Preparation time: 10 minutes
Cooking time: 10 minutes
Servings: 2

Ingredients:

- 4 free-range eggs
- 8-slices turkey breast, cooked
- 4 tablespoons salsa
- ¼ cup mozzarella cheese, grated
- ½ cup avocado, sliced
- ½ red bell pepper, sliced
- 2 x tortillas
- Salt and pepper to taste

Directions:

1. Whisk the eggs, then add some salt and pepper. Spray the inside of your air fryer tray with cooking spray and pour in the egg mixture.
2. Cook for 5-minutes at 390°F. Scrape into a clean bowl.
3. Divide the eggs between the two tortillas, followed by the turkey, avocado, pepper, cheese, and salsa. Roll up carefully. Spray inside of the air fryer again and place the burritos inside of it.
4. Cook at 350°F for 5-minutes. Serve warm.

Nutrition: Calories 289; Total Fat 12g; Carbs 7g; Protein 13g

345. **Turkey sausage patties**

Preparation time: 5 minutes
Cooking time: 4 minutes
Servings: 6
Ingredients:

- 1 teaspoon olive oil
- 1 small onion, diced
- 1 large garlic clove, chopped
- Salt and pepper to taste
- 1 tablespoon vinegar
- 1 tablespoon chives, chopped
- ¾ teaspoon paprika
- Pinch of nutmeg
- 1 lb. Lean ground turkey
- 1 teaspoon fennel seeds

Directions:

1. Preheat your air fryer to 375°F. Add half of the oil along with onion and garlic to air fryer.
2. Air fry for 1-minute then add fennel seeds then transfer to plate.
3. In a mixing bowl, mix paprika, ground turkey, nutmeg, chives, vinegar, salt pepper, and onion.
4. Mix well and form patties. Add the remaining oil to your air fryer and air fry patties for 3-minutes. Serve on buns.

Nutrition: Calories 302; Total Fat 12g; Carbs 12g; Protein 13g

346. **Mozzarella turkey rolls**

Preparation time: 5 minutes
Cooking time: 10 minutes
Servings: 4
Ingredients:

- 4 slices turkey breast
- 4 chive shoots (for tying rolls)
- 1 tomato, sliced
- ½ cup basil, fresh, chopped
- 1 cup mozzarella, sliced

Directions:

1. Preheat your air fryer to 390°F.
2. Place the slices of mozzarella cheese, tomato, and basil onto each slice of turkey.
3. Roll up and tie with chive shoot. Place into air fryer and cook for 10-minutes. Serve warm.

Nutrition: Calories 296; Total Fat 14g; Carbs 12g; Protein 12g

347. **Turkey balls stuffed with sage & onion**

Preparation time: 10 minutes
Cooking time: 15 minutes
Servings: 2
Ingredients:

- 5 ounces ground turkey
- 3 tablespoons breadcrumbs
- Salt and pepper to taste
- 1 teaspoon sage
- ½ small onion, diced
- 1 egg

Directions:

1. Add all the ingredients into large mixing bowl and combine well.
2. Form the mixture into small balls and put in air fryer and cook at 350°F for 15-minutes.
3. Serve with tartar sauce and mashed potatoes.

Nutrition: Calories 268; Total Fat 8g; Carbs 6g; Protein 19g

348. **Turkey loaf**

Preparation Time: 15 minutes
Cooking time: 40 minutes
Servings: 4
Ingredients:

- 1 egg
- ½ teaspoon dried savory dill
- 2/3 cup walnuts, finely chopped
- 1 ½ lbs. Turkey breast, diced
- ½ teaspoon ground allspice
- ¼ teaspoon black pepper
- 1 garlic clove, minced
- 1 tablespoon Dijon mustard
- 1 tablespoon liquid aminos
- 1 tablespoon tomato paste
- 2 tablespoons parmesan cheese, grated
- 1 tablespoon onion flakes

Directions:

1. Preheat your air fryer to 375°F. Grease a baking dish using cooking spray.
2. Whisk dill, egg, tomato paste, liquid aminos, mustard, garlic, allspice, salt, and pepper.
3. mix well and add diced turkey. Mix again and add cheese, walnuts and onion flakes.
4. Put mixture into baking dish and bake for 40-minutes in air fryer. Serve hot!

Nutrition: Calories 278; Total Fat 12g; Carbs 3g; Protein 13g

349. **Turkey, mushroom & egg casserole**

Preparation Time: 10 minutes
Cooking time: 15 minutes
Servings: 4
Ingredients:

- 6 eggs
- 1 ½ cups spinach
- 1 ¼ cups shredded cheddar cheese
- 2 onions, chopped
- ¼ cup cooked turkey, diced
- 4 mushrooms, diced
- Pinch of onion powder
- Salt and pepper to taste
- Pinch of garlic powder
- ¼ green bell pepper, chopped

Directions:

1. Preheat your air fryer to 400°F.
2. Whisk the eggs in mixing bowl. Add mushrooms, garlic powder, bell pepper, onion powder, onions, 1 cup cheese and cooked diced turkey. Mix well and add mixture to casserole dish.
3. sprinkle the top of mixture with remaining cheese. Add spinach on top.
4. Bake in air fryer for 15-minutes. Serve hot!

Nutrition: Calories 282; Total Fat 16g; Carbs 2g; Protein 12g

350. **Sage crumb chicken escalope**

Preparation Time: 10 minutes
Cooking time: 20 minutes
Servings: 4
Ingredients:

- 6 sage leaves
- ¼ cup parmesan cheese
- ½ cup breadcrumbs
- ½ cup almond flour
- 2 eggs, beaten
- 4 skinless chicken breasts, sliced

Directions:

1. Mix sage and parmesan in a bowl. Mix salt, pepper, and flour in another bowl.
2. Add to sage and parmesan mix. Mix with beaten eggs.
3. Dip chicken pieces into mixture, then cover with breadcrumbs.

4. Spray cooking spray in baking pan. Preheat your air fryer to 390°F and cook chicken for 20-minutes.

Nutrition: Calories 287; Total Fat 12g; Carbs 6g; Protein 13g

351. Easy blackened chicken

Preparation Time: 10 minutes
Cooking time: 11 minutes
Servings: 2
Ingredients:

- 2 medium-sized chicken breasts, skinless and boneless
- 1 tablespoon olive oil
- 3 tablespoons Cajun seasoning
- ½ teaspoon salt

Directions:

1. Rub the chicken breasts with Cajun seasoning, salt, and sprinkle with olive oil.
2. preheat your air fryer to 370°F and cook chicken breasts for 7-minutes.
3. Turnover and cook for an additional 4-minutes. Slice and serve.

Nutrition: Calories 298; Total Fat 12g; Carbs 3g; Protein 18g

352. Dijon lime chicken

Preparation Time: 5 minutes
Cooking time: 10 minutes
Servings: 6
Ingredients:

- 8 chicken drumsticks
- 3 tablespoons Dijon mustard
- 1 lime juice
- 1 lime zest
- ¾ teaspoon black pepper
- 1 clove garlic, crushed
- 1 tablespoon light mayonnaise
- 1 tablespoon olive oil
- Salt to taste
- 1 tablespoon parsley, chopped

Directions:

1. Preheat your air fryer to 375°F. Remove the skin from chicken. Season with salt. In a bowl, mix lime juice, Dijon mustard together.
2. Add lime zest, parsley, garlic, black pepper and mix well. Coat the chicken with lime mixture. Marinate for 15-minutes.
3. Add olive oil to air fryer. Add the chicken drumsticks and cook for 5-minutes.
4. Turn over drumsticks and cook for an additional 5-minutes. Serve hot with mayo.

Nutrition: Calories 290; Total Fat 13g; Carbs 2g; Protein 12g

353. Asian-style chicken

Preparation Time: 40 minutes
Cooking time: 15 minutes
Servings: 3
Ingredients:

- 1 lb. Chicken breasts, skinless, boneless, sliced
- 2 tablespoons sesame seeds
- 1 tablespoon olive oil
- ½ cup pineapple juice
- ½ cup soy sauce
- ¼ teaspoon ground black pepper
- 1 tablespoon grated ginger
- 3 garlic cloves, minced

Directions:

1. Mix all the ingredients in a bowl.
2. Set the chicken to marinate in fridge for at least 40-minutes.
3. Cook marinated chicken in air fryer at 380°F for 15-minutes.
4. Sprinkle cooked chicken with some sesame seeds and serve.

Nutrition: Calories 143; Total Fat 5g; Carbs 6g; Protein 18g

354. Pickle-brined fried chicken

Preparation Time: 8 hours
Cooking time: 27 minutes
Servings: 4
Ingredients:

- 4 chicken legs, bone-in, skin on, cut into drumsticks and thighs, about 3 ½ lbs.
- Pickle juice from 24-ounce jar of kosher dill pickles

- 1 teaspoon black pepper
- 1 teaspoon sea salt
- 1 cup breadcrumbs
- 2 tablespoons olive oil
- 2 eggs
- ½ cup almond flour
- 1/8 teaspoon cayenne pepper
- ½ teaspoon ground paprika

Directions:

1. Place chicken in a bowl and pour the pickle juice over it. Cover and transfer chicken to fridge to brine in pickle juice for 8-hours.
2. Remove the chicken from the fridge. Place flour in a bowl and season it with salt and pepper. In another bowl, whisk egg and olive oil.
3. Place the breadcrumbs in a third bowl, along with paprika, salt, pepper, and cayenne pepper. Preheat your air fryer to 370°F.
4. Remove the chicken from the pickle brine and pat dry. Coat pieces of chicken with flour, then egg mixture, and finally with breadcrumbs.
5. Place the breaded chicken on a baking sheet and spray each piece with cooking spray.
6. Air fry chicken in two batches. Place two pieces thighs and two drumsticks into air fryer basket. Air fry for 10-minutes.
7. Turn pieces of chicken over and cook for another 10-minutes. Remove chicken and set aside. Repeat with the second batch of chicken.
8. Lower the temperature to 340°F. Place the first batch of chicken on top of the second batch and air fry for an additional 7-minutes.

Nutrition: Calories 289; Total Fat 13g; Carbs 5g; Protein 12g

355. Tangy chicken strips

Preparation Time: 2 hours
Cooking time: 18 minutes
Servings: 4
Ingredients:

- 1 lb. Chicken strip
- Salt and pepper to taste
- 2 tablespoons soy sauce
- 6 tablespoons pineapple juice
- 2 tablespoons sesame oil
- 4 garlic cloves, minced
- 1 teaspoon ginger, minced

Directions:

1. Combine ingredients in a bowl, except chicken.
2. Skewer chicken and place in a bowl and marinate for 2-hours. Preheat your air fryer to 350°F.
3. Place marinated chicken in air fryer and cook for 18-minutes. Serve hot!

Nutrition: Calories 287; Total Fat 13g; Carbs 6g; Protein 15g

356. Veggie stuffed chicken breasts

Preparation Time: 10 minutes
Cooking Time: 25 minutes
Servings: 4
Ingredients:

- 4 chicken breasts; skinless and boneless
- 2 tbsp. Olive oil
- 3 tomatoes; chopped
- 1 red onion; chopped
- 1 zucchini; chopped
- 1 tsp. Italian seasoning
- 2 yellow bell peppers; chopped
- 1 cup mozzarella; shredded
- Salt and black pepper to the taste

Preparation:

1. Mix a slit on each chicken breast creating a pocket, season with salt and pepper and rub them with olive oil.
2. In a bowl, mix zucchini with Italian seasoning, bell peppers, tomatoes and onion and stir.
3. Stuff chicken breasts with this mix, sprinkle mozzarella over them, place them in your air fryer's basket and cook at 350 °F, for 15 minutes. Divide among plates and serve.

Nutrition: Calories 300; Fat 12; Fiber 7; Carbs 22; Protein 18

357. Duck and plum sauce

Preparation Time: 10 minutes
Cooking Time: 32 minutes
Servings: 2
Ingredients:

- 9 oz. Red plumps; stoned; cut into small wedges
- 2 tbsp. Sugar
- 2 tbsp. Red wine
- 2 duck breasts
- 1 tbsp. Butter; melted
- 1-star anise
- 1 tbsp. Olive oil
- 1 shallot; chopped
- 1 cup beef stock

Preparation:

1. Heat up a pan with the olive oil over medium heat, add shallot; stir and cook for 5 minutes;
2. Add sugar and plums; stir and cook until sugar dissolves.
3. Add stock and wine; stir, cook for 15 minutes; take off heat and keep warm for now.
4. Score duck breasts, season with salt and pepper, rub with melted butter, transfer to a heat proof dish that fits your air fryer, add star anise and plum sauce, introduce in your air fryer and cook at 360 °F, for 12 minutes. Divide everything on plates and serve.

Nutrition: Calories 400; Fat 25; Fiber 12; Carbs 29; Protein 44

358. Chicken breasts with passion fruit sauce

Preparation Time: 5 minutes
Cooking Time: 15 minutes
Servings: 4
Ingredients:

- 4 chicken breasts
- 4 passion fruits; halved, deseeded and pulp reserved
- 1 tbsp. Whiskey
- 2-star anise
- 2 oz. Maple syrup
- 1 bunch chives; chopped
- Salt and black pepper to the taste

Preparation:

1. Heat up a pan with the passion fruit pulp over medium heat, add whiskey, star anise, maple syrup and chives; stir well, simmer for 5-6 minutes and take off heat.
2. Season chicken with salt and pepper, put in preheated air fryer and cook at 360 °F, for 10 minutes; flipping halfway.
3. Divide chicken on plates, heat up the sauce a bit, drizzle it over chicken and serve.

Nutrition: Calories 374; Fat 8; Fiber 22; Carbs 34; Protein 37

359. Turkey, mushrooms and peas casserole

Preparation Time: 10 minutes
Cooking Time: 30 minutes
Servings: 4
Ingredients:

- 2 lbs. Turkey breasts; skinless, boneless
- 1 yellow onion; chopped
- 1 celery stalk; chopped.
- 1/2 cup peas
- 1 cup chicken stock
- 1 cup cream of mushrooms soup
- 1 cup bread cubes
- Salt and black pepper to the taste

Preparation:

1. In a pan that fits your air fryer, mix turkey with salt, pepper, onion, celery, peas and stock, introduce in your air fryer and cook at 360 °F, for 15 minutes.
2. Add bread cubes and cream of mushroom soup; stir toss and cook at 360 °F, for 5 minutes more.
3. Divide among plates and serve hot.

Nutrition: Calories 271; Fat 9; Fiber 9; Carbs 16; Protein: 7

360. Duck breasts and mango mix

Preparation Time: 1 hour
Cooking Time: 10 Minutes
Servings: 4
Ingredients:

- 4 duck breasts
- 3 garlic cloves; minced
- 2 tbsp. Olive oil
- 1½ tbsp. Lemongrass; chopped.
- 3 tbsp. Lemon juice
- Salt and black pepper to the taste
- For the mango mix:
- 1 mango; peeled and chopped
- 1 ½ tbsp. Lemon juice
- 1 tbsp. Coriander; chopped
- 1 red onion; chopped
- 1 tsp. Ginger; grated
- 3/4 tsp. Sugar
- 1 tbsp. Sweet chili sauce

Preparation:

1. In a bowl, mix duck breasts with salt, pepper, lemongrass, 3 tbsp. Lemon juice, olive oil and garlic; toss well, keep in the fridge for 1 hour, transfer to your air fryer and cook at 360 °F, for 10 minutes; flipping once.
2. Meanwhile; in a bowl, mix mango with coriander, onion, chili sauce, lemon juice, ginger and sugar and toss well.
3. Divide duck on plates, add mango mix on the side and serve.

Nutrition: Calories 465; Fat 11; Fiber 4; Carbs 29; Protein 38

361. Chicken and black olives sauce

Preparation Time: 10 minutes
Cooking Time: 8 minutes
Servings: 2
Ingredients:

- 1 chicken breast cut into 4 pieces
- 2 tbsp. Olive oil
- 3 garlic cloves; minced
- For the sauce:
- 1 cup black olives; pitted
- 2 tbsp. Olive oil
- 1/4 cup parsley; chopped
- 1 tbsp. Lemon juice
- Salt and black pepper to the taste

Preparation:

1. In your food processor, mix olives with salt, pepper, 2 tbsp. Olive oil, lemon juice and parsley, blend very well and transfer to a bowl.
2. Season chicken with salt and pepper, rub with the oil and garlic, place in your preheated air fryer and cook at 370 °F, for 8 minutes. Divide chicken on plates, top with olives sauce and serve.

Nutrition: Calories 270; Fat 12; Fiber 12; Carbs 23; Protein 22

362. Chicken breasts and BBQ chili sauce

Preparation Time: 10 minutes
Cooking Time: 20 minutes
Servings: 6
Ingredients:

- 6 chicken breasts; skinless and boneless
- 2 cups chili sauce
- 2 cups ketchup
- 1 cup pear jelly
- 1/4 cup honey
- 1 tsp. Garlic powder
- 1/2 tsp. Liquid smoke
- 1 tsp. Chili powder
- 1 tsp. Mustard powder
- 1 tsp. Sweet paprika
- Salt and black pepper to the taste

Preparation:

1. Season chicken breasts with salt and pepper, put in preheated air fryer and cook at 350 °F, for 10 minutes.
2. Meanwhile; heat up a pan with the chili sauce over medium heat, add ketchup, pear jelly, honey, liquid smoke, chili powder, mustard powder, sweet paprika, salt, pepper and the garlic powder; stir, bring to a simmer and cook for 10 minutes. Add air fried chicken breasts; toss well, divide among plates and serve.

Nutrition: Calories 473; Fat 13; Fiber 7; Carbs 39; Protein 33

363. Tea glazed chicken

Preparation Time: 10 minutes
Cooking Time: 30 minutes
Servings: 6
Ingredients:

- 6 chicken legs
- 6 black tea bags
- 1/4 tsp. Red pepper flakes
- 1 tbsp. Olive oil
- 1/2 cup pineapple preserves
- 1/2 cup apricot preserves
- 1 cup hot water
- 1 tbsp. Soy sauce
- 1 onion; chopped
- Salt and black pepper to the taste

Directions:

1. Put the hot water in a bowl, add tea bags, leave aside covered for 10 minutes; discard bags at the end and transfer tea to another bowl.
2. Add soy sauce, pepper flakes, apricot and pineapple preserves, whisk really well and take off heat.
3. Season chicken with salt and pepper, rub with oil, put in your air fryer and cook at 350 °F, for 5 minutes.
4. Spread onion on the bottom of a baking dish that fits your air fryer, add chicken pieces, drizzle the tea glaze on top, introduce in your air fryer and cook at 320 °F, for 25 minutes. Divide everything on plates and serve.

Nutrition: Calories 298; Fat 14; Fiber 1; Carbs 14; Protein 30

364. Duck and cherries

Preparation Time: 10 minutes
Cooking Time: 20 minutes
Servings: 4
Ingredients:

- 4 duck breasts; boneless, skin on and scored
- 1 tbsp. Ginger; grated
- 1 tsp. Cumin; ground
- 1/2 tsp. Clove; ground
- 2 cups cherries; pitted
- 1/2 cup sugar
- 1/4 cup honey
- 1/3 cup balsamic vinegar
- 1/2 cup yellow onion; chopped
- 1/2 tsp. Cinnamon powder
- 4 sage leaves; chopped
- 1 tsp. Garlic; minced
- 1 jalapeno; chopped
- 2 cups rhubarb; sliced
- Salt and black pepper to the taste

Preparation:

1. Season duck breast with salt and pepper, put in your air fryer and cook at 350 °F, for 5 minutes on each side.
2. Meanwhile; heat up a pan over medium heat, add sugar, honey, vinegar, garlic, ginger, cumin, clove, cinnamon, sage, jalapeno, rhubarb, onion and cherries; stir, bring to a simmer and cook for 10 minutes.
3. Add duck breasts; toss well, divide everything on plates and serve.

Nutrition: Calories 456; Fat 13; Fiber 4; Carbs 64; Protein 31

365. Chicken and radish mix

Preparation Time: 10 minutes
Cooking Time: 30 minutes
Servings: 4
Ingredients:

- 4 chicken things; bone-in
- 1 tbsp. Olive oil
- 3 carrots; cut into thin sticks
- 6 radishes; halved
- 2 tbsp. Chives; chopped
- 1 cup chicken stock
- 1 tsp. Sugar
- Salt and black pepper to the taste

Directions:

1. Heat up a pan that fits your air fryer over medium heat, add stock, carrots, sugar and radishes; stir gently, reduce heat to medium, cover pot partly and simmer for 20 minutes.
2. Rub chicken with olive oil, season with salt and pepper, put in your air fryer and cook at 350 °F, for 4 minutes.
3. Add chicken to radish mix; toss, introduce everything in your air fryer, cook for 4 minutes more, divide among plates and serve.

Nutrition: calories: 237; fat: 10; fiber: 4; carbs: 19; protein: 29

366. Pepperoni chicken

Preparation Time: 10 minutes
Cooking Time: 20 minutes
Servings: 6
Ingredients:

- 4 medium chicken breasts; skinless and boneless
- 14 oz. Tomato paste
- 1 tbsp. Olive oil
- 1 tsp. Oregano; dried
- 6 oz. Mozzarella; sliced
- 1 tsp. Garlic powder
- 2 oz. Pepperoni; sliced
- Salt and black pepper to the taste

Directions:

1. In a bowl, mix chicken with salt, pepper, garlic powder and oregano and toss.
2. Put chicken in your air fryer, cook at 350 °F, for 6 minutes and transfer to a pan that fits your air fryer.
3. Add mozzarella slices on top, spread tomato paste, top with pepperoni slices, introduce in your air fryer and cook at 350 °F, for 15 minutes more. Divide among plates and serve.

Nutrition: calories: 320; fat: 10; fiber: 16; carbs: 23; protein: 27

367. Duck breasts and raspberry sauce

Preparation Time: 10 minutes
Cooking Time: 15 minutes
Servings: 4
Ingredients:

- 2 duck breasts; skin on and scored
- 1 tbsp. Sugar
- 1 tsp. Red wine vinegar
- 1/2 cup raspberries
- 1/2 cup water
- 1/2 tsp. Cinnamon powder
- Salt and black pepper to the taste
- Cooking spray

Directions:

1. Season duck breasts with salt and pepper, spray them with cooking spray, put in preheated air fryer skin side down and cook at 350 °F, for 10 minutes.
2. Heat up a pan with the water over medium heat, add raspberries, cinnamon, sugar and wine; stir, bring to a simmer, transfer to your blender, puree and return to pan. Add air fryer duck breasts to pan as well; toss to coat, divide among plates and serve right away.

Nutrition: calories: 456; fat: 22; fiber: 4; carbs: 14; protein: 45

368. Chicken and peaches

Preparation Time: 20 minutes
Cooking Time: 20 minutes
Servings: 6
Ingredients:

- 1 whole chicken; cut into medium pieces
- 3/4 cup water
- 1/3 cup honey
- 1/4 cup olive oil
- 4 peaches; halved
- Salt and black pepper to the taste

Directions:

1. Put the water in a pot, bring to a simmer over medium heat, add honey, whisk really well and leave aside.
2. Rub chicken pieces with the oil, season with salt and pepper, place in your air fryer's basket and cook at 350 °F, for 10 minutes.

3. Brush chicken with some of the honey mix, cook for 6 minutes more, flip again, brush one more time with the honey mix and cook for 7 minutes more.
4. Divide chicken pieces on plates and keep warm.
5. Brush peaches with what's left of the honey marinade, place them in your air fryer and cook them for 3 minutes. Divide among plates next to chicken pieces and serve.

Nutrition: calories: 430; fat: 14; fiber: 3; carbs: 15; protein: 20

369. Herbed albacore
Preparation Time: 10 minutes
Cooking Time: 8 minutes
Servings: 4
Ingredients:
- Diced coriander, ½ cup
- Olive oil, ⅓ cup
- Diced purple onion, 1 small piece
- Balmy vinegar, 3 kitchen spoons
- Diced parsley, 2 kitchen spoons
- Diced sweet basil, 2 kitchen spoons
- Diced hot pepper, 1 piece
- Sushi albacore cutlets, 4 pieces
- Salt and black pepper to taste
- Cayenne pepper flecks, 1 teaspoon
- Diced sage, 1 teaspoon
- 3 garlic cloves, minced

Directions:
1. Barring the fish, put all the ingredients in a bowl
2. Mix and flip well
3. Insert the fish and flip, coat it properly
4. Set your air fryer to 360°F
5. Cook for 4 minutes
6. Flip, and cook for a further 4 minutes
7. Share into dishes then serve

Nutrition: Calories 306, fat 8, fiber 1, carbs 14, protein 16

370. Maple kipper
Preparation Time: 5 minutes
Cooking Time: 10 minutes
Servings: 2
Ingredients:
- Deboned kipper fish, 2
- Salt and black pepper to taste
- Mustard, 2 kitchen spoons
- Olive oil, 1 kitchen spoon
- Honey maple, 1 kitchen spoon

Directions:
1. Put the mustard with the oil in a bowl and mix
2. Add the honey maple, whisk well
3. Rub this mixture on the kipper
4. Set your air fryer to 370°F for 5 minutes
5. Flip, cook for a further 5 minutes
6. Serve instantly alongside a side salad.

Nutrition: Calories 290, fat 7, fiber 14, carbs 18, protein 17

371. Kipper and balmy orange gravy
Preparation Time: 5 minutes
Cooking Time: 15 minutes,
Servings: 4
Ingredients:
- Cubed, deboned kipper fish, 4
- 2 lemons, sliced
- Balmy vinegar, ¼ cup
- Sweet orange juice, ¼ cup
- A pinch of salt and black pepper

Directions:
1. Barring the fish, mix all the ingredient in a pan
2. Set your air fryer to about 360°F
3. Cook for 5 minutes
4. Insert the kipper
5. Flip lightly and cook in the air fryer 360°F for 10 minutes.
6. Share into dishes and serve immediately alongside a side salad.

Nutrition: Calories 227, fat 9, fiber 12, carbs 14, protein 11

372. Kipper and pansies
Preparation time: 30 minutes,

Servings: 4
Ingredients:
- Chopped purple onions, 2
- Olive oil, 2 kitchen spoons
- Trimmed and sliced pansies, 2
- Toasted and slice kernels, ¼ cup
- Salt and black pepper to taste
- Deboned kipper fish, 4
- Grilled pansies seeds, 5 teaspoons

Directions:
1. Apply salt and pepper seasoning to the fish
2. Rub 1 kitchen spoon of the oil over it
3. Set your air fryer to 350°F
4. Insert the fish and cook for 5-6 minutes
5. Flip and cook for about 5-6 minutes more
6. Share into dishes
7. Heat 1 kitchen spoon of oil in a pan at about 360°F
8. Insert the onions, swirl, and fry for 2 minutes.
9. Put in pansies seeds and bulbs, kernels, salt, and pepper
10. 1cook for 2-3 minutes more.
11. 1apply the mixture over the fish and dish immediately; enjoy!

Nutrition: Calories 284, fat 7, fiber 10, carbs 17, protein 16

373. Kipper strips and pinecone mix
Preparation Time: 15 minutes
Cooking Time: 15 minutes
Servings: 2
Ingredients:
- Canned pinecone portions, 8 ounces
- Shredded ginger, a ½ teaspoon
- Olive oil, a little sprinkle
- Pulverized garlic cloves, 2 teaspoons
- Balmy vinegar, i kitchen spoon
- Deboned kipper fish, medium-sized, 2 pieces
- Salt and black pepper to taste

Directions:
1. Rub oil in a pan place the fish in it
2. Insert all the other ingredients
3. Set your air fryer to 350°F
4. Insert the fish and cook for 10 minutes
5. Share into dishes and serve

Nutrition: Calories 236, fat 4, carbs 23, protein 6

374. Easy kipper strips and bell peppers
Preparation Time: 5 minutes
Cooking Time: 15 minutes
Servings: 6
Ingredients:
- Rough green olives, 1 cup
- Cayenne peppers, 3 pieces divided into average portions
- Smoke-dried pimento, a ½ teaspoon
- Salt and black pepper to taste
- Olive oil, 3 kitchen spoons
- Deboned and skinned kipper fish, 6 average pieces
- Diced coriander, 2 kitchen spoons

Directions:
1. Mix all the ingredients in a pan
2. Set your air fryer to 360°F
3. Insert the mixture and cook for 15 minutes.
4. Share the fish into dishes and serve.

Nutrition: Calories 281, fat 8, fiber 14, carbs 17, protein 16

375. Kipper and citrus dressing
Preparation Time: 5 minutes
Cooking Time: 10 minutes
Servings: 2
Ingredients:
- Deboned kipper fish, 2
- Orange peel, from ½ of the peel
- Citrus juice, from ½ an orange
- A pinch of salt and black pepper
- Mustard, 2 kitchen spoons
- Honey, 2 teaspoons
- Olive oil, 2 kitchen spoons
- Diced dill, 1 kitchen spoon

- Diced parsley, 2 kitchen spoons

Directions:
1. Place the citrus peel with the citrus juice, salt, pepper, mustard, honey, oil, dill, and parsley
2. Mix and whisk well
3. Insert the kipper into this mixture, and flip
4. Set your air fryer to 350°F
5. Insert the kipper and cook for 5 minutes
6. Flip, and cook for a further 5 minutes
7. Share the fish into dishes, sprinkle the citrus dressing on top, and serve.

Nutrition: Calories 272, fat 8, fiber 12, carbs 15, protein 16

376. Redfish paella
Preparation Time: 15 minutes
Cooking Time: 30 minutes
Servings: 4
Ingredients:
- Brown rice, 5 ounces
- Garden green beans, 2 ounces
- Chopped and deseeded cayenne pepper
- Chardonnay, 6 ounces
- Chicken broth, 3½ ounces
- Cubed redfish, 1 pound
- Oysters, 6
- Deveined and peeled prawn, 8
- Salt and black pepper to taste
- Olive oil, a little sprinkle

Directions:
1. Put all the ingredients in a pan and flip
2. Set your air fryer to 380°F
3. Insert the mixture and cook for 12 minutes
4. Stir, cook for a further 12 minutes
5. Share into dishes and serve

Nutrition: Calories 290, fat 12, fiber 2, carbs 16, protein 19

377. Kipper and capers
Preparation Time: 5 minutes
Cooking Time: 12 minutes
Servings: 4
Ingredients:
- Deboned kipper fish, 4 pieces
- Sapped capers, 1 kitchen spoon
- Diced dill, 1 kitchen spoon
- Salt and black pepper to taste
- Lemon juice, from 1 lemon
- Olive oil, 2 teaspoons

Directions:
1. Make a mixture of the capers, dill, salt, pepper, and the oil
2. Coat the fish with the resulting mixture
3. Set your air fryer to 360°F
4. Insert the fish and cook for 6 minutes
5. Flip, cook for a further 6 minutes
6. Share the fish into dishes, sprinkle the lemon juice atop, and serve

Nutrition: Calories 280, fat 11, fiber 1, carbs 12, protein 18

378. Kipper and jasmine rice
Preparation Time: 10 minutes
Cooking Time: 30 minutes
Servings: 2
Ingredients:
- Deboned wild kipper strips, 2
- Salt and black pepper to taste
- Jasmine rice, ½ cup
- Chicken broth, 1 cup
- Thawed margarine, 1 kitchen spoon
- Saffron, a ¼ teaspoon

Directions:
1. Barring the fish, place all ingredients in a pan
2. Flip and mix well
3. Set your air fryer 360°F
4. Insert the ingredients and cook for 15 minutes.
5. Insert the fish, place on the lid
6. Cook 12 minutes more at the same temperature

7. Share into dishes and serve immediately
Nutrition: Calories 271, fat 8, fiber 9, carbs 15, protein 8

379. Kipper and carrots
Preparation Time: 5 minutes
Cooking Time: 20 minutes
Servings: 2
Ingredients:
- Deboned kipper strips, 2
- Diced garlic cloves, 3
- Olive oil, 1 kitchen spoon
- Veggie broth, ¼ cup
- Baby carrots, 1 cup
- Salt and black pepper to taste

Directions:
1. Mix the ingredients in a pan
2. Set your air fryer to 370°F
3. Insert the mixture and cook for 20 minutes
4. Share into dishes and serve

Nutrition: Calories 200, fat 6, fiber 6, carbs 18, protein 11

380. Black cod & plum sauce
Preparation Time: 10 minutes
Cooking Time: 25 minutes
Servings: 2
Ingredients:
- 2 medium black cod fillets; skinless and boneless
- 1 red plum; pitted and chopped
- 2 tsp. Raw honey
- 1/4 tsp. Black peppercorns; crushed
- 1 egg white
- 1/2 cup red quinoa; already cooked
- 2 tsp. Whole wheat flour
- 4 tsp. Lemon juice
- 1/2 tsp. Smoked paprika
- 1 tsp. Olive oil
- 2 tsp. Parsley
- 1/4 cup water

Directions:
1. In a bowl; mix 1 tsp. Lemon juice with egg white, flour and 1/4 tsp. Paprika and whisk well.
2. Put quinoa in a bowl and mix it with ⅓ of egg white mix.
3. Put the fish into the bowl with the remaining egg white mix and toss to coat.
4. Dip fish in quinoa mix; coat well and leave aside for 10 minutes.
5. Heat up a pan with 1 tsp. Oil over medium heat; add peppercorns, honey and plum; stir, bring to a simmer and cook for 1 minute.
6. Add the rest of the lemon juice, the rest of the paprika and the water; stir well and simmer for 5 minutes.
7. Add parsley; stir, take sauce off heat and leave aside for now.
8. Put fish in your air fryer and cook at 380 °F, for 10 minutes. Arrange fish on plates, drizzle plum sauce on top and serve.

Nutrition: calories: 324; fat: 14; fiber: 22; carbs: 27; protein: 22

381. Fried branzino
Preparation Time: 10 minutes
Cooking Time: 10 minutes
Servings: 4
Ingredients:
- 4 medium branzino fillets; boneless
- 1/2 cup parsley; chopped
- 2 tbsp. Olive oil
- A pinch of red pepper flakes; crushed
- Zest from 1 lemon; grated
- Zest from 1 orange; grated
- Juice from 1/2 lemon
- Juice from 1/2 orange
- Salt and black pepper to the taste

Directions:
1. In large bowl; mix fish fillets with lemon zest, orange zest, lemon juice, orange juice, salt, pepper, oil and pepper flakes
2. Toss really well, transfer fillets to your preheated air fryer at 350° F and bake for 10 minutes; flipping fillets once.
3. Divide fish on plates, sprinkle with parsley and serve right away.

Nutrition: calories: 261; fat: 8; fiber: 12; carbs: 21; protein: 12

382. **French style cod**
Preparation Time: 10 minutes
Cooking Time: 22 minutes
Servings: 4
Ingredients:
- White wine, ½ c.
- De-boned cod, 2 lbs.
- Olive oil, 2 tbsps.
- Stewed canned tomatoes, 14 oz.
- Chopped yellow onion,
- Butter, 2 tbsps.
- Black pepper.
- Minced garlic cloves,
- Chopped parsley, 3 tbsps. .
- Salt.

Directions:
1. Set a pan with oil on fire to heat over medium heat.
2. Stir in onion and garlic to cook for 5 minutes.
3. Stir in wine to cook for 1 more minute.
4. Mix in tomatoes to boil for 2 minutes then stir in parsley and remove from heat.
5. Transfer the mix into a heat proof dish that fits the air fryer.
6. Add fish and season it with salt and pepper then cook for 14 minutes at 350°F.
7. Set the fish and tomatoes mix on plates and serve.

Nutrition: Calories: 231; fat: 8, fiber: 12, carbs: 26, protein: 14

383. **Cubed salmon chili**
Preparation Time: 10 minutes
Cooking Time: 10 minutes
Servings: 12
Ingredients:
- Olive oil, 2 tbsps.
- Black pepper.
- Chopped red chilies,
- Flour, 1/3 c.
- Egg,
- Water, ¼ c.
- Balsamic vinegar, ¼ c.
- Minced garlic cloves,
- Shredded coconut, 1¼ c.
- Honey, ½ c.
- Cubed salmon, 1 lb.
- Salt.

Directions:
1. Combine salt and flour in a mixing bowl.
2. Have another mixing bowl in place to combine black pepper and egg.
3. In a third bowl, put the coconut.
4. Pass the salmon cubes through flour, egg then coconut and place them into the air fryer.
5. Allow to cook for 8 minutes at 370°F and shake halfway.
6. Set the salmon cubes on plates.
7. Set a pan with water on fire to boil over medium high heat.
8. Stir in honey, vinegar, chilies and cloves to boil under low heat.
9. Drizzle the mix on salmon to serve.
10. Enjoy.

Nutrition: Calories: 220, fat: 12, fiber: 2, carbs: 14, protein: 13

384. **Creamy tuna cakes**
Preparation time: 15 minutes
Cooking time: 15 minutes
Servings: 4
Ingredients:
- 2: 6-ouncescans tuna, drained
- 1½ tablespoon almond flour
- 1½ tablespoons mayonnaise
- 1 tablespoon fresh lemon juice
- 1 teaspoon dried dill
- 1 teaspoon garlic powder
- ½ teaspoon onion powder
- Pinch of salt and ground black pepper

Directions:
1. Preheat the air fryer to 400°F and grease an air fryer basket.
2. Mix the tuna, mayonnaise, almond flour, lemon juice, dill, and spices in a large bowl.
3. Make 4 equal-sized patties from the mixture and arrange in the air fryer basket.
4. Cook for about 10 minutes and flip the sides.
5. Cook for 5 more minutes and dish out the tuna cakes in serving plates to serve warm.

Nutrition: Calories: 200, fat: 11g, carbohydrates: 9g, sugar: 8g, protein: 24g, sodium: 122mg

385. **Scallops with spinach**
Preparation time: 20 minutes
Cooking time: 10 minutes
Servings: 2
Ingredients:
- 1: 12-ouncespackage frozen spinach, thawed and drained
- 8 jumbo sea scallops
- Olive oil cooking spray
- 1 tablespoon fresh basil, chopped
- Salt and ground black pepper, as required
- ¾ cup heavy whipping cream
- 1 tablespoon tomato paste
- 1 teaspoon garlic, minced

Directions:
1. Preheat the air fryer to 350°F and grease an air fryer pan.
2. Season the scallops evenly with salt and black pepper.
3. Mix cream, tomato paste, garlic, basil, salt, and black pepper in a bowl.
4. Place spinach at the bottom of the air fryer pan, followed by seasoned scallops and top with the cream mixture.
5. Transfer into the air fryer and cook for about 10 minutes.
6. Dish out in a platter and serve hot.

Nutrition: Calories: 203, fat: 13g, carbohydrates: 13g, sugar: 7g, protein: 24g, sodium: 101mg

386. **Bacon wrapped scallops**
Preparation time: 15 minutes
Cooking time: 12 minutes
Servings: 4
Ingredients:
- 5 center-cut bacon slices, cut each in 4 pieces
- 20 sea scallops, cleaned and patted very dry
- Olive oil cooking spray
- 1 teaspoon lemon pepper seasoning
- ½ teaspoon paprika
- Salt and ground black pepper, to taste

Directions:
1. Preheat the air fryer to 400°F and grease an air fryer basket.
2. Wrap each scallop with a piece of bacon and secure each with a toothpick.
3. Season the scallops evenly with lemon pepper seasoning and paprika.
4. Arrange half of the scallops into the air fryer basket and spray with cooking spray.
5. Season with salt and black pepper and cook for about 6 minutes.
6. Repeat with the remaining half and serve warm.

Nutrition: Calories: 330, fat: 13g, carbohydrates: 5g, sugar: 0g, protein: 37g, sodium: 1118mg

387. **Glazed calamari**
Preparation time: 20 minutes
Cooking time: 13 minutes
Servings: 3
Ingredients:
- ½ pound calamari tubes, cut into ¼ inch rings
- 1 cup club soda
- 1 cup flour
- ½ tablespoon red pepper flakes, crushed
- Salt and black pepper, to taste
- For sauce
- ½ cup honey
- 2 tablespoons sriracha sauce
- ¼ teaspoon red pepper flakes, crushed

Directions:

1. Preheat the air fryer to 375°F and grease an air fryer basket.
2. Soak the calamari in the club soda in a bowl and keep aside for about 10 minutes.
3. Mix flour, red pepper flakes, salt, and black pepper in another bowl.
4. Drain the club soda from calamari and coat the calamari rings evenly with flour mixture.
5. Arrange calamari rings into the air fryer basket and cook for about 11 minutes.
6. Meanwhile, mix the honey, sriracha sauce and red pepper flakes in a bowl.
7. Coat the calamari rings with the honey sauce and cook for 2 more minutes.
8. Dish out the calamari rings onto serving plates and serve hot.

Nutrition: Calories: 307, fats: 4g, carbohydrates: 61g, sugar: 35g, proteins: 12g, sodium: 131mg

388. Buttered crab shells

Preparation time: 20 minutes
Cooking time: 10 minutes
Servings: 4

Ingredients:

- 4 soft crab shells, cleaned
- 1 cup buttermilk
- 3 eggs
- 2 cups panko breadcrumb
- 2 tablespoons butter, melted
- 2 teaspoons seafood seasoning
- 1½ teaspoons lemon zest, grated

Directions:

1. Preheat the air fryer to 375°F and grease an air fryer basket.
2. Place the buttermilk in a shallow bowl and whisk the eggs in a second bowl.
3. Mix the breadcrumbs, seafood seasoning, and lemon zest in a third bowl.
4. Soak the crab shells into the buttermilk for about 10 minutes, then dip in the eggs.
5. Dredge in the breadcrumb mixture and arrange the crab shells into the air fryer basket.
6. Cook for about 10 minutes and dish out in a platter.
7. Drizzle melted butter over the crab shells and immediately serve.

Nutrition: Calories: 521, fat: 18g, carbohydrates: 15g, sugar: 3g, protein: 48g, sodium: 1100mg

(**note:** seafood seasoning - mix the salt, celery seed, dry mustard powder, red pepper, black pepper, bay leaves, paprika, cloves, allspice, ginger, cardamom, and cinnamon together in a bowl until thoroughly combined.

389. Wasabi crab cakes

Preparation time: 20 minutes
Cooking time: 24 minutes
Servings: 6

Ingredients:

- 3 scallions, finely chopped
- 1 celery rib, finely chopped
- 1/3 cup plus ½ cup dry breadcrumbs, divided
- 2 large egg whites
- 1½ cups lump crab meat, drained
- 3 tablespoons mayonnaise
- 1 medium sweet red pepper, finely chopped
- ¼ teaspoon prepared wasabi
- Salt, to taste

Directions:

1. Preheat the air fryer to 375°F and grease an air fryer basket.
2. Mix scallions, red pepper, celery, 1/3 cup of breadcrumbs, egg whites, mayonnaise, wasabi, and salt in a large bowl.
3. Fold in the crab meat gently and mix well.
4. Place the remaining breadcrumbs in another bowl.
5. Make ¾-inch thick patties from the mixture and arrange half of the patties into the air fryer.
6. Cook for about 12 minutes, flipping once halfway through and repeat with the remaining patties.
7. Dish out and serve warm.

Nutrition: Calories: 112, fat: 4g, carbohydrates: 15g, sugar: 7g, protein: 9g, sodium: 253mg

390. Rice in crab shell

Preparation time: 20 minutes
Cooking time: 8 minutes
Servings: 2

Ingredients:

- 1 bowl cooked rice
- 4 tablespoons crab meat
- 2 tablespoons butter
- 2 tablespoons parmesan cheese, shredded
- 2 crab shells
- Paprika, to taste

Directions:

1. Preheat the air fryer to 390 °F and grease an air fryer basket.
2. Mix rice, crab meat, butter and paprika in a bowl.
3. Fill crab shell with rice mixture and top with parmesan cheese.
4. Arrange the crab shell in the air fryer basket and cook for about 8 minutes.
5. Sprinkle with more paprika and serve hot.

Nutrition: Calories: 285, fat: 33g, carbohydrates: 0g, sugar: 0g, protein: 33g, sodium: 153mg

391. Tuna zoodle casserole

Preparation time: 30 minutes
Cooking Time: 25 minutes
Servings: 4

Ingredients:

- 1 oz. Pork rinds, finely ground
- 2 medium zucchinis, spiralized
- 2: 5-oz.cans albacore tuna
- ¼ cup diced white onion
- ¼ cup chopped white mushrooms
- 2 stalks celery, finely chopped
- ½ cup heavy cream
- ½ cup vegetable broth
- 2 tbsp. Full-fat mayonnaise
- 2 tbsp. Salted butter
- ½ tsp. Red pepper flakes
- ¼ tsp. Xanthan gum

Directions:

1. In a large saucepan over medium heat, melt butter. Add onion, mushrooms and celery and sauté until fragrant, about 3–5 minutes.
2. Pour in heavy cream, vegetable broth, mayonnaise and xanthan gum. Reduce heat and continue cooking an additional 3 minutes, until the mixture begins to thicken.
3. Add red pepper flakes, zucchini and tuna. Turn off heat and stir until zucchini noodles are coated
4. Pour into 4-cup round baking dish. Top with ground pork rinds and cover the top of the dish with foil. Place into the air fryer basket. Adjust the temperature to 370 °F and set the timer for 15 minutes.
5. When 3 minutes remain, remove the foil to brown the top of the casserole. Serve warm.

Nutrition: calories: 339; protein: 17g; fiber: 8g; fat: 21g; carbs: 1g

392. Spicy avocado cod

Preparation time: 20 minutes
Cooking Time: 20 minutes
Servings: 2

Ingredients:

- 1 medium avocado; peeled, pitted and sliced
- ¼ cup chopped pickled jalapeños.
- 2: 3-oz.cod fillets
- ½ medium lime
- 1 cup shredded cabbage
- ¼ cup full-fat sour cream.
- 2 tbsp. Full-fat mayonnaise
- ½ tsp. Paprika
- ¼ tsp. Garlic powder.
- 1 tsp. Chili powder.
- 1 tsp. Cumin

Directions:

1. Take a large bowl, place cabbage, sour cream, mayonnaise and

jalapeños. Mix until fully coated. Let sit for 20 minutes in the refrigerator

2. Sprinkle cod fillets with chili powder, cumin, paprika and garlic powder. Place each fillet into the air fryer basket. Adjust the temperature to 370 degrees f and set the timer for 10 minutes.

3. Flip the fillets halfway through the cooking time. When fully cooked, fish should have an internal temperature of at least 145 °F

4. To serve, divide slaw mixture into two serving bowls, break cod fillets into pieces and spread over the bowls and top with avocado. Squeeze lime juice over each bowl. Serve immediately.

Nutrition: calories: 342; protein: 11g; fiber: 4g; fat: 22g; carbs: 17g

393. Ginger cod steaks
Preparation Time: 10 minutes
Cooking Time: 20 minutes
Servings: 2
Ingredients:

- Large cod steaks: 2 slices
- Turmeric powder: .25 tsp.
- Ginger powder: .5 tsp.
- Garlic powder: .5 tsp.
- Salt & pepper: 1 pinch
- Plum sauce: 1 tbsp.
- Ginger slices: as desired
- Kentucky kernel seasoned flour: +corn flour: 1 part of each

Directions:

1. Dry off the steaks and marinate using the pepper, salt, ginger powder, and turmeric powder for a few minutes.

2. Lightly coat the steaks with the corn flour/Kentucky mix.

3. Set the temperature in the fryer to 356°F for 15 minutes and increase to 400°F for 5 minutes. Time may vary depending on the size of the cod.

4. Prepare the sauce in wok. Brown the ginger slices and remove from the heat. Stir in the plum sauce adding water to thin as needed.

5. Serve the steaks with prepared sauce.
Nutrition: Calories: 140 Fat: 4g Carbs: 6g Protein: 17g

394. Honey & sriracha tossed calamari
Preparation Time: 10 minutes
Cooking Time: 15 minutes
Servings: 1-2
Ingredients:

- Calamari tubes - tentacles if you prefer: .5 lb.
- Club soda: 1 cup
- Four: 1 cup
- Salt - red pepper & black pepper: 2 dashes each
- Honey: .5 cup+ 1-2 tbsp. Sriracha
- Red pepper flakes: 2 shakes

Directions:

1. Fully rinse the calamari and blot it dry using bunch of paper towels. Slice into rings: 1/4 inch wide). Toss the rings into bowl. Pour in the club soda and stir until all are submerged. Wait for about 10 minutes.

2. Sift the salt, flour, red & black pepper. Set aside for now.

3. Dredge the calamari into the flour mixture and set on platter until ready to fry.

4. Spritz the basket of the Air Fryer with small amount of cooking oil spray. Arrange the calamari in the basket, careful not to crowd it too much.

5. Set the temperature at 375 °F and the timer for 11 minutes.

6. Shake the basket twice during the cooking process, loosening any rings that may stick.

7. Remove from the basket, toss with the sauce, and return to the fryer for two more minutes.

8. Serve with additional sauce as desired.

9. Make the sauce by combining honey, sriracha, and red pepper flakes in small bowl, mix until fully combined.
Nutrition: Calories: 290 Fat: 14g Carbs: 22g Protein: 10g

DINNER RECIPES

395. Mexican chicken wings
Preparation time: 10 minutes
Cooking time: 12 minutes
Servings: 5
Ingredients:

- 3 lb. Chicken wings
- 2 teaspoons olive oil
- 1 tablespoon taco seasoning mix

Directions:

1. Coat chicken wings with olive oil.
2. Sprinkle all sides with taco seasoning.
3. Prepare the air fryer to 350 °F.
4. Add the chicken wings to the air fryer.
5. Cook for 6 minutes per side.
6. Serve with salsa and sour cream.
Nutrition: Calories: 150 Fat: 0g Carbs: 2g Protein: 0g

396. Crispy chicken breast
Preparation time: 15 minutes
Cooking time: 15 minutes
Servings: 2
Ingredients:

- 1 egg, beaten
- ¼ cup all-purpose flour
- ¾ cup breadcrumbs
- 1 teaspoon dried oregano
- 2 teaspoon lemon zest
- ¼ cup parmesan cheese, grated
- Salt and pepper to taste
- ½ teaspoon cayenne pepper
- 2 chicken breast fillets

Directions:

1. Add the eggs to a bowl.
2. Add the flour to another bowl.
3. In the third bowl, mix the breadcrumbs, dried oregano, lemon zest, parmesan cheese, salt, pepper, and cayenne pepper.
4. Dip the chicken breast fillets in the first, second, and third bowls.
5. Add these to the air fryer basket.
6. Cook for 10 minutes at 375 °F.
7. Turn the chicken.
8. Cook for another 5 minutes.
Nutrition: Calories: 188 Fat: 6g Carbs: 5g Protein: 5g

397. Crunchy chicken tenderloins
Preparation time: 10 minutes
Cooking time: 15 minutes
Servings: 8
Ingredients:

- 1 egg, beaten
- 2 tablespoons vegetable oil
- ½ cup breadcrumbs
- 8 chicken tenderloins

Directions:

1. Ready your air fryer to 350 °F.
2. Add the egg to a bowl.
3. Mix the oil and breadcrumbs in another bowl.
4. Dip the chicken in egg and then in the oil mixture.
5. Add to the air fryer basket.
6. Cook for 15 minutes, flipping once or twice.
Nutrition: Calories: 291 Fat: 7g Carbs: 16g Protein: 38g

398. Chicken & broccoli
Preparation time: 10 minutes
Cooking time: 20 minutes
Servings: 4
Ingredients:

- 1 onion, sliced
- 2 cups broccoli florets
- 1 lb. Chicken breast fillet, sliced into cubes
- 2 tablespoons olive oil
- ½ teaspoon garlic powder
- 1 tablespoon ginger, minced
- 1 tablespoon reduced sodium soy sauce
- 1 teaspoon sesame seed oil
- 2 teaspoons rice vinegar

Directions:
1. Toss the onion, broccoli, and chicken in a bowl.
2. In another bowl, mix the rest of the ingredients.
3. Pour mixture into the first bowl.
4. Mix well.
5. Add mixture to the air fryer.
6. Cook at 380 °F for 20 minutes.

Nutrition: Calories: 191 Fat: 7g Carbs: 4g Protein: 25g

399.   Parmesan chicken
Preparation time: 10 minutes
Cooking time: 15 minutes
Servings: 2
Ingredients:
- 2 eggs, beaten
- 2 teaspoons paprika
- 1 ½ cups parmesan cheese, grated
- 2 tablespoons garlic paste
- 2 tablespoons dried Italian seasoning
- 2 chicken breast fillets, sliced in half
- Salt to taste
- Cooking spray

Directions:
1. Set and preheat your air fryer to 400 °F.
2. Combine paprika, cheese, garlic paste, and Italian seasoning in a bowl.
3. Add the eggs to a bowl.
4. Season chicken with salt.
5. Dip in egg and then in the paprika mixture.
6. Spray with oil.
7. Air fry for 15 minutes.

Nutrition: Calories: 370 Fat: 8g Carbs: 32g Protein: 32g

400.   Lemon chicken
Preparation time: 10 minutes
Cooking time: 20 minutes
Servings: 4
Ingredients:
- 6 chicken thighs
- 2 tablespoons olive oil
- 2 tablespoons lemon juice
- 1 tablespoon Italian herb seasoning blend
- Salt and pepper to taste
- 4 lemon slices for garnish

Directions:
1. Combine ingredients except garnish in a bowl.
2. Marinate for 30 minutes.
3. Place chicken in the air fryer basket.
4. Top with lemon slices and cook for 10 minutes per side at 350 °F.

Nutrition: Calories: 325 Fat: 23g Carbs: 2g Protein: 31g

401.   Roast chicken
Preparation time: 10 minutes
Cooking time: 50 minutes
Servings: 8
Ingredients:
- 1 whole chicken
- Chicken dry rub
- Cooking spray

Directions:
1. Spray chicken with oil.
2. Sprinkle with the dry rub.
3. Roast the chicken in the air fryer at 330 °F for 30 minutes.
4. Turn and roast for another 20 minutes.

Nutrition: Calories: 166 Fat: 6g Carbs: 1g Protein: 25g

402.   General Tso's chicken
Preparation time: 20 minutes
Cooking time: 35 minutes
Servings: 4
Ingredients:
- 1 lb. Chicken thigh fillets, sliced into smaller pieces
- Salt and pepper to taste
- 1 egg, beaten
- ¼ cup cornstarch
- Sauce
- 2 tablespoons reduced sodium soy sauce
- 1 ½ tablespoon vegetable oil
- 2 teaspoons rice vinegar
- 8 tablespoons chicken broth
- 2 teaspoons sugar
- 2 tablespoons ketchup
- 3 chiles de árbol, chopped and seeded
- 1 clove garlic, minced
- 1 tablespoon ginger, chopped

Directions:
1. Season chicken with salt and pepper.
2. Dip in egg and coat with cornstarch.
3. Set the air fryer at 400 °F and cook for 15 minutes, flipping once or twice.
4. In a pan over medium heat, simmer sauce ingredients for 15 minutes.
5. Add chicken to the pan.
6. Mix well.
7. Cook for 5 minutes.
8. Serve warm.

Nutrition: Calories: 397 Fat: 9g Carbs: 29g Protein: 46g

403.   Buttermilk fried chicken
Preparation time: 8 hours
Cooking time: 45 minutes
Servings: 6
Ingredients:
- Marinade
- 2 lb. Chicken
- 1 cup buttermilk
- ¼ cup hot sauce
- 1 teaspoon paprika
- 1 teaspoon garlic powder
- Salt and pepper to taste
- Breading
- 1 cup flour
- 1 teaspoon garlic powder
- 1 teaspoon paprika
- ½ cup cornstarch
- Salt and pepper to taste
- Cooking spray

Directions:
1. Mix the marinade ingredients in a bowl.
2. Cover and refrigerate for 8 hours.
3. Warm your air fryer to 375 °F.
4. In a bowl, mix the breading ingredients.
5. Add 2 tablespoons buttermilk batter to the flour bowl and mix well.
6. Dredge chicken with flour mixture.
7. Cook the chicken for 30 minutes.
8. Flip and cook for 15 minutes.

Nutrition: Calories: 335: Fat: 13g Carbs: 33g Protein: 24g

404.   Chicken and squash stew
Preparation Time: 5 minutes
Cooking Time: 17 minutes
Servings: 2
Ingredients:
- 2 chicken breasts, cubed
- Pepper, to taste
- ½ cup squash, cubed
- 1 tablespoon onions, sliced
- 1 tablespoon garlic, minced

- ½ teaspoon garlic salt
- 1 tablespoon carrots, diced
- 1½ cups chicken stock
- 1 tablespoon fresh cilantro, chopped

Directions:
1. Preheat the Air Fryer to 350°F/180°C.
2. Season the chicken cubes with pepper and place them in the Air Fryer Baking Pan.
3. Put cooking spray to the chicken and place the Air Fryer Baking Pan in the Basket.
4. Set the timer for 8 minutes.
5. Add the squash, onions, garlic, garlic salt and carrots to the Air Fryer Baking Pan and set the timer for 4 minutes.
6. Pour in the chicken stock and set the timer for five more minutes.
7. Top with the fresh cilantro.
8. Serve and enjoy!

Nutrition: Calories: 193 Fat: 3g Carbs: 28g Protein: 16g

405. Easy chili con carne
Preparation Time: 10 minutes
Cooking time: 20 minutes
Servings: 2
Ingredients:
- rashers bacon, chopped
- ½ pound ground beef
- 1 tablespoon onions, chopped
- 1 tablespoon garlic, minced
- 1 tablespoon red bell peppers, chopped
- 1 tablespoon green bell peppers, chopped
- 1 tablespoon tomato paste
- ½ teaspoon garlic salt
- pepper, to taste
- ¼ teaspoon paprika
- ¼ teaspoon chili flakes
- ½ cup tomato sauce
- ¼ cup cheddar cheese, grated
- 1 tablespoon fresh parsley, chopped
- ¼ cup tomatoes, diced

Directions:
1. Preheat the Air Fryer to 400°F/200°C.
2. Place the bacon and ground beef in the Air Fryer Baking Pan and set the timer for 5 minutes.
3. Add the onions, garlic, red and green bell peppers and tomato paste.
4. Season with the garlic salt, pepper, paprika and chili flakes and stir well to combine.
5. Set the timer for 10 minutes. Mix the chili midway through the cooking time to mix the flavors well together.
6. Stir in the tomato sauce.
7. Top with the cheddar cheese, fresh parsley and the diced tomatoes.
8. Cook for another 5 minutes or until the meat is cooked through.

Nutrition: Calories: 117 Fat: 3g Carbs: 16g Protein: 5g

406. Sweet chili pork bellies
Preparation Time: 10 minutes
Cooking time: 20 minutes
Servings: 4
Ingredients:
- 2 tablespoons olive oil
- 2 teaspoons lime juice
- 2 teaspoons honey
- 2 tablespoons garlic, minced
- 1 teaspoon paprika
- 1 teaspoon chili flakes
- 2 tablespoons fresh cilantro, chopped
- salt and pepper, to taste
- 1pound pork belly slices
- lime slices

Directions:
1 Preheat the Air Fryer to 400°F/200°C.

2. To make the sweet chili: Mix together the olive oil, lime juice, honey, minced garlic, paprika, chili flakes, fresh cilantro, salt and pepper.
3. Rub the pork belly slices evenly with the sweet chili.
4. Line the Air Fryer Basket with the lime slices and place the pork bellies on them.
5. Set the timer for 20 minutes or until the pork is cooked through. Halfway through the cooking time, flip the pork belly slices overusing a pair of kitchen tongs.
6. Serve and enjoy!

Nutrition: Calories: 258 Fat: 20g Carbs: 0g Protein: 19g

407. Chicken alfredo with kalamata olives
Preparation Time: 10 minutes
Cooking time: 23 minutes
Servings: 2
Ingredients:
- 2 rashers bacon, chopped
- 2 tablespoon garlic, minced
- 1 chicken breast, sliced
- 1 tablespoon kalamata olives, sliced
- ½ teaspoon garlic powder
- freshly ground black pepper
- ½ cup low fat cream
- ¼ cup chicken stock
- 1 tablespoon fresh parsley, chopped

Directions:
- Preheat the Air Fryer to 350°F/180°C.
- Place the chopped bacon in the Air Fryer Baking Pan and set the timer for 3 minutes.
- Add the minced garlic, chicken slices and kalamata olives.
- Season with the garlic powder and pepper.
- Return to the oven and set the time for 10 minutes.
- Combine the cream with the chicken stock and stir into the Air Fryer Baking Pan.
- Set the timer for 10 more minutes.
- Top with the fresh parsley. Serve and enjoy!

Nutrition: Calories: 488 Fat: 11g Carbs: 70g Protein: 30g

408. Flank steaks and peaches with truffle oil
Preparation time: 5 minutes
Cooking time: 8 minutes
Servings: 2
Ingredients:
- 2 flank steaks
- 1 teaspoon paprika
- Salt and pepper, to taste
- 4 peaches, pitted and halved
- 1 tablespoon truffle oil

Directions:
1. Preheat the air fryer to 350°F/180°C.
2. Season the steaks with the paprika, salt and pepper.
3. Spray the steaks with some cooking spray.
4. Arrange the steaks and peaches in the air fryer basket. Use the air fryer double layer rack if needed.
5. Set the timer for 8 minutes or until the steaks are cooked to your desired doneness.
6. Drizzle over with truffle oil.
7. Serve and enjoy!

Nutrition: Calories: 180 Fat: 9g Carbs: 0g Protein: 21g

409. Honey and pineapple beef stew
Preparation time: 40 minutes
Cooking time: 12 minutes
Servings: 2
Ingredients:
- 1-pound beef chunks
- 2 tablespoons olive oil
- Salt and pepper, to taste
- 1 teaspoon garlic powder
- 1 cup tomato sauce
- 2 tablespoons tomato paste
- ¼ cup olives, sliced
- ¼ cup onions, chopped

- ¼ cup honey
- 1 cup pineapple chunk
- ½ cup beef stock
- 2 tablespoons fresh basil, chopped

Directions:
1. Season the beef chunks the olive oil, salt, pepper and garlic powder. Set aside to chill in the fridge for 30 minutes.
2. Preheat the air fryer to 350°f/180°c.
3. Place the meat in the air fryer baking pan and add in the tomato sauce, tomato paste, olives, onions, honey and pineapple chunks.
4. Pour in the beef stock and stir well to combine.
5. Set the timer for 12 minutes or until desired doneness of meat. Halfway through the cooking time, stir the beef stew to allow even cooking.
6. Top with the fresh basil.
7. Serve and enjoy!

Nutrition: Calories: 370 Fat: 14g Carbs: 39g Protein: 23g

410. Creamy halibut chowder

Servings: 1
Preparation time: 5 minutes
Cooking time: 10 minutes

Ingredients:
- 1 halibut fillet, cut in cubes
- Salt and pepper, to taste
- ½ teaspoon olive oil
- ½ teaspoon lemon juice
- 1 cup fish stock
- ¼ cup cream
- ¼ cup mushrooms, sliced
- 1 tablespoon ginger, minced
- 1 tablespoon onion, chopped
- 1 tablespoon dill, chopped

Directions:
1. Preheat the air fryer to 350°f/180°c.
2. Place the halibut fillets in the air fryer baking pan and season with salt and pepper.
3. Drizzle with the olive oil and lemon juice.
4. Place the air fryer baking pan in the air fryer basket and set the timer for 2 minutes.
5. Pour in the fish stock and cream and add the mushrooms, ginger, and onions.
6. Stir well to combine.
7. Set the timer for 8 minutes.
8. Top with the fresh dill.
9. Serve and enjoy!

Nutrition: Calories: 198 Fat: 11g Carbs:12g Protein: 13

411. Snow peas with ginger salmon steaks

Servings: 1
Preparation time: 10 minutes
Cooking time: 8 minutes

Ingredients:
- 1 tablespoon ginger, minced
- 1 salmon steak
- Salt and pepper, to taste
- 1 teaspoon olive oil
- 1 tablespoon lemon juice
- ½ cup snow peas
- ½ small red bell pepper, seeds removed and sliced
- 1 tablespoon fresh cilantro, chopped

Directions:
1. Preheat the air fryer to 350°f/180°c.
2. Rub the ginger into the salmon steak and season with salt and pepper on both sides.
3. Drizzle over with the olive oil and lemon juice.
4. Place the fish in the air fryer baking pan with the snow peas, bell peppers, and fresh cilantro.
5. Season again with pepper.
6. Place the air fryer baking pan in the air fryer basket and set the timer for 8 minutes or until the salmon is cooked through.
7. Serve and enjoy!

Nutrition: Calories: 340 Fat: 20g Carbs: 9g Protein: 30g

412. Grilled cumin hanger steak

Preparation time: 15 minutes
Cooking time: 10 minutes
Servings: 2

Ingredients:
- 2 hanger steaks
- 1 teaspoon ground cumin
- 1 teaspoon paprika
- Salt and pepper, to taste
- 2 tablespoons olive oil
- 1 cup green peas
- ¼ cup mint leaves, chopped
- ¼ cup parmesan cheese, shavings

Directions:
1. Rub the steaks with cumin and paprika.
2. Season with salt and pepper and drizzle with 1 tablespoon of olive oil.
3. Rest for 10 minutes.
4. Attach the air fryer grill pan and preheat the air fryer to 350°f/180°c.
5. Arrange the steaks on the air fryer grill pan and set the timer for 5 minutes.
6. Remove the steaks from the air fryer grill pan and place the green peas and mint leaves on the air fryer grill pan.
7. Flip over the steaks and place them on top of the vegetables.
8. Drizzle with remaining olive oil and top with the parmesan cheese shavings.
9. Set the timer for 5 more minutes or until desired doneness of meat.
10. serve and enjoy!

Nutrition: Calories: 415 Fat: 11g Carbs: 26g Protein: 40g

413. Ginger fish stew

Preparation time: 35 minutes
Cooking time: 12 minutes
Servings: 2

Ingredients:
- 1 cod fillet, cut into small cubes
- 1 tablespoon sesame oil
- 1 teaspoon soy sauce
- White pepper, to taste
- ½ tablespoon fish oil
- 1 tablespoon ginger slice
- 1 tablespoon onion, sliced
- 1 tablespoon carrot, sliced
- 1 tablespoon garlic, sliced
- 1½ cups fish stock
- 1 head of bok choy, halved

Directions:
1. Marinade the fish fillets with half a tablespoon of sesame oil, the soy sauce, white pepper and fish oil for 30 minutes.
2. Preheat the air fryer to 350°f/180°c.
3. Place the fish fillets into the air fryer baking pan and add the ginger, onions, carrots and garlic.
4. Drizzle over with the remaining sesame oil.
5. Add water in the air fryer as recommended by the manufacturer's instructions for steaming food.
6. Set the timer for 7 minutes.
7. Flip the fish cubes and add in the fish stock.
8. Set the timer for 5 minutes.
9. Add the bok choy and cook for a minute more.
10. serve and enjoy!

Nutrition: Calories: 190 Fat: 1g Carbs: 5g Protein: 9g

414. Kimchi stuffed squid

Servings: 2
Preparation time: 5 minutes
Cooking time: 12 minutes

Ingredients:
- 1 large squid, cleaned
- 1 cup kimchi

Directions:
1. Preheat the air fryer to 350°f/180°c.
2. Stuff the squid with the kimchi and secure it with a toothpick.
3. Place the squid in the air fryer basket and spray it with some cooking spray.

4. Set the timer for 12 minutes or until the squid is cooked. Halfway through the cooking time, use kitchen tongs to rearrange the squid so that it will be cooked evenly.
5. Serve and enjoy!

Nutrition: Calories: 175 Fat: 2g Carbs: 30g Protein: 9g

415. Garlic and cream cheese rolled pork

Servings: 2
Preparation time: 15 minutes
Cooking time: 40 minutes
Ingredients:

- 2 tablespoons olive oil
- 3 tablespoons garlic, minced
- ½ teaspoon chili powder
- 1 teaspoon paprika
- 3 tablespoons fresh parsley, finely chopped
- Salt and pepper, to taste
- ¼ cup onions, chopped
- 1-pound pork belly
- ½ cup cream cheese
- 2 tablespoons chives, chopped

Directions:
1. Preheat the air fryer to 350°f/180°c.
2. Combine the olive oil, 2 tablespoons of garlic, chili powder, paprika, parsley, salt and pepper. Reserve a tablespoon of garlic for step
3. Add the onions and spread the mixture onto the pork belly.
4. Combine the cream cheese, the remaining minced garlic and chives and spread it over the onions on the pork.
5. Roll the meat firmly to form a log and secure with kitchen string.
6. Rub the reserved herb mixture onto the pork roll.
7. Place the pork roll seam-side down into the air fryer basket and set the timer for 40 minutes or until the pork is cooked through.
8. Serve and enjoy!

Nutrition: Calories: 350 Fat: 12g Carbs: 28g Protein: 32g

416. Appetizing egg curry

Preparation time: 20 minutes
Cooking time: 25 minutes
Servings: 4
Ingredients:

- 8 boiled eggs
- ½ teaspoon of salt
- ½ teaspoon of pepper
- 2 tablespoons of oil
- 1 tablespoon of garlic
- 1 tablespoon of ginger
- 6-7 peppercorns
- 2 onions
- 3 tomatoes
- 1 tablespoon of poppy seeds
- 1 tablespoon of coconut
- ½ teaspoon of paprika
- ½ teaspoon of red chili pepper

Directions:
1. Clean and chop eggs in the pieces.
2. Blend them with salt, pepper, garlic, ginger, poppy seeds, coconut, paprika and red chili pepper.
3. After that chop onions in the rings.
4. Cut tomatoes and peppercorns in the pieces.
5. Blend everything well.
6. Sprinkle the air fryer with oil.
7. Cook the meal in the air fryer for 15 minutes.
8. Then blend everything and cook for 10 minutes.
9. Serve hot with parsley.
10. 1enjoy with the meal.

Nutrition: Calories: 123 Fat: 3,5g Carbohydrates: 6,9g Protein: 2,8g

417. Flavorsome chicken ghee

Preparation time: 20 minutes
Cooking time: 30 minutes
Servings: 4
Ingredients:

- 1,5 lb. of chicken
- 1 cup of yogurt

- 1 teaspoon of red chili pepper
- ¼ teaspoon of turmeric
- 1/2 teaspoon of ginger
- ½ teaspoon of garlic
- 2 tablespoons of lime juice
- 7 tablespoons of ghee
- 10 curry leaves
- 2 tablespoons of coriander seeds
- ½ tablespoon of cumin seeds
- 2 tablespoons of oil

Directions:
1. Wash and clean chicken.
2. Chop it in the pieces.
3. Take the bowl and blend the red chili pepper, turmeric, ginger, chopped garlic, lime juice, ghee, coriander seeds, curry leaves and cumin seeds there.
4. Place chicken there and blend everything well.
5. After that sprinkle the air fryer with oil.
6. Preheat the air fryer to 350°F for 2-3 minutes.
7. Cook meal for 20 minutes.
8. Then blend everything and cook for 10 minutes.
9. Serve hot with vegetables.

Nutrition: Calories: 178 Fat: 5,2g Carbohydrates: 7,3g Protein: 4,2g

418. Tasty curry with meatballs

Preparation time: 25 minutes
Cooking time: 25 minutes
Servings: 4
Ingredients:

- 1 lb. of minced meat
- 2 onions
- 2 green chili peppers
- 2 tablespoons of ginger
- 3 tomatoes
- 3 cloves of garlic
- ½ teaspoon of dry herbs
- ½ teaspoon of oregano
- 1/3 teaspoon of turmeric
- 1 tablespoon of dill
- 1 tablespoon of parsley
- 3 tablespoons of oil

Directions:
1. Put meat in the bowl.
2. Add ginger, garlic, dry herbs, oregano, turmeric, parsley and dill there.
3. Mix everything well.
4. Then cut tomatoes in the pieces.
5. Add them to meat.
6. Chop onion in the rings.
7. Then blend all components.
8. Sprinkle the air fryer with oil.
9. Cook the meal for 15 minutes.
10. 1then mix everything.
11. 1cook for 10 minutes more.
12. 1serve hot.

Nutrition: Calories: 165 Fat: 5,3g Carbohydrates: 7,1g Protein: 4,5g

419. Spinach with meat

Preparation time: 25 minutes
Cooking time: 50 minutes
Servings: 4
Ingredients:

- 1 lb. of beef
- ½ teaspoon of pepper
- ½ teaspoon of salt
- 3 tablespoons of oil
- 1 ginger
- 4 onions
- 8 oz of spinach
- 3 cloves of garlic
- ½ cup of yogurt
- 4 tomatoes
- 2 tablespoons of coriander

- ¼ cup of butter
- 1 teaspoon of cumin

Directions:
1. Wash and clean the beef.
2. Chop meat in the pieces.
3. Take the bowl and place salt, pepper, chopped ginger, garlic, coriander, cumin and butter.
4. Then blend everything well and add meat there.
5. Chop onions in the rings.
6. Add them to spices and meat.
7. Cut spinach in the pieces.
8. Chop tomatoes and blend everything well.
9. Sprinkle the air fryer with oil.
10. 1cook the meal for 25 minutes at 300°F.
11. 1then blend everything well, cover with yogurt and cook for 25 minutes more.
12. 1serve hot with basil leaves.

Nutrition: Calories: 177 Fat: 5,2g Carbohydrates: 7,6g Protein: 4,9g

420. Mouthwatering chicken

Preparation time: 25 minutes
Cooking time: 20 minutes
Servings: 4

Ingredients:
- 1 lb. of chicken fillet
- ½ teaspoon of salt
- ½ teaspoon of pepper
- 3 tablespoons of oil
- 1 cup of flour
- 1 cup of breadcrumbs
- 2 eggs
- 2 tablespoons of sesame seeds
- 1 teaspoon of parsley
- ½ teaspoon of red pepper
- ½ teaspoon of paprika
- 1 teaspoon of lemon juice

Directions:
1. Cut meat in the parts.
2. Beat eggs.
3. Then rub meat with salt, pepper, sesame seeds, parsley, red pepper, paprika, lemon juice.
4. Place the piece of meat in flour, then in eggs.
5. After that blend the yummy components with breadcrumbs.
6. Sprinkle the air fryer with oil.
7. Preheat it to 350°F for 3 minutes.
8. Cook meat for 10 minutes.
9. Then shake and cook for 10 minutes.
10. 1serve the hot meal with pasta.
11. 1decorate with lemon and parsley.
12. 1enjoy with peppery chicken.

Nutrition: Calories: 168 Fat: 4,3g Carbohydrates: 7,8g Protein: 4,8g

421. Flavorsome bitter gourd

Preparation time: 25 minutes
Cooking time: 20 minutes
Servings: 4

Ingredients:
- 4 tablespoons of oil
- ½ teaspoon of pepper
- ½ teaspoon of salt
- ½ teaspoon of turmeric
- 8 oz of bitter gourd
- 4 onions
- ½ teaspoon of red chili pepper
- ½ teaspoon of onion powder
- ½ teaspoon of paprika
- 1/3 teaspoon of cumin
- 3 cloves of garlic

Directions:
1. Wash and clean the bitter gourd.
2. Cut it in the pieces.
3. Then rub them with pepper, salt, turmeric, red chili pepper, onion powder, paprika, cumin and chopped garlic.
4. Cut onions in the rings.

5. Blend everything well.
6. Sprinkle the air fryer with oil.
7. Preheat it to 350F.
8. Cook the meal for 10 minutes.
9. Then shake everything and cook for 10 minutes more.
10. 1serve hot with parsley.

Nutrition: Calories: 95 Fat: 2,1g Carbohydrates: 6,2g Protein: 1,1g

422. The piquant curry with flavorsome eggs

Preparation time: 25 minutes
Cooking time: 20 minutes
Servings: 4

Ingredients:
- 4 eggs
- ½ teaspoon of salt
- ½ teaspoon of pepper
- 3 tablespoons of oil
- 2 tablespoons of poppy seeds
- 2 tablespoons of mustard
- 1 teaspoon of red chili pepper
- ½ teaspoon of paprika
- ½ teaspoon of onion powder
- 4 cloves of garlic

Directions:
1. Beat eggs in the container.
2. Then add salt, pepper, poppy seeds, mustard, chili pepper, paprika, onion powder.
3. Blend the components of the meal.
4. Chop garlic in the pieces.
5. Then add to eggs.
6. After that grease the air fryer with oil.
7. Preheat it to 350°F.
8. Cook eggs for 10 minutes.
9. Then shake them and cook for 10 minutes.
10. 1serve hot with parsley and basil leaves.

Nutrition: Calories: 87 Fat: 2,2g Carbohydrates: 3,4g Protein: 1,6g

423. Spinach with groundnuts

Preparation time: 10 minutes
Cooking time: 15 minutes
Servings: 4

Ingredients:
- 1 tablespoon of ghee
- ½ tablespoon of red chili pepper
- ¼ tablespoon of cumin
- ½ teaspoon of salt
- ½ teaspoon of pepper
- 2 tomatoes
- 3 oz of groundnuts
- 6 oz of spinach
- 3 cloves of garlic
- ½ teaspoon of paprika
- ½ teaspoon of onion powder

Directions:
1. Wash and chop spinach in the pieces.
2. Then add red chili pepper, ghee, cumin, salt, pepper, groundnuts, garlic, paprika and onion powder.
3. Blend everything well.
4. After that chop tomatoes in the pieces.
5. Blend everything well.
6. Sprinkle the air fryer with oil.
7. Preheat it to 350°F for 3 minutes.
8. Cook the meal in the air fryer for 10 minutes.
9. Then shake well and cook for 5 minutes more.
10. 1serve hot with parsley and basil leaves.

Nutrition: Calories: 103 Fat: 2,1g Carbohydrates: 3,8g Protein: 1,1g

424. Piquant cheese in gravy

Preparation time: 15 minutes
Cooking time: 20 minutes
Servings: 4

Ingredients:
- 1 cup of breadcrumbs
- ½ teaspoon of pepper
- ½ teaspoon of salt

- 3 tablespoons of oil
- 2 tablespoons of yogurt
- ½ tablespoon of red chili pepper
- 1 tablespoon of ginger pasta
- 1 tablespoon of garlic pasta
- 1 tablespoon of honey
- 6 tomatoes
- 1 cup of cheese
- 4 tablespoons of cream
- 3 tablespoons of ketchup

Directions:
1. Slice tomatoes in the pieces.
2. Then add pepper, salt, red chili pepper, ginger pasta, honey, garlic pasta and ketchup.
3. Blend everything.
4. Sprinkle the air fryer with oil.
5. Preheat it to 360°F.
6. Then add breadcrumbs to tomatoes.
7. Blend the ingredients and cook them for 10 minutes.
8. Then add yogurt, cream and cheese.
9. Cook for 10 minutes more.
10. 1serve the hot meal.
11. 1decorate the scrumptious meal with parsley.

Nutrition: Calories: 137 Fat: 2,5g Carbohydrates: 5,2g Protein: 1,4g

425. Mutton in herbs and spices

Preparation time: 15 minutes
Cooking time: 45 minutes
Servings: 4
Ingredients:
- 1 lb. Of mutton
- 3 onions
- ½ teaspoon of pepper
- ½ teaspoon of salt
- 3 tablespoons of oil
- 2 tablespoons of ginger
- 2 tablespoons of garlic
- 6-7 tablespoons of ghee
- 4 oz of yogurt
- 1/3 teaspoon of red chili pepper
- ½ teaspoon of onion powder
- ½ teaspoon of rosemary
- 2 eggs

Directions:
1. Wash and clean meat.
2. Cut mutton in the tiny pieces.
3. Blend with pepper, salt, ginger, garlic, ghee, red chili pepper, onion powder and rosemary.
4. Beat eggs and add to meat.
5. Chop onions in the pieces and blend everything well.
6. Create cutlets.
7. Sprinkle the air fryer with oil.
8. Preheat to 350°F.
9. Cook cutlets for 25 minutes.
10. 1then cover them with yogurt.
11. 1cook for 20 minutes.
12. 1serve hot with parsley and pasta.

Nutrition: Calories: 156 Fat: 5,8g Carbohydrates: 5,6g Protein: 4,6g

426. Flavorsome and fiery aubergine

Preparation time: 15 minutes
Cooking time: 20 minutes
Servings: 4
Ingredients:
- 9 oz of aubergine
- 2 onions
- 5 cloves of garlic
- ½ teaspoon of salt
- ½ teaspoon of pepper
- 2 tablespoons of oil
- 1 tablespoon of sesame seeds
- 1 tablespoon of coriander seeds
- 1 tablespoon of cumin

- 4 tablespoons of butter
- ½ teaspoon of onion powder
- ½ teaspoon of dry herbs
- ½ teaspoon of parsley

Directions:
1. Wash and clean aubergine.
2. Then cut them in the pieces.
3. Rub vegetables with salt, pepper, garlic, sesame seeds, cumin, coriander seeds, butter, parsley, onion powder and dry herbs.
4. Chop onions in the rings.
5. Blend everything.
6. Sprinkle the air fryer with oil.
7. Preheat it for 5 minutes to 300°F.
8. Then cook the meal for 10 minutes.
9. Blend everything well and cook for 5 minutes.
10. 1serve hot with sauce.

Nutrition: Calories: 112 Fat: 3,2g Carbohydrates: 7,3g Protein: 1,2g

427. Mutton with ginger

Preparation time: 30 minutes
Cooking time: 45 minutes
Servings: 4
Ingredients:
- ½ teaspoon of salt
- ½ teaspoon of pepper
- 3 tablespoons of oil
- 1 lb. Of mutton
- 2 onions
- 2 big red peppers
- ½ teaspoon of dry herbs
- ½ teaspoon of garlic powder
- ½ teaspoon of cumin
- 1 tablespoon of lemon juice
- 1 tablespoon of ketchup
- 1 tablespoon of cream

Directions:
1. Rinse and clean mutton.
2. Then chop it in the pieces.
3. Cut onions and peppers and mix everything well.
4. Then add salt, pepper, dry herbs, garlic powder, cumin and blend everything well.
5. Sprinkle the air fryer with oil.
6. Preheat the air fryer to 300°F for 3 minutes.
7. Then place meat in the air fryer.
8. Cook for 20 minutes.
9. Then sprinkle with lemon juice, add ketchup and cream, blend everything well and cook for 25 minutes.
10. 1serve the hot mutton with parsley and basil leaves.

Nutrition: Calories: 136 Fat: 6,7g Carbohydrates: 7,1g Protein: 5,5g

428. Piquant and appetizing meat

Preparation time: 30 minutes
Cooking time: 45 minutes
Servings: 4
Ingredients:
- 1 lb. Of mutton
- ½ teaspoon of salt
- ½ teaspoon of pepper
- 5 onions
- 5 tomatoes
- 2 tablespoons of ginger
- 2 tablespoons of cumin
- ½ teaspoon of oregano
- ½ teaspoon of red chili pepper
- 1 teaspoon of paprika
- 2 tablespoons of mustard
- 2 tablespoons of lemon juice
- 1 teaspoon of garlic powder
- 2 tablespoons of oil

Directions:
1. Slice meat in the pieces.
2. Rub with salt, pepper, ginger, garlic, cumin, oregano, red chili pepper, paprika, mustard, lemon juice.

3. Grease the air fryer with oil.
4. Preheat the air fryer to 320°F for 2-3 minutes.
5. Cook meat for 25 minutes.
6. Then blend everything.
7. Cut onions and tomatoes in the pieces.
8. Add them later to mutton.
9. Blend the components.
10. 1cook for 20 minutes.
11. 1serve hot with vegetables and parsley.

Nutrition: Calories: 145 Fat: 6,8g Carbohydrates: 7,2g Protein: 5,9g

429.   Quinoa and spinach cakes
Preparation time: 5 minutes
Cooking time: 8 minutes
Servings:4

Ingredients:
- 2 c. Cooked quinoa
- 1 c. Chopped baby spinach
- 1 egg
- 2 tbsps. Minced parsley
- 1 teaspoon minced garlic
- 1 carrot, peeled and shredded
- 1 chopped onion
- ¼ c. Oat milk
- ¼ c. Parmesan cheese, grated
- 1 c. Breadcrumbs
- Sea salt
- Ground black

Directions:
1. In a mixing bowl, mix all ingredients. Season with salt and pepper to taste.
2. Preheat your air fryer to 390°F.
3. Scoop ¼ cup of quinoa and spinach mixture and place in the air fryer cooking basket. Cook in batches until browned for about 8 minutes.
4. Serve and enjoy!

Nutrition: calories 188 fat 4 g carbs 32g protein 1g.

430.   Spinach in cheese envelopes
Preparation time: 5 minutes
Cooking time: 12 minutes
Servings: 8

Ingredients:
- 1½ c. Almond flour
- 3 egg yolks
- 2 eggs
- ½ c. Cheddar cheese
- 2 c. Steamed spinach
- ¼ teaspoon salt
- ½ teaspoon pepper
- 3 c. Cream cheese
- ¼ c. Chopped onion

Directions:
1. Place cream cheese in a mixing bowl then whisks until soft and fluffy.
2. Add egg yolks to the mixing bowl then continue whisking until incorporated.
3. Stir in coconut flour to the cheese mixture then mix until becoming a soft dough.
4. Place the dough on a flat surface then roll until thin.
5. Cut the thin dough into 8 squares then keep.
6. Crash the eggs then place in a bowl.
7. Season with salt, pepper, and grated cheese, then mix well.
8. Add chopped spinach and onion to the egg mixture, then stir until combined.
9. Put spinach filling on a square dough then fold until becoming an envelope. Repeat with the remaining spinach filling and dough. Glue with water.
10. 1 preheat an air fryer to 425°F (218°C)
11. 1 arrange the spinach envelopes in the air fryer then cook for 12 minutes or until lightly golden brown.
12. 1 remove from the air fryer then serve warm. Enjoy!

Nutrition: calories 365 fat 36g protein 14g carbs 4g

431.   Chili roasted eggplant soba
Basic recipe

Preparation time: 10 minutes
Cooking time: 15 minutes
Servings: 4

Ingredients:
- 200g eggplants
- Kosher salt
- Ground black pepper
- Noodles:
- 8 oz. Soba noodles
- 1 c. Sliced button mushrooms
- 2 tbsps. Peanut oil
- 2 tbsps. Light soy sauce
- 1 tablespoon rice vinegar
- 2 tbsps. Chopped cilantro
- 2 chopped red chili pepper
- 1 teaspoon sesame oil

Directions:
1. In a mixing bowl, mix together ingredients for the marinade.
2. Wash eggplants and then slice into ¼-inch thick cuts. Season with salt and pepper, to taste.
3. Preheat your air fryer to 390°F.
4. Place eggplants in the air fryer cooking basket. Cook for 10 minutes.
5. Meanwhile, cook the soba noodles according to packaging directions. Drain the noodles.
6. In a large mixing bowl, combine the peanut oil, soy sauce, rice vinegar, cilantro, chili, and sesame oil. Mix well.
7. Add the cooked soba noodles, mushrooms, and roasted eggplants; toss to coat.
8. Transfer mixture into the air fryer cooking basket. Cook for another 5 minutes.
9. Serve and enjoy!

Nutrition: calories 318 fat 2g carbs 54g protein 13g.

432.   Fettuccini with roasted vegetables in tomato sauce
Preparation time: 10 minutes
Cooking time: 25 minutes
Servings: 4

Ingredients:
- 10 oz. Spaghetti, cooked
- 1 eggplant, chopped
- 1 chopped bell pepper
- 1 zucchini, chopped
- 4 oz. Halved grape tomatoes
- 1 teaspoon minced garlic
- 4 tbsps. Divided olive oil
- Kosher salt
- Ground black pepper
- 12 oz. Can diced tomatoes
- ½ teaspoon dried basil
- ½ teaspoon dried oregano
- 1 teaspoon Spanish paprika
- 1 teaspoon brown sugar

Directions:
1. In a mixing bowl, combine together eggplant, red bell pepper, zucchini, grape tomatoes, garlic, and 2 tablespoons olive oil. Add some salt and pepper, to taste.
2. Preheat your air fryer to 390°F.
3. Place vegetable mixture in the air fryer cooking basket and cook for about 10-12 minutes, or until vegetables are tender. Meanwhile, you can start preparing the tomato sauce.
4. In a saucepan, heat remaining 2 tablespoons olive oil. Stir fry garlic for 2 minutes. Add diced tomatoes and simmer for 3 minutes.
5. Stir in basil, oregano, paprika, and brown sugar. Season with salt and pepper, to taste. Let it cook for another 5-7 minutes. Once cooked, transfer the vegetables from air fryer to a mixing bowl.
6. Add the cooked spaghetti and prepared a sauce. Toss to combine well.
7. Divide among 4 serving plates.
8. Serve and enjoy!

Nutrition: calories 330 fat 14g carbs 43g protein 9g.

433. Tofu with peanut dipping sauce

Preparation time: 5 minutes
Cooking time: 8 minutes
Servings: 6

Ingredients:

- 16 oz. Cubed firm tofu
- 185g all-purpose flour
- ½ teaspoon Himalayan salt
- ½ teaspoon ground black pepper
- Olive oil spray
- For the dipping sauce:
- 1/3 c. Smooth low-sodium peanut butter
- 1 teaspoon minced garlic
- 2 tbsps. Light soy sauce
- 1 tablespoon fresh lime juice
- 1 teaspoon brown sugar
- 1/3 c. Water
- 2 tbsps. Chopped roasted

Directions:

1. In a bowl, mix all dipping sauce ingredients. Cover it with plastic wrap and keep refrigerated until ready to serve.
2. To make the fried tofu, season all-purpose flour with salt and pepper.
3. Coat the tofu cubes with the flour mixture. Spray with oil.
4. Preheat your air fryer to 390°F.
5. Place coated tofu in the cooking basket. Careful not to overcrowd them.
6. Cook until browned for approximately 8 minutes.
7. Serve with prepared peanut dipping sauce.
8. Enjoy!

Nutrition: calories 256 fat 11g carbs 22g protein 14 g.

434. Brown rice, spinach and tofu frittata

Preparation time: 5 minutes
Cooking time:55 minutes
Servings: 4

Ingredients:

- ½ cup baby spinach, chopped
- ½ cup kale, chopped
- ½ onion, chopped
- ½ teaspoon turmeric
- 1 ¾ cups brown rice, cooked
- 1 flax egg (1 tablespoon flaxseed meal + 3 tablespoon cold water1 package firm tofu
- 1 tablespoon olive oil
- 1 yellow pepper, chopped
- 2 tablespoons soy sauce
- 2 teaspoons arrowroot powder
- 2 teaspoons Dijon mustard
- 2/3 cup almond milk
- 3 big mushrooms, chopped
- 3 tablespoons nutritional yeast
- 4 cloves garlic, crushed
- 4 spring onions, chopped
- A handful of basil leaves, chopped

Directions:

1. Preheat the air fryer oven to 375°F. Grease pan that will fit inside the air fryer oven.
2. Prepare the frittata crust by mixing the brown rice and flax egg. Press the rice onto the baking dish until you form a crust. Brush with a little oil and cook for 10 minutes.
3. Meanwhile, heat olive oil in a skillet over medium flame and sauté the garlic and onions for 2 minutes.
4. Add the pepper and mushroom and continue stirring for 3 minutes.
5. Stir in the kale, spinach, spring onions, and basil. Remove from the pan and set aside.
6. In a food processor, pulse together the tofu, mustard, turmeric, soy sauce, nutritional yeast, vegan milk and arrowroot powder. Pour in a mixing bowl and stir in the sautéed vegetables.
7. Pour the vegan frittata mixture over the rice crust and cook in the air fryer oven for 40 minutes.

Nutrition: calories 226 fat 05g protein 16g

435. Coconut curry vegetable rice bowls

Preparation time: 5 minutes
Cooking time: 40minutes
Servings: 6

Ingredients:

- 2/3 cup uncooked brown rice
- 1 tsp. Curry powder
- 3/4 tsp. Salt divided
- 1 cup chopped green onion
- 1 cup sliced red bell pepper
- 1 tbsp. Grated ginger
- 1 1/2 tbsp. Sugar
- 1 cup matchstick carrots
- 1 cup chopped red cabbage
- 8 oz. Sliced water chestnuts
- 15 oz. No salt added chickpeas
- 13 oz. Coconut milk

Directions:

1. Add rice, water, curry powder, and 1/4 tsp. Of the salt in the instant pot. Pressure cook for 15 minutes. Sauté for 2 minutes and serve.

Nutrition: calories 1530 fat 110g carbs 250g protein 80g

436. Shrimp and corn

Preparation time: 10 minutes
Cooking time: 10 minutes
Servings: 2

Ingredients:

- 1½ pounds shrimp, peeled and deveined
- 2 cups corn
- A drizzle of olive oil
- ¼ cup chicken stock
- 1 tablespoon old bay seasoning
- Salt and black pepper to taste
- 1 teaspoon red pepper flakes, crushed
- 2 sweet onions, cut into wedges
- 8 garlic cloves, crushed

Directions:

1. Grease a pan that fits your air fryer with the oil.
2. Add all other ingredients to the oiled pan and toss well.
3. Place the pan in the fryer and cook at 390 °F for 10 minutes.
4. Divide everything into bowls and serve.

Nutrition: calories 261 fat 7 fiber 6 carbs 17 protein 11

437. Mussels bowls

Preparation time: 5 minutes
Cooking time: 12 minutes
Servings: 2

Ingredients:

- 2 pounds mussels, scrubbed
- 12 ounces black beer
- 1 tablespoon olive oil
- 1 yellow onion, chopped
- 8 ounces spicy sausage, chopped
- 1 tablespoon paprika

Directions:

1. Combine all the ingredients in a pan that fits your air fryer.
2. Place the pan in the air fryer and cook at 400 °F for 12 minutes.
3. Divide the mussels into bowls, serve, and enjoy!

Nutrition: calories 201 fat 6 fiber 7 carbs 17 protein 7

438. Fall-off-the-bone chicken

Preparation time: 10 minutes
Cooking time: 1hour and 10 minutes
Servings: 4

Ingredients:

- 1 tbsp. Packed brown sugar
- 1 tbsp. Chili powder
- 1 tbsp. Smoked paprika
- 1 tsp. Chopped thyme leaves
- ¼ tbsp. Kosher salt
- ¼ tbsp. Black pepper
- 1 whole small chicken

- 1 tbsp. Extra-virgin olive oil
- 2/3 c. Low-sodium chicken broth
- 2 tbsp. Chopped parsley

Directions:
1. Coat chicken with brown sugar, chili powder, sugar, pepper, paprika, and thyme.
2. Sauté chicken in oil for 3-4 minutes
3. Pour broth in the pot.
4. Pressure cook on high for 25 minutes
5. Garnish sliced chicken with parsley and serve.

Nutrition: calories 1212 fat 10g carbs 31g protein 15g

439. White chicken chili

Preparation time: 5 minutes
Cooking time: 30 minutes
Servings: 6

Ingredients:

- 1 tbsp. Vegetable oil
- 1 red bell pepper, diced
- .15 oz. Condensed cream of chicken soup
- 5 tbsp. Shredded cheddar cheese
- 2 green onions, sliced
- 1 cup kernel corn
- 1 tbsp. Chili powder
- 6 oz. (2boneless, skinless chicken breast)
- 15 oz. White cannellini beans
- 1 cup chunky salsa

Directions:
1. Sauté pepper, corn, and chili powder in oil for 2 minutes
2. Season chicken with salt and pepper.
3. Layer the beans, salsa, water, chicken, and soup over the corn mixture.
4. Pressure cook on high for 4 minutes
5. Shred chicken and return to pot.
6. Serve topped with cheese and green onions.

Nutrition: calories 1848 fat 70g carbs 204g protein 90g

440. Saffron shrimp mix

Preparation time: 10 minutes
Cooking time: 8 minutes
Servings: 2

Ingredients:

- 20 shrimp, peeled and deveined
- 2 tablespoons butter, melted
- Salt and black pepper to taste
- ¼ cup parsley, chopped
- ½ teaspoon saffron powder
- Juice of 1 lemon
- 4 garlic cloves, minced

Directions:
1. In a pan that fits your air fryer, mix the shrimp with all the other ingredients; toss well.
2. Place the pan in the fryer and cook at 380 °F for 8 minutes.
3. Divide between plates and serve hot.

Nutrition: calories 261 fat 7 fiber 9 carbs 16 protein 7

441. Beef Wellington

Preparation Time: 2 hours
Cooking Time: 35 minutes
Servings: 4

Ingredients:

- Homemade Chicken Liver Pate
- Homemade Short crust Pastry
- Beef Fillet
- 1 Medium Beaton Egg
- Salt & Pepper

Directions:
1. Bring out beef fillet, give it a clean, cut off any visible fat, season with salt and pepper and then seal it with the riotous film and surrounding area in the fridge for an hour.
2. Make your own batch of liver hen pate and self-made short crust pastry.
3. Roll out your short crust pastry and use a pastry brush with an egg whipped around the edges to make it sticky to seal.

4. Eliminate the cling film from the meat and put the meat in the center above the petite and push it slightly down.
5. Seal the pastry between the meat and the pate.
6. Score the crest of the pastry so that the meat is at risk of being inhaled.
7. Place the air fryer in the air fryer on the grill pan and prepare dinner at 160°C / 320°F for 35 minutes.
8. Rest for a few minutes, slice and serve with roasted potatoes.

Nutrition: Calories: 354 Fat: 22g Carbs: 12g Protein: 25g

442. Easy Air Fryer Pepperoni Pizza

Preparation Time: 15 minutes
Cooking Time: 15 minutes
Servings: 1
Ingredients:

- 1 Full Wheat
- Pizza 2 Tablespoon Pizza Sauce or Marinara If you don't like a thick sauce, you can make 1 tablespoon
- 1/8 cup mozzarella cheese, sliced
- 1/8 cup cheddar cheese, chopped if You decide only mozzarella cheese, pass over and use ¼ cup mozzarella
- slices pepperoni
- olive oil spray
- 1 tablespoon chopped parsley, optionally for pizza garnish

Directions:
1. Drizzle sauce on top of pita bread, then load pepperoni and chopped cheese on top.
2. Spray the pizza peel with olive oil spray.
3. Keep in an air fryer for eight minutes at 400 °F. Check on the pizza at the 6-7-minute mark to make sure it is not to your liking.
4. Remove pizza from the air fryer. Refrigerate before serving.
5. Crispy Crust Instructions For an extra-crisp crust, spray one side of the beaten bread with olive oil. Place in an air fryer for four minutes. This will allow one side to fully crisp.
6. Remove the beaten bread from the air fryer. Turn the pyre on the side which is less crisp. This should be the aspect that was the face-down in the air fryer.
7. Drizzle all over the chutney, then load pepperoni and chopped cheese on top.
8. Put the pizza again in the air fryer for 3-4 minutes until the cheese has melted. Use your judgment. You want to allow the pizza to cook for a few more minutes to reach its desired texture.
9. Remove pizza from the air fryer. Cool before serving.

Nutrition: Calories: 240 Fat: 11g Carbs: 30g Protein: 4g

443. Tofu with Sticky Orange Sauce

Preparation Time: 15 minutes
Cooking Time: 20 minutes
Servings:
Ingredients:

- 1-pound extra-firm tofu drained and pressed (or use super firm tofu)
- 1 teaspoon tamari
- 1 teaspoon cornstarch, (or arrowroot powder)

For sauce:

- 1 teaspoon orange zest
- 1/3 cup oranges juice
- 1/2 cup water
- 2 tablespoons cornstarch (or arrowroot powder)
- 1/4 teaspoon ground pepper flakes
- 1 teaspoon fresh ginger, minced
- 1 tablespoon garlic, minced
- 1 teaspoon pure maple syrup

Directions:
1. Cut tofu into dices.
2. Put tofu in a Ziploc bag. Add tamarind and seal the bag. Stir the bag until all the tofu is covered with tamarind.
3. Add a tablespoon of cornstarch to the bag. Stir again until the tofu is coated. Set the tofu aside for at least 15 minutes to marinate.
4. Meanwhile, add all the sauce elements to a small bowl and mix with a spoon.
5. Place the tofu in an air fryer. You in all probability want to do this in two batches.

6   Cook the tofu in 390°F steps for 10 minutes, adding it for 10 minutes.

7   After you finish cooking the batches of tofu, add it all to a pan on medium-high heat. Give the sauce a stir and pour over the tofu.

8   Mix tofu and sauce until it thickens, and the tofu becomes hot.

9   Serve directly with rice and boiled vegetables if desired.

Nutrition: Calories: 190 Fat: 3g Carbs: 16g Protein: 10g

444.   Bourbon Burger

Preparation Time: 20 minutes
Cooking Time: 30 minutes
Servings: 4
Ingredients:

- 1 tbsp bourbon
- 2 tablespoons brown sugar
- strips maple bacon reduced in half
- ¾ pound ground red meat 80% lean
- 1 tbsp minced onion
- 2 tbsp BBQ sauce
- 1/2 teaspoon salt
- freshly ground Black Pepper
- 2 Slices Colby Jack Cheese or Monterey Jack
- 2 Caesar Roll
- Salad and Tomato

Serve Zesty Burger Sauce:

- 2 tablespoons BBQ Sauce
- 2 tablespoons mayonnaise
- ¼ teaspoon ground Capsicum
- Fresh ground pepper

Directions:

1   Preheat the air fryer to 390F and pour a little water into the bottom of the air fryer.

2   Combine bourbon and brown sugar in a small bowl. Add the bacon strips in an air fryer basket and brush with brown sugar mixture. Air-fry at 390F for 4 minutes. Flip the bacon over, brushing with additional brown sugar and air-fry at 390° F for an additional 4 minutes until crispy.

3   While the bacon is cooking, make burger patties. In a large bowl combine ground beef, onion, BBQ sauce, salt, and pepper. Combine with your palms collectively and shape the meat into 2 patties.

4   Transfer the burger fryers to the air fryer basket and fry the burger for 15 to 20 minutes at 370°F for, depending on how you cook your burger (15 minutes for rare to medium-rare; well done 20 minutes). Flip the burger in the middle of the cooking process.

5   While the burger is air-frying, make the burger sauce by combining BBQ sauce, mayonnaise, paprika and freshly ground black pepper to style in a bowl.

6   When the burger is cooked to your liking, serve each patty with slices of Colby Jack cheese and air-fry for an additional minute, just to melt the cheese.

7   Spread the sauce inside the Kaiser Roll, place the burger on the rollers, top with bourbon bacon. , Enjoy salad and tomatoes!

Nutrition: Calories: 358 Fat: 11g Carbs: 37g Protein: 22g

445.   Fried Green Tomato

Preparation Time: 10 minutes
Cooking Time: 10 minutes
Servings: 4
Ingredients:

- 2 green tomatoes, (3 if they are small)
- salt and pepper
- 1/2 cup all-purpose flour
- 2 huge eggs
- 1/2 cup buttermilk
- 1 cup panko pieces
- 1 cup yellow cornmeal
- Olive Hua oil or vegetable oil

Directions:

1   Cut tomatoes into 1/4-inch slices. Dry with paper towels and season with salt and pepper.

2   Place the dough in a shallow dish or pie plate or use a paper plate for easy cleaning.

3   Collect eggs and buttermilk collectively in a shallow dish or bowl.

4   Mix poncho crumbs and cornmeal in a shallow dish or pie plate or use a paper plate for easy cleaning.

5   Preheat the air fryer to 400 °F.

6   Coat the tomato slices in the dough, dip in the egg mixture, and then press the Panko Crumb combination on each side. Sprinkle a little extra salt on them.

7   Smudge air fryer basket with oil and four tomato slices in the basket. Mist topped with oil. Air-fry for 5 minutes.

8   Flip the tomatoes, mist with oil and fry for more than 3 minutes.

9   Serve with Comeback Sauce if desired.

Nutrition: Calories: 194 Fat: 15g Carbs: 6g Protein: 4g

446.   Crispy Sweet Potato Tots

Preparation Time: 15 minutes
Cooking Time: 30 minutes
Servings: 4
Ingredients:

- 2 cups sweet potato puree
- 1/2 teaspoon salt
- 1/2 teaspoon cumin
- 1/2 teaspoon coriander
- 1/2 cup Panko breadcrumbs or regular breadcrumb

Directions:

1   Set air fryer to 390 ° F / 200 °C.

2   In a large bowl, mix all ingredients together.

3   Form into 1 tbsp of a toddler (a cookie scoop helps) and arrange on 1-2 plates.

4   Spray with spray oil and pass the rounds to coat the bottles with oil.

5   Carefully arrange the toddlers on the air fryer basket so that there is an area between them.

6   Cook for 6 to 7 minutes, and carefully flip them over. If the toes feel very soft and comfortable when you flip them, leave them for a few more minutes.

7   Cook for 5-7 additional minutes, until each leaf, is crisp but no longer burning.

8   Serve without delay with guacamole, ketchup or chipotle mayo pot

9   Arrange on a baking sheet. Freeze for several hours until frozen through the kits, then switch to a mass freezer bag and drain away with as much air as possible.

10   To cook dinner with frozen: warm air fryer at 390 ° F / 200 ° C.

11   Spray toddlers with spray oil to coat all sides.

12   Carefully prepare toddlers on the air fryer basket. Cook for 9 to 10 minutes, and carefully flip them over.

13   Cook for about 5 more minutes, until each aspect is crispy.

14   Serve now with ketchup, guacamole, or chipotle mayo.

15   To bake in the oven (for frozen or melted tots). Spray the baking pan with oil and prepare the. Spray children with oil.

16   Bake at 425 ° F for 20 minutes.

17   Boil them for 3-5 minutes to get crisp. Don't use parchment paper under the broiler anymore.

18   Allow cooling slightly earlier than disposing of baking sheets as they may additionally stick when heated.

Nutrition: Calories: 140 Fat: 5g Carbs: 23g Protein: 1g

447.   Baked Thai Peanut Chicken Egg Roll

Preparation Time: 15 minutes
Cooking Time: 35 minutes
Servings: 4
Ingredients:

- Egg Roll Wrappers
- 2c. Rotisserie poultry sliced
- 1/4 c. Thai Peanut Sauce
- 1 Medium Carrot Very Finely Sliced or Ribbon
- Naive Onion Sliced
- 1/4 Crimson Bell Pepper Julienned
- Non-stick Cooking Spray or Sesame Oil

Directions:

1   Preheat Air fryer 390° F or 425 ° F from the oven.

2   In a small bowl, toss poultry with Thai peanut sauce.

3   Lay the egg roll wrapper on an easy dry surface. Arrange 1/4 of carrots, bell peppers, and onions on top of the backside 1/3 of

the egg roll wrapper. Spoon half a cup of chicken mixture over the vegetables.

4   Moisten the outer edges of the cover with water. Fold the edges of the casing towards the core and roll tightly.

5   Repeat with the ultimate wrapper. (Keep the last wrapper included with a damp paper towel until ready for use.)

6   Spray the assembled egg rolls with non-stick cooking spray. Flip them over and spray the backside as well.

7   Place the egg rolls in the air fryer and bake them for 6-8 minutes at 390 °F or until they are crisp and golden brown.

8   (If you are baking an egg roll in an oven, lay the seam aspect down on the baking sheet with the cooking spray. Bake at 425°F for 15-20 minutes.)

9   Slice in half and dip. Serve with extra Thai peanut sauce for.

Nutrition: Calories: 237 Fat: 7g Carbs: 22g Protein: 22g

448.   Blue cheeseburgers

Preparation time: 10 minutes
Cooking time: 20 minutes
Servings 4
Ingredients
- Olive oil
- 1-pound lean ground beef
- ½ cup blue cheese, crumbled
- 1 teaspoon Worcestershire sauce
- ½ teaspoon freshly ground black pepper
- ½ teaspoon hot sauce
- ½ teaspoon minced garlic
- ¼ teaspoon salt
- 4 whole-wheat buns

Instructions
1. Spray a fryer basket lightly with olive oil.
2. In a large bowl, mix together the beef, blue cheese, Worcestershire sauce, pepper, hot sauce, garlic, and salt.
3. Form the mixture into 4 patties.
4. Place the patties in the fryer basket in a single layer, leaving a little room between them for even cooking.
5. Air fry for 10 minutes. Flip over and cook until the meat reaches an internal temperature of at least 160°f, an additional 7 to 10 minutes.
6. Place each patty on a bun and serve with low-calorie toppings like sliced tomatoes or onions.

Nutrition: Calories: 373; total fat: 14g; saturated fat: 7g; cholesterol: 78mg; carbohydrates: 25g; protein: 34g; fiber: 4g; sodium: 657mg

449.   Cheeseburger-stuffed bell peppers

Preparation time: 15 minutes
Cooking time: 20 minutes
Servings 4 / 360°F
Ingredients
- Olive oil
- 4 large red bell peppers
- 1-pound lean ground beef
- 1 cup diced onion
- Salt
- Freshly ground black pepper
- 1 cup cooked brown rice
- ½ cup shredded reduced-fat cheddar cheese
- ½ cup tomato sauce
- 2 tablespoons dill pickle relish
- 2 tablespoons ketchup
- 1 tablespoon Worcestershire sauce
- 1 tablespoon mustard
- ½ cup shredded lettuce
- ½ cup diced tomatoes

Instructions
1. Spray a fryer basket lightly with olive oil.
2. Cut about ½ inch off the tops of the peppers. Remove any seeds from the insides. Set aside.
3. In a large skillet over medium-high heat, cook the ground beef and onion until browned, about 5 minutes. Season with salt and pepper.

4. In a large bowl, mix together the ground beef mixture, rice, cheddar cheese, tomato sauce, relish, ketchup, Worcestershire sauce, and mustard.
5. Spoon the meat and rice mixture equally into the peppers.
6. Place the stuffed peppers into the fryer basket. Air fry until golden brown on top, 10 to 15 minutes.
7. Top each pepper with the shredded lettuce and diced tomatoes and serve.

Nutrition: Calories: 366; total fat: 11g; saturated fat: 5g; cholesterol: 75mg; carbohydrates: 33g; protein: 32g; fiber: 6g; sodium: 612mg

450.   Steak and veggie kebabs

Preparation Time: 2 Hours
Cooking Time: 15 Minutes
Servings 4
Ingredients
- ½ cup soy sauce
- 3 tablespoons lemon juice
- 2 tablespoons Worcestershire sauce
- 2 tablespoons Dijon mustard
- 1 teaspoon minced garlic
- ¾ teaspoon freshly ground black pepper
- 1-pound sirloin steak, cut into 1-inch cubes
- 1 medium red bell pepper, cut into big chunks
- 1 medium green bell pepper, cut into big chunks
- 1 medium red onion, cut into big chunks
- Olive oil

Directions
1. In a small bowl, whisk together the soy sauce, lemon juice, Worcestershire sauce, Dijon mustard, garlic, and black pepper. Divide the marinade equally between two large zip-top plastic bags.
2. Place the steak in one of the bags, seal, and refrigerate for at least 2 hours. Place the vegetables in the other bag, seal, and refrigerate for 1 hour.
3. If using wooden skewers, soak the skewers in water for at least 30 minutes.
4. Spray a fryer basket lightly with olive oil.
5. Thread the steak and veggies alternately onto the skewers.
6. Place the skewers in the fryer basket in a single layer. You may need to cook the skewers in batches.
7. Air fry for 8 minutes. Flip the skewers over, lightly spray with olive oil, and cook until the steak reaches your desired level of doneness, an additional 4 to 7 minutes. The internal temperature should read 125°F for rare, 135°F for medium rare, 145°F for medium and 150°F for medium well.

Nutrition: Calories: 271; total fat: 7g; saturated fat: 3g; cholesterol: 65mg; carbohydrates: 12g; protein: 38g; fiber: 2g; sodium: 2,147mg

451.   Korean BBQ beef bowls

Preparation Time: 2 Hours
Cooking Time: 25 Minutes
Servings 4
Ingredients
- ½ cup soy sauce
- 2 tablespoons brown sugar
- 2 tablespoons red wine vinegar or rice vinegar
- 1 tablespoon olive oil, plus more for spraying
- 1 tablespoon sesame oil
- 1-pound flank steak, sliced very thin against the grain
- 2 teaspoons cornstarch
- 2 cups cooked brown rice
- 2 cups steamed broccoli florets

Directions
1. In a large bowl, whisk together the soy sauce, brown sugar, vinegar, olive oil, and sesame oil. Add the steak, cover with plastic wrap, and refrigerate for at least 30 minutes or up to 2 hours.
2. Spray a fryer basket lightly with olive oil.
3. Remove as much marinade as possible from the steak. Reserve any leftover marinade.
4. Place the steak in the fryer basket in a single layer. You may need to cook the steak in batches.
5. Air fry for 10 minutes. Flip the steak over and cook until the steak reaches your desired level of doneness, an additional 7 to

10 minutes. The internal temperature should read 125°f for rare, 135°f for medium rare, 145°f for medium, and 150°f for medium well. Transfer the steak to a large bowl and set aside.

6. While the steak is cooking, in a small saucepan over medium-high heat, bring the remaining marinade to a boil.

7. In a small bowl, combine the cornstarch and 1 tablespoon of water to create a slurry. Add the slurry to the marinade, lower the heat to medium-low, and simmer, stirring, until the sauce starts to thicken, a few seconds to 1 minute.

8. Pour the sauce over the steak and stir to combine.

9. To assemble the bowls, spoon ½ cup brown rice and ½ cup of broccoli into each of four bowls and top with the steak.

Nutrition: Calories: 399; total fat: 15g; saturated fat: 1g; cholesterol: 45mg; carbohydrates: 36g; protein: 29g; fiber: 3g; sodium: 1,875mg

452. Beef roll-ups
Preparation time: 30 minutes, plus 30 minutes to marinate
Cooking time: 20 minutes
Servings 4
Ingredients
- 1½ pounds sirloin steak, cut into slices
- 2 tablespoons Worcestershire sauce
- ½ tablespoon garlic powder
- ½ tablespoon onion powder
- 2 medium bell peppers of any color, cut into thin strips
- ½ cup shredded mozzarella cheese
- Salt
- Freshly ground black pepper
- Olive oil

Directions
1. Using a meat mallet, pound the steaks very thin.
2. In a small bowl, combine the Worcestershire sauce, garlic powder, and onion powder to make a marinade.
3. Place the steaks and marinade in a large zip-top plastic bag, seal, and refrigerate for at least 30 minutes.
4. Soak 8 toothpicks in water for 15 to 20 minutes.
5. Place ¼ of the bell peppers and ¼ of the mozzarella cheese in the center of each steak. Season with salt and black pepper. Roll each steak up tightly and secure with 2 toothpicks.
6. Spray a fryer basket lightly with olive oil. Place the beef roll-ups in the fryer basket, toothpick side down, in a single layer. You may need to cook the roll-ups in batches.
7. Air fry for 10 minutes. Flip the steaks over and cook until the meat reaches an internal temperature of at least 150°f, an additional 7 to 10 minutes.
8. Let the roll-ups rest for 10 minutes before serving.

Nutrition: Calories: 378; total fat: 13g; saturated fat: 6g; cholesterol: 106mg; carbohydrates: 7g; protein: 56g; fiber: 1g; sodium: 297mg

453. Pork and apple skewers
Preparation Time: 15 Minutes
Cooking Time: 20 Minutes
Servings 4
Ingredients:
For the glaze
- ½ cup sugar-free apricot preserves
- tablespoons lemon juice
- 2 tablespoons Dijon mustard
- 2 teaspoons dried rosemary
- 1 teaspoon lemon zest
For the kebabs
- Olive oil
- 2 gala apples
- 1-pound pork tenderloin, cut into 1-inch pieces
- Salt
- Freshly ground black pepper

Directions:
1. In a small bowl, whisk together the apricot preserves, lemon juice, Dijon mustard, rosemary, and lemon zest. Set aside.
2. Spray a fryer basket lightly with olive oil.
3. Get the apple, remove core and slice into wedges

4. Cut each wedge of apple in half crosswise into chunks.
5. Rinse wooden skewers in water for at least 30 minutes before using.
6. Thread the pork and apples alternately onto the skewers. Spray lightly all over with olive oil and season with salt and pepper.
7. Place the skewers in the fryer basket in a single layer. You may need to cook the skewers in batches.
8. Air fry for 10 minutes. Generously brush the glaze onto the skewers.
9. Increase the temperature to 370°F and air fry for 5 minutes. Flip the skewers over, baste again with the glaze, and cook until the pork reaches an internal temperature of at least 145°F, an additional 3 to 5 minutes.

Nutrition: Calories: 200; total fat: 3g; saturated fat: 1g; cholesterol: 45mg; carbohydrates: 25g; protein: 24g; fiber: 3g; sodium: 254mg

454. Mesquite pork medallions
Preparation time: 10 minutes
Cooking time: 20 minutes
Servings 1
Ingredients
- 1 teaspoons olive oil, plus more for spraying
- 1-pound boneless pork tenderloin
- 2 tablespoons mesquite seasoning
- Spray a fryer basket lightly with olive oil.

Directions
1. Spray a fryer basket lightly with olive oil.
2. Dry the pork with a paper towel. Cut it into 10 (1/2-inch) medallions.
3. Put the pork with the mesquite seasoning and coat with the olive oil.
4. Place the pork in the fryer basket in a single layer, leaving room between each medallion. You may need to cook them in batches.
5. Air fry for 10 minutes. Flip the pork over and lightly spray with olive oil.

Nutrition: Calories: 124; total fat: 4g; saturated fat: 1g; cholesterol: 36mg; carbohydrates: 3g; protein: 19g; fiber: 0g; sodium: 206mg

455. Pork and ginger meatball bowl
Preparation time: 15 minutes
Cooking time: 15 minutes
Servings 4
Ingredients
- Olive oil
- 2 pounds lean ground pork
- 2 eggs, beaten
- 1 cup whole-wheat panko breadcrumbs
- 1 green onion, thinly sliced
- 2 teaspoons soy sauce
- 2 teaspoons minced garlic
- ½ teaspoon ground ginger
- 2 cups cooked rice noodles (cooked according to package directions
- 1 cup peeled and shredded carrots
- 1 cup peeled and thinly sliced cucumber
- 1 cup light Asian sesame dressing

Directions
1. Spray a fryer basket lightly with olive oil.
2. In a large bowl, mix together the pork, eggs, breadcrumbs, green onion, soy sauce, garlic, and ginger.
3. Using a small cookie scoop, form 24 meatballs.
4. Place the meatballs in a single layer in the fryer basket. Lightly spray meatballs with olive oil. You may need to cook the meatballs in batches.
5. Air fry until the meatballs reach an internal temperature of at least 145°F, 10 to 15 minutes, shaking the basket every 5 minutes for even cooking.
6. To assemble the bowls, place ½ cup rice noodles, ¼ cup carrots, and ¼ cup cucumber in 4 bowls. Drizzle each bowl with ¼ cup sesame dressing and top with 6 meatballs.

Nutrition: Calories: 642; total fat: 21g; saturated fat: 5g; cholesterol: 213mg; carbohydrates: 59g; protein: 56g; fiber: 5g; sodium: 1,304m

456. Coated avocado tacos

Preparation time: 10 minutes
Cooking time: 20 minutes
Servings: 12
Ingredients:

- 1 avocado
- Tortillas and toppings
- ½ cup panko breadcrumbs
- 1 egg
- Salt

Directions:
1. Scoop out the meat from each avocado shell and slice them into wedges.
2. Beat the egg in a shallow bowl and put the breadcrumbs in another bowl.
3. Dip the avocado wedges in the beaten egg and coat with breadcrumbs. Sprinkle them with a bit of salt. Arrange them in the cooking basket in a single layer.
4. Cook for 15 minutes at 392°F. Shake the basket halfway through the cooking process.
5. Put the cooked avocado wedges in tortillas and add your preferred toppings.

Nutrition: Calories: 179 fat: 07g Carbs: 229g protein: 94g

457. Roasted corn with butter and lime

Preparation time: 2 minutes
Cooking time: 20 minutes
Servings: 4

Ingredients:

- 4 corns
- ½ tsp. Pepper
- 1 tsp. Lime juice
- 1 tbsp. Chopped parsley
- 1 tbsp. Butter
- ¼ tsp. Salt

Directions:
1. Preheat air fryer to a temperature of 400°F.
2. Remove husk and transfer corns into air fryer and cook for 20 minutes.
3. After every 5 minutes shake the fryer basket.
4. When done rub butter. Sprinkle parsley, pepper, and salt. Drizzle lime juice on top. Serve!

Nutrition: Calories: 114 protein: 4 g fat: 26 g carbs: 124 g

458. Batter-fried scallions

Preparation time: 5 minutes
Cooking time: 5 minutes
Servings: 4
Ingredients:

- Trimmed scallion bunches,
- White wine, 1 cup
- Salt, 1 tsp.
- Flour, 1 cup
- Black pepper, 1 tsp.

Directions:
1. Set the air fryer to heat up to 3900f. Using a bowl, add and mix the white wine, flour and stir until it gets smooth. Add the salt, the black pepper and mix again. Dip each scallion into the flour mixture until it is properly covered and remove any excess batter. Grease your air fryer basket with nonstick cooking spray and add the scallions. At this point, you may need to work in batches.
2. Leave the scallions to cook for 5 minutes or until it has a golden-brown color and crispy texture, while still shaking it after every 2 minutes. Carefully remove it from your air fryer and check if it's properly done. Then allow it to cool before serving. Serve and enjoy.

Nutrition: Calories: 190 fat: 22g protein: 4g carbs: 9g

459. Heirloom tomato with baked feta

Preparation time: 20 minutes
Cooking time: 14 minutes
Servings: 4

Ingredients:

- 8 oz. Feta cheese
- Salt
- 2 heirloom tomatoes
- ½ cup sliced red onions
- 1 tbsp. Olive oil
- For the basil pesto
- ½ cup grated parmesan cheese
- Salt
- ½ cup olive oil
- 3 tbsps. Toasted pine nuts
- ½ cup chopped basil
- 1 garlic clove
- ½ cup chopped parsley

Directions:
1. Prepare the pesto.
2. Put the toasted pine nuts, garlic, salt, basil, and parmesan in a food processor. Process until combined.
3. Gradually add oil as you mix. Process until everything is blended.
4. Transfer to a bowl and cover. Refrigerate until ready to use.
5. Slice the feta and tomato into round slices with half an inch thickness. Use paper towels to pat them dry.
6. Spread a tbsp. Of pesto on top of each tomato slice.
7. Top with a slice of feta.
8. In a small bowl, mix a tbsp. Of olive oil and red onions.
9. Scoop the mixture on top of the feta layer. Arrange them in the cooking basket. Cook for 14 minutes at 390° F.
10. Transfer to a platter and add a tbsp. Of basil pesto on top of each. Sprinkle them with a bit of salt before serving.

Nutrition: calories: 493 fat: 423g carbs: 61g protein: 169g

460. Crispy potato skins

Preparation time: 5 minutes
Cooking time: 55 minutes
Servings: 2
Ingredients:

- 2 Yukon gold potatoes
- ¼ tsp. Sea salt
- ½ tsp. Olive oil
- 2 minced green onions, 4 bacon strips
- ¼ cup shredded cheddar cheese, 1/3 cup sour cream

Directions:
1. Rinse and scrub the potatoes until clean. Rub with oil and sprinkle with salt. Put them in the cooking basket. Cook for 35 minutes at 400°F. Transfer the cooked potatoes to a platter. Put the bacon strip in the cooking basket. Cook for 5 minutes at 400 °F.
2. Move to a plate and leave to cool. Crumble into bits.
3. Slice the potatoes in half.
4. Scoop out most of the meat. Arrange the potato skins with the skin facing side up in the cooking basket. Spray them with oil. Cook for 3 minutes at 400°F. Flip the potato skins. Fill each piece with cheese and crumbled bacon. Continue cooking for 2 more minutes. Transfer to a platter. Add a bit of sour cream on top. Sprinkle with minced onion and serve while warm.

Nutrition: Calories: 483 fat: 73g Carbs: 98g protein: 152g

461. Beets and carrots

Preparation time: 1 minute
Cooking time: 12 minutes
Servings: 4
Ingredients:

- 4 carrots whole
- 4 sliced young beetroots
- ¼ tsp. Black pepper
- 1 tsp. Olive oil
- ¼ tsp. Salt
- 1 tbsps. Lemon juice

Directions:
1. Preheat air fryer to a temperature of 400°F (200°C)

2. Transfer beetroots and carrots to air fryer basket and sprinkle salt and pepper. Drizzle olive oil and toss to combine.
3. Leave to cook for 12 minutes. Shake the basket of fryer after halftime. Remove from the air fryer and drizzle lemon juice. Serve and enjoy!

Nutrition: Calories: 71 protein: 92 g fat: 43 g carbs: 106 g

462. Mac and cheese balls
Preparation time: 20 minutes
Cooking time: 25 minutes
Servings: 6
Ingredients:
- ½ shredded pound mozzarella cheese
- 2 eggs
- 3 cup seasoned panko breadcrumbs
- Salt
- 2 tbsps. All-purpose flour
- 1 lb. Grated cheddar cheese
- 1 lb. Elbow macaroni
- 2 cup heated cream
- Pepper
- 2 tbsps. Unsalted butter
- 2 tbsps. Egg wash
- ½ lb. Shredded parmesan cheese

Directions:
1. Prepare the macaroni in relation to the directions on the package.
2. Rinse with cold water and drain. Transfer to a bowl and set aside.
3. Melt butter in a saucepan over medium flame. Add flour and whisk for a couple of minutes. Stir the heated cream until there are no more lumps. Cook until thick. Remove from the stove. Stir in the cheeses until melted. Season with salt and pepper.
4. Top the cheese mixture onto the cooked macaroni. Gently fold until combined. Transfer to a shallow pan and refrigerate for 2 hours.
5. Use your hands to form meatball-sized balls from the mixture. Arrange them in a tray lined with wax paper. Freeze overnight.
6. Prepare the egg wash by combining 2 tbsps. Of cream and eggs in a shallow bowl.
7. Dip the frozen mac and cheese balls in the egg wash and coat them with panko breadcrumbs. Gently press to make the coating stick.
8. Arrange them in the cooking basket. Cook for 8 minutes at 400°F.

Nutrition: Calories: 907 Fat: 423g Carbs: 874g Protein: 499g

463. Broccoli crisps
Preparation time: 10 minutes
Cooking time: 12 minutes
Servings: 4
Ingredients:
- Large chopped broccoli head,
- Salt, 1 tsp.
- Olive oil, 2 tbsps.
- Black pepper, 1 tsp.

Directions:
1. Set the air fryer to heat up to 360°F.
2. Using a bowl, add and toss the broccoli florets with olive oil, salt, and black pepper.
3. Add the broccoli florets and cook it for 12 minutes, then shake after 6 minutes.
4. Carefully remove it from your air fryer and allow it to cool off.
5. Serve and enjoy!

Nutrition: Calories: 120 fat: 19g protein: 5g carbs: 3g

464. Maple syrup bacon
Preparation time: 5 minutes
Cooking time: 10 minutes
Servings: 2
Ingredients:
- Maple syrup.
- Thick bacon slices, 1

Directions:
1. Preheat your air fryer to 400°f.
2. Place the bacon on the flat surface and brush with the maple syrup.
3. Move to the air fryer to cook for 10 minutes.

4. Serve and enjoy!

Nutrition: Calories: 91 carbs: 0g protein: 8g fat: 2g

465. Low-Carb Pizza Crust
Preparation Time: 10 minutes
Cooking Time: 20 minutes
Servings: 4
Ingredients
- 1 tbsp. full-fat cream cheese
- ½ cup whole-milk mozzarella cheese, shredded
- 2 tbsp. flour
- 1 egg white

Directions:
1. Prepare the cream cheese, mozzarella, and flour in a microwaveable bowl and heat in the microwave for half a minute. Mix well to create a smooth consistency. Add in the egg white and stir to form a soft ball of dough.
2. With slightly wet hands, press the dough into a pizza crust about six inches in diameter.
3. Arrange sheet of parchment paper in the bottom of your fryer and lay the crust on top. Cook for ten minutes at 350°F, turning the crust over halfway through the cooking time.
4. Top the pizza base with the toppings of your choice and enjoy!

Nutrition: Calories: 260 Fat: 21g Carbs: 6g Protein: 9g

466. Colby Potato Patties
Preparation Time: 5 minutes
Cooking Time: 15 minutes
Servings: 8
Ingredients
- 2 lb. white potatoes, peeled and grated
- ½ cup scallions, finely chopped
- ½ tsp. freshly ground black pepper
- 1tbsp. fine sea salt
- ½ tsp. hot paprika
- 2 cups Colby cheese, shredded
- ¼ cup canola oil
- 1 cup crushed crackers

Directions:
1. Boil the potatoes until soft. Dry them off and peel them before mashing thoroughly, leaving no lumps.
2. Combine the mashed potatoes with scallions, pepper, salt, paprika, and cheese.
3. Shape mixture into balls with your hands and press with your palm to flatten them into patties.
4. In shallow dish, combine the canola oil and crushed crackers. Coat the patties in the crumb mixture.
5. Cook the patties at 360°F for about 10 minutes, in multiple batches if necessary.
6. Serve with tabasco mayo or the sauce of your choice.

Nutrition: Calories: 130 Fat: 7g Carbs: 17g Protein: 1g

467. Turkey Garlic Potatoes
Preparation Time: 10 minutes
Cooking Time: 45 minutes
Servings: 2
Ingredients
- unsmoked turkey strips
- small potatoes
- 1 tsp. garlic, minced
- 2 tsp. olive oil
- Salt to taste
- Pepper to taste

Directions:
1. Peel the potatoes and cube them finely.
2. Coat in 1 teaspoon of oil and cook in the Air Fryer for 10 minutes at 350°F.
3. In separate bowl, slice the turkey finely and combine with the garlic, oil, salt and pepper. Pour the potatoes into the bowl and mix well.

4. Lay the mixture on some silver aluminum foil, transfer to the fryer and cook for about 10 minutes.
5. Serve with raita.

Nutrition: Calories: 210 Fat: 4g Carbs: 22g Protein: 22g

468. Scrambled Eggs
Preparation Time: 5 minutes
Cooking Time: 15 minutes
Servings: 2
Ingredients

- 2 tbsp. olive oil, melted
- eggs, whisked
- oz. fresh spinach, chopped
- 1 medium-sized tomato, chopped
- 1 tsp. fresh lemon juice
- ½ tsp. coarse salt
- ½ tsp. ground black pepper
- ½ cup of fresh basil, roughly chopped

Directions:
1. Grease the Air Fryer baking pan with the oil, tilting it to spread the oil around. Pre-heat the fryer at 280°F.
2. Mix the remaining ingredients, apart from the basil leaves, whisking well until everything is completely combined.
3. Cook in the fryer for 8 - 12 minutes.
4. Top with fresh basil leaves before serving with little sour cream if desired.

Nutrition: Calories: 140 Fat: 10g Carbs: 2g Protein: 12g

469. Bacon-Wrapped Onion Rings
Preparation Time: 10 minutes
Cooking Time: 15 minutes
Servings: 8
Ingredients

- 1 large onion, peeled
- slices sugar-free bacon
- 1 tbsp. sriracha

Directions:
1. Chop up the onion into slices a quarter-inch thick. Gently pull apart the rings. Take a slice of bacon and wrap it around an onion ring. Repeat with the rest of the ingredients.
2. Place each onion ring in your fryer.
3. Cut the onion rings at 350°F for ten minutes, turning them halfway through to ensure the bacon crisps up.
4. Serve hot with the sriracha.

Nutrition: Calories: 280 Fat: 19g Carbs: 25g Protein: 3g

470. Grilled Cheese
Preparation Time: 5 minutes
Cooking Time: 25 minutes
Servings: 2
Ingredients

- slices bread
- ½ cup sharp cheddar cheese
- ¼ cup butter, melted

Directions:
1. Pre-heat the Air Fryer at 360°F.
2. Put cheese and butter in separate bowls.
3. Apply the butter to each side of the bread slices with a brush.
4. Spread the cheese across two of the slices of bread and make two sandwiches. Transfer both to the fryer.
5. Cook for 5 – 7 minutes or until a golden-brown color is achieved and the cheese is melted.

Nutrition: Calories: 170 Fat: 8g Carbs: 17g Protein: 5g

471. Peppered Puff Pastry
Preparation Time: 10 minutes
Cooking Time: 25 minutes
Servings: 4
Ingredients

- 1 ½ tbsp. sesame oil
- 1 cup white mushrooms, sliced

- 2 cloves garlic, minced
- 1 bell pepper, seeded and chopped
- ¼ tsp. sea salt
- ¼ tsp. dried rosemary
- ½ tsp. ground black pepper, or more to taste
- oz. puff pastry sheets
- ½ cup crème fraiche
- 1 egg, well whisked
- ½ cup parmesan cheese, preferably freshly grated

Directions:
1. Pre-heat your Air Fryer to 400°F.
2. Heat the sesame oil over moderate temperature and fry the mushrooms, garlic, and pepper until soft and fragrant.
3. Sprinkle on the salt, rosemary, and pepper.
4. In the meantime, unroll the puff pastry and slice it into 4-inch squares.
5. Spread the crème fraiche across each square.
6. Spoon equal amounts of the vegetables into the puff pastry squares. Enclose each square around the filling in triangle shape, pressing the edges with your fingertips.
7. Brush each triangle with some whisked egg and cover with grated Parmesan.
8. Cook for 22-25 minutes.

Nutrition: Calories: 259 Fat: 18g Carbs: 21g Protein: 3g

472. Horseradish Mayo & Gorgonzola Mushrooms
Preparation Time: 10 minutes
Cooking Time: 15 minutes
Servings: 5
Ingredients

- ½ cup of breadcrumbs
- 2 cloves garlic, pressed
- 2 tbsp. fresh coriander, chopped
- 1/3 tsp. kosher salt
- ½ tsp. crushed red pepper flakes
- 1 ½ tbsp. olive oil
- 2 medium-sized mushrooms, stems removed
- ½ cup Gorgonzola cheese, grated
- ¼ cup low-fat mayonnaise
- 1 tsp. prepared horseradish, well-drained
- 1 tbsp. fresh parsley, finely chopped

Directions:
1. Combine the breadcrumbs together with the garlic, coriander, salt, red pepper, and the olive oil.
2. Take equal-sized amounts of the bread crumb mixture and use them to stuff the mushroom caps. Add the grated Gorgonzola on top of each.
3. Put the mushrooms in the Air Fryer grill pan and transfer to the fryer.
4. Grill them at 380°F for 8-12 minutes, ensuring the stuffing is warm throughout.
5. In the meantime, prepare the horseradish mayo. Mix together the mayonnaise, horseradish and parsley.
6. When the mushrooms are ready, serve with the mayo.

Nutrition: Calories: 140 Fat: 13g Carbs: 6g Protein: 0g

473. Crumbed Beans
Preparation Time:
Cooking Time: 10 minutes
Servings: 4
Ingredients

- ½ cup flour
- 1 tsp. smoky chipotle powder
- ½ tsp. ground black pepper
- 1 tsp. sea salt flakes
- 2 eggs, beaten
- ½ cup crushed saltines
- oz. wax beans

Directions:

1. Combine the flour, chipotle powder, black pepper, and salt in a bowl. Put the eggs in second bowl. Place the crushed saltines in third bowl.
2. Wash the beans with cold water and discard any tough strings.
3. Coat the beans with the flour mixture, before dipping them into the beaten egg. Lastly cover them with the crushed saltines.
4. Spritz the beans with cooking spray.
5. Air-fry at 360°F for 4 minutes. Give the cooking basket a good shake and continue to cook for 3 minutes. Serve hot.

Nutrition: Calories: 200 Fat: 8g Carbs: 27g Protein: 4g

474. Croutons
Preparation Time: 5 minutes
Cooking Time: 10 minutes
Servings: 4
Ingredients
- 2 slices friendly bread
- 1 tbsp. olive oil

Directions:
1. Cut the slices of bread into medium-size chunks.
2. Coat the inside of the Air Fryer with the oil. Set it to 390degreesF and allow it to heat up.
3. Place the chunks inside and shallow fry for at least 8 minutes.
4. Serve with hot soup.

Nutrition: Calories: 186 Fat: 7g Carbs: 25g Protein: 4g

475. Cheese Lings
Preparation Time: 5 minutes
Cooking Time: 25 minutes
Servings: 6
Ingredients
- 1 cup flour
- small cubes cheese, grated
- ¼ tsp. chili powder
- 1 tsp. butter
- Salt to taste
- 1 tsp. baking powder

Directions:
1. Put all ingredients to form a dough, along with a small amount water as necessary.
2. Divide the dough into equal portions and roll each one into a ball.
3. Pre-heat Air Fryer at 360°F.
4. Transfer the balls to the fryer and air fry for 5 minutes, stirring periodically.

Nutrition: Calories: 489 Fat: 20g Carbs: 69g Protein: 8g

476. Vegetable & Cheese Omelet
Preparation Time: 5 minutes
Cooking Time: 15 minutes
Servings: 2
Ingredients
- tbsp. plain milk
- eggs, whisked
- 1 tsp. melted butter
- Kosher salt
- freshly ground black pepper, to taste
- 1 red bell pepper, deveined and chopped
- 1 green bell pepper, deveined and chopped
- 1 white onion, finely chopped
- ½ cup baby spinach leaves, roughly chopped
- ½ cup Halloumi cheese, shaved

Directions:
1. Grease the Air Fryer baking pan with some canola oil.
2. Place all of the ingredients in the baking pan and stir well.
3. Transfer to the fryer and cook at 350°F for 13 minutes.
4. Serve warm.

Nutrition: Calories: 300 Fat: 3g Carbs: 6g Protein: 12g

477. Rosemary Cornbread
Preparation Time: 10 minutes

Cooking Time: 1 hour
Servings: 6
Ingredients
- 1 cup cornmeal
- 1 ½ cups flour
- ½ tsp. baking soda
- ½ tsp. baking powder
- ¼ tsp. kosher salt
- 1 tsp. dried rosemary
- ¼ tsp. garlic powder
- 2 tbsp. sugar
- 2 eggs
- ¼ cup melted butter
- 1 cup buttermilk
- ½ cup corn kernels

Directions:
1. In bowl, combine all the dry ingredients.
2. Get another bowl, mix together all the wet ingredients. Combine the two.
3. Fold in the corn kernels and stir vigorously.
4. Pour the batter into a lightly greased round loaf pan that is lightly greased.
5. Cook for 1 hour at 380°F.

Nutrition: Calories: 200 Fat: 8g Carbs: 28g Protein: 3g

478. Flatbread
Preparation Time: 10 minutes
Cooking Time: 20 minutes
Servings: 1
Ingredients
1 cup mozzarella cheese, shredded
¼ cup blanched finely ground flour
1 oz. full-fat cream cheese, softened
Directions:
1. Microwave the mozzarella for half a minute until melted. Combine with the flour to achieve a smooth consistency, before adding the cream cheese. Keep mixing to create a dough, microwaving the mixture again if the cheese begins to harden.
2. Divide the dough into two equal pieces. Between two sheets of parchment paper, roll out the dough until it is about a quarter-inch thick. Cover the bottom of your fryer with another sheet of parchment.
3. Transfer the dough into the fryer and cook at 320°F for seven minutes. You may need to complete this step in two batches.
4. Make sure to turn the flatbread halfway through cooking. Take care when removing it from the fryer and serve warm.

Nutrition: Calories: 220 Fat: 5g Carbs: 38g Protein: 7g

479. Popcorn Broccoli
Preparation Time: 10 minutes
Cooking Time: 10 minutes
Servings: 1
Ingredients
- egg yolks
- ¼ cup butter, melted
- 2 cups coconut flower
- Salt and pepper
- 2 cups broccoli florets

Directions:
1. 1.Whisk egg yolks in empty bowl and melted butter together. Throw in the coconut flour, salt and pepper, then stir again to combine well.
2. 2.Pre-heat the fryer at 400°F.
3. 3.Dip each broccoli floret into the mixture and place in the fryer. Cook for six minutes, in multiple batches if necessary. Take care when removing them from the fryer and enjoy!

Nutrition: Calories: 60 Fat: 3g Carbs: 6g Protein: 3g

480. Creamy potatoes
Preparation time: 5 minutes
Cooking time: 20 minutes
Servings: 4
Ingredients:

- 2 gold potatoes, cut into medium pieces
- 1 tablespoon olive oil
- Salt and black pepper to taste
- 3 tablespoons sour cream

Directions:
1. In a baking dish that fits your air fryer, mix all the ingredients and toss.
2. Place the dish in the air fryer and cook at 370 °F for 20 minutes.
3. Divide between plates and serve as a side dish.

Nutrition: calories 201, fat 8, fiber 9, carbs 18, protein 5

481. Mint-butter stuffed mushrooms

Preparation Time: 5 minutes
Cooking Time: 12 minutes
Servings 3
Ingredients

- 3 garlic cloves, minced
- 1 teaspoon ground black pepper, or more to taste
- 1/3 cup seasoned breadcrumbs
- 1½ tablespoons fresh mint, chopped
- 1 teaspoon salt, or more to taste
- 1½ tablespoons melted butter
- 14 medium-sized mushrooms, cleaned, stalks removed

Directions
1. Mix all of the above ingredients, minus the mushrooms, in a mixing bowl to prepare the filling.
2. Then, stuff the mushrooms with the prepared filling.
3. Air-fry stuffed mushrooms at 375 °F for about 12 minutes. Taste for doneness and serve at room temperature as a vegetarian appetizer.

Nutrition:290 calories; 17g fat; 14g carbs; 28g protein; 3g sugars

482. Ricotta and leafy green omelet

Preparation Time: 5 minutes
Cooking Time: 15 minutes
Servings 2
Ingredients

- 1/3 cup ricotta cheese
- 5 eggs, beaten
- 1/2 red bell pepper, seeded and sliced
- 1 cup mixed greens, roughly chopped
- 1/2 green bell pepper, seeded and sliced
- 1/2 teaspoon dried basil
- 1/2 chipotle pepper, finely minced
- 1/2 teaspoon dried oregano

Directions
1. Lightly coat the inside of a baking dish with a pan spray.
2. Then, throw all ingredients into the baking dish; give it a good stir.
3. Bake at 325 °F for 15 minutes.

Nutrition:409 calories; 25g fat; 9g carbs; 29g protein; 3g sugars

483. Mayo brussels sprouts

Preparation time: 5 minutes
Cooking time: 15 minutes
Servings: 4
Ingredients:

- 1-pound brussels sprouts, trimmed and halved
- Salt and black pepper to taste
- 6 teaspoons olive oil
- ½ cup mayonnaise
- 2 tablespoons garlic, minced

Directions:
1. In your air fryer, mix the sprouts, salt, pepper, and oil; toss well.
2. Cook the sprouts at 390 °F for 15 minutes.
3. Transfer them to a bowl; then add the mayonnaise and the garlic and toss.
4. Divide between plates and serve as a side dish.

Nutrition: calories 202, fat 6, fiber 8, carbs 12, protein 8

484. Pantano Romanesco with goat cheese

Preparation Time: 6 minutes
Cooking Time: 14 minutes
Servings 4
Ingredients

- 6 ounces goat cheese, sliced

- 2 shallots, thinly sliced
- 2 Pantano Romanesco tomatoes, cut into 1/2-inch slices
- 1 ½ tablespoons extra-virgin olive oil
- 3/4 teaspoon sea salt
- Fresh parsley, for garnish
- Fresh basil, chopped

Directions
1. Preheat your air fryer to 380 °F.
2. Now, pat each tomato slice dry using a paper towel. Sprinkle each slice with salt and chopped basil. Top with a slice of goat cheese.
3. Top with the shallot slices; drizzle with olive oil. Add the prepared tomato and feta "bites" to the air fryer food basket.
4. Cook in the air fryer for about 14 minutes. Lastly, adjust seasonings to taste and serve garnished with fresh parsley leaves. Enjoy!

Nutrition:237 calories; 24g fat; 9g carbs; 13g protein; 9g sugars

485. Swiss chard and cheese omelet

Preparation Time: 7 minutes
Cooking Time: 18 minutes
Servings 2
Ingredients

- 1 teaspoon garlic paste
- 1 ½ tablespoons olive oil
- 1/2 cup crème fraiche
- 1/3 teaspoon ground black pepper, to your liking
- 1/3 cup swiss cheese, crumbled
- 1 teaspoon cayenne pepper
- 1/3 cup swiss chard, torn into pieces
- 5 eggs
- 1/4 cup yellow onions, chopped
- 1 teaspoon fine sea salt

Directions
1. Crack your eggs into a mixing dish; then, add the crème fraiche, salt, ground black pepper, and cayenne pepper.
2. Next, coat the inside of a baking dish with olive oil and tilt it to spread evenly. Scrape the egg/cream mixture into the baking dish. Add the other ingredients; mix to combine well.
3. Bake for 18 minutes at 292 °F. Serve immediately.

Nutrition:388 calories; 27g fat; 6g carbs; 29g protein; 6g sugars

486. Mom's jacket potatoes

Preparation Time: 5 minutes
Cooking Time: 20 minutes
Servings 4
Ingredients

- 1/3 cup cottage cheese, softened
- 1/3 cup Parmigiano-Reggiano cheese, grated
- 1 teaspoon black pepper
- 1 ½ heaping tablespoons roughly chopped cilantro leaves
- 1/3 cup green onions, finely chopped
- 5 average-sized potatoes
- 2 ½ tablespoons softened butter
- 1 teaspoon salt

Directions
1. Firstly, stab your potatoes with a fork. Cook them in the air fryer basket for 20 minutes at 345 °F.
2. While the potatoes are cooking, make the filling by mixing the rest of the above ingredients.
3. Afterward, open the potatoes up and stuff them with the prepared filling. Bon appétit!

Nutrition:270 calories; 19g fat; 32g carbs; 8g protein; 8g sugars

487. Green beans and shallots

Preparation time: 5 minutes
Cooking time: 25 minutes
Servings: 4
Ingredients:

- 1½ pounds green beans, trimmed
- Salt and black pepper to taste
- ½ pound shallots, chopped
- ¼ cup walnuts, chopped
- 2 tablespoons olive oil

Directions:

1. In your air fryer, mix all ingredients and toss.
2. Cook at 350 °F for 25 minutes.
3. Divide between plates and serve as a side dish.

Nutrition: calories 182, fat 3, fiber 6, carbs 11, protein 5

488. Italian mushroom mix

Preparation time: 5 minutes
Cooking time: 15 minutes
Servings: 4

Ingredients:
- 1-pound button mushrooms, halved
- 2 tablespoons parmesan cheese, grated
- 1 teaspoon Italian seasoning
- A pinch of salt and black pepper
- 3 tablespoons butter, melted

Directions:
1. In a pan that fits your air fryer, mix all the ingredients and toss.
2. Place the pan in the air fryer and cook at 360 °F for 15 minutes.
3. Divide the mix between plates and serve.

Nutrition: calories 194, fat 4, fiber 4, carbs 14, protein 7

489. Herbed roasted potatoes

Preparation Time: 5 minutes
Cooking Time: 17 minutes
Servings 4

Ingredients
- 1 teaspoon crushed dried thyme
- 1 teaspoon ground black pepper
- 2 tablespoons olive oil
- 1/2 tablespoon crushed dried rosemary
- 3 potatoes, peeled, washed and cut into wedges
- 1/2 teaspoon seasoned salt

Directions
1. Lay the potatoes in the air fryer cooking basket; drizzle olive oil over your potatoes.
2. Then, cook for 17 minutes at 353 °F.
3. Toss with the seasonings and serve warm with your favorite salad on the side.

Nutrition: 208 calories; 1g fat; 38g carbs; 6g protein; 5g sugars

490. Easy frizzled leeks

Preparation Time: 25 minutes
Cooking Time: 18 minutes
Servings 6

Ingredients
- 1/2 teaspoon porcini powder
- 1 1/2 cup rice flour
- 1 tablespoon vegetable oil
- 3 medium-sized leeks, slice into julienne strips
- 2 large-sized dishes with ice water
- 2 teaspoons onion powder
- Fine sea salt and cayenne pepper, to taste

Directions
1. Allow the leeks to soak in ice water for about 25 minutes; drain well.
2. Place the rice flour, salt, cayenne pepper, onions powder, and porcini powder into a resealable bag. Add the celery and shake to coat well.
3. Drizzle vegetable oil over the seasoned leeks. Air fry at 390 °F for about 18 minutes; turn them halfway through the cooking

time. Serve with homemade mayonnaise or any other sauce for dipping. Enjoy!

Nutrition: 291 calories; 6g fat; 53g carbs; 7g protein; 3g sugars

491. Oyster mushroom and lemongrass omelet

Preparation Time: 7 minutes
Cooking Time: 35 minutes
Servings 2

Ingredients
- 3 king oyster mushrooms, thinly sliced
- 1 lemongrass, chopped
- 1/2 teaspoon dried marjoram
- 5 eggs
- 1/3 cup swiss cheese, grated
- 2 tablespoons sour cream
- 1 1/2 teaspoon dried rosemary
- 2 teaspoons red pepper flakes, crushed
- 2 tablespoons butter, melted
- 1/2 red onion, peeled and sliced into thin rounds
- ½ teaspoon garlic powder
- 1 teaspoon dried dill weed
- Fine sea salt and ground black pepper, to your liking

Directions
1. Get the onion then peeled and sliced into thin rounds
2. Melt the margarine in a skillet that is placed over a medium flame. Then, sweat the onion, mushrooms, and lemongrass until they have softened; reserve.
3. Then, preheat the air fryer to 325° F. Then, crack the eggs into a mixing bowl and whisk them well. Then, fold in the sour cream and give it a good stir.
4. Now, stir in the salt, black pepper, red pepper, rosemary, garlic powder, marjoram, and dill.
5. Grease the inside of an air fryer baking dish with a thin layer of a cooking spray. Pour the egg/seasoning mixture into the baking dish; throw in the reserved mixture. Top with the Swiss cheese.
6. Set the timer for 35 minutes; cook until a knife inserted in the center comes out clean and dry

Nutrition: 362 calories; 29g fat; 2g carbs; 19g protein; 8g sugars

492. Spinach and cheese stuffed baked potatoes

Preparation Time: 10 minutes
Cooking Time: 14 minutes
Servings 4

Ingredients
- 3 tablespoons extra-virgin olive oil
- 2/3 cup sour cream, at room temperature
- 1½ cup baby spinach leaves, torn into small pieces
- 3 pounds russet potatoes
- 2 garlic cloves, peeled and finely minced
- 1/4 teaspoon fine sea salt, or more to taste
- 1/4 teaspoon freshly cracked black pepper, or more to taste
- 1/3 cup cheddar cheese, freshly grated

Directions
1. Firstly, stab the potatoes with a fork. Preheat the air fryer to 345° F. Now, cook the potatoes for 14 minutes.
2. Meanwhile, make the filling by mixing the rest of the above items.
3. Afterward that, open the potatoes up and stuff them with the prepared filling. Bon appétit!

Nutrition: 327 calories; 7g fat; 59g carbs; 4g protein; 2g sugars

CASSEROLES

493.   Cheesy spinach casserole
Preparation time: 10 minutes
Cooking time: 20 minutes
Servings: 4
Ingredients:

- 1 can (15ounces / 383g spinach, drained and squeezed)
- 1 cup cottage cheese
- 2 large eggs, beaten
- ¼ cup crumbled feta cheese
- 2 tablespoons all-purpose flour
- 2 tablespoons butter, melted
- 1 clove minced garlic
- 1 1/2 teaspoons onion powder
- 1/8 teaspoon ground nutmeg
- Cooking spray

Directions:
1. Put oil to the pie pan and set aside.
2. Combine spinach, cottage cheese, eggs, feta cheese, flour, butter, garlic, onion powder, and nutmeg in a bowl. Stir until all ingredients are well incorporated. Pour into the prepared pie pan.
3. Cook at the corresponding preset mode or air fry at 375°F (191°C until the center is set, 18 to 20 minutes).
4. Serve warm.

Nutrition: Calories: 176 Fat: 10g Carbs: 3g Protein: 18g

494.   Creamy cheesy tomato casserole
Preparation time: 5 minutes
Cooking time: 30 minutes
Servings: 4
Ingredients:

- 5 eggs
- 2 tablespoons heavy cream
- 3 tablespoons chunky tomato sauce
- 2 tablespoons grated parmesan cheese

Directions:
1. Prepare a mixing bowl, then add the eggs and cream.
2. Mix in the tomato sauce and add the cheese.
3. Spread into a glass baking dish and cook at 350 °F for 30 minutes.
4. Top with extra cheese and serve.

Nutrition: Calories: 50 Fat: 5g Carbs: 3g Protein: 4g

495.   Fast cheesy green bean casserole
Preparation time: 4 minutes
Cooking time: 6 minutes
Servings: 4
Ingredients:

- 1 tablespoon melted butter
- 1 cup green beans
- 6 ounces cheddar cheese, shredded
- 7 ounces parmesan cheese, shredded
- ¼ cup heavy cream
- Sea salt, to taste

Directions:
1. Put melted butter in the baking pan.
2. Add the green beans, salt, cheddar, and black pepper to the prepared baking pan. Stir to mix well, then spread the parmesan and cream on top.
3. Place baking pan in the fryer and cook for 6 minutes at 400 °F. Wait until the beans are soft and the cheese melts.
4. Serve immediately.

Nutrition: Calories: 223 Fat: 13g Carbs: 19g Protein: 5g

496.   Cheesy pastrami casserole
Preparation time: 10 minutes
Cooking time: 8 minutes
Servings: 2
Ingredients:

- 1 cup pastrami, sliced
- 1 bell pepper, chopped
- ¼ cup Greek yogurt

- 2 spring onions, chopped
- ½ cup cheddar cheese, grated
- 4 eggs
- ¼ teaspoon ground black pepper
- Sea salt, to taste
- Cooking spray

Directions:
1. Spritz a baking pan with cooking spray.
2. Put all ingredients in a mixing bowl. Stir to mix well. Pour the mixture into the baking pan.
3. Arrange the baking pan in the air fryer. Cook for 8 minutes at 330 °F (166°C) or until the eggs are set and the edges are lightly browned. Check the doneness during the last 2 minutes of the baking.
4. Remove the baking pan from the air fryer and allow it to cool for 10 minutes before serving.

Nutrition: Calories: 382 Fat: 25g Carbs: 20g Protein: 20g

497.   Cheesy chicken ham casserole
Preparation time: 15 minutes
Cooking time: 15 minutes
Servings: 4 6
Ingredients:

- 2 cups diced cooked chicken
- 1 cup diced ham
- ¼ teaspoon ground nutmeg
- ½ cup half-and-half
- ½ teaspoon ground black pepper
- 6 slices swiss cheese
- Cooking spray

Directions:
1. Spritz a baking pan with cooking spray.
2. Combine the chicken, ham, nutmeg, half-and-half, and ground black pepper in a large bowl. Stir to mix well.
3. Add half of the mixture into the baking pan, then top the mixture with 3 slices of swiss cheese, then pour in the remaining mixture and top with remaining cheese slices.
4. Arrange the baking pan in the air fryer and cook at the corresponding preset mode or air fry at 350°F (177°C) for 15 minutes or until the egg is set and the cheese melts.
5. Serve immediately.

Nutrition: Calories: 293 Fat: 16g Carbs: 22g Protein: 15g

498.   Cheesy sausage and broccoli casserole
Preparation time: 10 minutes
Cooking time: 20 minutes
Servings: 8
Ingredients:

- 10 eggs
- 1 cup cheddar cheese, shredded and divided
- ¾ cup heavy whipping cream
- 1 (12ounce / 340g package cooked chicken sausage
- 1 cup broccoli, chopped
- 2 cloves garlic, minced
- ½ tablespoon salt
- ¼ tablespoon ground black pepper
- Cooking spray

Directions:
1. Spritz a baking pan with cooking spray.
2. Whisk the eggs with cheddar and cream in a large bowl to mix well.
3. Combine the cooked sausage, broccoli, salt, garlic, and ground black pepper in a separate bowl. Stir to mix well.
4. Put sausage mixture into the baking pan, then spread the egg mixture over to cover.
5. Put the baking pan in the air fryer. Cook at the corresponding preset mode or air fry at 400°F (204°C until the eggs are set).
6. Serve immediately.

Nutrition: Calories: 370 Fat: 20g Carbs: 32g Protein: 17g

499.   Curry chicken and mushroom casserole
Preparation time: 15 minutes

Cooking time: 20 minutes
Servings: 4
Ingredients:

- 4 chicken breasts
- 1 tablespoon curry powder
- 1 cup of coconut milk
- Salt, to taste
- 1 broccoli, cut into florets
- 1 cup mushrooms
- ½ cup shredded parmesan cheese
- Cooking spray

Directions:

1. Spritz a casserole dish with cooking spray.
2. Cube the chicken breasts and combine them with curry powder and coconut milk in a bowl. Season with salt.
3. Add the broccoli and mushroom and mix well.
4. Pour the mixture into the casserole dish. Top with the cheese.
5. Move it to the air fryer. Adjust to 350 °F and cook for about 20 minutes.
6. Serve warm.

Nutrition: Calories: 285 Fat: 16g Carbs: 23g Protein: 13g

500. Lush chicken and vegetable casserole

Preparation time: 15 minutes
Cooking time: 15 minutes
Servings: 4
Ingredients:

- 4 boneless and skinless chicken breasts
- 2 carrots, sliced
- 1 yellow bell pepper, cut into strips
- 1 red bell pepper, cut into strips
- 15 ounces (425 g) broccoli florets
- 1 cup snow peas
- 1 scallion, sliced
- Cooking spray

Sauce:

- 1 teaspoon sriracha
- 3 tablespoons soy sauce
- 2 tablespoons oyster sauce
- 1 tablespoon rice wine vinegar
- 1 teaspoon cornstarch
- 1 tablespoon grated ginger
- 2 garlic cloves, minced
- 1 teaspoon sesame oil
- 1 tablespoon brown sugar

Directions:

1. Cut the chicken breasts into cubes.
2. Spritz a baking pan with cooking spray.
3. Combine the chicken, carrot, and bell peppers in a large bowl. Stir to mix well.
4. Prepare a separate bowl and put the ingredients for the sauce. Stir to mix well.
5. Pour the chicken mixture into the baking pan, then pour the sauce over. Stir to coat well.
6. Cook at the corresponding preset mode or air fry at 370°F (188°C)for 5 minutes, then add the broccoli and snow peas to the pan and cook for 8 more minutes or until the vegetables are tender.
7. Remove the casserole from the air fryer and sprinkle with sliced scallion before serving.

Nutrition: Calories: 195 Fat: 6g Carbs: 19g Protein: 17g

501. Garlicky beef and mushroom casserole

Preparation time: 10 minutes
Cooking time: 25 minutes
Servings: 4
Ingredients:

- 1 1/2pounds (680 g) beef steak
- 1 ounce (28 g) dry onion soup mix
- 2 cups sliced mushrooms
- 1 (15ounce / 411g can cream of mushroom soup
- 1/2 cup beef broth
- 1/4 cup red wine

- 3 garlic cloves, minced
- 1 whole onion, chopped

Directions:

1. Put the beef steak in a large bowl, then sprinkle with dry onion soup mix. Toss to coat well.
2. Combine the mushrooms with mushroom soup, beef broth, red wine, garlic, and onion in a large bowl. Stir to mix well.
3. Transfer the beef steak to a baking pan, then pour in the mushroom mixture.
4. Adjust the air fryer to 360 °F. Cook until the mushrooms are soft, and the beef is well browned.
5. Remove the baking pan from the air fryer and serve immediately.

Nutrition: Calories: 322 Fat: 19g Carbs: 12g Protein: 24g

502. Cauliflower and pumpkin casserole

Preparation time: 15 minutes
Cooking time: 50 minutes
Servings: 6
Ingredients:

- 1 cup chicken broth
- 2 cups cauliflower florets
- 1 cup canned pumpkin purée
- 1/4 cup heavy cream
- 1 teaspoon vanilla extract
- 2 large eggs, beaten
- 1/3 cup melted unsalted butter
- 1/4 cup of sugar
- 1 teaspoon fine sea salt
- Chopped fresh parsley leaves for garnish
- Topping:
- ½ cup blanched almond flour
- 1 cup chopped pecans
- ⅓ cup unsalted butter, melted
- ½ cup of sugar

Directions:

1. Pour the chicken broth into a baking pan basket, then add the cauliflower.
2. Place the baking pan in the air fryer—bake for 20 minutes or until soft.
3. To make the topping, put the ingredients in a large bowl. Stir to mix well.
4. Pat the cauliflower with paper towels, then place in a food processor and pulse with pumpkin purée, heavy cream, vanilla extract, eggs, butter, sugar, and salt until smooth.
5. Clean the baking pan and grease with more butter, then pour the purée mixture in the pan. Spread the topping over the mixture.
6. Prepare the baking pan in the air fryer. Set to 350 °F (177ºC) for 30 minutes or until the topping is lightly browned.
7. Remove the casserole from the air fryer and serve with fresh parsley on top.

Nutrition: Calories: 83 Fat: 3g Carbs: 11g Protein: 5g

503. Corn and bell pepper casserole

Preparation time: 10 minutes
Cooking time: 20 minutes
Servings: 4
Ingredients:

- 1 cup corn kernels
- ¼ cup bell pepper, finely chopped
- ½ cup low-fat milk
- 1 large egg, beaten
- ½ cup yellow cornmeal
- ½ cup all-purpose flour
- ½ teaspoon baking powder
- 2 tablespoons melted unsalted butter
- 1 tablespoon granulated sugar
- Pinch of cayenne pepper
- ¼ teaspoon kosher salt
- Cooking spray

Directions:

1. Spritz a baking pan with cooking spray.
2. Prepare all ingredients in a large bowl. Stir to mix well. Pour the mixture into the baking pan.

3. Place the pan in the air fryer. Cook at the corresponding preset mode or air fry at 330°F(166°C) for 20 minutes or until lightly browned and set.
4. Remove the baking pan from the air fryer and serve immediately.

Nutrition: Calories: 154 Fat: 9g Carbs: 15g Protein: 5g

504. Grits and asparagus casserole

Preparation time: 5 minutes
Cooking time: 30 minutes
Servings: 4
Ingredients:

- 10 fresh asparagus spears
- 2 cups cooked grits, cooled to room temperature
- 2 teaspoons Worcestershire sauce
- 1 egg, beaten
- ½ teaspoon garlic powder
- ¼ teaspoon salt
- 2 slices provolone cheese, crushed
- Cooking spray

Directions:

1. Spritz a baking pan with cooking spray.
2. Cut the asparagus into one inch pieces
3. Set the asparagus in the air fryer basket. Spritz the asparagus with cooking spray. Air fry for 5 minutes or until lightly browned and crispy.
4. Meanwhile, combine the grits, Worcestershire sauce, egg, garlic powder, and salt in a bowl. Stir to mix well.
5. Pour half of the grits mixture in the prepared baking pan then spread with fried asparagus.
6. Spoon half of grits mixture into air fryer baking pan and top with asparagus. Spread the cheese over the asparagus.
7. Position the baking pan in the air fryer. Cook at the corresponding preset mode or air fry at 390°f until the egg is set and lightly browned.
8. Serve immediately.

Nutrition: Calories: 224 Fat: 15g Carbs: 14g Protein: 8g

CHICKEN AND POULTRY

505. Tandoori chicken

Preparation time: 30 minutes
Cooking time: 15 minutes
Servings: 2
Ingredients:
For the tandoori chicken:

- 1/2 chicken, halved
- 2 cloves garlic, peeled, minced
- 1/2 tbsp fresh ginger, minced
- 1/4 cup yogurt (Greek)
- 1/2 tsp chili powder
- 1/2 tsp salt or to taste
- 1/2 tsp turmeric powder
- Drops of orange food coloring
- 1/2 tsp garam masala
- Cooking spray or oil for basting

To serve (optional:

- Lemon wedges to serve
- A handful fresh cilantro, chopped, to garnish
- Sliced onions to serve

Directions:

1. Add garlic, chili, ginger, powder, salt, food coloring, turmeric powder, yogurt, and garam masala into a bowl and mix well.
2. Marinate the chicken with this mixture. Refrigerate for about 30 minutes.
3. Place the chicken pieces (without the marinade in the air fryer basket).
4. Spray a little cooking spray or brush with oil. Flip sides and spray again with cooking spray.
5. Air fry in a preheated fryer at 400 °F for 12 minutes. Flip sides after 6 minutes of cooking, spraying some more oil over the chicken.
6. Air fry until the internal temperature of the meat shows 165 °F on a meat cooking thermometer.
7. Serve with sliced onions and lemon wedges.

Nutrition: Calories: 178 Fat: 6 g Carb: 2 g Protein: 25 g

506. Baked Thai peanut chicken egg rolls

Preparation time: 10 minutes
Cooking time: 8 minutes
Servings: 2
Ingredients:

- 2 egg roll wrappers
- 2 tbsps. Thai peanut sauce
- 2 green onions, chopped
- 1/2 cup shredded rotisserie chicken
- 1 small carrot, very thinly sliced
- 1/8 red peppers, sliced

Directions:

1. Place chicken in a bowl. Spread Thai peanut sauce over the chicken.
2. Place the egg roll wrappers on your countertop. Divide equally—carrot, onion, and bell pepper—and place on the wrappers' bottom third. Divide the chicken and place over the vegetables.
3. Brush the edges of the wrappers with water. Fold the sides slightly over the filling and then roll the wrappers tightly. Cover with moist paper towels until ready to fry.
4. Spray the egg rolls all over with cooking spray. Place in the air fryer basket.
5. Air fry in a preheated fryer at 390 °F for 6–8 minutes or until crisp.
6. Chop into 2 halves and serve with Thai peanut sauce.

Nutrition: Calories: 235 Fat: 2 g Carb: 17 g Protein: 21 g

507. Chick fila chicken sandwich

Preparation time: 10 minutes
Cooking time: 14 minutes
Servings: 3
Ingredients:

- 1 chicken breast, skinless, boneless, half an inch in thickness
- 1 egg
- 1/2 cup flour (all-purpose)
- 1 tbsp potato starch
- 1/2 tsp sea salt
- 1/4 tsp garlic powder
- 1/2 tbsp extra virgin olive oil
- 2–3 hamburger buns, toasted, buttered
- 1/4 cup dill pickle juice
- 1/4 cup milk
- 1 tbsp powdered sugar
- 1/2 tsp paprika
- Ground pepper as per taste
- ⅛ tsp ground celery seeds
- Dill pickle chips to serve
- Cayenne pepper as per taste (optional
- Mayonnaise to serve

Directions:

1. Chop chicken into 2–3 parts.
2. Add chicken and pickle juice into a Ziplock bag and seal it. Turn the bag a few times so that the chicken is well coated with the pickle juice. Chill for 30–60 minutes.
3. Add egg and milk to a bowl and whisk well.
4. Add flour, potato starch, and all the spices in another shallow bowl.
5. First, dip chicken in the egg mixture. Shake to drop off excess egg.
6. Next, dredge in the flour mixture. Shake to drop off excess flour. This step is necessary.

7. Put oil in the air fryer basket. Add the chicken pieces to the air fryer basket. Spray some cooking spray over the chicken.
8. Air fry in a preheated air fryer at 340 °F for 12 minutes. Flip sides after 6 minutes of cooking, spraying some more oil over the chicken.
9. Increase the temperature to 400 °F. Cook for 2 minutes. Turn to sides and cook the other side for 2 minutes.
10. 1place the chicken on the bottom half of the burger buns. Drop some mayonnaise over it. Place dill pickle chips and sprinkle cayenne pepper if using and serve.

Nutrition: Calories: 281 Fat: 6 g Carb: 38 g Protein: 15 g

508. **Chicken fried rice**
Preparation time: 5 minutes
Cooking time: 20 minutes
Servings: 3
Ingredients:
- 1/2 cups cold rice
- 1/2 tbsps. Soy sauce
- 1 green onion, sliced
- 3/4 cup frozen vegetables of your choice
- 1/2 tsp vegetable oil
- 1/2 tsp sesame oil
- Salt as per taste
- 1/2 tbsp chili sauce (optional

Directions:
1. Add all of ingredients into a bowl and toss well.
2. Transfer into the air fryer baking accessory.
3. Place the baking accessory in the air fryer.
4. air fry in a preheated fryer at 340 °f for 12–15 minutes. Stir every 5 minutes.
5. Serve hot.

Nutrition: Calories: 420 Fat: 2 g Carb: 80 g Protein: 15 g

509. **Southwest chicken salad**
Preparation time: 20 minutes
Cooking time: 30 minutes
Servings: 2
Ingredients:
For chicken:
- 1/2 boneless, skinless chicken breasts, thawed
- 1/2 tbsp avocado oil
- 1/4 tsp cumin powder
- 1/8 tsp garlic powder
- 1 tbsp lime juice (freshly squeezed
- 1/4 tsp chili powder
- 1/8 tsp onion powder
- 1/8 tsp salt or to taste
For salad:
- 2 cups green leaf lettuce
- Small avocado
- 1/2 cup black beans, drained, rinsed
- 1/2 cup corn
- 1/2 cup halved cherry tomatoes
- Southwestern dressing or any other dressing of your choice, as required

Directions:
1. Add chicken, oil, and lime juice into a bowl. Stir until the chicken is well coated with the mixture.
2. Add and stir all the spices into a bowl. Sprinkle all over the chicken. Cover it well and place it in the refrigerator for 20–30 minutes.
3. Discard the marinating mixture and place the chicken in the air fryer basket.
4. Bake in a preheated air fryer at 400 °F for 25 minutes. Flip sides after about 12–13 minutes of baking. Cook till the temperature of the chicken internally is 165 °F.
5. Remove chicken from the air fryer and place it on your cutting board. When cool enough to handle, chop or shred the chicken.
6. Put all salad ingredients into a bowl. Add chicken and toss well. Pour dressing on top and toss well.
7. Serve.

Nutrition (without dressing: Calories: 271 Fat: 6 g Carb: 21 g Protein: 29 g

510. **Chicken shawarma bowl**

Preparation time: 10 minutes
Cooking time: 12–15 minutes
Servings: 2
Ingredients:
- For chicken shawarma:
- 1/2 chicken thighs, skinless, boneless, chopped into bitesize pieces
- 1/2 tsp kosher salt
- 1 tsp oregano herbs (dry)
- 1/2 tsp cumin powder
- 1/4 tsp ground allspice
- 1 tbsp vegetable oil
- 1/2 tsp cinnamon powder
- 1/2 tsp coriander powder
- For the bowl:
- 3/4 cup halved grape tomatoes
- 1/2 small english cucumber, sliced
- 1/2 cup pitted olives
- 1/2 cup cooked cauliflower rice
- 1 cup salad greens
- Dry roasted chickpeas to garnish (optional
- For the dressing (optional:
- 1/2 cup nonfat yogurt (greek
- A pinch oregano
- 1–2 tbsp. Lime juice

Directions:
1. Add oregano, salt, and all the spices into a bowl and mix well.
2. Place chicken in a bowl. Drizzle oil over it. Sprinkle spice mixture over it and toss well.
3. Set aside at room temperature for 30–60 minutes.
4. Transfer into the air fryer basket.
5. Air fry in a preheated air fryer at 350 °F for about 12–15 minutes or until crisp. Shake the basket halfway through frying.
6. For the dressing, prepare the dressing ingredients into a mixing bowl and whisk well.
7. To assemble, take 2 serving bowls. Divide salad greens among the bowls. Place cauliflower rice, tomatoes, cucumber, chicken shawarma, and olives in whatever manner you desire.
8. Drizzle the yogurt dressing on top if desired. Garnish with roasted garbanzo beans if using and serve.

Nutrition: Calories: 313 Fat: 17 g Carb: 12 g Protein: 29 g

511. **Potato chip chicken**
Preparation time: 15 minutes
Cooking time: 15 minutes
Servings: 2
Ingredients:
- 1/2 chicken breasts, thinly sliced
- 2 ounces potato chips, crushed
- 1 egg
- 1/2 tsp all-purpose seasoning (optional)

Directions:
1. Add cooking spray to the air fryer basket.
2. Beat egg in a shallow, wide dish.
3. Place crushed chips on a plate.
4. First, dip chicken slices in the egg. Shake to drop off excess egg. Next, dredge in chips. Press to adhere and place in the air fryer.
5. Air fry in a preheated air fryer at 400 °F for 12–15 minutes or until brown and cooked through. Turn the chicken halfway through cooking. The outer covering should be brown and crisp as well.

Nutrition: Calories: 314 Fat: 15 g Carb: 14 g Protein: 28 g

512. **Calzones**
Preparation time: 15 minutes
Cooking time: 12 minutes
Servings: 4
Ingredients:
- 2 tsp olive oil
- 6 ounces spinach leaves (small
- 4 ounces shredded rotisserie chicken breast
- 3 ounces shredded mozzarella
- 1/2 cup minced red onion

- 2/3 cup marinara sauce
- 12 ounces fresh, prepared whole-wheat pizza dough

Directions:
1. Place a nonstick pan over medium high heat. Add oil. When the oil heats, add onion and sauté until translucent.
2. Mix well spinach and cook until it wilts. Turn the heat off.
3. Add marinara sauce and chicken and mix well.
4. Make 8 equal portions of the dough. Shape into balls.
5. Dust your countertop with some flour. Roll the balls of dough into circles of 6 inches in diameter.
6. Divide the chicken mixture among the rolled dough and place it on one half of the circle. Close the second half over the filling. Crimp the edges to seal.
7. Spray calzones with cooking spray and place in the air fryer.
8. Bake in a preheated air fryer at 350 °F for 12–15 minutes or until golden brown. Turn the calzones halfway through baking.
9. Cool for a few minutes and serve.

Nutrition: Calories: 348 Fat: 12 g Carb: 44 g Protein: 21 g

513.   **Barbecue chicken**
Preparation time: 10 minutes
Cooking time: 20 minutes
Servings: 4
Ingredients:
- ⅓ cup no salt added tomato sauce
- 2 tablespoons low sodium grainy mustard
- 2 tablespoons apple cider vinegar
- 1 tablespoon honey
- 2 garlic cloves, minced
- 1 jalapeño pepper, minced
- 3 tablespoons minced onion
- 4 (5ounce / 142g) lowsodium boneless, skinless chicken breasts

Directions:
1. Press preheat, set the temperature at 370ºF (188ºC).
2. Put together the tomato sauce, mustard, cider vinegar, honey, garlic, jalapeño, and onion.
3. Brush the chicken breasts with some sauce and air fry for 10 minutes.
4. Remove the air fryer basket and turn the chicken; brush with more sauce. Air fry for 5 minutes more.
5. Remove the air fryer basket and turn the chicken again; brush with more sauce. Air fry for 3 to 5 minutes more, or until the chicken reaches an internal temperature of 165ºF.
6. Discard any remaining sauce. Serve immediately.

Nutrition: Calories: 209 Fat: 10g Carbs: 0g Protein: 26g

514.   **Chicken Manchurian**
Preparation time: 10 minutes
Cooking time: 20 minutes
Servings: 2
Ingredients:
- 1pound boneless, skinless chicken breasts
- ¼ cup ketchup
- 1 tablespoon tomato-based chili sauce
- 1 tablespoon soy sauce
- 1 tablespoon rice vinegar
- 2 teaspoons vegetable oil
- 1 teaspoon hot sauce, such as tabasco
- ½ teaspoon garlic powder
- ¼ teaspoon cayenne pepper
- 2 scallions, thinly sliced
- Cooked white rice, for serving

Directions:
1. Slice the chicken into one inch.
2. Press preheat and set the temperature at 350ºF(177ºc).
3. In a bowl, combine the chicken, ketchup, chili sauce, soy sauce, vinegar, oil, hot sauce, garlic powder, cayenne, and three quarters of the scallions and toss until evenly coated.
4. Scrape the chicken and sauce into a metal cake pan and place the pan in the air fryer.
5. Cook until the chicken is bake and the sauce is reduced to a thick glaze, about 20 minutes, flipping the chicken pieces halfway through.

6. Remove the pan from the air fryer. Spoon the chicken and sauce over rice and top with the remaining scallions. Serve immediately.

Nutrition: Calories: 352 Fat: 33g Carbs: 12g Protein: 4g

515.   **Chicken with pineapple and peach**
Preparation time: 10 minutes
Cooking time: 15 minutes
Servings: 4
Ingredients:
- 1 pound (454 g) low sodium boneless, skinless chicken breasts, cut into 1inch pieces
- 1 medium red onion, chopped
- 1 (8ounce / 227g) can pineapple chunks, drained, ¼ cup juice reserved
- 1 tablespoon peanut oil or safflower oil
- 1 peach, peeled, pitted, and cubed
- 1 tablespoon cornstarch
- ½ teaspoon ground ginger
- ¼ teaspoon ground allspice
- Brown rice, cooked (optional)

Directions:
1. Choose to preheat and set the temperature at 380ºF (193ºC).
2. In a medium metal bowl, mix the chicken, red onion, pineapple, and peanut oil. Bake in the air fryer for 9 minutes. Remove and stir.
3. Add the peach and return the bowl to the air fryer. Bake for 3 minutes more. Remove and stir again.
4. Mix the pineapple juice, the cornstarch, ginger, and allspice well. Put to the chicken mixture and stir to combine.
5. Bake for 2 to 3 minutes more or until the chicken reaches an internal temperature of 165ºF (74ºC) on a meat thermometer, and the sauce is slightly thickened.
6. Serve immediately with brown rice, if desired.

Nutrition: Calories: 330 Fat: 4g Carbs: 5g Protein: 18g

516.   **China spicy turkey thighs**
Preparation time: 10 minutes
Cooking time: 25 minutes
Servings: 6
Ingredients:
- 2 pounds (907 g) turkey thighs
- 1 teaspoon Chinese five spice powder
- ¼ teaspoon Sichuan pepper
- 1 teaspoon pink Himalayan salt
- 1 tablespoon Chinese rice vinegar
- 1 tablespoon mustard
- 1 tablespoon chili sauce
- 2 tablespoons soy sauce
- Cooking spray

Directions:
1. Press Preheat set the temperature at 360ºF (182ºC). Put cooking spray in the air fryer basket.
2. Rub the turkey thighs with five spice powder, Sichuan pepper, and salt on a clean work surface.
3. Put the turkey thighs in the preheated air fryer and spritz with cooking spray.
4. Air fry for 22 minutes or until well browned. Flip the thighs at least three times during the cooking.
5. Meanwhile, heat the remaining ingredients in a saucepan over medium high heat. Cook for 3 minutes or until the sauce is thickened and reduces to two thirds.
6. Transfer the thighs onto a plate and baste with sauce before serving.

Nutrition: Calories: 250 Fat: 4g Carbs: 2g Protein: 48g

517.   **Coconut chicken meatballs**
Preparation time: 10 minutes
Cooking time: 14 minutes
Servings: 4
Ingredients:
- 1pound (454 g) ground chicken
- 2 scallions, finely chopped
- 1 cup chopped fresh cilantro leaves
- ¼ cup unsweetened shredded coconut

- 1 tablespoon hoisin sauce
- 1 tablespoon soy sauce
- 2 teaspoons sriracha or other hot sauce
- 1 teaspoon toasted sesame oil
- ½ teaspoon kosher salt
- 1 teaspoon black pepper

Directions:
1. Select preheat, set the temperature at 350°F (177°C).
2. In a large bowl, gently mix the chicken, scallions, cilantro, coconut, hoisin, soy sauce, sriracha, sesame oil, salt, and pepper until thoroughly combined (the mixture will be wet and sticky.
3. Place a sheet of parchment paper in the air fryer basket. Using a small scoop or teaspoon, drop rounds of the mixture in a single layer onto the parchment paper.
4. Air fry for 10 minutes, turning the meatballs halfway through the cooking time. Increase the temperature to 400°f (204°C) and air fry for 4 minutes more to brown the meatballs.
5. Transfer the meatballs to a serving platter. Repeat with any remaining chicken mixture. Serve.

Nutrition: Calories: 321 Fat: 22g Carbs: 9g Protein: 21g

518. Garlic soy chicken thighs
Preparation time: 10 minutes
Cooking time: 30 minutes
Servings: 2
Ingredients:
- 2 tablespoons chicken stock
- 2 tablespoons reduced sodium soy sauce
- 1½ tablespoons sugar
- garlic cloves, smashed and peeled
- 2 large scallions, cut into 2 to 3inch batons, plus more, thinly sliced, for garnish
- 2 bone in, skin on chicken thighs (7 to 8 ounces / 198 to 227 g each)

Directions:
1. Press "preheat" set the temperature at 375F (191C).
2. In a metal cake pan, combine the chicken stock, soy sauce, and sugar and stir until the sugar dissolves.
3. Add the garlic cloves, scallions, and chicken thighs, turning the thighs to coat them in the marinade, then resting them skin side up.
4. Put the pan in the fryer and bake, flipping the thighs every 5 minutes after the first 10 minutes, until the chicken is cooked through and the marinade is reduced to a sticky glaze over the chicken, about 30 minutes.
5. Take the pan from the air fryer and serve the chicken thighs warm, with any remaining glaze spooned over the top, and sprinkled with more sliced scallions.

Nutrition: Calories: 250 Fat: 19g Carbs: 2g Protein: 23g

519. Lettuce chicken tacos with peanut sauce
Preparation time: 10 minutes
Cooking time: 6 minutes
Servings: 4
Ingredients:
- 1pound (454 g) ground chicken
- 2 cloves garlic, minced
- ¼ cup diced onions
- ¼ teaspoon of sea salt
- Cooking spray
- Peanut sauce:
- ¼ cup creamy peanut butter, at room temperature
- 2 tablespoons tamari
- 1½ teaspoons hot sauce
- 2 tablespoons lime juice
- 2 tablespoons grated fresh ginger
- 2 tablespoons chicken broth
- 2 teaspoons sugar

For serving:
- 2 small heads butter lettuce, leaves separated
- Lime slices (optional

Directions:
1. Press preheat mode and set the temperature at 350°f (177°c). Spritz a baking pan with cooking spray.

2. Combine the ground chicken, garlic, and onions in the baking pan, then sprinkle with salt. Use a fork to break the ground chicken and combine them well.
3. Place the pan in the preheated air fryer. Bake in the preheated air fryer for 5 minutes or until the chicken is lightly browned. Stir them halfway through the cooking time.
4. Meanwhile, get the ingredients for the sauce and mix well in a small bowl.
5. Pour the sauce in the pan of chicken, then cook for 1 more minute or until heated through.
6. Unfold the lettuce leaves on a large serving plate, then divide the chicken mixture on the lettuce leaves. Drizzle with lime juice and serve immediately.

Nutrition: Calories: 287 Fat: 16g Carbs: 21g Protein: 19g

520. Pomegranate glazed chicken with couscous salad
Preparation time: 25 minutes
Cooking time: 20 minutes
Servings: 4
Ingredients:
- 3 tablespoons plus 2 teaspoons pomegranate molasses
- ½ teaspoon ground cinnamon
- 1 teaspoon minced fresh thyme
- Salt and ground black pepper, to taste
- 2 (12ounce / 340g) bonein split chicken breasts, trimmed
- ¼ cup chicken broth
- ¼ cup of water
- ½ cup couscous
- 1 tablespoon minced fresh parsley
- 2 ounces (57 g) cherry tomatoes, quartered
- 1 scallion, white part minced, green part sliced thin on bias
- 1 tablespoon extra-virgin olive oil
- 1ounce (28 g) feta cheese, crumbled
- Cooking spray

Directions:
1. Press "preheat" set the temperature at 350°f (177°)c. Spritz the air fryer basket with cooking spray.
2. Combine 3 tablespoons of pomegranate molasses, cinnamon, thyme, and ⅛ teaspoon of salt in a small bowl. Stir to mix well. Set aside.
3. Place the chicken breasts in the preheated air fryer, skin side down, and spritz with cooking spray. Sprinkle with salt and ground black pepper.
4. Air fry for 10 minutes, then brush the chicken with half of the pomegranate molasses mixture and flip. Air fry for 5 more minutes.
5. Brush the chicken with the remaining pomegranate molasses mixture and flip. Air fry for another 5 minutes or until the chicken breasts' internal temperature reaches at least 165°f (74°c).
6. Meanwhile, pour the broth and water into a pot and bring to a boil over medium high heat. Add the couscous and sprinkle with salt.
7. Put cover and let it simmer until the liquid is almost absorbed.
8. Mix well the remaining ingredients, except for the cheese, with cooked couscous in a large bowl. Scatter with the feta cheese.
9. When the air frying is complete, remove the chicken from the air fryer and allow it to cool for 10 minutes. Serve with vegetable and couscous salad.

Nutrition: Calories: 496 Fat: 21g Carbs: 48g Protein: 30g

521. Strawberry glazed turkey
Preparation time: 10 minutes
Cooking time: 37 minutes
Servings: 2
Ingredients:
- 2 pounds (907 g) turkey breast
- 1 tablespoon olive oil
- Salt and ground black pepper, to taste
- 1 cup fresh strawberries

Directions:
1. Choose to preheat, set the temperature at 375°f (191°c).
2. Rub the turkey bread with olive oil on a clean work surface, then sprinkle with salt and ground black pepper.

3. Transfer the turkey to the preheated air fryer and air fry for 30 minutes or until the turkey reaches at least 165°f (74°c). Flip the turkey breast halfway through.
4. Meanwhile, prepare the strawberries in a food processor and pulse until smooth.
5. When the frying of the turkey is complete spread the puréed strawberries over the turkey and fry for 7 more minutes. Serve immediately.

Nutrition: Calories: 269 Fat: 4g Carbs: 10g Protein: 49g

522. Thai curry meatballs
Preparation time: 10 minutes
Cooking time: 10 minutes
Servings: 4
Ingredients:
- 1pound (454 g) ground chicken
- ¼ cup chopped fresh cilantro
- 1 teaspoon chopped fresh mint
- 1 tablespoon fresh lime juice
- 1 tablespoon Thai red, green, or yellow curry paste
- 1 tablespoon fish sauce
- 2 garlic cloves, minced
- 2 teaspoons minced fresh ginger
- ½ teaspoon kosher salt
- ½ teaspoon black pepper
- ¼ teaspoon red pepper flakes

Directions:
1. Press "preheat" set the temperature at 400°f (204°c).
2. In a large bowl, gently mix the ground chicken, cilantro, mint, lime juice, curry paste, fish sauce, garlic, ginger, salt, black pepper, and red pepper flakes until thoroughly combined.
3. Form the mixture into 16 meatballs.
4. Set out the meatballs in a single layer in the air fryer basket. Air fry for 10 minutes, turning the meatballs halfway through the cooking time. Serve immediately.

Nutrition: Calories: 300 Fat: 20g Carbs: 16g Protein: 21g

523. Chicken pasta
Preparation time: 10 minutes
Cooking time: 15 minutes
Servings: 4
Ingredients:
- 1 lb. Bitesize chicken breasts, boneless and skinless
- 1 tbsp garlic, minced
- 2 bell peppers, seeded and diced
- 2 tbsp olive oil
- 1 onion, diced
- 1 cup chicken stock
- 3 tbsp fajita seasoning
- 8 oz penne pasta, dry
- 7 oz can tomato

Directions:
1. Add olive oil and set pot on sauté mode.
2. Add chicken and half fajita seasoning in the pot and sauté chicken for 35 minutes.
3. Add garlic, bell pepper, onions, and remaining fajitas seasoning and sauté for 2 minutes.
4. Add tomatoes, stock, and pasta and stir well.
5. Seal the pot with a pressure-cooking lid and cook on high for 6 minutes.
6. Once done, release pressure using a quick release. Remove lid.
7. Set pot on sauté mode and cook for 12 minutes. Serve and enjoy.

Nutrition: Calories 462 Fat 30g Carbohydrates 14g Protein 37g

524. Sweet & tangy tamarind chicken
Preparation time: 10 minutes
Cooking time: 15 minutes
Servings: 4
Ingredients:
- 2 lbs. Chicken breasts, skinless, boneless, and cut into pieces
- 1 tbsp ketchup
- 1 tbsp vinegar
- 2 tbsp ginger, grated
- 1 garlic clove, minced
- 3 tbsp olive oil
- 1 tbsp arrowroot powder
- 1/2 cup tamarind paste
- 2 tbsp brown sugar
- 1 tsp salt

Directions:
1. Add oil into the inner pot and set on sauté mode.
2. Add ginger and garlic and sauté for 30 seconds.
3. Add chicken and sauté for 4 minutes.
4. Mix the tamarind paste, brown sugar, ketchup, vinegar, and salt and pour over chicken and stir well.
5. Seal the pot with a pressure-cooking lid and cook on high for 8 minutes.
6. Once done, release pressure using a quick release. Remove lid.
7. Get small bowl and put arrowroot powder with 2 tbsp water, then pour it into the pot.
8. Set pot on sauté mode and cook chicken for 12 minutes. Serve and enjoy.

Nutrition: Calories 132 Fat 2g Carbohydrates 35g Protein 2g

525. Tasty butter chicken
Preparation time: 10 minutes
Cooking time: 8 minutes
Servings: 6
Ingredients:
- 3 lbs. Chicken breasts, boneless, skinless, and cut into cubes
- 1/2 cup butter, cut into cubes
- 2 tbsp tomato paste
- 1 tsp turmeric powder
- 2 tbsp garam masala
- 1 tbsp ginger paste
- 1 tbsp garlic paste
- 1 onion, diced
- 1/4 cup fresh cilantro, chopped
- 1/2 cup heavy cream
- 1 1/4 cup tomato sauce
- 2/3 cup chicken stock
- 1 1/2 tsp olive oil
- 1 tsp kosher salt

Directions:
1. Add 3 tbsp butter and oil in the inner pot of instant pot duo crisp and set pot on sauté mode.
2. Add garlic paste and onion and sauté for a minute.
3. Add chicken, tomato sauce, stock, tomato paste, turmeric, garam masala, ginger paste, salt, and stir to combine.
4. Seal the pot with a pressure-cooking lid and cook on high for 5 minutes.
5. Once done, release pressure using a quick release. Remove lid.
6. Set pot on sauté mode. Add remaining butter and heavy cream and cook for 2 minutes.
7. Stir well and serve.

Nutrition: Calories 643 Fat 33 g Carbohydrates 2 g Protein 64 g

526. Dijon chicken
Preparation time: 10 minutes
Cooking time: 50 minutes
Servings: 4
Ingredients:
- 1 1/2 lbs. Chicken thighs, skinless and boneless
- 2 tbsp Dijon mustard
- 1/4 cup French mustard
- 4 tbsp maple syrup
- 2 tsp olive oil

Directions:
1. In a large bowl, mix maple syrup, olive oil, Dijon mustard, and French mustard.
2. Add chicken to the bowl and mix until chicken is well coated.
3. Transfer chicken into the instant pot air fryer basket and place basket in the pot.
4. Seal the pot with an air fryer lid, select bake mode, and cook at 375° f for 50 minutes.
5. Serve and enjoy.

Nutrition: Calories 112 Fat 5g Carbohydrates 3g Protein 18g

527. Mustard chicken

Preparation time: 10 minutes
Cooking time: 20 minutes
Servings: 4
Ingredients:

- 1 lbs. Chicken tenders
- 1 garlic clove, minced
- 1/2 oz fresh lemon juice
- 2 tbsp fresh tarragon, chopped
- 1/2 cup whole grain mustard
- 1/2 tsp paprika
- 1/2 tsp pepper
- 1/4 tsp kosher salt

Directions:

1. Add all ingredients except chicken to the large bowl and mix well.
2. Add chicken to the bowl and stir until well coated.
3. Place the dehydrating tray in a multilevel air fryer basket and place the basket in the instant pot.
4. Place chicken tenders on dehydrating tray.
5. Seal pot with air fryer lid and select bake mode, then set the temperature to 380° f and timer for 20 minutes. Turn chicken halfway through.
6. Serve and enjoy.

Nutrition: Calories 242 Fat 5 g Carbohydrates 1 g Protein 32 g

528. Creamy Italian chicken

Preparation time: 10 minutes
Cooking time: 10 minutes
Servings: 8
Ingredients:

- 2 lbs. Chicken breasts, skinless and boneless
- 1 cup chicken stock
- 1/4 cup butter
- 14 oz can cream of chicken soup
- 8 oz cream cheese
- 1 tbsp Italian seasoning

Directions:

1. Add the chicken stock into the inner pot of instant pot duo crisp.
2. Add cream of chicken soup, Italian seasoning, and butter into the pot and stir well.
3. Seal the pot with a pressure-cooking lid and cook on high for 10 minutes.
4. Once done, release pressure using a quick release. Remove lid.
5. Put and stir the cheese until melted.
6. Serve and enjoy.

Nutrition: Calories 313 Fat 5g Carbohydrates 7g Protein 52g

529. Orange curried chicken stir-fry

Preparation time: 10 minutes
Cooking time: 18 minutes
Servings: 4
Ingredients:

- 1 yellow bell pepper, cut into 1½inch pieces
- 1 small red onion, sliced
- Olive oil for misting
- ¼ cup chicken stock
- 2 tablespoons honey
- ¼ cup of orange juice
- 1 tablespoon cornstarch
- 3 to 3 teaspoons curry powder
- 3/4 lb. Chicken thighs boneless

Directions:

1. Cut the boneless chicken to one inch each piece.
2. Put the chicken thighs, pepper, and red onion in the instant crisp air fryer basket and mist with olive oil.
3. Air frying. Lock the air fryer lid. Cook for 1to 14 minutes or until the chicken is cooked to 165°f, shaking the basket halfway through cooking time.
4. Get the chicken and vegetables from the air fryer basket and set aside.
5. In a 6inch metal bowl, combine the stock, honey, orange juice, cornstarch, curry powder, and mix well. Add the chicken and vegetables, stir, and put the bowl in the basket.

6. Return the basket to the instant crisp air fryer and cook for 2 minutes.
7. Remove and stir, then cook for 2 to 3 minutes or until the sauce is thickened and bubbly.

Nutrition: Calories: 437Fat: 9gCarbs: 54gProtein: 34g

530. Chicken tikka kebab

Preparation time: 8 hours
Cooking time: 17 minutes
Servings: 4
Ingredients:

- 1 lb. Chicken thighs boneless skinless, cubed
- 1 tablespoon oil
- 1/2 cup red onion, cubed
- 1/2 cup green bell pepper, cubed
- 1/2 cup red bell pepper, cubed
- Lime wedges to garnish
- Onion rounds to garnish
- For marinade:
- 1/2 cup yogurt Greek
- 3/4 tablespoon ginger, grated
- 3/4 tablespoon garlic, minced
- 1 tablespoon lime juice
- 2 teaspoon red chili powder mild
- 1/2 teaspoon ground turmeric
- 1 teaspoon garam masala
- 1 teaspoon coriander powder
- 1/2 tablespoon dried fenugreek leaves
- 1 teaspoon salt

Directions:

1. Fold in chicken, then mix well to coat and refrigerate for 8 hours.
2. Add bell pepper, onions, and oil to the marinade and mix well.
3. Arrange chicken, peppers, and onions on the skewers.
4. Set the air fryer basket in the instant pot duo.
5. Put on the air fryer lid and seal it.
6. Hit the "air fry button" and select 10 minutes of cooking time, then press "start."
7. Once the instant pot duo beeps and remove its lid.
8. Flip the skewers and continue air frying for 7 minutes. Serve.

Nutrition: Calories 241 Fat 12g Carbohydrate 5g Protein 28g

531. Honey cashew butter chicken

Preparation time: 10 minutes
Cooking time: 7 minutes
Servings: 3
Ingredients:

- 1 lb. Chicken breast, cut into chunks
- 2 tbsp rice vinegar
- 2 tbsp honey
- 2 tbsp coconut aminos
- 1/4 cup cashew butter
- 2 garlic cloves, minced
- 1/4 cup chicken broth
- 1/2 tbsp sriracha

Directions:

1. Add chicken into the inner pot of instant pot duo crisp.
2. In a small bowl, mix cashew butter, garlic, broth, sriracha, vinegar, honey, and coconut aminos and pour over chicken.
3. Seal the pot with a pressure-cooking lid and cook on high for 7 minutes.
4. Once done, release pressure using a quick release. Remove lid.
5. Stir well and serve.

Nutrition: Calories 252 Fat 12g Carbohydrates 24g Protein 16g

532. Chicken mac and cheese

Preparation time: 10 minutes
Cooking time: 9 minutes
Servings: 6
Ingredients:

- 2 1/2 cup macaroni
- 2 cup chicken stock
- 1 cup cooked chicken, shredded
- 1 1/4 cup heavy cream
- 8 tablespoon butter

- 2 2/3 cups cheddar cheese, shredded
- 1/3 cup parmesan cheese, shredded
- 1 bag Ritz crackers
- 1/4 teaspoon garlic powder
- Salt and pepper to taste

Directions:
1. Add chicken stock, heavy cream, chicken, 4 tablespoon butter, and macaroni to the instant pot duo.
2. Put on the pressure-cooking lid and seal it.
3. Hit the "pressure button" and select 4 minutes of cooking time, then press "start."
4. Crush the crackers and mix them well with tablespoons melted butter.
5. Once the instant pot duo beeps, do a quick release and remove its lid.
6. Put on the air fryer lid and seal it.
7. Hit the "air fryer button" and select 5 minutes of cooking time, then press "start."
8. Once the instant pot duo beeps, remove its lid. Serve.

Nutrition: Calories 366 Fat 5g Carbohydrate 35gg Protein 41g

533. Duck breasts with endives
Preparation time: 10 minutes
Cooking time: 25 minutes
Servings: 4
Ingredients:
- Duck breasts – 2
- Salt and black pepper to taste
- Sugar – 1 tbsp.
- Olive oil – 1 tbsp.
- Endives – 6, julienned
- Cranberries – 2 tbsps.
- White wine – 8 ounces
- Garlic – 1 tbsp. Minced
- Heavy cream – 2 tbsps.

Directions:
1. Cut the duck breasts and season with salt and pepper.
2. Cook in the fryer at 350°f for 20 minutes. Flip once.
3. At the same time, heat a pan with oil over medium heat.
4. Add endives and sugar. Stir and cook for 2 minutes. Add salt, pepper, wine, garlic, cream, and cranberries.
5. Stir-fry for 3 minutes—divide duck breasts among plates.
6. Drizzle with the endives sauce and serve.

Nutrition: Calories: 550 Fat: 23g Carbs: 51g Protein: 38g

534. Pork chop fries
Preparation time: 10 minutes
Cooking time: 15 minutes
Serve: 4
Ingredients:
- 1 lb. Pork chops, cut into fries
- 1/2 cup parmesan cheese, grated
- Oz pork rinds, crushed
- 1/2 cup ranch dressing
- Pepper
- Salt

Directions:
1. In a shallow dish, mix crushed pork rinds, parmesan cheese, pepper, and salt.
2. Add pork chop pieces and ranch dressing into the Ziplock bag, seal bag and shake well.
3. Remove pork chop pieces from Ziplock bag and coat with crushed pork rind mixture.
4. Place the cooking tray in the air fryer basket—line the air fryer basket with parchment paper.
5. Select bake mode.
6. Set time to 15 minutes and temperature 400° f, then press start.
7. The air fryer display will prompt you to add food once the temperature is reached, then place breaded pork chop fries in the air fryer basket.
8. Serve and enjoy.

Nutrition: Calories 608 Fat 44 g Carbohydrates 7 g Protein 52 g

535. Herb pork chops
Preparation time: 10 minutes
Cooking time: 15 minutes

Serve: 4
Ingredients:
- 4 pork chops
- 2 tsp oregano
- 2 tsp thyme
- 2 tsp sage
- 1 tsp garlic powder
- 1 tsp paprika
- 1 tsp rosemary
- Pepper
- Salt

Directions:
1. Spray pork chops with cooking spray.
2. Mix together garlic powder, paprika, rosemary, oregano, thyme, sage, pepper, and salt and rub over pork chops.
3. Select air fry mode.
4. Set time to 15 minutes and temperature 360° f, then press start.
5. The air fryer display will prompt you to add food once the temperature is reached.
6. Put the pork chops in the air fryer basket. Turn pork chops halfway through.
7. Serve and enjoy.

Nutrition: Calories 266 Fat 22 g Carbohydrates 2 g Sugar 3 g Protein 14 g

536. Spicy parmesan pork chops
Preparation time: 10 minutes
Cooking time: 9 minutes
Servings: 2
Ingredients:
- 2 pork chops, boneless
- 1 tsp paprika
- 3 tbsp parmesan cheese, grated
- 1/3 cup almond flour
- 1 tsp Cajun seasoning
- 1 tsp dried mixed herbs

Directions:
1. In a shallow bowl, mix parmesan cheese, almond flour, paprika, mixed herbs, and Cajun seasoning.
2. Spray pork chops with cooking spray and coat with parmesan cheese.
3. Select air fry mode.
4. Set time to 9 minutes and temperature 350° f, then press start.
5. The air fryer display will show add food once the temperature is reached, then place breaded pork chops in the air fryer basket. Turn pork chops halfway through.
6. Serve and enjoy.

Nutrition: Calories 359 Fat 22 g Carbohydrates 6 g Sugar 3 g Protein 24 g

537. Moist pork chops
Preparation time: 10 minutes
Cooking time: 14 minutes
Servings: 2
Ingredients:
- 2 pork chops
- 1 tsp paprika
- 1 tsp garlic powder
- 1 tsp olive oil
- Pepper
- Salt

Directions:
1. Graze pork chops with olive oil and season with garlic powder, paprika, pepper, and salt.
2. Select air fry mode.
3. Set time to 14 minutes and temperature 360° f, then press start.
4. Once the temperature is reached, the fryer will prompt add food. Place pork chops in the basket. Turn pork chops halfway through.
5. Serve and enjoy.

Nutrition: Calories 284 Fat 24 g Carbohydrates 6 g Sugar 5 g Protein 14 g

538. Pecan Dijon pork chops
Preparation time: 10 minutes
Cooking time: 12 minutes
Servings: 6
Ingredients:

- 1 egg
- 6 pork chops, boneless
- 2 garlic cloves, minced
- 1 tbsp water
- 1 tsp Dijon mustard
- 1 tsp garlic powder
- 1 tsp onion powder
- 2 tsp Italian seasoning
- 1/3 cup arrowroot
- 1 cup pecans, finely chopped
- 1/4 tsp salt

Directions:
1. Mix egg with garlic, water, and Dijon mustard in an empty mixing bowl.
2. In a separate shallow bowl, mix arrowroot, pecans, Italian seasoning, onion powder, garlic powder, and salt.
3. Dip pork chop in the egg mixture and coat with arrowroot mixture.
4. Place the cooking tray in the air fryer basket.
5. Select air fry mode.
6. Set time to 12 minutes and temperature 400° f, then press start.
7. The air fryer display will prompt you to add food once the temperature is reached. Add the coated pork chops in the air fryer basket.
8. Turn pork chops halfway through. Serve and enjoy.

Nutrition: Calories 410 Fat 31 g Carbohydrates 8 g Sugar 1 g Protein 24 g

539. Stuffed pork chops
Preparation time: 10 minutes
Cooking time: 35 minutes
Servings: 4
Ingredients:
- 4 pork chops, boneless and thick cut
- 2 tbsp olives, chopped
- 2 tbsp sundried tomatoes, chopped
- 1/2 cup feta cheese, crumbled
- 2 garlic cloves, minced
- 2 tbsp fresh parsley, chopped

Directions:
1. In a bowl, combine feta cheese, garlic, parsley, olives, and sundried tomatoes.
2. Stuff cheese mixture all the pork chops. Season pork chops with pepper and salt.
3. Select bake mode.
4. Set time to 35 minutes and temperature 375° f, then press start.
5. The air fryer display will prompt you to add food once the temperature is reached, then place stuffed pork chops in the air fryer basket. Serve and enjoy.

Nutrition: Calories 314 Fat 24 g Carbohydrates 9 g Protein 29 g

540. Cajun herb pork chops
Preparation time: 10 minutes
Cooking time: 9 minutes
Servings: 2
Ingredients:
- 2 pork chops, boneless
- 1 tsp herb de Provence
- 1 tsp paprika
- 1/2 tsp Cajun seasoning
- 3 tbsp parmesan cheese, grated
- 1/3 cup almond flour

Directions:
1. Mix together almond flour, Cajun seasoning, herb de Provence, paprika, and parmesan cheese.
2. Spray both the pork chops with cooking spray.
3. Coat both the pork chops with almond flour mixture.
4. Select bake mode.
5. Set time to 8 minutes and temperature 350° f, then press start.
6. Add pork chops in the air fryer basket. Turn pork chops halfway through.
7. Serve and enjoy.

Nutrition: Calories 332 Fat 23 g Carbohydrates 2 g Sugar 3 g Protein 24 g

541. Thai pork chops
Preparation time: 2 hours

Cooking time: 12 minutes
Servings: 2
Ingredients:
- 2 pork chops
- 1 tsp black pepper
- 3 tbsp lemongrass, chopped
- 1 tbsp shallot, chopped
- 1 tbsp garlic, chopped
- 1 tsp liquid stevia
- 1 tbsp sesame oil
- 1 tbsp fish sauce
- 1 tsp soy sauce

Directions:
1. Add pork chops in a mixing bowl.
2. Pour remaining ingredients over the pork chops and mix well.
3. Place in refrigerator for 2 hours.
4. Select air fry mode.
5. Set time to 12 minutes and temperature 400° f, then press start.
6. The air fryer display will prompt you to add food once the temperature is reached, then place marinated pork chops in the air fryer basket. Serve and enjoy.

Nutrition: Calories 340 Fat 28 g Carbohydrates 3 g Sugar 4 g Protein 13 g

542. Creole seasoned pork chops
Preparation time: 10 minutes
Cooking time: 12 minutes
Servings: 6
Ingredients:
- 1 1/2 lbs. Pork chops, boneless
- 1/4 cup parmesan cheese, grated
- 1/3 cup almond flour
- 1 tsp paprika
- 1 tsp creole seasoning
- 1 tsp garlic powder

Directions:
1. Add all ingredients except pork chops into the Ziplock bag.
2. Add pork chops into the bag. Seal bag and shake well.
3. Remove pork chops from the Ziplock bag.
4. Select air fry mode.
5. Set time to 12 minutes and temperature 360° f, then press start.
6. Put the pork chops in the basket once the display prompt you to add food.
7. Serve and enjoy.

Nutrition: Calories 405 Fat 31 g Carbohydrates 2 g Sugar 2 g Protein 21 g

543. Air fried pork bites
Preparation time: 10 minutes
Cooking time: 15 minutes
Servings: 4
Ingredients:
- 1 lb. Pork belly, cut into 1inch cubes
- 1 tsp soy sauce
- Pepper
- Salt

Directions:
1. In a bowl, toss pork cubes with soy sauce, pepper, and salt.
2. Select air fry mode.
3. Set time to 15 minutes and temperature 400° f, then press start.
4. The air fryer display will prompt you to add food once the temperature is reached, then place pork cubes in the air fryer basket.
5. Serve and enjoy.

Nutrition: Calories 524 Fat 35 g Carbohydrates 1 g Sugar 0 g Protein 54 g

544. Coconut pork chops
Preparation time: 10 minutes
Cooking time: 14 minutes
Servings: 4
Ingredients:
- 4 pork chops
- 1 tbsp coconut oil
- 1 tbsp coconut butter
- 2 tsp parsley
- 2 tsp garlic, grated
- Pepper

- Salt

Directions:
1. In a large bowl, mix with seasonings, garlic, butter, and coconut oil.
2. Add and mix well pork chops to the bowl. Place in refrigerator overnight. Select air fry mode.
3. Set time to 14 minutes and temperature 350° f, then press start.
4. Once the temperature is reached the air fryer display will prompt you to add food.
5. then place marinated pork chops in the air fryer basket. Turn pork chops halfway through.
6. Serve and enjoy.

Nutrition: Calories 299 Fat 28 g Carbohydrates 3 g Sugar 3 g Protein 13 g

545.   Pork kebabs
Preparation time: 4 hours
Cooking time: 15 minutes
Serve: 6
Ingredients:
- 2 lbs. Country style pork ribs, cut into cubes
- 1/4 cup soy sauce
- 1/2 cup olive oil
- 1 tbsp Italian seasoning

Directions:
1. Add soy sauce, oil, Italian seasoning, pork cubes into the Ziplock bag, seal bag, and place in the refrigerator for 4 hours.
2. Remove pork cubes from marinade and place the cubes on wooden skewers.
3. Place the cooking tray in the air fryer basket.
4. Line the air fryer basket with parchment paper. Select bake mode.
5. Set time to 15 minutes and temperature 380° f, then press start.
6. The air fryer display will prompt you to add food once the temperature is reached, then place pork skewers in the air fryer basket.
7. Serve and enjoy.

Nutrition: Calories 438 Fat 39 g Carbohydrates 1 g Protein 31 g

546.   Spicy pork patties
Preparation time: 10 minutes
Cooking time: 10 minutes
Serve: 2
Ingredients:
- 1/2 lb. Ground pork
- 1 tbsp Cajun seasoning
- 1 egg, lightly beaten
- 1/2 cup almond flour
- Pepper
- Salt

Directions:
1. Add all ingredients and mix into the large bowl until well combined.
2. Make two equal shapes of patties from the meat mixture.
3. Select air fry mode.
4. Set time to 10 minutes and temperature 360° f, then press start.
5. The air fryer display will prompt you to add food once the temperature is reached, then place patties in the air fryer basket.
6. Serve and enjoy.

Nutrition: Calories 234 Fat 7 g Carbohydrates 7 g Protein 34 g

547.   Lemon pepper pork
Preparation time: 5 minutes
Cooking time: 15 minutes
Servings: 4
Ingredients:
- 4 pork chops, boneless
- 1 tsp lemon pepper seasoning
- Salt

Directions:
1. Season pork chops with lemon pepper seasoning and salt.
2. Select air fry mode.
3. Set time to 15 minutes and temperature 400° f, then press start.
4. The air fryer display will prompt you to add food once the temperature is reached.
5. Add pork chops in the air fryer basket.
6. Serve and enjoy.

Nutrition: Calories 257 Fat 19 g Carbohydrates 3 g Protein 18 g

548.   Boozy pork loin chops
Preparation time: 5 minutes
Cooking time: 18 minutes
Servings: 6
Ingredients:
- 2 tablespoons vermouth
- 6 center cut loin pork chops
- 1/2 tablespoon fresh basil, minced
- 1/3 teaspoon ground black pepper
- 2 tablespoons whole grain mustard
- 1 teaspoon fine kosher salt

Directions:
1. Toss pork chops with other ingredients until they are well coated on both sides.
2. Air fry your chops for 18 minutes at 405° f, turning once or twice.
3. Mound your favorite salad on a serving plate; top with pork chops and enjoy.

Nutrition: Calories 393 Fat 14g Carbs 6g Protein 56g

549.   Classic smoked pork chops
Preparation time: 10 minutes
Cooking time: 20 minutes
Servings: 6
Ingredients:
- 6 pork chops
- Hickory smoked salt, to savor
- Ground black pepper, to savor
- 1 teaspoon onion powder
- 1/2 teaspoon garlic powder
- 1/2 teaspoon cayenne pepper
- 1/3 cup almond meal

Directions
1. Gently put all ingredients into a zip top plastic bag; shake them up to coat well.
2. Spritz the chops with a pan spray (canola spray) works well here and transfer them to the air fryer cooking basket.
3. Roast them for 20 minutes at 375 °f. Serve with sautéed vegetables.

Nutrition: 332 calories 17g fat 8g carbs 48g protein

550.   Pork ribs with red wine sauce
Preparation time: 3 hours
Cooking time: 25 minutes
Servings: 4
Ingredients:
- For the pork ribs:
- 1 ½ pounds pork ribs
- 2 tablespoons olive oil
- 1/2 teaspoon freshly cracked black peppercorns
- 1/2 teaspoon hickory smoked salt
- 1 tablespoon Dijon mustard
- 2 tablespoons coconut aminos
- 2 tablespoons lime juice
- 1 clove garlic, minced
- For the red wine sauce:
- 1 ½ cups beef stock
- 1 cup red wine
- 1 teaspoon balsamic vinegar
- 1/4 teaspoon salt

Directions:
1. Place all ingredients for the pork ribs in a large sized mixing dish. Cover and marinate in your refrigerator overnight or at least 3 hours.
2. Air fry the pork ribs for 10 minutes at 320° f.
3. Meanwhile, make the sauce. Add a beef stock to a deep pan preheated over a moderate flame; boil until it is reduced by half.
4. Add the remaining ingredients and increase the temperature to high heat. Let it cook for further 10 minutes or until your sauce is reduced by half.
5. Serve the pork ribs with red wine sauce. Bon appétit!

Nutrition: Calories 438 Fat 23g Carbs 3g Protein 32g

551. Pork with buttery broccoli

Preparation time: 15 minutes
Cooking time: 30 minutes
Servings: 4

Ingredients:

- 1 ½ pounds blade steaks skinless, boneless
- Kosher salt
- Ground black pepper, to taste
- 2 garlic cloves, crushed
- 2 tablespoons coconut aminos
- 1 tablespoon oyster sauce
- 2 tablespoon lemon juice
- 1pound broccoli, broken into florets
- 2 tablespoons butter, melted
- 1 teaspoon dried dill weed
- 2 tablespoons sunflower seeds, lightly toasted

Directions:

1. Start by preheating your air fryer to 385° f. Spritz the bottom and sides of the cooking basket with cooking spray.
2. Now, season the pork with salt and black pepper. Add the garlic, coconut aminos, oyster sauce, and lemon juice.
3. Cook for 20 minutes then turn over halfway through the cooking time.
4. Toss the broccoli with the melted butter and dill. Add the broccoli to the cooking basket and cook at 400° f for 6 minutes, shaking the basket periodically.
5. Serve the warm pork with broccoli and garnish with sunflower seeds.

Nutrition: Calories 346 Fat 11g Carbs 4g Protein 32g

552. Pork sausage with mashed cauliflower

Preparation time: 10 minutes
Cooking time: 30 minutes
Servings: 6

Ingredients:

- 1pound cauliflower, chopped
- 1/2 teaspoon tarragon
- 1/3 cup Colby cheese
- 1/2 teaspoon ground black pepper
- 1/2 onion, peeled and sliced
- 1 teaspoon cumin powder
- 1/2 teaspoon sea salt
- 3 beaten eggs
- 6 pork sausages, chopped

Directions

1. Boil the cauliflower until tender. Then, purée the cauliflower in your blender.
2. Transfer to a mixing dish along with the other ingredients.
3. Divide the prepared mixture among six lightly greased ramekins; now, place ramekins in your air fryer.
4. Bake in the preheated air fryer for 27 minutes at 365° f. Eat warm.

Nutrition: Calories 506 Fat 42g Carbs 6g Protein 28g

553. Farmhouse pork with vegetables

Preparation time: 10 minutes
Cooking time: 45 minutes
Servings: 6

Ingredients:

- 1 ½ pounds pork belly
- 2 bell peppers, sliced
- 2 cloves garlic, finely minced
- 4 green onions, quartered, white and green parts
- 1/4 cup cooking wine
- Kosher salt
- Ground black pepper, to taste
- 1 teaspoon cayenne pepper
- 1 tablespoon coriander
- 1 teaspoon celery seeds

Directions

1. Boil the pork belly for approximately 15 minutes. Then, cut it into chunks.

2. Arrange the pork chunks, bell peppers, garlic, and green onions in the air fryer basket. Drizzle everything with cooking wine of your choice.
3. Sprinkle with salt, black pepper, cayenne pepper, fresh coriander, and celery seeds. Toss to coat well.
4. Roast in the preheated air fryer at 330° f for 30 minutes.
5. Serve on individual serving plates. Bon appétit!

Nutrition: Calories 589 Fat 67g Carbs 5g Protein 19g

554. Spicy pork sausage with eggs

Preparation time: 15 minutes
Cooking time: 30 minutes
Servings: 6

Ingredients:

- 1 seeded green bell pepper, thinly sliced
- 6 medium-sized eggs
- 1 habanero pepper, seeded and minced
- 1/2 teaspoon sea salt
- 2 teaspoons fennel seeds
- 1 thinly sliced red bell pepper, seeded
- 1 teaspoon tarragon
- 1/2 teaspoon freshly cracked black pepper
- 6 pork sausages

Directions

1. Place the sausages and all peppers in the air fryer cooking basket. Cook at 335° f for 9 minutes.
2. Divide the eggs among 6 ramekins; sprinkle each egg with the seasonings.
3. Cook for 11 more minutes at 395° f. Serve warm with sausages. Enjoy!

Nutrition: Calories 468 Fat 39g Carbs 6g Protein 26g

555. Spicy pork meatballs

Preparation time: 15 minutes
Cooking time: 15 minutes
Servings: 4

Ingredients:

- 1pound ground pork
- 1 cup scallions, finely chopped
- 2 cloves garlic, finely minced
- 1 ½ tablespoons Worcester sauce
- 1 tablespoon oyster sauce
- 1 teaspoon turmeric powder
- 1/2 teaspoon freshly grated ginger root
- 1 small sliced red chili, for garnish

Directions

1. Prepare all the ingredients apart from red chili. Mix using the hands to ensure an even mixture.
2. Roll into equal balls and transfer them to the air fryer cooking basket.
3. Set the timer for 15 minutes and push the power button. Air fry at 350° f.
4. Sprinkle with sliced red chili; serve immediately with your favorite sauce for dipping. Enjoy!

Nutrition: Calories 354 Fat 26g Carbs 8g Protein 30g

556. Meatballs with herbs and mozzarella

Preparation time: 10 minutes
Cooking time: 15 minutes
Servings: 4

Ingredients:

- 1/2pound ground pork
- 1/2pound ground beef
- 1 shallot, chopped
- 2 garlic cloves, minced
- 1 tablespoon coriander, chopped
- 1 teaspoon fresh mint, minced
- Sea salt
- Ground black pepper, to taste
- 1/2 teaspoon mustard seeds
- 1 teaspoon fennel seeds
- 1 teaspoon ground cumin
- 1 cup mozzarella, sliced

Directions

1. Get a bowl and mix all ingredients, except the mozzarella.

2. Shape the mixture into balls and transfer them to a lightly greased cooking basket.
3. Cook the meatballs in the preheated air fryer at 380° for 10 minutes. Check the meatballs halfway through the cooking time.
4. Top with sliced mozzarella and bake for 3 minutes more.
5. To serve, arrange on a nice serving platter. Bon appétit!

Nutrition: Calories 311 Fat 15g Carbs 5g Protein 31g

557. Spicy and creamy pork gratin

Preparation time: 10 minutes
Cooking time: 20 minutes
Servings: 4
Ingredients:

- 2 tablespoons olive oil
- 2 pounds pork tenderloin, cut into serving size pieces
- 1 teaspoon coarse sea salt
- 1/2 teaspoon freshly ground pepper
- 1/4 teaspoon chili powder
- 1 teaspoon dried marjoram
- 1 tablespoon mustard
- 1 cup ricotta cheese
- 1 ½ cups chicken broth

Directions

1. Ready your air fryer to 350° f.
2. Heat the olive oil in a pan over medium high heat. Once hot, cook the pork for 6 to 7 minutes, flipping it to ensure even cooking.
3. Arrange the pork in a lightly greased casserole dish. Season with salt, black pepper, chili powder, and marjoram.
4. In a mixing dish, thoroughly combine the mustard, cheese, and chicken broth. Pour the mixture over the pork chops in the casserole dish.
5. Bake for another 15 minutes or until bubbly and heated through.

Nutrition: 433 calories 24g fat 6g carbs 55g protein

558. Cheesy ground pork casserole

Preparation time: 10 minutes
Cooking time: 20 minutes
Servings: 4
Ingredients:

- 1 pound lean ground pork
- 1/2 pound ground beef
- 1/4 cup tomato puree
- Sea salt
- Ground black pepper, to taste
- 1 teaspoon smoked paprika
- 1/2 teaspoon dried oregano
- 1 teaspoon dried basil
- 1 teaspoon dried rosemary
- 2 eggs
- 1 cup cottage cheese, crumbled, at room temperature
- 1/2 cup cotija cheese, shredded

Directions

1. Lightly grease a casserole dish with a nonstick cooking oil. Add the ground meat to the bottom of your casserole dish.
2. Add the tomato puree. Sprinkle with salt, black pepper, paprika, oregano, basil, and rosemary.
3. Mix egg with cheese in a mixing bowl. Place on top of the ground meat mixture. Place a piece of foil on top.
4. Bake in the preheated air fryer at 350° f for 10 minutes; remove the foil and cook an additional 6 minutes. Bon appétit!

Nutrition: 449 calories 23g fat 6g carbs; 4g protein

559. Spanish Pinchos Morunos

Preparation time: 2 hours
Cooking time: 20 minutes
Servings: 4
Ingredients:

- 2 pounds center cut loin chop, cut into bitesize pieces
- 1 teaspoon oregano
- 1/2 teaspoon ground turmeric
- 1/2 teaspoon ground coriander
- 1 teaspoon ground cumin
- 2 teaspoons sweet Spanish paprika
- Sea salt

- Freshly ground black pepper, to taste
- 2 garlic cloves, minced
- 2 tablespoons extra virgin olive oil
- 1/4 cup dry red wine
- 1 lemon, 1/2 juiced 1/2 wedges

Directions

1. Get all ingredients, except the lemon wedges, then mix well in a large ceramic dish. Allow it to marinate for 2 hours in your refrigerator.
2. Discard the marinade. Now, thread the pork pieces on to skewers and place them in the cooking basket.
3. Preheat the air fryer at 360 ° f.
4. Cook for 15 minutes and shaking the basket every 5 minutes. Work in batches.
5. Serve immediately garnished with lemon wedges. Enjoy.

Nutrition: Calories 432 Fat 23g Carbs 4g Protein 49g

560. Bolognese sauce with a twist

Preparation time: 10 minutes
Cooking time: 14 minutes
Servings: 4
Ingredients:

- 1 teaspoon kosher salt
- 1/3 teaspoon cayenne pepper
- 1½ pounds ground pork
- 1/3 cup tomato paste
- 3 cloves garlic, minced
- 1/2 medium-sized white onion, peeled and chopped
- 1/3 tablespoon fresh cilantro, chopped
- 1/2 tablespoon extra-virgin olive oil
- 1/3 teaspoon freshly cracked black pepper
- 1/2 teaspoon grated fresh ginger

Directions:

1. Begin by preheating your air fryer to 395 ° f.
2. Then, thoroughly combine all the ingredients until the mixture is uniform.
3. Transfer the meat mixture to the air fryer baking dish and cook for about 14 minutes.
4. Serve with zucchini noodles and enjoy.

Nutrition: Calories 490 Fat 33g Carbs 2g Protein 29g

561. Spicy Chicken Tenders with Aioli Sauce

Preparation Time: 10 minutes
Cooking Time: 12 minutes
Servings: 4
Ingredients:

- 3 chicken breasts, skinless, cut into strips
- 4 tbsp olive oil
- 1 cup breadcrumbs
- Salt and black pepper to taste
- ½ tbsp garlic powder
- ½ tbsp ground chili
- ½ cup mayonnaise
- 2 tbsp olive oil
- ½ tbsp ground chili

Directions:

1. Mix breadcrumbs, salt, pepper, garlic powder and chili, and spread onto a plate. Spray the chicken with oil. Roll the strips in the breadcrumb mixture until well coated. Spray with a little bit of oil.
2. Arrange an even layer of strips into your air fryer and cook for 6 minutes at 360° F, turning once halfway through. To prepare the hot aioli: combine mayo with oil and ground chili. Serve hot.

Nutrition: Calories: 490 Fat: 21g Carbs: 34g Protein: 39g

562. Marinara Sauce Cheese Chicken

Preparation Time: 10 minutes
Cooking time: 15 minutes
Servings: 2
Ingredients:

- 2 chicken breasts, skinless, beaten, ½-inch thick
- 1 egg, beaten
- ½ cup breadcrumbs
- A pinch of salt and black pepper
- 2 tbsp marinara sauce

- 2 tbsp Grana Padano cheese, grated
- 2 slices mozzarella cheese

Directions:
1. Dip the breasts into the egg, then into the crumbs and arrange in the fryer; cook for 5 minutes at 400° F.
2. Then, turn over and drizzle with marinara sauce, Grana Padano and mozzarella.
3. Cook for 5 more minutes at 400 F.

Nutrition: Calories: 265 Fat: 10g Carbs: 10g Protein: 32g

563. Honey Thighs with Garlic

Preparation Time: 10 minutes
Cooking time: 30 minutes
Servings: 4

Ingredients:
- 4 thighs, skin-on
- 3 tbsp honey
- 2 tbsp Dijon mustard
- ½ tbsp garlic powder
- Salt and black pepper to taste

Directions:
1. In a bowl, mix honey, mustard, garlic, salt, and black pepper.
2. Coat the thighs in the mixture and arrange them in your air fryer.
3. Cook for 16 minutes at 400 F, turning once halfway through.

Nutrition: Calories: 294 Fat: 7g Carbs: 19g Protein: 34g

564. Buttery Chicken with Monterrey Jack Cheese

Preparation Time: 10 minutes
Cooking time: 15 minutes
Servings: 4

Ingredients:
- ½ cup Italian breadcrumbs
- 2 tbsp grated Parmesan cheese
- 1 tbsp butter, melted
- 4 chicken thighs
- ½ cup marinara sauce
- ½ cup shredded Monterrey Jack cheese

Directions:
1. Spray the air fryer basket with cooking spray. In a bowl, mix the crumbs and Parmesan cheese. Pour the butter into another bowl. Brush the thighs with butter. Dip each one into the crumbs mixture, until well-coated.
2. Arrange two chicken thighs in the air fryer, and lightly spray with cooking oil.
3. Cook for 5 minutes at 380° F. Flip over, top with a few tbsp marinara sauce and shredded Monterrey Jack cheese. Cook until no longer pink in the center, for 4 minutes. Repeat with the remaining thighs.

Nutrition: Calories: 290 Fat: 11g Carbs: 36g Protein: 14g

565. Chicken Breasts with Rosemary

Preparation Time: 10minutes
Cooking time: 20 minutes
Servings: 2

Ingredients:
- 2 tbsp Dijon mustard
- 1 tbsp maple syrup
- 2 tsp minced fresh rosemary
- ¼ tsp salt
- ⅛ tsp black pepper
- 2 chicken breasts, boneless, skinless

Directions:
1. In a bowl, mix mustard, maple syrup, rosemary, salt, and pepper. Rub mixture onto chicken breasts.
2. Spray generously the air fryer basket generously with cooking spray.
3. Arrange the breasts inside and cook for 20 minutes, turning once halfway through.

Nutrition: Calories: 183 Fat: 8g Carbs: 1g Protein: 23g

566. Thyme Whole Chicken with Pancetta and Lemon

Preparation Time: 15 minutes
Cooking time: 30 minutes
Servings: 4

Ingredients:
- 1 small whole chicken
- 1 lemon
- 4 slices pancetta, roughly chopped
- 1 onion, chopped
- 1 sprig fresh thyme
- Olive oil
- Salt and black pepper

Directions:
1. In a bowl, mix pancetta, onion, thyme, salt, and black pepper. Pat dry the chicken with a dry paper towel. Insert the pancetta mixture into chicken's cavity and press tight.
2. Put in the whole lemon and rub the top and sides of the chicken with salt and black pepper. Spray the air fryer's basket with olive oil and arrange the chicken inside.
3. Cook for 30 minutes on 400° F, turning once halfway through.

Nutrition: Calories: 383 Fat: 16g Carbs: 1g Protein: 55g

567. Green Chicken Drumsticks with Coconut Cream

Preparation Time: 10 minutes
Cooking time: 15 minutes
Servings: 4

Ingredients:
- 4 chicken drumsticks, boneless, skinless
- 2 tbsp green curry paste
- 3 tbsp coconut cream
- Salt and black pepper
- ½ fresh jalapeno chili, finely chopped
- A handful of fresh parsley, roughly chopped

Directions:
1. In a bowl, add drumsticks, paste, cream, salt, black pepper and jalapeno; coat the chicken well.
2. Arrange the drumsticks in the air fryer and cook for 6 minutes at 400° F, flipping once halfway through.
3. Serve with fresh cilantro.

Nutrition: Calories: 412 Fat: 23g Carbs: 16g Protein: 37g

568. Creamy Chicken Nuggets

Preparation Time: 5 minutes
Cooking time: 10 minutes
Servings: 4

Ingredients:
- 2 chicken breasts, skinless, boneless, cut into nuggets
- 4 tbsp sour cream
- ½ cup breadcrumbs
- ½ tbsp garlic powder
- ½ tsp cayenne pepper
- Salt and black pepper to taste

Directions:
1. In a bowl, add sour cream and place the chicken. Stir well.
2. Mix the breadcrumbs, garlic, cayenne, salt, and black pepper and scatter onto a plate.
3. Roll up the chicken in the breadcrumbs to coat well.
4. Grease the air with oil. Arrange the nuggets in an even layer and cook for 10 minutes on 360° F, turning once halfway through cooking.

Nutrition: Calories: 215 Fat: 13g Carbs: 10g Protein: 13g

569. Herby Stuffed Chicken

Preparation Time: 15 minutes
Cooking time: 50 minutes
Servings: 2

Ingredients:
- 1 small chicken
- 1 ½ tbsp olive oil
- Salt and black pepper to taste to season
- 1 cup breadcrumbs
- ⅓ cup chopped sage
- ⅓ cup chopped thyme
- 2 cloves garlic, crushed
- 1 brown onion, chopped
- 3 tbsp butter
- 2 eggs, beaten

Directions:
1. Rinse the chicken gently, pat dry with a paper towel and remove any excess fat with a knife; set aside. On a stove top, place a pan.

Add the butter, garlic and onion and sauté to brown. Add the eggs, sage, thyme, pepper, and salt.

2. Mix well. Cook for 20 seconds and turn the heat off. Stuff the chicken with the mixture into the cavity. Then, tie the legs of the spatchcock with a butcher's twine and brush with olive oil. Rub the top and sides of the chicken generously with salt and pepper. Preheat the Air Fryer to 390° F.

3. Place the spatchcock into the fryer basket and roast for 25 minutes. Turn the chicken over and continue cooking for 10-15 minutes more; check throughout the cooking time to ensure it doesn't dry or overcooks. Remove onto a chopping board and wrap with aluminum foil; let rest for 10 minutes. Serve with a side of steamed broccoli.

Nutrition: Calories: 185 Fat: 8g Carbs: 4g Protein: 17g

570.   Chili Chicken Wings
Preparation Time: 16 hours
Cooking time: 16 minutes
Servings: 4
Ingredients:
- 2 lb. chicken wings
- 1 tbsp olive oil
- 3 cloves garlic, minced
- 1 tbsp chili powder
- ½ tbsp cinnamon powder
- ½ tsp allspice
- 1 habanero pepper, seeded
- 1 tbsp soy sauce
- ½ tbsp white pepper
- ¼ cup red wine vinegar
- 3 tbsp lime juice
- 2 Scallions, chopped
- ½ tbsp grated ginger
- ½ tbsp chopped fresh thyme
- ⅓ tbsp sugar
- ½ tbsp salt

Directions:
1. In a bowl, add the olive oil, soy sauce, garlic, habanero pepper, allspice, cinnamon powder, cayenne pepper, white pepper, salt, sugar, thyme, ginger, scallions, lime juice, and red wine vinegar; mix well.
2. Add the chicken wings to the marinade mixture and coat it well with the mixture. Cover the bowl with cling film and refrigerate the chicken to marinate for 16 hours. Preheat the Air Fryer to 400° F. Remove the chicken from the fridge, drain all the liquid, and pat each wing dry using a paper towel.
3. Place half of the wings in the basket and cook for 16 minutes. Shake halfway through. Remove onto a serving platter and repeat the cooking process for the remaining wings. Serve with blue cheese dip or ranch dressing.

Nutrition: Calories: 191 Fat: 9g Carbs: 13g Protein: 0g

571.   Spice and Juicy Chicken Breasts
Preparation Time: 10 minutes
Cooking time: 25 minutes
Servings: 3
Ingredients:
- 2 chicken breasts
- Salt and black pepper to taste
- 1 cup flour
- 3 eggs
- ½ cup apple cider vinegar
- ½ tbsp ginger paste
- ½ tbsp garlic paste
- 1 tbsp sugar
- 2 red chilies, minced
- 2 tbsp tomato puree
- 1 red pepper
- 1 green pepper
- 1 tbsp paprika
- 4 tbsp water

Directions:

1. Preheat the Air Fryer to 350° F. Put the chicken breasts on a clean flat surface. Cut them in cubes. Pour the flour in a bowl, crack the eggs in, add the salt and pepper; whisk. Put the chicken in the flour mixture; mix to coat.
2. Place the chicken in the fryer's basket, spray with cooking spray, and fry for 8 minutes. Pull out the fryer basket, shake to toss, and spray again with cooking spray. Keep cooking for 7 minutes or until golden and crispy.
3. Remove the chicken to a plate. Put the red, yellow, and green peppers on a chopping board. Using a knife, cut open and deseed them; cut the flesh in long strips. In a bowl, add the water, apple cider vinegar, sugar, ginger and garlic puree, red chili, tomato puree, and smoked paprika; mix with a fork.
4. Place a skillet over medium heat on a stovetop and spray with cooking spray. Add the chicken and pepper strips. Stir and cook until the peppers are sweaty but still crunchy. Pour the chili mixture on the chicken, stir, and bring to simmer for 10 minutes; turn off the heat. Dish the chicken chili sauce into a serving bowl and serve.

Nutrition: Calories: 173 Fat: 2g Carbs: 9g Protein: 29g

572.   Chicken Kabobs with Garlic Sauce
Preparation Time: 10 minutes
Cooking time: 20 minutes
Servings: 3
Ingredients:
- 3 chicken breasts
- Salt to season
- 1 tbsp chili powder
- ¼ cup maple syrup
- ½ cup soy sauce
- 2 red peppers
- 1 green pepper
- 7 mushrooms
- 2 tbsp sesame seeds
- 1 garlic clove
- 2 tbsp olive oil
- Zest and juice from 1 lime
- A pinch of salt
- ¼ cup fresh parsley, chopped

Directions:
1. Put the chicken breasts on a clean flat surface and cut them in 2-inch cubes with a knife. Add them to a bowl, along with the chili powder, salt, maple syrup, soy sauce, sesame seeds, and spray them with cooking spray. Toss to coat and set aside. Place the peppers on the chopping board. Use a knife to open, deseed and cut in cubes.
2. Likewise, cut the mushrooms in halves. Start stacking up the Ingredients: - stick 1 red pepper, then green, a chicken cube, and a mushroom half. Repeat the arrangement until the skewer is full. Repeat the process until all the ingredients are used. Preheat the Air Fryer to 330° F.
3. Brush the kabobs with soy sauce mixture and place them into the fryer basket. Grease with cooking spray and grill for 20 minutes; flip halfway through.
4. Meanwhile, mix all salsa Verde Ingredients: in your food processor and blend until you obtain a chunky paste. Remove the kabobs when ready and serve with a side of salsa Verde.

Nutrition: Calories: 250 Fat: 5g Carbs: 5g Protein: 30g

573.   Zucchini Stuffed Lemony Chicken
Preparation Time: 20 minutes
Cooking time: 2 hours
Servings: 6
Ingredients:
- 1 whole chicken, 3 lb.
- 2 red and peeled onions
- 2 tbsp olive oil
- 2 apricots
- 1 zucchini
- 1 apple
- 2 cloves finely chopped garlic
- Fresh chopped thyme
- Salt and black pepper to taste

- 5 oz honey
- juice from 1 lemon
- 2 tbsp olive oil
- Salt and black pepper to taste

Directions:
1. For the stuffing, chop all Ingredients: into tiny pieces. Transfer to a large bowl and add the olive oil. Season with salt and black pepper. Fill the cavity of the chicken with the stuffing, without packing it tightly.
2. Place the chicken in the Air Fryer and cook for 35 minutes at 340 F. Warm the honey and the lemon juice in a large pan; season with salt and pepper. Reduce the temperature of the Air Fryer to 320 F.
3. Brush the chicken with some of the honey-lemon marinade and return it to the fryer. Cook for another 70 minutes; brush the chicken every 20-25 minutes with the marinade. Garnish with parsley and serve with potatoes.

Nutrition: Calories: 179 Fat: 4g Carbs: 21g Protein: 19g

574. Drumsticks with Blue Cheese Sauce

Preparation Time: 2 hours
Cooking time: 25 minutes
Servings: 4
Ingredients:
- 1 lb. mini drumsticks
- 3 tbsp butter
- 3 tbsp paprika
- 2 tbsp powdered cumin
- ¼ cup hot sauce
- 1 tbsp maple syrup
- 2 tbsp onion powder
- 2 tbsp garlic powder
- ½ cup mayonnaise
- 1 cup crumbled blue cheese
- 1 cup sour cream
- 1 ½ tbsp garlic powder
- 1 ½ tbsp onion powder
- Salt and black pepper to taste
- 1 ½ tbsp cayenne pepper
- 1 ½ tbsp white wine vinegar
- 2 tbsp buttermilk
- 1 ½ Worcestershire sauce

Directions:
1. Start with the drumstick sauce; place a pan over medium heat on a stove top. Melt the butter, and add the hot sauce, paprika, garlic, onion, maple syrup, and cumin; mix well. Cook the mixture for 5 minutes or until the sauce reduces. Turn off the heat and let cool. Put the drumsticks in a bowl, pour half of the sauce over, and mix it.
2. Save the remaining sauce for serving. Refrigerate the drumsticks for 2 hours. Meanwhile, make the blue cheese sauce: in a jug, add the sour cream, blue cheese, mayonnaise, garlic powder, onion powder, buttermilk, cayenne pepper, vinegar, Worcestershire sauce, pepper, and salt. Using a stick blender, blend the Ingredients: until they are well mixed with no large lumps. Adjust the salt and pepper taste as desired. Preheat the Air Fryer to 350° F.
3. Remove the drumsticks from the fridge and place them in the fryer basket; cook for 15 minutes. Turn the drumsticks with tongs every 5 minutes to ensure that they are evenly cooked. Remove the drumsticks to a serving bowl and pour the remaining sauce over. Serve with the blue cheese sauce and a side of celery sticks.

Nutrition: Calories: 210 Fat: 13g Carbs: 1g Protein: 22g

575. Chili Lime Chicken Lollipop

Preparation Time: 15 minutes
Cooking time: 10 minutes
Servings: 3
Ingredients:
- 1 lb. mini chicken drumsticks
- ½ tbsp soy sauce
- 1 tbsp lime juice
- Salt and black pepper to taste

- 1 tbsp cornstarch
- ½ tbsp minced garlic
- ½ tbsp chili powder
- ½ tbsp chopped cilantro
- ½ tbsp garlic-ginger paste
- 1 tbsp vinegar
- 1 tbsp chili paste
- ½ tbsp beaten egg
- 1 tbsp paprika
- 1 tbsp flour
- 2 tbsp maple syrup

Directions:
1. Mix garlic ginger paste, chili powder, maple syrup, paprika powder, chopped coriander, plain vinegar, egg, garlic, and salt, in a bowl.
2. Add the chicken drumsticks and toss to coat; Stir in cornstarch, flour, and lime juice.
3. Preheat the Air Fryer to 350° F. Remove each drumstick, shake off the excess marinade, and place in a single layer in the basket; cook for 5 minutes.
4. Slide out the basket, spray the chicken with cooking spray and continue to cook for 5 minutes. Remove onto a serving platter and serve with tomato dip and a side of steamed asparagus.

Nutrition: Calories: 150 Fat: 5g Carbs: 1g Protein: 25g

576. Almond Turkey with Lemon and Eggs

Preparation Time: 15 minutes
Cooking time: 35 minutes
Servings: 3
Ingredients:
- 1 lb. turkey breasts
- Salt and black pepper to taste to season
- ¼ cup chicken soup cream
- ¼ cup mayonnaise
- 2 tbsp lemon juice
- ¼ cup slivered almonds, chopped
- ¼ cup breadcrumbs
- 2 tbsp chopped green onion
- 2 tbsp chopped pimentos
- 2 Boiled eggs, chopped
- ½ cup diced celery

Directions:
1. Preheat the Air Fryer to 390° F. Place the turkey breasts on a clean flat surface and season with salt and pepper.
2. Grease with cooking spray and place them in the fryer's basket; cook for 13 minutes. Remove turkey back onto the chopping board, let cool, and cut into dices. In a bowl, add the celery, chopped eggs, pimentos, green onions, slivered almonds, lemon juice, mayonnaise, diced turkey, and chicken soup cream and mix well.
3. Grease a 5 X 5 inches casserole dish with cooking spray, scoop the turkey mixture into the bowl, sprinkle the breadcrumbs on it, and spray with cooking spray. Put the dish in the fryer basket and bake the Ingredients: at 390° F for 20 minutes. Remove and serve with a side of steamed asparagus.

Nutrition: Calories: 214 Fat: 6g Carbs: 18g Protein: 21g

577. Party Chicken Wings with Sesame

Preparation Time: 10 minutes
Cooking time: 12 minutes
Servings: 4
Ingredients:
- 1 lb. chicken wings
- 2 tbsp sesame oil
- 2 tbsp maple syrup
- Salt and black pepper
- 3 tbsp sesame seeds

Directions:
1. In a bowl, add wings, oil, maple syrup, salt and pepper, and stir to coat well.
2. In another bowl, add the sesame seeds and roll the wings in the seeds to coat thoroughly.
3. Arrange the wings in an even layer inside your air fryer and cook for 12 minutes on 360° F, turning once halfway through.

Nutrition: Calories: 230 Fat: 17g Carbs: 0g Protein: 19g

578. **Buttermilk Chicken Bites**
Preparation Time: 10 minutes
Cooking time: 12 minutes
Servings: 4
Ingredients:

- 2 chicken breasts, skinless, cut into 2 pieces each
- 1 egg, beaten
- ¼ cup buttermilk
- 1 cup corn flakes, crushed
- Salt and black pepper to taste

Directions:

1. In a bowl, whisk egg and buttermilk. Add in chicken pieces and stir to coat.
2. In a plate, spread the cornflakes out and mix with salt and pepper. Coat the chicken pieces in the cornflakes. Spray the air fryer with cooking spray.
3. Arrange the chicken in an even layer in the air fryer; cook for 12 minutes at 360° F, turning once halfway through.

Nutrition: Calories: 230 Fat: 9g Carbs: 20g Protein: 18g

579. **Savory Chicken Burgers**
Preparation Time: 10 minutes
Cooking time: 10 minutes
Servings: 4
Ingredients:

- 1 lb. ground chicken
- ½ onion, chopped
- 2 garlic cloves, chopped
- 1 egg, beaten
- ½ cup breadcrumbs
- ½ tbsp ground cumin
- ½ tbsp paprika
- ½ tbsp cilantro seeds, crushed
- Salt and black pepper to taste

Directions:

1. In a bowl, mix chicken, onion, garlic, egg, breadcrumbs, cumin, paprika, cilantro, salt, and black pepper, with hands; shape into 4 patties.
2. Grease the air fryer with oil and arrange the patties inside. Do not layer them. Cook in batches if needed.
3. Cook for 10 minutes at 380° F, turning once halfway through.

Nutrition: Calories: 250 Fat: 13g Carbs: 5g Protein: 26g

580. **Creamy Chicken With Prosciutto**
Preparation Time: 10 minutes
Cooking time: 15 minutes
Servings: 2
Ingredients:

- 2 chicken breasts
- 1 tbsp olive oil
- Salt and black pepper to taste to season
- 1 cup semi-dried tomatoes, sliced
- ½ cup brie cheese, halved
- 4 slices thin prosciutto

Directions:

1. Preheat the Air Fryer to 365° F. Put the chicken on a chopping board and cut a small incision deep enough to make stuffing on both. Insert one slice of cheese and 4 to 5 tomato slices into each chicken.
2. Lay the prosciutto on the chopping board. Put the chicken on one side and roll the prosciutto over the chicken making sure that both ends of the prosciutto meet under the chicken.
3. Drizzle olive oil and sprinkle with salt and pepper. Place the chicken in the basket and cook for 10 minutes. Turn the breasts over and cook for another 5 minutes. Slice each chicken breast in half and serve with tomato salad.

Nutrition: Calories: 414 Fat: 16g Carbs: 16g Protein: 41g

581. **Chicken Tenders with Tarragon**
Preparation Time: 10 minutes
Cooking time: 12 minutes
Servings: 2
Ingredients:

- 2 chicken tenders

- Salt and black pepper to taste
- ½ cup dried tarragon
- 1 tbsp butter

Directions:

1. Preheat the Air Fryer to 390° F. Lay out a 12 X 12 inch cut of foil on a flat surface. Place the chicken breasts on the foil, sprinkle the tarragon on both, and share the butter onto both breasts. Sprinkle with salt and pepper.
2. Loosely wrap the foil around the breasts to enable air flow. Place the wrapped chicken in the basket and cook for 12 minutes. Remove the chicken and carefully unwrap the foil. Serve with the sauce extract and steamed veggies.

Nutrition: Calories: 201 Fat: 4g Carbs: 9g Protein: 27g

582. **Herby Chicken with Lime**
Preparation Time: 20 minutes
Cooking time: 30 minutes
Servings: 4
Ingredients:

- 1 (2½ lb.) whole chicken, on the bone
- Salt and black pepper to taste to season
- 1 tbsp chili powder
- 1 tbsp garlic powder
- 4 tbsp oregano
- 2 tbsp cilantro powder
- 2 tbsp cumin powder
- 2 tbsp olive oil
- 4 tbsp paprika
- 1 lime, juiced

Directions:

1. In a bowl, pour the oregano, garlic powder, chili powder, ground cilantro, paprika, cumin powder, pepper, salt, and olive oil. Mix well to create a rub for the chicken and rub onto it. Refrigerate for 20 minutes.
2. Preheat the Air Fryer to 350° F.
3. Remove the chicken from the refrigerator; place in the fryer basket and cook for 20 minutes.
4. Use a skewer to poke the chicken to ensure that it is clear of juices. If not, cook the chicken further for 5 to 10 minutes; let to rest for 10 minutes. After, drizzle the lime juice over and serve with green salad.

Nutrition: Calories: 150 Fat: 6g Carbs: 5g Protein: 20g

583. **Chicken Wrapped In Bacon**
Preparation Time: 10 minutes
Cooking time: 15 minutes
Servings: 2 to 4
Ingredients:

- 2 chicken breasts
- 8 oz onion and chive cream cheese
- 1 tbsp butter
- 6 turkey bacon
- Salt to taste
- 1 tbsp fresh parsley, chopped
- juice from ½ lemon

Directions:

1. Preheat the Air Fryer to 390° F. Stretch out the bacon slightly and lay them on in 2 sets; 3 bacon strips together on each side.
2. Place the chicken breast on each bacon set and use a knife to smear the cream cheese on both. Share the butter on top and sprinkle with salt.
3. Wrap the bacon around the chicken and secure the ends into the wrap.
4. Place the wrapped chicken in the fryer's basket and cook for 14 minutes. Turn the chicken halfway through. Remove the chicken onto a serving platter and top with parsley and lemon juice. Serve with steamed greens.

Nutrition: Calories: 200 Fat: 20g Carbs: 9g Protein: 39g

584. **Fruity Chicken Breasts with BBQ Sauce**
Preparation Time: 10 minutes
Cooking time: 20 minutes
Servings: 2
Ingredients:

- 2 large chicken breasts, cubed

- 2 green bell peppers, sliced
- ½ onion, sliced
- 1 can drain pineapple chunks
- ½ cup barbecue sauce

Directions:
1. Preheat the Air Fryer to 370° F.
2. Thread the green bell peppers, the chicken, the onions and the pineapple chunks on the skewers.
3. Brush with barbecue sauce and fry for 20 minutes, until thoroughly cooked and slightly crispy.

Nutrition: Calories: 255 Fat: 4g Carbs: 9g Protein: 32g

585. Broccoli Chicken Casserole

Preparation Time: 15 minutes
Cooking time: 25 minutes
Servings: 3

Ingredients:
- 3 chicken breasts
- Salt and black pepper to taste
- 1 cup shredded Cheddar cheese
- 1 broccoli head
- ½ cup mushroom soup cream
- ½ cup croutons

Directions:
1. Preheat the Air Fryer to 390° F. Place the chicken breasts on a clean flat surface and season with salt and pepper.
2. Grease with cooking spray and place them in the fryer basket. Close the Air Fryer and cook for 13 minutes. Meanwhile, place the broccoli on the chopping board and use a knife to chop.
3. Remove them onto the chopping board, let cool, and cut into bite-size pieces. In a bowl, add the chicken, broccoli, cheddar cheese, and mushroom soup cream; mix well.
4. Scoop the mixture into a 3 X 3cm casserole dish, add the croutons on top and spray with cooking spray.
5. Put the dish in the basket and cook for 10 minutes. Serve with a side of steamed greens.

Nutrition: Calories: 142 Fat: 3g Carbs: 9g Protein: 20g

586. Asian Spicy Turkey

Preparation Time: 10 minutes
Cooking time: 35 minutes
Servings: 6

Ingredients:
- 1 tablespoon sesame oil
- 2 pounds turkey thighs
- 1 teaspoon Chinese Five-spice powder
- 1 teaspoon pink Himalayan salt
- 1/4 teaspoon Sichuan pepper
- 1 tablespoon Chinese rice vinegar
- 2 tablespoons soy sauce
- 1 tablespoon chili sauce
- 1 tablespoon mustard

Directions:
1. Preheat your Air Fryer to 360° F.
2. Brush the sesame oil all over the turkey thighs. Season them with spices.
3. Cook for 23 minutes, turning over once or twice. Make sure to work in batches to ensure even cooking
4. In the meantime, combine the remaining Ingredients: in a wok (or similar type pan that is preheated over medium-high heat). Cook and stir until the sauce reduces by about a third.
5. Add the fried turkey thighs to the wok; gently stir to coat with the sauce.
6. Let the turkey rest for 10 minutes before slicing and serving. Enjoy!

Nutrition: 279 Calories; 12g Fat; 4g Carbs; 29g Protein; 4g Sugars; 2g Fiber

587. Spicy Chicken Drumsticks with Herbs

Preparation Time: 10 minutes
Cooking time: 35 minutes
Servings: 6

Ingredients:
- 6 chicken drumsticks
- Sauce:
- 6 ounces hot sauce

- 3 tablespoons olive oil
- 3 tablespoons tamari sauce
- 1 teaspoon dried thyme
- 1/2 teaspoon dried oregano

Directions:
1. Spritz the sides and bottom of the cooking basket with a nonstick cooking spray.
2. Cook the chicken drumsticks at 380° F for 35 minutes, flipping them over halfway through.
3. Meanwhile, heat the hot sauce, olive oil, tamari sauce, thyme, and oregano in a pan over medium-low heat; reserve.
4. Drizzle the sauce over the prepared chicken drumsticks; toss to coat well and serve. Bon appétit!

Nutrition: 280 Calories; 17g Fat; 6g Carbs; 21g Protein; 4g Sugars; 5g Fiber

588. Classic Chicken with Peanuts

Preparation Time: 10 minutes
Cooking time: 15 minutes
Servings: 4

Ingredients:
- 1 ½ pounds chicken tenderloins
- 2 tablespoons peanut oil
- 1/2 cup parmesan cheese, grated
- Sea salt and ground black pepper, to taste
- 1/2 teaspoon garlic powder
- 1 teaspoon red pepper flakes
- 2 tablespoons peanuts, roasted and roughly chopped

Directions:
1. Start by preheating your Air Fryer to 360 ° F.
2. Brush the chicken tenderloins with peanut oil on all sides.
3. In a mixing bowl, thoroughly combine grated parmesan cheese, salt, black pepper, garlic powder, and red pepper flakes. Dredge the chicken in the breading, shaking off any residual coating.
4. Lay the chicken tenderloins into the cooking basket. Cook for 12 to 13 minutes or until it is no longer pink in the center. Work in batches; an instant-read thermometer should read at least 165° F.
5. Serve garnished with roasted peanuts. Bon appétit!

Nutrition: 354 Calories; 14g Fat; 3g Carbs; 40g Protein; 4g Sugars; 7g Fiber

589. Turkey with Paprika and Tarragon

Preparation Time: 10 minutes
Cooking time: 40 minutes
Servings: 6

Ingredients:
- 2 pounds turkey tenderloins
- 2 tablespoons olive oil
- Salt and ground black pepper, to taste
- 1 teaspoon smoked paprika
- 2 tablespoons dry white wine
- 1 tablespoon fresh tarragon leaves, chopped

Directions:
1. Brush the turkey tenderloins with olive oil. Season with salt, black pepper, and paprika.
2. Afterwards, add the white wine and tarragon.
3. Cook the turkey tenderloins at 350 ° F for 30 minutes, flipping them over halfway through. Let them rest for 5 to 9 minutes before slicing and serving. Enjoy!

Nutrition: 217 Calories; 5g Fat; 2g Carbs; 37g Protein; 5g Sugars; 3g Fiber

590. Italian-Style Chicken with Roma Tomatoes

Preparation Time: 10 minutes
Cooking time: 35 minutes
Servings: 8

Ingredients:
- 2 teaspoons olive oil, melted
- 3 pounds chicken breasts, bone-in
- 1/2 teaspoon black pepper, freshly ground
- 1/2 teaspoon salt
- 1 teaspoon cayenne pepper
- 2 tablespoons fresh parsley, minced
- 1 teaspoon fresh basil, minced
- 1 teaspoon fresh rosemary, minced
- 4 medium-sized Roma tomatoes, halved

Directions:

1. Start by preheating your Air Fryer to 370 ° F. Brush the cooking basket with 1 teaspoon of olive oil.
2. Sprinkle the chicken breasts with all seasonings listed above.
3. Cook for 25 minutes or until chicken breasts are slightly browned. Work in batches.

4. Arrange the tomatoes in the cooking basket and brush them with the remaining teaspoon of olive oil. Season with sea salt.
5. Cook the tomatoes at 350° F for 10 minutes, shaking halfway through the cooking time. Serve with chicken breasts. Bon appétit!

Nutrition: 315 Calories; 11g Fat; 7g Carbs; 36g Protein; 7g Sugars; 9g Fiber

BEEF, STEAK AND LAMB RECIPES

591. Braised beef shanks
Preparation time: 15 minutes
Cooking time: 6 hours
Servings: 4
Ingredients:

- 2 pounds beef shanks
- 5 garlic cloves, minced
- 2 fresh rosemary sprigs
- 1 tablespoon fresh lime juice
- Salt and ground black pepper, as required
- 1 cup beef broth

Directions:
1. Lightly grease a Dutch oven that will fit in the air fryer oven.
2. In the pan, add all ingredients and mix well.
3. Arrange the Dutch oven over the wire rack.
4. Select "slow cooker" of air fryer oven and set on "low".
5. Set the timer for 6 hours and press "start/stop" to begin cooking.
6. Once done, get the Dutch oven.
7. Open the lid and serve hot.

Nutrition: Calories: 449 Fat: 22g Carbs: 13g Protein: 33g

592. Spiced beef brisket
Preparation time: 15 minutes
Cooking time: 6 hours
Servings: 12
Ingredients:

- 1 tablespoon olive oil
- 1 large yellow onion, sliced
- 3 garlic cloves, minced
- 1 (4pound)beef brisket
- ½ teaspoon red pepper flakes, crushed
- ½ teaspoon smoked paprika
- ½ teaspoon ground cumin
- Salt and ground black pepper, as required
- 2 cups beef broth

Directions:
1. In an oven safe pan that will fit in the air fryer oven, place all ingredients and stir to combine.
2. Cover the pan with a lid.
3. Arrange the pan over the wire rack.
4. Select slow cooker of air fryer oven and set on low.
5. Set the timer for 6 hours and press "start/stop" to begin cooking.
6. Remove the pan from the oven once done and place the brisket onto a cutting board for about 10-15 minutes before slicing.
7. Cut into desired sized slices and serve.

Nutrition: Calories: 188 Fat: 11g Carbs: 3g Protein: 18g

593. Rosemary beef chuck roast
Preparation time: 10 minutes
Cooking time: 45 minutes
Servings: 6
Ingredients:

- 1 (2pound)beef chuck roast
- 1 tablespoon olive oil
- 2 teaspoons dried rosemary, crushed
- Salt, as required

Directions:
1. .in a bowl, add the oil, herbs and salt and mix well.
2. Coat the beef roast with herb mixture generously.
3. Arrange the beef roast onto the greased enamel roasting pan.

4. Select air fry of air fryer oven and adjust the temperature to 360 ° f.
5. Set 45 minutes and press "start/stop" to begin preheating.
6. When the unit beeps to show that it is preheated, insert the roasting pan in the oven.
7. Get the pan from the oven and place the roast onto a cutting board.
8. With a piece of foil, cover the beef roast for about 20 minutes before slicing.
9. With a sharp knife, cut the beef roast into desired size slices and serve.

Nutrition: Calories: 358 Fat: 19g Carbs: 6g Protein: 34g

594. Beef round roast with carrots
Preparation time: 15 minutes
Cooking time: 8 hours
Servings: 6
Ingredients:

- 1 (2pound)beef round roast
- 3 large carrots, peeled and chopped
- 1 large yellow onion, sliced thinly
- 1 cup tomato sauce
- 1 teaspoon ground cumin
- ½ teaspoon ground cinnamon
- Salt and ground black pepper, as required

Directions:
1. In an oven safe pan that will fit in the air fryer oven, place all ingredients and stir to combine.
2. Cover the pan with a lid.
3. Arrange the pan over the wire rack.
4. Select slow cooker of air fryer oven and set on "low".
5. Set the timer for 8 hours and press "start/stop" to begin cooking.
6. Take the pan from the oven and place the roast onto a cutting board for about 10-15 minutes before slicing.
7. Cut into desired sized slices and serve.

Nutrition: Calories: 269 Fat: 11g Carbs: 18g Protein: 21g

595. Beef taco casserole
Preparation time: 15 minutes
Cooking time: 25 minutes
Servings: 6
Ingredients:

- 2 pounds ground beef
- 2 tablespoons taco seasoning
- 1 cup cheddar cheese, shredded
- 1 cup cottage cheese
- 1 cup salsa

Directions:
1. In a bowl, add the beef and taco seasoning and mix well.
2. Add the cheeses and salsa and stir to combine.
3. Put beef mixture into a baking dish and slightly press to smooth the top surface.
4. Select "bake" of air fryer oven and adjust the temperature to 370° f. Press start and cook for 25 minutes
5. When the unit beeps to show that it is preheated, arrange the baking dish over the wire rack.
6. Take out the baking dish from oven and set aside for about 5 minutes before serving.

Nutrition: Calories: 549 Fat: 23g Carbs: 55g Protein: 31g

596. Spiced flank steak
Preparation time: 1 hour
Cooking time: 12 minutes

Servings: 6
Ingredients:

- 2 tablespoons balsamic vinegar
- 2 tablespoons olive oil
- 3 garlic cloves, minced
- 1 teaspoon red chili powder
- 1 teaspoon ground cumin
- 1 teaspoon onion powder
- Salt and ground black pepper, as required
- 1 (2poundflank steak

Directions:

1. Add vinegar, spices, salt and black pepper in a large bowl. Mix well.
2. Add the steak and coat with mixture generously.
3. Cover the bowl and place in the refrigerator for at least 1 hour.
4. Remove the steak from bowl and place onto the greased enamel roasting pan.
5. Select "broil" air fryer oven and set the timer for 12 minutes.
6. Press "start/stop" to begin preheating.
7. When the unit beeps to show that it is preheated, insert the roasting pan in the oven.
8. Place the steak onto a cutting board once done cooking.
9. Cut the steak into desired sized slices and serve.

Nutrition: Calories: 197 Fat: 9g Carbs: 2g Protein: 23g

597. Buttered striploin steak
Preparation time: 10 minutes
Cooking time: 12 minutes
Servings: 2
Ingredients:

- 2 (7ounces) strip loin steaks
- 1½ tablespoons butter, softened
- Salt and ground black pepper, as required

Directions:

1. Coat each steak evenly with butter and then, season with salt and black pepper.
2. Arrange the steaks into the greased air fry basket.
3. Select "air fry" of air fryer oven and adjust the temperature to 392° f.
4. Set the timer for 12 minutes and press "start/stop" to begin preheating.
5. When the unit beeps to show that it is preheated, insert the air fry basket in the oven.
6. Place the steaks onto serving plates.
7. Serve hot.

Nutrition: Calories: 210 Fat: 16g Carbs: 0g Protein: 16g

598. Steak with bell peppers
Preparation time: 15 minutes
Cooking time: 12 minutes
Servings: 4
Ingredients:

- 1 teaspoon dried oregano, crushed
- 1 teaspoon onion powder
- 1 teaspoon garlic powder
- 1 teaspoon red chili powder
- 1 teaspoon paprika
- Salt, as required
- 1¼ pounds flank steak, cut into thin strips
- 3 green bell peppers, seeded and cubed
- 1 red onion, sliced
- 2 tablespoons olive oil
- 34 tablespoons feta cheese, crumbled

Directions:

1. In a large bowl, mix the oregano and spices.
2. Add the steak strips, bell peppers, onion, and oil and mix until well combined.
3. Arrange the steak mixture into the greased air fry basket.
4. Select "air fry" of air fryer oven and adjust the temperature to 390° f.
5. Set the timer for 12 minutes and press "start/stop" to begin preheating.
6. When the unit beeps to show that it is preheated, insert the air fry basket in the oven.
7. Arrange the steak mixture onto serving plates.
8. Serve immediately with the topping of feta.

Nutrition: Calories: 218 Fat: 7g Carbs: 6g Protein: 30g

599. Leg of lamb with brussels sprout
Preparation time: 15 minutes
Cooking time: 1 hour and 30 minutes
Servings: 6
Ingredients:

- 2¼ pounds leg of lamb
- 3 tablespoons olive oil, divided
- 1 tablespoon fresh rosemary, minced
- 1 tablespoon fresh lemon thyme
- 1 garlic clove, minced
- Salt and ground black pepper, as required
- 1½ pounds brussels sprouts, trimmed
- 2 tablespoons honey

Directions:

1. Cut the leg of lamb at several places using a sharp knife.
2. In a bowl, mix 2 tablespoons of oil, herbs, garlic, salt, and black pepper.
3. Generously coat the leg of lamb with oil mixture.
4. Place leg of lamb into the prepared air fry basket.
5. Select "air fry" of air fryer oven and adjust the temperature to 300° f.
6. Set the timer for 75 minutes and press "start/stop" to begin preheating.
7. When the unit beeps to show that it is preheated, insert the air fry basket in the oven.
8. Meanwhile, coat the brussels sprout evenly with the remaining oil and honey.
9. Arrange the brussels sprout into the air fry basket with leg of lamb.
10. Select "air fry" of air fryer oven and adjust the temperature to 392 ° f.
11. Regulate the timer for 15 minutes and press "start/stop" to begin cooking.
12. Insert the air fry basket in the oven. Once done,
13. Transfer the leg of lamb onto a platter.
14. With a foil piece, cover the leg of lamb for about 10 minutes before slicing.
15. Cut the leg of lamb into desired size pieces and serve alongside the brussels sprout.

Nutrition: Calories: 220 Fat: 15g Carbs: 0g Protein: 22g

600. Herbed rack of lamb
Preparation time: 15 minutes
Cooking time: 15 minutes
Servings: 4
Ingredients:

- 4 tablespoons olive oil
- 2 teaspoons garlic, minced
- 2 tablespoons dried rosemary
- 1 tablespoon dried thyme
- Salt and ground black pepper, as required
- 1 rack of lamb

Directions:

1. Prepare a large bowl. Add all ingredients except for rack of lamb and mix well.
2. Rub the rack of lamb with herb mixture generously.
3. Arrange the rack of lamb into the greased air fry basket.
4. Select "air fry" of air fryer oven and adjust the temperature to 360° f.
5. Adjust timer for 10 minutes and press "start/stop" to begin preheating.
6. When the unit beeps to show that it is preheated, insert the air fry basket in the oven.
7. Put out the rack onto a cutting board for at least 10 minutes.
8. Cut the rack into chops and serve.

Nutrition: Calories: 293 Fat: 15g Carbs: 4g Protein: 32g

601. Crumbed rack of lamb
Preparation time: 15 minutes
Cooking time: 30 minutes
Servings: 5
Ingredients:

- 1 tablespoon butter, melted
- 1 garlic clove, finely chopped
- 1 (1¾pound rack of lamb
- Salt and ground black pepper, as required
- 1 egg
- 1/2 cup panko breadcrumbs
- 1 tablespoon fresh thyme, minced
- 1 tablespoon fresh rosemary, minced

Directions:

1. In a bowl, mix the butter, garlic, salt, and black pepper.
2. Coat the rack of lamb with garlic mixture evenly.
3. In a shallow dish, beat the egg.
4. In another dish, mix the breadcrumbs and herbs.
5. Dip the rack of lamb in beaten egg and then, coat with breadcrumbs mixture.
6. Arrange the rack of lamb into the greased air fry basket.
7. Select "air fry" of air fryer oven and adjust the temperature to 212 ° f.
8. Adjust timer for 25 minutes and press "start/stop" to begin preheating.
9. When the unit beeps to show that it is preheated, insert the air fry basket in the oven.
10. Place the rack onto a cutting board for at least 10 minutes.
11. Cut the rack into individual chops and serve.

Nutrition: Calories: 696 Fat: 56g Carbs: 7g Protein: 22g

602. Sweet and Sour Delicious Pork

Preparation Time: 15 minutes
Cooking Time: 20 minutes
Servings: 4
Ingredients

- 1 pound 5 oz pork tenderloin, trimmed of fat, cut into strips
- 1 tablespoon corn flour (+ extra for coating)
- 4 oz red wine
- 10 oz tomato sauce or passata
- 1 tablespoon tomato paste or tomato puree
- 5 oz unsweetened apple juice
- 2 tablespoons brown sugar
- 2 sliced onions
- 2 cloves finely chopped garlic (optional)
- 2 tablespoons red wine vinegar
- 2 tablespoons olive oil
- Salt and freshly ground pepper to taste

Directions

1. Mix in a large bowl corn flour with red wine until smooth than add there: tomato sauce, apple juice, vinegar, sugar, tomato paste, season and mix thoroughly. Set bowl aside.
2. Coat chopped meat in corn flour and set aside.
3. Slice onions and put them into air fryer. Pour the olive oil over them. Cook for 5 minutes.
4. Add coated with flour pork and finely chopped garlic (optional). Cook for another 5 minutes.
5. Stir the pork to separate the pieces and add them to the sweet and sour sauce. Cook for 10 minutes or until the pork tender and the sauce thick.
6. Season to taste.

Nutrition: Calories: 291 Fat: 7g Carbs: 37g Protein: 22g

603. Country Fried Steak

Preparation Time: 10 minutes
Cooking Time: 12-15 minutes
Servings: 2
Ingredients

- 2 pieces 6-ounce sirloin steak pounded thin
- 4 eggs, beaten
- 1 ½ cup all-purpose flour
- 1 ½ cup breadcrumbs
- 1 teaspoon onion powder
- 1 teaspoon garlic powder
- 1 teaspoon salt
- ½ teaspoon pepper

Directions

1. Combine the breadcrumbs, onion, and garlic powder, salt and pepper.

2. In other bowls place flour and beat eggs.
3. Dip the steak in this order: flour, eggs, and seasoned breadcrumbs.
4. Cook breaded steak for 6-7 minute at 380° F, turn over once and cook for another 5-7 minutes until becomes golden and crispy.

Nutrition: Calories: 250 Fat: 17g Carbs: 13g Protein: 9g

604. Easy Cooking Pork Chop

Preparation Time: 15 minutes
Cooking Time: 15 minutes
Servings: 2
Ingredients

- 2 middle pieces pork chop
- 1 tablespoon plain flour
- 1 egg, beaten
- 2 tablespoon olive oil
- 3 tablespoon breadcrumbs
- Salt and ground pepper for seasoning

Directions

1. Season pork chop with salt and ground pepper from both sides.
2. In three different bowls place plain flour, beaten egg, and breadcrumbs.
3. Coat each pork chop from both sides first with flour then with egg and with breadcrumbs.
4. Preheat the Air Fryer to 380°F
5. Place coated pork chops into the Fryer and cook for 10 minutes from one side and 5 minutes from another side.
6. Serve with cooked rice and mashed potatoes.

Nutrition: Calories: 164 Fat: 6g Carbs: 0g Protein: 26g

605. Char Siu

Preparation Time: 5 minutes
Cooking Time: 15 minutes
Servings: 2
Ingredients

- 1-pound pork
- 3 tablespoon hoisin sauce
- 3 tablespoon sugar
- 3 tablespoon soy sauce
- 2 tablespoon corn syrup
- 2 tablespoon mirin
- 2 tablespoon olive oil
- Salt and pepper to taste

Directions

1. Cut pork into 2-inch stripes.
2. Mix all ingredients besides oil together in a large bowl and then put the meat into marinade. Set aside at least for 40 minutes.
3. Discard marinade and sprinkle pork with olive oil.
4. Cook in the air fryer preheated to 380° F for 15 minutes.
5. Serve.

Nutrition: Calories: 210 Fat: 14g Carbs: 0g Protein: 20g

606. Pork Satay with Peanut Sauce

Preparation Time: 20 minutes
Cooking Time: 10 minutes
Servings: 3-4
Ingredients

- 1-pound pork chops, cut into 1-inch cubes
- 2 garlic, minced
- 1 tablespoon fresh ginger, grated
- 2 teaspoons chili paste
- 2-3 tablespoons sweet soy sauce
- 2 tablespoons vegetable oil
- 1 shallot, finely chopped
- 1 teaspoon ground coriander
- ½ cup coconut milk
- 4 oz unsalted butter

Directions

1. Mix half of the garlic in a dish with the ginger, 1 teaspoon hot pepper sauce, 1 tablespoon soy sauce, and 1 tablespoon oil. Add the meat to the mixture and leave to marinate for 15 minutes.
2. Preheat the air fryer to 380° F. Put the marinated meat in the air fryer basket cook for 12 minutes until brown and done. Turn once while cooking.

3. Meanwhile, make the peanut sauce. Heat 1 tablespoon of the oil in a saucepan and gently sauté the shallot with garlic. Add the coriander and cook for 1-2 minutes more. Mix the coconut milk and the peanuts with 1 teaspoon hot pepper sauce and 1 tablespoon soy sauce with the shallot mixture and gently boil for 5 minutes, stirring constantly.
4. Serve the meat with sauce and enjoy!

Nutrition: Calories: 288 Fat: 25g Carbs: 27g Protein: 23g

607. Zero Oil Pork Chops

Preparation Time: 5 minutes
Cooking Time: 15 minutes
Servings: 2

Ingredients

- 2 pieces pork chops
- 1 tablespoon of plain flour
- 1 large egg
- 2 tablespoon breadcrumbs
- Salt and black pepper to taste

Directions

1. First, you need to preheat the air fryer to 360° F.
2. Then, season pork chops with salt and black pepper and set aside.
3. Beat the egg in the plate. In another plate place the flour and in the third plate - breadcrumbs.
4. Cover each pork chop with the flour on both sides, then, dip in the egg, then, cover with breadcrumbs. Make sure that meat covered from all sides.
5. Place pork chops in the air fryer and cook for 15 minutes, until they are tender and crispy. Turn once while cooking, to cook the meat from both sides.
6. Serve with fresh vegetables or mashed potatoes.

Nutrition: Calories: 33 Fat: 0g Carbs: 0g Protein: 6g

608. Delicious Pork Tenderloin

Preparation Time: 15 minutes
Cooking Time: 15 minutes
Servings: 2

Ingredients

- 1-pound pork tenderloin
- 1 medium red or yellow pepper, sliced
- 1 large red onion, sliced
- 2 tablespoon Provencal herbs
- 1 tablespoon Olive oil
- ½ tablespoon mustard
- Ground black pepper
- Salt, to taste

Directions

1. In the large bowl mix sliced pepper and onion, Provencal herbs, salt and ground pepper to taste. Also, add olive oil to this mixture.
2. Cut the pork tenderloin into 4-6 large pieces, scrub with salt, ground pepper, and mustard.
3. Preheat your Air Fryer to 370-390° F.
4. Place vegetable mixture to the air fryer.
5. Coat meat pieces with olive oil and place them up to the vegetables.
6. Cook for 15 minutes until meat and vegetables will become roasted.
7. Turn the meat and vegetable in the middle of cooking process.

Nutrition: Calories: 130 Fat: 4g Carbs: 3g Protein: 23g

609. Drunken Ham with Mustard

Preparation Time: 10 minutes
Cooking Time: 40 minutes
Servings: 4

Ingredients

- 1 joint of ham, approximately 1-2 pounds
- 2 tablespoon honey
- 2 tablespoon French mustard
- 8 oz whiskey
- 1 teaspoon Provencal herbs
- 1 tablespoon salt

Directions

1. In a large casserole dish that fits in your Air Fryer prepare the marinade: combine the whiskey, honey and mustard.

2. Place the ham in the oven dish and turn it in the marinade.
3. Preheat the Air Fryer to 380° F and cook the ham for 15 minutes.
4. Add another shot of whiskey and turn in the marinade again. Cook the ham for 25 minutes until done.
5. Serve with potatoes and fresh vegetables.

Nutrition: Calories: 240 Fat: 4g Carbs: 12g Protein: 17g

610. Empanadas with Pumpkin and Pork

Preparation Time: 15 minutes
Cooking Time: 25 minutes,
Servings: 3

Ingredients

- 1-pound ground pork
- 1 small onion, chopped
- 1 cup pumpkin purée
- 1 red chili pepper, minced
- A pinch of cinnamon
- ½ teaspoon dried thyme
- 2 tablespoons olive oil
- 3 tablespoons water
- Salt and freshly ground black pepper
- 1 package of 10 empanada discs, thawed

Directions

1. First, you need to prepare filling. Preheat your sauté pan over medium-high heat. Add ground pork and chopped onions and sauté for about 5 minutes. The pork should be brown, and the onions are soft. Drain the fat from the pan and discard.
2. Then, add the pumpkin purée, water, red chili pepper, cinnamon, thyme to the sauté pan. Season with salt and pepper and combine evenly. Simmer the mixture for 10 minutes. Remove the pan from the heat and set aside to chill.
3. Place the empanada discs on a flat surface and brush the edges with water. Place couple tablespoons of the filling in the center of each disc. Fold the dough over the filling to form a half moon. Brush both sides of the empanadas with olive oil.
4. Preheat the air fryer to 360° F.
5. Place 3 to 5 empanadas into the air fryer basket depending of the size of your empanadas. Do not overload the air fryer. Cook for 14 minutes, turning over after 8 minutes. Serve warm.

Nutrition: Calories: 260 Fat: 11g Carbs: 39g Protein: 3g

611. Easy Steak Sticks

Preparation Time: 5 minutes
Cooking Time: 20 minutes
Servings: 3

Ingredients

- 1-pound steak
- 2 tablespoon olive oil
- 1 teaspoon dried thyme
- 1 teaspoon dried parsley
- A pinch of chili powder
- Salt and pepper to taste
- Sesame seeds for garnish

Directions

1. Cut the steak into 1-inch strips.
2. In the mixing bowl combine the olive oil and dried herbs. Add chili powder and stir to combine.
3. Preheat the air fryer to 370° F.
4. Lay meat strips to the working surface. Evenly season meat with salt and black pepper. Skewer the steak strips to the skewers. Dip the meat in the oil mixture and place to the air fryer basket. Cook for 15-20 minutes, until brown and crispy.
5. Serve with cooked rice or mashed potatoes. You can also garnish the meat with sesame seeds and freshly chopped herbs of your choice.

Nutrition: Calories: 190 Fat: 9g Carbs: 0g Protein: 25g

612. Pork Loin with Potatoes and Herbs

Preparation Time: 10 minutes
Cooking Time: 30 minutes
Servings: 4

Ingredients

- 2-pound pork loin
- 2 large potatoes, large dice
- ½ teaspoon garlic powder

- ½ teaspoon red pepper flakes
- 1 teaspoon dried parsley, crushed
- ½ teaspoon black pepper, freshly ground
- A pinch of salt
- Balsamic glaze to taste

Directions

1. Sprinkle the pork loin with garlic powder, red pepper flakes, parsley, salt, and pepper.
2. Preheat the air fryer to 370° F and place the pork loin, then the potatoes next to the pork in the basket of the air fryer and close. Cook for about 20-25 minutes.
3. Remove the pork loin from the air fryer. Let it rest for a few minutes before slicing.
4. Place the roasted potatoes to the serving plate. Slice the pork. Place 4-5 slices over the potatoes and drizzle the balsamic glaze over the pork.

Nutrition: Calories: 127 Fat: 4g Carbs: 2g Protein: 20g

613. Pork Chops Fried

Preparation Time: 20 minutes;
Cook time: 25 minutes
Servings: 3

Ingredients

- 3-4 pieces pork chops (cut in 1-inch thick, roughly 10 oz each)
- ¼ cup olive oil, divided
- 1 tablespoon cilantro, chopped
- 1 tablespoon parsley, chopped
- 1 tablespoon rosemary, chopped
- 1 tablespoon Dijon mustard
- 1 tablespoon coriander, ground
- 1-2 teaspoon salt to taste
- 1 teaspoon sugar

Directions

1. In the large mixing bowl combine 1/4 cup olive oil, 1 tablespoon cilantro, parsley, rosemary, Dijon mustard, coriander. Add some salt and black pepper. Dip the meat to the mixture, then transfer to a re-sealable bag and refrigerate for 2-3 hours.
2. Preheat the Air Fryer to 390°F.
3. Remove the pork chops out of the refrigerator and let sit at room temp for 30 minutes prior to cooking.
4. Reheat the Air Fryer to 390°F.
5. Cook 1 to 2 pork chops in the Air Fryer for 10-12 minutes. Please note thinner cuts will cook faster. Take 2 minutes off the cooking time for thinner cuts. The pork chop will be done when it has reached an internal temperature of 140°F
6. Serve with mashed potatoes or another garnish you prefer.

Nutrition: Calories: 170 Fat: 7g Carbs: 0g Protein: 25g

614. Chinese Roast Pork

Preparation Time: 5 minutes
Cooking Time: 25 minutes
Servings: 4

Ingredients

- 2 pounds of pork shoulder
- 2 tablespoons sugar
- 1 tablespoon honey
- 1/3 cup of soy sauce
- 1/2 tablespoon salt

Directions

1. Cut the meat in large pieces. Place to a large bowl and add all ingredients to make a marinade. Stir to combine well to coat all the meat pieces.
2. Preheat the air fryer to 350° F. Transfer marinated meat and cook for about 10 minutes, stirring couple times while cooking.
3. Increase the temperature to 400° F and cook for another 3-5 minutes until completely cooked.

Nutrition: Calories: 219 Fat: 8g Carbs: 18g Protein: 18g

615. Mouth Watering Pork Tenderloin with Bell Pepper

Preparation Time: 7 minutes
Cooking Time: 15 minutes
Servings: 3

Ingredients

- 1-pound pork tenderloin

- 2 medium-sized yellow or red bell peppers, cut into strips
- 1 little onion, sliced
- 2 teaspoons Provencal herbs
- Salt and black pepper to taste
- 1 tablespoon olive oil

Directions

1. In the large mixing bowl combine sliced bell peppers, onions, and Provencal herbs. Season with salt and pepper to taste. Sprinkle with the olive oil and set aside.
2. Cut the pork tenderloin into 1-inch cubes and rub with salt and black pepper.
3. Preheat the air fryer to 370° F.
4. On the bottom of the air fryer basket lay seasoned meat and coat with vegetable mixture. Fry for 15 minutes, turning the meat and veggies once while cooking.
5. Serve with mashed potatoes.

Nutrition: Calories: 140 Fat: 6g Carbs: 3g Protein: 19g

616. Cheesy Pork Fillets

Preparation Time: 8 minutes
Cooking Time: 20 minutes
Servings: 3

Ingredients

- 3 pork filets
- 2 large eggs, beaten
- 1 cup all-purpose flour
- 3 slices swiss cheese
- Salt and black pepper to taste

Directions

1. Preheat the air fryer to 380° F.
2. Dip pork fillets in egg and top each fillet with cheese slice. Season with salt and pepper and cover each piece with little more egg and then coat in all-purpose flour.
3. Place these "patties" in the air fryer and cook for 20 minutes, turning once during cooking.
4. When ready, serve hot and enjoy!

Nutrition: Calories: 384 Fat: 23g Carbs: 5g Protein: 36g

617. Beef with Broccoli

Preparation Time: 20 minutes
Cooking Time: 25 minutes
Servings: 3

Ingredients

- 2 ½ tablespoons - cornstarch, divided
- ½ cup water
- ½ teaspoon garlic, minced
- 2 8oz New York Steaks
- 1 ½ tablespoons vegetable oil
- 4 cups broccoli florets
- 1 onion, cut into wedges
- 1/3 cup reduced sodium soy sauce
- 2 tablespoons - brown sugar
- 1 teaspoon - ground ginger

Directions

1. Mix in a large bowl: cornstarch, water, minced garlic.
2. Cut beef into 6mm wide strips and coated in the mixture.
3. Put beef into air fryer, pour with oil and cook for 10 minutes. Then remove and set aside.
4. Add broccoli and onion to air fryer, pour with oil and cook for 8 minutes.
5. Combine in a bowl ginger, brown sugar, soy sauce, remaining cornstarch and water.
6. Add beef and sauce mixture to the air fryer and cook for 6-8 minutes.

Nutrition: Calories: 251 Fat: 18g Carbs: 10g Protein: 7g

618. Healthy Beef Schnitzel

Preparation Time: 10 minutes
Cooking Time: 12 minutes
Servings: 2

Ingredients

- 3 tablespoons olive oil
- 2 oz breadcrumbs
- 2 whisked eggs
- 2 thin beef schnitzels

- 1 lemon to serve

Directions
1. Preheat air fryer to 360°F
2. In the large bowl mix olive oil and breadcrumbs. Keep moving until the mixture become loose and friable.
3. Dip the beef schnitzel into the egg.
4. Then dip the schnitzel into crumb mixture. Make sure it is evenly covered with crumbs.
5. Lay schnitzel to the bottom of fryer basket and cook for nearly 12 minutes. (Time of Directions may vary depending on the thickness of the schnitzel.
6. Serve with lemon and enjoy!

Nutrition: Calories: 252 Fat: 12g Carbs: 21g Protein: 16g

619. Ground Beef
Preparation Time: 6 minutes
Cooking Time: 14 minutes
Servings: 3

Ingredients
- 2 tablespoons olive oil
- 1 medium onion, chopped
- 1-pound ground beef
- 1 bunch fresh spinach
- Salt and black pepper, to taste

Directions
1. Grease the baking tray with the olive oil.
2. Preheat the air fryer to 330° F. Add chopped onion to the tray and cook in the fryer for 2-3 minutes, stirring often. Add ground beef, mix well and cook for another 10 minutes, stirring occasionally.
3. Add chopped spinach, season with salt and pepper, stir to combine. Cook for 2-4 minutes until ready.
4. Serve and enjoy!

Nutrition: Calories: 231 Fat: 15g Carbs: 0g Protein: 23g

620. Crispy Beef Cubes
Preparation Time: 10 minutes
Cooking Time: 18 minutes
Servings: 4

Ingredients
- 1-pound beef loin
- 1 jar (16 oz) cheese pasta sauce
- 6 tablespoons breadcrumbs
- Salt and black pepper, to taste
- 1 tablespoon extra-virgin olive oil

Directions
1. Cut beef into 1-inch cubes and transfer to a mixing bowl and coat with pasta sauce.
2. In another bowl combine breadcrumbs, olive oil, salt and pepper. Mix well.
3. Place beef cubes to a breadcrumb mixture and coat from all sides.
4. Preheat the air fryer to 380° F. Cook beef cubes for 12-15 minutes, stirring occasionally, until ready and crispy.
5. Serve hot.

Nutrition: Calories: 554 Fat: 23g Carbs: 43g Protein: 44g

621. Rolled Up Tender Beef
Preparation Time: 10 minutes
Cooking Time: 20 minutes
Servings: 4

Ingredients
- 2-pound beef steak
- 5-6 slices Cheddar cheese
- ½ cup fresh baby spinach
- 4 tablespoons Pesto
- 2 tablespoons unsalted butter
- 1 teaspoon salt
- ¼ teaspoon black pepper
- 1 tablespoon olive oil

Directions
1. Open beef steak and spread the butter over the meat. Then cover it with pesto.
2. Layer cheese slices, baby spinach and season with salt and pepper. Roll up the meat and secure with toothpicks. Season with salt and pepper again.

3. Preheat the air fryer to 390° F and sprinkle frying basket with olive oil.
4. Place beef roll in the air fryer and cook for 15-20 minutes, turning couple times to roast from all sides.
5. Slice beef roll and serve with mashed potatoes or steamed rice.

Nutrition: Calories: 187 Fat: 8g Carbs: 16g Protein: 14g

622. Veal Rolls with Sage
Preparation Time: 15 minutes
Cooking Time: 15 minutes
Servings: 4

Ingredients
- 15 oz meat or chicken stock
- 7 oz dry white wine
- 4 veal cutlets
- Freshly ground pepper
- 8 fresh sage leaves
- 4 slices ham
- 2 tablespoons butter

Directions
1. Preheat the air fryer to 380° F.
2. Boil the meat stock and the wine in a wide pan on medium heat until it has reduced to one-third of the original amount.
3. Sprinkle salt and pepper on the cutlets and cover them with the sage leaves. Firmly roll the cutlets and wrap a slice of ham around each cutlet. Thinly brush the entire cutlets with butter and place them in the basket.
4. Slide the basket into the air fryer and cook for 10 minutes. Roast the veal rolls until nicely brown. Lower the temperature to 302° F and cook for another 5 minutes.
5. Mix the remainder of the butter with the reduced stock and season the gravy with salt and pepper. Thinly slice the veal rolls and serve them with the gravy. Serve.

Nutrition: Calories: 227 Fat: 11g Carbs: 4g Protein: 27g

623. Air Fryer Chipotle Beef
Preparation Time: 10 minutes
Cooking Time: 30 minutes
Servings: 6

Ingredients
- 3 pounds beef eye
- 4 garlic cloves, minced
- 1 tablespoon ground cumin
- 2 teaspoons salt
- 1 small onion
- 3 tablespoons chipotles in adobo sauce
- 1 cup water
- ½ teaspoons ground cloves
- ½ teaspoons black pepper
- 1 tablespoon olive oil
- 1 tablespoon ground oregano

Directions
1. Add garlic cloves, cumin, lime juice, oregano, onion, chipotles, water and cloves in a food processor. Blend until it becomes smooth.
2. Cut the beef into medium size pieces. Season the meat with salt and black pepper. Preheat the air fryer to 400° F. Sprinkle some oil in it. Add the beef and cook for about 5 minutes.
3. Add the mixture from food processor to the air fryer. Stir to coat the beef perfectly and cook for 25 minutes, stirring occasionally. Cook until ready and serve.

Nutrition: Calories: 190 Fat: 14g Carbs: 10g Protein: 7g

624. Greek Meatballs with Feta
Preparation Time: 10 minutes
Cooking Time: 10 minutes
Servings: 2

Ingredients
- ½ pound ground beef
- 1 slice white bread, crumbled
- ¼ cup feta cheese, crumbled
- 1 tablespoon fresh oregano, chopped
- 1 tablespoon fresh parsley, chopped
- ½ teaspoon ground black pepper
- A pinch of salt

Directions

1. In the large mixing bowl combine ground beef, breadcrumbs, fresh herbs, ground pepper and salt. Mix well to receive smooth paste.
2. Divide the mixture into 8-10 equal pieces.
3. Wet your hands and roll meatballs.
4. Preheat the Air Fryer to 370-390°F
5. Place meatballs into the Fryer and cook for 8-10 minutes, depending on the size of your meatballs.
6. Serve with rice or pasta.

Nutrition: Calories: 294 Fat: 11g Carbs: 26g Protein: 23g

625. Rib Eye Steak

Preparation Time: 5 minutes
Cooking Time: 15-20 minutes
Servings: 4

Ingredients

- 2 pounds rib eye steak
- 1 tablespoon steak rub
- 1 tablespoon olive oil

Directions

1. Preheat your Air Fryer to 390-400° F.
2. Season the steak on both sides with rub and sprinkle with olive oil.
3. Cook the steak for about 7-8 minutes, rotate the steak and cook for another 6-7 minute until golden brown and ready.

Nutrition: Calories: 360 Fat: 32g Carbs: 0g Protein: 18g

626. Fried Beef with Potatoes and Mushrooms

Preparation Time: 20 minutes
Cooking Time: 15 minutes
Servings: 3

Ingredients

- 1-pound beef steak
- 1 medium onion, sliced
- 8 oz mushrooms, sliced
- ½ pound potatoes, diced
- Sauce you prefer (Barbecue or Teriyaki)
- Salt and black pepper for seasoning

Directions

1. Wash vegetables, chop onion and mushrooms, dice potatoes.
2. Sprinkle them with salt and pepper.
3. Cut beef steak into 1-inch pieces.
4. In the large mixing bowl combine onion, potatoes, mushrooms and beef. Marinate with sauce and set aside for 15-20 minutes.
5. Preheat the Air Fryer to 350-370°F
6. Put meat and vegetables into the Fryer and cook for 15 minutes.
7. After cooking replace the meal to the serving plate and sprinkle with fresh chopped parsley.

Nutrition: Calories: 336 Fat: 16g Carbs: 22g Protein: 25g

627. Homemade Cheese Stuffed Burgers

Preparation Time: 10 minutes
Cooking Time: 20 minutes
Servings: 2

Ingredients

- 1 pound finely ground beef
- 2 oz cheddar cheese
- Salt and ground pepper to taste

Directions

1. Take the large mixing bowl and put minced beef. Break it up and season with salt and black pepper.
2. Divide the mince into 4 balls.
3. Cut the cheese into 4 equal pieces.
4. Take half mince from one of the balls and form it into a circle about 2.5 inch wide.
5. Push a piece of the cheese into the center of the mince ball.
6. From the remaining half of mince make the circle with the same width and put on the top. Carefully join the base with cheese and the top and then gently form the burger with your hands.
7. Preheat the Air Fryer to 370°F
8. Cook burgers in the Air Fryer for about 15-20 minutes until they become ready turning halfway through the cooking time.

Nutrition: Calories: 297 Fat: 23g Carbs: 3g Protein: 19g

628. Beef Meatballs in Red Sauce

Preparation Time: 15 minutes
Cooking Time: 10 minutes

Servings: 3

Ingredients

- 12 oz. (3/4 pounds) ground beef
- 1 small onion
- 1 tablespoon finely chopped fresh parsley
- 1 egg
- ½ tablespoon finely chopped fresh thyme leaves
- 3 tablespoons breadcrumbs
- Pepper and salt to taste
- You can also use 10 oz. tomato sauce

Directions

1. All ingredients put into large bowl and mix. This mixture shapes in 10-12 balls
2. Cook in Air fryer on 390°F for 8 minutes.
3. After that, add tomato sauce and back to the Air fryer on 330°F and cook again for 5 minutes.
4. This meal is actually meatballs, and red sauce is optional. You can serve balls without red sauce if you like.

Nutrition: Calories: 341 Fat: 15g Carbs: 19g Protein: 28g

629. Meat Rolls with Sage

Preparation Time: 15 minutes
Cooking Time: 15 minutes
Servings: 3-4

Ingredients

- 4 veal cutlets
- 2 cups beef stock
- 1 cup dry white wine
- 8 fresh sage leaves
- 4 slices cured ham
- 1 tablespoon butter
- Freshly ground pepper
- A pinch of salt

Directions

1. Preheat the Air Fryer to 390° F. Pour the beef stock and the wine in a wide pan and bring to a boil over medium heat until it has reduced to one-third of the original amount.
2. Sprinkle salt and pepper on the cutlets and cover them with the sage leaves. Firmly roll the cutlets and wrap a slice of ham around each cutlet.
3. Thinly cover the entire cutlets with butter and place them in the Air Fryer basket. Put the basket in the Fryer and cook for about 10 minutes until nicely brown.
4. Lower the temperature to 320° F and additionally for 5 minutes until almost done. Mix the remainder of the butter with the reduced stock and season the gravy with salt and pepper.
5. Thinly slice the veal rolls and serve them with the gravy. Tastes great with tagliatelle and green beans.

Nutrition: Calories: 180 Fat: 15g Carbs: 1g Protein: 10g

630. Gentle Thyme Meatloaf

Preparation Time: 15 minutes
Cooking Time: 25 minutes
Servings: 3

Ingredients

- 1-pound ground beef
- 1 egg, beaten
- 3 tablespoons breadcrumbs
- 2 oz salami, chopped
- 1 medium onion, chopped
- 2 tablespoons olive oil
- 1 tablespoon fresh thyme
- Ground pepper and salt to taste

Directions

1. In the large bowl mix ground beef, one egg, breadcrumbs, chopped salami and chopped onion. Add thyme, ground pepper and salt to taste. Stir to combine.
2. Place the beef mixture in the heatproof dish and grease the top with olive oil.
3. Preheat the Air Fryer to 370°F
4. Put the dish with mixture into the Air Fryer cooking basket and set the timer for 25 minutes. Cook until become nicely brown and done.

5. After Directions cut the meatloaf into wedges you like and serve with potatoes or vegetable salad.

Nutrition: Calories: 331 Fat: 18g Carbs: 14g Protein: 27g

FISH AND SEAFOODS

631. Cod steaks with plum sauce
Preparation time: 10 minutes
Cooking time: 20 minutes
Servings: 2
Ingredients:
- 2 big cod steaks
- Salt and black pepper to the taste
- ½ teaspoon garlic powder
- ½ teaspoon ginger powder
- ¼ teaspoon turmeric powder
- 1 tablespoon plum sauce
- Cooking spray

Directions:
1. Season cod steaks with salt and pepper, spray them with cooking oil, add garlic powder, ginger powder and turmeric powder and rub well.
2. Place cod steaks in your air fryer and cook at 360 ° f for 15 minutes, flipping them after 7 minutes.
3. Heat a pan over medium heat, add plum sauce, stir and cook for 2 minutes.
4. Divide cod steaks on plates, drizzle plum sauce all over and serve.
5. Enjoy!

Nutrition: calories 250, fat 7, fiber 1, carbs 14, protein 12

632. Lemony Saba fish
Preparation time: 10 minutes
Cooking time: 8 minutes
Servings: 1
Ingredients:
- 4 Saba fish fillets, boneless
- Salt and black pepper to the taste
- 3 red chili pepper, chopped
- 2 tablespoons lemon juice
- 2 tablespoon olive oil
- 2 tablespoon garlic, minced

Directions:
1. Put salt and pepper to fish fillets with salt then put in a bowl.
2. Add lemon juice, oil, chili and garlic toss to coat, transfer fish to your air fryer.
3. Cook for 8 minutes at 360° f, flipping halfway.
4. Divide among plates and serve with some fries.
5. Enjoy!

Nutrition: calories 300, fat 4, fiber 8, carbs 15, protein 15

633. Asian halibut
Preparation time: 30 minutes
Cooking time: 10 minutes
Servings: 3
Ingredients:
- 1-pound halibut steaks
- 2/3 cup soy sauce
- ¼ cup sugar
- 2 tablespoons lime juice
- ½ cup mirin
- ¼ teaspoon red pepper flakes, crushed
- ¼ cup orange juice
- ¼ teaspoon ginger, grated
- 1 garlic clove, minced

Directions:
1. Put soy sauce in a pan, heat up over medium heat, add mirin, sugar, lime and orange juice, pepper flakes, ginger and garlic, stir well, bring to a boil and take off heat.
2. Bring half of the marinade to a bowl. Add halibut, toss to coat and leave aside in the fridge for 30 minutes.

3. Transfer halibut to your air fryer and cook at 390 ° f for 10 minutes, flipping once.
4. Divide halibut steaks on plates, drizzle the rest of the marinade all over and serve hot.
5. Enjoy!

Nutrition: calories 286, fat 5, fiber 12, carbs 14, protein 23

634. Cod fillets and peas
Preparation time: 10 minutes
Cooking time: 10 minutes
Servings: 4
Ingredients:
- 4 cod fillets, boneless
- 2 tablespoons parsley, chopped
- 2 cups peas
- 4 tablespoons wine
- ½ teaspoon oregano, dried
- ½ teaspoon sweet paprika
- 2 garlic cloves, minced
- Salt and pepper to the taste

Directions:
1. In your food processor mix garlic with parsley, salt, pepper, oregano, paprika, and wine, blend well.
2. Rub fish with half of this mix, place in your air fryer and cook at 360 ° f for 10 minutes.
3. Meanwhile, put peas in a pot, add water to cover, add salt, bring to a boil over medium high heat.
4. Cook for 10 minutes, drain and divide among plates.
5. Also divide fish on plates, spread the rest of the herb dressing all over and serve.
6. Enjoy!

Nutrition: calories 261, fat 8, fiber 12, carbs 20, protein 22

635. Coconut coated fish cakes with mango sauce
Preparation: 20 minutes
Cooking time: 14 minutes
Servings: 4
Ingredients:
- 18 ounces of white fish fillet
- 1 green onion, finely chopped
- 1 mango, peeled, cubed
- 4 tablespoons of ground coconut
- 1½ ounces of parsley, finely chopped
- 1½ teaspoons of ground fresh red chili
- 1 lime, juice and zest
- 1 egg
- 1 teaspoon of salt

Directions:
1. Add ½ ounce of parsley, ½ teaspoon of ground chili, half of the lime juice and zest to the mango cubes and mix thoroughly.
2. Using a food processor, puree the fish and add the salt, egg, and lime zest, lime juice and chili. Stir in the green onions, 2 tablespoons of coconut and the rest of the parsley.
3. Put the rest of the coconut in a shallow dish. Mold the fish mixture into 12 round cakes. Place the cakes in the coconut to coat them.
4. Put half of the cakes into the fryer basket and bake for 7 minutes at 356°f. Remove when cakes are golden and bake the second batch of cakes.
5. Serve the cakes with the mango salsa.

Nutrition: Calories: 200 Fat: 13g Carbs: 8g Protein: 14g

636. Teriyaki glazed halibut steak
Preparation: 30 minutes
cooking time: 1015 minutes
servings: 3
Ingredients
- 1-pound halibut steak for the marinade:

~ 130 ~

- 2/3 cup low sodium soy sauce
- ½ cup mirin
- 2 tablespoons lime juice
- ¼ cup sugar
- ¼ cup orange juice
- ¼ teaspoon ginger ground
- ¼ teaspoon crushed red pepper flakes
- 1 each garlic clove (smashed)

Directions
1. Place all the ingredients for the teriyaki glaze/marinade in a saucepan. Bring to a boil and lessen by half, then let it cool.
2. When it cools, pour half of the glaze/marinade into a Ziploc bag together with the halibut then refrigerate for 30 minutes.
3. Preheat the air fryer to 390°f. Place the marinated halibut into the air fryer and cook 10-12 minutes. Brush some of the glaze that's left over the halibut steak.
4. Spread over white rice with basil/mint chutney.

Nutrition: Calories: 280 Fat: 7g Carbs: 14g Protein: 37g

637. Tabasco shrimp
Preparation time: 10 minutes
Cooking time: 10 minutes
Servings: 4
Ingredients:
- 1-pound shrimp, peeled and deveined
- 1 teaspoon red pepper flakes
- 2 tablespoon olive oil
- 1 teaspoon tabasco sauce
- 2 tablespoons water
- 1 teaspoon oregano, dried
- Salt and black pepper to the taste
- ½ teaspoon parsley, dried
- ½ teaspoon smoked paprika

Directions:
1. In a bowl, mix oil with water, tabasco sauce, pepper flakes, oregano, parsley, salt, pepper, paprika and shrimp and toss well to coat.
2. Transfer shrimp to your preheated air fryer at 370° f and cook for 10 minutes shaking the fryer once.
3. Divide shrimp on plates and serve with a side salad.
4. Enjoy!

Nutrition: calories 200, fat 5, fiber 6, carbs 13, protein 8

638. Italian barramundi fillets and tomato salsa
Preparation time: 10 minutes
Cooking time: 8 minutes
Servings: 4
Ingredients:
- 2 barramundi fillets, boneless
- 1 tablespoon olive oil+ 2 teaspoons
- 2 teaspoons Italian seasoning
- ¼ cup green olives, pitted and chopped
- ¼ cup cherry tomatoes, chopped
- ¼ cup black olives, chopped
- 1 tablespoon lemon zest
- 2 tablespoons lemon zest
- Salt and black pepper to the taste
- 2 tablespoons parsley, chopped

Directions:
1. Rub fish with salt, pepper, Italian seasoning and 2 teaspoons olive oil.
2. Once the air fryer is ready at 360° f, cook the fillet for 8 minutes.
3. In a bowl, mix tomatoes with black olives, green olives, salt, pepper, lemon zest and lemon juice, parsley and 1 tablespoon olive oil and toss well
4. Divide fish on plates, add tomato salsa on top and serve.
5. Enjoy!

Nutrition: calories 270, fat 4, fiber 2, carbs 18, protein 27

639. Flavored Jamaican salmon
Preparation time: 10 minutes
Cooking time: 10 minutes
Servings: 4
Ingredients:
- 2 teaspoons sriracha sauce

- 4 teaspoons sugar
- 3 scallions, chopped
- Salt and black pepper to the taste
- 2 teaspoons olive oil
- 4 teaspoons apple cider vinegar
- 3 teaspoons avocado oil
- 4 medium salmon fillets, boneless
- 4 cups baby arugula
- 2 cups cabbage, shredded
- 1 and ½ teaspoon Jamaican jerk seasoning ¼ cup pepitas, toasted
- 2 cups radish, julienned

Directions:
1. In a bowl, mix sriracha with sugar, whisk and transfer 2 teaspoons to another bowl.
2. Combine 2 teaspoons sriracha mix with the avocado oil, olive oil, vinegar, salt and pepper and whisk well.
3. Sprinkle jerk seasoning over salmon, rub with sriracha and sugar mix and season with salt and pepper.
4. Take it to the air fryer and cook at 360° f for 10 minutes, flipping once.
5. In a bowl, mix radishes with cabbage, arugula, salt, pepper, sriracha and vinegar mix and toss well.
6. Divide salmon and radish mix on plates, sprinkle pepitas and scallions on top and serve.
7. Enjoy!

Nutrition: calories 290, fat 6, fiber 12, carbs 17, protein 10

640. Stuffed calamari
Preparation time: 10 minutes
Cooking time: 25 minutes
Servings: 4
Ingredients:
- 4 big calamari, tentacles separated and chopped, and tubes reserved
- 2 tablespoons parsley, chopped
- 5 ounces kale, chopped
- 2 garlic cloves, minced
- 1 red bell pepper, chopped
- 1 tablespoon olive oil
- 2 ounces canned tomato puree
- 1 yellow onion, chopped
- Salt and black pepper to the taste

Directions:
1. Heat the pan with the oil over medium heat, add onion and garlic, stir and cook for 2 minutes.
2. Add bell pepper, tomato puree, calamari tentacles, kale, salt and pepper, stir, cook for 10 minutes and take off heat. Stir and cook for 3 minutes.
3. Stuff calamari tubes with this mix, secure with toothpicks, put in your air fryer and cook at 360 ° f for 20 minutes.
4. Divide calamari on plates, sprinkle parsley all over and serve.
5. Enjoy!

Nutrition: calories 322, fat 10, fiber 14, carbs 14, protein 22

641. Snapper fillets and veggies
Preparation time: 10 minutes
Cooking time: 14 minutes
Servings: 2
Ingredients:
- 2 red snapper fillets, boneless
- 1 tablespoon olive oil
- ½ cup red bell pepper, chopped
- ½ cup green bell pepper, chopped
- ½ cup leeks, chopped
- Salt and black pepper to the taste
- 1 teaspoon tarragon, dried
- A splash of white wine

Directions:
1. Put a hot proof dish that fits your air fryer, mix fish fillets with salt, pepper, oil, green bell pepper, red bell pepper, leeks, tarragon and wine.
2. Toss well everything, introduce in preheated air fryer at 350° f and cook for 14 minutes, flipping fish fillets halfway.

3. Divide fish and veggies on plates and serve warm.
4. Enjoy!
Nutrition: calories 300, fat 12, fiber 8, carbs 29, protein 12

642. **Lemon sole and swiss chard**
Preparation time: 10 minutes
Cooking time: 14 minutes
Servings: 4
Ingredients:
- 1 teaspoon lemon zest, grated
- 4 white bread slices, quartered
- ¼ cup walnuts, chopped
- ¼ cup parmesan, grated
- 4 tablespoons olive oil
- 4 sole fillets, boneless
- Salt and black pepper to the taste
- 4 tablespoons butter
- ¼ cup lemon juice
- 3 tablespoons capers
- 2 garlic cloves, minced
- 2 bunches swiss chard, chopped

Directions:
1. In your food processor, mix bread with walnuts, cheese and lemon zest and pulse well.
2. Add half of the olive oil, pulse well again and leave aside for now.
3. Heat up a pan with the butter over medium heat, add lemon juice, salt, pepper and capers, stir well, add fish and toss it.
4. Transfer fish to your preheated air fryer's basket, top with bread mix you've made at the beginning and cook at 350° f for 14 minutes.
5. Meanwhile, heat up another pan with the rest of the oil, add garlic, swiss chard, salt and pepper, stir gently, cook for 2 minutes and take off heat.
6. Divide fish on plates and serve with sautéed chard on the side.
7. Enjoy!
Nutrition: calories 321, fat 7, fiber 18, carbs 27, protein 12

643. **Prawns**
Preparation Time: 10 minutes
Cooking Time: 10 minutes
Servings: 4
Ingredients:
- 1 lb. prawns, peeled
- 1 lb. bacon slices
Directions:
1. Preheat the Air Fryer to 400°F.
2. Wrap the bacon slices around the prawns and put them in fryer's basket.
3. Air fry for 5 minutes and serve hot.
Nutrition: Calories: 35 Fat: 2g Carbs: 0g Protein: 4g

644. **Mango shrimp skewers**
Preparation Time: 10 minutes
Cooking Time: 15 minutes
Servings:4
Ingredients:
- 2 tbsp olive oil
- ½ tsp garlic powder
- 1 tsp dry mango powder
- 2 tbsp fresh lime juice
- salt and black pepper to taste

Directions:
1. In a bowl, mix well the garlic powder, mango powder, lime juice, salt, and pepper. Add the shrimp and toss to coat. Cover and allow to marinate for minutes.
2. Preheat your Air Fryer to 390° F. Spray the air fryer basket with cooking spray.
3. Transfer the marinated shrimp to the cooking basket and drizzle the olive oil.
4. Cook for 5 minutes, Slide out the fryer basket and shake the shrimp; cook for 5 minutes.
5. Cool for 5 minutes and serve.
Nutrition: Calories: 261 Fat: 8g Carbs: 0g Protein: 28g

645. **Easy Creamy Shrimp Nachos**
Preparation Time: 10 minutes

Cooking Time: 10 Minutes
Servings: 4
Ingredients:
- 1-pound shrimp, cleaned and deveined
- 1 tablespoon olive oil
- 2 tablespoons fresh lemon juice
- 1 teaspoon paprika
- 1/4 teaspoon cumin powder
- 1/2 teaspoon shallot powder
- 1/2 teaspoon garlic powder
- Coarse sea salt
- ground black pepper, to taste
- 1 (9ounce bag corn tortilla chips
- 1/4 cup pickled jalapeño, minced
- 1 cup Pepper Jack cheese, grated
- 1/2 cup sour cream

Directions:
1. Roll the shrimp with the olive oil, lemon juice, paprika, cumin powder, shallot powder, garlic powder, salt, and black pepper.
2. Cook in the preheated Air Fryer at 390° F for 5 minutes.
3. Place the tortilla chips on the aluminum foil lined cooking basket. Top with the shrimp mixture, jalapeño and cheese. Cook for another minute until cheese has melted.
4. Serve garnished with sour cream and enjoy!
Nutrition: Calories: 534 Fat: 34g Carbs: 26g Protein: 27g

646. **Fried Crawfish**
Preparation Time: 5 minutes
Cooking Time: 5 minutes
Servings: 4
Ingredients:
- 1pound crawfish
- 1 tablespoon avocado oil
- 1 teaspoon onion powder
- 1 tablespoon rosemary, chopped

Directions:
1. Preheat the air fryer to 340°F.
2. Place the crawfish in the air fryer basket and sprinkle with avocado oil and rosemary. Add the onion powder and stir the crawfish gently.
3. Cook the meal for 5 minutes.

Nutrition: Calories: 370 Fat: 21g Carbs: 27g Protein: 17g

647. **Prawn Burgers**
Preparation Time: 10 minutes
Cooking Time: 6 minutes
Servings: 2
Ingredients:
- ½ cup prawns, peeled, deveined and finely chopped
- ½ cup breadcrumbs
- 23 tablespoons onion, finely chopped
- 3 cups fresh baby greens
- ½ teaspoon ginger, minced
- ½ teaspoon garlic, minced
- ½ teaspoon red chili powder
- ½ teaspoon ground cumin
- ¼ teaspoon ground turmeric
- Salt and ground black pepper, as required

Directions:
1. Preheat the Air fryer to 390° F and grease an Air fryer basket.
2. Mix the prawns, breadcrumbs, onion, ginger, garlic, and spices in a bowl.
3. Make small sized patties from the mixture and transfer to the Air fryer basket.
4. Cook for about 6 minutes and dish out in a platter.
5. Serve immediately warm alongside the baby greens.
Nutrition: Calories: 184 Fat: 3g Carbs: 13g Protein: 26g

648. **Jumbo Shrimp**
Preparation Time: 5 minutes
Cooking Time: 10 Minutes
Servings: 4

Ingredients:

- 12 jumbo shrimps
- ½ tsp. garlic salt
- ¼ tsp. freshly cracked mixed peppercorns

For the Sauce:

- 1 tsp. Dijon mustard
- 4 tbsp. mayonnaise
- 1 tsp. lemon zest
- 1 tsp. chipotle powder
- ½ tsp. cumin powder

Directions:

1. Dust garlic salt over the shrimp and coat with the cracked peppercorns.
2. Fry the shrimp in the cooking basket at 395degreesF for 5 minutes.
3. Turn the shrimp over and allow to cook for a further 2 minutes.
4. In the meantime, mix together all ingredients for the sauce with a whisk.
5. Serve over the shrimp.

Nutrition: Calories: 148 Fat: 4g Carbs: 2g Protein: 24g

649. Sardine Cakes
Preparation Time: 5 minutes
Cooking Time: 10 minutes
Servings: 5
Ingredients:

- 12 oz sardines, trimmed, cleaned
- ¼ cup coconut flour
- 1 egg, beaten
- 2 tablespoons flax meal
- 1 teaspoon ground black pepper
- 1 teaspoon salt
- Cooking spray

Directions:

1. Chop the sardines roughly and put them in the bowl. Add coconut flour, egg, flax meal, ground black pepper, and salt.
2. Mix up the mixture with the help of the fork. Then make 5 cakes from the sardine mixture.
3. Preheat the air fryer to 390°F. Add cooking spray to the air fryer basket and place the cakes inside.
4. Cook them for 5 minutes from each side.

Nutrition: Calories: 24 Carbs: 2g Protein: 1g

650. Mahi-mahi And Broccoli Cakes
Preparation Time: 5 minutes
Cooking Time: 11 minutes
Servings: 4
Ingredients:

- ½ cup broccoli, shredded
- 1 tablespoon flax meal
- 1 egg, beaten
- 1 teaspoon ground coriander
- 1 oz Monterey Jack cheese, shredded
- ½ teaspoon salt
- 6 oz Mahi-mahi, chopped
- Cooking spray

Directions:

1. In the mixing bowl mix up flax meal, egg, ground coriander, salt, broccoli, and chopped Mahi-mahi.
2. Stir the ingredients gently with the help of the fork and add shredded Monterey Jack cheese. Stir the mixture until homogenous.
3. Then make 4 cakes. Preheat the air fryer to 390°F. Place the Mahi-mahi cakes in the air fryer and spray them gently with cooking spray.
4. Cook the fish cakes for 5 minutes and then flip on another side. Cook the fish cakes for 6 minutes more.

Nutrition: Calories: 150 Fat: 7g Carbs: 9g Protein: 13g

651. Greek style Monkfish With Vegetables
Preparation Time: 10 minutes
Cooking Time: 20 Minutes
Servings: 2
Ingredients:

- 2 teaspoons olive oil

- 1 cup celery, sliced
- 2 bell peppers, sliced
- 1 teaspoon dried thyme
- 1/2 teaspoon dried marjoram
- 1/2 teaspoon dried rosemary
- 2 monkfish fillets
- 1 tablespoon soy sauce
- 2 tablespoons lime juice
- Coarse salt
- Ground black pepper, to taste
- 1 teaspoon cayenne pepper
- 1/2 cup piited and sliced Kalamata olives

Directions:

1. Heat the olive oil for minute. Once hot, sauté the celery and peppers until tender, about 4 minutes.
2. Sprinkle with thyme, marjoram, and rosemary and set aside.
3. Toss the fish fillets with the soy sauce, lime juice, salt, black pepper, and cayenne pepper.
4. Position fish fillets in a lightly greased cooking basket and bake at 390° F for 8 minutes.
5. Turn them over, add the olives, and cook an additional 4 minutes. Serve with the sautéed vegetables on the side. Bon appétit!

Nutrition: Calories: 210 Fat: 13g Carbs: 9g Protein: 16g

652. Wrapped Scallops
Preparation Time: 5 minutes
Cooking Time: 7 minutes
Servings: 4
Ingredients:

- 1 teaspoon ground coriander
- ½ teaspoon ground paprika
- ¼ teaspoon salt
- 16 oz scallops
- 4 oz bacon, sliced
- 1 teaspoon sesame oil

Directions:

1. Sprinkle the scallops with ground coriander, ground paprika, and salt.
2. Then wrap the scallops in the bacon slices and secure with toothpicks.
3. Sprinkle the scallops with sesame oil. Preheat the air fryer to 400°F.
4. Put the scallops in the air fryer basket and cook them for 7 minutes.

Nutrition: Calories: 110 Fat: 9g Carbs: 1g Protein: 5g

653. Butter Mussels
Preparation Time: 5 minutes
Cooking Time: 2 minutes
Servings:5
Ingredients:

- 2pounds mussels
- 1 shallot, chopped
- 1 tablespoon minced garlic
- 1 tablespoon butter, melted
- 1 teaspoon sunflower oil
- 1 teaspoon salt
- 1 tablespoon fresh parsley, chopped
- ½ teaspoon chili flakes

Directions:

1. Clean and wash mussels and put them in the big bowl.
2. Add shallot, minced garlic, butter, sunflower oil, salt, and chili flakes. Shake the mussels well. Preheat the air fryer to 390°F.
3. Put the mussels in the air fryer basket and cook for 2 minutes.
4. Then transfer the cooked meal in the serving bowl and top it with chopped fresh parsley.

Nutrition: Calories: 300 Fat: 15g Carbs: 10g Protein: 31g

654. Greek style Grilled Scallops
Preparation Time: 2 hours
Cooking Time: 15 minutes
Servings:3
Ingredients:

- ¼ cup Greek yogurt

- A pinch of saffron threads
- 1 ½ teaspoons rice vinegar
- Salt and pepper to taste
- 12 large sea scallops
- 2 tablespoons olive oil

Directions:
1. Arrange all ingredients in a Ziploc and allow the scallops to marinate in the fridge for at least 2 hours.
2. Preheat the air fryer at 3900°F.
3. Place the grill pan accessory in the air fryer.
4. Grill the scallops for 15 minutes.
5. Serve on bread and drizzle with more olive oil if desired.

Nutrition: Calories: 392 Fat: 29g Carbs: 5g Protein: 29g

655. Spiced Coco lime Skewered Shrimp
Preparation Time: 10 minutes
Cooking Time: 12 minutes
Servings:6
Ingredients:
- 1 lime, zested and juiced
- 1/3 cup chopped fresh cilantro
- 1/3 cup shredded coconut
- 1/4 cup olive oil
- 1/4 cup soy sauce
- 1pound uncooked medium shrimp, peeled and deveined
- 2 garlic cloves
- 2 jalapeno peppers, seeded

Directions:
1. In food processor, process until smooth the soy sauce, olive oil, coconut oil, cilantro, garlic, lime juice, lime zest, and jalapeno.
2. In a shallow dish, mix well shrimp and processed marinade. Toss well to coat and marinate in the ref for 3 hours.
3. Thread shrimps in skewers. Place on skewer rack in air fryer.
4. For 6 minutes, cook on 360°F. If needed, cook in batches.
5. Serve and enjoy.

Nutrition: Calories: 169 Fat: 11g Carbs: 5g Protein: 13g

656. Tuna Au Gratin With Herbs
Preparation Time: 10 minutes
Cooking Time: 20 minutes
Servings: 4
Ingredients:
- 1 tablespoon butter, melted
- 1 medium sized leek, thinly sliced
- 1 tablespoon chicken stock
- 1 tablespoon dry white wine
- 1-pound tuna
- 1/2 teaspoon red pepper flakes, crushed
- Sea salt
- ground black pepper, to taste
- 1/2 teaspoon dried rosemary
- 1/2 teaspoon dried basil
- 1/2 teaspoon dried thyme
- 2 small ripe tomatoes, pureed
- 1 cup Parmesan cheese, grated

Directions:
1. Melt 2 tablespoon of butter in a sauté pan over medium high heat.
2. Now, cook the leek and garlic until tender and aromatic.
3. Add the stock and wine to deglaze the pan.
4. Preheat the Air Fryer to 370° F.
5. Grease a casserole dish with the remaining 1/2 tablespoon of melted butter. Place the fish in the casserole dish. Add the seasonings. Top with the sautéed leek mixture.
6. Add the tomato puree. Cook for 10 minutes in the preheated Air Fryer.
7. Top with grated Parmesan cheese; cook an additional 7 minutes until the crumbs are golden. Bon appétit!

Nutrition: Calories: 240 Fat: 1g Carbs: 30g Protein: 4g

657. Shrimp And Pine Nuts Mix
Preparation Time: 5 minutes
Cooking Time: 12 minutes
Servings: 4
Ingredients:

- ½ cup parsley leaves
- ½ cup basil leaves
- 2 tablespoons lemon juice
- 1/3 cup pine nuts
- ¼ cup parmesan, grated
- A pinch of salt and black pepper
- ½ cup olive oil
- 1 and ½ pounds shrimp, peeled and deveined
- ¼ teaspoon lemon zest, grated

Directions:
1. Prepare all ingredients except the shrimp in blender and pulse well.
2. In a bowl, mix the shrimp with the pesto and toss.
3. Put the shrimp in your air fryer's basket and cook at 360° F for minutes, flipping the shrimp halfway.
4. Divide the shrimp into bowls and serve.

Nutrition: Calories: 365 Fat: 21g Carbs: 0g Protein: 0g

658. Cheesy Shrimps
Preparation Time: 5 minutes
Cooking Time: 5 Minutes
Servings: 4
Ingredients:
- 14 oz shrimps, peeled
- 2 eggs, beaten
- ¼ cup heavy cream
- 1 teaspoon salt
- 1 teaspoon ground black pepper
- 4 oz Monterey jack cheese, shredded
- 5 tablespoons coconut flour
- 1 tablespoon lemon juice, for garnish

Directions:
1. In the mixing bowl mix up heavy cream, salt, and ground black pepper. Add eggs and whisk the mixture until homogenous.
2. After this, mix up coconut flour and Monterey jack cheese. Dip the shrimps in the heavy cream mixture and coat in the coconut flour mixture.
3. Then dip the shrimps in the egg mixture again and coat in the coconut flour.
4. Preheat the air fryer to 400°F. Arrange the shrimps in the air fryer in one layer and cook them for 5 minutes.
5. Repeat the same step with remaining shrimps.
6. Sprinkle the bang-bang shrimps with lemon juice.

Nutrition: Calories: 210 Fat: 11g Carbs: 9g Protein: 8g

659. Coconut lime shrimp
Preparation time: 5 minutes
Cooking time: 10 minutes
Servings: 4
Ingredients:
- 1-pound shrimp, cleaned and deveined
- 1 cup unsweetened, shredded coconut
- 1 tablespoon lime zest, grated
- ½ teaspoon cayenne powder
- 1 cup flour
- 1 tablespoon cornstarch
- 1 teaspoon salt
- 1 teaspoon pepper
- 1 egg white

Directions:
1. Set the air fryer to 350°F.
2. In a bowl, combine the unsweetened shredded coconut, lime zest, and cayenne powder.
3. In a second bowl, combine the flour, cornstarch, salt, and pepper.
4. Place the egg white in a third bowl.
5. One at a time, dip each shrimp first in the flour mixture, then the egg white, and then in the coconut mixture, patting on the coconut with your fingers to make sure it sticks.
6. Place the shrimp in the basket of the air fryer.
7. Cook for 10 minutes, turning once halfway through.

Nutrition: Calories 353, Total fat 13 g, Saturated fat 4 g, Total carbohydrate 39 g, Dietary fiber 9 g, Sugars 1 g, protein 21 g

660. Prosciutto wrapped shrimp

Preparation time: 1o minutes
Cooking time: 10 minutes
Servings: 4
Ingredients:

- 1-pound shrimp, cleaned and deveined
- 2 teaspoons lemon juice
- ½ teaspoon salt
- 1 teaspoon black pepper
- ½ teaspoon garlic powder
- ½ pound prosciutto, or enough to wrap each shrimp with one piece

Directions:

1. Set the air fryer to 350°F.
2. Season the shrimp with the lemon juice, salt, black pepper, and garlic powder.
3. Take one piece of prosciutto and wrap it completely around one piece of shrimp.
4. Repeat until all the shrimp is wrapped and place it in the basket of the air fryer.
5. Cook for 10 minutes, or until the shrimp is cooked all the way through.

Nutrition: Calories 261, Total fat 10 g, Saturated fat 4 g, Total carbohydrate 0 g, Dietary fiber 0 g, sugars 0 g, Protein 30 g

661. Shrimp spring rolls

Preparation time: 10 minutes
Cooking time: 15 minutes
Servings: 4
Ingredients:

- 1 tablespoon peanut oil
- 1 teaspoon sesame oil
- 2 cloves garlic, crushed and minced
- 1 teaspoon fresh ginger, grated
- ¼ cup water chestnuts, cut into small strips
- ½ cup carrots, shredded
- ½ cup cabbage, shredded
- ¼ cup scallions, sliced
- 1 tablespoon soy sauce
- 1 teaspoon five spice powder
- 1 teaspoon salt
- 1 teaspoon pepper
- ¼ pound shrimp, cleaned, deveined and sliced
- ½ cup bean sprouts
- 12-14 spring roll wrappers
- 1 egg, lightly beaten

Directions:

1. Heat the peanut oil and sesame oil in a large skillet over medium heat.
2. Add the garlic, ginger, chestnuts, carrots, cabbage, scallions, and soy sauce.
3. Season the mixture with five spice powder, salt, and pepper. Sauté the mixture for 3-5 minutes.
4. Add the shrimp and bean sprouts. Cook just until the shrimp is pink, and then remove the skillet from the heat.
5. Lay the spring roll wrappers out on the counter or other flat surface.
6. Brush the ends with the beaten egg mixture.
7. Place a generous spoonful of the mixture onto each spring roll wrapper.
8. Roll each one up, fold in the ends, and press the edge to seal.
9. Lightly brush the spring roll with the egg mixture again, if desired.
10. Set the air fryer to 390°F.
11. Place the spring rolls in the basket of the air fryer and cook for 5 minutes.
12. Serve with your favorite dipping sauce, if desired.

Nutrition: Calories 179, Total fat 1 g, Saturated fat 8 g. Total carbohydrate 25 g, Dietary fiber 3 g, Sugars 28 g, Protein 7 g

662. Flakey fried whitefish

Preparation time: 15 minutes
Cooking time: 15 minutes
Servings: 4

Ingredients:

- 1-pound whitefish fillets, cut into 3-4-inch pieces
- 2 teaspoons fresh lemon juice
- 1 teaspoon salt
- 1 teaspoon black pepper
- ½ cup flour
- 2 eggs, lightly beaten
- 1 cup panko breadcrumbs
- 1 tablespoon fresh tarragon, chopped
- 1 tablespoon fresh parsley chopped
- 1 tablespoon olive oil

Directions:

1. Set the air fryer to 390°F.
2. Sprinkle the whitefish fillets with lemon juice and season them with salt and black pepper.
3. Place the flour in one bowl and the eggs in a second bowl.
4. In a third bowl, combine the panko breadcrumbs, tarragon, parsley, and olive oil. Mix until the olive oil is worked through the crumbs.
5. Dust a piece of whitefish with the flour, and then dip it into the egg mixture.
6. Next, place it into the panko mixture and use your hands to pat the crumbs onto the fish. Repeat until all the pieces are coated.
7. Place the whitefish pieces in the basket of the air fryer.
8. Cook for 12-15 minutes, or until the fish is cooked through.

Nutrition: Calories 378, Total fat 18 g, Saturated fat 6 g, Total carbohydrate 21 g, Dietary fiber 9 g, sugars 1 g, Protein 30 g

663. Cod with simple olive caper sauce

Preparation time: 10 minutes
Cooking time: 15 minutes
Servings: 4
Ingredients:

- 1-pound cod pieces
- 1 tablespoon plus 1 teaspoon olive oil
- 1 teaspoon lemon juice
- 1 teaspoon salt
- 1 teaspoon black pepper
- 1 cup cherry tomatoes, halved
- 2 cloves garlic, crushed and minced
- ¼ cup kalamata olives, diced
- 1 tablespoon capers
- ¼ cup fresh basil, chopped

Directions:

1. Set the air fryer to 355°F.
2. Lightly brush the cod with 1 teaspoon of the olive oil.
3. Sprinkle the cod with lemon juice and season it with salt and black pepper.
4. Place the cod in the basket of the air fryer.
5. Cook for 12 minutes, or until the cod is flakey and tender.
6. While the cod is cooking, heat the remaining olive oil in a large skillet over medium.
7. Add the tomatoes and cook for 2-3 minutes, or until they begin to break down and release their juices.
8. Next, add the garlic, olives, capers, and basil to the skillet. Cook, stirring frequently, for 4-5 minutes.
9. Remove the cod from the air fryer and transfer it to serving plates.
10. Top the cod with the olive caper sauce before serving.

Nutrition: Calories 167, Total fat 2 g, Saturated fat 8 g, Total carbohydrate 2 g, Dietary fiber 8 g, Sugars 0 g, Protein 27 g

664. Sesame soy striped bass

Preparation time: 15 minutes
Cooking time: 10 minutes
Servings: 4
Ingredients:

- 1-pound striped bass steaks
- 1 cup soy sauce
- ½ cup mirin
- 2 tablespoons sesame oil
- 2 tablespoons brown sugar
- 1 tablespoon lime juice
- 1 tablespoon garlic chili paste

- ¼ cup apple juice

Directions:
1. Place the bass steaks in a shallow baking dish.
2. In a bowl, combine the soy sauce, mirin, sesame oil, brown sugar, lime juice, garlic chili paste, and apple juice. Use a whisk to blend.
3. Cover the steaks with the sesame soy sauce, cover, and refrigerate for one hour.
4. Set the air fryer to 390°f.
5. Remove the bass from the marinade and blot up any extra.
6. Place the steaks in the air fryer and cook for approximately 10 minutes, or until the fish is cooked through and flakey.
7. Remove the bass from the air fryer and let it rest several minutes before serving.

Nutrition: Calories 310, Total fat 12 g, Saturated fat 7 g, total carbohydrate 21 g, Dietary fiber 5 g, Sugars 13 g, protein 28 g

665. Crab and herb croquettes

Preparation time: 15 minutes
Cooking time: 15 minutes
Servings: 4
Ingredients:
- 1 tablespoon olive oil
- ½ cup red onion, diced
- ¼ cup celery, diced
- ¼ cup red bell pepper, diced
- 3 cloves garlic, crushed and minced
- 1 teaspoon salt
- 1 teaspoon black pepper
- 1 tablespoon fresh tarragon, chopped
- 1 tablespoon fresh parsley, chopped
- 1-pound lump crab meat, shredded
- ¼ cup sour cream
- 2 eggs
- ½ cup flour
- 1 cup panko breadcrumbs
- 1 teaspoon fresh lemon zest
- 1-2 teaspoon crushed red pepper flakes

Directions:
1. Place the olive oil in a skillet over medium heat.
2. Add the red onion, celery, red bell pepper, and garlic. Cook, stirring frequently, for approximately 5 minutes, or until the vegetables begin to become tender.
3. Season the mixture with salt, black pepper, tarragon, and parsley. Remove the skillet from the heat and allow it to cool enough so the mixture can be handled.
4. Next, transfer the vegetables to a bowl and add the lump crab meat, sour cream, and 1 egg. Mix well.
5. Set the air fryer to 390°f.
6. Place the flour in a bowl. In a second bowl, lightly beat the remaining egg.
7. In a blender or food processor, combine the panko breadcrumbs, lemon zest, and crushed red pepper flakes. Transfer the contents to a third bowl.
8. Take the large spoonful of the lump crab mixture and form them into golf ball sized fritters.
9. Dip each one first into the flour, then the egg, and finally the panko mixture.
10. Place them in the air fryer and cook for 10 minutes.
11. Serve with your favorite seafood dipping sauce.

Nutrition: Calories 334, total fat 13 g, saturated fat 1 g, total carbohydrate 23 g, dietary fiber 4 g, sugars 4 g, protein 33 g

666. Garlic tarragon buttered salmon

Preparation time: 30 minutes
Cooking time: 20 minutes
Servings: 4
Ingredients:
- ¼ cup butter
- 1 tablespoon shallot, diced
- 1 tablespoon fresh tarragon, chopped
- 1 teaspoon fresh lemon zest
- 1-pound salmon fillets
- 1 teaspoon salt

- 1 teaspoon black pepper
- Fresh lemon slices for garnish

Directions:
1. Set the air fryer to 350°f.
2. Melt the butter in a saucepan over medium heat.
3. Once the butter has melted, add the shallot, tarragon, and lemon zest. Cook, stirring frequently, for 2-3 minutes. Remove it from the heat and set it aside.
4. Season the salmon fillets with salt and black pepper.
5. Liberally brush both sides of each piece of salmon with the garlic tarragon butter.
6. Place the salmon pieces in the air fryer and cook for 15 minutes, turning once halfway through.
7. Remove the salmon from the air fryer and garnish with any remaining butter sauce and fresh lemon slices.

Nutrition: Calories 276, Total fat 15 g, Saturated fat 1 g, Total carbohydrate 4 g, dietary fiber 0 g, Sugars 0 g, Protein 21 g

667. Fish and seafood recipes

Preparation time: 25 minutes
Cooking time: 20 minutes   servings: 4
Ingredients :
- ½ pounds jumbo shrimp, cleaned, shelled and deveined
- 1-pound cherry tomatoes
- Tablespoons butter, melted
- 1 tablespoons sriracha sauce
- Sea salt and ground black pepper, to taste
- 1/2 teaspoon dried oregano
- 1/2 teaspoon dried basil
- 1 teaspoon dried parsley flakes
- 1/2 teaspoon marjoram
- 1/2 teaspoon mustard seeds

Directions
1. Toss all ingredients in a mixing bowl until the shrimp and tomatoes are covered on all sides.
2. Soak the wooden skewers in water for 15 minutes.
3. Thread the jumbo shrimp and cherry tomatoes onto skewers. Cook in the preheated air fryer at 400 ° f for 5 minutes, working with batches.

Nutrition: 247 calories; 4g fat; 6g carbs; 34g protein; 5g sugars; 8g fiber

668. Crumbed fish fillets with tarragon

Preparation time: 25 minutes
Cooking time: 20 minutes   servings: 4
Ingredients :
- 2 eggs, beaten
- 1/2 teaspoon tarragon
- 4 fish fillets, halved
- 2 tablespoons dry white wine
- 1/3 cup parmesan cheese, grated
- Teaspoon seasoned salt
- 1/3 teaspoon mixed peppercorns
- 1/2 teaspoon fennel seed

Directions
1. Add the parmesan cheese, salt, peppercorns, fennel seeds, and tarragon to your food processor; blitz for about 20 seconds.
2. Drizzle fish fillets with dry white wine. Dump the egg into a shallow dish.
3. Now, coat the fish fillets with the beaten egg on all sides; then, coat them with the seasoned cracker mix.
4. Air-fry at 345° f for about 17 minutes.

Nutrition: 305 calories; 17g fat; 3g carbs; 22g protein; 3g sugars; 1g fiber

669. Smoked and creamed white fish

Preparation time: 20 minutes
Cooking time: 15 minutes   servings: 4
Ingredients:
- 1/2 tablespoon yogurt
- 1/3 cup spring garlic, finely chopped
- Fresh chopped chives, for garnish
- 3 eggs, beaten
- 1/2 teaspoon dried dill weed
- Teaspoon dried rosemary
- 1/3 cup scallions, chopped
- 1/3 cup smoked whitefish, chopped

- 1 ½ tablespoon crème fraiche
- 1 teaspoon kosher salt
- 1 teaspoon dried marjoram
- 1/3 teaspoon ground black pepper, or more to taste
- Cooking spray

Directions
1. Firstly, spritz four oven-safe ramekins with cooking spray. Then, divide smoked whitefish, spring garlic, and scallions among greased ramekins.
2. Crack an egg into each ramekin; add the crème, yogurt, and all seasonings.
3. Now, air-fry approximately 13 minutes at 355° f. Taste for doneness and eat warm garnished with fresh chives.

Nutrition: 249 calories; 21g fat; 6g carbs; 3g protein; 1g sugars; 7g fiber

670. Tangy cod fillets
Preparation time: 20 minutes
Cooking time: 15 minutes
Servings: 2

Ingredients :
- ½ tablespoons sesame oil
- 1/2 heaping teaspoon dried parsley flakes
- 1/3 teaspoon fresh lemon zest, finely grated
- Medium-sized cod fillets
- 1 teaspoon sea salt flakes
- A pinch of salt and pepper
- 1/3 teaspoon ground black pepper, or more to savor
- 1/2 tablespoon fresh lemon juice

Directions
1. Set the air fryer to cook at 375° f. Season each cod fillet with sea salt flakes, black pepper, and dried parsley flakes. Now, drizzle them with sesame oil.
2. Place the seasoned cod fillets in a single layer at the bottom of the cooking basket; air-fry approximately 10 minutes.
3. While the fillets are cooking, prepare the sauce by mixing the other ingredients. Serve cod fillets on four individual plates garnished with the creamy citrus sauce.

Nutrition: 291 calories; 11g fat; 7g carbs; 46g protein; 2g sugars; 5g fiber

671. Fish and cauliflower cakes
Preparation time: 2 hours 20 minutes
Cooking time: 13 minutes
Servings: 4

Ingredients :
- 1/2-pound cauliflower florets
- 1/2 teaspoon English mustard
- 2 tablespoons butter, room temperature
- 1/2 tablespoon cilantro, minced
- 2 tablespoons sour cream
- 2 ½ cups cooked white fish
- Salt and freshly cracked black pepper, to savor

Directions
1. Boil the cauliflower until tender. Then, purée the cauliflower in your blender. Transfer to a mixing dish.
2. Now, stir in the fish, cilantro, salt, and black pepper.
3. Add the sour cream, English mustard, and butter; mix until everything's well incorporated. Using your hands, shape into patties.
4. Place in the refrigerator for about 2 hours. Cook for 13 minutes at 395° f. Serve with some extra English mustard.

Nutrition: 285 calories; 11g fat; 3g carbs; 31g protein; 6g sugars; 3g fiber

672. Marinated scallops with butter and beer
Preparation time: 1 hour 10 minutes
Cooking time: 7 minutes
Servings: 4

Ingredients :
- 2 pounds sea scallops
- 1/2 cup beer
- 4 tablespoons butter
- 2 sprigs rosemary, only leaves
- Sea salt and freshly cracked black pepper, to taste

Directions
1. In a ceramic dish, mix the sea scallops with beer; let it marinate for 1 hour.

2. Meanwhile, preheat your air fryer to 400° f. Melt the butter and add the rosemary leaves. Stir for a few minutes.
3. Discard the marinade and transfer the sea scallops to the air fryer basket. Season with salt and black pepper.
4. Cook the scallops in the preheated air fryer for 7 minutes, shaking the basket halfway through the cooking time. Work in batches.

Nutrition: 471 calories; 23g fat; 9g carbs; 54g protein; 2g sugars; 1g fiber

673. Fijian coconut fish
Preparation time: 20 minutes + marinating time
Cooking time: 15 minutes
Servings: 2

Ingredients :
- Cup coconut milk
- Tablespoons lime juice
- Tablespoons shoyu sauce
- Salt and white pepper, to taste
- 1 teaspoon turmeric powder
- 1/2 teaspoon ginger powder
- 1/2 Thai bird's eye chili, seeded and finely chopped
- 1-pound tilapia
- 2 tablespoons olive oil

Directions
1. In a mixing bowl, thoroughly combine the coconut milk with the lime juice, shoyu sauce, salt, pepper, turmeric, ginger, and chili pepper. Add tilapia and let it marinate for 1 hour.
2. Brush the air fryer basket with olive oil. Discard the marinade and place the tilapia fillets in the air fryer basket.
3. Cook the tilapia in the preheated air fryer at 400 ° f for 6 minutes; turn them over and cook for 6 minutes more. Work in batches.
4. Serve with some extra lime wedges if desired.

Nutrition: 426 calories; 25g fat; 4g carbs; 52g protein; 5g sugars; 4g fiber

674. Mushroom and tilapia
Preparation time: 10 minutes
Cooking time: 16 minutes
Servings: 4

Ingredients:
- ½ cup yellow onion, sliced thin
- 4 ounces filets tilapia
- 2 tablespoons olive oil
- 2 cups mushroom, sliced
- 4 tablespoons soy sauce
- 2 cloves garlic, minced
- Tablespoon honey
- Tablespoons rice vinegar
- And ½ teaspoon salt
- 1 tablespoon red chili flakes

Directions:
1. Preheat your air fryer to 350° f in "air fry" mode
2. Season the fish with half the salt
3. Drizzle with half the oil
4. Cook for 15 minutes
5. Take a large skillet and add remaining oil and heat it
6. Add the onion, garlic, and mushroom when it is hot
7. Cook until onions are soft
8. Stir in the soy sauce, honey, vinegar, and chili flakes
9. Simmer for 1 minute
10. 1 serve with mushroom sauce and enjoy!

Nutrition: Calories: 300 Fat: 10 g Saturated fat: 2 g Carbohydrates: 12 g Fiber: 4 g Sodium: 609 mg Protein: 45 g

675. Bacon-wrapped shrimp
Preparation time: 5 minutes
Cooking time: 5 minutes
servings: 4

Ingredients
- 1¼ pound tiger shrimp, peeled and deveined
- Pound bacon

Directions:
1. Preparing the ingredients. Wrap each shrimp with a slice of bacon.
2. Refrigerate for about 20 minutes.
3. Preheat the air fryer oven to 390° f.

4. Air frying. Arrange the shrimp in the oven rack/basket. Place the rack on the middle-shelf of the air fryer oven. Cook for about 5-7 minutes.

Nutrition: Calories 70 Total fat 5g Total carbs 0g Fiber 0g Protein 7g Sugar 0g Sodium 150mg

676. Fried scallops with saffron cream sauce

Preparation time: 5 minutes;
Cooking time: 2 minutes;
Servings: 4

Ingredients:
- Olive oil for greasing
- 24 scallops, cleaned
- 2/3 cup heavy cream
- Tbsp freshly squeezed lemon juice
- ¼ tsp dried crushed saffron threads

Directions:
1. Insert the dripping pan in the bottom part of the air fryer and preheat the oven at air fry mode 400° f for 2 to 3 minutes.
2. Lightly brush the rotisserie basket with some olive oil and fill with the scallops.
3. Close and fit the basket in the oven using the rotisserie lift and set the timer for 2 minutes or until the scallops are golden brown on the outside.
4. Meanwhile, in a medium bowl, quickly whisk the heavy cream lemon juice and saffron threads.
5. When the scallops are ready, transfer to a serving plate and drizzle the sauce on top.
6. Enjoy immediately.

Nutrition: Calories 77, total fat 73g, total carbs 05g, fiber 0g, protein 15g, sugar 66g, sodium 31mg

677. Grilled salmon with butter and wine

Preparation time: 45 minutes
Cooking time: 10 minutes servings: 4

Ingredients :
- 2 cloves garlic, minced
- 4 tablespoons butter, melted
- Sea salt and ground black pepper, to taste
- Teaspoon smoked paprika
- 1/2 teaspoon onion powder
- 1 tablespoon lime juice
- 1/4 cup dry white wine
- 4 salmon steaks

Directions
1. Place all ingredients in a large ceramic dish. Cover and let it marinate for 30 minutes in the refrigerator.
2. Arrange the salmon steaks on the grill pan. Bake at 390° for 5 minutes, or until the salmon steaks are easily flaked with a fork.
3. Flip the fish steaks, baste with the reserved marinade, and cook another 5 minutes.

Nutrition: 516 calories; 26g fat; 4g carbs; 67g protein; 7g sugars; 5g fiber

678. Zesty ranch fish fillets

Preparation time: 10 minutes;
Cooking time: 13 minutes; servings: 4

Ingredients:
- ¾ cup finely crushed cornflakes or panko breadcrumbs
- 3 tbsp dry ranch-style dressing mix
- Tsp fresh lemon zest
- ½ tbsp olive oil
- Eggs, beaten
- White fish fillets
- Lemon wedges to garnish

Directions:
1. Insert the dripping pan in the bottom part of the air fryer and preheat the oven at air fry mode at 400° f for 2 to 3 minutes.
2. Mix the cornflakes, dressing mix, lemon zest, and oil on a shallow plate and then pour the eggs on another.
3. Working in two batches, dip the fish into the egg, drip off excess egg, and coat well in the cornflakes mixture on both sides.
4. Place the fish on the cooking tray and fix the tray on the middle rack of the oven. Close the oven and set the timer for 13 minutes and cook until the fish is golden brown and the fish flaky within.
5. Transfer to a serving plate and serve with the lemon wedges.

Nutrition: Calories 409, total fat 284g, total carbs 79g, fiber 5g, protein 455g, sugar 41g, sodium 322mg

FRUIT AND VEGETABLES

679. Toasty pepper bites

Preparation time: 6 minutes
Cooking time: 15-30 minutes
Serving: 4

Ingredients
- 1 medium-sized red bell pepper cut into small pieces
- 1 medium-sized yellow bell pepper cut up into small pieces
- 1 medium-sized green bell pepper cut up into small pieces
- 3 tablespoons of balsamic vinegar
- 2 tablespoon of olive oil
- 1 tablespoon of minced garlic
- 1/2 teaspoon of dried basil
- 1/2 a teaspoon of dried parsley
- Kosher salt as needed
- Pepper as needed

Directions:
1. Take a mixing bowl and add all of the diced-up bell peppers
2. Mix them well and add olive oil, garlic, balsamic vinegar, basil and parsley
3. Mix them well
4. Season with salt and pepper
5. Stir well
6. Cover and allow it to chill for 30 minutes
7. Preheat your fryer to 390 °f
8. Transfer the peppers to your frying basket and cook for 10-15 minutes
9. Serve and enjoy!

Nutrition: Calories: 148 Carbohydrate: 17g Protein: 5g Fat: 7g

680. Platter of brussels and pine nuts

Preparation time: 10 minutes
Cooking time: 35 minutes
Serving: 6

Ingredients
- 15 ounces of brussels sprouts
- 1 tablespoon of olive oil
- 1 and a 3/4 ounce of drained raisins
- Juice of 1 orange
- 1 and a 3/4-ounce toasted pine nuts

Directions:
1. Take a pot of boiling water and add sprouts, boil for 4 minutes
2. Transfer them to cold water and drain them, store them in a freezer and allow them to cool
3. Take raising and soak them in orange juice for 20 minutes
4. Preheat your fryer to 392 degrees Fahrenheit
5. Take a pan and pour oil and stir fry your sprouts
6. Transfer the sprouts to the cooking basket and roast for 15 minutes
7. Serve the sprouts with a garnish of raisins, pine nuts, orange juice
8. Enjoy!

Nutrition: Calories: 267 Fat: 25g Dietary fiber: 6g Protein: 7g

681. Veggie crisps and cheesy pesto

Preparation time: 10 minutes
Cooking time: 50 minutes
Serving: 6

Ingredients
- For the vegetable crisps
- 2 parsnips
- 2 beetroot

- 1 medium-sized peeled sweet potato
- 1 tablespoon of olive oil
- ½ a teaspoon of chili powder
- For the cheesy pesto twist
- 1 pack of 11 ounces all butter puff pastry
- 1 tablespoon of flour
- About 1 and a ¾ ounce of cream cheese
- 4 tablespoons of pesto
- 1 beaten egg
- 1 and a ¾ ounce of grated parmesan cheese

Directions:
1. Preheat your air fryer to a temperature of 464 ° f
2. Take a peeler and shave off super thin slices of parsnips, sweet potato, and beetroot
3. Take out the air fryer cooking basket and toss in the cut vegetables in the oil and mix it up with chili powder. Finally, season them with pinches of salt and pepper
4. Cook them in the air fryer until it has reached a golden-brown texture (usually takes 20 minutes, keeping in mind that you are going to have to shake from time to time.
5. When dealing with the cheesy pesto twists, you are going to first want to roll up the pastry into rectangle shaped on a surface that is scattered with flour
6. Keep in mind that the vertical side should be longer than the horizontal side
7. Take a knife and cut them in middle
8. On one half of the cut, spread the cream cheese and pesto then turn one half on top the other creating a sort of sandwich
9. Again, cut it in the middle and create about 2 long rectangles. Then slice each of the rectangles into stripes that are 1cm thick
10. 1gently twist each of the strips, pulling then consequently in order to lengthen the shape
11. 1once the twists are ready, brush them up with the beaten egg and spread a generous amount of parmesan
12. 1put them in the cooking basket and cook them for 2025 minutes until a golden-brown texture has been achieved
13. 1serve either hot or cold depending on your preference

Nutrition Calories: 473 Fat: 23g Dietary fiber: 7g Protein: 5g

682. **Surfing zucchini fries**
Preparation time: 10 minutes
Cooking time: 1520 minutes
Serving: 4
Ingredients
- 3 medium-sized zucchinis sliced up into sticks
- 2 egg whites
- ½ a cup of seasoned breadcrumbs
- 2 tablespoon of grated parmesan cheese
- Cooking spray
- ¼ teaspoon of garlic powder
- Salt as required
- Pepper as required

Directions:
1. Preheat your fryer to 425 °f
2. Take the fryer basket and place a cooling rack inside
3. Coat it with cooking spray
4. Take a bowl and add egg whites and beat it
5. Season with some pepper and salt
6. Take another bowl and add garlic powder, breadcrumbs, and cheese
7. Take your zucchini sticks and dredge them into the egg followed by the breadcrumbs
8. Transfer the zucchini to your cooking tray and spray some oil
9. Bake for 20 minutes
10. 1serve with ranch sauce and enjoy!

Nutrition Calories: 367 Protein: 4g Fat: 28g Dietary fiber: 3g

683. **Beautiful baked apples**
Preparation time: 5 minutes
Cooking time: 10 minutes
Serving: 8
Ingredients
- 4 pieces of apple
- ¾ ounce of butter
- 2 tablespoons of brown sugar

- 1 and ¾ ounce of fresh breadcrumbs
- 1 and a ½ ounce of mixed seeds
- Zest of 1 orange
- 1 teaspoon cinnamon

Directions:
1. Prepare the apples by scoring the skin around the circumference and coring them using a knife
2. Take the cored apples and stuff them with the listed ingredients
3. Preheat your fryer to 356 °f
4. Transfer the apples to your frying basket and bake for 10 minutes
5. Serve hot and enjoy!

Nutrition Calories: 53 Fat: 4g Protein: 3g Dietary fiber: 4g

684. **Unexpectedly awesome banana split**
Preparation time: 10 minutes
Cooking time: 15 minutes
Serving: 4
Ingredients
- 3 tablespoons of butter
- Bananas as required
- 3 egg whites
- ½ a cup of corn flour
- 3 tablespoons of cinnamon sugar
- 1 cup of panko breadcrumbs

Directions:
1. Firstly, take a saucepan and melt the butter over moderate temperatures
2. Add the breadcrumbs to the molten butter and stir it for about 34 minutes
3. When they have acquired a nice golden-brown texture, remove them from the pan and place them in a bowl
4. Take another bowl and beat the eggs properly
5. Take another bowl and place the flour their
6. Peel the bananas gently slice them into two
7. Roll up the banana slices in the flour, followed by the eggs and finally the breadcrumbs
8. Once all of the bananas have been processed, take out the air fryer basket and place them in the basket
9. Gently dust it off with cinnamon sugar
10. 1let the bananas cook for about 10 minutes at a temperature of 280 ° f
11. 1in the meantime, take a bowl and scoop up some vanilla, strawberry and chocolate ice cream.
12. 1once the bananas are done, take them out from the fryer and gently place them on the sides of the ice cream
13. 1top it off with nuts and whipped cream for decoration

Nutrition Calories: 510 Fat: 120g Protein: 71g Dietary fiber: 92g

685. **Mini zucchini's and feta**
Preparation time: 10 minutes
Cooking time: 40 minutes
Serving: 4
Ingredients
- 12-ounce thawed puff pastry
- 4 large eggs
- ¼ cup milk
- 1 medium-sized thinly sliced zucchini
- 4 oz. Drained and crumbled feta cheese
- 2 tablespoon chopped fresh dill
- Olive oil spray
- Kosher salt as needed
- Freshly ground black pepper

Directions:
1. Preheat your fryer to 360 °f
2. Take a bowl and whisk eggs, season with salt and pepper
3. Add zucchini, feta, and dill to the mix
4. Stir well
5. Take 8 pieces of muffin tins and grease them up
6. Roll out the pastry and cut them into the bottom part of your tins (and the sides
7. Divide the egg mix amongst the tins and cook in batches (giving each batch about 15-20 minutes
8. Enjoy!

Nutrition Calories:201 Carbohydrate: 13g Protein: 11g Fat: 12g

686. Paneer and Cheese Balls

Preparation Time: 10 minutes
Cooking Time: 15 minutes
Servings 4
Ingredients:

- 7 oz. of paneer
- 2 oz. of cheese of your choice, cut into small cubes
- 2 tbsps. of all-purpose flour
- 1 tbsp. of cornstarch
- 2 onions, finely chopped
- 1 whole finely chopped ginger (about 100gr)
- 1 tsp. of chili powder
- salt
- a few coriander leaves, finely chopped
- vegetable oil for frying

Directions:

1. In a bowl, mix the flour, cornstarch, onion, ginger, and chili powder, salt, and coriander leaves thoroughly.
2. After that, take a small portion of the whole mixture, stay calm and roll it up against your palm, turning it into a flat and circular shape if possible.
3. Directly at the middle of the shape, take one of the cheese cubes which you had set aside and place it inside stuffing it.
4. Once stuffed, slowly start to roll down the edges and turn the overall structure into a good-looking, healthy ball by rolling it on your palm, as if you are playing with dices.
5. You are going to have to turn all of your mixtures into a ball, there is a lot of work is ahead of you, repeat the process until all of the mixtures has run out.
6. Preheat the Air Fryer to 350°f.
7. Place the balls in the Fryer and cook until golden brown, 10-15 minutes. Serve with ketchup or chutney.

Nutrition: Calories: 150 Fat: 9g Carbs: 17g Protein: 2g

687. Samosas

Preparation Time: 15 minutes
Cooking Time: 45 minutes
Servings 4
Ingredients:

- 2 russet potatoes, peeled and cubed
- ½ cup of green peas
- 2 tsps. of garam masala powder
- 1 tsp. of ginger garlic paste
- 1 tsp. of chili powder
- 1 tsp. of turmeric
- salt
- ½ tsp. of cumin seed
- vegetable oil for frying and brushing
- 2 cups of all-purpose flour
- 1 tsp. of carom seed
- 2 tsps. of ghee (melted butter will also work)

Directions:

1. Prepare the crust:
2. In a bowl, combine the flour, carom seed, ghee, and as much water as necessary to make a smooth dough. Knead the dough briefly and chill in the refrigerator for 30 min.
3. While the dough chills, prepare the filling: in a medium saucepan, cover the potatoes with water and bring to a boil. Add the peas and continue to boil until the vegetables are tender. Drain and mash them well.
4. Add the garam masala, ginger garlic paste, chili powder, and turmeric to the potato mixture. Season with salt to taste and mix well.
1. In a small sauté pan, heat 2 tbsps. of oil over medium heat. Add the cumin seeds toast until aromatic and sizzling. Add the cumin to the potato mixture, mix well again, and set aside.
2. Remove the dough from the refrigerator, roll out on a counter, and cut into several squares.
3. Place a spoonful of filling in each square and fold the samosa to resemble the photograph above, carefully sealing the edges.
4. Preheat the Air Fryer to 350°f.
5. Brush the samosas with oil, place in the Fryer, and cook until golden, 18-20 min.

Nutrition: Calories: 308 Fat: 18 g Carbohydrate: 32 g Dietary Fiber: 2 g

688. Vegetable Spring Rolls

Preparation Time: 10 minutes
Cooking Time: 35 minutes
Servings: 10
Ingredients:

- 2 cups of cabbage, shredded
- 1 large carrot, cut into thin matchsticks
- 2 large onions, cut into thin matchsticks
- ½ bell pepper, cut into thin matchsticks —any color will work
- 2inch piece ginger, grated
- 8 cloves garlic, minced
- 2 tbsps. of cooking oil plus more for brushing
- a few pinches sugar
- a few pinches salt
- 1 tsp. of soy sauce
- 1 tbsp. of black pepper
- 23 green onions, thinly sliced
- 10 spring roll wrappers
- 2 tbsps. of cornstarch
- water

Directions:

1. Filling: Get a large bowl then, add the cabbage, carrot, onion, bell pepper, ginger, and garlic.
2. In a medium sauté pan, heat 2 tbsps. oil over high heat adds the filling mixture, stirring in a few pinches of sugar and salt (the sugar helps the vegetables maintain their color).
3. Cook for 23 min, add the soy sauce and black pepper, mix well, and remove from heat. Stir in green onions. Set aside.
4. In a bowl, combine the cornstarch and enough water to make a creamy paste.
5. Fill the rolls: place a tbsp. alternatively, so of filling in the center of each wrapper and roll tightly, dampening the edges with the cornstarch paste to ensure a good seal. Repeat until all the wrappers and filling are used. Alternatively, cut the wrappers into smaller sizes and make mini spring rolls—fun!
6. Briefly, preheat the Air Fryer to 350°f.
7. Brush the rolls with oil, arrange in the Fryer, and cook until crisp and golden, about 20 min, flipping once at the halfway point.

Nutrition: Calories: 154 Fat: 8 g Carbohydrate: 4.3 g Dietary Fiber: 2.4 g

689. Semolina Cutlets

Preparation Time: 5 minutes
Cooking Time: 15 minutes
Servings: 2
Ingredients:

- 5 cups of milk
- 1½ cups of your favorite vegetables
- 1 cup of semolina
- salt and pepper
- oil for frying

Directions:

1. Cook the vegetables until softened, 23 minutes. Season with salt and pepper.
2. Add the semolina to the milk mixture, continuing to cook until thickened, about 10 minutes. Remove from heat, spread in a thin layer on a parchment lined baking sheet, and chill in the refrigerator until firm, 34 hours.
3. When ready to cook, remove the baking sheet from the refrigerator, and cut the semolina mixture into cutlets using a sharp knife.
4. Briefly, preheat the Air Fryer to 350°f.
5. Brush the cutlets with oil, arrange in the Fryer, and bake until golden, about 10 minutes.
6. Serve with hot sauce!

Nutrition: Calories: 327 Fat: 1.2 g Carbohydrate: 66.2 g Dietary Fiber: 4.8 g Protein: 12.1 g

690. Onion Pakora

Preparation Time: 5 minutes
Cooking Time: 20 minutes
Servings: 6
Ingredients:

- 1 cup of graham flour

- ¼ cup of rice flour
- 2 tsps. vegetable oil
- 4 onions, finely chopped
- 2 green chili peppers, finely chopped
- 1 tbsp. of fresh coriander, chopped
- ¼ tsp. of carom
- 1/8 tsp. of chili powder
- turmeric
- salt

Directions:
1. Put the flours and oil in a bowl. Mix well, adding water as necessary to create a thick, dough like consistency.
2. Add the onions, peppers, coriander, carom, chili powder, and turmeric. Season with salt and mix well.
3. Briefly, preheat the Air Fryer to 350°f.
4. Roll the vegetable mixture into small balls, arrange in the Fryer, and cook until browned, about 6 minutes.
5. Serve with hot sauce and enjoy!

Nutrition: Calories: 119 Fat: 2 g Carbohydrate: 21 g Dietary Fiber: 6 g Protein: 6 g

691.   Vegan Fried Ravioli
Preparation Time: 10 minutes
Cooking Time: 10 minutes
Servings: 4
Ingredients:
- ½ cup of panko breadcrumbs
- 1 tsp. of dried oregano
- Pinch salt & pepper
- 2 tsps. of nutritional yeast flakes
- 1 tsp. of dried basil
- 1 tsp. of garlic powder
- ¼ cup of liquid from a can of chickpeas or other beans*
- 8 oz. of frozen or thawed vegan ravioli**
- Spritz cooking spray
- ½ cup of marinara for dipping

Directions:
1. Mix panko bread. Crumbs, nutritional yeast garlic powder, flakes, dried basil, dried oregano, pepper, and salt.
2. Put aquafaba into a small separate bowl.
3. Dip ravioli into aquafaba and shake off excess liquid then dredge in bread crumb mixture.
4. Put ravioli into the air fryer basket. Proceed until all of the ravioli has been breaded.
5. Sprinkle the ravioli with cooking spray.
6. Set Air Fryer to 390°f and air fry for 6 minutes. Flip each ravioli over.
7. Get ravioli from Air Fryer and serve with marinara for dipping.

Nutrition: Calories: 150 Fat: 3g Carbohydrates: 27 g Protein: 5g

692.   Avocado Fries
Preparation Time: 5 minutes
Cooking Time: 15 minutes
Servings: 4
Ingredients:
- ½ tsp. of salt
- ½ cup of panko breadcrumbs
- 1 Haas avocado – peeled, pitted, and sliced
- aquafaba from 1 (15 oz.) can white beans or garbanzo beans.

Directions:
1. In a bowl, toss together the panko and salt. Pour the aquafaba into another bowl.
2. Dredge the avocado slices in the aquafaba in the panko to get a nice, even coating.
3. Arrange the slices in a layer in the Air Fryer basket. A single layer is important.
4. Air Fry for 10 minutes at 390°f (without preheating.), shaking after 5 minutes.
5. Serve with your favorite sauce.

To bake:
1. Preheat the oven to 400°f. Arrange the slices in a single Air fry for 10 minutes at 390°f (without preheating.), shaking after 5 minutes.
2. Lay out on a greased baking sheet. Bake for 20 minutes.

3. Serve with your favorite dipping sauce!

Nutrition: Calories: 711 Fat: 59g Carbohydrates: 21 g Protein: 26g Dietary Fiber: 3.56 g

693.   Crispy Veggie Fries
Preparation Time: 10 minutes
Cooking Time: 10 minutes
Servings: 3
Ingredients:
- 2 tbsps. of nutritional yeast flakes, divided
- 1 cup of panko breadcrumbs
- Salt and pepper
- 1 cup of rice flour
- 2 tbsps. of Follow Your Heart Vegan Egg powder*
- 2/3 cup of cold water
- Assorted veggies of choice, cut into bitesize chunks or French fry shapes (such as cauliflower, green beans, sweet onions, zucchini or squash)

Directions:
1. Set up 3 dishes on the counter: Place rice flour in one dish and in another dish whisk the 2/3 cup water, 1 tbsp. of the nutritional yeast flakes and Vegan Egg powder. Whisk until smooth.
2. In the last dish, mix 1 tbsp. of nutritional yeast, the panko breadcrumbs, and pinches of salt and pepper.
3. One veggie fry at a time, dip in the rice flour, followed by Vegan Egg mixture, finally the breadcrumb mixture, pressing gently to set coating. Make as many veggie fries as desired.
4. Lightly spray the Air Fryer basket (or a parchment lined baking sheet. Place the veggie fries in the basket, give them a quick splash of oil and set the fryer at 380°f for 8 minutes.

Nutrition: Calories: 134 Fat: 6.6 g Carbohydrates: 13g Protein: 1.5 g Dietary Fiber: 20 g

694.   Air fried carrots, yellow squash & zucchini
Preparation time: 7 minutes
Cooking time: 35 minutes
Servings: 4
Ingredients:
- 1 tbsp. Chopped tarragon leaves
- ½tsp. White pepper
- 1 tsp. Salt
- 1pound yellow squash
- 1pound zucchini
- 6 tsp. Olive oil
- ½pound carrots

Directions:
1. Stem and root the end of squash and zucchini and cut in ¾inch halfmoons. Peel and cut carrots into 1inch cubes.
2. Combine carrot cubes with 2 tsp. Of olive oil, tossing to combine. Pour into air fryer basket and cook 5 minutes at 400°f.
3. As carrots cook, drizzle remaining olive oil over squash and zucchini pieces, then season with pepper and salt. Toss well to coat.
4. Add squash and zucchini when the timer for carrots goes off. Cook 30 minutes, making sure to toss 23 times during the cooking process.
5. Once done, take out veggies and toss with tarragon. Serve up warm!

Nutrition: calories: 122 fat: 9g protein: 6g sugar: 0g

695.   Cheesy cauliflower fritters
Preparation time: 5 minutes
Cooking time: 14 minutes
Servings: 8
Ingredients:
- ½c. Chopped parsley
- 1 c. Italian breadcrumbs
- 1 3 c. Shredded mozzarella cheese
- 1 3 c. Shredded sharp cheddar cheese
- 1 egg
- 2 minced garlic cloves
- 3 chopped scallions
- 1 head of cauliflower

Directions:

1. Cut cauliflower up into florets. Wash well and pat dry. Place into a food processor and pulse 20-30 seconds till it looks like rice.
2. Place cauliflower rice in a bowl and mix with pepper, salt, egg, cheeses, breadcrumbs, garlic, and scallions.
3. With hands, form 15 patties of the mixture. Add more breadcrumbs if needed.
4. With olive oil, spritz patties, and place into your air fryer in a single layer.
5. Cook 14 minutes at 390°f, flipping after 7 minutes.

Nutrition: calories: 209 fat: 17g protein: 6g sugar: 5g

696.   Zucchini parmesan chips

Preparation time: 5 minutes
Cooking time: 8 minutes
Servings: 10

Ingredients:

- ½tsp. Paprika
- ½c. Grated parmesan cheese
- ½c. Italian breadcrumbs
- 1 lightly beaten egg
- 2 thinly sliced zucchinis

Directions:

1. Use a very sharp knife or mandolin slicer to slice zucchini as thinly as you can. Pat off extra moisture.
2. Beat egg with a pinch of pepper and salt and a bit of water.
3. Combine paprika, cheese, and breadcrumbs in a bowl.
4. Dip slices of zucchini into the egg mixture and then into breadcrumb mixture. Press gently to coat.
5. With olive oil cooking spray, mist coated zucchini slices. Place into your air fryer in a single layer.
6. Cook 8 minutes at 350°f.
7. Sprinkle with salt and serve with salsa.

Nutrition: calories: 211 fat: 16g protein: 8g sugar: 0g

697.   Crispy roasted broccoli

Preparation time: 45 minutes
Cooking time: 10 minutes
Servings: 2

Ingredients:

- ¼tsp. Masala
- ½tsp. Red chili powder
- ½tsp. Salt
- ¼tsp. Turmeric powder
- 1 tbsp. Chickpea flour
- 2 tbsp. Yogurt
- 1pound broccoli

Directions:

1. Cut broccoli up into florets. Soak in bowl of water with 2 teaspoons of salt for at least half an hour to remove impurities.
2. Take out broccoli florets from water and let drain. Wipe down thoroughly.
3. Mix all other ingredients together to create a marinade.
4. Toss broccoli florets in the marinade. Cover and chill 15-30 minutes.
5. Preheat air fryer to 390°f. Place marinated broccoli florets into the fryer. Cook 10 minutes.
6. 5 minutes into cooking shake the basket. Florets will be crispy when done.

Nutrition: calories: 96 fat: 3g protein: 7g sugar: 5g

698.   Crispy jalapeno coins

Preparation time: 10 minutes
Cooking time: 810 minutes
Servings: 810

Ingredients:

- 1 egg
- 23 tbsp. Coconut flour
- 1 sliced and seeded jalapeno
- Pinch of garlic powder
- Pinch of onion powder
- Pinch of Cajun seasoning (optional)
- Pinch of pepper and salt

Directions:

1. Ensure your air fryer is preheated to 400°f.
2. Mix together all dry ingredients.

3. Pat jalapeno slices dry. Dip coins into egg wash and then into dry mixture. Toss to thoroughly coat.
4. Add coated jalapeno slices to air fryer in a singular layer. Spray with olive oil.
5. Cook just till crispy.

Nutrition: calories: 128 fat: 8g protein: 7g sugar: 0g

699.   Spaghetti squash tots

Preparation time: 5 minutes
Cooking time: 15 minutes
Servings: 810

Ingredients:

- ¼tsp. Pepper
- ½tsp. Salt
- 1 thinly sliced scallion
- 1 spaghetti squash

Directions:

1. Wash and cut squash in half lengthwise. Scrape out the seeds.
2. With a fork, remove spaghetti meat by strands and throw out skins.
3. In a clean towel, toss in squash and wring out as much moisture as possible. Place in a bowl and with a knife slice through meat a few times to cut up smaller.
4. Add pepper, salt, and scallions to squash and mix well.
5. Create "tot" shapes with your hands and place in air fryer. Spray with olive oil.
6. Cook 15 minutes at 350°f until golden and crispy!

Nutrition: calories: 231 fat: 18g protein: 5g sugar: 0g

700.   Cinnamon butternut squash fries

Preparation time: 10 minutes
Cooking time: 10 minutes
Servings: 2

Ingredients:

- 1 pinch of salt
- 1 tbsp. Powdered unprocessed sugar
- ½tsp. Nutmeg
- 2 tsp. Cinnamon
- 1 tbsp. Coconut oil
- 10 ounces precut butternut squash fries

Directions:

1. In a plastic bag, pour in all ingredients. Coat fries with other components till coated and sugar is dissolved.
2. Spread coated fries into a single layer in the air fryer. Cook 10 minutes at 390°f until crispy.

Nutrition: calories: 175 fat: 8g protein: 1g sugar: 5g

701.   Cheesy artichokes

Preparation time: 10 minutes
Cooking time: 14 minutes
Servings: 4

Ingredients:

- 4 artichokes, trimmed and halved
- 1 cup cheddar cheese, shredded
- 2 tablespoons olive oil
- A pinch of salt and black pepper
- 3 garlic cloves, minced
- 1 teaspoon garlic powder

Directions:

1. In your air fryer's basket, combine the artichokes with the oil, cheese and the other ingredients, toss and cook at 400° f for 14 minutes.
2. Divide everything between plates and serve.

Nutrition: calories 191, fat 8, fiber 2, carbohydrates 12, protein 8

702.   Paprika tomatoes

Preparation time: 10 minutes
Cooking time: 15 minutes
Servings: 4

Ingredients:

- 1pound cherry tomatoes, halved
- 1 tablespoon sweet paprika
- 2 tablespoons olive oil
- 2 garlic cloves, minced
- 1 tablespoon lime juice
- 1 tablespoon chives, chopped

Directions:

1. In your air fryer's basket, combine the tomatoes with the paprika and the other ingredients, toss and cook at a temperature of 370° f for 15 minutes.
2. Divide between plates and serve.

Nutrition: calories 131, fat 4, fiber 7, carbohydrates 10, protein 8

703. Avocado and tomato salad

Preparation time: 10 minutes
Cooking time: 12 minutes
Servings: 4

Ingredients:

- 1pound tomatoes, cut into wedges
- 2 avocados, peeled, pitted and sliced
- 2 tablespoons avocado oil
- 1 red onion, sliced
- 1 tablespoon balsamic vinegar
- Salt and black pepper to the taste
- 1 tablespoon cilantro, chopped

Directions:

1. In your air fryer, combine the tomatoes with the avocados and the other ingredients, toss and cook at 360° f for 12 minutes.
2. Divide between plates and serve.

Nutrition: calories 144, fat 7, fiber 5, carbohydrates 8, protein 6

704. Sesame broccoli mix

Preparation time: 5 minutes
Cooking time: 14 minutes
Servings: 4

Ingredients:

- 1pound broccoli florets
- 1 tablespoon sesame oil
- 1 teaspoon sesame seeds, toasted
- 1 red onion, sliced
- 1 tablespoon lime juice
- 1 teaspoon chili powder
- Salt and black pepper to the taste

Directions:

1. In your air fryer, combine the broccoli with the oil, sesame seeds and the other ingredients, toss and cook at 380° f for 14 minutes.
2. Divide between plates and serve.

Nutrition: calories 141, fat 3, fiber 4, carbohydrates 4, protein 2

705. Cabbage sauté

Preparation time: 5 minutes
Cooking time: 15 minutes
Servings: 4

Ingredients:

- 1pound red cabbage, shredded
- 1 tablespoon balsamic vinegar
- 2 red onions, sliced
- 1 tablespoon olive oil
- 1 tablespoon dill, chopped
- Salt and black pepper to the taste

Directions:

1. Heat up air fryer with oil at 380° f, add the cabbage, onions and the other ingredients, toss and cook for 15 minutes.
2. Divide between plates and serve.

Nutrition: calories 100, fat 4, fiber 2, carbohydrates 7, protein 2

706. Tomatoes and kidney beans

Preparation time: 10 minutes
Cooking time: 20 minutes
Servings: 4

Ingredients:

- 1pound cherry tomatoes, halved
- 1 cup canned kidney beans, drained
- 2 tablespoons balsamic vinegar
- 2 tablespoons olive oil
- 3 garlic cloves, minced
- Salt and black pepper to the taste
- 1 tablespoon chives, chopped

Directions:

1. In your air fryer, combine the cherry tomatoes with the beans and the other ingredients, toss and cook at 380° f for 20 minutes.
2. Divide between plates and serve.

Nutrition: calories 101, fat 3, fiber 3, carbohydrates 4, protein 2

707. Glazed mushrooms

Preparation time: 10 minutes
Cooking time: 15 minutes
Servings: 4

Ingredients:

- ½cup low sodium soy sauce
- 4 tablespoons fresh lemon juice
- 1 tablespoon maple syrup
- 4 garlic cloves, finely chopped
- Ground black pepper, as required
- 20 ounces fresh cremini mushrooms, halved

Directions:

1. Add the soy sauce, lemon juice, maple syrup, garlic and black pepper and mix well. Set aside.
2. Place the mushroom into the greased baking pan in a single layer.
3. Select "air fry" of digital air fryer oven and then adjust the temperature to 350° f.
4. Set the timer for 15 minutes and press "start/stop" to begin cooking.
5. When the unit beeps to show that it is preheated, insert the baking pan in the oven.
6. After 10 minutes of cooking, in the pan, add the soy sauce mixture and stir to combine.
7. When cooking time is complete, remove the mushrooms from oven and serve hot.

Nutrition: calories 70 total fat 3 g total carbohydrates 15 g protein 9 g

708. Garlic corn

Preparation time: 5 minutes
Cooking time: 15 minutes
Servings: 4

Ingredients:

- 2cups corn
- 3garlic cloves, minced
- 1tablespoon olive oil
- Juice of 1 lime
- 1teaspoon sweet paprika
- Salt and black pepper to the taste
- 2tablespoons dill, chopped

Directions:

1. Mix the corn with the garlic and the other ingredients in a pan that fits the air fryer, toss, put the pan in the machine and cook at 390° f for 15 minutes.
2. Divide everything between plates and serve.

Nutrition: calories 180, fat 3, fiber 2, carbohydrates 4, protein 6

SNACK RECIPES

709. Barbeque corn sandwich
Preparation Time: 15 minutes
Cooking Time: 45 minutes
Servings: 4
Ingredients:
- 1 capsicum
- 1 cap sweet corn kernels
- 2 tablespoon butter (room temperature)
- 4 slices of white bread (cut the edges and slice the bread horizontally)

For the sauce:
- 1/3 cup stock or water
- ¼ teaspoon mustard powder
- Salt and black pepper to taste
- 1 ½ tablespoon tomato ketchup
- ¼ cup onion (chopped)
- 1 teaspoon olive oil
- 1 Garlic flakes (crushed)
- ½ tablespoon sugar
- ½ tablespoon Worcestershire sauce
- ½ tablespoon red chili sauce

Directions:
1. Heat oil in a pan over medium high flame. Add garlic and onions and cook for 4 minutes while stirring often.
2. Add the sugar, chili sauce, mustard, stock, Worcestershire sauce, and tomato ketchup. Mix well and bring to a boil. Turn the heat to low black pepper. Season with salt and black pepper. Set aside.
3. Place other pans over medium flame. Melt butter and roast the corn kernels.
4. Roast and turn them over until black patches develop.
5. Remove the skin and seeds. Chop it finely and transfer to a bowl. Add the barbecue sauce and roasted corn kernels. Mix well spread the mixture on a slice of bread and put another slice on top.
6. Put the sandwich in the cooking basket. Cook for 15 minutes at 355° F. Flip the sandwich halfway through the cooking process.
7. Serve along with chutney while hot.
Nutrition: Calories: 142 Protein: 4 grams Fat: 8 grams Carbohydrates: 19 grams

710. Simple coffee cake
Preparation Time: 15 minutes
Cooking Time: 30 minutes
Servings: 2
Ingredients:
- ¼ cup butter
- ½ teaspoon instant coffee
- 1 tablespoon black coffee, brewed
- 1 egg
- A ¼ cup of sugar
- ¼ cup flour
- 1 teaspoon of cocoa powder
- A pinch of salt
- Powdered sugar, for icing

Directions:
1. Preheat the air fryer to 330° F. and grease a small ring cake pan.
2. Beat the sugar and egg along in a very bowl.
3. Beat in cocoa, instant and black coffee; stir in salt and flour.
4. Transfer the batter to the prepared pan. Cook for 15 minutes.
Nutrition: Calories: 418 Protein: 1 grams Fat: 25 grams Carbohydrates: 48 grams

711. Quick zucchini cakes
Preparation Time: 10 minutes
Cooking Time: 22 minutes
Servings: 12
Ingredients:
- ½ cup whole wheat flour
- 1 yellow onion; chopped
- Cooking spray
- ½ cup dill; chopped
- 1 egg
- 2 garlic cloves; minced
- 3 zucchinis; grated
- Salt and black pepper to the taste

Directions:
1. In a bowl; mix zucchinis with garlic, onion, flour, salt, pepper, egg, and dill.
2. Stir well, shape small patties out of this mix, spray them with cooking spray; place them in your air fryer's basket and cook at 370° F, for 6 minutes on each side.
3. Serve them as a snack right away.
Nutrition: Calories: 60 Protein: 2 grams Fat: 1-gram Carbohydrates: 6 grams

712. Lime cheesecake
Preparation Time: 15 minutes
Cooking Time: 4 hours 14 minutes
Servings: 10
Ingredients:
- 2 tablespoons butter, melted
- 2 teaspoons sugar
- 4 ounces flour
- ¼ cup coconut, shredded
- For the filling:
- 1-pound cream cheese
- Zest from 1 lime, grated
- Juice from 1 lime
- 2 cups hot water
- 2 sachets lime jelly

Directions:
1. In a bowl, mix coconut with flour, butter, and sugar, stir well and press this on the bottom of the pan that fits your air fryer.
2. Meanwhile, put the hot water in a bowl, add jelly sachets and until it dissolves.
3. Put cream cheese in a bowl, add jelly, lime juice, and zest and whisk really well.
4. Add this over the crust, spread, introduce in the air fryer and cook at 300° F. for 4 minutes.
5. Keep in the fridge for 4 hours before serving.
6. Enjoy!
Nutrition: Calories: 260 Protein: 7 grams Fat: 23 grams Carbohydrates: 5 grams

713. Marvelous lemon biscuits
Preparation Time: 10 minutes
Cooking Time: 10 minutes
Servings: 4
Ingredients:
- ½ cup softened unsalted butter
- 5 cups of coconut flour
- 1 lemon juice and zest
- 2 cups of coconut milk
- 2 teaspoons of yeast
- A ¼ cup of granulated sugar
- 1 teaspoon of salt
- 1 teaspoon of baking soda
- 1 teaspoon of baking powder

Directions:
1. Preheat your air fryer to 360° f.
2. Using a bowl, add and stir the coconut flour, yeast, baking soda, baking powder, salt, and granulated sugar.
3. Add and stir in the coconut milk, lemon juice, lemon zest, unsalted butter and mix it properly until it has soft dough's texture.
4. Roll out the pastry and cut it into biscuits.
5. Place the biscuits on a baking sheet and cook it for 5 minutes at a 360° f.
6. Remove and allow it to cool off until it is cool enough to eat.
7. Sprinkle it with icing sugar.
8. Serve and enjoy!

Nutrition: Calories: 170 Protein: 2 grams Fat: 7 grams Carbohydrates: 26 grams

714. **Banana fritters**
Preparation Time: 10 minutes
Cooking Time: 15 minutes
Servings: 8
Ingredients:

- 8 bananas
- 3 tablespoons vegetable oil
- 3 tablespoons corn flour
- 1 egg white
- ¾ cup breadcrumbs

Directions:
1. Preheat the air fryer to 350° f. And combine the oil and breadcrumbs, in a small bowl. Coat the bananas with the corn flour first, brush them with egg white, and dip them in the breadcrumb mixture.
2. Arrange on a lined baking sheet and cook for 8 minutes.

Nutrition: Calories: 203 Protein: 4 grams Fat: 3 grams Carbohydrates: 35 grams

715. **Tasty banana snack**
Preparation Time: 10 minutes
Cooking Time: 15 minutes
Servings: 8
Ingredients:

- 16 baking cups crust
- 1 banana; peeled and sliced into 16 pieces
- ¼ cup peanut butter
- A ¾ cup of chocolate chips
- 1 tablespoon vegetable oil

Directions:
1. Put chocolate chips in a small pot, heat up over low heat; stir until it melts and takes off heat.
2. In a bowl; mix peanut butter with coconut oil and whisk well.
3. Spoon 1 teaspoon chocolates mix in a cup, add 1 banana slice and top with 1 teaspoon butter mix.
4. Repeat with rest of the cups, place them all into a dish that fits your air fryer, cook at 320° f. For 5 minutes; transfer to a freezer and keep there until you serve them as a snack.

Nutrition: Calories: 70 Protein: 1-gram Fat: 4 grams Carbohydrates: 10 grams

716. **Strawberry cobbler**
Preparation Time: 10 minutes
Cooking Time: 25 minutes
Servings: 6
Ingredients:

- A ¾ cup of sugar
- 6 cups strawberries, halved
- 1/8 teaspoon baking powder
- 1 tablespoon lemon juice
- ½ cup flour
- A pinch of baking soda
- A ½ cup of water
- 3 and ½ tablespoon olive oil
- Cooking spray

Directions:
1. In a bowl, mix strawberries with half of the sugar, sprinkle some flour, add lemon juice, whisk and pour into the baking dish that fits your air fryer and greased with cooking spray.
2. In another bowl, mix flour with the rest of the sugar, baking powder and soda and stir well.
3. Add the olive oil and mix until the whole thing with your hands.
4. Add ½ cup water and spread over strawberries.
5. Introduce in the fryer at 355° f. And bake for 25 minutes.
6. Leave cobbler aside to cool down, slice and serve.
7. Enjoy!

Nutrition: Calories: 221 Protein: 9 grams Fat: 3 grams Carbohydrates: 6 grams

717. **Super yummy brownies**
Preparation Time: 10 minutes
Cooking Time: 25 minutes
Servings: 4
Ingredients:

- 4ounces of softened unsalted butter
- 8ounces of bittersweet chocolate chips
- 3 eggs
- 1 cup of granulated sugar
- ½ teaspoon of salt
- 1 cup of all-purpose flour

Directions:
1. Preheat your air fryer to 350° F.
2. Grease a heat safe dish that is convenient with your air fryer.
3. Using a saucepan, soften the butter and chocolate.
4. Then using a large bowl, add and mix all the ingredients properly.
5. Add the brownie batter to the greased heat safe dish and smoothen the surface.
6. Place it in your air fryer and cook it for 25 minutes or until a toothpick comes out clean in the center.
7. Remove the brownies and allow it to chill it is cool enough to eat, thereafter cut it into squares. Serve and enjoy!

Nutrition: Calories: 130 Protein: 2 grams Fat: 5 grams Carbohydrates: 21 grams

718. **Grilled scallion cheese sandwich**
Preparation Time: 10 minutes
Cooking Time: 20 minutes
Servings: 1
Ingredients:

- 2 teaspoons butter (room temperature
- ¾ cup grated cheddar cheese
- 2 slices of bread
- 1 tablespoon grated parmesan cheese
- 2 scallions (thinly sliced

Directions:
1. Spread a teaspoon of butter on a slice of bread. Place it in the cooking basket with the buttered side facing down.
2. Add scallions and cheddar cheese on top. Spread the rest of the butter in the other slice of bread. Place it on top of the sandwich and sprinkle with parmesan cheese.
3. Cook for 10 minutes at 356° f.
4. Serve and enjoy!

Nutrition: Calories: 511 Protein: 26 grams Fat: 34 grams Carbohydrates: 19 grams

719. **Berry crumble**
Preparation Time: 10 minutes
Cooking Time: 30 minutes
Servings: 6
Ingredients:

- 12 oz. Fresh strawberries
- 7 oz. Fresh raspberries
- 5 oz. Fresh blueberries
- 5 tablespoons cold butter
- 2 tablespoons lemon juice
- 1 cup flour
- A ½ cup of sugar
- 1 tablespoon water
- A pinch of salt

Directions:
1. Gently mass the berries, but make sure there are chunks left. Mix with the lemon juice and 2 tablespoons of the sugar.
2. Place the berry mixture at the bottom of a prepared round cake. Combine the flour with the salt and sugar, in a bowl.
3. Add the water and rub the butter with your fingers until the mixture becomes crumbled.
4. Arrange the crisp batter over the berries. Cook in the air fryer at 390° f for 20 minutes. Serve chilled.

Nutrition: Calories: 261 Protein: 6 grams Fat: 6 grams Carbohydrates: 47 grams

720. **Plum cake**
Preparation Time: 15 minutes
Cooking Time: 1 hour and 56minutes
Servings: 8
Ingredients:

- 7 ounces flour
- 1 package dried yeast
- 1 ounces butter, soft

- 1 egg, whisked
- 5 tablespoons sugar
- 3 ounces warm milk
- 1 and ¾ pounds plums, pitted and cut into quarters
- Zest from 1 lemon, grated
- 1ounce almond flakes

Directions:
1. In a bowl, mix yeast with butter, flour, and 3 tablespoons sugar and stir well.
2. Add milk and egg and whisk for 4 minutes until you obtain dough.
3. Arrange the dough in a spring form the pan that fits your air fryer and which you've greased with some butter, cover and leave aside for 1 hour.
4. Arrange plumps on top of the butter, sprinkle the rest of the sugar, introduce in the sugar, introduce in your air fryer at 350° f. Bake for 36 minutes, cool down, sprinkle almond flakes and lemon zest on top, slice and serve.
5. Enjoy!

Nutrition: Calories: 192 Protein: 7 grams Fat: 4 grams Carbohydrates: 6 grams

721. Banana chips

Preparation time: 5 minutes
Cooking time: 5 minutes
Servings: 8
Ingredients:
- ¼ cup peanut butter, soft
- 1 banana, peeled and sliced into 16 pieces
- 1 tablespoon vegetable oil

Directions:
1. Put the banana slices in your air fryer's basket and drizzle the oil over them.
2. Cook at 360° f for 5 minutes.
3. Transfer to bowls and serve them dipped in peanut butter.

Nutrition: calories 100, fat 4, fiber 1, carbs 10, protein 4

722. Lemony apple bites

Preparation time: 5 minutes
Cooking time: 5 minutes
Servings: 4
Ingredients:
- 3 big apples, cored, peeled and cubed
- 2 teaspoons lemon juice
- ½ cup caramel sauce

Directions:
1. In your air fryer, mix all the ingredients; toss well.
2. Cook at 340° f for 5 minutes.
3. Divide into cups and serve as a snack.

Nutrition: Calories 190 Fat 4 Fiber 2 carbs 14 Protein 6

723. Basil and cilantro crackers

Preparation time: 10 minutes
Cooking time: 16 minutes
Servings: 6
Ingredients:
- ½ teaspoon baking powder
- Salt and black pepper to taste
- 1¼ cups flour
- 1 garlic clove, minced
- 2 tablespoons basil, minced
- 2 tablespoons cilantro, minced
- 4 tablespoons butter, melted

Directions:
1. Add all the ingredients to a bowl and stir until you obtain a dough.
2. Spread this on a lined baking sheet that fits your air fryer.
3. Place the baking sheet in the fryer at 325° f and cook for 16 minutes.
4. Cool down, cut, and serve.

Nutrition: Calories 171 Fat 4 Fiber 2 Carbs 14 Protein 6

724. Balsamic zucchini slices

Preparation time: 5 minutes
Cooking time: 50 minutes
Servings: 6
Ingredients:
- 3 zucchinis, thinly sliced
- Salt and black pepper to taste
- 2 tablespoons avocado oil
- 2 tablespoons balsamic vinegar

Directions:
1. Add all the ingredients to a bowl and mix.
2. Put the zucchini mixture in your air fryer's basket and cook at 220° f for 50 minutes.
3. Serve as a snack and enjoy!

Nutrition: Calories 40 Fat 4 Fiber 2 Carbs 14 Protein 6

725. Turmeric carrot chips

Preparation time: 5 minutes
Cooking time: 25 minutes
Servings: 4
Ingredients:
- 4 carrots, thinly sliced
- Salt and black pepper to taste
- ½ teaspoon turmeric powder
- ½ teaspoon chat masala
- 1 teaspoon olive oil

Directions:
1. Place all ingredients in a bowl and toss well.
2. Put the mixture in your air fryer's basket and cook at 370° f for 25 minutes, shaking the fryer from time to time.
3. Serve as a snack.

Nutrition: Calories 161 Fat 4 fiber 2 carbs 14 protein 6

726. Lentils snack

Preparation time: 5 minutes
Cooking time: 12 minutes
Servings: 4
Ingredients:
- 15 ounces canned lentils, drained
- ½ teaspoon cumin, ground
- 1 tablespoon olive oil
- 1 teaspoon sweet paprika
- Salt and black pepper to taste

Directions:
1. Place all ingredients in a bowl and mix well.
2. Transfer the mixture to your air fryer and cook at 400° f for 12 minutes.
3. Divide into bowls and serve as a snack or a side, or appetizer!

Nutrition: Calories 151 Fat 4 Fiber 2 Carbs 14 Protein 6

727. Salmon tarts

Preparation time: 20 min
Cooking time: 10 minutes
Servings: 15
Ingredients
- 15 mini tart cases
- 4 eggs, lightly beaten
- ½ cup heavy cream
- Salt and black pepper
- 3 oz smoked salmon
- 6 oz cream cheese, divided into 15 pieces
- 6 fresh dill

Directions
1. Mix together eggs and cream in a pourable measuring container. Arrange the tarts into the air fryer. Pour in mixture into the tarts, about halfway up the side and top with a piece of salmon and a piece of cheese. Cook for 10 minutes at 340° f, regularly check to avoid overcooking. Sprinkle dill and serve chilled.

Nutrition: Calories 415 Fat 4 Fiber 2 Carbs 14 protein 6

728. Bacon & chicken wrapped jalapenos

Preparation time: 40 min
Cooking time: 30 minutes
Servings: 4
Ingredients
- Jalapeno peppers, halved lengthwise and seeded
- 4 chicken breasts, butterflied and halved
- 6 oz cream cheese
- 6 oz cheddar cheese
- 16 slices bacon
- 1 cup breadcrumbs

- Salt and pepper to taste
- 2 eggs
- Cooking spray

Directions
1. Season the chicken with pepper and salt on both sides. In a bowl, add cream cheese, cheddar, a pinch of pepper and salt. Mix well.
2. Take each jalapeno and spoon in the cheese mixture to the brim. On a working board, flatten each piece of chicken and lay 2 bacon slices each on them.
3. Place a stuffed jalapeno on each laid out chicken and bacon set and wrap the jalapenos in them.
4. Preheat the air fryer to 350° f. Add the eggs to a bowl and pour the breadcrumbs in another bowl. Also, set a flat plate aside.
5. Take each wrapped jalapeno and dip it into the eggs and then in the breadcrumbs. Place them on the flat plate.
6. Lightly grease the fryer basket with cooking spray. Arrange 45 breaded jalapenos in the basket and cook for 7 minutes.
7. Prepare a paper towel lined plate; set aside. Once the timer beeps, open the fryer, turn the jalapenos, and cook further for 4 minutes.
8. Once ready, remove them onto the paper towel lined plate. Repeat the cooking process for the remaining jalapenos.
9. Serve with a sweet dip for an enhanced taste.

Nutrition: Calories 192 Fat 4 Fiber 2 carbs 14 Protein 6

729. Mouthwatering salami sticks
Preparation time: 2 hrs. 10 min
Cooking time: 20 minutes
Servings: 3
Ingredients
- 1 lb. Ground beef
- 3 tbsp sugar
- A pinch garlic powders
- A pinch chili powders
- Salt to taste
- 1 tsp liquid smoke

Directions
1. Place the meat, sugar, garlic powder, chili powder, salt and liquid smoke in a bowl. Mix with a spoon. Mold out 4 sticks with your hands, place them on a plate, and refrigerate for 2 hours. Cook at 350° f. For 10 minutes, flipping once halfway through.

Nutrition: Calories 428 Carbs 12g Fat 16g Protein 42g

730. Sour cream sausage balls
Preparation time: 50 min
Cooking time: 25 minutes
Servings: 8
Ingredients
- 1 ½ lb. Ground sausages
- 2 ¼ cups cheddar cheese, shredded
- 1 ½ cup flour
- ¾ tsp baking soda
- 4 eggs
- ¾ cup sour cream
- 1 tsp dried oregano
- 1 tsp smoked paprika
- 2 tsp garlic powder
- ½ cup liquid coconut oil

Directions
1. In a pan over medium heat, add the sausages and brown for 34 minutes. Drain the excess fat and set aside.
2. In a bowl, sift in baking soda, and flour. Set aside.
3. In another bowl, add eggs, sour cream, oregano, paprika, coconut oil, and garlic powder.
4. Whisk to combine well. Combine the egg and flour mixtures using a spatula.
5. Add the cheese and sausages. Fold in and let it sit for 5 minutes to thicken. Rub your hands with coconut oil and mold out bite size balls out of the batter.
6. Place them on a tray and refrigerate for 15 minutes. Then, add them in the air fryer, without overcrowding.
7. Cook for 10 minutes per round, at 400° f, in batches if needed.

Nutrition: Calories 457 Carbs 12g Fat 16g Protein 42g

731. Air fried fish and chips
Preparation Time: 15 minutes

Cooking Time: 30 minutes
Servings: 4
Ingredients:
- 6 ounces (4 nos.) Tilapia fillets, skinless
- 13 ounces (2 nos.) Russet potatoes, scrubbed
- 1 cup panko breadcrumbs, whole-wheat
- ½ cup of malt vinegar
- 2 eggs, large
- 1 cup all-purpose flour
- 2 tablespoons water
- 1¼ teaspoons salt, divided
- Vegetable cooking oil spray

Directions:
1. Scrub wash the potatoes and pat dry.
2. Cut the potatoes in spiral shapes.
3. Spritz some cooking oil in the air fryer basket and place the potato chips in the air fryer basket.
4. Put the air fryer basket in the inner pot of the instant pot air fryer. Spray some cooking oil on the chips and close the crisp cover.
5. In the air fry mode, set the temperature at 375 ° f and timer for 10 minutes.
6. Press start to begin cooking. Halfway through the cooking, open the crisp lid and shake the air fryer basket for even cooking.
7. Spry some more cooking oil and close the crisp lid to resume cooking. Once the cooking is over, season it with salt.
8. In the meantime, using a medium bowl, combine flour and salt.
9. Whisk the eggs and water in a shallow dish in the meantime.
10. Mix the panko breadcrumbs and ½ teaspoon salt in the third shallow dish.
11. Cut the fillets in long strips and dredge them in the flour mix, then dip in the egg mix and lastly dredge in the panko breadcrumbs. Press the coating gently, so that the coating can hold in the fish strips firmly.
12. Spritz some cooking oil in the air fryer basket and place the coated fillets in the air fryer basket.
13. Place the air fryer basket in the inner pot of the instant pot air fryer. Spray some cooking oil on the fillets. Close the crisp lid.
14. In the air fry mode, set the temperature at 375 ° f and timer to 10 minutes. Press start to begin cooking.
15. Do not overcrowd the air fryer basket, cook it in batches.
16. Halfway through the cooking, open the crisp cover and flip the fillet chips. Spray some cooking oil if required.
17. Close the crisp lid, so that it can resume cooking from where you have stopped.
18. After cooking, serve hot with an equal portion of potatoes with 2 tablespoons of malt vinegar as dipping.

Nutrition: Calories 415 Carbohydrates: 46g Fat 7g, protein: 44g Sodium: 754mg Sugars: 2g Saturated fat: 2g Calcium: 23mg

732. Plantain chips
Preparation Time: 5 minutes
Cooking Time: 15 minutes
Servings: 2
Ingredients:
- 9¾ ounces (1 no.) Green plantain
- ½ teaspoon of sea salt
- Canola oil spray

Directions:
1. Trim and cut the plantain into round slices, make sure to keep them very thin in thickness.
2. Spray some cooking oil in the air fryer basket and place the plantain slices into it.
3. Spritz some cooking oil on the plantain slices. Sprinkle some sea salt
4. Place the air fryer basket in the inner pot of the instant pot air fryer. Close the crisp lid.
5. In the air fry mode, select the temperature at 350degrees f and timer for 18 minutes. Press start to begin the cooking.
6. Halfway through the cooking, open the crisp lid and shake the air fryer basket. Spritz some more cooking oil if required.
7. To prevent burning, keep checking the slices every 5 minutes.
8. Close the crisp lid to resume the cooking. You don't have to worry about its cooking setting, as the appliance can remember

the last cooking option and resume cooking from the point where you have interrupted the cooking.

9. When cooked, shake the basket and empty the slices in a plate using tongs.
10. Serve with your favorite condiment.

Nutrition: Calories 415 Carbohydrates: 46g Fat 7g, protein: 44g Sodium: 754mg Sugars: 2g Saturated fat: 2g Calcium: 23mg

733. Fried pickles
Preparation time: 15 minutes
Cooking time: 3 minutes
Servings: 6
Ingredients:
- 1 large egg
- ¾ cup almond milk
- pinch of cayenne
- 1 cup xanthium gum, divided
- ½ cup almond meal
- 2 tbsp fresh dill, chopped
- 2 tsp paprika
- 2 tsp black pepper
- 1 tsp salt
- 36 dill pickle slices, cold
- canola oil
- ranch dressing, for dipping

Directions:
1. Whisk together cayenne, milk, and egg.
2. Spread half cup xanthium gum in a shallow dish.
3. Mix the remaining ½ cup xanthium gum with almond meal, salt, pepper, dill, and paprika.
4. Dredge the pickle slices first through the xanthium gum then dip them in egg wash.
5. Coat them with almond meal mixture and shake off the excess.
6. Place them in the fryer basket and spray them with oil.
7. Return the basket to the fryer and air fry the pickles for 3 minutes at 370° f working in batches as to not crowd the basket.
8. Serve warm.

Nutrition: calories 138 total fat 12 g saturated fat 9 g cholesterol 31 mg mg total carbs 8 g fiber 8 g sugar 9 g protein 4 g

734. Crusted mozzarella sticks
Preparation time: 15 minutes
Cooking time: 5 minutes
Servings: 12
Ingredients:
- 12 mozzarella sticks string cheese, cut in half
- 2 large eggs, beaten
- ½ cup almond flour
- ½ cup parmesan cheese
- 1 tsp Italian seasoning
- ½ tsp garlic salt

Directions:
1. Mix almond flour with Italian seasoning, garlic salt, and parmesan cheese.
2. Whisk eggs in a separate bowl and keep them aside.
3. Dip the mozzarella sticks in eggs then coat with cheese mixture.
4. Spread them on a baking sheet lined with wax paper.
5. Freeze the sticks for 30 minutes then place them in the air fryer basket.
6. Return the basket to the fryer then air fry them for 5 minutes at 400°f.
7. Let them sit for 1 minute then transfer to a plate.
8. Serve.

Nutrition: calories 362 total fat 19 g saturated fat 9 g cholesterol 49 mg mg total carbs 1 g fiber 4 g sugar 1 g protein 23 g

735. Sesame nuggets
Preparation time: 15 minutes
Cooking time: 12 minutes
Servings: 6
Ingredients:
- 1 lb. chicken, cubed
- pinch sea salt
- 1 tsp sesame oil
- ¼ cup coconut flour

- ½ tsp ground ginger
- 4 egg whites
- 6 tbsp toasted sesame seeds
- cooking spray of choice

Directions:
1. Let your air fryer preheat to 400° f.
2. Meanwhile, toss the chicken cubes with sesame oil and salt.
3. Mix coconut flour with ground ginger in a Ziploc bag then place the chicken in it.
4. Zip the bag and shake well to coat the chicken well.
5. Whisk egg whites in a bowl then dip the coated chicken in egg whites.
6. Coat them with sesame seeds and shake off the excess.
7. Place the nuggets in the air fryer basket and return the basket to the fryer.
8. Air fry the nuggets for 6 minutes then flip them.
9. Spray the nuggets with cooking oil and cook for another 6 minutes.
10. Serve fresh.

Nutrition: calories 130 total fat 13 g saturated fat 4 g cholesterol 173 mg total carbs 9 g fiber 1 g sugar 2 g protein 77 g

736. Fried parmesan zucchini
Preparation time: 15 minutes
Cooking time: 16 minutes
Servings: 4
Ingredients:
- 2 medium zucchinis, sliced
- 1 large egg
- ½ cup grated parmesan cheese
- ¼ cup almond flour
- ½ tsp garlic powder
- 1 tsp Italian seasoning
- avocado oil spray

Directions:
1. Whisk egg in a shallow bowl and mix cheese, flour, Italian seasoning, and garlic powder in another.
2. Dip the zucchini slices in the egg then cheese mixture. Shake off the excess.
3. Place the slices in the air fryer basket and spray them with avocado oil.
4. Return the basket to the air fryer and air fry the slices for 8 minutes at 370° f.
5. Flip the zucchini slices and spray them with more oil.
6. Air fry them for 8 minutes more.
7. Cook them in batches.
8. Serve.

Nutrition: calories 139 total fat 6 g saturated fat 6 g cholesterol 67 mg total carbs 1 g fiber 3 g sugar 2 g protein 12 g

737. Radish chips
Preparation time: 15 minutes
Cooking time: 18 minutes
Servings: 6
Ingredients:
- 1 lb. bag of radish slices
- avocado oil or olive oil, enough to coat radishes
- salt, to taste
- pepper, to taste
- garlic powder, to taste
- onion powder, to taste

Directions:
1. Toss the washed radish slices with oil, salt, pepper, onion powder, and garlic powder.
2. Spread these slices in the air fryer basket and return the basket to the fryer.
3. Air fry them for 5 minutes at 370° f then toss them well.
4. Air fry the slices again for 5 more minutes.
5. Adjust seasoning with more spices and cooking oil.
6. Air fry these slices again for 5 minutes then toss them.
7. Cook for another 3 minutes.
8. Serve them.

Nutrition: calories 72 total fat 6 g saturated fat 4 g cholesterol 37 mg total carbs 6 g fiber 6 g sugar 6 g protein 8 g

738. Crispy blooming onion

Preparation time: 15 minutes
Cooking time: 10 minutes
Servings: 1
Ingredients:
- 1 large onion
- 2 ½ cups almond flour
- 4 tsp old bay seasoning
- 2 eggs, beaten
- ½ cup coconut milk

Directions:
1. Slice the top of the onion while keeping its base intact.
2. Wash it well and drain all the water out of it.
3. Carve several slits vertically from top to bottom at equal distances. Make sure to keep the cut up to one inch above the base.
4. Spread the onion layers like flower petals and set it aside.
5. Preheat the air fryer to 400° f.
6. Whisk eggs with the milk in one bowl and mix flour with seasoning in another.
7. Dust the onion flower with flour mixture then dip it in the egg mixture.
8. Sprinkle the remaining flour mixture over it and shake off the excess.
9. Place the onion flower in the air fryer basket and return the basket to the fryer.
10. Air fry the onion for 10 minutes in the preheated air fryer.
11. Serve.

Nutrition: calories 158 total fat 16 g saturated fat 6 g cholesterol 131 mg total carbs 14 g fiber 3 g sugar 4 g protein 6 g

739.   Popcorn chicken
Preparation time: 2 hours
Cooking time: 8 minutes
Servings: 10
Ingredients:
- Marinade
- 2 lbs. chicken breast tenders, diced
- 2 cups almond milk
- 1 tsp salt
- ½ tsp black pepper
- ½ tsp ground paprika
- Dry ingredients
- 3 cups almond flour
- 3 tsp salt
- 2 tsp black pepper
- 2 tsp paprika
- oil spray

Directions:
1. Add all the ingredients for the marinade in a Ziplock bag.
2. Place the chicken in it then zip the bag. Shake it well then refrigerate for 2 hours or more.
3. Meanwhile, mix all the dry ingredients in a shallow container.
4. Remove the chicken from the marinade and dredge the pieces through the dry mixture.
5. Shake off the excess then place the pieces in the air fryer basket.
6. Spray them with cooking oil then return the basket to the air fryer.
7. Air fry them for 8 minutes at 370°f and toss them when cooked halfway through.
8. Serve immediately.

Nutrition: calories 242 total fat 19 g saturated fat 16 g cholesterol 36 mg total carbs 6 g fiber 2 g sugar 6 g protein 28 g

740.   Breaded mushrooms
Preparation time: 15 minutes
Cooking time: 7 minutes
Servings: 2
Ingredients:
- ½ lb. button mushrooms
- 1 cup almond flour
- 1 egg
- 1 cup almond meal
- 3 oz grated Parmigiano Reggiano cheese
- salt and pepper, to taste

Directions:
1. Let your air fryer preheat to 360° f.
2. Toss almond meal with cheese in a shallow bowl.
3. Whisk egg in one bowl and spread flour in another.
4. Wash mushrooms then pat dry. Coat each mushroom with flour.
5. Dip each of them in the egg then finally in the breadcrumbs mixture.
6. Shake off the excess and place the mushrooms in the air fryer basket.
7. Spray them with cooking oil and return the basket to the fryer.
8. Air fry these mushrooms for 7 minutes in the preheated air fryer.
9. Toss the mushrooms once cooked halfway through then continue cooking.
10. Serve warm.

Nutrition: calories 140 total fat 2 g saturated fat 2 g cholesterol 82 mg total carbs 9 g fiber 6 g sugar 1 g protein 3 g

741.   Monkey bread
Preparation time: 15 minutes
Cooking time: 7 minutes
Servings: 4
Ingredients:
- 1 cup almond flour
- 1 cup nonfat Greek yogurt
- 1 tsp swerve sugar substitute½ tsp cinnamon

Directions:
1. Combine yogurt with flour to create a smooth dough in a mixing bowl.
2. Divide the dough into 8 equal pieces and roll them into small balls.
3. Mix cinnamon with swerve sugar in a shallow bowl.
4. Roll each ball in the cinnamon mixture and coat well.
5. Place these balls in the air fryer basket and return the basket to the fryer basket.
6. Cook these bread balls for 7 minutes at 375° f on air fry mode.
7. Serve.

Nutrition: calories 73 total fat 3 g saturated fat 3 g cholesterol 3 mg total carbs 2 g fiber 9 g sugar 5 g protein 3 g

742.   Stuffed jalapeno
Preparation time: 10 minutes
Cooking time: 10 minutes
Servings: 4
Ingredients
- 1 lb. Ground pork sausage
- 1 (8 oz.) package cream cheese, softened
- 1 cup shredded parmesan cheese
- 1 lb. Large fresh jalapeno peppers halved lengthwise and seeded
- 1 (8 oz.) bottle ranch dressing

Directions:
1. In mix pork sausage ground with ranch dressing and cream cheese in a bowl. But the jalapeno in half and remove their seeds.
2. Divide the cream cheese mixture into the jalapeno halves. Place the jalapeno pepper in a baking tray.
3. Set the baking tray inside the air fryer toaster oven and close the lid. Select the bake mode at 350 ° f temperature for 10 minutes. Serve warm.

Nutrition: calories: 168 protein: 4g carbs: 11g fat: 22g

743.   Garlicky bok choy
Preparation time: 10 minutes
Cooking time: 10 minutes
Servings: 2
Ingredients
- Bunches baby bok choy
- Spray oil
- 1 tsp garlic powder

Directions:
1. 1toss bok choy with garlic powder and spread them in the air fryer basket. Spray them with cooking oil.
2. Set the air fryer basket inside the air fryer toaster oven and close the lid.
3. Select the air fry mode at 350 ° f temperature for 6 minutes. Serve fresh.

Nutrition: calories: 81 protein: 4g carbs: 7g fat: 3g

744.   Chia seed crackers
Preparation time: 15 minutes

Cooking time: 45 minutes

Servings: 48

Ingredients

- 1 cup raw chia seed
- 3/4 teaspoon salt
- 1/4 teaspoon garlic powder
- 1/4 teaspoon onion powder
- 1 cup cold water

Directions:

1. 1put the chia seeds in a bowl. Add salt, garlic powder, and onion powder.
2. 2pour into the water. Stir. Cover with plastic wrap. Store in the fridge overnight. Preheat the air fryer toaster oven to 95 ° c.
3. Cover a baking sheet with a silicone mat or parchment. Transfer the soaked linseed to a prepared baking sheet.
4. Scatter it out with a spatula in a thin, flat rectangle about 1 cm thick. Rate the rectangle in about 32 small rectangles.
5. Bake in the preheated air fryer toaster oven up to the chia seeds have darkened and contract slightly, about 3 hours. Let it cool. Break individual cookies.

Nutrition: calories 120 fat 9 g carbs 9 g protein 9g

745. **Baked eggplant chips**

Preparation time: 5 minutes

Cooking time: 15 minutes

Servings: 4

Ingredients

- Medium eggplant, cut into 1/4-inch slices
- 1/2 cup crushed cornflakes.
- 1/8 teaspoon ground black pepper
- Tablespoons grated goat cheese
- Egg whites

Directions:

1. Preheat the air fryer toaster oven to 245 ° f. Mix the crushed cornflakes, pepper and goat cheese in a small container.
2. Set aside the egg whites in a different container. Dip the eggplant slices in the egg white and cover the crushed cornflakes mixture.
3. Place on a greased baking sheet.
4. Bake in the preheated air fryer toaster oven for 5 minutes, then turn and bake for another 5 to 10 minutes until golden yellow and crispy.

Nutrition: calories 92 fat 1 g carbs 19 g protein 9g

746. **Flax seed chips**

Preparation time: 5 minutes

Cooking time: 15 minutes

Servings: 4

Ingredients

- 1 cup almond flour
- 1/2 cup flax seeds
- 1 1/2 teaspoons seasoned salt
- 1 teaspoon sea salt
- 1/2 cup water

Directions:

1. Preheat the air fryer toaster oven to 170°c. Combine almond flour, flax seeds, 1 1/2 teaspoons seasoned salt and sea salt in a container.
2. Stir in the water up to the dough is completely mixed.
3. Shape the dough into narrow size slices the size of a bite and place them on a baking sheet. Sprinkle the rounds with seasoned salt.
4. bake in preheated air fryer toaster oven up to crispy, about 15 minutes.
5. Cool fully and store in an airtight box or in a sealed bag.

Nutrition: calories 129 fat 1g carbs 19 g protein 9g

747. **Salted hazelnuts**

Preparation time: 15 minutes

Cooking time: 10 minutes

Servings: 8

Ingredients

- Cups dry roasted hazelnuts, no salt added
- Tablespoons coconut oil
- 1 teaspoon garlic powder
- 1 sprig fresh thyme, chopped
- 1 1/2 teaspoons salt

Directions:

1. 1preheat the air fryer toaster oven to 175 ° c. Mix the hazelnuts, coconut oil, garlic powder and thyme in a bowl until the nuts are fully covered. Sprinkle with salt. Spread evenly on a baking sheet. Bake in the preheated air fryer toaster oven for 10 minutes.

Nutrition: calories 237 fat 23 g carbs 9 g protein 4g

748. **Apricots stuffed with walnuts**

Preparation time: 10 minutes

Cooking time: 15 minutes

Servings: 6

Ingredients

- Fresh apricots
- Tablespoons mini semi-sweet chocolate chips
- 1/4 cup walnuts
- 1/2 cup apple cider vinegar

Directions:

1. Cut each apricot in half. Combine the chocolate chips, walnuts and apple cider vinegar in a small bowl. Put about 2 teaspoons of the filling mixture in each half of the apricots.
2. Place the assembled mold in the oven on the wire rack. Position set air fry at 200 ° c for 15 minutes.
3. Cook golden brown and crispy.

Nutrition: calories 99 fat 6 g carbs 13 protein 5g

749. **Rutabaga chips**

Preparation time: 10 minutes

Cooking time: 5 minutes

Servings: 20

Ingredients

- 1 tablespoon coconut oil
- 1 rutabaga, sliced paper thin (peel optional
- 1/2 teaspoon salt

Directions:

1. 1pour coconut oil into a plastic bag (a bag of products works well. Add rutabaga slices and shake to cover them. Cover a large plate with oil or oil spray. Place the air fryer basket onto the baking pan. Put the assembled pan into rack position   arrange to air fry at 350°f for 05 minutes

Nutrition: calories 80 fat 5 g carbs 12 g protein 1g

750. **Peanut banana chips**

Preparation time: 5 minutes

Cooking time: 15 minutes

Servings: 8

Ingredients

- ¼ cup peanut butter, soft
- 1 banana, peeled and sliced into 16 pieces
- 1 tablespoon vegetable oil

Directions:

1. 1put the banana slices in your air fryer's basket and drizzle the oil over them.
2. 2cook at 360° f for 5 minutes.
3. 3transfer to bowls and serve them dipped in peanut butter.

Nutrition: calories 100, fat 4, fiber 1, carbs 10, protein 4

751. **Chives radish snack**

Preparation time: 5 minutes

Cooking time: 10 minutes

Servings: 4

Ingredients

- 16 radishes, sliced
- A drizzle of olive oil
- Salt and black pepper to taste
- 1 tablespoon chives, chopped

Directions:

1. in a bowl, mix the radishes, salt, pepper, and oil; toss well.
2. place the radishes in your air fryer's basket and cook at 350° f for 10 minutes.
3. divide into bowls and serve with chives sprinkled on top.

Nutrition: calories 100, fat 1, fiber 2, carbs 4, protein 1

752. **Hot chicken wing**

Preparation time: 10 minutes

Cooking time: 40 minutes

Servings: 4

Ingredients

- 15 chicken wings

- Salt and pepper to taste
- ⅓ cup hot sauce
- ⅓ cup butter
- ½ tbsp vinegar

Directions
1. 1preheat the air fryer to 360° f. Season the vignettes with pepper and salt. Add them to the air fryer and cook for 35 minutes. Toss every 5 minutes. Once ready, remove them into a bowl. Over low heat melts the butter in a saucepan. Add the vinegar and hot sauce. Stir and cook for a minute.
2. 2turn the heat off. Pour the sauce over the chicken. Toss to coat well. Transfer the chicken to a serving platter. Serve with blue cheese dressing.

Nutrition: calories 563; carbs 2g; fat 28g; protein 35g

753. Roasted lima beans

Preparation time: 5 minutes
Cooking time: 40 minutes
Servings: 4
Ingredients
- 1 can (12 ounce) lima beans
- Tablespoons coconut oil
- Salt
- Garlic salt (optional)
- Paprika (optional)

Directions:
1. 1dry the lima beans with a kitchen towel to not wet them. In a bowl, mix the lima beans with coconut oil and sprinkle with salt, garlic salt and paprika.
2. Place the air fryer basket onto the baking pan.
3. Put the assembled pan into rack position arrange to air fry at 350°f for 5 minutes

Nutrition: calories 161 fat 5 g carbs 12 g protein 1g

754. Cheesy bombs in bacon

Preparation time: 10 minutes
Cooking time: 10 minutes
Servings: 8
Ingredients
- Bacon slices, cut in half
- 16 oz mozzarella cheese, cut into 8 pieces
- Tbsp butter, melted

Directions
1. 1wrap each cheese string with a slice of bacon and secure the ends with toothpicks. Set aside.
2. 2grease the crisp basket with the melted butter and add in the bombs. Close the crisping lid, select air fry mode, and set the temperature to 370° f and set the time to 10 minutes.
3. 3at the 5-minute mark, turn the bombs. When ready, remove to a paper-lined plate to drain the excess oil. Serve on a platter with toothpicks.

Nutrition: calories 230; fat 15g; sodium 310mg; carbs 2g; protein 24g

755. Brazilian snack pao de queijo

Preparation time: 15 minutes
Cooking time: 20 minutes
Servings: 4
Ingredients
- Cups all-purpose flour
- 1 cup milk
- Eggs, cracked into a bowl
- Cups grated parmesan cheese
- ½ cup olive oil

Directions
1. 1grease the crisp basket with cooking spray and set aside.
2. 2put the cooker on medium and select sear/sauté mode.
3. 3add the milk, oil, and salt, and let boil. Add the flour and mix it vigorously with a spoon.
4. 4let the mixture cool. Once cooled, use a hand mixer to mix the dough well, and add the eggs and cheese while still mixing. The dough should be thick and sticky.
5. 5use your hands to make 14 balls out of the mixture and put them in the greased basket. Put the basket in the pot and close the crisping lid.
6. 6select air fry, set the temperature to 380° f and set the timer to 15 minutes.

7. at the 7-minute mark, shake the balls. Serve with lemon aioli, garlic mayo or ketchup.

Nutrition: calories 625; fat 34g; sodium 304mg; carbs 54g; protein 26g

756. Bacon chicken roll

Preparation time: 5 minutes
Cooking time: 25 minutes
Servings: 4
Ingredients:
- 6 chicken breast ribs, cleaned
- 6 slices of bacon
- Garlic, salt, and black pepper to taste
- Wood sticks

Direction:
1. Preheat the air fryer. Set the time of 5 minutes and the temperature to 200°c. At the end of that time, the air fryer will turn off.
2. Season the chicken with garlic, pepper, and salt to taste. Place each chicken roll on a slice of bacon and roll it. Prick with a stick to secure.
3. Place in the basket of the air fryer. Set the time of 20 minutes and press the power button. Shake the basket halfway through to get golden rolls evenly.
4. Once ready, transfer to a plate and serve

Nutrition: Calories: 217 Proteins: 20g Carbohydrates: 8g

757. Rosemary russet potato chips

Preparation time: 10 minutes
Cooking time: 1 hour
Servings: 4
Ingredients:
- ½ tsp. Salt
- 4 russet potatoes
- 1 tbsp. Olive oil
- 2 tsps. Chopped rosemary

Directions:
1. Rinse the potatoes and scrub to clean. Peel and cut them in a lengthwise manner similar to thin chips.
2. Put them in a bowl and soak in water for 30 minutes.
3. Pat the potato chips with paper towels to dry.
4. Toss the chips in a bowl with olive oil. Transfer them to the cooking basket.
5. Cook for 30 minutes at 330°f. Shake several times during the cooking process.
6. Toss the cooked chips in a bowl with salt and rosemary while warm.

Nutrition: Calories: 322 Fat: 69g Carbs: 66g Protein: 5g

758. Coconut chicken bites

Preparation time: 10 minutes
Cooking time: 10 minutes
Servings: 4
Ingredients:
- Chicken tenders,
- Panko breadcrumbs, ¾ cup
- Black pepper.
- Cooking spray.
- Shredded coconut, ¾ cup
- Garlic powder, 2 tsps.
- Eggs,
- Salt.

Directions:
1. In a bowl, mix eggs with garlic powder, salt and pepper, and whisk well.
2. In another bowl, mix coconut with panko and stir well.
3. Dip chicken tenders in the egg mixture and then coat well with coconut mixture.
4. Spray chicken bits using cooking spray.
5. Move them to the air fryer basket and cook at 350° f for 10 minutes.
6. Serve.

Nutrition: Calories: 252 Fat: 4g Carbs: 14g Protein: 24g

759. Mini popovers

Preparation time: 10 minutes
Cooking time: 15 minutes
Servings: 4

Ingredients
- 1 tsp butter melted
- 2 eggs at room temperature
- 1 cup of milk at room temperature
- 1 cup all-purpose flour
- Salt and pepper to taste

Directions:
1. Generously coat a mini popover with nonstick spray.
2. Add all the ingredients to a blender and process it at medium speed.
3. Fill each mold with 2 tsp batter. Place a drip pan at the bottom of the cooking chamber.
4. Using the display panel select air fry and adjust it to 400 °f and a time of 20 minutes then touch start.
5. When the display panel indicates 'add food' place the egg bite mold on the lower side of the cooking tray.
6. When the display indicates turn food. Do not touch anything. When the popovers are brown open the cooking chamber and pierce them to release steam and cook for a minute or so.
7. Serve immediately.

Nutrition: Calories 53 Fat 1g Carbs 9g Proteins 2g

760. Mac and cheese bites
Preparation time: 1 hour
Cooking time: 10 minutes
Servings: 4

Ingredients:
- 3 pieces bacon
- 3 cloves garlic
- 1/2 can beer
- 3/4 cups milk
- 2 cups elbow macaroni noodles
- 1-1/2 cups shredded cheddar cheese
- 1/4 cup grated parmesan cheese
- 3 eggs
- 1/2 cup flour
- 1/2 cup breadcrumbs
- Salt & pepper, to taste

Directions:
1. Cook the macaroni in a pot of boiling, salted water to al dente.
2. Meanwhile, dice your bacon and chop your garlic into fine pieces.
3. Cook the bacon until it begins to crisp, then add garlic and sauté for another minute.
4. Slowly mix in 3 tablespoons of flour until the mixture begins to turn into a paste.
5. Slowly add the milk and beer, making sure to stir continuously for about 5 minutes or until the sauce starts to take on a thicker consistency.
6. Add salt, pepper, and cheeses and mix until the cheese is completely melted.
7. Drain the macaroni. Place the macaroni in a bowl and mix in the cheese sauce until the macaroni is evenly coated throughout.
8. Place the mixture in the fridge for 45 minutes so it can set.
9. Beat the egg, place the breadcrumbs on a plate, and put the rest of the flour in a bowl or plate.
10. When the macaroni is set, remove it from the fridge. Take small handfuls and roll them into a ball.
11. Roll them in flour, dip them in egg, and then roll them in breadcrumbs until evenly coated.
12. Place them on the bottom of your basket making sure to give each ball room around it.
13. Cook in the air fryer at 360°f for 10 minutes.

Nutrition: Calories: 483 Fiber: 7 g Fat: 25 g Carbs: 38 g Protein: 26 g.

761. Crispy apple and pear with oatmeal
Preparation time: 5 minutes
Cooking time: 30 minutes
Servings: 4

Ingredients:
- ¼ cup plus 2 tbsp quick-cooking oatmeal
- 3 tbsp common flour
- 2 tbsp packed brown sugar
- ½ tsp ground condiments for pumpkin pies, divided
- 1½ tbsp butter in small pieces
- 1 medium apple (8 ounces) golden delicious, peeled, without center and chopped
- 1 medium pear (8 ounces, peeled and chopped)
- 1 tsp lemon juice
- 4 ounces mascarpone cheese
- ½ tbsp of sugar
- ½ tsp vanilla essence

Direction:
1. Preheat the air fryer to a temperature of 350°f. Combine oatmeal, flour, brown sugar, and ¼ teaspoon of pumpkin pie seasonings in a medium bowl.
2. Add the butter, and using your fingers or kneader, incorporating it until it becomes crumb; set it aside.
3. Mix the apple pieces and pears, sprinkle with lemon juice and pumpkin pie seasonings. Pour this mixture into a 1-quart oven-safe container that fits comfortably inside the basket.
4. Spray the reserved oatmeal mixture over the fruit pieces evenly. Cook for 30 minutes or until the fruit becomes soft. Remove the container from the fryer and let it cool slightly.
5. While the crunch is cooling, mix the mascarpone cheese, sugar, and vanilla in a small bowl. Put a portion of the mascarpone cheese mixture on the crunch.

Nutrition: Calories: 81 Fat: 3g Carbohydrates: 12g Protein: 1g

762. Pesto crackers
Preparation time: 10 minutes
Cooking time: 17 minutes
Servings: 6

Ingredients:
- Basil pesto, 2 tbsps.
- Dried basil, ¼ tsp.
- Black pepper.
- Minced garlic clove,
- Baking powder, ½ tsp.
- Salt.
- Flour, 1 ¼ cup
- Butter, 3 tbsps.

Directions:
1. Mix butter, pesto, basil, cayenne, garlic, flour, baking powder, salt and pepper in a bowl and make a dough.
2. Set the dough on a lined baking sheet.
3. Bake in the air fryer at 325° f for 17 minutes.
4. Cool and cut into crackers then serve.

Nutrition: Calories: 200 Fat: 20g Carbs: 4g Protein: 7g

763. Buns with carrots and nuts
Preparation time: 5 minutes
Cooking time: 20 minutes
Servings: 4

Ingredients:
- ½ cup whole-grain flower
- ¼ cup of sugar
- ½ tsp baking soda
- ¼ tsp cinnamon
- ⅛ tsp nutmeg
- ½ cup grated carrots
- 2 tbsp chopped walnuts
- 2 tbsp grated coconut
- 2 tbsp golden raisins
- 1 egg
- 1 tbsp milk
- ½ tsp vanilla essence
- ¼ cup applesauce

Direction:
1. Preheat the fryer to a temperature of 350°f. Grease the bottom of 4 muffin molds or glass cups for custard, or magazine with muffin papers.
2. Combine flour, sugar, baking soda, cinnamon, and nutmeg in a medium bowl. Add carrots, nuts, coconut, and raisins to the flour mixture.
3. Beat together the egg, milk, and vanilla in a small bowl. Add the applesauce. Put the flour mixture and stir until well incorporated.
4. Fill the prepared molds or cups with an equal amount of dough and then put them inside the basket.

5. Cook for 15 minutes, then let them cool in the molds for 5 minutes before removing.

Nutrition: Calories: 195 Fat: 104g Carbohydrates: 225g Protein: 22g Sugar: 115g Cholesterol: 67mg

764. Bread corn sandwich
Preparation time: 15 minutes
Cooking time: 30 minutes
Servings: 4
Ingredients:
- 4 slices of white bread
- 2 tbsp. Butter
- 1 c. Sweet corn kernels
- 1 capsicum
- ¼c. Chopped onion
- Black pepper
- 1 crushed garlic flake
- 1 ½ tbsps. Tomato ketchup
- ½ tbsp. Red chili sauce
- 1 tsp. Olive oil
- 1/3 c. Stock or water
- ¼ tsp. Mustard powder
- Salt
- ½ tbsp. Sugar
- ½ tbsp. Worcestershire sauce

Directions:
1. Set the pan with oil on fire over medium-high heat
2. Add garlic and onions and cook for 4 minutes while stirring often.
3. Add the sugar, chili sauce, mustard, stock, Worcestershire sauce, and tomato ketchup.
4. Combine then allow to cook
5. Reduce the heat then simmer for 10 minutes.
6. Season with salt and black pepper. Set aside.
7. Place another pan over medium flame. Melt butter and roast the corn kernels.
8. Lightly rub a bit of oil on the capsicum.
9. Roast and turn them over until black patches develop.
10. Remove the seeds and skin.
11. Finely chop and transfer to a bowl.
12. Add the barbecue sauce and roasted corn kernels. Mix well.
13. Set the mixture on a slice of bread and put another slice on top.
14. Put the sandwich in the cooking basket.
15. Cook for 15 minutes at 356°f.
16. Flip the sandwich halfway through the cooking process.
17. Serve along with chutney while hot.

Nutrition: Calories: 142 Fat: 8g Carbs: 19g Protein: 4g

765. Cumin and squash chili
Preparation time: 10 minutes
Cooking time: 16 minutes
Servings: 4
Ingredients:
- 1 medium butternut squash
- 2 teaspoons cumin seeds
- 1 large pinch chili flakes
- 1 tablespoon olive oil
- 1 and ½ ounces pine nuts
- 1 small bunch fresh coriander, chopped

Directions:
1. Take the squash and slice it
2. Remove seeds and cut into smaller chunks
3. Take a bowl and add chunked squash, spice and oil
4. Mix well
5. Pre-heat your fryer to 360° f and add the squash to the cooking basket in "air fry" mode
6. Roast for 20 minutes, making sure to shake the basket from time to time to avoid burning
7. Take a pan and place it over medium heat, add pine nuts to the pan and dry toast for 2 minutes
8. Sprinkle nuts on top of the squash and serve
9. Enjoy!

Nutrition: Calories: 339 Fat: 4 g Saturated fat: 1 g Carbohydrates: 40 g Fiber: 17 g Protein: 17 g

766. Pizza toast
Preparation time: 10 minutes
Cooking time: 5 minutes
Servings: 4
Ingredients:
- 4 Texas toast slices
- 8 oz mozzarella cheese, shredded
- ½ jar pizza sauce
- 4 basil leaves

Directions:
1. Arrange toast slices on instant vortex air fryer oven drip pan and air fry at 380° f for 2 minutes.
2. After 2 minutes remove the pan from the air fryer oven.
3. Add pizza sauce, mozzarella cheese, and basil leaves on each toast slice.
4. Return pan in air fryer oven and air fry until cheese is melted.
5. Serve and enjoy.

Nutrition: Calories 260 Fat 11 g Carbohydrates 21 g Sugar 2 g Protein 19 g Cholesterol 30 mg

767. Rosemary Cauliflower
Preparation Time: 5 minutes
Cooking Time: 25 minutes
Servings: 1
Ingredients:
- 1 large head of cauliflower, torn into smaller bits
- 2 eggs, beaten
- ¼ teaspoon black pepper
- ¼ teaspoon garlic powder
- ¼ teaspoon rosemary (dried or fresh)

Directions:
1. Ready and set the air fryer to 390 °f.
2. Place the spices in with the beaten egg and stir to combine.
3. Then transfer the cauliflower to the egg mixture. Coat well.
4. Place the cauliflower in the air fryer and cook for 25 minutes.
5. Serve with a sour cream dip and salad.

Nutrition: Calories: 32 Fat: 2g Carbs: 2g Protein: 1g

768. Beet Burgers
Preparation Time: 10 minutes
Cooking Time: 25 minutes
Servings: 4
Ingredients:
- 2 cups shredded red beets
- 1 cup chickpea flour
- 1 egg, beaten
- ¼ teaspoon black pepper
- ¼ teaspoon garlic powder

Directions:
1. Turn on and set air fryer to 390 °f.
2. Combine the chickpea flour with the pepper and garlic powder.
3. Then stir in the beets and the egg.
4. Use a large wooden spoon or your hands to combine well.
5. Use your hands to form burger patties.
6. Place the beet burgers in the air fryer and cook for 25 minutes.
7. Serve with low carb or gluten free bread, mayonnaise and pickles and salad.

Nutrition: Calories: 160 Fat: 3g Carbs: 27g Protein: 5g

769. Peanut Carrot Burgers
Preparation Time: 10 minutes
Cooking Time: 25 minutes
Servings: 4
Ingredients:
- 2 cups shredded carrots
- 1 cup peanut flour
- 1 egg, beaten
- ¼ teaspoon black pepper
- ¼ teaspoon garlic powder

Directions:
1. Warm up the air fryer to 390 °f.
2. Combine the peanut flour with the pepper and garlic powder.
3. Then stir in the carrots and the egg. Use a large wooden spoon or your hands to mix well.
4. Use your hands to form burger patties.
5. Place the carrot burgers in the air fryer and cook for 25 minutes.

6. Serve with low carb or gluten free bread, mayonnaise and pickles and salad.

Nutrition: Calories: 190 Fat: 7g Carbs: 7g Protein: 2g

770. **Lemon Lentil Burgers**

Preparation Time: 10 minutes
Cooking Time: 25 minutes
Servings: 4
Ingredients:

- 2 cups cooked green lentils
- 2 tablespoons lemon juice
- 1 cup chickpea flour
- 1 egg, beaten
- ¼ teaspoon black pepper
- ¼ teaspoon garlic powder

Directions:

1. Foreheat air fryer to 390 °f.
2. Place all of the ingredients in a food processor and pulse for a few seconds.
3. Use your hands to form burger patties.
4. Arrange burger patties in the air fryer and cook for 25 – 30 minutes.
5. Serve with low carb or gluten free bread and salad.

Nutrition: Calories: 89 Fat: 0.6g Carbs: 17g Protein: 4g

771. **White Bean Cheese Balls**

Preparation Time: 10 minutes
Cooking Time: 25 minutes
Servings: 4
Ingredients:

- 2 cups cooked white beans
- 1 cup chickpea flour
- 1 egg, beaten
- ¼ teaspoon black pepper
- ¼ teaspoon garlic powder
- 2 cups mozzarella cheese

Directions:

1. Warm the air fryer to 390 °f.
2. Combine all of the ingredients in a food processor and pulse (or stir by hand for a thicker consistency).
3. Use your hands to form balls.
4. Cooke the balls for 25 minutes.
5. Serve with a tomato sauce or salsa dip. Also delicious with homemade guacamole.

Nutrition: Calories: 67 Fat: 0.7g Carbs: 13g Protein: 6g

772. **Tomato and Cheese Black Bean Sticks**

Preparation Time: 5 minutes
Cooking Time: 25 minutes
Servings: 4
Ingredients:

- 2 cups cooked black beans
- 1 cup chickpea flour
- 1 egg, beaten
- ¼ teaspoon black pepper
- ¼ teaspoon garlic powder
- 2 cups mozzarella cheese
- 1 tomato, chopped

Directions:

1. Get ready your air fryer to 390 °f.
2. Combine all of the ingredients in a food processor and pulse (or stir by hand for a thicker consistency).
3. Form sticks using hands.
4. Cook for 25 minutes.
5. Serve with guacamole.

Nutrition: Calories: 59 Fat: 0.4g Carbs: 12g Protein: 3g

773. **Lentil Cheese Balls**

Preparation Time: 5 minutes
Cooking Time: 25 minutes
Servings: 6
Ingredients:

- 2 cups cooked red lentils
- 2 cups cream cheese
- 1 cup swiss cheese
- 1 teaspoon garlic powder
- 2 cups chickpea flour

Directions:

1. Turn on and warm up air fryer to 390 °f.
2. Combine the lentils, cream cheese, swiss cheese and garlic powder in a dish. Mix well using a large spoon or your hands.
3. Once the mixture is evenly distributed, use your hands to form balls.
4. Roll the balls in the chickpea flour.
5. Put balls in the air fryer and cook for 25 minutes. Serve with dip and salad.

Nutrition: Calories: 62 Fat: 2.1g Carbs: 7g Protein: 4g

774. **Fried Spinach Dip**

Preparation Time: 5 minutes
Cooking Time: 25 minutes
Servings: 4
Ingredients:

- 2 cups sour cream
- 1 cup cream cheese
- 1 garlic clove, chopped
- 1 cups Havarti cheese, grated
- 1 cup frozen spinach, thawed and drained
- 1 tablespoon chickpea flour
- 1 teaspoon black pepper
- 1 teaspoon garlic powder

Directions:

1. Set up air fryer to 390 °f.
2. Mix the sour cream, cream cheese, chopped garlic, spinach, chickpea flour, black pepper and garlic powder in a mixing bowl.
3. Transfer to a heat safe dish. Cover with the Havarti cheese.
4. Cook in the air fryer for 25 minutes.
5. Serve the dip with raw veggies, chips or use as a delicious sandwich condiment.

Nutrition: Calories: 134 Fat: 7g Carbs: 16g Protein: 3g

775. **Pistachio and Quinoa Burgers**

Preparation Time: 10 minutes
Cooking Time: 25 minutes
Servings: 4
Ingredients:

- 2 cups cooked quinoa
- 1 cup pistachio
- 1 teaspoon garlic powder
- 1 cup cream cheese
- 1 egg, beaten

Directions:

1. Switch on and adjust air fryer to 390 °f.
2. Place all of the ingredients in a food processor and pulse for a few seconds or stir by hand.
3. Use hands to form burger patties.
4. Place in the air fryer and cook the burger patties for 25 – 30 minutes.
5. Serve with low carb or gluten free bread and salad.

Nutrition: Calories: 250 Fat: 3g Carbs: 43g Protein: 13g

776. **Sweet Apple Walnut Balls**

Preparation Time: 5 minutes
Cooking Time: 15 minutes
Servings: 1
Ingredients:

- 2 cups grated apples
- 1 cup walnut
- 1 cup date
- 1 tablespoon butter (substitute with coconut oil for a vegan version)
- 1 teaspoon cinnamon

Directions:

1. Preheat to 390 degrees F.
2. Place all of the ingredients in a food processor and pulse for a few seconds or stir by hand.
3. Use your hands to form balls.
4. Lay out balls in the air fryer and cook for 15 minutes.
5. Serve as a snack, sweet appetizer or with ice cream as a dessert.

Nutrition: Calories: 66 Fat: 5g Carbs: 5.6g Protein: 1.4g

777. **Almond Plum Balls**
Preparation Time: 5 minutes
Cooking Time: 15 minutes
Servings: 1
Ingredients:

- 2 cups chopped plums
- 1 cup almond
- 1 cup date
- 1 tablespoon butter (substitute with coconut oil for a vegan version)
- 1 teaspoon cinnamon
- 1 pinch nutmeg

Directions:

1. Adjust air fryer to 390 °f.
2. Place all of the ingredients in a food processor and pulse for a few seconds or stir by hand.
3. Use hands to form balls. Then, put and cook in air fryer for 15 minutes.
4. Serve as a snack, sweet appetizer or with ice cream as a dessert.

Nutrition: Calories: 195 Fat: 9g Carbs: 20g Protein: 8g

778. **Sunflower Seed Broccoli Cheese Balls**
Preparation Time: 10 minutes
Cooking Time: 15 minutes
Servings: 1
Ingredients:

- 2 cups broccoli
- 1 cup sunflower seed
- 1 cup mozzarella cheese (grated)
- 1 teaspoon garlic powder

Directions:

1. Get ready with your air fryer to 390 °f.
2. Place all of the ingredients in a food processor and pulse for a few seconds or stir by hand.
3. Use your hands to form balls.
4. Place in the fryer and cook for 15 minutes.

Nutrition: Calories: 216 Fat: 10g Carbs: 15gProtein: 16g

779. **Tofu Egg Rolls**
Preparation Time: 10 minutes
Cooking Time: 10 minutes
Servings: 4
Ingredients:

- 5 sheets of rice "paper" (egg roll sheets)
- 2 eggs, beaten
- 1 tablespoon onion powder
- 1 tablespoon garlic powder
- 1 ½ cups tofu cut into cube
- ½ cup cream cheese
- ½ cup shredded purple cabbage
- ½ cup pineapple
- ½ cup shredded carrots

Directions:

1. Preheat your fryer to 390 °f.
2. Mix the cheese, carrots, cabbage, tofu, pineapple and the onion and garlic powder.
3. Dip each rice "paper" in lukewarm water and remove quickly. Spread flat on a clean surface.
4. Distribute the tofu mix evenly among the rice sheets.
5. Wrap up and fold over the rice rolls. Dip in the egg mix.
6. Place on a greased, heat safe form and cook in the Air fryer for 10 minutes.

Nutrition: Calories: 130 Fat: 3g Carbs: 18g Protein: 7g

780. **Avocado Egg Rolls**
Preparation Time: 10 minutes
Cooking Time: 10 minutes
Servings: 4
Ingredients:

- 5 egg roll sheets
- 2 eggs, beaten
- Three large avocados
- ½ cup herbed cream cheese
- 1 cup cubed mango

Directions:

1. 1.Preheat your Air fryer to 300 °f.
2. 2.Mix the cheese, avocado and mango.
3. 3.Dip each roll sheet in lukewarm water and remove quickly. Spread flat on a clean surface.
4. 4.Distribute the mango avocado mix evenly among the rice sheets.
5. Wrap up and fold over the rice rolls.
6. Dip in the egg mix.
7. Place on a greased, heat safe form and cook in the Air fryer for 10 minutes.

Nutrition: Calories: 148 Fat: 8g Carbs: 17g Protein: 3g

781. **Mango Tofu**
Preparation Time: 30 minutes
Cooking Time: 10 minutes
Servings: 1
Ingredients:

- 1 package firm tofu with moisture squeezed out
- 2 cups mango chunks, processed in a food processor to a puree
- 1 tablespoon honey

Directions:

1. Set fryer to 390 °f.
2. Combine all of the ingredients except the tofu in a mixing bowl.
3. Add the tofu and leave to marinade overnight if possible.
4. Fry in the Air fryer for 10 minutes.

Nutrition: Calories: 360 Fat: 12g Carbs: 67g Protein: 19g

782. **Strawberry Cheesecake Rolls**
Preparation Time: 15 minutes
Cooking Time: 20 minutes
Servings: 12
Ingredients:

- 1/3 Cup Strawberries, Sliced Fresh
- 1 Tablespoon Strawberry Preserves
- 4 Ounces Cream Cheese
- 8 Ounce Can Crescent Rolls
- Cooking Oil

Directions:

1. Roll out dough into a large rectangle, cutting twelve rectangles from it. You'll need to make two cuts lengthwise and three cuts crosswise.
2. Put your cream cheese in a microwave safe bowl, and then microwave for fifteen minutes so that it softens.
3. In a medium bowl combine your strawberry preserves and cream cheese, mixing well.
4. Scoop two teaspoons of this mixture onto each piece and spread it out. Just make sure you don't go to the edges of the dough. Add fresh strawberries to each.
5. Roll each rectangle up to create a roll, and then spray your air fryer basket down with cooking oil.
   Put your rolls in the basket, but do not stack them. If you do, they'll cook together, so it's better to cook them in batches.
6. Cook for eight minutes and allow them to cool for two to three minutes before removing them from your air fryer basket.
7. Repeat until all of your remaining rolls are cooked and allow them to cool before serving.

Nutrition: Calories: 98 Protein: 3g Fat: 5 g Carbs: 12 g

783. **Berry Mix**
Preparation Time: 6 minutes
Cooking Time: 6 minutes
Servings: 4
Ingredients:

- 2 Tablespoons Lemon Juice, Fresh
- 1 ½ Tablespoons Champagne Vinegar
- 1 ½ Tablespoons Maple Syrup
- 1 lb. Strawberries, Halved
- 1 Tablespoon Olive Oil
- 1 ½ Cups Blueberries, Fresh
- ¼ Cup Basil Leaves, Fresh & Torn

Directions:

1. Start by getting a pan that fits into your air fryer and mix all ingredients together until well combined.
2. Heat your air fryer to 310 °f and cook for 6 minutes.
3. Sprinkle with basil before serving either warm or chilled.

Nutrition: Calories: 163 Protein: 2.1 g Fat: 4 g Carbs: 10 g

784. **Blueberry Scones**
Preparation Time: 10 minutes
Cooking Time: 10 minutes
Servings: 10
Ingredients:
- 2 Teaspoon Vanilla Extract, Pure
- 2 Teaspoon Baking Powder
- 5 Tablespoons Sugar
- ½ Cup Butter
- ½ Cup Heavy Cream
- 2 Eggs
- 1 Cup White Flour
- 1 Cup Blueberries

Directions:
1. Start by mixing your baking soda, salt, flour, and blueberries. Stir well.
2. Get a bowl and mix your heavy cream, vanilla extract, butter, eggs and sugar.
3. Stir well, and then combine both measures together to form a dough.
4. Shape ten triangles from this mixture, and then preheat your air fryer to 320°f.
5. Cook for ten minutes and serve chilled.

Nutrition: Calories: 260 Fat: 11g Carbs: 37g Protein: 3g

785. **Easy Macaroons**
Preparation Time: 10 minutes
Cooking Time: 8 minutes
Servings: 20
Ingredients:
- 2 Tablespoons Sugar
- 1 Teaspoon Vanilla Extract, Pure
- 2 Cups Coconut, Shredded
- 4 Egg Whites

Directions:
1. Get out a bowl and mix your sugar and egg whites together using a mixer, and then add in your vanilla extract and coconut.
2. Shape into small balls, and then cook for 8 minutes in your air fryer at 340°f.
3. Allow to cool before serving.

Nutrition: Calories: 55 Protein: 1g Fat: 6g Carbs: 2g

786. **Black Tea Cake**
Preparation Time: 15 minutes
Cooking Time: 30 minutes
Servings: 12
Ingredients:
- 4 Eggs
- 2 Cups Sugar
- ½ Cup Butter
- 6 Tablespoons Black Tea Powder
- 2 Cups Whole Milk
- ½ Cup Olive Oil
- 2 Teaspoons Vanilla Extract, Pure
- 3 ½ Cups Flour
- 1 Teaspoon Baking Soda
- 3 Teaspoons Baking Powder

Cream:
- 6 Tablespoons Honey
- 1 Cup Butter, Softened
- 4 Cups Sugar

Directions:
1. Begin by putting the milk in a pot, heating it over medium heat. Add in your tea and stir well. Take it off heat, allowing it to cool down.
2. Get out a bowl and mix a half a cup of butter with two cups of sugar, vegetable oil, eggs, vanilla extract, baking soda, baking powder, and your flour. Mix well.
3. Proud this mixture into two round pans that have been greased.
4. Cook in your air fryer at 330°f for 25 minutes.
5. In a bowl mix your honey, four cups of sugar and a cup of butter. Stir until it's well combined.
6. Spread your cream all over the top of the cake once its cooled and cool it down before serving.

Nutrition: Calories: 200 Protein: 2g Fat: 4gCarbs: 6g

787. **Lentil Cookies**
Preparation Time: 15 minutes
Cooking Time: 15 minutes
Servings: 36
Ingredients:
- 1 Cup Water
- 1 Cup Whole Wheat Flour
- 1 Cup Lentils, Canned, Drained & Mashed
- 1 Cup White Flour
- 1 Teaspoon Cinnamon Powder
- 1 Teaspoon Baking Powder
- 1 Cup Butter, Softened
- ½ Teaspoon Nutmeg, Ground
- ½ Cup Brown Sugar
- 1 Cup Rolled Oats
- ½ Cup White Sugar
- 1 Egg
- 2 teaspoons Almond Extract
- 1 Cup Raisins
- 1 Cup Coconut, Unsweetened & Shredded

Directions:
1. Get out a bowl and mix your white and whole wheat flour with your baking powder, salt, cinnamon and nutmeg. Stir until well combined.
2. In another bowl mix your white sugar, brown sugar and butter, mixing for two minutes using a kitchen mixer.
3. Add in your lentils, almond extract, egg, flour mix, oats, raisins, and coconut. Stir until everything is well combined.
4. Scoop dough onto a baking sheet that fits in air fryer. You'll need to cook in batches.
5. Cook at 350°f for 15 minutes and serve once cooled.

Nutrition: Calories: 154 Protein: 7g Fat: 2gCarbs: 4g

788. **Date & Lentil Brownies**
Preparation Time: 10 minutes
Cooking Time: 20 minutes
Servings: 8
Ingredients:
- 28 Ounces Lentils, Canned, Rinsed & Drained
- 12 Dates
- 1 Tablespoon Honey, Raw
- 1 Banana, Peeled & Chopped
- ½ Teaspoon Baking Soda
- 4 Tablespoons Almond Butter
- 2 Tablespoons Cocoa Powder

Directions:
1. Start by mixing your butter, banana, cocoa, baking soda, honey and lentils in a food processor.
2. Blend well before adding in your dates and pulsing a few more times.
3. Pour this into a greased pan that will fit into your air fryer.
4. Make sure that it's spread evenly, and then cook at 360°f for fifteen minutes.
5. Allow them to cool before slicing to serve.

Nutrition: Calories: 162 Protein: 4g Fat: 4g Carbs: 3g

789. **Dark Chocolate & Oatmeal Cookies**
Preparation Time: 15 minutes
Cooking Time: 10 minutes
Servings: 30
Ingredients:
- 3 Tablespoons Butter, Unsalted
- 1 Cup Oatmeal, Quick Cooking
- 2 Ounces Dark Chocolate, Chopped
- 2 Egg Whites
- ½ Cup Brown Sugar, Packed
- 1 Teaspoon Vanilla Extract, Pure
- ½ Cup Pastry Flour, Whole Wheat
- ¼ Cup Cranberries, Dried
- ½ Teaspoon Baking Soda

Directions:

1. Start by getting out a metal medium bowl and mix together your dark chocolate and butter. Bake for one to three minutes in your air fryer. Your chocolate should melt, and then stir the mixture smooth.
2. Add in your brown sugar, vanilla and egg whites, beating until smooth.
3. Add in your oatmeal, baking soda and pastry flour. Stir in your cranberries and make a dough.
4. Form thirty-one-inch balls and cook in batches of eight in your air fryer for seven to ten minutes.
5. Allow them to cool before serving.

Nutrition: Calories: 55 Protein: 1g Fat: 2g Carbs: 8g

790. Maple Cupcakes
Preparation Time: 15 minutes
Cooking Time: 20 minutes
Servings: 4
Ingredients:
- 4 Teaspoons Maple Syrup
- ½ Apple, Cored & Chopped
- ¾ Cup White Flour
- ½ Teaspoon Baking Powder
- 1 Teaspoon Vanilla Extract, Pure
- 4 Tablespoons Butter
- ½ Cup Applesauce
- 4 Eggs
- 2 Teaspoons Cinnamon, Ground

Directions:
1. Start by heating up a pan with butter, placing it over medium heat. Add in your maple syrup, applesauce, vanilla and eggs.
2. Stir well and then take off heat. Allow the mixture to cool down, and then add in your baking powder, apples, cinnamon and flour.
3. Whisk well, and then pour into a cupcake pan that fits in your air fryer. You may have to do this n batches.
4. Heat your air fryer to 350°f and cook for twenty minutes. Allow your cupcakes to cool before serving.

Nutrition: Calories: 150 Protein: 4g Fat: 3g Carbs: 5g

791. Ricotta Lemon Cake
Preparation Time: 15 minutes
Cooking Time: 30 minutes
Servings: 4
Ingredients:
- 8 Eggs, Whisked
- 1/2 lb. Sugar
- 3 lbs. Ricotta Cheese
- 1 Lemon, Zested
- 1 Orange, Zested
- Butter for Greasing

Directions:
1. Start by getting out a bowl and mix your sugar, cheese, eggs, orange zest and lemon zest together. Stir well, and then grease a baking pan that fits in your air fryer.
2. Spread the batter in it, and then cook at 390°f for thirty minutes. Reduce your heat to 380°f and cook for an additional forty minutes.
3. Allow to cool down before serving.

Nutrition: Calories: 110 Protein: 4g Fat: 3g Carbs: 3g

792. Cinnamon Pineapple
Preparation Time: 10 minutes
Cooking Time: 20 minutes
Servings: 2
Ingredients:
- 4 Pineapple Slices
- 2 Tablespoons Sugar
- 1 Teaspoon Cinnamon

Directions:
1. Start by adding your sugar and cinnamon into a zipper top bag and shake well. Add in your pineapple slices, shaking until they're well coated.
2. Allow it to marinate in the fridge for twenty minutes, and then preheat your air fryer for five minutes.
3. Place your pineapple pieces in the air fryer once it's heated to 360, and then grill for ten minutes. Flip and grill for an additional ten minutes.

Nutrition: Calories: 276 Protein: 4.6g Fat: 5.3g Carbs: 4.2g

793. Blueberry Pudding
Preparation Time: 15 minutes
Cooking Time: 35 minutes
Servings: 6
Ingredients:
- 3 Tablespoons Maple syrup
- 2 Tablespoons Rosemary, Fresh & Chopped
- 2 Cups Flour
- 2 Cups Rolled Oats
- 8 Cups Blueberries, fresh
- 1 Stick Butter, Melted
- 1 Cup Walnuts, Chopped

Directions:
1. Start by spreading your blueberries in a greased pan that fits in your air fryer.
2. Get out a food processor and mix your flour, walnuts, butter, oats, maple syrup and rosemary. Blend well, and then place this over your blueberries.
3. Cook at 350°f for twenty-five minutes. Allow it to cool before slicing to serve.

Nutrition: Calories: 150 Protein: 4g Fat: 3g Carbs: 7g

794. Green Sandwich
Preparation Time: 15 minutes
Cooking Time: 10 to 13 minutes
Servings 4
Ingredients:
- 1½ cups chopped mixed greens
- 2 garlic cloves, thinly sliced
- 2 teaspoons olive oil
- 2 slices low sodium Swiss cheese
- 4 slices low sodium whole wheat bread
- Cooking spray

Directions:
1. In a nonstick round baking pan, mix the greens, garlic, and olive oil.
2. Detach the rotating blade of the air fryer and slide the baking pan into the air fryer. Cook at the corresponding preset mode or Air Fry at 400°f (204° C) for 4 to 5 minutes. Stirring once, until the vegetables are tender. Drain, if necessary.
3. Make 2 sandwiches, dividing half of the greens and 1 slice of Swiss cheese between 2 slices of bread. Lightly spray the outsides of the sandwiches with cooking spray.
4. Cook at the corresponding preset mode or bake the sandwiches in the air fryer for 6 to 8 minutes, turning with tongs halfway through, until the bread is toasted and the cheese melts.
5. Cut each sandwich in half and serve.

Nutrition: Calories: 245 Fat: 2g Carbs: 28g Protein: 8g

795. Eggplant Sandwich
Preparation Time: 10 minutes
Cooking Time: 9 to 12 minutes
Servings 4
Ingredients:
- 1 baby eggplant, peeled and chopped
- 1 red bell pepper, sliced
- ½ cup diced red onion
- ½ cup shredded carrot
- 1 teaspoon olive oil
- 1/3 cup Greek yogurt
- ½ teaspoon dried tarragon
- 2 lows odium whole wheat pita breads, halved crosswise

Directions:
1. Stir together the eggplant, red bell pepper, red onion, carrot, and olive oil in the air fryer basket. Cook at the corresponding preset mode or Air Fry at 390°F (199°C) for 7 to 9 minutes or until the vegetables are tender. Drain if necessary.
2. In a small bowl, carefully mix the yogurt and tarragon until well combined.
3. Stir the yogurt mixture into the vegetables. Stuff one fourth of this mixture into each pita pocket.
4. Detach the rotating blade of the air fryer basket and place the sandwiches in. Cook at the corresponding preset mode or bake

for 2 to 3 minutes, or until the bread is toasted. Flip the sandwiches halfway through.

5. Serve immediately.

Nutrition: Calories: 423 Fat: 18g Carbs: 42g Protein: 22g

796.　Bacon Sandwich

Preparation Time: 10 minutes
Cooking Time: 6 minutes
Servings 4
Ingredients:

- 1/3 cup spicy barbecue sauce
- 2 tablespoons honey
- 8 slices cooked bacon, cut into thirds
- 1 red bell pepper, sliced
- 1 yellow bell pepper, sliced
- 3 pita pockets, cut in half
- 1¼ cups torn butter lettuce leaves
- 2 tomatoes, sliced

Directions:

1. In a small bowl, put the barbecue sauce and the honey. Brush this mixture lightly onto the bacon slices and the red and yellow pepper slices.
2. Put the peppers into the air fryer basket. Cook at the corresponding preset mode or Air Fry at 350° F (177° C) for 4 minutes.
3. Add the bacon, and Air Fry for 2 more minutes or until the bacon is browned and the peppers are tender.
4. Fill the pita with the bacon, peppers, any remaining barbecue sauce, lettuce, and tomatoes, and serve immediately.

Nutrition: Calories: 450 Fat: 29g Carbs: 26g Protein: 20g

797.　Tuna Sandwich

Preparation Time: 8 minutes
Cooking Time: 4 to 8 minutes
Servings 4
Ingredients:

- 1 can chunk light tuna, drained
- ¼ cup mayonnaise
- 2 tablespoons mustard
- 1 tablespoon lemon juice
- 2 green onions, minced
- 4 slices of whole or wheat bread
- 3 tablespoons softened butter
- 6 thin slices cheese

Directions:

1. Put together the tuna, mayonnaise, mustard, lemon juice, and green onions. Set aside.
2. Arrange the bread, butter side up, in the air fryer.
3. Cook at 390° F (199° C) for 2 to 4 minutes, or until golden brown.
4. Put one slice of cheese on top of each bread and return to the air fryer. Cook until the cheese melts and starts to brown.
5. Take out from the air fryer, top with the tuna mixture, and serve.

Nutrition: Calories: 240 Fat: 5g Carbs: 27g Protein: 25g

798.　Shrimp Sandwich

Preparation Time: 10 minutes
Cooking Time: 5 to 7 minutes
Servings 4
Ingredients:

- 1¼ cups shredded Colby, Cheddar, or Havarti cheese
- 1 (6ounce / 170g) can tiny shrimp, drained
- 3 tablespoons mayonnaise
- 2 tablespoons minced green onion
- 4 slices whole grain or wheat bread
- 2 tablespoons softened butter

Directions:

1. Mix well the cheese, shrimp, mayonnaise, and green onion in a bowl.
2. Put mixture on two of the slices of bread. Top with the other slices of bread to make two sandwiches. Spread the sandwiches lightly with butter.
3. Detach the rotating blade of the air fryer basket. Arrange the sandwiches in the basket.

4. Cook at the corresponding preset mode or Air Fry at 400°F (204°C) for 5 to 7 minutes, or until the bread is browned and crisp and the cheese is melted. Flip the sandwiches halfway through with tongs.
5. Cut in half and serve warm.

Nutrition: Calories: 401 Fat: 19g Carbs: 35g Protein: 19g

799.　Chicken Sandwich

Preparation Time: 10 minutes
Cooking Time: 9 to 11 minutes
Servings 4
Ingredients:

- 2 boneless, skinless chicken breasts, cut into 1inch cubes
- 1 small red onion, sliced
- 1 red bell pepper, sliced
- 1/3 cup Italian salad dressing, divided
- ½ teaspoon dried thyme
- 4 pita pockets, split
- 2 cups torn butter lettuce
- 1 cup chopped cherry tomatoes

Directions:

1. Place the chicken, onion, and bell pepper in the air fryer basket. Drizzle with 1 tablespoon of the Italian salad dressing, add the thyme, and toss.
2. Cook at the corresponding preset mode or Air Fry at 380°F (193°C) for 9 to 11 minutes, or until the chicken is 165°F (74°C) on a food thermometer.
3. Move the chicken and vegetables to a bowl. Toss with the remaining salad dressing.
4. Complete sandwiches with pita pockets, butter lettuce, and cherry tomatoes. Serve immediately.

Nutrition: Calories: 495 Fat: 14g Carbs: 58g Protein: 31g

800.　Sloppy Joes

Preparation Time: 10 minutes
Cooking Time: 17 minutes
Servings: 4 large sandwiches
Ingredients:

- 1 pound (454 g) very lean ground beef
- 1 teaspoon onion powder
- 1/3 cup ketchup
- ¼ cup water
- ½ teaspoon celery seed
- 1 tablespoon lemon juice
- 1½ teaspoons brown sugar
- 1¼ teaspoons lows odium Worcestershire sauce
- ½ teaspoon salt (optional)
- ½ teaspoon vinegar
- 1/8 teaspoon dry mustard
- Hamburger or slider buns, for serving
- Cooking spray

Directions:

1. Break the raw ground beef into small chunks and pile into the basket with cooking spray.
2. Cook at the corresponding preset mode or Air Fry at 390°F (199°C) for 10 minutes or until meat is well browned.
3. Remove the meat from the air fryer, drain, and use a knife and fork to crumble into small pieces.
4. Give the air fryer basket a quick rinse to remove any bits of meat. Detach the rotating blade.
5. Place all the remaining ingredients, except for the buns, in a nonstick round baking pan and mix together. Add the meat and stir well.
6. Arrange the pan in the air fryer. Cook at the corresponding preset mode or Bake at 330°F (166°C) for 5 minutes. Stir and bake for 2 more minutes.
7. Scoop onto buns. Serve hot.

Nutrition: Calories: 380 Fat: 29g Carbs: 5g Protein: 21g

801.　Avocado and Cabbage Tacos

Preparation Time: 15 minutes
Cooking Time: 6 minutes
Servings 4
Ingredients:

- ¼ cup all-purpose flour

- ¼ teaspoon salt, plus more as needed
- ¼ teaspoon ground black pepper
- 2 large egg whites
- 1¼ cups panko breadcrumbs
- 2 tablespoons olive oil
- 2 avocados, peeled and halved, cut into ½inchthick slices
- ½ small red cabbage, thinly sliced
- 1 deseeded jalapeño, thinly sliced
- 2 green onions, thinly sliced
- ½ cup cilantro leaves
- ¼ cup mayonnaise
- Juice and zest of 1 lime
- 4 corn tortillas, warmed
- ½ cup sour cream
- Cooking spray

Directions:
1. Pour the flour in a large bowl and sprinkle with salt and black pepper, then stir to mix well.
2. Whisk the egg whites in a separate bowl. Combine the panko with olive oil on a shallow dish.
3. Dredge the avocado slices in the bowl of flour, then into the egg to coat. Shake the excess off, then roll the slices over the panko.
4. Arrange the avocado slices in the basket and spritz the cooking spray.
5. Cook at the corresponding preset mode or Air Fry at 400°F (204°C) for 6 minutes or until tender and lightly browned.
6. Combine the cabbage, jalapeño, onions, cilantro leaves, mayo, lime juice and zest, and a touch of salt in a separate large bowl. Toss to mix well.
7. Unfold the tortillas on a clean work surface, then spread with cabbage slaw and air fried avocados. Top with sour cream and serve.

Nutrition: Calories: 279 Fat: 416g Carbs: 32g Protein: 5g

802. Mango Salsa Cod Tacos
Preparation Time: 15 minutes
Cooking Time: 17 minutes
Servings: 6
Ingredients:
- 1 egg
- 5 ounces (142 gr) Mexican beer
- ¾ cup all-purpose flour
- ¾ cup cornstarch
- ¼ teaspoon chili powder
- ½ teaspoon ground cumin
- ½ pound (227 gr) cod, cut into large pieces
- 6 corn tortillas
- Cooking spray

For the Salsa:
- 1 mango, peeled and diced

- ¼ red bell pepper, diced
- ½ small jalapeño, diced
- ¼ red onion, minced
- Juice of half a lime
- Pinch chopped fresh cilantro
- ¼ teaspoon salt
- ¼ teaspoon ground black pepper

1. Whisk the egg with beer in a bowl. Combine the flour, cornstarch, chili powder, and cumin in a separate bowl.
2. Dredge the cod in the egg mixture first, then in the flour mixture to coat well. Shake the excess off.
3. Detach the rotating blade and arrange the cod in the air fryer and spritz with cooking spray.
4. Cook at the corresponding preset mode or Air Fry at 380°F (193°C) for 17 minutes or until golden brown and crunchy. Flip the cod halfway through.
5. Combine salsa ingredients in a small bowl. Stir to mix well.
6. Unfold the tortillas on a clean work surface, then divide the fish on the tortillas and spread the salsa on top. Fold to serve.

Nutrition: Calories: 61 Fat: 0.3g Carbs: 15g Protein: 1.1g

803. Golden Cod Tacos
Preparation Time: 5 minutes
Cooking Time: 15 minutes
Servings 4
Ingredients:
- 2 eggs
- 1¼ cups Mexican beer
- 1½ cups coconut flour
- 1½ cups almond flour
- ½ tablespoon chili powder
- 1 tablespoon cumin
- Salt, to taste
- 1-pound (454 g) cod fillet, slice into large pieces
- 4 toasted corn tortillas
- 4 large lettuce leaves, chopped
- ¼ cup salsa
- Cooking spray

Directions:
1. Break the eggs in a bowl, then pour in the beer. Whisk to combine well.
2. Combine the coconut flour, almond flour, chili powder, cumin, and salt in a separate bowl. Stir to mix well.
3. Dunk the cod pieces in the egg mixture, then shake the excess off and dredge into the flour mixture to coat well.
4. Arrange the cod in the air fryer. Cook at the corresponding preset mode or Air Fry at 375°F (191°C) for 15 minutes or until golden brown.
5. Unwrap the toasted tortillas on a large plate, then divide the cod and lettuce leaves on top. Baste with salsa and wrap to serve.

Nutrition: Calories: 488 Fat: 22g Carbs: 42g Protein: 33g

APPETIZER RECIPES

804. Salty lemon artichokes
Preparation time: 15 minutes
Cooking time: 45 minutes
Servings: 2
Ingredients:
- 1 lemon
- 2 artichokes
- 1 teaspoon kosher salt
- 1 garlic head
- 2 teaspoons olive oil

Directions:
1. Cut off the edges of the artichokes.
2. Cut the lemon into the halves.
3. Peel the garlic head and chop the garlic cloves roughly.
4. Then place the chopped garlic in the artichokes.
5. Sprinkle the artichokes with the olive oil and kosher salt.
6. Then squeeze the lemon juice into the artichokes.
7. Wrap the artichokes in the foil.

8. Preheat the air fryer to 330° f.
9. Place the wrapped artichokes in the air fryer and cook it for 45 minutes
10. 1 when the artichokes are cooked – discard the foil and serve.
11. 1 enjoy!

Nutrition: calories 133 fat 5 fiber 7, carbs 27, protein 6

805. Maple carrot fries
Preparation time: 10 minutes
Cooking time: 12 minutes
Servings: 6
Ingredients:
- 1 lb. Carrot, peeled and cut into sticks
- 1 teaspoon maple syrup
- 1 teaspoon olive oil
- ½ teaspoon ground cinnamon
- Salt, to taste

Directions:
1. In a bowl, add all the ingredients and mix well.

2. Press "power button" of air fry oven and turn the dial to select the "air fry" mode.
3. Press the time button and again turn the dial to set the cooking time to 12 minutes
4. Now push the temp button and rotate the dial to set the temperature at 400° f.
5. Press "start/pause" button to start.
6. When the unit beeps to show that it is preheated, open the lid.
7. Arrange the carrot fries in "air fry basket" and insert in the oven.
8. Serve warm.

Nutrition: calories 41 total fat 8 g saturated fat 1 g cholesterol 0 mg sodium 79 mg carbs 3 g fiber 2 g sugar 4 g protein 6 g

806. Sugary carrot strips

Preparation time: 10 minutes
Cooking time: 10 minutes
Servings: 2
Ingredients:

- 2 carrots
- 1 teaspoon brown sugar
- 1 teaspoon olive oil
- 1 tablespoon soy sauce
- 1 teaspoon honey
- ½ teaspoon ground black pepper

Directions:
1. Peel the carrot and cut it into the strips.
2. Then put the carrot strips in the bowl.
3. Sprinkle the carrot strips with the olive oil, soy sauce, honey, and ground black pepper.
4. Shake the mixture gently.
5. Preheat the air fryer to 360° f.
6. Cook the carrot for 10 minutes
7. After this, shake the carrot strips well.
8. Enjoy!

Nutrition: calories 67, fat 4 fiber 7, carbs 13 protein 1

807. Onion green beans

Preparation time: 10 minutes
Cooking time: 12 minutes
Servings: 2
Ingredients:

- 11 oz. Green beans
- 1 tablespoon onion powder
- 1 tablespoon olive oil
- ½ teaspoon salt
- ¼ teaspoon chili flakes

Directions:
1. Wash the green beans carefully and place them in the bowl.
2. Sprinkle the green beans with the onion powder, salt, chili flakes, and olive oil.
3. Shake the green beans carefully.
4. Preheat the air fryer to 400° f.
5. Put the green beans in the air fryer and cook it for 8 minutes
6. After this, shake the green beans and cook them for 4 minutes more at 400° f.
7. When the time is over – shake the green beans.
8. Serve the side dish and enjoy!

Nutrition: calories 1205 fat 2, fiber 5 carbs 19 protein 2

808. Mozzarella radish salad

Preparation time: 10 minutes
Cooking time: 20 minutes
Servings: 2
Ingredients:

- 8 oz. Radish
- 4 oz. Mozzarella
- 1 teaspoon balsamic vinegar
- ½ teaspoon salt
- 1 tablespoon olive oil
- 1 teaspoon dried oregano

Directions:
1. Wash the radish carefully and cut it into the halves.
2. Preheat the air fryer to 360° f.
3. Put the radish halves in the air fryer basket.
4. Sprinkle the radish with the salt and olive oil.
5. Cook the radish for 20 minutes

6. Shake the radish after 10 minutes of cooking.
7. When the time is over – transfer the radish to the serving plate.
8. Chop mozzarella roughly.
9. Sprinkle the radish with mozzarella, balsamic vinegar, and dried oregano.
10. 1 stir it gently with the help of 2 forks.
11. 1 serve it immediately.

Nutrition: calories 241 fat 12, fiber 1 carbs 4 protein 19

809. Cremini mushroom satay

Preparation time: 10 minutes
Cooking time: 6 minutes
Servings: 2
Ingredients:

- 7 oz. Cremini mushrooms
- 2 tablespoon coconut milk
- 1 tablespoon butter
- 1 teaspoon chili flake
- ½ teaspoon balsamic vinegar
- ½ teaspoon curry powder
- ½ teaspoon white pepper

Directions:
1. Wash the mushrooms carefully.
2. Then sprinkle the mushrooms with the chili flakes, curry powder, and white pepper.
3. Preheat the air fryer to 400° f.
4. Toss the butter in the air fryer basket and melt it.
5. Put the mushrooms in the air fryer and cook it for 2 minutes
6. Shake the mushrooms well and sprinkle with the coconut milk and balsamic vinegar.
7. Cook the mushrooms for 4 minutes more at 400° f.
8. Then skewer the mushrooms on the wooden sticks and serve.
9. Enjoy!

Nutrition: calories 116 fat 5 fiber 3 carbs 6 protein 3

810. Eggplant ratatouille

Preparation time: 15 minutes
Cooking time: 15 minutes
Servings: 2
Ingredients:

- 1 eggplant
- 1 sweet yellow pepper
- 3 cherry tomatoes
- 1/3 white onion, chopped
- ½ teaspoon garlic clove, sliced
- 1 teaspoon olive oil
- ½ teaspoon ground black pepper
- ½ teaspoon Italian seasoning

Directions:
1. Preheat the air fryer to 360° f.
2. Peel the eggplants and chop them.
3. Put the chopped eggplants in the air fryer basket.
4. Chop the cherry tomatoes and add them to the air fryer basket.
5. Then add chopped onion, sliced garlic clove, olive oil, ground black pepper, and Italian seasoning.
6. Chop the sweet yellow pepper roughly and add it to the air fryer basket.
7. Shake the vegetables gently and cook it for 15 minutes
8. Stir the meal after 8 minutes of cooking.
9. Transfer the cooked ratatouille in the serving plates.
10. Enjoy!

Nutrition: calories 149 fat 7,fiber 17, carbs 29 protein 1

811. Quinoa pilaf

Preparation time: 2 minutes
Cooking time: 10 minutes
Servings: 4
Ingredients:

- 2 cups quinoa
- 2 garlic cloves; minced.
- 3 cups water
- 2 tsp. Turmeric
- 1 handful parsley; chopped.
- 2 tsp. Cumin, ground.
- 2 tbsp extra virgin olive oil

- Salt to the taste

Directions:
1. Set your instant pot on sauté mode; add oil and heat it up.
2. Add garlic, stir and cook it for 30 seconds.
3. Add water, quinoa, cumin, turmeric and salt; then stir well. Close the lid and cook at high for 1 minute
4. Release the pressure naturally for 10 minutes, then release remaining pressure by turning the valve to 'venting', fluff quinoa with a fork, transfer to plates, season it with more salt if needed, sprinkle parsley on top and serve as a side dish.

Nutrition: calories 110 protein 13g carbs 15g fat 5g

812. Mashed squash
Preparation time: 10 minutes
Cooking time: 20 minutes
Servings: 4

Ingredients:
- 2 acorn squash, cut into halves and seeded
- 1/4 tsp. Baking soda
- 2 tbsp butter
- 1/2 cup water
- 1/2 tsp. Nutmeg grated
- 2 tbsp brown sugar
- Salt and black pepper to the taste

Directions:
1. Sprinkle squash halves with salt, pepper and baking soda and place them in the steamer basket of your instant pot
2. Add 1/2 cup water to the pot, close the lid and cook at high for 20 minutes
3. Quickly release the pressure, take squash and leave aside on a plate to cool down
4. Scrape flesh from the squash and put in a bowl.
5. Add salt, pepper to the taste, butter, sugar and nutmeg and mash everything with a potato mashes. Stir well and serve.

Nutrition: calories 250 protein 14g carbs 12g fat 10g

813. Apple and butternut mash
Preparation time: 17 minutes
Cooking time: 8 minutes
Servings: 4

Ingredients:
- 1 butternut squash, peeled and cut into medium chunks
- 1/2 tsp. Apple pie spice
- 2 tbsp brown butter
- 2 apples, sliced
- 1 cup water
- 1 yellow onion, thinly sliced
- Salt to the taste

Directions:
1. Put squash, onion and apple pieces in the steamer basket of your instant pot, put the water in the pot, close the lid and cook at high for 8 minutes
2. Quickly release the pressure and transfer squash, onion and apple pieces to a bowl.
3. Mash using a potato masher, add salt, apple pie spice and brown butter, stir well and serve warm

Nutrition: calories 321 protein 33g carbs 28g fat 10g

814. Sweet carrot puree
Preparation time: 6 minutes
Cooking time: 4 minutes
Servings: 4

Ingredients:
- 1 ½ lb. Carrots; peeled and chopped.
- 1 tsp. Brown sugar
- 1 tbsp soft butter
- 1 tbsp honey
- 1 cup water
- Salt to the taste

Directions:
1. Put carrots in your instant pot, add the water, close the lid and cook at high for 4 minutes
2. Release the pressure naturally, drain carrots and place them in a bowl.
3. Mash them using a hand blender, add butter salt and honey
4. Blend again well, add sugar on top and serve right away

Nutrition: calories 421 protein 43g carbs 30g fat 15g

815. Israeli couscous dish
Preparation time: 10 minutes
Cooking time: 5 minutes
Servings: 10

Ingredients:
- 16 oz. Harvest grains blend
- 2 ½ cups chicken stock
- 2 tbsp butter
- Parsley leaves; chopped for serving
- Salt and black pepper to the taste

Directions:
1. Set your instant pot on sauté mode; add butter and melt it.
2. Add grains and stock and stir
3. Close the instant pot lid and cook at high for 5 minutes
4. Quickly release the pressure, fluff couscous with a fork, season it with salt and pepper to the taste, divide among plates, sprinkle parsley on top and serve.

Nutrition: calories 390 protein 32g carbs 24g fat 14g

816. Mashed turnips dish
Preparation time: 10 minutes
Cooking time: 5 minutes
Servings: 4

Ingredients:
- 4 turnips; peeled and chopped.
- 1 yellow onion; chopped.
- 1/4 cup sour cream
- 1/2 cup chicken stock
- Salt and black pepper to the taste

Directions:
1. In your instant pot, mix turnips with stock and onion
2. Stir, close the lid and cook at high for 5 minutes
3. Release the pressure naturally, drain turnips and transfer them to a bowl.
4. Puree them using your mixer and add salt, pepper to the taste and sour cream
5. Blend again and serve right away.

Nutrition: calories 260 protein 40g carbs 31g fat 16g

817. Onions & parsnips
Preparation time: 12 minutes
Cooking time: 28 minutes
Servings: 4

Ingredients:
- 1 yellow onion thinly sliced.
- 1 ½ cups beef stock
- 2 ½ lb. Parsnips; chopped.
- 1 thyme spring
- 4 tbsp pastured lard
- Salt and black pepper to the taste

Directions:
1. Set your instant pot on sauté mode; add 3 tablespoon lard and heat it up
2. Add parsnips, stir and cook it for 15 minutes
3. Add stock and thyme; then stir well. Close the lid and cook at high for 3 minutes
4. Quickly release the pressure, transfer the parsnips mix to your blender, add salt and pepper to the taste and pulse very well. Set the pot on sauté mode again, add the rest of the lard and heat it up.
5. Add onion, stir and cook it for 10 minutes
6. Transfer blended parsnips to plates, top with sautéed onions and serve.

Nutrition: calories 142 protein 253g carbs 13g fat 12g

818. Roasted cashews
Preparation time: 5 minutes
Cooking time: 5 minutes
Servings: 6

Ingredients:
- 1½ cups raw cashew nuts
- 1 teaspoon butter, melted
- Salt and freshly ground black pepper, as needed

Directions:
1. In a bowl, mix together all the ingredients.

2. Press "power button" of air fry oven and turn the dial to select the "air fry" mode.
3. Press the time button and again turn the dial to set the cooking time to 5 minutes
4. Now push the temp button and rotate the dial to set the temperature at 355 ° f.
5. Press "start/pause" button to start.
6. When the unit beeps to show that it is preheated, open the lid.
7. Arrange the cashews in "air fry basket" and insert in the oven.
8. Shake the cashews once halfway through.

Nutrition: calories 202 total fat 15 g saturated fat 5 g cholesterol 2 mg sodium 37 mg carbs 12 g fiber 1 g sugar 7 g protein 3 g

819. Steamed pot stickers
Preparation time: 20 minutes
Cooking time: 10 minutes
Servings: 30 pot stickers
Ingredients:
- ½ cup finely chopped cabbage
- ¼ cup finely chopped red bell pepper
- 2 green onions, finely chopped
- 1 egg, beaten
- 2 tablespoons cocktail sauce
- 2 teaspoons low-sodium soy sauce
- 30 wonton wrappers
- 3 tablespoons water, plus more for brushing the wrappers

Directions:
1. in a small bowl, combine the cabbage, pepper, green onions, egg, cocktail sauce, and soy sauce, and mix well.
2. put about 1 teaspoon of the mixture in the center of each wonton wrapper. Fold the wrapper in half, covering the filling; dampen the edges with water, and seal. You can crimp the edges of the wrapper with your fingers, so they look like the pot stickers you get in restaurants. Brush them with water.
3. put 3 tablespoons water in the pan under the air fryer basket. Cook the pot stickers in 2 batches for 9 to 10 minutes or until the pot stickers are hot and the bottoms are lightly browned.

Nutrition (3 pot stickers: calories: 291; total fat: 2g; saturated fat: 0g; cholesterol: 35mg; sodium: 649mg; carbohydrates: 57g; fiber: 3g; protein: 10g

820. Spinach dip with bread knots
Preparation time: 12 minutes
cooking time: 16 to 21 minutes
servings: 6
Ingredients:
- Nonstick cooking spray
- 1 (8-ouncepackage cream cheese, cut into cubes
- ¼ cup sour cream
- ½ cup frozen chopped spinach, thawed and drained
- ½ cup grated swiss cheese
- 2 green onions, chopped
- ½ (11-ouncecan refrigerated breadstick dough
- 2 tablespoons melted butter
- 3 tablespoons grated parmesan cheese

Directions:
1. spray a 6-by-6-by-2-inch pan with nonstick cooking spray.
2. in a medium bowl, combine the cream cheese, sour cream, spinach, swiss cheese, and green onions, and mix well. Spread into the prepared pan and bake for 8 minutes or until hot.
3. while the dip is baking, unroll six of the breadsticks and cut them in half crosswise to make 12 pieces.
4. gently stretch each piece of dough and tie into a loose knot; tuck in the ends.
5. when the dip is hot, remove from the air fryer and carefully place each bread knot on top of the dip, covering the surface of the dip. Brush each knot with melted butter and sprinkle parmesan cheese on top.
6. bake for 8 to 13 minutes or until the bread knots are golden brown and cooked through.

Nutrition: calories: 264; total fat: 23g; saturated fat: 14g; cholesterol: 68mg; sodium: 270mg; carbohydrates: 7g; fiber: 0g; protein: 8g

821. Arancini
Preparation time: 15 minutes
cooking time: 16 to 22 minutes
servings: 16 arancini

Ingredients:
- 2 cups cooked and cooled rice or leftover risotto
- 2 eggs, beaten
- 1½ cups panko breadcrumbs, divided
- ½ cup grated parmesan cheese
- 2 tablespoons minced fresh basil
- 16 ¾-inch cubes mozzarella cheese
- 2 tablespoons olive oil

Directions:
1. in a medium bowl, combine the rice, eggs, ½ cup of the breadcrumbs, parmesan cheese, and basil. Form this mixture into 16 1½-inch balls.
2. poke a hole in each of the balls with your finger and insert a mozzarella cube. Form the rice mixture firmly around the cheese.
3. on a shallow plate, combine the remaining 1 cup breadcrumbs with the olive oil and mix well. Roll the rice balls in the breadcrumbs to coat.
4. cook the arancini in batches for 8 to 11 minutes or until golden brown.

Nutrition (2 arancini: calories: 378; total fat: 11g; saturated fat: 4g; cholesterol: 57mg; sodium: 361mg; carbohydrates: 53g; fiber: 2g; protein: 16g

822. Pesto bruschetta
Preparation time: 10 minutes
cooking time: 4 to 8 minutes
servings: 4
Ingredients:
- 8 slices French bread, ½ inch thick
- 2 tablespoons softened butter
- 1 cup shredded mozzarella cheese
- ½ cup basil pesto
- 1 cup chopped grape tomatoes
- 2 green onions, thinly sliced

Directions:
1. spread the bread with the butter and place butter-side up in the air fryer basket. Bake for 3 to 5 minutes or until the bread is light golden brown.
2. remove the bread from the basket and top each piece with some of the cheese. Return to the basket in batches and bake until the cheese melts, about 1 to 3 minutes.
3. meanwhile, combine the pesto, tomatoes, and green onions in a small bowl.
4. when the cheese has melted, remove the bread from the air fryer and place on a serving plate. Top each slice with some of the pesto mixture and serve.

Nutrition: calories: 462; total fat: 25g; saturated fat: 10g; cholesterol: 38mg; sodium: 822mg; carbohydrates: 41g; fiber: 3g; protein: 19g

823. Fried tortellini with spicy dipping sauce
Preparation time: 8 minutes
cooking time: 20 minutes
servings: 4
Ingredients:
- ¾ cup mayonnaise
- 2 tablespoons mustard
- 1 egg
- ½ cup flour
- ½ teaspoon dried oregano
- 1½ cups breadcrumbs
- 2 tablespoons olive oil
- 2 cups frozen cheese tortellini

Directions:
1. in a small bowl, combine the mayonnaise and mustard and mix well. Set aside.
2. in a shallow bowl, beat the egg. In a separate bowl, combine the flour and oregano. In another bowl, combine the breadcrumbs and olive oil, and mix well.
3. drop the tortellini, a few at a time, into the egg, then into the flour, then into the egg again, and then into the breadcrumbs to coat. Put into the air fryer basket, cooking in batches.
4. air-fry for about 10 minutes, shaking halfway through the cooking time, or until the tortellini are crisp and golden brown on the outside. Serve with the mayonnaise.

Nutrition: calories: 698; total fat: 31g; saturated fat: 4g; cholesterol: 66mg; sodium: 832mg; carbohydrates: 88g; fiber: 3g; protein: 18g

824. Waffle fry poutine

Preparation time: 10 minutes
cooking time: 15 to 17 minutes
servings: 4
Ingredients:

- 2 cups frozen waffle cut fries
- 2 teaspoons olive oil
- 1 red bell pepper, chopped
- 2 green onions, sliced
- 1 cup shredded swiss cheese
- ½ cup bottled chicken gravy

Directions:

1. toss the waffle fries with olive oil and place in the air fryer basket. Air-fry for 10 to 12 minutes or until the fries are crisp and light golden brown, shaking the basket halfway through the cooking time.
2. transfer the fries to a 6-by-6-by-2-inch pan and top with the pepper, green onions, and cheese. Air-fry for 3 minutes until the vegetables are crisp and tender.
3. remove the pan from the air fryer and drizzle the gravy over the fries. Air-fry for 2 minutes or until the gravy is hot. Serve immediately.

Nutrition: calories: 347; total fat: 19g; saturated fat: 7g; cholesterol: 26mg; sodium: 435mg; carbohydrates: 33g; fiber: 4g; protein: 12g

825. Beef and mango skewers

Preparation time: 10 minutes
cooking time: 5 minutes
servings: 4
Ingredients:

- ¾ pound beef sirloin tip, cut into 1-inch cubes
- 2 tablespoons balsamic vinegar
- 1 tablespoon olive oil
- 1 tablespoon honey
- ½ teaspoon dried marjoram
- Pinch salt
- Freshly ground black pepper
- 1 mango

Directions:

1. put the beef cubes in a medium bowl and add the balsamic vinegar, olive oil, honey, marjoram, salt, and pepper. Mix well, then massage the marinade into the beef with your hands. Set aside.
2. to prepare the mango, stand it on end and cut the skin off, using a sharp knife. Then carefully cut around the oval pit to remove the flesh. Cut the mango into 1-inch cubes.
3. thread metal skewers alternating with three beef cubes and two mango cubes.
4. grill the skewers in the air fryer basket for 4 to 7 minutes or until the beef is browned and at least 145°f.

Nutrition: calories: 242; total fat: 9g; saturated fat: 3g; cholesterol: 76mg; sodium: 96mg; carbohydrates: 13g; fiber: 1g; protein: 26g

826. Spicy kale chips with yogurt sauce

Preparation time: 10 minutes
cooking time: 5 minutes
servings: 4
Ingredients:

- 1 cup Greek yogurt
- 3 tablespoons lemon juice
- 2 tablespoons honey mustard
- ½ teaspoon dried oregano
- 1 bunch curly kale
- 2 tablespoons olive oil
- ½ teaspoon salt
- ⅛ teaspoon pepper

Directions:

1. in a small bowl, combine the yogurt, lemon juice, honey mustard, and oregano, and set aside.
2. remove the stems and ribs from the kale with a sharp knife. Cut the leaves into 2- to 3-inch pieces.
3. toss the kale with olive oil, salt, and pepper. Massage the oil into the leaves with your hands.
4. air-fry the kale in batches until crisp, about 5 minutes, shaking the basket once during cooking time. Serve with the yogurt sauce.

Nutrition: calories: 154; total fat: 8g; saturated fat: 2g; cholesterol: 3mg; sodium: 378mg; carbohydrates: 13g; fiber: 1g; protein: 8g

827. Phyllo artichoke triangles

Preparation time: 15 minutes
cooking time: 9 minutes
servings: 18 triangles
Ingredients:

- ¼ cup ricotta cheese
- 1 egg white
- ⅓ cup minced drained artichoke hearts
- 3 tablespoons grated mozzarella cheese
- ½ teaspoon dried thyme
- 6 sheets frozen phyllo dough, thawed
- 2 tablespoons melted butter

Directions:

1. in a small bowl, combine ricotta cheese, egg white, artichoke hearts, mozzarella cheese, and thyme, and mix well.
2. cover the phyllo dough with a damp kitchen towel while you work so it doesn't dry out. Using one sheet at a time, place on the work surface and cut into thirds lengthwise.
3. put about 1½ teaspoons of the filling on each strip at the base. Fold the bottom right-hand tip of phyllo over the filling to meet the other side in a triangle, then continue folding in a triangle. Brush each triangle with butter to seal the edges. Repeat with remaining phyllo dough and filling.
4. bake, 6 at a time, for about 3 to 4 minutes or until the phyllo is golden brown and crisp.

Nutrition (3 triangles: calories: 271; total fat: 17g; saturated fat: 7g; cholesterol: 19mg; sodium: 232mg; carbohydrates: 23g; fiber: 5g; protein: 9g

PASTA AND RICE RECIPES

828. Mexican Rice

Preparation Time: 5 minutes
Cooking Time: 14 to 16 minutes
Servings 4 to 6
Ingredients:

- 1 tablespoon olive oil
- ¼ cup diced onion
- 2 cups long grain white rice
- 1 cup salsa
- 2 1/3 cups chicken stock
- 1 teaspoon salt

Directions:

1. Press the Sauté button on the Instant Pot and heat the olive oil. Add the diced onion and sauté for 2 to 3 minutes until translucent.
2. Add the white rice and cook for an additional 2 to 3 minutes. Stir in the remaining ingredients.
3. Lock the lid and cook for 10 minutes at High Pressure.
4. Once cooking is complete, do a natural pressure release for 10 minutes, then release any remaining pressure. Carefully open the lid.
5. Down the rice with the spatula or fork. Serve warm.

Nutrition: Calories: 199 Fat: 8g Carbs: 29g Protein: 3g

829. Spanish Rice

Preparation Time: 5 minutes
Cooking Time: 14 minutes
Servings 4 to 6

Ingredients:

- 2 tablespoons butter
- 2 cups long grain rice
- 8 ounces (227 g) tomato sauce
- 1½ cups chicken stock or water
- 1 teaspoon chili powder
- 1 teaspoon cumin
- ½ teaspoon onion powder
- ½ teaspoon garlic powder
- ½ teaspoon salt

Directions:

1. Set your Instant Pot to Sauté and melt the butter.
2. Add the rice and sauté for about 4 minutes, stirring occasionally.
3. Add the remaining ingredients to the Instant Pot and stir.
4. Secure the lid and set the cooking time for 10 minutes at High Pressure.
5. When the timer beeps, perform a natural pressure release for 10 minutes, then release any remaining pressure. Carefully remove the lid.
6. Use spatula or fork to fluff the rice. Serve warm.

Nutrition: Calories: 141 Fat: 8g Carbs: 13g Protein: 2g

830. Carrot and Pea Rice

Preparation Time: 10 minutes
Cooking Time: 23 minutes
Servings 4 to 6
Ingredients:

- 1 tablespoon olive oil
- 1 clove garlic, minced
- ¼ cup chopped shallots
- 2 cups chicken broth
- 1½ cups basmati rice, rinsed
- 1 cup frozen peas
- ½ cup chopped carrots
- 2 teaspoons curry powder
- Salt and ground black pepper, to taste

Directions:

1. Set your Instant Pot to Sauté and heat the olive oil.
2. Add the garlic and shallots and sauté for about 3 minutes until fragrant, stirring occasionally.
3. Add the remaining ingredients to the Instant Pot and stir to incorporate.
4. Lock the lid. Select the Rice mode and set the cooking time for 20 minutes at High Pressure.
5. Once cooking is complete, do a natural pressure release for 10 minutes, then release any remaining pressure. Carefully remove the lid.
6. Serve warm.

Nutrition: Calories: 190 Fat: 0g Carbs: 42g Protein: 5g

831. Pesto Farfalle with Cherry Tomatoes

Preparation Time: 5 minutes
Cooking Time: 8 to 9 minutes
Servings 2 to 4
Ingredients:

- 1½ cup farfalle
- cups water
- ¾ cup vegan pesto sauce
- 1 cup cherry tomatoes, quartered

Directions:

1. Place the farfalle and water in your Instant Pot.
2. Secure the lid and cook for 7 minutes at High Pressure.
3. Once cooking is complete, do a quick pressure release. Carefully remove the lid.
4. Drain the pasta and transfer it back to the pot.
5. Stir in the sauce.
6. Press the Sauté button on your Instant Pot and cook for 1 to 2 minutes.
7. Add in the tomatoes and stir to combine.
8. Transfer to a serving dish and serve immediately.

Nutrition: Calories: 370 Fat: 12g Carbs: 45g Protein: 12g

832. Pasta Carbonara

Preparation Time: 10 minutes
Cooking Time: 8 to 9 minutes

Servings 4
Ingredients:

- 1-pound (454 g) pasta dry such as rigatoni, penne or cavatappi
- cups water
- ¼ teaspoon kosher salt
- large eggs
- 1 cup grated Parmesan cheese
- Ground black pepper, to taste
- 8 ounces (227 g) bacon pancetta or guanciale
- tablespoons heavy cream

Directions:

1. Place the pasta, water, and salt in your Instant Pot.
2. Secure the lid. Press the Manual button and cook for 5 minutes at High Pressure.
3. Meantime beat together the eggs, cheese and black pepper in a mixing bowl until well mixed.
4. Cook the bacon on medium heat in a frying pan for 3 minutes until crispy.
5. Once cooking is complete, do a quick pressure release. Carefully remove the lid.
6. Select the Sauté mode. Transfer the bacon to the pot and cook for 30 seconds.
7. Stir in the egg mixture and heavy cream.
8. Secure the lid and let stand for 5 minutes.
9. Transfer to a serving dish and serve.

Nutrition: Calories: 409 Fat: 9g Carbs: 43g Protein: 13g

833. Lemony Parmesan Risotto with Peas

Preparation Time: 10 minutes
Cooking Time: 15 minutes
Servings 4
Ingredients:

- 1 tablespoon extra-virgin olive oil
- 2 tablespoons butter, divided
- 1 yellow onion, chopped
- 1½ cups Arborio rice
- 2 tablespoons lemon juice
- 3½ cups chicken stock, divided
- 1½ cups frozen peas, thawed
- 2 tablespoons parsley, finely chopped
- 2 tablespoons parmesan, finely grated
- 1 teaspoon grated lemon zest
- Salt and ground black pepper, to taste

Directions:

1. Press the Sauté button on your Instant Pot. Add and heat the oil and 1 tablespoon of butter.
2. Put onion and cook for 5 minutes, stirring occasionally. Mix in the rice and cook for an additional 3 minutes, stirring occasionally.
3. Stir in the lemon juice and 3 cups of stock.
4. Lock the lid. Select the Manual function and set the cooking time for 5 minutes at High Pressure.
5. Once cooking is complete, do a quick pressure release. Carefully open the lid.
6. Select the Sauté function again. Fold in the remaining ½ cup of stock and the peas and sauté for 2 minutes.
7. Add the remaining 1 tablespoon of butter, parsley, parmesan, lemon zest, salt, and pepper and stir well. Serve.

Nutrition: Calories: 317 Fat: 5g Carbs: 54g Protein: 11g

834. Rice Bowl with Raisins and Almonds

Preparation Time: 5 minutes
Cooking Time: 20 minutes
Servings 4
Ingredients:

- 1 cup brown rice
- 1 cup water
- 1 cup coconut milk
- ½ cup coconut chips
- ½ cup maple syrup
- ¼ cup raisins
- ¼ cup almonds
- A pinch of cinnamon powder
- Salt, to taste

Directions:

1. Place the rice and water into the Instant Pot and give a stir.
2. Set the cooking time for 15 minutes at High Pressure and secure the lid.
3. When the timer beeps, perform a quick pressure release. Carefully remove the lid.
4. Stir in the coconut milk, coconut chips, maple syrup, raisins, almonds, cinnamon powder, and salt.
5. Lock the lid and set the cooking time for 5 minutes at High Pressure.
6. 6.Once cooking is complete, do a quick pressure release. Open the lid.
7. Serve warm.

Nutrition: Calories: 261 Fat: 6g Carbs: 45g Protein: 6g

835.   Vegetable Basmati Rice

Preparation Time: 10 minutes
Cooking Time: 9 to 10 minutes
Servings 6 to 8
Ingredients:

- tablespoons olive oil
- 3 cloves garlic, minced
- 1 large onion, finely chopped
- 3 tablespoons chopped cilantro stalks
- 1 cup garden peas, frozen
- 1 cup sweet corn, frozen
- 2 cups basmati rice, rinsed
- 1 teaspoon turmeric powder
- ¼ teaspoon salt
- 3 cups chicken stock
- 2 tablespoons butter (optional)

Directions:

1. Press the Sauté button on the Instant Pot and heat the olive oil.
2. Add the garlic, onion, and cilantro and sauté for 5 to 6 minutes, stirring occasionally, or until the garlic is fragrant.
3. Stir in the peas, sweet corn, and rice. Scatter with the turmeric and salt. Put in the chicken stock and stir to combine.
4. Cook for 4 minutes at High Pressure.
5. Once cooking is complete, do a quick pressure release. Carefully open the lid.
6. You can add the butter, if desired. Serve warm.

Nutrition: Calories: 210 Fat: 0g Carbs: 48g Protein: 4g

836.   Chicken and Broccoli Rice

Preparation Time: 5 minutes
Cooking Time: 20 minutes
Servings 4 to 6
Ingredients:

- 2 tablespoons butter
- 2 cloves garlic, minced
- 1 onion, chopped
- 1½ pounds (680 g) boneless chicken breasts, sliced
- Salt and ground black pepper, to taste
- 11/3 cups chicken broth
- 11/3 cups long grain rice
- ½ cup milk
- 1 cup broccoli florets
- ½ cup grated Cheddar cheese

Directions:

1. Set your Instant Pot to Sauté and melt the butter.
2. Add the garlic, onion, and chicken pieces to the pot. Season with salt and pepper to taste.
3. Sauté for 5 minutes, stirring occasionally, or until the chicken is lightly browned.
4. Stir in the chicken broth, rice, milk, broccoli, and cheese.
5. Cook for 15 minutes at High Pressure.
6. When the timer beeps, perform a natural pressure release for 10 minutes, then release any remaining pressure. Carefully remove the lid.
7. Divide into bowls and serve.

Nutrition: Calories: 249 Fat: 5g Carbs: 23g Protein: 0g

837.   Stick of Butter Rice

Preparation Time: 5 minutes
Cooking Time: 24 minutes
Servings 4 to 6

Ingredients:

- 1 stick (½ cup) butter
- 2 cups brown rice
- 1½ cups French onion soup
- 1 cups vegetable stock

Directions:

1. Set your Instant Pot to Sauté and melt the butter.
2. Add the rice, onion soup, and vegetable stock to the Instant Pot and stir until combined.
3. Lock the lid and cook 22 minutes at High Pressure.
4. When the timer beeps, perform a natural pressure release for 10 minutes, then release any remaining pressure. Carefully remove the lid.
5. Serve warm.

Nutrition: Calories: 390 Fat: 23g Carbs: 39g Protein: 4g

838.   Jasmine Rice with Cauliflower and Pineapple

Preparation Time: 5 minutes
Cooking Time: 20 minutes
Servings 4 to 6
Ingredients:

- cups water
- 2 cups jasmine rice
- 1 cauliflower, florets separated and chopped
- ½ pineapple, peeled and chopped
- 2 teaspoons extra virgin olive oil
- Salt and ground black pepper, to taste

Directions:

1. Stir together all the ingredients in the Instant Pot.
2. Make sure to lock the lid and cook for 20 minutes at Low Pressure.
3. When the timer beeps, perform a natural pressure release for 10 minutes, then release any remaining pressure. Carefully remove the lid.
4. Fluff with the rice spatula or fork, then serve.

Nutrition: Calories: 106 Fat: 1g Carbs: 21g Protein: 3g

839.   Brown Rice and Black Bean Casserole

Preparation Time: 5 minutes
Cooking Time: 28 minutes
Servings 4 to 6
Ingredients:

- 2 cups uncooked brown rice
- 1 cup black beans, soaked for at least 2 hours and drained
- ounces (170 g) tomato paste
- cups water
- 1 teaspoon garlic
- 2 teaspoons chili powder
- 2 teaspoons onion powder
- 1 teaspoon salt, or more to taste

Directions:

1. Prepare all ingredients into the Instant Pot and stir to mix well.
2. Choose the Manual mode and set the cooking time for 28 minutes at High Pressure.
3. When the timer beeps, perform a quick pressure release. Carefully remove the lid.
4. Taste and add more salt, if needed. Serve immediately.

Nutrition: Calories: 270 Fat: 12g Carbs: 29g Protein: 14g

840.   Chipotle Style Rice

Preparation Time: 10 minutes
Cooking Time: 30 minutes
Servings 4 to 6
Ingredients:

- 2 cups brown rice, rinsed
- 2¾ cups water
- small bay leaves
- 1 lime, juiced
- 1½ tablespoons olive oil
- 1 teaspoon salt
- ½ cup chopped cilantro

Directions:

1. 1.Place the rice, water, and bay leaves into the Instant Pot and stir.

2. 2.Lock the lid. Select the Rice mode and set the cooking time for 30 minutes at High Pressure.
3. 3.When the timer beeps, perform a natural pressure release for 10 minutes, then release any remaining pressure. Carefully remove the lid.
4. 4.Add the lime juice, olive oil, salt, and cilantro and stir to mix well. Serve immediately.

Nutrition: Calories: 130 Fat: 3g Carbs: 23g Protein: 2g

BREAD RECIPES

841.   Cream bread
Preparation time: 20 minutes
Cooking time: 55 minutes
Servings: 12
Ingredients:
- 1 cup milk
- ¾ cup whipping cream
- 1 large egg
- 4½ cups bread flour
- ½ cup all-purpose flour
- 2 tablespoons milk powder
- 1 teaspoon salt
- ¼ cup fine sugar
- 3 teaspoons dry yeast

Directions:
1. In the baking pan of a bread machine, place all the ingredients in the order recommended by the manufacturer.
2. Place the baking pan in bread machine and close with the lid.
3. Select the dough cycle and press start button.
4. Once the cycle is completed, remove the paddles from bread machine but keep the dough inside for about 45-50 minutes to proof.
5. Set the temperature of air fryer to 375°f. Grease 2 loaf pans.
6. Remove the dough from pan and place onto a lightly floured surface.
7. Divide the dough into four equal-sized balls and then, roll each into a rectangle.
8. Tightly, roll each rectangle like a swiss roll.
9. Place two rolls into each prepared loaf pan.
10. Set aside for about 1 hour.
11. Arrange the loaf pans into an air fryer basket.
12. Air fry for about 50-55 minutes or until a toothpick inserted in the center comes out clean.
13. Remove the pans from air fryer and place onto a wire rack for about 10-15 minutes.
14. Then, remove the bread rolls from pans and place onto a wire rack until they are completely cool before slicing.
15. Cut each roll into desired size slices and serve.

Nutrition: Calories: 215 Carbohydrate: 39 g Protein: 5 g Fat: 1 g Sugar: 2 g

842.   Sunflower seeds bread
Preparation time: 15 minutes
Cooking time: 18 minutes
Servings: 4
Ingredients:
- 2/3 cup whole-wheat flour
- 2/3 cup plain flour
- 1/3 cup sunflower seeds
- ½ sachet instant yeast
- 1 teaspoon salt
- 2/3-1 cup lukewarm water

Directions:
1. In a bowl, mix the flours, sunflower seeds, yeast, and salt.
2. Slowly, add in the water, stirring continuously until a soft dough ball form.
3. Now, move the dough onto a lightly floured surface and knead for about 5 minutes using your hands.
4. Make a ball from the dough and place into a bowl.
5. With a plastic wrap, cover the bowl and place at a warm place for about 30 minutes.
6. Set the temperature of air fryer to 390°f. Grease a cake pan. (6"x 3")
7. Coat the top of dough with water and place into the prepared cake pan.

8. Arrange the cake pan into an air fryer basket.
9. Air fry for about 18 minutes or until a toothpick inserted in the center comes out clean.
10. Remove from air fryer and place the pan onto a wire rack for about 10-15 minutes.
11. Carefully, take out the bread from pan and put onto a wire rack until it is completely cool before slicing.
12. Cut the bread into desired size slices and serve.

Nutrition: Calories: 177 Carbohydrate: 33 g Protein 5 g Fat 4 g Sugar 2 g

843.   Date bread
Preparation time: 15 minutes
Cooking time: 22 minutes
Servings: 10
Ingredients:
- 2½ cup dates, pitted and chopped
- ¼ cup butter
- 1 cup hot water
- 1½ cups flour
- ½ cup brown sugar
- ½ teaspoon salt
- 1 egg

Directions:
1. In a large bowl, add the dates, butter and top with the hot water.
2. Set aside for about 5 minutes.
3. In a separate bowl, mix the flour, brown sugar, baking powder, baking soda, and salt.
4. In the same bowl of dates, mix well the flour mixture, and egg.
5. Set the temperature of air fryer to 340°f. Grease an air fryer nonstick pan.
6. Place the mixture into the prepared pan.
7. Arrange the pan into an air fryer basket.
8. Air fry for about 22 minutes or until a toothpick inserted in the center comes out clean.
9. Remove from air fryer and place the pan onto a wire rack for about 10-15 minutes.
10. Carefully, take out the bread from pan and put onto a wire rack until it's completely let it cool before slicing.
11. Cut the bread into desired size slices and serve.

Nutrition: Calories: 269 Carbohydrate: 51 g protein: 6 g Fat: 4 g Sugar: 33 g

844.   Yogurt banana bread
Preparation time: 15 minutes
Cooking time: 35 minutes
Servings: 5
Ingredients:
- ½ cup all-purpose flour
- ¼ cup whole-wheat flour
- ½ teaspoon salt
- 1 large egg
- 1 cup granulated sugar
- 1/2 cup plain yogurt
- 1/2 cup vegetable oil
- 1 teaspoon pure vanilla extract
- 3 ripe bananas, peeled and mashed
- 3 tablespoons turbinado sugar

Directions:
1. In a bowl, sift together the flours, baking soda, and salt.
2. In another large bowl, mix well the egg, granulated sugar, yogurt, oil, and vanilla extract.
3. Add in the bananas and beat until it blends well.
4. Now, add the flour mixture and mix until just combined.
5. Set the temperature of air fryer to 310°f.

6. Place the mixture evenly into a cake pan and sprinkle with the turbinado sugar.
7. Arrange the cake pan into an air fryer basket.
8. Air fry for about 30-35 minutes or until a toothpick inserted in the center comes out clean, turning the pan once halfway through.
9. Carefully, take out the bread from pan and put onto a wire rack until it is completely cool before slicing.
10. Cut the bread into desired size slices and serve

Nutrition: Calories: 317 Carbohydrate: 42 g Protein: 3 g Fat: 16 g Sugar: 26 g Sodium: 106 mg

845.   Soda bread
Preparation time: 15 minutes
Cooking time: 30 minutes
Servings: 10
Ingredients:
- 3 cups whole-wheat flour
- 1 tablespoon sugar
- 2 teaspoon caraway seeds
- 1/2 teaspoon sea salt
- ¼ cup chilled butter, cubed into small pieces
- 1 large egg, beaten
- 1½ cups buttermilk

Directions:
1. In a large bowl, mix the flour, sugar, caraway seeds, baking soda and salt and mix well.
2. With a pastry cutter, cut in the butter flour until coarse crumbs like mixture is formed.
3. Make a well in the center of flour mixture.
4. In the well, add the egg, followed by the buttermilk and with a spatula, mix until well combined.
5. With floured hand, shape the dough into a ball.
6. Place the dough onto a floured surface and lightly knead it.
7. Shape the dough into a 6-inch ball.
8. With a serrated knife, score an x on the top of the dough.
9. Press "power button" of air fry oven and turn the dial to select the "air crisp" mode.
10. Press the "time button" and again turn the dial to set the cooking time to 30 minutes.
11. Now push the "temp button" and rotate the dial to set the temperature at 350°f.
12. Press "start/pause" button to start.
13. When the unit beeps to show that it's preheated, open the lid.
14. Arrange the dough in lightly greased air fry basket and insert in the oven.
15. Place the pan onto a wire rack to cool for about 10 minutes.
16. Carefully, invert the bread onto wire rack to cool completely before slicing.
17. Cut the bread into desired-sized slices and serve.

Nutrition: Calories: 205 Fat: 9 g Saturated fat: 3 g Sodium: 392 mg Carbs: 38 g Fiber: 2 g Sugar: 1 g Protein: 9 g

846.   Baguette bread
Preparation time: 15 minutes
cooking time: 20 minutes
Servings: 8
Ingredients:
- ¾ cup warm water
- ¾ teaspoon quick yeast
- ½ teaspoon demerara sugar
- 1 cup bread flour
- ½ cup whole-wheat flour
- ½ cup oat flour
- 1¼ teaspoons salt

Directions:
1. In a large bowl, place the water and sprinkle with yeast and sugar.
2. Set aside for 5 minutes or until foamy.

3. Add the bread flour and salt mix until a stiff dough form.
4. Put the dough onto a floured surface and with your hands, knead until smooth and elastic.
5. Now, shape the dough into a ball.
6. Place the dough into a slightly oiled bowl and turn to coat well.
7. With a plastic wrap, cover the bowl and place in a warm place for about 1 hour or until doubled in size.
8. With your hands, punch down the dough and form into a long slender loaf.
9. Place the loaf onto a lightly greased baking sheet and set aside in warm place, uncovered, for about 30 minutes.
10. Press "power button" of air fry oven and turn the dial to select the "air bake" mode.
11. Press the "time button" and again turn the dial to set the cooking time to 20 minutes.
12. Now push the "temp button" and rotate the dial to set the temperature at 450°f.
13. Press "start/pause" button to start.
14. When the unit beeps to show that it's preheated, open the lid.
15. Carefully, arrange the dough onto the "wire rack" and insert in the oven.
16. Carefully, invert the bread onto wire rack to cool completely before slicing.
17. Cut the bread into desired-sized slices and serve.

Nutrition: Calories: 114 Fat: 8 g Carbs: 28 g Fiber: 1 g Sugar: 3 g Protein: 8 g

847.   Yogurt bread
Preparation time: 20 minutes
Cooking time: 40 minutes
servings: 10
Ingredients:
- 1½ cups warm water, divided
- 1½ teaspoons active dry yeast
- 1 teaspoon sugar
- 3 cups all-purpose flour
- 1 cup plain Greek yogurt
- 2 teaspoons kosher salt

Directions:
1. Add ½ cup of the warm water, yeast and sugar in the bowl of a stand mixer, fitted with the dough hook attachment and mix well.
2. Set aside for about 5 minutes.
3. Add the flour, yogurt, and salt and mix on medium-low speed until the dough comes together.
4. Then, mix on medium speed for 5 minutes.
5. Place the dough into a bowl.
6. With a plastic wrap, cover the bowl and place in a warm place for about 2-3 hours or until doubled in size.
7. Place the dough onto a greased parchment paper-lined rack.
8. With a kitchen towel, cover the dough and let rest for 15 minutes.
9. With a very sharp knife, cut a 4 x ½-inch deep cut down the center of the dough.
10. Press "power button" of air fry oven and turn the dial to select the "air roast" mode.
11. Press the "time button" and again turn the dial to set the cooking time to 40 minutes.
12. Now push the "temp button" and rotate the dial to set the temperature at 325°f.
13. Press "start/pause" button to start.
14. When the unit beeps to show that it's preheated, open the lid.
15. Carefully, arrange the dough onto the "wire rack" and insert in the oven.
16. Carefully, invert the bread onto wire rack to cool completely before slicing.
17. Cut the bread into desired-sized slices and serve.

Nutrition: Calories: 157 Fat: 7 g Carbs: 31 g Fiber: 1 g Sugar: 2 g Protein: 5 g

848. Spicy seafood risotto

Preparation Time: 10 minutes
Cooking Time: 25 minutes
Servings: 3
Ingredients

- 1 ½ cups cooked rice, cold
- 3 tablespoons shallots, minced
- 2 garlic cloves, minced
- 1 tablespoon oyster sauce
- 2 tablespoons dry white wine
- 2 tablespoons sesame oil
- Salt and ground black pepper, to taste
- 2 eggs
- 4 ounces lump crab meat
- 1 teaspoon ancho chili powder
- 2 tablespoons fresh parsley, roughly chopped

Directions
1. Mix the cold rice, shallots, garlic, oyster sauce, dry white wine, sesame oil, salt, and black pepper in a lightly greased baking pan. Stir in the whisked eggs.
2. Cook in the preheated air fryer at 370° for 13 to 16 minutes.
3. Add the crab and ancho chili powder to the baking dish; stir until everything is well combined. Cook for 6 minutes more.
4. Serve at room temperature, garnished with fresh parsley. Bon appétit!

Nutrition: 445 calories; 17g fat; 48g carbs; 24g protein; 5g sugars

849. Mexican-style brown rice casserole

Preparation Time: 15 minutes
Cooking Time: 50 minutes
Servings: 4
Ingredients

- 1 tablespoon olive oil
- 1 shallot, chopped
- 2 cloves garlic, minced
- 1 habanero pepper, minced
- 2 cups brown rice
- 3 cups chicken broth
- 1 cup water
- 2 ripe tomatoes, pureed
- Sea salt and ground black pepper, to taste
- 1/2 teaspoon dried Mexican oregano
- 1 teaspoon red pepper flakes
- 1 cup Mexican cotija cheese, crumbled

Directions
1. In a nonstick skillet, heat the olive oil over a moderate flame. Once hot, cook the shallot, garlic, and habanero pepper until tender and fragrant; reserve.
2. Heat the brown rice, vegetable broth and water in a pot over high heat. Bring it to a boil; turn the stove down to simmer and cook for 35 minutes.
3. Grease a baking pan with nonstick cooking spray.
4. Spoon the cooked rice into the baking pan. Add the sautéed mixture. Spoon the tomato puree over the sautéed mixture. Sprinkle with salt, black pepper, oregano, and red pepper.
5. Cook in the preheated air fryer at 380° f for 8 minutes. Top with the cotija cheese and bake for 5 minutes longer or until cheese is melted. Enjoy!

Nutrition: 433 calories; 4g fat; 76g carbs; 11g protein; 8g sugars

850. Japanese chicken and rice salad

Preparation Time: 15 minutes
Cooking Time: 45 minutes
Servings: 4
Ingredients

- 1-pound chicken tenderloins
- 2 tablespoons shallots, chopped
- 1 garlic clove, minced
- 1 red bell pepper, chopped
- 1 ½ cups brown rice
- 1 cup baby spinach
- 1/2 cup snow peas
- 2 tablespoons soy sauce
- 1 teaspoon yellow mustard
- 1 tablespoon rice vinegar
- 1 tablespoon liquid from pickled ginger
- 1 teaspoon agave syrup
- 2 tablespoons black sesame seeds, to serve
- 1/4 cup mandarin orange segments

Directions
1. Start by preheating your air fryer to 380 degrees f. Then, add the chicken tenderloins to the baking pan and cook until it starts to get crisp or about 6 minutes.
2. Add the shallots, garlic, and bell pepper. Cook for 6 minutes more. Wait for the chicken mixture to cool down completely and transfer to a salad bowl.
3. Bring 3 cups of water and 1 teaspoon of salt to a boil in a saucepan over medium-high heat. Stir in the rice and reduce the heat to simmer; cook about 20 minutes.
4. Let your rice sit in the covered saucepan for another 10 minutes. Drain the rice and allow it to cool completely.
5. Stir the cold rice into the salad bowl; add the baby spinach and snow peas. In a small mixing dish, whisk the soy sauce, mustard, rice vinegar, liquid from pickled ginger, and agave syrup.
6. Dress the salad and stir well to combine. Garnish with black sesame seeds and mandarin orange. Enjoy!

Nutrition: 387 calories; 7g fat; 69g carbs; 24g protein; 9g sugars

851. Risotto balls with bacon and corn

Preparation Time: 15 minutes
Cooking Time: 30 minutes
Servings: 6
Ingredients

- 4 slices Canadian bacon
- 1 tablespoon olive oil
- 1/2 medium-sized leek, chopped
- 1 teaspoon fresh garlic, minced
- Sea salt and freshly ground pepper, to taste
- 1 cup white rice
- 4 cups vegetable broth
- 1/3 cup dry white wine
- 2 tablespoons tamari sauce
- 1 tablespoon oyster sauce
- 1 tablespoon butter
- 1 cup sweet corn kernels
- 1 bell pepper, seeded and chopped
- 2 eggs lightly beaten
- 1 cup breadcrumbs
- 1 cup parmesan cheese, preferably freshly grated

Directions
1. Cook the Canadian bacon in a nonstick skillet over medium-high heat. Let it cool, finely chop and reserve.
2. Heat the olive oil in a saucepan over medium heat. Now, sauté the leeks and garlic, stirring occasionally, about 5 minutes. Add the salt and pepper.
3. Stir in the white rice. Continue to cook approximately 3 minutes or until translucent. Add the warm broth, wine, tamari sauce, and oyster sauce; cook until the liquid is absorbed.
4. Remove the saucepan from the heat; stir in the butter, corn, bell pepper, and reserved Canadian bacon. Let it cool completely. Then, shape the mixture into small balls.
5. In a shallow bowl, combine the eggs with the breadcrumbs and parmesan cheese. Dip each ball in the eggs/crumb mixture.
6. Cook in the preheated air fryer at 395° f for 10 to 12 minutes, shaking the basket periodically. Serve warm.

Nutrition: 435 calories; 16g fat; 44g carbs; 23g protein; 1g sugars

852. Cheese and bacon crescent ring

Preparation Time: 10 minutes
Cooking Time: 25 minutes

Servings: 4
Ingredients
- 1 (8-ounce) can crescent dough sheet
- 1 ½ cups Monterey jack cheese, shredded
- 4 slices bacon, cut chopped
- 4 tablespoons tomato sauce
- 1 teaspoon dried oregano

Directions
1. Unroll the crescent dough sheet and separate into 8 triangles. Arrange the triangles on a piece of parchment paper; place the triangles in the ring so it should look like the sun.
2. Place the shredded Monterey jack cheese, bacon, and tomato sauce on the half of each triangle, at the center of the ring. Sprinkle with oregano.
3. Bring each triangle up over the filling. Press the overlapping dough to flatten. Transfer the parchment paper with the crescent ring to the air fryer basket.
4. Bake at 355° f for 20 minutes or until the ring is golden brown. Bon appétit!

Nutrition: 506 calories; 38g fat; 36g carbs; 27g protein; 9g sugars

853. Paella-style Spanish rice
Preparation Time: 10 minutes
Cooking Time: 35 minutes
Servings: 2
Ingredients
- 2 cups water
- 1 cup white rice, rinsed and drained
- 1 cube vegetable stock
- 1 chorizo, sliced
- 2 cups brown mushrooms, cleaned and sliced
- 2 cloves garlic, finely chopped
- 1/2 teaspoon fresh ginger, ground
- 1 long red chili, minced
- 1/4 cup dry white wine
- 1/2 cup tomato sauce
- 1 teaspoon smoked paprika
- Kosher salt and ground black pepper, to taste
- 1 cup green beans

Directions
1. In a medium saucepan, bring the water to a boil. Add the rice and vegetable stock cube. Stir and reduce the heat. Cover and let it simmer for 20 minutes.
2. Then, place the chorizo, mushrooms, garlic, ginger, and red chili in the baking pan. Cook at 380° f for 6 minutes, stirring periodically.
3. Add the prepared rice to the casserole dish. Add the remaining ingredients and gently stir to combine.
4. Cook for 6 minutes, checking periodically to ensure even cooking. Serve in individual bowls and enjoy!

Nutrition: 546 calories; 14g fat; 97g carbs; 16g protein; 5g sugars

854. Buckwheat and potato flat bread
Preparation Time: 10 minutes
Cooking Time: 20 minutes
Servings: 4
Ingredients
- 4 potatoes, medium-sized
- 1 cup buckwheat flour
- 1/2 teaspoon salt
- 1/2 teaspoon red chili powder
- 1/4 cup honey

Directions
1. Put the potatoes into a large saucepan; add water to cover by about 1 inch. Bring to a boil. Then, lower the heat, and let your potatoes simmer about 8 minutes until they are fork tender.
2. Mash the potatoes and add the flour, salt, and chili powder. Create 4 balls and flatten them with a rolling pin
3. Bake in the preheated air fryer at 390° f for 6 minutes. Serve warm with honey.

Nutrition: 334 calories; 2g fat; 73g carbs; 4g protein; 15g sugars

855. Couscous and black bean bowl
Preparation Time: 10 minutes
Cooking Time: 35 minutes

Servings: 4
Ingredients
- 1 cup couscous
- 1 cup canned black beans, drained and rinsed
- 1 tablespoon fresh cilantro, chopped
- 1 bell pepper, sliced
- 2 tomatoes, sliced
- 2 cups baby spinach
- 1 red onion, sliced
- Sea salt and ground black pepper, to taste
- 1 teaspoon lemon juice
- 1 teaspoon lemon zest
- 1 tablespoon olive oil
- 4 tablespoons tahini

Directions
1. Put the couscous in a bowl; pour the boiling water to cover by about 1 inch. Cover and set aside for 5 to 8 minutes; fluff with a fork.
2. Place the couscous in a lightly greased cake pan. Transfer the pan to the air fryer basket and cook at 360° f about 20 minutes. Make sure to stir every 5 minutes to ensure even cooking.
3. Transfer the prepared couscous to a mixing bowl. Add the remaining ingredients; gently stir to combine. Bon appétit!

Nutrition: 352 calories; 12g fat; 49g carbs; 16g protein; 7g sugars

856. Delicious coconut granola
Preparation Time: 15 minutes
Cooking Time: 40 minutes
Servings: 12
Ingredients
- 2 cups rolled oats
- 2 tablespoons butter
- 1 cup honey
- 1/2 teaspoon coconut extract
- 1/2 teaspoon vanilla extract
- 1/4 cup sesame seeds
- 1/4 cup pumpkin seeds
- 1/2 cup coconut flakes

Directions
1. Thoroughly combine all ingredients, except the coconut flakes; mix well.
2. Spread the mixture onto the air fryer trays. Spritz with nonstick cooking spray.
3. Bake at 230° f for 25 minutes; rotate the trays, add the coconut flakes, and bake for a further 10 to 15 minutes.
4. This granola can be stored in an airtight container for up to 3 weeks. Enjoy!

Nutrition: 192 calories; 1g fat; 32g carbs; 3g protein; 28g sugars

857. Savory cheesy cornmeal biscuits
Preparation Time: 15 minutes
Cooking Time: 35 minutes
Servings: 6
Ingredients
- 2 cups all-purpose flour
- 1 teaspoon baking soda
- 1 teaspoon baking powder
- 1 teaspoon granulated sugar
- 1/4 teaspoon ground chipotle
- Sea salt, to taste
- A pinch of grated nutmeg
- 1 stick butter, cold
- 6 ounces canned whole corn kernels
- 1 cup Colby cheese, shredded
- 2 tablespoons sour cream
- 2 eggs, beaten

Directions
1. In a mixing bowl, combine the flour, baking soda, baking powder, sugar, ground chipotle, salt, and a pinch of nutmeg.
2. Cut in the butter until the mixture resembles coarse crumbs. Stir in the corn, Colby cheese, sour cream, and eggs; stir until everything is well incorporated.

3. Turn the dough out onto a floured surface. Knead the dough with your hands and roll it out to 1-inch thickness. Using 3-inch round cutter, cut out the biscuits.
4. Transfer the cornmeal biscuits to the lightly greased air fryer basket. Brush the biscuits with cooking oil.
5. Bake in the preheated air fryer at 400° f for 17 minutes. Continue cooking until all the batter is used. Bon appétit!

Nutrition: 444 calories; 27g fat; 36g carbs; 14g protein; 6g sugars

858. Asian-style shrimp pilaf
Preparation Time: 15 minutes
Cooking Time: 45 minutes
Servings: 3
Ingredients
- 1 cup koshihikari rice, rinsed
- 1 yellow onion, chopped
- 2 garlic cloves, minced
- 1/2 teaspoon fresh ginger, grated
- 1 tablespoon shoyu sauce
- 2 tablespoons rice wine
- 1 tablespoon sushi seasoning
- 1 tablespoon caster sugar
- 1/2 teaspoon sea salt
- 5 ounces frozen shrimp, thawed
- 2 tablespoons katsuobushi flakes, for serving

Directions
1. Place the koshihikari rice and 2 cups of water in a large saucepan and bring to a boil. Cover turn the heat down to low and continue cooking for 15 minutes more. Set aside for 10 minutes.
2. Mix the rice, onion, garlic, ginger, shoyu sauce, wine, sushi seasoning, sugar, and salt in a lightly greased baking dish.
3. Cook in the preheated air fryer at 370°f for 13 to 16 minutes.
4. Add the shrimp to the baking dish and gently stir until everything is well combined. Cook for 6 minutes more.
5. Serve at room temperature, garnished with katsuobushi flakes. Enjoy!

Nutrition: 368 calories; 3g fat; 64g carbs; 9g protein; 19g sugars

DESSERT RECIPES

859. Honey roasted pears with ricotta
Preparation time: 7 minutes
cooking time: 18 to 23 minutes
servings: 4
Ingredients
- 2 large bosc pears, halved and seeded (see tip
- 3 tablespoons honey
- 1 tablespoon unsalted butter
- ½ teaspoon ground cinnamon
- ¼ cup walnuts, chopped
- ¼ cup part skim low-fat ricotta cheese, divided

Directions
1. 1 in a 6 by 2 inch pan, place the pears cut side up.
2. 2 in a small microwave safe bowl, melt the honey, butter, and cinnamon. Brush this mixture over the cut sides of the pears.
3. 3 pour 3 tablespoons of water around the pears in the pan. Roast the pears for 18 to 23 minutes, or until tender when pierced with a fork and slightly crisp on the edges, basting once with the liquid in the pan.
4. 4 carefully remove the pears from the pan and place on a serving plate. Drizzle each with some liquid from the pan, sprinkle the walnuts on top, and serve with a spoonful of ricotta cheese.

Nutrition calories: 138; fat: 4g (26% of calories from fat; saturated fat: 3g; protein: 2g; carbohydrates: 25g; sodium: 17mg; fiber: 3g;

860. Grilled spiced fruit
Preparation time: 10 minutes
cooking time: 3 to 5 minutes
servings: 4
Ingredients
- 2 peaches, peeled, pitted, and thickly sliced
- 3 plums, halved and pitted
- 3 nectarines, halved and pitted
- 1 tablespoon honey
- ½ teaspoon ground cinnamon
- ¼ teaspoon ground allspice

Directions
1. Pinch cayenne pepper
2. Thread the fruit, alternating the types, onto 8 bamboo or metal skewers that fit into the air fryer.
3. In a small bowl, stir together the honey, cinnamon, allspice, and cayenne. Brush the glaze onto the fruit.
4. Grill the skewers for 3 to 5 minutes, or until lightly browned and caramelized. Cool for 5 minutes and serve.

Nutrition calories: 121; fat: 1g (7% of calories from fat; saturated fat: 0g; protein: 3g; carbohydrates: 30g; sodium: 0mg; fiber: 4g;

861. Caramelized peaches with blueberries
Preparation time: 10 minutes
cooking time: 7 to 11 minutes
servings: 6

Directions
1. Place the peaches, cut side up, in the air fryer basket. Sprinkle evenly with the brown sugar. Bake for 7 to 11 -minutes, or until they start to brown around the edges and become tender.
2. Meanwhile, in a small bowl, stir together the yogurt, vanilla, and cinnamon.
3. When the peaches are done, transfer them to a serving plate. Top with the yogurt mixture and the blueberries. Serve immediately.

Nutrition calories: 98; fat: 1g (10% calories from fat; saturated fat: 0g; protein: 5g; carbohydrates: 20g; sodium: 20mg; fiber: 4g;

862. Stuffed apples
Preparation time: 13 minutes
cooking time: 12 to 17 minutes
servings: 4
Ingredients
- 4 medium apples, rinsed and patted dry (see tip
- 2 tablespoons freshly squeezed lemon juice
- ¼ cup golden raisins
- 3 tablespoons chopped walnuts
- 3 tablespoons dried cranberries
- 2 tablespoons packed brown sugar
- ⅓ cup apple cider

Directions
1. Cut a strip of peel from the top of each apple and remove the core, being careful not to cut through the bottom of the apple. Sprinkle the cut parts of the apples with lemon juice and place in a 6by2inch pan.
2. In a small bowl, stir together the raisins, walnuts, cranberries, and brown sugar. Stuff one fourth of this mixture into each apple.
3. Pour the apple cider around the apples in the pan.
4. Bake in the air fryer for 12 to 17 minutes, or until the apples are tender when pierced with a fork. Serve immediately.

Nutrition calories: 122; fat: 4g (25% of calories from fat; saturated fat: 0g; protein: 1g; carbohydrates: 22g; sodium: 8mg; fiber: 1g;

863. Apple peach crisp
Preparation time: 10 minutes
cooking time: 10 to 12 minutes
servings: 4
Ingredients
- 1 apple, peeled and chopped
- 2 peaches, peeled, pitted, and chopped
- 2 tablespoons honey
- ½ cup quick cooking oatmeal
- ⅓ cup whole-wheat pastry flour
- 3 tablespoons packed brown sugar
- 2 tablespoons unsalted butter, at room temperature
- ½ teaspoon ground cinnamon

Directions

1. in a 6by2inch pan, thoroughly mix the apple, peaches, and honey.
2. in a medium bowl, stir together the oatmeal, pastry flour, brown sugar, butter, and cinnamon until crumbly. Sprinkle this mixture over the fruit.
3. bake for 10 to 12 minutes, or until the fruit is bubbly and the topping is golden brown. Serve warm.

Nutrition calories: 237; fat: 7g (26% calories from fat; saturated fat: 4g; protein: 3g; carbohydrates: 44g; sodium: 1mg; fiber: 5g;

864. Strawberry rhubarb crumble

Preparation time: 10 minutes
cooking time: 12 to 17 minutes
servings: 6

Ingredients

- 1½ cups sliced fresh strawberries
- ¾ cup sliced rhubarb
- ⅓ cup sugar
- ⅔ cup quick cooking oatmeal
- ½ cup whole-wheat pastry flour
- ¼ cup packed brown sugar
- ½ teaspoon ground cinnamon

Directions

1. 3 tablespoons unsalted butter, melted
2. 1 in a 6 by 2 inch metal pan, combine the strawberries, -rhubarb, and sugar.
3. 2 in a medium bowl, mix the oatmeal, pastry flour, brown sugar, and cinnamon.
4. 3 stir the melted butter into the oatmeal mixture until crumbly. Sprinkle this over the fruit. Bake for 12 to 17 -minutes, or until the fruit is bubbling and the topping is golden brown. Serve warm.

Nutrition calories: 206; fat: 7g (30% calories from fat; saturated fat: 4g; protein: 3g; carbohydrates: 36g; sodium: 1mg; fiber: 4g;

865. Mixed berry crumble

Preparation time: 10 minutes
cooking time: 11 to 16 minutes
servings: 4

Ingredients

- ½ cup chopped fresh strawberries
- ½ cup fresh blueberries
- ⅓ cup frozen raspberries
- 1 tablespoon freshly squeezed lemon juice
- 1 tablespoon honey
- ⅔ cup whole-wheat pastry flour (see tip)
- 3 tablespoons packed brown sugar
- 2 tablespoons unsalted butter, melted

Directions

1. In a 6 by 2 inch pan, combine the strawberries, blue-berries, and raspberries. Drizzle with the lemon juice and honey.
2. In a small bowl, mix the pastry flour and brown sugar.
3. Stir in the butter and mix until crumbly. Sprinkle this mixture over the fruit.
4. Bake for 11 to 16 minutes, or until the fruit is tender and bubbly and the topping is golden brown. Serve warm.

Nutrition calories: 199; fat: 6g (27% of calories from fat; saturated fat: 4g; protein: 3g; carbohydrates: 35g; sodium: 1mg; fiber: 4g;

866. Apple blueberry hand pies

Preparation time: 20 minutes
cooking time: 7 to 9 minutes
servings: 4

Ingredients

- 1 medium granny smith apple, peeled and finely chopped
- ½ cup dried blueberries
- 1 tablespoon freshly squeezed orange juice
- 1 tablespoon packed brown sugar
- 2 teaspoons cornstarch
- 4 sheets frozen phyllo dough, thawed
- 8 teaspoons unsalted butter, melted
- 8 teaspoons sugar
- Nonstick cooking spray, for coating the phyllo dough

Directions

1. In a medium bowl, mix the apple, blueberries, orange juice, brown sugar, and cornstarch.
2. Place 1 sheet of phyllo dough on a work surface with the narrow side facing you. Brush very lightly with 1 -teaspoon of butter and sprinkle with 1 teaspoon of sugar. Fold the phyllo sheet in half from left to right.
3. Place one fourth of the fruit filling at the bottom of the sheet in the center. Fold the left side of the sheet over the filling. Spray lightly with cooking spray.
4. Fold the right side of the sheet over the filling. Brush with 1 teaspoon of butter and sprinkle with 1 teaspoon of sugar.
5. Fold the bottom right corner of the dough up to meet the left side of the pastry sheet to form a triangle. Continue folding the triangles over to enclose the filling, as you would fold a flag. Seal the edge with a bit of water.
6. Spray lightly with cooking spray. Repeat with the remaining 3 sheets of the phyllo, butter, sugar, and cooking spray, making four pies.
7. Place the pies in the air fryer basket. Bake for 7 to 9 -minutes, or until golden brown and crisp. Remove the pies and let cool on a wire rack before serving.

Nutrition calories: 239; fat: 8g (30% calories from fat; saturated fat: 5g; protein 2g; carbohydrates: 42g; sodium: 34mg; fiber: 5g;

867. Oatmeal carrot cookie cups

Preparation time: 10 minutes
cooking time: 8 to 10 minutes
servings: 16 cups

Ingredients

- 3 tablespoons unsalted butter, at room temperature
- ¼ cup packed brown sugar
- 1 tablespoon honey
- 1 egg white
- ½ teaspoon vanilla extract
- ⅓ cup finely grated carrot (see tip
- ½ cup quick cooking oatmeal
- ⅓ cup whole-wheat pastry flour
- ½ teaspoon baking soda
- ¼ cup dried cherries

Directions

1. In a medium bowl, beat the butter, brown sugar, and honey until well combined.
2. Add the egg white, vanilla, and carrot. Beat to combine.
3. Stir in the oatmeal, pastry flour, and baking soda.
4. Stir in the dried cherries.
5. Double up 32 mini muffin foil cups to make 16 cups. Fill each with about 4 teaspoons of dough. Bake the cookie cups, 8 at a time, for 8 to 10 minutes, or until light golden brown and just set. Serve warm.

Nutrition calories: 127; fat: 5g (35% calories from fat; saturated fat: 3g; protein: 2g; carbohydrates: 20g; sodium: 88mg; fiber: 1g;

868. Dark chocolate oatmeal cookies

Preparation time: 10 minutes
cooking time: 8 to 13 minutes
servings: 30 cookies

Ingredients

- 3 tablespoons unsalted butter
- 2 ounces dark chocolate, chopped (see tip
- ½ cup packed brown sugar
- 2 egg whites
- 1 teaspoon pure vanilla extract
- 1 cup quick cooking oatmeal
- ½ cup whole-wheat pastry flour
- ½ teaspoon baking soda
- ¼ cup dried cranberries

Directions

1. In a medium metal bowl, mix the butter and dark -chocolate. Bake in the air fryer for 1 to 3 minutes, or until the butter and chocolate melt. Stir until smooth.
2. Beat in the brown sugar, egg whites, and vanilla until smooth.
3. Stir in the oatmeal, pastry flour, and baking soda.
4. Stir in the cranberries. Form the dough into about 30 (1inchballs. Bake the dough balls, in batches of 8, in the air fryer basket for 7 to 10 minutes, or until set.

5. Carefully remove the cookies from the air fryer and cool on a wire rack. Repeat with the remaining dough balls.

Nutrition: calories: 55; fat: 2g (33% of calories from fat; saturated fat: 1g; protein: 1g; carbohydrates: 8g; sodium: 25mg; fiber: 1g;

869. Tasty banana and cinnamon cake

Preparation Time: 10 minutes
Cooking Time: 30 minutes
Servings: 4
Ingredients:

- Butter, soft 1 tbsp.
- Egg 1
- Brown sugar ⅓ cup.
- Honey 2 tbsp.
- Banana; peeled and mashed 1
- White flour 1 cup.
- Baking powder 1 tsp.
- Cinnamon powder ½ tsp.
- Cooking spray

Directions :

1. Take a cake pan and spritz some cooking spray on it. Leave the pan aside.
2. Add butter with sugar, banana, honey, egg, cinnamon, baking powder, flour in a bowl and whisk all the ingredients together.
3. Now, take the greased cake pan and pour this batter into the pan.
4. Set your air fryer at 350° f for 30 minutes and introduce the pan into the fryer to cook for the given time.
5. Let the cake cool down in room temperature.
6. Cut cakes into slices, serve and enjoy this delicious cake.

Nutrition: Calories 232, fat 4, fiber 1, carbs 34, protein 4

870. Delicious banana bread

Preparation Time: 15 minutes
Cooking Time: 40 minutes
Servings: 6
Ingredients:

- Sugar ¾ cup.
- Butter 1/3 cup.
- Vanilla extract 1 tsp.
- Egg 1
- Bananas ; mashed 2
- Baking powder 1 tsp.
- Flour 1 and ½ cups.
- Baking soda ½ tsps.
- Milk 1/3 cup.
- Cream of tartar 1 and ½ tsps.
- Cooking spray

Directions:

1. Take a bowl and mix milk with cream of tartar, sugar, butter, egg, vanilla, bananas and stir everything together.
2. Gather another bowl to add flour with baking powder and baking soda.
3. Blend these two mixtures together and grease a cake pan with the cooking spray.
4. Pour the batter into the greased cake pan and place it into the air fryer to cook at 320°f for 40 minutes.
5. Take the bread out of the fryer and let it cool down in room temperature.
6. Slice the bread evenly and enjoy by serving it immediately.

Nutrition: Calories 292, fat 7, fiber 8, carbs 28, protein 4

871. Easy to make air fried bananas

Preparation Time: 10 minutes
Cooking Time: 10 minutes
Servings: 4
Ingredients:

- Butter 3 tbsp.
- Eggs 2
- Bananas ; peeled and halved 8
- Corn flour ½ cup.
- Cinnamon sugar 3 tbsp .
- Panko 1 cup.

Directions:

1. Take a pan to melt the butter over medium high heat.
2. Add panko into the pan and give it a stir.
3. Let it cook for 4 minutes and then transfer to a bowl.
4. Coat the bananas with flour, egg, panko mix and arrange them properly in your air fryer basket.
5. Sprinkle some cinnamon sugar on top and set the fryer at 280°f for 10 minutes to cook.
6. Once cooked, serve immediately.

Nutrition: Calories 164, fat 1, fiber 4, carbs 32, protein 4

872. Lentils and dates brownies with honey and banana flavor

Preparation Time: 10 minutes
Cooking Time: 15 minutes
Servings: 8
Ingredients:

- Canned lentils rinsed and drained 28 ounces.
- Dates 12
- Honey 1 tbsp.
- Banana, peeled and chopped 1
- Baking soda ½ tsp.
- Almond butter 4 tbsp.
- Cocoa powder 2 tbsp.

Directions:

1. In a container of your food processor, add lentils, butter, banana, cocoa, baking soda, honey and blend it really well.
2. In it then add some dates, some more pulse before pouring it into a greased pan that fits your air fryer and spread evenly. Now bring it to fryer and let it bake for 15 minutes at 360°f.
3. After it's done, take the brownies mix out of the oven and let it cool.
4. Lastly, cut them into pieces before arranging them on a platter to serve.

Nutrition: Calories 162, fat 4, fiber 2, carbs 3, protein 4

873. Ginger flavored cheesecake

Preparation Time: 15 minutes
Cooking Time: 20 minutes
Servings: 6
Ingredients:

- Butter ; melted 2 tsps.
- Ginger cookies ; crumbled ½ cup.
- Cream cheese ; soft 16 ounces.
- Eggs 2
- Sugar ½ cup.
- Rum 1 tsp.
- Vanilla extract ½ tsp.
- Nutmeg ; ground ½ tsp.

Directions:

1. Take a pan and grease it well with butter.
2. Spread cookie crumbs on the bottom evenly.
3. Gather a mixer bowl to beat cream cheese with nutmeg, vanilla, rum and eggs.
4. Blend these ingredients together extremely well and spread it over cookie crumbs.
5. Set your air fryer at 340° f for 20 minutes and put the pan into the fryer to cook.
6. Leave cheesecake to cool down completely and then put it in the fridge for 2 hours.
7. Slice into equal pieces and serve cold right away to enjoy it the most in the summer heat.

Nutrition: Calories 412, fat 12, fiber 6, carbs 20, protein 6

874. Coffee cheesecakes with mascarpone cheese on top

Preparation Time: 15 minutes
Cooking Time: 20 minutes
Servings: 6
Ingredients:

- For the cheesecakes:
- Butter 2 tbsp.
- Cream cheese 8 ounces.
- Coffee 3 tbsp.
- Eggs 3
- Sugar 1/3 cup.

- Caramel syrup 1 tbsp.
- For the frosting:
- Caramel syrup 3 tbsp.
- Butter 3 tbsp.
- Mascarpone cheese, soft 8 ounces.
- Sugar 2 tbsp.

Directions:
1. take a blender and in it add cream cheese, eggs, 2 tbsp butter, coffee, 1 tbsp caramel syrup, ⅓ cup sugar and mix it well. Now take a cupcake pan which fits in your air fryer and spoon the mixture in it before bringing it to the fryer and cook and let it bake for 20 minutes at 320° f.
2. after it's done, take out the pan and leave it aside to cool down and then let it freeze in your fridge for another 3 hours.
3. in the meantime, take another bowl and mix 2 tbsp sugar and mascarpone cheese and blend it well. After 3 hours take out the cake and ice it with this batter and serve them.

Nutrition: Calories 254, fat 23, fiber 0, carbs 21, protein 5

875. Tasty lime cheesecake
Preparation Time: 15 minutes
Cooking Time: 4 hours and 4 minutes
Servings: 10
Ingredients:
- Butter, melted 2 tbsp.
- Sugar 2 tsps.
- Flour 4 ounces.
- Coconut ; shredded ¼ cup.
- For the filling:
- Cream cheese 1 pound.
- Lime zest ; grated 1 lime.
- Lime juice 1 lime.
- Hot water 2 cups.
- Lime jelly 2 sachets.

Directions:
1. Gather a bowl to mix coconut with flour, butter and sugar and stir everything well.
2. Press this mixture on the bottom of a pan that fits your air fryer.
3. In the meantime, put hot water in a bowl and add jelly sachets to it. Mix it until it dissolves completely.
4. Take another bowl and whisk cream cheese with jelly, lime juice and zest together.
5. Spread this over the crust and place the pan in your air fryer.
6. Set your fryer at 300°f for 4 minutes and cook.
7. Refrigerate the cake for 4 hours and then enjoy having it all cold.

Nutrition: Calories 260, fat 23, fiber 2, carbs 5, protein 7

876. Sweet potato cheesecake
Preparation Time: 10 minutes
Cooking Time: 4 minutes
Servings: 4
Ingredients:
- Butter, melted 4 tbsp.
- Mascarpone, soft 6 ounces.
- Cream cheese, soft 8 ounces.
- Graham crackers, crumbled 2/3 cup.
- Milk ¾ cup.
- Vanilla extract 1 tsp.
- Sweet potato puree 2/3 cup.
- Cinnamon powder ¼ tsps.

Directions:
1. gather a bowl and in it add butter, crumbled crackers, and stir it really well.
2. take a cake pan that fits your air fryer and now, press it on the bottom of the cake pan before you keep it in the fridge.
3. take another bowl and in it mix cream cheese with mascarpone, sweet potato puree, milk, cinnamon, vanilla and whisk it really well until it forms a smooth consistency.
4. now spread this mixture over the crust and bring it in your air fryer and let it cook for 4 minutes at 300°f.
5. after it's done and well cooked, take it out and keep it in the fridge to completely cool down before serving it.

Nutrition: Calories 172, fat 4, fiber 6, carbs 8, protein 3

877. Mandarin pudding with honey on top
Preparation Time: 15 minutes
Cooking Time: 40 minutes
Servings: 8
Ingredients:
- Mandarin ; peeled and sliced 1
- Juice from mandarins 2
- Brown sugar 2 tbsp.
- Butter ; soft 4 ounces.
- Eggs ; whisked 4 ounces.
- Sugar ¾ cup.
- White flour ¾ cup.
- Almonds ; ground ¾ cup.
- Honey for serving.

Directions:
1. Take out a loaf pan and grease it with some butter.
2. Sprinkle some brown sugar on the bottom and arrange the mandarin slices.
3. Gather a bowl and mix butter with sugar, eggs, almonds, flour and mandarin juice.
4. Stir this well and spoon this over mandarin slices.
5. Place the pan in your air fryer to cook at 360°f for 40 minutes.
6. Transfer the pudding on a plate and drizzle some honey on top.

Nutrition: Calories 162, fat 3, fiber 2, carbs 3, protein 6

878. Passion fruit pudding
Preparation Time: 10 minutes
Cooking Time: 40 minutes
Servings: 6
Ingredients:
- Paleo passion fruit curd 1 cup.
- Passion fruits, pulp and seeds 4
- Maple syrup 3 and ½ ounces.
- Eggs 3
- Ghee melted 2 ounces.
- Almond milk 3 and ½ ounces.
- Almond flour ½ cup.
- Baking powder ½ tsp.

Directions:
1. First, take a bowl and in it mix half of the fruit curd with passion fruits seeds and pulp, and give it a really good stir before dividing it into 6 heatproof ramekins.
2. Keep aside the bowl and gather another bowl now to whisk eggs with maple syrup, ghee, rest of the curd, baking powder, milk, flour, and again stir it really well.
3. Now divide this mix into the ramekins before you introduce in the fryer and cook it for 40 minutes at 200 0f.
4. Once it's done, take it out and leave the puddings to cool down before you serve it.

Nutrition: Calories 430, fat 22, fiber 3, carbs 7, protein 8

879. Chocolate pumpkin cake
Preparation Time: 10 minutes
Cooking Time: 30 minutes
Servings: 12
Ingredients:
- White flour ¾ cup.
- Whole wheat flour ¾ cup.
- Baking soda 1 tsp.
- Pumpkin pie spice ¾ tsp.
- Sugar ¾ cup.
- Banana ; mashed 1
- Baking powder ½ tsp.
- Canola oil 2 tbsp.
- Greek yogurt ½ cup.
- Canned pumpkin puree 8 ounces.
- Cooking spray
- Egg 1
- Vanilla extract ½ tsp.
- Chocolate chips 2/3 cup.

Directions:
1. take a bowl and add white flour with whole wheat flour, salt, baking soda and powder and pumpkin spice.

2. stir all these ingredients together well.
3. gather another bowl to mix sugar with oil, banana, yoghurt, pumpkin puree, vanilla and egg. Blend these ingredients together with the help of a hand mixer.
4. combine these two mixtures together and additionally put some chocolate chips into it.
5. transfer this batter into a greased Bundt pan that fits your air fryer.
6. place the pan in your air fryer and cook for 30 minutes at 330°f.
7. cool down the cake before you cut it and serve.

Nutrition: Calories: 232, fat 7, fiber 7, carbs 29, protein 4

880. **Walnut and raisin stuffed apples**

Preparation time: 5 minutes

cooking time: 20 minutes

servings: 2

Ingredients:
- 3 tablespoons crushed walnuts
- 2 tablespoons raisins
- 2 granny smith apples, cored, bottom intact
- 1 teaspoon cinnamon
- From the cupboard:
- 3 tablespoons sugar
- 2 tablespoons butter, under room temperature

Directions:
1. Preheat air fryer to 350°f (180°c). Spritz the air fryer basket with cooking spray.
2. Combine all the ingredients, except for the apples, in a bowl. Stir to mix well.
3. Place the apples in the air fryer basket, bottom side down, then spoon the mixture in the core hollows of the apples.
4. Cook for 20 minutes or until the apples are wilted. Serve warm.

Nutrition Calories: 322; fat: 18g; carbs: 33g; protein: 7g

881. **Coconut cupcakes**

Preparation time: 20 minutes

cooking time: 10 minutes

servings: 4

Ingredients:
- 2 eggs
- ½ cup coconut flour
- ⅓ cup coconut milk
- 1 teaspoon vanilla extract
- ½ cup coconut chips, for garnish
- From the cupboard:
- 1 tablespoon coconut oil, melted
- Special equipment:

Directions:
1. A 4cup muffin tin, coated with melted butter
2. Whisk together the eggs, flour, milk, vanilla, and coconut oil in a bowl. Let sit for 20 minutes under room temperature, then spoon the mixture in a 4cup muffin tin.
3. Preheat the air fryer to 230°f (110°c).
4. Arrange the muffin tin in the air fryer, then cook for 4 to 5 minutes or until the edges of the cupcakes are lightly browned.
5. Remove the cupcakes from the basket and serve with coconut chips on top.

Nutrition Calories: 177; fat: 19g; carbs: 6g; protein: 7g

882. **Easy lemon curd**

Preparation time: 9 minutes

cooking time: 21 minutes

servings: 2

Ingredients:
- 1 egg
- 1 egg yolk
- ¾ lemon, juiced
- From the cupboard:
- 3 tablespoons sugar
- 3 tablespoons butter
- Special equipment:
- A medium ramekin

Directions:
1. Preheat the air fryer to 220°f (104°c).

2. Mix the butter and sugar in a medium ramekin, then gradually fold in the egg and yolk. Stir until the mixture is smooth and yellow. Then mix in the lemon juice.
3. Put the ramekin in the air fryer and cook for 6 minutes, then increase the temperature of the air fryer to 320°f (160°c) and cook for an additional 15 minutes or until a toothpick inserted in the ramekin comes out clean.
4. Remove the ramekin from the air fryer and pour the mixture in a bowl. Wrap the bowl in plastic and refrigerate for at least 8 hours. Serve chilled.

Tip: replace the lemon juice with other extracts, such as vanilla extract or berry extract, to make a unique taste of curds.

Nutrition Calories: 262; fat: 27g; carbs: 17g; protein: 4g

883. **Honey and peanut butter banana toast**

Preparation time: 10 minutes

cooking time: 9 minutes

servings: 4

Ingredients:
- 4 slices white bread
- 4 tablespoons peanut butter
- 2 bananas, peeled and thinly sliced
- 1 teaspoon ground cinnamon
- 4 tablespoons honey
- From the cupboard:
- 2 tablespoons butter, softened

Directions:
1. Preheat the air fryer to 375°f (190°c).
2. On a clean work surface, coat the bottom side of a slice of bread with ½ tablespoon of butter, then smear 1 tablespoon of peanut butter on top of the bread with a knife.
3. Arrange the slices of half of a banana on peanut butter. Sprinkle with ¼ teaspoon of cinnamon and drizzle with 1 tablespoon of honey. Repeat with the remaining ingredients.
4. Arrange them in the preheated air fryer and cook for 5 minutes, then increase the temperature to 400°f (205°c) and cook for 4 more minutes or until the bread is toast and the banana slices are golden brown. You may need to work in batches to avoid overcrowding.
5. Serve the banana toast on a plate warm.

Tip: you can cut the bread slices in half to make it easier to fit the air fryer basket.

Nutrition Calories: 330; fat: 16g; carbs: 41g; protein: 6g

884. **Chocolate fondants with easy praline**

Preparation time: 10 minutes

cooking time: 15 minutes

servings: 4

Ingredients:
- ¾ cup dark chocolate
- ½ cup peanut butter, crunchy
- 4 eggs, room temperature
- ⅛ cup flour, sieved
- From the cupboard:
- ½ cup sugar, divided
- 1 teaspoon salt
- ¼ cup water
- 2 tablespoons butter, diced

Directions:
1. Make the praline: combine half of the sugar, salt, and water in a saucepan, then bring to a boil over mediumlow heat. Keep stirring.
2. Reduce the heat to low and simmer for 5 to 6 minutes or until the liquid reduces in half.
3. Pour the mixture in a baking pan. Allow to cool until hardened, then break them into pieces and set aside until ready to serve.
4. Preheat the air fryer to 300°f (150°c).
5. Bring a small pot of water to a boil over medium heat, then put a heatproof bowl over the pot.
6. Make the fondants: combine the chocolate, peanut butter, and butter in the heatproof bowl. Keep stirring until the well mixed.
7. Remove the bowl from the pot and let stand for a few minutes. Whisk in the eggs, flour, and remaining sugar.
8. Spritz 4 small loaf pans with cooking spray, then spoon the chocolate mixture in the pans.

9. Put the pans in the preheated air fryer and cook for 7 minutes or until a toothpick inserted in the center comes out clean.

Tip: the reason to heat the chocolate mixture in a heatproof bowl over a pot of boiling water is to control the heating temperature under 212°f (100°c).

Nutrition Calories: 620; fat: 41g; carbs: 44g; protein: 10g

885. Simple blueberry turnovers

Preparation time: 15 minutes
cooking time: 20 minutes
servings: 8

Ingredients:
- 1 (17ounce / 482gbox frozen puff pastry dough, thawed, cut into 8 squares in total
- 1 (10ounce / 284gcan blueberry pie filling
- 1 egg white, beaten

Directions:
1. Preheat the air fryer to 370°f (188°c). Spritz the air fryer basket with cooking spray.
2. Make the turnovers: unfold the puff pastry squares on a clean work surface, spoon 1 tablespoon of the filling on each square.
3. Brush the edges of the squares with egg white. Fold the squares over the filling diagonally to form triangles, then press the edges to seal with a fork.
4. Arrange the turnovers in the air fryer basket and spritz with cooking spray. You may need to work in batches to avoid overcrowding.
5. Cook for 8 minutes or until golden brown. Flip the turnovers halfway through the cooking time.
6. Allow to cool for a few minutes, then remove the turnovers from the air fryer and serve.
7. Tip: thaw the puff pastry dough in the refrigerator for 4 hours, or at room temperature for 40 minutes. Do not microwave the frozen puff pastry dough.

Nutrition Calories: 224; fat: 10g; carbs: 20g; protein: 0g

886. Cream cheese and pineapple wontons

Preparation time: 5 minutes
cooking time: 40 minutes
servings: 10

Ingredients:
- 1 cup finely chopped fresh pineapple
- 8 ounces (227 g) cream cheese, softened
- 20 wonton wrappers

Directions:
1. Preheat the air fryer to 380°f (193°c). Spritz the air fryer basket with cooking spray.
2. Combine the pineapple and cream cheese in a bowl. Stir well to mix.
3. On a clean work surface, unfold the wonton wrappers, then divide the mixture into the center of the wrappers.
4. Fold the wrappers over the mixture diagonally to form triangles, then fold 2 bottom corners up toward each other. Press to vent the air remains in the wontons, then press the open edges to seal with a fork.
5. Arrange the wontons in the preheated air fryer and spritz with cooking spray. You may need to work in batches to avoid overcrowding.
6. Cook for 10 minutes, then flip the wontons and cook for 6 minutes more or until the wontons are golden brown. Check the doneness of the wontons periodically.
7. Remove the wontons from the air fryer basket. Allow to cool before serving.

Tip: replace the filling of cream cheese and pineapple with the mixture of shrimp meat, a little piece of soup cube, and chopped cucumber to make a unique taste of wonton.

Nutrition Calories: 137; fat: 0g; carbs: 10g; protein: 0g

887. Banana s'mores

Preparation time: 10 minutes
cooking time: 6 minutes
servings: 4

Ingredients:
- 4 unpeeled bananas
- 3 tablespoons mini marshmallows
- 3 tablespoons graham cracker cereal
- 3 tablespoons mini peanut butter chips
- 3 tablespoons mini semisweet chocolate chips

Directions:
1. Preheat the air fryer to 400°f (205°c). Spitz the air fryer basket with cooking spray.
2. Slice into the skin and meat of bananas lengthwise along the inside of the curve, keep the bottom of the skin intact.
3. Open the bananas to form pockets, then fill the pockets with remaining ingredients. Press them in bananas to avoid leaking.
4. Arrange the bananas in the preheated air fryer and cook for 6 minutes or until the bananas are soft and the skin is charred.
5. Gently remove the bananas from the air fryer basket with tongs. Allow to cool for a few minutes before serving.

Tip: arrange the bananas on the side of the air fryer basket to keep them upright with the filling facing up.

Nutrition Calories: 213; fat: 5g; carbs: 48g; protein: 3g

888. Crispy chocolate meringue cookies

Preparation time: 10 minutes
cooking time: 1 hour
Servings 8

Ingredients:
- 3 large egg whites
- ¼ teaspoon cream of tartar
- ¼ cup swerve confectioners' style sweetener
- 2 tablespoons unsweetened cocoa powder
- Special equipment:
- A piping bag with a ¾inch tip

Directions:
1. Preheat the air fryer to 225°f (107°c). Line a 6inch pie pan with parchment paper.
2. Whisk the egg whites and tartar cream with a hand mixer to form soft peaks, then mix in the sweetener and keep whisking until stiff peaks form. Fold in the cocoa powder.
3. Gently pour the mixture in a piping bag with a ¾inch tip, then pipe sixteen 1inch cookies on the pie pan. Keep a space between each two cookies.
4. Put the pan in the preheated air fryer and cook for an hour or until the cookies are crispy.
5. Allow the cookies to cool for 20 minutes, then remove the pie pan from the air fryer and serve.

Tip: if you don't have a piping bag, you can snip a resealable plastic bag to make a ¾inch hole.

Nutrition Calories: 12; fat: 3g; carbs: 0g; protein: 0g

889. Easy cinnamon twists

Preparation time: 10 minutes
cooking time: 10 to 20 minutes
servings: 9

Ingredients:
- 1 sheet puff pastry, cut into 18 strips
- 1 teaspoon ground cinnamon
- From the cupboard:
- ¼ cup granulated sugar

Directions:
1. Preheat the air fryer to 330°f (166°c). Spritz the air fryer basket with cooking spray.
2. Form the puff pastry strips into twists, then put the twists in the air fryer basket. You need to work in batches to avoid overcrowding.
3. Cook for 4 minutes or until lightly browned. Flip the twists halfway through the cooking time.
4. Meanwhile, mix the cinnamon and sugar in a bowl.
5. Transfer the cooked twists in the bowl of cinnamon mixture with tongs. Allow to cool for 5 minutes, then toss to coat well and serve.

Tip: you can baste the twists with chocolate glaze for a better palate.

Nutrition Calories: 99; fat: 0g; carbs: 10g; protein: 0g

890. Salty Cheese and Vegetable Pie

Preparation Time: 30 minutes
Cooking Time: 40 minutes
Servings: 6

Ingredients:
- 2 round sheets of puff pastry
- 1 husked broccoli
- 25g butter
- 3 sliced leeks

- 200ml milk cream
- 15g sliced onion
- 15g cut tarragon
- 2 tablespoons of mustard
- Salt and pepper
- 200g sliced gorgonzola cheese
- 1 beaten egg

Directions:
1. With one of the sheets, cover the previously greased Air Fryer mold. Cover with waxed paper, prick the dough and add legumes to avoid deforming.
2. Take the Air Fryer programmed at 180°c for 5 to 10 minutes. Meanwhile, place the broccoli in boiling water for 1 minute and Reserve up in cold water.
3. In a pan melt the butter and sauté the leek. Add the cream of milk, chives, tarragon, mustard, salt, and pepper. Mix well and remove from heat.
4. Pour the mixture into the mold, add broccoli and gorgonzola.
5. Paint the edges of the dough with egg and cover with the second sheet of puff pastry pressing the edges. To paint with egg and to take to the Air Fryer to 180°c by 25 - 30 minutes covering with aluminum paper to average cooking.
6. Let stand, unmold and cool. Serve up fresh

Nutrition: Calories: 469 Fat: 25g Carbs: 54g Protein: 8g

891. Avocado Brownie
Preparation Time: 15 minutes
Cooking Time: 25 minutes
Servings: 6
Ingredients:
- 400g black chocolate coating
- 4 eggs
- 2 avocados
- 80g honey
- 20g cocoa powder
- 25g sugar
- 25g wheat flour

Directions:
1. Melt the chocolate and leave it to rest. Cut the avocado in half, remove the bone and extract the meat.
2. Grind the avocado and add to the chocolate with the rest of the ingredients.
3. Stir until everything is well integrated and prepare the mold of the Air Fryer with waxed paper.
4. Pour the mixture into the mold and give small blows to remove the air.
5. Program it at 180°c for 20 - 25 minutes. Let stand, unmold and let cool before serving

Nutrition: Calories: 139 Fat: 8g Carbs: 16g Protein: 3g

892. Brownie with Marshmallows
Preparation Time: 10 minutes
Cooking Time: 25 minutes
Servings: 6
Ingredients:
- 450g sugar
- 130g cocoa powder
- 225g butter
- 1 teaspoon vanilla essence
- Salt
- 4 egg
- 170g wheat flour
- 20 large marshmallows

Directions:
1. Melt the butter. Mix cocoa with sugar and beat with but ter. Add vanilla, salt, and eggs one by one mixing well.
2. Add the flour and mix until homogeneous. Prepare the mold of the Air Fryer with waxed paper and pour the mixture.
3. Cover over with the marshmallows and set at 180°c for 15 to 25 minutes.
4. Half the time covers with aluminum foil. Let cool and Serve up.

Nutrition: Calories: 160 Fat: 8g Carbs: 20g Protein: 2g

893. Red Wine Muffins
Preparation Time: 15 minutes

Cooking Time: 15 minutes
Servings: 6
Ingredients:
- 2 eggs
- 125g sugar
- Olive oil
- 50ml red wine
- A spoonful of hot water
- 75g cocoa powder
- 125g wheat flour
- 1 envelope of instant yeast

Directions:
1. Sift flour, cocoa, and yeast. In a bowl add eggs, sugar and mix with a blender until fluffy.
2. Incorporate oil, wine, and water while continuing to beat.
3. Add them dry and mix gently until homogenizing.
4. Place paper cups in a cupcake mold suitable for the Air Fryer.
5. Fill the mold up to ¾ of its capacity, take the Air Fryer programmed at 180°c for 10 - 15 minutes.
6. Allow to cool and Serve up with tea, coffee or milk.

Nutrition: Calories: 234 Fat: 11g Carbs: 31g Protein: 3g

894. Tea Cupcake
Preparation Time: 15 minutes
Cooking Time: 30 minutes
Servings: 6
Ingredients:
- 300g of water
- 2 teaspoons black tea
- 200g of nuts
- 4 eggs
- 300g sugar
- 250g sunflower oil.
- Vanilla
- 3 tablespoons of cocoa powder
- ½ teaspoon lemon juice
- 500g flour
- 1 envelope of instant yeast

Directions:
1. Prepare tea and Reserve up. Place the chopped nuts, the cold tea, eggs, sugar, and oil, vanilla, cocoa and lemon juice, mix 15 seconds at speed 5 in the processor.
2. Add flour and yeast, mix 20 seconds at speed 4.
3. Once you obtain a homogeneous mass, prepare a suitable mold, greased and bring Air Fryer for 20 to 25 minutes at 180°c.
4. Check the cooking and puncture with a stick, if necessary, put another 10 minutes, covered with a piece of aluminum foil

Nutrition: Calories: 160 Fat: 6g Carbs: 21g Protein: 2g

895. Rustic Cheesecake
Preparation Time: 15 minutes
Cooking Time: 35 minutes
Servings: 1
Ingredients:
- 100 g of unsalted butter.
- 75 g of sugar.
- 1 pinch of salt.
- 1 egg.
- 100 g of flour.
- 80 g of rye flour.
- 1 teaspoon instant yeast
- 250 g of cream cheese
- 1 egg.
- 40 g of sugar.
- 1 teaspoon vanilla sugar
- 1 pinch of salt.
- 200 g of currants

Directions:
1. Prepare a mold. Mix butter and sugar in a bowl; beat with a hand mixer until fluffy. Add egg, salt and beat.
2. Add the two flours, yeast and mix. There must be a manageable mass. Cover the bottom and walls of the mold with this mass.

3. Mix cream cheese, egg, sugar and salt, mix to eliminate lumps. Pour into the base that is in the mold. Place the currants to taste.
4. Bring the Air Fryer for 20 to 25 minutes at a temperature of 180° c.
5. Check the cooking, place aluminum foil and reprogram for 10 more minutes, or until golden brown.

Nutrition: Calories: 380 Fat: 28g Carbs: 50g Protein: 10g

896. Lemon Cake with Cheese Meringue

Preparation Time: 15 minutes
Cooking Time: 25 minutes
Servings: 4
Ingredients:

- Grated and juice of 1 lemon
- 3 eggs
- 1 cup of vegetable oil
- 2 cups flour
- 1 and ¾ cups of sugar
- 1 tablespoon baking powder
- 300g of cream cheese
- 1 can of condensed milk
- White chocolate.
- Vanilla essence to taste.
- 1 tablespoon of unflavored gelatin.
- 2 cups of milk cream.

Directions:

1. Place lemon, egg, oil, sugar, flour and baking powder in the blender. Process until a homogeneous paste is obtained.
2. Prepare the mold of the Air Fryer with wax paper and pour the mixture. Program it at 180°c for 20 to 25 minutes. Let stand, unmold and cool.
3. Meanwhile, dissolve the gelatin in water and set aside. Bring the chocolate cheese until melted.
4. Remove from the heat and add condensed milk next to the vanilla while stirring. Add the gelatin while mixing.
5. Apart whisk the cream to the point of snow and add to the previous mixture in an enveloping way.
6. Decorate the cake with the Preparation and refrigerate. Serve up cold with coffee or tea.

Nutrition: Calories: 430 Fat: 9g Carbs: 65g Protein: 9g

897. Creamy Sponge Cake

Preparation Time: 15 minutes
Cooking Time: 35 minutes
Servings: 1
Ingredients:

- 125g of cream cheese
- 30g of butter
- 70ml of milk
- 3 buds
- ½ teaspoon of salt
- Lemon juice
- 30g wheat flour
- 30g cornstarch
- 60g of sugar

Directions:

1. Prepare a mold. Place butter, cream cheese and milk in the processor. Add egg yolks and mix. Add salt and lemon juice.
2. Sift flour and cornstarch, keep mixing. Beat the whites until stiff, add the powdered sugar, little by little.
3. Join the two mixtures in three parts, with enveloping movements from top to bottom, until integrating.
4. Place in the mold and take the Air Fryer to a temperature of 160° c, for 20 - 25 minutes, check the cooking with a toothpick and cover with aluminum foil, cook for 10 minutes more if necessary.

Nutrition: Calories: 111 Fat: 5g Carbs: 14g Protein: 1g

898. Banana Inverted Cake

Preparation Time: 15 minutes
Cooking Time: 25 minutes
Servings: 1
Ingredients:

- 3 bananas cut horizontally
- 150g of butter
- ½ cup of brown sugar
- 1 cup of sugar
- Cinnamon
- Hot rum
- 2 eggs
- Vanilla
- 1 cup of milk
- 1 and ½ cup of flour
- 1 tablespoon baking powder
- 1 tablespoon of baking soda

Directions:

1. Place the bananas in the mold of the Air Fryer. Melt 50g butter in butter with ½ cup of sugar and cinnamon.
2. Then add the hot rum and light a fire with a match, when turning off remove from the heat and pour over the bananas.
3. Separate with a blender, mix butter and sugar until creamy. Add eggs, vanilla, and milk while stirring.
4. Sift flour, baking powder, baking soda and add it to the previous mix.
5. Beat in an enveloping way until it is integrated and poured over the bananas.
6. Program the Air Fryer at 180°c for 20 to 25 minutes, then cover with aluminum foil and program for 15 - 20 minutes.
7. Allow to cool and unmold by turning the mold. Serve up fresh.

Nutrition: Calories: 198 Fat: 9g Carbs: 28g Protein: 2g

899. Yogurt Cake

Preparation Time: 20 minutes
Cooking Time: 15 minutes
Servings: 1
Ingredients:

- 3 eggs
- 1 vanilla yogurt
- 2 cups sugar
- 3 cups rising flour
- 1 cup of oil
- Vanilla

Directions:

1. Beat the eggs with sugar until dissolved and add yogurt while stirring. Add oil little by little along with the vanilla.
2. Sift the flour and add it gently for 7 minutes.
3. Prepare the mold of the Air Fryer with waxed paper and pour the mixture. Schedule at 180°C for 15 - 20 minutes.
4. Cover with aluminum foil and program for 10 - 15 more minutes.
5. Let cool, unmold and serve.

Nutrition: Calories: 361 Fat: 11g Carbs: 59g Protein: 10g

900. Grandma's Cake

Preparation Time: 20 minutes
Cooking Time: 20 – 25 minutes
Servings: 1
Ingredients:

- 4 eggs
- 150g sugar
- 125g melted butter
- 1 teaspoon vanilla essence
- 500ml milk
- 125g flour
- Salt
- Powdered sugar

Directions:

1. Separate egg whites and egg yolks.
2. Beat the yolks with sugar until well-integrated.
3. Add butter, flour, milk and mix well until homogeneous. Apart, beat the whites with salt to the point of snow.
4. Incorporate the previous mixture in an enveloping manner until it is well integrated.
5. Prepare the mold of the Air Fryer with waxed paper and pour the mixture.
6. Schedule at 180°C for 15 - 20 minutes.
7. Cover with aluminum foil and program for 20 to 25 minutes.
8. Let cool unmold and Serve up with icing sugar.

Nutrition: Calories: 260 Fat: 8g Carbs: 40g Protein: 5g

901. Leeks Pie
Preparation Time: 10 minutes
Cooking Time: 15 minutes
Servings: 1
Ingredients:
- 400g leeks in sheets
- 150g grated cheese
- 500ml milk
- 4 slices of bread
- 4 eggs
- 1 tablespoon butter
- Salt and pepper

Directions:
1. Place the leeks in water and cook until tender.
2. Drain, cut finely and Reserve up.
3. Sauté the leeks in butter for a few minutes and Reserve up.
4. In a pot place milk and bring to the fire. Before boiling add bread, remove from heat and let cool. Add to the leeks and add cheese.
5. Beat eggs well and add to the mixture, stirring well and seasoning.
6. Prepare the mold of the Air Fryer with waxed paper and pour the mixture.
7. Take the Air Fryer and set at 180°C for 10 - 15 minutes. Serve up hot.

Nutrition: Calories: 198 Fat: 14g Carbs: 15g Protein: 3g

902. Pineapple Galette
Preparation Time: 10 minutes
Cooking Time: 40 minutes
Servings 2
Ingredients:
- ¼ medium size pineapple, peeled, cored, and cut crosswise into ¼inchthick slices
- 2 tablespoons dark rum
- 1 teaspoon vanilla extract
- ½ teaspoon kosher salt
- Finely grated zest of ½ lime
- 1 store bought sheet puff pastry, cut into an 8inch round
- 3 tablespoons granulated sugar
- 2 tablespoons unsalted butter, cubed and chilled
- Coconut ice cream, for serving

Directions:
1. Preheat the air fryer to 310°F (154°C).
2. In a small bowl, combine the pineapple slices, rum, vanilla, salt, and lime zest and let stand for at least 10 minutes to allow the pineapple to soak in the rum.
3. Meanwhile, press the puff pastry round into the bottom and up the sides of a round metal cake pan and use the tines of a fork to dock the bottom and sides.
4. Position the pineapple slices on the bottom of the pastry in more or less a single layer, then sprinkle with the sugar and dot with the butter.
5. Drizzle with the leftover juices from the bowl. Put the pan in the air fryer and bake until the pastry is puffed and golden brown and the pineapple is lightly caramelized on top.
6. Unmold the galette from the pan and serve warm with coconut ice cream.

Nutrition: Calories: 17 Fat: 5g Carbs: 29g Protein: 3g

903. Ricotta Lemon Poppy Seed Cake
Preparation Time: 15 minutes
Cooking Time: 55 minutes
Servings 4
Ingredients:
- 1 cup almond flour
- ½ cup sugar
- 3 large eggs
- ¼ cup heavy cream
- ¼ cup full fat ricotta cheese
- ¼ cup coconut oil, melted
- 2 tablespoons poppy seeds
- 1 teaspoon baking powder
- 1 teaspoon pure lemon extract
- 1 lemon Grated zest and juice, plus more zest for garnish

Directions:
1. Preheat the air fryer to 325°F (163°C).
2. Generously butter a round baking pan. Line the bottom of the pan with parchment paper cut to fit.
3. In a large bowl, combine the almond flour, sugar, eggs, cream, ricotta, coconut oil, poppy seeds, baking powder, lemon extract, lemon zest, and lemon juice. Beat well until blended and fluffy.
4. Pour the batter into the prepared pan. Cover the pan tightly with aluminum foil. Set the pan in the air fryer basket and bake for 45 minutes.
5. Remove the foil and bake for 10 to 15 minutes more until a knife (do not use a toothpick) inserted into the center of the cake comes out clean.
6. Remove the cake from pan and let it cool on the rack for 15 minutes before slicing.
7. Top with additional lemon zest, slice and serve.

Nutrition: Calories: 317 Fat: 12g Carbs: 48g Protein: 6g

904. Cardamom and Vanilla Custard
Preparation Time: 5 minutes
Cooking Time: 25 minutes
Servings 2
Ingredients:
- 1 cup whole milk
- 1 large egg
- 2 tablespoons plus 1 teaspoon sugar
- ¼ teaspoon vanilla bean paste
- ¼ teaspoon ground cardamom, plus more for sprinkling

Directions:
1. Preheat the air fryer to 350°F (177°C).
2. In a medium bowl, beat together the milk, egg, sugar, vanilla, and cardamom.
3. Put two ramekins in the air fryer basket. Divide the mixture between the ramekins. Sprinkle lightly with cardamom. Cover each ramekin tightly with aluminum foil. Bake for 25 minutes.
4. Let the custards cool on a wire rack for 5 to 10 minutes.
5. Serve warm or refrigerate until cold and serve chilled.

Nutrition: Calories: 280 Fat: 16g Carbs: 30g Protein: 2g

905. Orange Cake
Preparation Time: 10 minutes
Cooking Time: 23 minutes
Servings 8
Ingredients:
- Nonstick baking spray with flour
- 1¼ cups all-purpose flour
- 1/3 cup yellow cornmeal
- ¾ cup white sugar
- 1 teaspoon baking soda
- ¼ cup safflower oil
- 1¼ cups orange juice, divided
- 1 teaspoon vanilla
- ¼ cup powdered sugar

Directions:
1. Preheat the air fryer to 350°F (177°C).
2. Put flour, cornmeal, sugar, baking soda, safflower oil, 1 cup of the orange juice, and vanilla in a bowl and mix well.
3. Pour the batter into the baking pan and place in the air fryer. Bake for 23 minutes or until a toothpick inserted in the center of the cake comes out clean.
4. Remove the cake from the basket and place on a cooling rack. Using a toothpick, make about 20 holes in the cake.
5. In a small bowl, combine remaining 1/4 cup of orange juice and the powdered sugar and stir well. Drizzle this mixture over the hot cake slowly so the cake absorbs it.

Nutrition: Calories: 198 Fat: 10g Carbs: 27g Protein: 1g

906. Black Forest Pies
Preparation Time: 10 minutes
Cooking Time: 15 minutes
Servings 6
Ingredients:
- 3 tablespoons milk or dark chocolate chips
- 2 tablespoons thick, hot fudge sauce
- 2 tablespoons chopped dried cherries

- 1 (10by15inch) sheet frozen puff pastry, thawed
- 1 egg white, beaten
- 2 tablespoons sugar
- ½ teaspoon cinnamon

Directions:
1. Preheat the air fryer to 350°F (177°C).
2. Mix in the chocolate chips, fudge sauce, and dried cherries.
3. Roll out the puff pastry on a floured surface. Cut into 6 squares with a sharp knife.
4. Divide the chocolate chip mixture into the center of each puff pastry square. Fold the squares in half to make triangles. Firmly press the edges with the tines of a fork to seal.
5. Brush the triangles on all sides sparingly with the beaten egg white. Sprinkle the tops with sugar and cinnamon.
6. Put in the air fryer basket and bake for 15 minutes or until the triangles are golden brown. The filling will be hot, so cool for at least 20 minutes before serving.

Nutrition: Calories: 330 Fat: 18g Carbs: 40g Protein: 4g

907.   Graham Cracker Cheesecake
Preparation Time: 10 minutes
Cooking Time: 20 minutes
Servings 8
Ingredients:

- 1 cup graham cracker crumbs
- 3 tablespoons softened butter
- 1½ (8ounce / 227g) packages cream cheese, softened
- 1/3 cup sugar
- 2 eggs
- 1 tablespoon flour
- 1 teaspoon vanilla
- ¼ cup chocolate syrup

Directions
1. Combine the cream cheese and sugar in a medium bowl and mix well. Beat eggs slowly. Add the flour and vanilla.
2. Put butter and graham in a small bowl to make the crust. Mix well. Press into the bottom of a baking pan and put in the freezer to set.
3. Preheat the air fryer to 450°F (232°C).
4. Remove 2/3 cup of the filling to a small bowl and stir in the chocolate syrup until combined.
5. Pour the vanilla filling into the pan with the crust. Drop the chocolate filling over the vanilla filling by the spoonful. With a clean butter knife, stir the fillings in a zigzag pattern to marbleize them.
6. Bake for 20 minutes or until the cheesecake is just set.
7. Cool on a wire rack for 1 hour, then chill in the refrigerator until the cheesecake is firm. Serve immediately.

Nutrition: Calories: 499 Fat: 33g Carbs: 39g Protein: 8g

908.   Banana and Walnut Cake
Preparation Time: 10 minutes
Cooking Time: 25 minutes
Servings 6
Ingredients:

1. 1-pound (454 g) bananas, mashed
2. 8 ounces (227 g) flour
3. 6 ounces (170 g) sugar
4. ounces (99 g) walnuts, chopped
5. ounces (71 g) butter, melted
6. 2 eggs, lightly beaten
7. ¼ teaspoon baking soda

Directions:
1. reheat the air fryer to 355°F (179°C).
2. In a bowl, combine the sugar, butter, egg, flour, and baking soda with a whisk. Stir in the bananas and walnuts.
3. Transfer the mixture to a greased baking dish. Put the dish in the air fryer and bake for 10 minutes.
4. Reduce the temperature to 330°F (166°C) and bake for another 15 minutes. Serve hot.

Nutrition: Calories: 481 Fat: 19g Carbs:74g Protein: 5g

909.   Cinnamon and Pecan Pie
Preparation Time: 10 minutes
Cooking Time: 25 minutes
Servings 4
Ingredients:

- 1 pie dough
- ½ teaspoons cinnamon
- ¾ teaspoon vanilla extract
- 2 eggs
- ¾ cup maple syrup
- 1/8 teaspoon nutmeg
- 3 tablespoons melted butter, divided
- 2 tablespoons sugar
- ½ cup chopped pecans

Directions:
1. Preheat the air fryer to 370°F (188°C).
2. In a small bowl, coat the pecans in 1 tablespoon of melted butter.
3. Transfer the pecans to the air fryer and air fry for about 10 minutes.
4. Put the pie dough in greased pie pan and add the pecans on top.
5. In a bowl, mix the rest of the ingredients. Pour this over the pecans.
6. Put the pan in the air fryer and bake for 25 minutes.
7. Serve immediately.

Nutrition: Calories: 576 Fat: 28g Carbs: 76g Protein: 5g

910.   Pineapple and Chocolate Cake
Preparation Time: 10 minutes
Cooking Time: 35 to 40 minutes
Servings 4
Ingredients:

- 2 cups flour
- 4 ounces (113 g) butter, melted
- ¼ cup sugar
- ½ pound (227 g) pineapple, chopped
- ½ cup pineapple juice
- 1 ounce (28 g) dark chocolate, grated
- 1 large egg
- 2 tablespoons skimmed milk

Directions:
1. Preheat the air fryer to 370°F (188°C).
2. Grease cake tin with a little oil or butter.
3. In a bowl, combine the butter and flour to create crumbly consistency.
4. Add the sugar, chopped pineapple, juice, and grated dark chocolate and mix well.
5. In separate bowl, combine the egg and milk. Add this mixture to the flour mixture and stir well until soft dough forms.
6. Gently put the mixture into the cake tin and transfer to the air fryer.
7. Bake for 35 to 40 minutes. Serve immediately.

Nutrition: Calories: 225 Fat: 3g Carbs: 6g Protein: 2g

911.   Chocolate and Peanut Butter Lava Cupcakes
Preparation Time: 10 minutes
Cooking Time: 10 to 13 minutes
Servings 8
Ingredients:

- Nonstick baking spray with flour
- 1 1/3 cups chocolate cake mix
- 1 egg
- 1 egg yolk
- ¼ cup safflower oil
- ¼ cup hot water
- 1/3 cup sour cream
- 3 tablespoons peanut butter
- 1/2 tablespoon powdered sugar

Directions:
1. Preheat the air fryer to 350°F (177°C).
2. Spray each muffin cups lightly with nonstick spray; set aside.
3. Mix well cake mix, egg, egg yolk, safflower oil, water, and sour cream, and beat until combined.
4. In a small bowl, combine the peanut butter and powdered sugar and mix well. Form this mixture into 8 balls.
5. Spoon about 1/4 cup of the chocolate batter into each muffin cup and top with a peanut butter ball. Spoon remaining batter on top of the peanut butter balls to cover them.

6. Arrange the cups in the air fryer basket, leaving some space between each. Bake for 10 to 13 minutes or until the tops look dry and set.
7. Let the cupcakes cool for about 10 minutes, then serve warm.

Nutrition: Calories: 194 Fat: 9g Carbs: 24g Protein: 4g

912.   Chocolate Molten Cake
Preparation Time: 5 minutes
Cooking Time: 10 minutes
Servings 4
Ingredients:

- ounces (99 g) butter, melted
- 3½ tablespoons sugar
- ounces (99 g) chocolate, melted
- 1½ tablespoons flour
- 2 eggs

Directions:

1. Preheat the air fryer to 375°F (191°C).
2. Grease four ramekins with a little butter.
3. Rigorously combine the eggs, butter, and sugar before stirring in the melted chocolate. Slowly fold in the flour.
4. Put equal amount of the mixture into each ramekin.
5. Put them in the air fryer and bake for 10 minutes
6. Put the ramekins upside down on plates and let the cakes fall out. Serve hot.

Nutrition: Calories: 290 Fat: 11g Carbs: 45g Protein: 3g

913.   Chocolate soufflé
Preparation Time: 15 minutes
Cooking Time: 15 minutes
Servings: 2
Ingredients

- 1/3 cup Milk
- 2 tbsp. Butter soft to melted
- 1 tbsp. Flour
- 2 tbsp. Splenda
- 1 Egg Yolk
- 1/4 cup Sugar Free Chocolate Chips
- 2 egg whites
- 1/2 teaspoon of cream of tartar
- 1/2 teaspoon of Vanilla Extract

Directions

1. Grease the ramekins with spray oil or softened butter.
2. Sprinkle with any sugar alternative, make sure to cover them.
3. Let the air fryer preheat to 325 – 330° F
4. Melt the chocolate in a microwave safe bowl. Mix every 30 seconds until fully melted.
5. Melt the one and a half tablespoons of butter over low medium heat. In a small sized skillet.
6. Once the butter has melted, then whisk in the flour. Keep whisking until thickened. Then turn the heat off.
7. Add the egg whites with cream of tartar, with the whisk attachment, in a stand mixer, mix until peaks forms.
8. Meanwhile, combine the ingredients in a melted chocolate bowl, add the flour mixture and melted butter to chocolate, and blend. Add in the vanilla extract, egg yolks, remaining sugar alternative.
9. Fold the egg white peaks gently with the ingredients into the bowl.
10. Add the mix into ramekins about 3/4 full of five-ounce ramekins
11. Let it bake for 12-14 minutes, or until done.

Nutrition: calories: 288kcal; carbohydrates: 5g; protein: 6g; fat: 24g;

914.   Carrot cake
Preparation Time: 15 minutes
Cooking Time: 40 minutes
Servings: 8
Ingredients

- All-purpose Flour: 1 ¼ cups
- Pumpkin Pie Spice: 1 tsp
- Baking Powder: one teaspoon
- Splenda: 3/4 cup
- Carrots: 2 cups–grated
- 2 Eggs
- Baking Soda: half teaspoon
- Canola Oil: ¾ cup

Directions

1. Let the air fryer preheat to 350° F. Spray the pan with oil spray.
2. And add flour over that.
3. Put baking powder, flour, pumpkin pie spice, and baking soda.
4. In another bowl, mix the eggs, oil, and sugar alternative. Now combine the dry to wet ingredients.
5. Add half of the dry ingredients first mix and the other half of the dry mixture.
6. Add in the grated carrots.
7. Lay cake batter to the greased cake pan.
8. Place the cake pan in the basket of the air fryer.
9. Let it Air fry for half an hour, but do not let the top too brown.
10. If the top is browning, add a piece of foil over the top of the cake.
11. Air fry it until a toothpick comes out clean, 35 - 40 minutes in total.
12. Let the cake cool down before serving.

Nutrition: calories: 287; carbohydrates: 19g; protein: 4g; fat: 22g;

915.   Cheesecake muffins
Preparation Time: 20 minutes
Cooking Time: 28 minutes
Servings: 18
Ingredients

- Splenda: 1/2 cup
- 1 1/2 Cream Cheese
- 2 Eggs
- Vanilla Extract: 1 tsp

Directions

1. Let the oven preheat to 300° F.
2. Spray the muffin pan with oil.
3. In a bowl, add the sugar alternative, vanilla extract, and cream cheese. Mix well
4. Add in the eggs gently, one at a time. Do not over mix the batter.
5. Let it bake for 25 to 30 minutes, or until cooked.
6. Take out from the air fryer and let them cool before adding frosting.
7. Serve and enjoy.

Nutrition: calories: 93kcal; carbohydrates: 1g; protein: 2g; fat: 9g;

916.   Chocolate donut holes
Preparation Time: 15 minutes
Cooking Time: 15 minutes
Servings: 3
Ingredients

- 6 tbsp. Splenda
- 1 Cup any flour
- Baking Soda: half tsp.
- 6 tbsp. Unsweetened Cocoa Powder
- 3 tbsp. of Butter
- 1 Egg
- Baking Powder: half tsp.
- 2 tbsp. of Unsweetened Chocolate chopped
- 1/4 cup Plain Yogurt

Directions

1. In a big mixing bowl, combine the baking powder, baking soda, and flour.
2. Then add in the cocoa powder and sugar alternative.
3. In a mug or microwave safe bowl, melt the butter and the unsweetened chocolate.
4. Mix every 15 seconds and make sure they melt together and combine well.
5. Set it aside to cool it down.
6. In that big mixing bowl from before, add in the yogurt and the egg. Put melted butter and chocolate mixture. Enclose bowl with plastic wrap and let it chill in the refrigerator for 30 minutes.
7. To make the donut balls, take out the batter from the fridge.
8. With the help of a tablespoon, scoop out sufficient batter so a donut ball will form with your hands.
9. You can use oil on your hands if the dough is too sticky.
10. Spray the oil on the air fryer basket and sprinkle with flour and let it preheat to 350° F.
11. Work in batches and add the balls in one single layer.
12. Let it bake for 10 to 12 minutes until they are done. Take out from air fryer, let it cool and serve hot or cold.

Nutrition: calories 22kcal; carbohydrates: 1g; protein: 1g; fat: 2g

917. Peanut butter cookies

Preparation Time: 20 minutes
Cooking Time: 9 minutes
Servings: 23

Ingredients

- All natural 100% peanut butter: 1 cup
- One whisked egg
- Liquid stevia drops: 1 teaspoon
- Sugar alternative: 1 cup

Directions

1. Mix all the ingredients into a dough. Make 24 balls with your hands from the combined dough.
2. On a cookie sheet or cutting board, press the dough balls with the help of a fork to form a crisscross pattern.
3. Add six cookies to the basket of air fryer in a single layer. Make sure the cookies are separated from each other. Cook in batches
4. Let them Air Fry, for 8-10 minutes, at 325. Take the basket out from the air fryer.
5. Let the cookies cool for one minute, then with care, take the cookies out.
6. Keep baking the rest of the peanut butter cookies in batches.
7. Let them cool completely and serve.

Nutrition: 1 cookie; calories: 198kcal; carbohydrates: 7g; protein: 9g; fat: 17g;

918. Lemon slice & bake cookies

Preparation Time: 5 minutes
Cooking Time: 5 minutes
Servings: 24

Ingredients

- 1/2 teaspoon of salt
- 1/2 cup of coconut flour
- 1/2 cup of unsalted butter softened
- 1/2 teaspoon of liquid vanilla stevia
- 1/2 cup of swerve granular sweetener
- 1 tablespoon lemon juice
- Lemon extract: 1/4 tsp, it is optional
- 2 egg yolks

For icing

- 3 tsp of lemon juice
- 2/3 cup of Swerve confectioner's sweetener

Directions

1. In a stand mixer bowl, add baking soda, coconut flour, salt and Swerve, mix until well combined
2. Then add the butter softened) to the dry ingredients, mix well. Add all the remaining ingredients but do not add in the yolks yet. Adjust the seasoning of lemon flavor and sweetness to your liking, add more if needed.
3. Add the yolk and combine well.
4. Spread big piece of plastic wrap on a flat surface, put the batter in the center, roll around the dough and make it into a log form, for almost 12 inches. Keep this log in the fridge for 23 hours or overnight, if possible.
5. Let the oven preheat to 325°F. generously spray the air fryer basket, take the log out from plastic wrap only unwrap how much you want to use it, and keep the rest in the fridge.
6. Cut in 1/4-inch cookies, place as many cookies in the air fryer basket in one single, do not overcrowd the basket.
7. Bake for 3five minutes, or until the cookies' edges become brown. Let it cool in the basket for two minutes, then take out from the basket. And let them cool on a wire rack.

Once all cookies are baked, pour the icing over. Serve and enjoy.

Nutrition: calories 66, fat 6g, carbohydrates 2g, fiber 1g, sugar 1g, protein 1g

919. Thumbprint cookies

Preparation Time: 15 minutes
Cooking Time: 10 minutes
Servings: 10

Ingredients

- One teaspoon of baking powder
- One cup of almond flour
- Three tablespoons of natural low-calorie sweetener
- One large egg
- Three and a half tablespoons raspberry reduced sugar) preserving

- Four tablespoons of softened cream cheese

Directions

1. In a large bowl, add egg, baking powder, flour, sweetener, and cream cheese, mix well until a dough wet form.
2. Chill the dough in the fridge for almost 20 minutes, until dough is cool enough
3. And then form into balls.
4. Let the air fryer preheat to 400° F, add the parchment paper to the air fryer basket.
5. Make ten balls from the dough and put them in the prepared air fryer basket.
6. With your clean hands, make an indentation from your thumb in the center of every cookie. Add one teaspoon of the raspberry preserve in the thumb hole.
7. Bake in the air fryer for seven minutes, or until light golden brown to your liking.
8. Let the cookies cool completely in the parchment paper for almost 15 minutes, or they will fall apart.
9. Serve with tea and enjoy.

Nutrition: 116 calories, protein 7g, carbohydrates 1g, fat 6g

920. Tahini oatmeal chocolate chunk cookies

Preparation Time: 10 minutes
Cooking Time: 5 minutes
Servings: 8

Ingredients

- 1/3 cup of tahini
- 1/4 cup of walnuts
- 1/4 cup of maple syrup
- 1/4 cup of Chocolate chunks
- 1/4 tsp of sea salt
- 2 tablespoons of almond flour
- 1 teaspoon of vanilla, it is optional
- 1 cup of gluten free oat flakes
- 1 teaspoon of cinnamon, it is optional

Directions

1. Let the air fryer Preheat to 350° F.
2. In a big bowl, add the maple syrup, cinnamon if used, the tahini, salt, and vanilla if used. Mix well, then add in the walnuts, oat flakes, and almond meal. Then fold the chocolate chips gently.
3. Now the mix is ready, take a full tablespoon of mixture, separate into eight amounts. Wet clean damp hands press them on a baking tray or with a spatula.
4. Place four cookies, or more depending on your air fryer size, line the air fryer basket with parchment paper in one single layer.
5. Let them cook for 56 minutes at 350° f, air fry for more minutes if you like them crispy.

Nutrition: calories: 185, fat: 12g, carbohydrates: 15g, protein 12 g

921. Apple cider vinegar donuts

Preparation Time: 10 minutes
Cooking Time: 10 minutes
Servings: 8

Ingredients

For Muffins

- Coconut flour: 1 cup
- Four eggs, large
- Coconut oil: 4 tbsp., melted
- Baking soda: 1 tsp
- Apple cider vinegar: 2/3 cup
- Cinnamon: 1 tsp
- Honey: 3 tbsp.
- A pinch of salt

For Drizzle

- Coffee Syrup Turmeric Pumpkin Spice

Directions

1. Let the air fryer preheat to 350°f. spray oil on a baking tray, spray a generous amount of grease with melted coconut oil
2. Put apple cider vinegar, honey, melted coconut oil, salt mix well, then crack the eggs and whisk it all together.
3. In another bowl, sift the coconut flour, baking soda, and cinnamon so that the dry ingredients will combine well.
4. Now add the wet ingredients to dry ingredients until completely combined. Do not worry if the batter is kind of wet.

5. Pour the batter into the prepared donut baking pan. And add the batter into cavities. With the help of your hands, spread the batter in the cavity evenly.
6. Let it bake for ten minutes or 8 minutes at 350°f, or until light golden brown.
7. Make sure halfway cooking if they are not getting too brown, with a toothpick check to see if the donuts are cooked, and a toothpick comes out clean.
8. Take out from the oven and let them cool for at least ten minutes to harden up, then remove otherwise. They will fall apart since they are very tender.
9. Before serving, drizzle with coffee syrup turmeric pumpkin spice).
10. Serve right away and enjoy.

Nutrition: calories 179, fat 12, carbohydrates 9g, fiber 2g, protein 5g

922. Pumpkin pie
Preparation Time: 10 minutes
Cooking Time: 50 minutes
Servings: 6
Ingredients:
- 2 cups ginger snaps, ground
- 32 ounces canned pumpkin
- 1 cup egg whites
- 1 cup sugar
- teaspoons pumpkin pie spice blend
- 2 cans (12 ounce each evaporated skim milk)

Directions:
1. Grease an ovenproof pie pan with cooking spray. Place the ground cookies in the pan. Spread all over and press lightly.
2. In a large bowl, mix together the rest of the ingredients. Pour over the cookies.
3. Place the dish in a preheated air fryer.
4. Bake in an air fryer at 350°f for about 40-45 minutes. Remove from the air fryer.
5. Cool and refrigerate. Slice into wedges and serve.

Nutrition: Calories: 270 Fat: 12g Carbs: 31g Protein: 4g

923. Gulab Jamun
Preparation Time: 15 minutes
Cooking Time: 20 minutes
Servings: 10
Ingredients:
For jamun:
- 1 cup milk powder
- 1 cup milk
- 1 cup flour
- 2 tablespoons baking powder

For syrup:
- 2 cups sugar
- cups water
- 1 teaspoon rose extract, or a tablespoon rose water

Directions:
1. Mix together all the ingredients of jamun and form smooth dough. Divide into 20 -25 equal portions and shape into small balls. Place the balls in the air fryer basket and place the basket in the air fryer.
2. Cook in a preheated air fryer at 350°f for 5 minutes or until they turn golden brown.
3. Meanwhile make the syrup as follows: Pour water into a saucepan and place the pan over medium heat. Add sugar and bring to the boil. Stir until the sugar is completely dissolved.
4. Remove from heat and cool slightly. Add rose extract and stir. Place fried balls in it and let it soak in it for at least an hour.
5. Serve warm or at room temperature but not chilled

Nutrition: Calories: 143 Fat: 7g Carbs: 17g Protein: 2g

924. Apple Pie
Preparation Time: 15 minutes
Cooking Time: 1 hour and 5 minutes
Servings: 4
Ingredients:
- 2 medium sized apples, peeled, cored, sliced
- 2 pie crust (store bought)
- ½ cup sugar
- 2 tablespoons unsalted butter

- ½ teaspoon ground cinnamon

Directions:
1. Place one piecrust on a pie plate. Mix together cinnamon and sugar.
2. Lay the apple slices in layers over the piecrust in layers. Sprinkle sugar mixture over each layer and sprinkle a few butter pieces over each layer. Cover with the other piecrust.
3. Place the piecrust in a preheated air fryer. Bake in a preheated oven at 390°f for about 10 minutes. Lower temperature to 350°f and bake for about 30 minutes.
4. Slice and serve warm.

Nutrition: Calories: 290 Fat: 16g Carbs: 33g Protein: 3g

925. Lemon Sponge Cake
Preparation Time: 10 minutes
Cooking Time: 25 minutes
Servings: 6
Ingredients:
- 1-cup flour
- ¼ pound butter at room temperature
- ½ cup + 1 tablespoon caster sugar
- ½ teaspoon baking powder
- 2 small eggs
- ½ teaspoon lemon zest, grated
- A little melted butter for greasing the baking dish

Directions:
1. Add all the ingredients of the cake into a blender and blend until smooth and creamy.
2. Grease a baking dish with melted butter. Pour the batter into the dish.
3. Place the dish in a preheated air fryer and bake at 350°f for 15 minutes or until a toothpick when inserted in the center comes out clean. Do not check before the timer goes off.
4. Remove the dish from the air fryer and let it cool.
5. Run a knife all around the cake and remove the cake from the dish.
6. Slice and serve.

Nutrition: Calories: 195 Fat: 2g Carbs: 39g Protein: 4g

926. Oreo Biscuit Cake
Preparation Time: 8 minutes
Cooking Time: 16 minutes
Servings: 6
Ingredients:
- 25 Oreo biscuits, ground finely
- 2 teaspoons baking powder
- 1 teaspoon baking soda
- 2 cups milk
- 2 tablespoons almonds, slivered

Directions:
1. Add all the ingredients of the cake except almonds into a blender and blend until smooth and creamy. Transfer into a bowl. Add almonds and fold gently.
2. Grease a baking dish with melted butter. Pour the batter into the dish.
3. Place the dish in a preheated air fryer and bake at 390°f for 8 minutes or until a toothpick when inserted in the center comes out clean. Do not check before the timer goes off.
4. Remove the dish from the air fryer and let it cool.
5. Run a knife all around the cake and remove the cake from the dish.
6. Slice and serve.

Nutrition: Calories: 340 Fat: 14g Carbs: 50g Protein: 5g

927. Chocolate Covered Macaroons
Preparation Time: 15 minutes
Cooking Time: 30 minutes
Servings: 8
Ingredients:
- 2 large egg whites
- 2 cups shredded coconut, unsweetened
- 1-½ ounces milk chocolate
- A large pinch salt
- 1 teaspoon almond extract
- ½ cup sugar
- tablespoons butter

Directions:

1. Place shredded coconut on a parchment paper lined baking sheet. Bake in a preheated air fryer about 4 minutes until lightly toasted.
2. Whisk egg white until frothy and doubled. Add sugar and salt and whisk again. Add almond extract and toasted coconut.
3. Divide and shape into small balls and place on the lined baking sheet.
4. Bake at 390°f for about 15 minutes until golden.

Nutrition: Calories: 71 Fat: 5g Carbs: 6.2g Protein: 1g

928. Blueberry Custard

Preparation Time: 10 minutes
Cooking Time: 35 minutes
Servings: 4
Ingredients:

- eggs
- 1 ¼ cups milk
- 1 ½ tablespoons butter, melted
- 2 tablespoons honey
- 1/3 cup all-purpose flour
- ½ cup blueberries
- ½ teaspoon ground nutmeg
- 1 ½ tablespoons confectioners' sugar
- ½ teaspoon vanilla extract
- ¼ teaspoon salt

Directions:

1. Add butter to a baking dish that is smaller than the air fryer and that fits into the air fryer. Swirl the dish so as to spread butter all over the dish. Alternately, you can grease ramekins.
2. Blend together eggs, honey, milk, vanilla, flour and salt until smooth. Pour in the dish.
3. Sprinkle blueberries all over.
4. Place the dish in the air fryer.
5. Bake in a preheated air fryer 390°F for about 20-25 minutes until golden.
6. Remove from air fryer and cool for a while.
7. Sprinkle nutmeg and confectioners' sugar and serve.

Nutrition: Calories: 285 Fat: 8g Carbs: 35g Protein: 18g

929. Peach Tarts

Preparation Time: 20 minutes
Cooking Time: 50 minutes
Servings: 12
Ingredients:

- 2 sheets 14-ounce package) frozen puff pastry, thaw according to directions on the package
- ½ cup sugar
- 2 pounds peaches, pitted, chopped into wedges
- 2 tablespoons honey
- Freshly ground black pepper to taste
- A large pinch sea salt

Directions:

1. Cut each puff pastry sheet into 6 squares of 4 inches each. Arrange the squares on a baking sheet that is lined with parchment paper. Prick the squares all over with a fork.
2. Place the fruit of your choice at the center leaving 1/2-inch border on all the sides.
3. Sprinkle sugar and pepper.
4. Place the baking sheet in the air fryer.
5. Bake in a preheated air fryer at 350°F for 25 - 30 minutes. Sprinkle salt just before serving.
6. Drizzle honey and serve immediately.

Nutrition: Calories: 280 Fat: 16g Carbs: 32g Protein: 4g

930. Red Velvet Cupcakes

Preparation Time: 20 minutes
Cooking Time: 45 minutes
Servings: 12
Ingredients:
For cake:

- eggs
- 1 ½ cups peanut butter
- teaspoons beet powder
- 1 ½ cups icing sugar
- Cocoa 2 teaspoons

- cups flour

For frosting:

- 2 cups hard butter
- teaspoons vanilla essence
- 1 ½ cups icing sugar
- 2 cups cream cheese
- ½ cup strawberry sauce optional

For garnishing:

- A little chocolate crushed or shaved
- strawberries, thinly sliced

Directions:

1. Add all the ingredients of the cake into a mixing bowl and beat with an electric mixer. Pour into greased cupcake molds up to 3/4th
2. Place the molds in a preheated air fryer. Bake in an air fryer at 350F for 5 minutes and then at 340F for 10-12 minutes.
3. For frosting: Whisk together with an electric beater, butter, icing sugar and vanilla until smooth. Add rest of the ingredients and whisk.
4. Top the cakes with the frosting and place strawberry slices and chocolate over it and serve.

Nutrition: Calories: 180 Fat: 15g Carbs: 30g Protein: 2g

931. Blackberry and Apricot Crumble

Preparation Time: 15 minutes
Cooking Time: 30 – 35 minutes
Servings: 6
Ingredients:

- oz blackberries, fresh
- oz apricots, fresh
- ½ cup sugar
- 1 ½ cup flour
- Salt, as per taste
- 2 tablespoon lemon juice
- ½ tablespoon butter, cold

Directions:

1. Cut the apricots in half and remove reseed them. Dice the apricots in cubes and place them in a salad bowl.
2. Add around 1 1/2 tablespoon of sugar, blackberries and lemon juice to the bowl and mix well.
3. Take an oven safe dish and grease it well. Pour the above mixture into this dish and spread carefully.
4. In another bowl add salt and flour and mix well. Add the remaining sugar to the above bowl and mix again.
5. Add around 1 tablespoon cold water and butter to the flour mixture and knead. A crumbly mixture should form.
6. Keep the fryer on preheat mode at 200° C for about 3-5 minutes.
7. Spread the flour mixture over the fruits carefully. Press down lightly to set it.
8. Put the oven dish in the fryer basket and cook for about 15-22 minutes or until crumble turns golden brown.

Nutrition: Calories: 317 Fat: 11g Carbs: 47g Protein: 4g

932. Peanut Cookies

Preparation Time: 10 minutes
Cooking Time: 22 minutes
Servings: 12
Ingredients:

- 1 ¾ cups all-purpose flour
- ½ cup peanut butter
- tablespoons vegetable oil
- A pinch of salt
- ¼ cup caster sugar
- 1 egg yolk, beaten

Directions:

1. Add flour, peanut butter, oil, salt, and sugar into a bowl and mix well using your hands until dough is formed.
2. Line the air fryer basket with baking sheet.
3. Divide the dough and form small balls. Roll each ball into cookies and place on the baking sheet. Brush with yolk.
4. Place the basket in a preheated air fryer and bake at 340°F for 10-12 minutes.
5. If you like it crunchier, then bake for a couple of minutes more.

Nutrition: Calories: 134 Fat: 7g Carbs: 16g Protein: 2g

933. Chocolate banana packets
Preparation Time: 5 minutes
Cooking Time: 15 minutes
Servings: 1
Ingredients:

- Miniature marshmallows 2 tablespoons
- Cereal, cinnamon, crunchy, slightly crushed 2 tablespoons
- Banana, peeled 1 piece
- Chocolate chips, semi-sweet 2 tablespoons

Directions:

1. Preheat air fryer to 390 °F.
2. Slightly open banana by cutting lengthwise. Place on sheet of foil.
3. Fill sliced banana with chocolate chips and marshmallows. Close foil packet.
4. Air-fry for fifteen to twenty minutes.
5. Open packet and top banana with crushed cereal.
6. Nutrition: calories 270 fat 0 g protein 0 g carbohydrates 50 g

934. Creamy strawberry mini wraps
Preparation Time: 10 minutes
Cooking Time: 15 minutes
Servings: 12
Ingredients:

- Cream cheese, softened 4 ounces
- Strawberry jam 12 teaspoon
- Pie crust, refrigerated 1 box
- Powdered sugar 1/3 cup

Directions:

1. Preheat air fryer to 350 °F.
2. Roll out pie crusts and cut out 12 squares.
3. Beat together powdered sugar and cream cheese.
4. Shape each dough square into a diamond before filling with cream cheese mixture 1 tablespoon. Top each with strawberry jam 1 teaspoon) and cover with dough sides.
5. Place mini wraps on baking sheet and air-fry for fifteen minutes.

Nutrition: calories 190 fat 5 g protein 0 g carbohydrates 20 g

935. Heavenly butter cake bars
Preparation Time: 15 minutes
Cooking Time: 35 minutes
Servings: 12
Ingredients:

- Butter, melted 1/2 cup
- Cream cheese 8 ounces
- Vanilla 1 teaspoon
- Cake mix, super moist, French vanilla 15 ¼ ounces
- Eggs 3 pieces
- Powdered sugar 1 pound

Directions:

1. Preheat air fryer to 325 °F.
2. Use parchment to line baking dish.
3. Blend in the cake mix with egg and melted butter to form soft dough. Press into baking dish.
4. Beat together 2 eggs, cream cheese, vanilla, and sugar. Spread on top of cake mix layer.
5. Air-fry for forty-five minutes. Let cool before slicing.

Nutrition: calories 294 fat 13 g protein 8 g carbohydrates 36 g

936. Tasty shortbread cookies
Preparation Time: 25 minutes
Cooking Time: 1 hr. 5 minutes
Servings: 4
Ingredients:

- Powdered sugar 3/4 cup
- Flour, all-purpose 2 ½ cups
- Butter, softened 1 cup
- Vanilla 1 teaspoon

Directions:

1. Preheat air fryer to 325 °F.
2. Combine butter, vanilla and powdered sugar with flour to form a soft dough.
3. Roll out dough and cut out 4 circles. Place on cookie sheet.
4. Air-fry for fourteen to sixteen minutes.

Nutrition: calories 70 fat 0 g protein 0 g carbohydrates 0 g

937. Air-fried mini pies
Preparation Time: 20 minutes
Cooking Time: 55 minutes
Servings: 12
Ingredients:

- Pie filling 4 cups
- Pie crusts, refrigerated 2 packages
- Egg, whisked 1 piece

Directions:

1. Preheat air fryer to 325 °F.
2. Mist cooking spray onto 12 muffin cups.
3. Roll out pie crust and cut out twelve 4-inch circles. Press each onto bottom of a muffin cup. Cut remaining dough into thin strips.
4. Add pie filling 1/4 cup to each dough cup. Cover each with dough strips laid in a lattice pattern.
5. Brush whisked egg on tops of pies and air-fry for thirty to forty minutes.

Nutrition: calories 193 fat 4 g protein 7 g carbohydrates 29 g

938. Pumpkin pie minis
Preparation Time: 25 minutes
Cooking Time: 20 minutes
Servings: 12
Ingredients:

- Nutmeg 1/4 teaspoon
- Brown sugar 3/8 cup
- Pumpkin puree 1 cup
- Cinnamon 1/2 teaspoon
- Heavy cream 1 tablespoon
- Egg, large 1 piece
- Pie crust, refrigerated 1 package

Directions:

1. Preheat air fryer to 325 °F.
2. Combine pumpkin, heavy cream, spices, and brown sugar.
3. Unroll dough pieces and cut out twenty-four 2.5-inch circles. Place 12 circles on sheet of parchment. Top each with pie filling 1 tablespoon and cover with another circle.
4. Press to seal and brush all mini pies with whisked egg 1 piece. Dust all over with mixture of cinnamon and sugar.
5. Air-fry for twenty minutes.

Nutrition: calories 180 fat 0 g protein 0 g carbohydrates 20 g

939. Mouthwatering walnut apple pie bites
Preparation Time: 10 minutes
Cooking Time: 15 minutes
Servings: 8
Ingredients:

- Brown sugar 4 tablespoons
- Butter, melted 1 tablespoon
- Apple, tart juicy, red, washed, sliced into 8 portions, skin on 1 piece
- Cinnamon 3 teaspoons
- Crescent rolls, refrigerated 1 can
- Walnuts, chopped finely 1 ounce

Directions:

1. Preheat air fryer to 325 °F.
2. Roll out crescent rolls onto baking sheet misted with cooking spray.
3. Brush melted butter on rolls before sprinkling with cinnamon and brown sugar. Add 3/4 of finely chopped walnuts on top; press gently to adhere.
4. Top each of wide ends with a slice of apple, then roll up. Graze melted butter on top of rolls before sprinkling with cinnamon and remaining 1/4 of finely chopped walnuts.
5. Air-fry for fifteen minutes.

Nutrition: calories 47 fat 75 g protein 6 g carbohydrates 6 g

940. Gooey apple pie cookies
Preparation Time: 15 minutes
Cooking Time: 20 minutes
Servings: 12
Ingredients:

- Egg, slightly beaten 1 piece
- Caramel sauce 1 jar
- Flour, all-purpose 2 tablespoons
- Pie crusts, refrigerated 1 package
- Apple pie filling 1 can

- Cinnamon sugar 3 tablespoons

Directions:
1. Preheat air fryer to 325 °F.
2. Roll out dough and spread thinly with caramel sauce. Chop up apple pie filling and spread over caramel sauce.
3. Cover with strips from other rolled out dough, laid to form a lattice pattern. Cut out 3-inch cookies and arrange on baking sheet.
4. Air-fry for twenty to twenty-five minutes.

Nutrition: calories 218 fat 5 g protein 1 g carbohydrates 42 g

941. Apple pie with cinnamon roll crust

Preparation Time: 15 minutes
Cooking Time: 55 minutes
Servings: 16
Ingredients:
Crust:

- Butter, unsalted, melted 1 tablespoon
- Egg, beaten 1 piece) + water 1 teaspoon—to make egg wash
- Pie crust, refrigerated 1 package
- Cinnamon, ground 2 teaspoons

Pie:

- Butter, unsalted, at room temp. 1 stick)
- Apples, Granny Smith, small, peeled, cored, sliced thinly 7 pieces
- Sugar, light brown 1 cup
- Flour, all purpose, unbleached 1 cup
- Granulated sugar

Icing:

- Vanilla 1/4 teaspoon
- Milk 2 teaspoons
- Powdered sugar 1/2 cup
- Cinnamon, ground 1/4 teaspoon

Directions:
1. Preheat air fryer to 375 °F.
2. Unroll pie crust; brush top with butter before sprinkling with cinnamon. Roll up and slice into half-inch rounds.
3. Press mini rolls into pie plate and brush tops with egg wash. Top with sliced apples. Cover with crumbly mixture of flour, brown sugar, and butter. Sprinkle with granulated sugar.
4. Air-fry for forty to forty-five minutes.
5. Finish by icing with whisked mixture milk, powdered sugar, cinnamon, and vanilla.

Nutrition: calories 255 fat 10 g protein 5 g carbohydrates 30 g

942. Sugar cookie cake

Preparation Time: 5 minutes
Cooking Time: 35 minutes
Servings: 24
Ingredients:

- Condensed milk, sweetened 14 ounces
- Cinnamon, ground 1 teaspoon
- Butter, salted, melted 3/4 cup
- Cookie butter 14 ounces
- Eggs 3 pieces
- Sugar cookie mix, prepared 17 ½ ounces

Directions:
1. Preheat air fryer to 325 °F. Mist cooking spray onto baking dish.
2. Combine cookie butter with eggs, cinnamon, and condensed milk. Spread on baking dish and top with even layer of fry cookie mix.
3. Drizzle melted butter on top and air-fry for thirty-five minutes.
4. Let cool before slicing and serving.

Nutrition: calories 295 fat 15 g protein 0 g carbohydrates 30 g

943. Lemon cake

Preparation time: 10 minutes
Cooking time: 15 minutes
Servings: 2
Ingredients:

- ¼ cup butter
- tablespoons sugar
- 1 egg
- 1 tablespoon lemon juice
- ¼ cup flour
- ¼ teaspoon salt

- 1 tablespoon lemon rind

Directions:
1. Preheat the air fryer to 325°f/170°c.
2. Cream the butter and sugar in a bowl.
3. Mix in the egg and lemon juice.
4. Mix together the flour and salt and gradually add to the mixture.
5. Fold in the lemon rind.
6. Pour the batter into the air fryer baking pan and place the air fryer baking pan in the air fryer basket.
7. Set the timer for 15 minutes.
8. Remove from the air fryer and allow to cool.
9. Serve and enjoy!

Nutrition: Calories 100, Fat 4, Fiber 1, Carbs 12, Protein 1

944. Pomegrante and kiwi cake

Preparation time: 10 minutes
Cooking time: 15 minutes
Servings: 2
Ingredients:

- ¼ cup butter
- tablespoons sugar
- 1 egg
- 1 tablespoon pomegranate extract
- ¼ cup flour
- ¼ teaspoon salt
- ¼ cup pomegranate puree
- 1 cup whipped cream
- 1 cup kiwis, sliced

Directions:
1. Preheat the air fryer to 325°f/170°c.
2. Cream the butter and sugar in a bowl.
3. Mix in the egg and pomegranate extract.
4. Mix together the flour and salt and gradually add to the mixture.
5. Fold in the pomegranate puree and mix well to combine.
6. Pour the batter into the air fryer baking pan and place the air fryer baking pan in the air fryer basket.
7. Set the timer for 15 minutes.
8. Remove from the air fryer and allow to cool.
9. Top with the whipped cream and kiwi slices.
10. Serve and enjoy!

Nutrition: Calories 210, Fat 5, Fiber 1, Carbs 14, Protein 3

945. Granola cookies

Preparation time: 10 minutes
Cooking time: 15 minutes
Servings: makes 30 cookies
Ingredients:

- ½ cup caster sugar
- ½ cup cooking oil
- ½ cup ground almonds
- 2 cups plain flour
- 1 teaspoon baking powder
- 1 teaspoon baking soda
- ¼ cup granola

Directions:
1. Preheat the air fryer to 275°f/140°c.
2. Mix together the caster sugar, cooking oil and ground almonds in a stand mixer.
3. Mix together flour, baking powder and baking soda and gradually add to the ground almond mixture.
4. Fold in the granola.
5. Line the air fryer basket and air fryer double layer rack with parchment paper. Drop teaspoon full of batter onto the parchment papers.
6. Set the timer for 15 minutes.
7. Allow the cookies to cool in the air fryer for a few minutes before transferring to a serving plate.
8. Serve and enjoy!

Nutrition: Calories 133, Fat 2, Fiber 2, Carbs 13, Protein 2

946. Chocolate chip mint tea scones

Preparation time: 15 minutes
Cooking time: 10 minutes
Servings: 4
Ingredients:

- 2 cups flour

- 2½ teaspoons baking powder
- 2 tablespoons cocoa powder
- ½ teaspoon salt
- 1 teaspoon sugar
- 1 teaspoon peppermint oil
- 1 tablespoon butter, melted
- 1 egg
- ¾ cup milk, plus more for brushing
- ¼ cup chocolate chips
- ¼ cup dark chocolate, melted

Directions:
1. Preheat the air fryer to 375°f/190°c.
2. In a mixing bowl, combine flour, baking powder, cocoa powder, salt, sugar and peppermint oil.
3. Add the butter and mix until the consistency of the mixture resembles breadcrumbs. Make a well in the center of the mixture.
4. Mix together the egg and the milk and pour into the well.
5. Mix until a dough form.
6. Transfer the dough to a floured work surface and knead lightly.
7. Add the chocolate chips.
8. Make scones using round cookie cutters.
9. Arrange the scones in the air fryer basket and use the air fryer double layer rack if needed.
10. Brush the scones with a little milk.
11. Set the timer for 10 minutes.
12. Remove the scones from the air fryer and allow to cool.
13. Drizzle over with the melted chocolate.
14. Serve and enjoy!

Nutrition: Calories 100, Fat 4, Fiber 1, Carbs 12, Protein 1

947.   Nutella crunch pie
Preparation time: 10 minutes plus 1-hour chilling time
Cooking time: 5 minutes
Servings: 2
Ingredients:
- 8-inch pie dough
- ½ cup Nutella
- ½ cup cocoa puffs
- whipped cream, to top

Directions:
1. Preheat the air fryer to 325°f/190°c.
2. Place the pie dough on a work surface lightly dusted with flour.
3. Grease the pie pan with cooking spray.
4. Cut out an 8-inch pie dough and line the pie pan.
5. Fold the edges of the pie dough so that they sit on the rim of the pie pan.
6. Place the pan in the air fryer basket and set the timer for 5 minutes.
7. Remove the pan from the air fryer and allow to cool completely.
8. Spread the Nutella on the crust.
9. Add the cocoa puffs into the crust.
10. Top with the whipped cream
11. Chill the pie for an hour.
12. Serve and enjoy!

Nutrition: Calories 87, Fat 2, Fiber 1, Carbs 2, Protein 1

948.   Strawberry and lime cookies
Preparation time: 10 minutes
Cooking time: 8 minutes
Servings: 2
Ingredients:
- 1¼ cups all-purpose flour
- ½ cup cake flour
- ½ teaspoon baking powder
- ¼ teaspoon baking soda
- ¾ teaspoon salt
- 1 teaspoon granulated sugar
- 1 teaspoon lime juice
- 1 teaspoon strawberry extract
- tablespoons unsalted butter, melted
- ¾ cup cold buttermilk

Directions:
1. Preheat the air fryer to 400°f/200°c.

2. Sift the all-purpose flour, cake flour, baking powder, baking soda and salt in a bowl.
3. Mix in the sugar, lime juice and strawberry extract.
4. Mix in the butter and buttermilk and mix until a dough form
5. Roll the dough on a lightly floured work surface to ½-inch thick.
6. Use cookie cutters to cut out cookies from the dough.
7. Arrange the cookies in the air fryer basket and use the air fryer double layer rack if needed.
8. Set the timer to 8 minutes and cook the cookies until they are golden brown.
9. Serve and enjoy!

Nutrition: Calories 150, Fat 5, Fiber 5, Carbs 12, Protein 1

949.   Mango jam cookies
Preparation time: 15 minutes plus 30 minutes chilling time
Cooking time: 6 minutes
Servings: 2
Ingredients:
- 1 cup plain flour
- 2 tablespoons cornstarch
- 2 tablespoons icing sugar
- tablespoons custard powder
- ⅛ teaspoon salt
- ½ cup unsalted butter, chilled
- 1 egg yolk
- Cold water, if needed
- 1 cup ready-made mango jam
- 1 teaspoon lemon juice

Directions:
1. Sift together the plain flour, cornstarch, icing sugar, custard powder and salt in a bowl.
2. Rub in the butter until the mixture resembles breadcrumbs.
3. Mix in the egg yolk and knead to form a dough. Add some cold water if the dough is too dry.
4. Divide the dough into 2 equal portions and wrap each portion with plastic wrap.
5. Chill in the refrigerator for at least 30 minutes.
6. While the dough is chilling, make the mango filling by mixing the mango jam with the lemon juice with a fork until the jam becomes a smoother consistency.
7. Preheat the air fryer to 300°f/150°c.
8. Roll out the dough onto a lightly floured work surface until ¼-inch thick.
9. Cut out cookies using cookies cutters.
10. Arrange the cookies in the air fryer basket and use the air fryer double layer rack if needed.
11. Set the timer for 6 minutes or until the cookies are golden brown.
12. Remove the cookies from the air fryer and allow to cool.
13. Spread each cookie with the mango jam.
14. Serve and enjoy!

Nutrition: Calories 100, Fat 4, Fiber 1, Carbs 12, Protein 1

950.   Peach and mango tartlets
Preparation time: 15 minutes plus 30 minutes chilling time
Cooking time: 30 minutes
Servings: makes about 20 tartlets
Ingredients:
- 1 cup plain flour
- 2 tablespoons cornstarch
- 2 tablespoons icing sugar
- tablespoons custard powder
- ½ cup unsalted butter, chilled
- 1 egg yolk, beaten
- 1 cup mango, diced
- 1 cup peach, sliced
- 1 teaspoon lemon juice

Directions:
1. Sift together the flour, cornstarch, icing sugar and custard powder.
2. Rub in the butter until it resembles breadcrumbs.
3. Mix in the egg yolk and knead to form a dough.
4. Wrap the dough in plastic wrap and chill for at least 30 minutes.
5. Mix the mangoes, peaches and lemon juice and set aside.
6. Preheat the air fryer to 300°f/150°c.

7   Roll out the dough on a lightly floured surface to ¼-inch thick.
8   Cut out circles using a cookie cutter to the size that fits the mini tart molds.
9   Arrange the mini tartlets in the air fryer basket and use the air fryer double layer rack if needed.
10 Set the timer for 6 minutes or until they are golden brown.
11 Remove from the air fryer and fill with the fruits.
12 Serve and enjoy!

Nutrition: Calories 100, Fat 4, Fiber 1, Carbs 12, Protein 1

951.   Figs and coconut butter mix
Preparation time: 6 minutes
Cooking time: 4 minutes
Servings: 3
Ingredients:
- 2 tablespoons coconut butter
- figs, halved
- ¼ cup sugar
- 1 cup almond, toasted and chopped

Directions:
1   Put butter in a pan that fits your air fryer and melt over medium high heat.
2   Add figs, sugar and almonds, toss, introduce in your air fryer and cook at 300 ° for 4 minutes.
3   Divide into bowls and serve cold.
4   Enjoy!

Nutrition: Calories 170, Fat 4, Fiber 5, Carbs 7, Protein 9

952.   pears and espresso cream
Preparation time: 10 minutes
Cooking time: 30 minutes
Servings: 4
Ingredients:
- pears, halved and cored
- 2 tablespoons lemon juice
- 1 tablespoon sugar
- 2 tablespoons water
- 2 tablespoons butter
- For the cream:
- 1 cup whipping cream
- 1 cup mascarpone
- 1/3 cup sugar
- 2 tablespoons espresso, cold

Directions:
1   In a bowl, mix pears halves with lemon juice, 1 tablespoons sugar, butter and water, toss well, transfer them to your air fryer and cook at 360 degrees f for 30 minutes.
2   Meanwhile, in a bowl, mix whipping cream with mascarpone, 1/3 cup sugar and espresso, whisk really well and keep in the fridge until pears are done.
3   Divide pears on plates, top with espresso cream and serve them.
4   Enjoy!

Nutrition: Calories 211, Fat 5, Fiber 7, Carbs 8, Protein 7

953.   Poppyseed cake
Preparation time: 10 minutes
Cooking time: 30 minutes
Servings: 6
Ingredients:
- 1 and ¼ cups flour
- 1 teaspoon baking powder
- ¾ cup sugar
- 1 tablespoon orange zest, grated
- 2 teaspoons lime zest, grated
- ½ cup butter, soft
- 2 eggs, whisked
- ½ teaspoon vanilla extract
- 2 tablespoons poppy seeds
- 1 cup milk
- For the cream:
- 1 cup sugar
- ½ cup passion fruit puree
- tablespoons butter, melted
- egg yolks

Directions:

1   In a bowl, mix flour with baking powder, ¾ cup sugar, orange zest and lime zest and stir.
2   Add ½ cup butter, eggs, poppy seeds, vanilla and milk, stir using your mixer, pour into a cake pan that fits your air fryer and cook at 350° f for about 30 minutes.
3   Meanwhile, heat up a pan with 3 tablespoons butter over medium heat, add sugar and stir until it dissolves.
4   Take off heat, add passion fruit puree and egg yolks gradually and whisk really well.
5   Take cake out of the fryer, cool it down a bit and cut into halves horizontally.
6   Spread ¼ of passion fruit cream over one half, top with the other cake half and spread ¼ of the cream on top.
7   Serve cold.
8   Enjoy!

Nutrition: Calories 211, Fat 6, Fiber 7, Carbs 12, Protein 6

954.   Blueberry Pie
Preparation Time: 5 minutes
Cooking Time: 18 minutes
Servings: 4
Ingredients:
- 2 frozen pie crusts
- 2 (21-ounce) jars blueberry pie filling
- 1 teaspoon milk
- 1 teaspoon sugar

Directions:
1   Thaw one crust for 30 minutes on the countertop. Place one crust into the bottom of a 6-inch pie pan.
2   Pour the pie filling into the bottom crust, then cover it with the other crust, being careful to press the bottom and top crusts together around the edge to form a seal.
3   Trim off any excess pie dough. Cut venting holes in the top crust with a knife or a small decoratively shaped cookie cutter.
4   Brush the top crust with milk, then sprinkle the sugar over it. Place the pie in the air fryer basket.
5   Set the temperature of your AF to 310°F. Set the timer and bake for 15 minutes.
6   Check the pie after 15 minutes. If it needs additional time, reset the timer and bake for an additional 3 minutes.
7   Using silicone oven mitts, remove the pie from the air fryer and let cool for 15 minutes before serving.

Nutrition: Calories: 320 Fat: 16g Carbs: 41g Protein: 3g

955.   Chocolate Bundt Cake
Preparation Time: 5 minutes
Cooking Time: 30 minutes
Servings: 4
Ingredients:
- 1¾ cups all-purpose flour
- 2 cups sugar
- ¾ cup unsweetened cocoa powder
- 1 teaspoon baking soda
- 1 teaspoon baking powder
- ½ cup vegetable oil
- 1 teaspoon salt
- 2 teaspoons vanilla extract
- 2 large eggs
- 1 cup milk
- 1 cup hot water

Directions:
1   Spray a 6-inch Bundt pan with cooking spray.
2   Prepare the flour, sugar, cocoa powder, baking soda, baking powder, oil, salt, vanilla, eggs, milk, and hot water.
3   Pour the cake batter into the prepared pan and set the pan in the air fryer basket.
4   Set the temperature of your AF to 330°F and bake for 20 minutes.
5   Using silicone oven mitts, remove the Bundt pan from the air fryer. Set the pan on a wire cooling rack.
6   Put plate over the top of the Bundt pan. Carefully flip the plate and the pan over and set the plate on the counter.
7   Lift the Bundt pan off the cake.

Nutrition: Calories: 176 Fat: 9g Carbs: 22g Protein: 3g

956. Raspberry Cream Roll-Ups

Preparation Time: 10 minutes
Cooking Time: 25 minutes
Servings: 4
Ingredients:

- 1 cup of fresh raspberries, rinsed and patted dry
- ½ cup of cream cheese, softened to room temperature
- ¼ cup of brown sugar
- ¼ cup of sweetened condensed milk
- 1 egg
- 1 teaspoon of corn starch
- spring roll wrappers
- ¼ cup of water

Directions:

1. Cover the basket of the Air fryer with a lining of tin foil, leaving the edges uncovered to allow air to circulate through the basket. Preheat the air fryer to 350 degrees.
2. Bring out a mixing bowl, put cream cheese, brown sugar, condensed milk, cornstarch, and egg.
3. Beat or whip thoroughly, until all ingredients are completely mixed and fluffy, thick and stiff.
4. Spoon even amounts of the creamy filling into each spring roll wrapper, then top each dollop of filling with several raspberries.
5. Roll up the wraps around the creamy raspberry filling and seal the seams with a few dabs of water. Place each roll on the foil-lined Air fryer basket, seams facing down.
6. Set the air fryer timer to 10 minutes. During cooking, shake the handle of the fryer basket to ensure a nice even surface crisp.
7. After 10 minutes, when the Air fryer shuts off, the spring rolls should be golden brown and perfect on the outside, while the raspberries and cream filling will have cooked together in a glorious fusion. Remove with tongs and serve hot or cold.

Nutrition: Calories: 164 Fat: 1g Carbs: 33g Protein: 7g

957. Banana-Choco Brownies

Preparation Time: 5 minutes
Cooking Time: 30 minutes
Servings: 12
Ingredients:

- 2 cups almond flour
- 2 teaspoons baking powder
- ½ teaspoon baking powder
- ½ teaspoon baking soda
- ½ teaspoon salt
- 1 over-ripe banana
- large eggs
- ½ teaspoon stevia powder
- ¼ cup coconut oil
- 1 tablespoon vinegar
- 1/3 cup almond flour
- 1/3 cup cocoa powder

Directions:

1. Preheat the air fryer for 5 minutes.
2. Prepare a food processor and process all ingredients. Pulse until well-combined.
3. Pour into a baking dish that will fit in the air fryer.
4. Arrange in the air fryer basket and cook for 30 minutes at 350°F or if a toothpick inserted in the middle comes out clean.

Nutrition: Calories: 75 Fat:6.5g Protein:1.7g Sugar:2g

958. Fudge Brownies

Preparation Time: 5 minutes
Cooking Time: 20 minutes
Servings: 6
Ingredients:

- tablespoons (1 stick) unsalted butter, melted
- 1 cup sugar
- 1 teaspoon vanilla extract
- 2 large eggs
- ½ cup all-purpose flour
- ½ cup cocoa powder
- 1 teaspoon baking powder

Directions:

1. Spray a 6-inch air fryer–safe baking pan with cooking spray or grease the pan with butter.
2. Get a medium bowl, mix together the butter and sugar, then add the vanilla and eggs and beat until well combined.
3. Add the flour, cocoa powder, and baking powder and mix until smooth. Pour the batter into the prepared pan.
4. Set the temperature of your AF to 350°F and bake for 20 minutes. Once the center is set, use silicon oven mitts to remove the pan from the air fryer.
5. Let cool slightly before serving.

Nutrition: Calories: 110 Fat: 7g Carbs: 3g Protein: 2g

959. Cinnamon Toast

Preparation Time: 5 minutes
Cooking Time: 5 minutes
Servings: 6
Ingredients:

- 2 tsp. pepper
- 1 ½ tsp. vanilla extract
- 1 ½ tsp. cinnamon
- ½ C. sweetener of choice
- 1 C. coconut oil
- slices whole wheat bread

Directions:

1. Melt coconut oil and mix with sweetener until dissolved. Mix in remaining ingredients minus bread till incorporated.
2. Spread mixture onto bread, covering all area.
3. Place coated pieces of bread in your Air fryer.
4. Cook 5 minutes at 400°F. Remove and cut diagonally. Enjoy.

Nutrition: Calories: 124 Fat:2g Protein:0g Sugar:4g

960. Easy Baked Chocolate Mug Cake

Preparation Time: 5 minutes
Cooking Time: 15 minutes
Servings: 3
Ingredients:

- ½ cup cocoa powder
- ½ cup stevia powder
- 1 cup coconut cream
- 1 package cream cheese, room temperature
- 1 tablespoon vanilla extract
- tablespoons butter

Directions:

1. Preheat the air fryer for 5 minutes. In a mixing bowl, combine all ingredients using hand mixer to mix everything until fluffy.
2. Pour into greased mugs. Place the mugs in the fryer basket.
3. Bake for 15 minutes at 350°F.Place in the fridge to chill before serving.

Nutrition: Calories: 744 Fat:69.7g Protein:13.9 Sugar:4g

961. Easy Chocolate-Frosted Doughnuts

Preparation Time: 5 minutes
Cooking Time: 5 minutes
Servings: 6
Ingredients:

- 1 (16.3-ounce / 8-count) package refrigerated biscuit dough
- ¾ cup powdered sugar
- ¼ cup unsweetened cocoa powder
- ¼ cup milk

Directions:

1. Unroll the biscuit dough onto a cutting board and separate the biscuits.
2. Using a 1-inch biscuit cutter or cookie cutter, cut out the center of each biscuit.
3. Place the doughnuts into the air fryer. (You may have to cook your doughnuts in more than one batch.)
4. 2Set the temperature of your AF to 330°F. Set the timer and bake for 5 minutes.
5. Using tongs, remove the doughnuts from the air fryer and let them cool slightly before glazing.
6. Meanwhile, in a small mixing bowl, combine the powdered sugar, unsweetened cocoa powder, and milk and mix until smooth.
7. Dip your doughnuts into the glaze and use a knife to smooth the frosting evenly over the doughnut.
8. Let the glaze set before serving.

Nutrition: Calories: 233 Fat: 8g Carbohydrate: 37g Sugar: 15g

962.   Angel Food Cake
Preparation Time: 10 minutes
Cooking Time: 30 minutes
Servings: 12
Ingredients:
- ¼ cup butter, melted
- 1 cup powdered erythritol
- 1 teaspoon strawberry extract
- egg whites
- 2 teaspoons cream of tartar
- A pinch of salt

Directions:
1 Preheat the air fryer for 5 minutes.
2 Blend egg whites and tartar. Use a hand mixer and whisk until white and fluffy.
3 Add the rest of the ingredients except for the butter and whisk for another minute.
4 Pour into a baking dish.
5 Cook for 30 minutes at 400°F or if a toothpick inserted in the middle comes out clean. Drizzle with melted butter once cooled.

Nutrition: Calories: 140 Fat: 0g Protein: 3g Carbs: 32g

963.   Fried Peaches
Preparation Time: 2 hours
Cooking Time: 15 minutes
Servings: 4
Ingredients:
- ripe peaches (1/2 a peach = 1 serving)
- 1 1/2 cups flour
- Salt
- 2 egg yolks
- 3/4 cups cold water
- 1 1/2 tablespoons olive oil
- 2 tablespoons brandy
- egg whites
- Cinnamon/sugar mix

Directions:
1 Mix flour, egg yolks, and salt in a mixing bowl. Slowly mix in water, then add brandy. Set the mixture aside for 2 hours and go do something for 1 hour 45 minutes.
2 Boil a large pot of water and cut and X at the bottom of each peach. While the water boils fill another large bowl with water and ice then plunge it in the ice bath.
3 Now the peels should basically fall off the peach. Beat the egg whites and mix into the batter mix. Dip each peach in the mix to coat.
4 Cook at 360°F for 10 Minutes.
5 Prepare a plate with cinnamon/sugar mix, roll peaches in mix and serve.

Nutrition: Calories: 68 Fat: 5g Protein: 1g Carbs: 6g

964.   Apple Dumplings
Preparation Time: 10 minutes
Cooking Time: 25 minutes
Servings: 4
Ingredients:
- 2 tbsp. melted coconut oil
- 2 puff pastry sheets
- 1 tbsp. brown sugar
- 2 tbsp. raisins
- 2 small apples of choice

Directions:
1 Ensure your air fryer is preheated to 356°F.
2 Core and peel apples and mix with raisins and sugar.
3 Place a bit of apple mixture into puff pastry sheets and brush sides with melted coconut oil.
4 Place into the Air fryer. Cook 25 minutes, turning halfway through. Will be golden when done.

Nutrition: Calories: 163 Fat: 9g Carbs: 21g Protein: 1g

965.   Poppy Seed Balls
Preparation Time: 20 minutes
Cooking time: 8 minutes
Servings: 14
Ingredients:
- ½ cup heavy cream
- 1 cup coconut flour
- ¼ teaspoon salt
- ½ teaspoon ground cinnamon
- tablespoon poppy seeds
- ¼ teaspoon ground ginger
- 1 teaspoon butter
- ½ teaspoon baking powder
- ½ teaspoon apple cider vinegar
- tablespoon stevia extract

Directions:
1 Mix the coconut flour, salt, ground cinnamon, poppy seeds, ground ginger, and baking powder together in a bowl.
2 Gently melt butter and add to the dried mixture.
3 Add apple cider vinegar and stevia extract.
4 Add heavy cream and knead to a soft dough.
5 Make the log from the dough and cut into 11 balls.
6 Preheat the air fryer to 365° F.
7 Put the poppy seed balls in the air fryer basket.
8 Cook the balls for 3 minutes.
9 Shake them a little and cook for 5 minutes more.
10 1Check if the balls are cooked using a toothpick.
11 Cool before serving.

Nutrition: calories 63, fat 4.2, fiber 4.1, carbs 7.4, protein 1.7

966.   Pecan Bars
Preparation Time: 18 minutes
Cooking time: 23 minutes
Servings: 8
Ingredients:
- 1 cup almond flour
- ¼ cup hot water
- ¼ teaspoon salt
- tablespoon stevia extract
- 1 teaspoon vanilla extract
- tablespoon butter
- tablespoon pecans, crushed
- ½ teaspoon baking powder
- ½ teaspoon apple cider vinegar
- ½ teaspoon sesame oil

Directions:
1 Soften the butter.
2 Combine the soft butter and almond flour in a bowl.
3 Then add salt, stevia extract, vanilla extract, water, baking powder, and apple cider vinegar.
4 Drizzle the almond flour mixture with sesame oil and knead until well combined.
5 Then add the crushed pecans and knead the dough for 2 minutes more.
6 Preheat the air fryer to 350° F.
7 Cover the air fryer tray with parchment paper and place the almond flour dough.
8 Flatten it to cover the surface.
9 Cover with more parchment paper and cook for 20 minutes.
10 Remove the cover and cook for 3 minutes more.
11 1Cool before cutting into 8 bars.

Nutrition: calories 157, fat 14.3, fiber 2.2, carbs 4.1, protein 3.7

967.   Macadamia Nut Brownies
Preparation Time: 15 minutes
Cooking time: 25 minutes
Servings: 16
Ingredients:
- eggs
- 1/3 cup macadamia nuts, crushed
- tablespoon butter, melted
- 1 cup coconut flour
- ½ teaspoon baking powder
- 1 teaspoon fresh lemon juice
- oz. dark chocolate, melted
- tablespoon swerves

Directions:
1 Break eggs into a mixer bowl and mix.
2 Add melted butter and keep mixing for 2 minutes.

3   Add coconut flour, baking powder, fresh lemon juice, melted dark chocolate, and swerve.
4   Mix using a silicon spatula.
5   Add the crushed macadamia nuts and stir carefully.
6   Preheat the air fryer to 355° F.
7   Pour the brownie dough into the air fryer basket tray and cook for 25 minutes.
8   Cooked brownies should be soft but well cooked.
9   Slice the brownies into 12 pieces.

Nutrition: calories 112, fat 7.6, fiber 3.4, carbs 7.5, protein 2.4

968.   Coconut-Sunflower Bars

Preparation Time: 15 minutes
Cooking time: 16 minutes
Servings: 8
Ingredients:

- tablespoon sunflower seeds
- 1 tablespoon coconut flakes
- ½ cup almond flour
- 2 tablespoon coconut milk
- 2 tablespoon butter
- ¼ teaspoon salt
- 2 tablespoon stevia extract
- 1 egg

Directions:
1   Crush the sunflower seeds and combine them with the coconut flakes.
2   Then add the almond flour and salt.
3   Stir the dried ingredients carefully.
4   Crack the egg into the mixture.
5   Add the coconut milk, butter, and stevia extract.
6   Mix using a spatula or use a hand mixer.
7   Preheat the air fryer to 355° F.
8   Pour the coconut mixture into the air fryer tray and cook for 16 minutes.
9   If the mixture is too thick – increase the time of cooking by 2-3 minutes.
10   Cool the cooked mixture.
11   Cut it into 8 small bars.

Nutrition: calories 90, fat 8.2, fiber 1, carbs 2, protein 2.5

969.   Green Avocado Pudding

Preparation Time: 10 minutes
Cooking Time: 3minutes
Servings: 3
Ingredients:

- 1 tablespoon cocoa powder
- 1 avocado, pitted
- teaspoon stevia extract
- ¼ teaspoon vanilla extract
- ¼ teaspoon salt
- tablespoon almond milk

Directions:
1   Preheat the air fryer to 360° F.
2   Strip avocado and mash, it with a fork.
3   Then combine with the stevia extract, vanilla extract, salt, and almond milk.
4   Add the cocoa powder.
5   Use a hand mixer to combine.
6   Pour the pudding mixture into the air fryer basket.
7   Cook for 3 minutes.
8   Allow to cool before serving.

Nutrition: calories 199, fat 19.3, fiber 5.6, carbs 8.2, protein 2.2

970.   Sunflower Cookies

Preparation Time: 15 minutes
Cooking time: 10 minutes
Servings: 8
Ingredients:

- oz. sunflower seed butter
- ½ teaspoon salt
- 1 tablespoon stevia extract
- tablespoon coconut flour
- ¼ teaspoon salt
- ¼ teaspoon olive oil

Directions:

1   Combine the sunflower seed butter and coconut flour together.
2   Sprinkle the mixture with salt and stevia extract.
3   Add olive oil and mix well.
4   Mix until you have a well combined dough.
5   Separate the dough into 8 balls and flatten gently.
6   Preheat the air fryer to 365° F.
7   Put the flattened balls into the air fryer rack.
8   Cook for 10 minutes.
9   Allow to cool before serving.

Nutrition: calories 126, fat 9.2, fiber 2.3, carbs 8.6, protein 4.2

971.   Keto Vanilla Mousse

Preparation Time: 15 minutes
Cooking time: 6 minutes
Servings: 4
Ingredients:

- 1 teaspoon vanilla extract
- ½ cup cream cheese
- ½ cup almond milk
- ¼ cup blackberries
- teaspoon stevia extract
- 2 tablespoon butter
- ¼ teaspoon cinnamon

Directions:
1   Preheat the air fryer to 320° F.
2   Combine butter, vanilla extract, and almond milk and transfer the mixture to the air fryer.
3   Cook the mixture for 6 minutes or well combined.
4   Then stir it carefully and chill to room temperature.
5   Crush the blackberries.
6   Whisk the cream cheese using a hand whisker for 2 minutes.
7   Add the crushed blackberries and whisk for 1 minute more.
8   Add cinnamon and stevia extract.
9   Stir gently.
10   Combine the almond butter liquid and cream cheese mixture together.
11   Mix using a hand mixer.
12   When well mixed pour into a glass vessel.
13   Place it in the fridge and cool.

Nutrition: calories 228, fat 23.1, fiber 1.2, carbs 3.5, protein 3.1

972.   Avocado Brownies

Preparation Time: 15 minutes
Cooking time: 20 minutes
Servings: 6
Ingredients:

- 1avocado, pitted
- teaspoon Erythritol
- ¼ teaspoon vanilla extract
- 1 oz. dark chocolate
- tablespoon almond flour
- ½ teaspoon stevia powder
- 1 egg
- 1 teaspoon coconut oil
- ¼ teaspoon baking powder
- ¼ teaspoon salt

Directions:
1   Peel the avocado and chop it roughly.
2   Put the avocado in a blender.
3   Melt the dark chocolate and add it to the blender.
4   Add vanilla extract and blend the mixture until smooth.
5   Add almond flour, stevia powder, coconut oil, baking powder, salt, and Erythritol.
6   Crack the egg in the mixture and blend until smooth.
7   Preheat the air fryer to 355 F.
8   Pour the avocado brownie mixture into the air fryer tray and flatten using a spatula.
9   Cook the brownie dough for 20 minutes.
10   Cut into 6 brownie bars and allow to cool.

Nutrition: calories 131, fat 11.2, fiber 2.8, carbs 8.3, protein 2.7

973.   Cheesecake Mousse

Preparation Time: 20 minutes
Cooking time: 4 minutes
Servings: 12
Ingredients:

- ¼ cup heavy cream
- 1 egg
- ½ cup cream cheese
- 1/3 cup Erythritol
- ¼ teaspoon lime zest
- scoop stevia

Directions:
1. Crack the egg into a mixer bowl and whisk.
2. Add the heavy cream and keep whisking until the mixture is fluffy.
3. Then add cream cheese, lime zest, stevia, and Erythritol.
4. Whisk well.
5. Preheat the air fryer to 310° F.
6. Pour the cheesecake mixture into the air fryer tray and cook for 14 minutes, stirring every 4 minutes.
7. Whisk carefully using a hand whisker.
8. Cool before serving.

Nutrition: calories 43, fat 4.8, fiber 0, carbs 7.1, protein 1.3

974. Sweet Bacon Cookies
Preparation Time: 10 minutes
Cooking time: 7 minutes
Servings: 6
Ingredients:

- slices bacon, cooked, chopped
- tablespoon peanut butter
- ¼ teaspoon baking soda
- tablespoon swerves
- ½ teaspoon vanilla extract
- ¼ teaspoon ground ginger

Directions:
1. Take a large bowl and combine the baking soda, peanut butter, swerve, vanilla extract, and ground ginger together.
2. Add chopped bacon and mix the dough with a spatula.
3. When the dough is well mixed make the log and cut into 6 parts.
4. Roll the balls from the dough and flatten them gently.
5. Preheat the air fryer to 350° F.
6. Place the cookies in the air fryer and cook for 7 minutes.
7. Cool before serving.

Nutrition: calories 109, fat 8.8, fiber 0.8, carbs 3.8, protein 5.2

975. Sunflower Seed Pie
Preparation Time: 20 minutes
Cooking time: 20 minutes
Servings: 6
Ingredients:

- ½ cup sunflower seeds
- 1 cup almond flour
- ¼ cup heavy cream
- eggs
- 1 teaspoon butter
- ½ teaspoon vanilla extract
- ½ teaspoon ground ginger
- scoop stevia
- ½ teaspoon baking powder

Directions:
1. Split eggs in a large bowl and whisk them.
2. Add heavy cream, butter, almond flour, vanilla extract, ground ginger, stevia, and baking powder.
3. Mix the dough gently with a hand mixer.
4. Then add the sunflower seeds and stir the dough with a spatula.
5. Leave the pie dough for 10 minutes to rest.
6. Preheat the air fryer to 360° F.
7. Transfer the dough to the air fryer dish.
8. Cook the pie for 20 minutes.
9. Then let the pie chill well before serving.

Nutrition: calories 180, fat 14.8, fiber 2.4, carbs 5.4, protein 6.8

976. Coconut Pie
Preparation Time: 25 minutes
Cooking time: 10 minutes
Servings: 4
Ingredients:

- 1 cup almond flour
- tablespoon butter

- ¼ teaspoon salt
- 1 scoop stevia
- 1 tablespoon ice water
- eggs
- ½ cup heavy cream
- 1 teaspoon butter
- 2 tablespoon coconut flakes
- 1 teaspoon vanilla extract

Directions:
1. Preheat the air fryer to 360° F.
2. Combine the almond flour and 3 tablespoons of the butter in a bowl.
3. Add salt and stevia.
4. Blend well.
5. When the mixture starts to become smooth add ice water and blend for 2 minutes.
6. Cover the air fryer crust with parchment paper and place the dough.
7. Roll it is using your fingertips.
8. Place the piecrust in the air fryer and cook for 7 minutes.
9. Meanwhile, crack the eggs in a bowl and whisk them.
10. Add 1 teaspoon of butter and heavy cream and whisk well for 3 minutes.
11. Add coconut flakes and vanilla extract. Whisk it for 1 minute more.
12. When the pie crust is cooked remove it from the air fryer to cool.
13. Pour the whisked heavy cream mixture in the air fryer and cook it for 3 minutes at 365° F. Whisk carefully.
14. Pour the cooked heavy cream mixture over the piecrust.
15. Chill until the filling of the pie is a little bit solid then serve.

Nutrition: calories 190, fat 17.3, fiber 1.6, carbs 3.6, protein 5.3

977. Cream Cheese Muffins
Preparation Time: 15 minutes
Cooking time: 10 minutes
Servings: 8
Ingredients:

- 1 egg
- 1 cup cream cheese
- 1 cup almond flour
- ¼ teaspoon salt
- 1 teaspoon baking soda
- 1 teaspoon apple cider vinegar
- teaspoon swerves
- 2 tablespoon coconut flakes

Directions:
1. Break egg in a bowl and add cream cheese.
2. Whisk the mixture well.
3. Sprinkle the cream cheese mixture with the almond flour, salt, baking soda, and apple cider vinegar.
4. Add swerve and coconut flakes.
5. Use a hand mixer to make the dough.
6. Preheat the air fryer to 360° F.
7. Fill 1/2 part of every muffin mold with the muffin dough and put the muffins in the air fryer.
8. Cook for 10 minutes.
9. Allow to cool before serving.

Nutrition: calories 135, fat 12.8, fiber 0.5, carbs 2.3, protein 3.7

978. Tangerine Cake
Preparation Time: 10 minutes
Cooking Time: 20 minutes
Servings: 8
Ingredients:

- ¾ cup sugar 2 cups flour
- ¼ cup olive oil
- ½ cup milk
- 1 teaspoon juice vinegar
- ½ teaspoon vanilla concentrate
- Juice and get-up-and-go from 2 lemons
- Juice and get-up-and-go from 1 tangerine
- Tangerine slices, for serving

Directions:

1 In a bowl, blend flour in with sugar and mix.
2 In another bowl, blend oil in with milk, vinegar, vanilla concentrate, lemon squeeze and pizzazz and tangerine get-up-and-go and whisk quite well.
3 Add flour, mix well, empty this into a cake skillet that accommodates the air fryer cooker, present in the fryer and cook at 360°F for about 20 minutes.
4 Serve immediately with tangerine slices on top. Enjoy the recipe!

Nutrition: calories 190, fat 1, fiber 1, carbs 4, protein 4

979. Mandarin Pudding
Preparation Time: 20 minutes
Cooking Time: 40 minutes
Servings: 8
Ingredients:
- 1 mandarin, stripped and cut Juice from 2 mandarins
- 1 tablespoon darker sugar 4 ounces margarine, delicate
- 2 eggs, whisked
- ¾ cup sugar
- ¾ cup white flour
- ¾ cup almonds, ground Honey for serving

Directions:
1 Grease a portion skillet with some margarine, sprinkle dark colored sugar on the base and mastermind mandarin cuts.
2 In a bowl, blend spread in with sugar, eggs, almonds, flour and mandarin juice, mix, spoon this over mandarin cuts, place container in the air fryer cooker and cook at 360 Deg. Fahrenheit for about 40 minutes.
3 Transfer pudding to a plate and present with honey on top.
4 Enjoy the recipe!

Nutrition: calories 162, fat 3, fiber 2, carbs 3, protein 6

980. Cocoa and Almonds Bars
Preparation Time: 30 minutes
Cooking Time: 4 minutes
Servings: 6
Ingredients:
- ¼ cup cocoa nibs
- 1 cup almonds, drenched and depleted
- 2 tablespoons cocoa powder
- ¼ cup hemp seeds
- ¼ cup goji berries
- ¼ cup coconut, destroyed
- dates, hollowed and drenched

Directions:
1 Put almonds in your food processor, mix, include hemp seeds, cocoa nibs, cocoa powder, goji, coconut and mix quite well.
2 Add dates, mix well once more, spread on a lined heating sheet that accommodates the air fryer cooker and cook at 320 °F for about 4 minutes.
3 Cut into two halves and keep in the cooler for 30 minutes before serving.
4 Enjoy the recipe!

Nutrition: calories 140, fat 6, fiber 3, carbs 7, protein 19

981. Dark Colored Butter Cookies
Preparation Time: 10 minutes
Cooking Time: 10 minutes
Servings: 6
Ingredients:
- 1 and ½ cups spread
- 2 cups dark colored sugar
- 2 eggs, whisked
- cups flour
- 2/3 cup walnuts, hacked
- 2 teaspoons vanilla concentrate
- 1 teaspoon preparing pop
- ½ teaspoon preparing powder

Directions:
1 Heat up a dish with the spread over medium heat, mix until it liquefies, include dark colored sugar and mix until this disintegrates.
2 In a bowl, blend flour in with walnuts, vanilla concentrate, preparing pop, heating powder and eggs and mix well.

3 Add dark colored margarine, mix well and organize spoonful of this blend on a lined heating sheet that accommodates the air fryer cooker.
4 Introduce in the fryer and cook at 340°F for about 10 minutes.
5 Leave cookies to chill off and serve. Enjoy the recipe!

Nutrition: calories 144, fat 5, fiber 6, carbs 19, protein 2

982. Tomato Cake
Preparation Time: 10 minutes
Cooking Time: 30 minutes
Servings: 4
Ingredients:
1 and ½ cups flour
- 1 teaspoon cinnamon powder
- 1 teaspoon preparing powder
- 1 teaspoon preparing pop
- ¾ cup maple syrup
- 1 cup tomatoes hacked
- ½ cup olive oil
- 2 tablespoon apple juice vinegar

Directions:
1 1.In a bowl, blend flour in with preparing powder, heating pop, cinnamon and maple syrup and mix well.
3 In another bowl, blend tomatoes in with olive oil and vinegar and mix well.
4 Combine the 2 blends, mix well, fill a lubed round skillet that accommodates the air fryer cooker, present in the fryer and cook at 360°F for about 30 minutes.
5 Leave cake to chill off, cut and serve.
2 Enjoy the recipe!

Nutrition: calories 153, fat 2, fiber 1, carbs 25, protein 4

983. Cashew Bars
Preparation Time: 10 minutes
Cooking Time: 15 minutes
Servings: 6
Ingredients:
- 1/3 cup honey
- ¼ cup almond meal
- 1 tablespoon almond spread
- 1 and ½ cups cashews, hacked
- dates, slashed
- ¾ cup coconut, destroyed
- 1 tablespoon chia seeds

Directions:
1. In a bowl, blend honey in with almond meal and almond spread and mix well.
2. Add cashews, coconut, dates and chia seeds and mix well once more.
3. Spread this on a lined heating sheet that accommodates the air fryer cooker and press well.
4. Introduce in the fryer and cook at 300°F for about 15 minutes.
5. Leave blend to chill off, cut into medium bars and serve. Enjoy!

Nutrition: calories 121, fat 4, fiber 7, carbs 5, protein 6

984. Orange Cookies
Preparation Time: 10 minutes
Cooking Time: 12 minutes
Servings: 8
Ingredients:
- cups flour
- 1 teaspoon heating powder
- ½ cup margarine, delicate
- ¾ cup sugar
- 1 egg, whisked
- 1 teaspoon vanilla concentrate
- 1 tablespoon orange pizzazz, ground

For the filling:
- ounces cream cheddar, delicate
- ½ cup margarine
- 2 cups powdered sugar

Directions:
1 In a bowl, blend cream cheddar with 1/2 cup spread and 2 cups powdered sugar, mix well utilizing your blender and leave aside until further notice.

2   In another bowl, blend flour in with heating powder.
3   In a third bowl, blend 1/2 cup spread with 3/4 cup sugar, egg, vanilla concentrate and orange pizzazz and whisk well.
4   Combine flour with orange blend, mix well and scoop 1 tablespoon of the blend on a lined heating sheet that accommodates the air fryer cooker.
5   Repeat with the remainder of the orange player, present in the fryer and cook at 340°F for about 12 minutes.
6   Leave cookies to chill off, spread cream filling on half of them top with different cookies and serve.

Nutrition: calories 124, fat 5, fiber 6, carbs 8, protein 4

985. Cornflakes French Toast
Preparation Time: 10 minutes
Cooking Time: 20 minutes
Servings: 1
Ingredients:

- Bread cuts (dark colored or white)
- egg white for each
- 1 tsp. sugar for each
- Crushed cornflakes

Directions:

1   Set up two cuts and cut them along the corner to corner.
2   Dunk the bread triangles into this blend and afterward cover them with the squashed cornflakes.
3   Pre-heat the Air-Fryer at 180° C for 4 minutes. Look for the covered bread triangles in the fry crate and close it.
4   Let them cook at a similar temperature for an additional 20 minutes at any rate.
5   Part of the way through the procedure, turn the triangles over with the goal that you get a uniform cook.
6   Serve these cuts with chocolate sauce.

Nutrition: Calories: 240 Fat: 3g Carbs: 30g Protein: 1g

986. Peaches Cake
Preparation Time: 45 minutes
Cooking Time: 35 minutes
Servings: 4
Ingredients:

- 1 pie mixture
- and ¼ pounds peaches, hollowed and cleaved
- 2 tablespoons cornstarch
- ½ cup sugar
- 2 tablespoons flour
- A spot of nutmeg, ground
- 1 tablespoon dim rum
- 1 tablespoon lemon juice
- 2 tablespoons spread, dissolved

Directions:

1   Roll pie batter into a pie dish that accommodates the air fryer cooker and press well.
2   In a bowl, blend peaches in with cornstarch, sugar, flour, nutmeg, rum, lemon squeeze and margarine and mix well.
3   Pour and spread this into pie container, present in the air fryer cooker and cook at 350°F for about 35 minutes.
4   Serve warm or cold.

Nutrition: calories 231, fat 6, fiber 7, carbs 9, protein 5

987. Plum And Current Tart
Preparation Time: 10 minutes
Cooking Time: 35 minutes
Servings: 6
Ingredients:
For the disintegrate:

- ¼ cup almond flour
- ¼ cup millet flour
- 1 cup dark colored rice flour
- ½ cup genuine sweetener
- tablespoons margarine, delicate 3 tablespoons milk

For the filling:

- 1-pound little plums, pitted and divided 1 cup white currants
- tablespoons cornstarch
- tablespoons sugar

- ½ teaspoon vanilla concentrate
- ½ teaspoon cinnamon powder
- ¼ teaspoon ginger powder
- 1 teaspoon lime juice

Directions:

1   In a bowl, blend darker rice flour with 1/2 cup sugar, millet flour, almond flour, spread and milk and mix until you get a sand like mixture.
2   Reserve 1/4 of the mixture press the remainder of the batter into a tart container that accommodates the air fryer cooker and keep in the refrigerator for 30 minutes.
3   Meanwhile, in a bowl, blend plums with currants, 3 tablespoons sugar, cornstarch, vanilla concentrate, cinnamon, ginger and lime squeeze and mix well.
4   Pour this over tart outside layer, disintegrate reserved mixture on top, present in the air fryer cooker and cook at 350 °F for about 35 minutes.
5   Leave tart to chill off, cut and serve. Enjoy the recipe!

Nutrition: calories 200, fat 5, fiber 4, carbs 8, protein 6

988. Plum Bars
Preparation Time: 10 minutes
Cooking Time: 16 minutes
Servings: 8
Ingredients:

- cups dried plums
- tablespoons water
- 2 cup moved oats
- 1 cup dark colored sugar
- ½ teaspoon preparing pop
- 1 teaspoon cinnamon powder
- 2 tablespoons spread, liquefied
- 1 egg, whisked
- Cooking spray

Directions:

1   In your food processor, blend plums with water and mix until you get a clingy spread.
2   In a bowl, blend oats in with cinnamon, preparing pop, sugar, egg and margarine and whisk truly well.
3   Press portion of the oats blend in a preparing dish that accommodates the air fryer cooker showered with cooking oil, spread plums blend and top with the other portion of the oats blend.
4   Introduce in the air fryer cooker and cook at 350 °F for about 16 minutes.
5   Leave blend aside to chill off, cut into medium bars and serve.

Nutrition: calories 111, fat 5, fiber 6, carbs 12, protein 6

989. Chocolate Brandy Cake
Preparation Time: 15 minutes
Cooking Time: 35 minutes
Servings: 8
Ingredients:

- 1 egg
- ½ cup milk
- ¼ cup vegetable oil
- 1 tsp vanilla extract
- ½ cup brandy
- 1/3 cup brown sugar
- ½ cup flour
- ¼ cup cocoa powder
- ¾ tsp. baking soda
- ¾ tsp. baking powder
- ½ tsp salt

Directions:

1   Preheat the fryer to 320° F.
2   Put the egg, milk, vanilla, and brandy in a bowl. Stir until combined.
3   In a second bowl, combine the remaining ingredients. Gradually add the liquid ingredients to the flour mixture and stir just until combined. The batter should be thing.
4   Spray a cake pan, which fits into the air fryer basket, with nonstick spray. Pour the batter into the pan. Cover with foil. Poke a few holes into the foil top and bake for 30 minutes.

5   Remove the foil and bake for 5 more minutes. Remove from the air frying and cool completely before serving.

6   Enjoy!

Nutrition: Calories: 380 Fat: 12g Carbs: 61g Protein: 0g

990. Chocolate Cherry Tart

Preparation Time: 15 minutes
Cooking Time: 40 minutes
Servings: 8
Ingredients:

- 1 cup dark chocolate, melted
- tbsp. sugar
- 1 tsp. almond extract
- ¼ cup flour
- 1 cup cherries, pit removed and cut in half
- 1 tube premade sugar cookie dough

Directions:

1   Preheat air fryer to 325° F.

2   Press the sugar cooking dough into a tart pan. Bake for 10 minutes.

3   In a bowl, combine the cherries, almond extract, flour, and sugar.

4   Pour the chocolate into the bottom of the baked cookie shell. Top with cherry mixture.

5   Bake for 30 minutes.

6   Cool completely before serving. Enjoy!

Nutrition: Calories: 181 Fat: 10g Carbs: 22g Protein: 2g

991. Chocolate Caramel Peanut Cake

Preparation Time: 15 minutes
Cooking Time: 20 minutes
Servings: 8
Ingredients:

- 1 Box chocolate cake mix
- eggs
- ½ cup oil
- ½ cup water
- 1 cup caramel sauce
- 1 cup heavy cream
- 1 tbsp. powdered sugar
- 1 cup chocolate syrup
- ½ cup chopped peanuts

Directions:

1   Turn on the air fryer to 320° F

2   Mix together the cake mixes, egg, oil, and water. Place in a cake pan that fits in the air fryer and bake for 20 minutes.

3   Remove the cake from the fryer. Spread the caramel sauce on top while still hot. Refrigerate until cold.

4   Mix well heavy cream and powdered sugar on high speed in a mixing bowl. Whip until fluffy. Spread over cooled cake. Sprinkle peanuts on top.

5   Serve and enjoy!

Nutrition: Calories: 544 Fat: 33g Carbs: 51g Protein: 9g

992. Cinnamon Doughnuts

Preparation Time: 10 minutes
Cooking Time: 20 minutes
Servings: 10
Ingredients:

- ½ cup sugar
- 2¼ cups cake flour
- 1½ tsp baking powder
- tbsp. butter, cold
- 1 tsp salt
- 2 beaten egg yolks
- 1 egg white
- ½ cup sour cream
- ½ cup vegetable oil
- 1 cup sugar
- 2 tsp. cinnamon

Directions:

1   Preheat fryer to 320° F.

2   In a bowl, combine the sugar and butter. Stir until the mixture is crumbly. Add the egg yolks and whites. stir until smooth.

3   In another bowl, add the flour, the baking powder and the salt.

4   Add half the flour and half the sour cream mixture to the sugar mixture. Stir well then add remaining flour and sour cream. Refrigerate for 1 hour.

5   On a lightly floured surface, roll the dough 1/2-inch-thick and cut into small circles.

6   Brush with the oil and set in the fryer basket. Cook for 10 minutes. Sprinkle with cinnamon while still hot. Serve and enjoy.

Nutrition: Calories: 130 Fat: 7g Carbs: 16g Protein: 1g

993. Chocolate Orange Fudge Cake

Preparation Time: 15 minutes
Cooking Time: 25 minutes
Servings: 4
Ingredients:

- tbsp. flour
- tbsp. sugar
- 2 cups dark chocolate, melted
- 2 cups butter, melted
- 1 tbsp. orange zest
- 1 tbsp. orange juice
- 2 large eggs

Directions:

1   Warm up the air fryer to 320° F. Spray the pan which fits in the air fryer with not stick spray.

2   Combine the chocolate and butter, whisk until smooth.

3   In a second bowl, combine the sugar and egg. Whisk well.

4   Add the sugar mixture, orange zest, and orange juice into the chocolate mixture. Add the flour and mix well.

5   Pour into the cake pan. Bake for 20 minutes.

6   Remove cake from the fryer and flip upside down. Tap the pan and remove the cake from the pan.

7   Serve and enjoy!

Nutrition: Calories: 285 Fat: 15g Carbs: 0g Protein: 4g

994. Triple Chocolate Cheesecake

Preparation Time: 10 minutes
Cooking Time: 25 minutes
Servings: 6
Ingredients:

- cups crushed Oreo cookies
- tbsp. of melted butter
- 1 cup cream cheese
- ½ cup sugar
- eggs
- ½ cup of sour cream
- ½ cup heavy cream
- ½ cup cream de cacao liqueur
- ¼ cup flour
- 1 tsp vanilla extract
- 1 cup semi-sweet chocolate chips
- ¼ cup cocoa powder

Directions:

1   Turn on the air fryer to 320° F.

2   Combine the Oreos and butter until well combined.

3   Spray a springform pan which will fit into the air fryer basket with nonstick spray. Press the Oreo mixture into the pan.

4   Whip together the cream cheese, sugar, liqueur, chocolate chips, flour, cocoa, vanilla, sour cream, and egg until smooth. Pour over the crust into an even layer.

5   Bake for 30 minutes, or until a toothpick inserted into the center of the cake comes out clean.

6   Cool completely, enjoy!

Nutrition: Calories:150 Fat: 2g Carbs: 20g Protein: 5g

995. Chocolate Chiffon Cake

Preparation Time: 10 minutes
Cooking Time: 35 minutes
Servings: 10
Ingredients:

- egg yolks
- ½ cup sugar
- ½ cup milk
- ½ cup vegetable oil
- ¼ cup cake flour
- ½ tsp baking powder

- ¼ cup cocoa powder
- egg whites
- 1/3 tsp cream of tartar

Directions:
1. Ready the fryer to 320° F.
2. Mix the yolks egg yolks and half the sugar in a small bowl.
3. In a second bowl combine the milk and olive oil. Mix well. Add in the flour, baking powder, and cocoa powder.
4. Add the yolk mixture to the flour mixture. Mix well until very smooth.
5. Put in the mixing bowl the egg whites and cream of tartar. Mix on high until soft peaks form. Add remaining sugar and mix on high speed until stiff peaks form.
6. Gradually add the egg white mixture to the cake batter and carefully stir. Pour into a cake pan.
7. Bake until a toothpick put into the center comes out clean. Cool completely before slicing. Serve and enjoy!

Nutrition: Calories: 274 Fat: 11g Carbs: 41g Protein: 4g

996. Dark Chocolate Truffles
Preparation Time: 15 minutes
Cooking Time: 15 minutes
Servings: 10
Ingredients:
- cups dark chocolate chips, melted
- ¼ cup coconut oil
- tbsp. orange juice
- 1 tsp vanilla extract
- ½ cup honey
- 1 tbsp. heavy cream
- tbsp. flour
- ¼ cup cocoa powder

Directions:
1. Preheat fryer to 240° F.
2. Combine all ingredients except cocoa powder until smooth. Mixture will be thick.
3. Shape into balls and roll to the cocoa powder.
4. Bake for 10 minutes.
5. Cool, serve, and enjoy!

Nutrition: Calories: 180 Fat: 12g Carbs: 16g Protein: 2g

997. Rum Cake
Preparation Time: 15 minutes
Cooking Time: 35 minutes
Servings: 8
Ingredients:
- 1 cup walnuts, chopped
- 1 package yellow cake mix
- 1 package vanilla pudding mix
- large eggs
- ½ cup water
- ½ cup vegetable oil
- ½ cup dark rum

Directions:
1. Turn on the air fryer to 330 ° F. Spray a cake pan that will fit into the air fryer with non-stick spray.
2. Combine all ingredients and mix well. Pour into prepared cake pan.
3. Bake for 30 minutes.
4. Cool completely before serving.
5. Enjoy!

Nutrition: Calories: 225 Fat: 12g Carbs: 24g Protein: 3g

998. Palmier Biscuits
Preparation Time: 10 minutes
Cooking Time: 15 minutes
Servings: 8
Ingredients:
- 1 lb. pre-made puff pastry
- tbsp. sugar
- 1 tsp. vanilla extract
- 1 large egg white

Directions:
1. Preheat air fryer to 350° F. Line a baking sheet with parchment paper.

2. Combine the vanilla and sugar together.
3. Cut the puff pastry into two equal rectangles. Brush each with the egg white and sprinkle with sugar. Only use about half of the sugar. Place rectangles on top of each other. .
4. Cut into strips and sprinkle with remaining sugar. Bake for 15 minutes. Enjoy!

Nutrition: Calories: 109 Fat: 4g Carbs: 12g Protein: 1g

999. Lazy Dump Cake
Preparation Time: 15 minutes
Cooking Time: 40 minutes
Servings: 6
Ingredients:
- (15oz) cans sliced peaches in heavy syrup
- 1 box vanilla cake mix
- ½ cup butter
- 1 tsp. ground cinnamon

Directions:
1. Prepare the air fryer to 350° F.
2. Pour the peaches into a baking pan sprayed with nonstick spray.
3. Combine the butter, cinnamon, and cake mix just until crumbly. Pour over top of the peaches.
4. Bake for 30 minutes. Serve warm.
5. Enjoy!

Nutrition: Calories: 195 Fat: 11g Carbs: 26g Protein: 3g

1000. Cherry Coconut Cake
Preparation Time: 10 minutes
Cooking Time: 30 minutes
Servings: 8
Ingredients:
- cups flour
- 1 tsp baking powder
- ½ tsp. baking soda
- ½ cup butter
- ¾ cup sugar
- 2 egg yolks
- 2 egg whites
- ½ cup shredded sweetened coconut
- ¾ cups sliced maraschino cherries
- ½ cup orange juice

Directions:
1. Set the air fryer to 320°F. Grease a cake pan that will fit into the air fryer.
2. Mix the butter with a mixer on high speed until creamy. Add the sugar and beat again until light and fluffy
3. Add the yolks and keep beating until well combined. Stir in the coconut and the cherries.
4. Add the flour and orange juice, mix just until combined.
5. In a second bowl, beat the egg whites until stiff peaks form. Fold into the coconut cake batter.
6. Pour into the prepared cake pan and bake for 30 minutes.
7. Cool completely. Serve and enjoy.

Nutrition: Calories: 379 Fat: 12g Carbs: 66g Protein: 2g

1001. Pineapple Cobbler
Preparation Time: 10 minutes
Cooking Time: 30 minutes
Servings: 7
Ingredients:
- ½ cup butter, cut into small cubes
- 1 box yellow cake mix
- (15oz) cans pineapple chunks, drained
- ¼ cup brown sugar
- 1 cup maraschino cherries, cut in half

Directions:
1. Put the air fryer to 390° F.
2. Spread the pineapple and cherries in an even layer.
3. Sprinkle the cake mix and sugar on top. Scatter the butter cubed over the cake mix.
4. Bake for 30 minutes or until golden brown. Serve warm.
5. Enjoy!

Nutrition: Calories: 314 Fat: 12g Carbs: 50g Protein: 3g

CONCLUSION

Life is so much more comfortable with an air fryer oven; you can effortlessly cook any recipes from your cookbook. You can cook in an air fryer the whole day and won't be able to get enough of the incredible innovation. It is designed beautifully and makes sure to create less hassle for the people who do not have enough time to cook.

Anyone can make the recipes out of the air fryer. You need to know the right measurements, and you will have a great recipe ready for you. Once you know how to cook with an air fryer, you would want to cook in it every time. There are various recipes found in this book to try, so get started now without wasting any time!

The air fryer is an innovative way to cook food that is both healthy and easy. The air fryer ensures healthy food without using too much oil. Instead of oil, this excellent kitchen appliance uses circulating hot air to cook food. The method is fast, convenient, and can be surprisingly good, but only if you are equipped with the right recipes.

This air fryer cookbook includes various types of delicious recipes that are suitable for all tastes. Every recipe is full of flavor, simple to make, and a healthier alternative to traditionally cooked foods. This is filled with recipes for delicious and crispy delights. The air fryer can create fried food fast without added fat, calories, or guilt.

If you want to cut down on your carbs and follow a diet that would rapidly encourage you to lose more weight and stay healthy, choosing a diet is a personal and intimate matter. It largely depends on your body's physiology and your requirements and expectations regarding which diet might be the best one for you.

Regardless of which diet you choose, keep in mind that the air fryer will significantly amplify the joy of the experience by allowing you to cook healthy meals that will seamlessly complement your lifestyle and your diet choice.

It is undoubtedly a multipurpose kitchen appliance that is highly recommended to everybody. It presents one with a palatable atmosphere to enjoy fried delicious but healthy, cheaper, and more convenient foods. The use of this kitchen appliance ensures that the making of some of your favorite snacks and meals will be carried out in a stressfree manner without hassling around, which invariably legitimizes its worth and gives you value for your money.

You should never limit yourself, go on, and try new things! Explore new recipes! Experiment with different ingredients, seasonings, and various methods. Create some new recipes and keep your mind open. By so doing, you will be able to get the best out of your air fryer.

The air fryer truly is not an appliance that should be kept on the shelf. Instead, try it out and give it a shot when you are worked up about one of your desirable recipes or if you are starting to get used to the air frying method.

There are no limits with the air fryer, and we will explore some more recipes as well. In addition to all the great options that we talked about before, you will find that there are tasty desserts that can make those sweet teeth in no time, and some great sauces and dressing to always be in control over the foods you eat.

There are just so many options to choose from that it won't take long before you find a whole bunch of recipes to use, and before you start to wonder why you didn't get the air fryer so much sooner. There are lot of things to appreciate with air fryer, and it becomes an even better tool to use when you have the right recipes in place and can use them.

Printed in Great Britain
by Amazon

58185817R00113